W9-CNS-716

Network+

Certification

Training Kit

PUBLISHED BY
Microsoft Press
A Division of Microsoft Corporation
One Microsoft Way
Redmond, Washington 98052-6399

Library of Congress Cataloging-in-Publication Data
Network+ Certification Training Kit / Microsoft Corporation.
      p. cm.
    Includes index.
    ISBN 0-7356-1346-X
    1. Computer networks--Certification--Study guides.   I. Microsoft Corporation.

  TK5105.5 .N48 2001
  004.6'076--dc21   2001030326

Printed and bound in the United States of America.

1 2 3 4 5 6 7 8 9   QWT   6 5 4 3 2 1

Distributed in Canada by Penguin Books Canada Limited.

A CIP catalogue record for this book is available from the British Library.

Microsoft Press books are available through booksellers and distributors worldwide. For further information about international editions, contact your local Microsoft Corporation office or contact Microsoft Press International directly at fax (425) 936-7329. Visit our Web site at mspress.microsoft.com. Send comments to *tkinput@microsoft.com*.

For Microsoft Press:
Acquisitions Editor: Thomas Pohlmann
Project Editor: Karen Szall
Technical Editor: James W. Johnson

Author: Craig Zacker

For J&L Publishing:
Project Manager/Layout: Linda Robinson
Manuscript Editor: Uma Kukathas
Electronic Artist: David Holter
Proofreader: Paul Vautier

Body Part No. X08-03774

Contents

About This Book

Welcome to the *Network+ Certification Training Kit.* This training kit introduces the basic concepts of computer networking. It is designed to prepare you to take the Network+ Certification exam administered by the Computing Technology Industry Association (CompTIA). The Network+ Certification program covers the networking technologies most commonly used today. It measures the technical knowledge of networking professionals. Passing the Network+ Certification exam means you are certified as possessing the basic knowledge and skills needed to work in the computer networking field. However, this book is not just about getting you through the exam. The lessons in these chapters also provide you with knowledge you will really use when working on networks.

Each chapter in this book is divided into lessons. Most lessons include hands-on procedures that allow you to practice or demonstrate a particular concept or skill. Each chapter ends with a short summary of all lessons and a set of review questions to test your knowledge of the lesson material.

Intended Audience

This book is for people aspiring to have careers as network administrators or support technicians who want an objective assessment of their skills, and who would like certification of their accomplishments. The audience for this book ranges from people with little or no actual experience in network administration to individuals who are working in entry-level to intermediate positions in the field. This book can also help you prepare to take the related Network+ Examination NK-N10-001.

Prerequisites

There are no official prerequisites for taking the Network+ Certification exam or for using this book, but you are expected to be familiar with the workings of personal computers and have at least a basic idea of what a data network is and why it's useful. In some ways, the Network+ Certification exam can be thought of as the next step after CompTIA's A+ Certification examination That exam measures a user's knowledge of personal computers and their qualifications to work as a computer service technician. The A+ Certification exam is not a prerequisite for this self-paced training course, but the knowledge gained in preparing for and taking that exam would certainly help you in your preparation for the Network+ Certification exam.

About The CD-ROM

The Supplemental Course Materials compact disc contains a variety of informational aids that may be used throughout this book. This includes video demonstrations that supplement some of the key concepts covered in the book. You should view these demonstrations when suggested, and then use them as a review tool while you work through the material.

The CD-ROM also contains an eBook for this training kit and for the *Microsoft Encyclopedia of Networking*. The eBooks require an HTML (Hypertext Markup Language) browser. If Microsoft Internet Explorer is installed on your system, click eLibrary on the user interface menu and follow the prompts. You will be given the option of installing either or both of the eBooks. (If AutoRun is disabled on your machine, refer to the Readme.txt file on the CD-ROM.) The demonstrations are stored as HTML files with embedded Microsoft Windows Media Player files. If your machine has standard multimedia support and an HTML browser, you can view these demonstrations by double-clicking them.

For specific information about what is included on the companion CD-ROM and how to access this information, see the Readme.txt file on the CD-ROM.

Features of This Book

Starting with Chapter 4, each chapter has a "Before You Begin" section, which prepares you for completing the chapter.

The chapters are broken into lessons. Some lessons contain practice exercises that give you an opportunity to use the information presented or to explore the part of the application being described.

The "Chapter Summary" section at the end of the chapter lists the most important points discussed in the text.

The "Chapter Review" section at the end of the chapter allows you to test yourself on what you have learned in that chapter.

Appendix A, "Questions and Answers" contains all the book's questions and provides the appropriate answers.

Notes

Several types of notes appear throughout the lessons.

- Notes marked **Note** contain supplemental information.
- Notes marked **Tip** contain explanations of possible results or alternative methods.

- Notes marked **Important** contain information that is essential to completing a task.
- Notes marked **Caution** and **Warning** contain warnings about possible loss of data.

Conventions

The following conventions are used throughout this book.

Notational Conventions

- Characters or commands that you type appear in **bold** type.
- *Italic* in syntax statements indicates placeholders for variable information. *Italic* is also used for book titles and defined words.
- Names of files and folders appear in Title caps, except when you are to type them directly. Unless otherwise indicated, you can use all lowercase letters when you type a file name in a dialog box or at a command prompt.
- File name extensions appear in all lowercase.
- Acronyms appear in all uppercase.
- Monospace type represents code samples, examples of screen text, or entries that you might type at a command prompt or in initialization files.
- Square brackets [ ] are used in syntax statements to enclose optional items. For example, [*filename*] in command syntax indicates that you can choose to type a file name with the command. Type only the information within the brackets, not the brackets themselves.
- Braces { } are used in syntax statements to enclose required items. Type only the information within the braces, not the braces themselves.
- Icons represent specific sections in the book as follows:

Icon	Represents
	A multimedia presentation. You will find the applicable multimedia presentation on the course compact disc.
	An exercise containing questions about the lesson just presented. Answers to the exercises are contained in Appendix A, "Questions and Answers," at the end of the book.
	Chapter review questions. These questions at the end of each chapter allow you to test what you have learned in the lessons. You will find the answers to the review questions in Appendix A, "Questions and Answers," at the end of the book.

Keyboard Conventions

- A plus sign (+) between two key names means that you must press those keys at the same time. For example, "Press ALT+TAB" means that you hold down ALT while you press TAB.

- A comma (,) between two or more key names means that you must press each of the keys consecutively, not together. For example, "Press ALT, F, X" means that you press and release each key in sequence. "Press ALT+W, L" means that you first press ALT and W together, and then release them and press L.

- You can choose menu commands with the keyboard. Press the ALT key to activate the menu bar, and then sequentially press the keys that correspond to the highlighted or underlined letter of the menu name and the command name. For some commands, you can also press a key combination listed in the menu.

- You can select or clear check boxes or option buttons in dialog boxes with the keyboard. Press the ALT key, and then press the key that corresponds to the underlined letter of the option name. Or you can press TAB until the option is highlighted, and then press the spacebar to select or clear the check box or option button.

- You can cancel the display of a dialog box by pressing the ESC key.

Chapter and Appendix Overview

This self-paced training course combines notes, exercises, multimedia presentations, and review questions to teach you the fundamentals of data networking you will need to prepare you for the Network+ exam. The course is designed to be completed from beginning to end, but you can choose a customized track and complete only the sections that interest you. (See the next section, "Finding the Best Starting Point for You" for more information.) If you choose the customized track option, see the "Before You Begin" sections in the chapters.

The book is divided into the following chapters:

- The section you are reading, "About This Book," contains a self-paced training overview and introduces the components of this training course. Read this section thoroughly to get the greatest educational value from this course and to plan which lessons you will complete.

- Chapter 1, "Networking Basics," examines some of the basic networking vocabulary and architectural concepts that form the foundation for the rest of the book. The layers of the Open Systems Interconnection (OSI) reference model and the protocols that run at the various layers are an essential part of understanding how a network functions.

- Chapter 2, "Network Hardware," introduces the physical building blocks of a local area network (LAN), including the cables that connect the computers together, the network interface adapter that provides each computer with its interface to the network, and the hubs that connect the various network devices together.

- Chapter 3, "Network Connections," explains how to combine relatively small LANs into large enterprise networks using more complex hardware devices, such as bridges, routers, and switches.

- Chapter 4, "Networking Software," covers the networking capabilities of the operating systems, client software, and directory services that run on the computers connected to a LAN.

- Chapter 5, "Data-Link Layer Protocols," discusses protocols like Ethernet and Token Ring, which operate at the data-link layer of the OSI reference model and are responsible for the final packaging of application data before it's transmitted over the network.

- Chapter 6, "Network Layer Protocols," examines the protocols at the third layer of the OSI reference model, such as Internet Protocol (IP) and Internetwork Packet Exchange (IPX), which are responsible for addressing and routing network packets to their final destinations.

- Chapter 7, "Transport Layer Protocols," covers protocols such as Transmission Control Protocol (TCP) and User Datagram Protocol (UDP), which operate at the transport layer of the OSI model and provide additional services such as packet acknowledgment and segmentation.

- Chapter 8, "TCP/IP Fundamentals," provides an overview of the various protocols in the TCP/IP suite and some of the fundamental principles of TCP/IP communications, such as IP addressing and subnet masking.

- Chapter 9, "TCP/IP Routing," discusses the process by which TCP/IP packets are routed through complex internetworks (such as the Internet) to their destinations.

- Chapter 10, "TCP/IP Applications," lists some of the important services used by TCP/IP networks and the utilities that network administrators can use to maintain them.

- Chapter 11, "TCP/IP Configuration," examines the process of configuring a TCP/IP client to participate on a network, including the most common parameters found in all operating systems that support the protocols.

- Chapter 12, "Remote Network Access," covers the mechanisms that enable users to access a network from a remote location, including direct connections and virtual private networks (VPNs).

- Chapter 13, "Network Security," discusses some of the basic security precautions used on most networks, such as password policies and firewalls.

- Chapter 14, "Planning the Network," examines the network planning process that takes place before any hardware or software products are purchased or installed.

- Chapter 15, "Installing a Network," provides the information you need to install both internal and external network cables and connect them to the computers, hubs, and other hardware components.

- Chapter 16, "Network Maintenance," covers some of the most essential maintenance chores required by a professional network, such as the performance of regular backups, virus protection, and software upgrades.

- Chapter 17, "Network Troubleshooting Procedures," explains how to identify and recognize the various components you might find on a network and examines the logical progressions that the troubleshooting process takes on the way to finding a solution to a problem.

- Chapter 18, "Network Troubleshooting Tools," describes some of the indicators that network administrators use to know when a problem exists, some of the hardware and software tools you can use to troubleshoot network problems, and some of the resources where you can find additional networking information.

- Chapter 19, "Network Troubleshooting Scenarios," contains a comprehensive account of an actual networking problem and the steps that a network support technician can take to isolate, diagnose, and resolve it.

- Appendix A, "Questions and Answers," lists all of the exercise and review questions from the book, showing the page number where the question appears and the suggested answer.

- The Glossary provides definitions of key networking terms used throughout the book.

Finding the Best Starting Point For You

Because this book is self-paced, you can skip some lessons and revisit them later. The following tables provide a list of the skills measured on certification exam *Network+ Examination* NK-N10-001. The table lists the skills, as defined in the objectives for the exam, and where in this book you will find the lesson relating to a particular skill.

The exam objectives group the skills into two general areas: knowledge of networking technology and knowledge of networking practices.

Note Exam objectives are subject to change without prior notice.

Knowledge of Networking Technology

Basic Knowledge

Skill Being Measured	Location in Book
Understand network structure.	Chapter 1, Lesson 1; Chapter 2, Lesson 1
Describe network operating systems, clients, and directory services.	Chapter 4
Define IPX, IP, and NetBEUI.	Chapter 6
Describe fault tolerance and its implementation methods.	Chapter 14, Lesson 2
Describe the OSI model and identify protocols, services, and functions that relate to each layer.	Chapter 1, Lesson 2
Recognize and describe types and characteristics of network media: coaxial, fiber-optic, Category 3, Category 5, unshielded twisted pair (UTP), shielded twisted pair, 10Base2, 100VG AnyLan, RJ45, Bayonet-Neill-Concelman (BNC), and so on.	Chapter 5, Lesson 1
Describe the basic attributes, purposes, and functions of network elements, including:	Chapter 1, Lesson 1; Chapter 2, Lessons 1 and 2; Chapter 3, Lesson 3

Full- and half-duplexing

WANs and LANs

Servers, workstations, and hosts

Server-based and peer-to-peer networking

Cabling, network interface cards (NICs), and routers

Broadband and baseband transmission

Use of gateways as default IP routers and the means by which to connect dissimilar systems or protocols

Physical Layer

Skill Being Measured	Location in Book
Configure and troubleshoot NICs.	Chapter 2, Lesson 2; Chapter 18, Lesson 3
Describe and differentiate the following network components:	Chapter 2, Lessons 1 and 3; Chapter 3, Lesson 2
Hubs	
Multistation access units (MAUs)	
Transceivers	
Repeaters	

Data-Link Layer

Skill Being Measured	Location in Book
Define bridges and why they are used.	Chapter 3, Lesson 1
Explain the IEEE Project 802 specifications, including 802.2, 802.3, and 802.5.	Chapter 5, Lessons 1 and 2
Describe the function and characteristics of MAC addresses.	Chapter 5, Lesson 1

Network Layer

Skill Being Measured	Location in Book
Define the following routing and network-layer concepts:	Chapter 6, Lesson 1; Chapter 9, Lessons 1 and 2
Routing, including static and dynamic routing	
The difference between a router and a brouter	
The difference between routable and nonroutable protocols	
Default gateways and subnetworks	
The reason for employing unique network IDs	

Transport Layer

Skill Being Measured	Location in Book
Describe the difference between connectionless and connection transport.	Chapter 7, Lesson 1
Describe the purpose of name resolution.	Chapter 10, Lesson 1

TCP/IP Fundamentals

Skill Being Measured	Location in Book
Demonstrate knowledge of the following TCP/IP fundamentals:	Chapter 8, Lesson 1; Chapter 9, Lesson 1; Chapter 10, Lesson 1; Chapter 11, Lesson 1
IP default gateways	
Dynamic Host Configuration Protocol (DHCP), Domain Name Ssystem (DNS), Windows Internet Naming Service (WINS), and host files	
Main TCP/IP protocols including TCP, UDP, Post Office Protocol 3 (POP3), Simple Mail Transfer Protocol (SMTP), Simple Network Management Protocol (SNMP), File Transfer Protocol (FTP), Hypertext Transfer Protocol (http), and IP	
Broad acceptance of TCP/IP operating systems and hosts worldwide	
Internet DNS hierarchies	
Demonstrate knowledge of the concepts of TCP/IP addressing, including:	Chapter 7, Lesson 1; Chapter 8, Lesson 2
A, B, and C classes of IP addresses and their default subnet mask	
The use of port number (HTTP, FTP, SMTP), and the port numbers commonly assigned to a given service	
Demonstrate knowledge of TCP/IP configuration concepts, including:	Chapter 11, Lesson 1; Chapter 13, Lesson 3
The definition of IP proxy and why the proxy is used	
The identity of the normal configuration parameters for a workstation	

TCP/IP Utilities

Skill Being Measured	Location in Book
Explain how and when to use the following TCP/IP utilities to test, validate, and troubleshoot IP connectivity:	Chapter 10, Lesson 2
Address Resolution Protocol (ARP)	
Telnet	
NBTSTAT	
TRACERT	
NETSTAT	
Ipconfig/winipcfg	
FTP	
PING	

Remote Connectivity

Skill Being Measured	Location in Book
Describe PPP and SLIP.	Chapter 5, Lesson 3
Explain the purpose and function of Point-to-Point Protocol (PPTP) and the conditions under which it is useful.	Chapter 12, Lesson 1
Describe the attributes, advantages, and disadvantages of Integrated Services Digital Network (ISDN) and the Public Switched Telephone Network (PSTN), or the Plain Old Telephone Service (POTS).	Chapter 12, Lesson 1
Describe modem configurations, including serial port interrupt request (IRQ), input/output (I/O) address, and maximum port speed.	Chapter 12, Lesson 1
Specify the requirements for a remote connection.	Chapter 12, Lesson 1

Security

Skill Being Measured	Location in Book
Describe issues to consider when selecting a security mode, including user and share level.	Chapter 13, Lesson 2
Describe standard password practices and procedures.	Chapter 13, Lesson 1
Explain the need to employ data encryption to protect network data.	Chapter 11, Lesson 1
Explain the purpose of a firewall.	Chapter 13, Lesson 2

Knowledge of Networking Practices

Implementing and Installing the Network

Skill Being Measured	Location in Book
Demonstrate awareness that administrative and test accounts, passwords, IP addresses, IP configurations, relevant Standard Operating Procedures, and so on, must be obtained before network implementation.	Chapter 14, Lesson 3
Evaluate environmental factors that affect networks.	Chapter 14, Lesson 1
Recognize, visually or by description, common peripheral ports, external small computer system interface (SCSI) devices (especially DB-25 connectors), and common network componentry, including:	Chapter 17, Lesson 1

    Print servers

    Peripherals

    Hubs

    Routers

    Brouters

    Bridges

    Patch panels

    Uniterrupted power supply (UPS) devices

    NICs

    Token Ring media filters

Demonstrate awareness of compatibility and cabling issues including:	Chapter 14, Lesson 1; Chapter 17, Lesson 1

    The consequences of trying to install an analog modem in a digital jack

    Variations in the use of RJ45 connectors, depending on the cabling

    The implications of using patch cables

Maintaining and Supporting a Network

Skill Being Measured	Location in Book
Describe the types of test documentation that are usually available for a vendor's patches, fixes, upgrades, and so on.	Chapter 16, Lesson 3; Chapter 18, Lesson 1
Demonstrate an awareness of the issues in a given network maintenance scenario, including the following:	Chapter 16

Standard backup procedures and backup media storage practices

The need for periodic application of software patches and other fixes to the network

The need to install anti-virus software on the server and workstations

The need to frequently update virus signatures

Troubleshooting the Network

Skill Being Measured	Location in Book
Identify the following steps as a systematic approach to identifying the extent of a network problem and, given a problem scenario, select the appropriate next step.	Chapter 17, Lesson 2; Chapter 19, Lesson 1

1. Determine whether the problem exists across the network.
2. Determine whether the problem is workstation, workgroup, LAN or WAN.
3. Determine whether the problem is consistent and replicable, and use standard troubleshooting methods.

Skill Being Measured	Location in Book
Identify the following steps as a systematic approach to determining whether a problem is attributable to the operator or the system, and, given a problem scenario, select the appropriate next step.	Chapter 17, Lesson 2

1. Identify the exact issue.
2. Recreate the problem.
3. Isolate the cause.
4. Formulate a correction.
5. Implement the correction.
6. Test
7. Document the problem and the solution.
8. Provide feedback.

Identify the following steps as a systematic approach to determining whether a problem is attributable to the operator or the system, and, given a problem scenario, select the appropriate next step.

1. Have a second operator perform the same task on an equivalent workstation.

2. Have a second operator perform the same task on the original operator's workstation.

3. Ascertain whether operators are following standard operating procedure.

Given a network troubleshooting scenario, demonstrate awareness of the need to check for physical and logical indicators of trouble, including:

Link lights

Power lights

Error displays

Error logs and displays

Performance monitors

Given a network problem scenario, including symptoms, determine the most likely cause or causes of the problem based on the available information. Select the most appropriate course of action based on this inference. Issues can include:

Recognizing abnormal physical conditions

Isolating and correcting problems in cases where there is fault in the physical media (patch cable)

Checking the status of servers

Checking for configuration problems with DNS, WINS, HOST file

Checking for viruses

Checking the validity of the account name and password

Rechecking operator logon procedures

Selecting and running appropriate diagnostics

Identify the purpose and function of common network tools, including:

Crossover cable

Hardware loopback

Tone generator

Tone locator (fox and hound)

Getting Started

This self-paced training course contains demonstration videos that enhance and supplement the text. The following sections discuss the hardware and software required to view the demonstration videos on the companion CD-ROM.

Hardware Requirements

Each computer must have the following minimum configuration.

- Multimedia PC with 16-bit sound system
- 16 MB RAM for Windows 95 or Windows 98
- 32 MB RAM for Windows ME or Windows NT
- 64 MB RAM for Windows 2000
- An additional 70 MB minimum of hard disk space to install Internet Explorer 5.5 from this CD-ROM, if Internet Explorer is not already installed
- Standard multimedia player, such as Windows Media Player or compatible software
- 4 MB of available hard drive space is required for Windows Media Player
- A double-speed CD-ROM drive or better
- Super VGA display with at least 256 colors
- Microsoft Mouse or compatible pointing device

Software Requirements

The following software is required to view the demonstration videos in this course:

- Microsoft Windows 95, Windows 98, Windows Me, Windows NT 4 with Service Pack 3 or later, or Windows 2000
- Microsoft Internet Explorer 4.01 or later
- Microsoft Windows Media Player

To view the eBook version of the book, you will need Microsoft Internet Explorer 4.01 or later. A version of Microsoft Internet Explorer 5.5 is supplied on the companion CD-ROM. For more information, see the Readme.txt file on the companion CD-ROM.

To view the demonstration videos on the companion CD-ROM, you will need a machine with standard multimedia support and an HTML browser. Microsoft Windows Media Player is supplied on the companion CD-ROM.

Note You must have the Supplemental Course Materials CD-ROM inserted in your CD-ROM drive to run the eBook.

The Network+ Certification Program

Network+ Certification is a testing program sponsored by the Computing Technology Industry Association (ComTIA) that certifies the knowledge of networking technicians who have accumulated 18 to 24 months of experience in the information technology (IT) industry.

The development of the Network+ Certification program began in 1995, when a group of technology-industry companies came together to create the IT Skills Project. This committee was formed to direct CompTIA in identifying, classifying, and publishing skills standards for networking professionals employed in three types of organizations: IT companies, channel partners, and business/government firms. Acting on the committee's recommendations, CompTIA defined these job skills through an industry-wide survey. Results and analyses of this survey were used as a foundation for the Network+ Certification program.

Earning the Network+ certification means that you possess the knowledge needed to configure and install the TCP/IP client. This exam covers a wide range of vendor and product-neutral networking technologies.

Benefits of Certification

For most individuals entering the computer industry, Network+ Certification is only the first step. Or it can be thought of as the next step after CompTIA's A+ Certification examination, which measures your knowledge of personal computers and your qualifications to work as a computer service technician. Passing the Network+ examination certifies you as possessing the basic knowledge and skills needed to work in the computer networking field. If you are interested in becoming a Microsoft Certified Systems Engineer (MCSE), the *Network+ Certification Training Kit* provides just the foundation you need to get on your way with confidence.

With Network+ Certification, you will receive many benefits, including:

- **Recognized proof of professional achievement** The Network+ credential asserts that the holder has reached a level of competence commonly accepted and valued by the industry.
- **Enhanced job opportunities** Many employers give hiring preference to applicants with Network+ certification.
- **Opportunity for advancement** The Network+ credential can be a plus when an employer awards job promotions.
- **Training requirement** Network+ certification is being adopted as a prerequisite to enrollment in certain vendors' training courses.
- **Customer confidence** As the general public learns about Network+ certification, customers will request that only certified technicians be assigned to their accounts.

- **Improved productivity** Certified employees perform work faster and more accurately. Statistics show that certified employees can work up to 75 percent faster than noncertified employees.
- **Customer satisfaction** When employees have credentials that prove their competency, customer expectations are more likely to be met. More business can be generated for the employer through repeat sales to satisfied customers.

The Network+ Exam

The text in this book prepares you to master the skills needed to pass the Network+ exam. By mastering all course work, you will be able to complete the Network+ Certification exam with the confidence you need to ensure success. Individuals are permitted to take the exam as many times as they like.

The exam is broken down into two sections. The first section contains nine subsections and the second section contains three subsections. The following table lists the sections and the extent to which they are represented.

I.	**Knowledge of Networking Technology**	**77%**
1.	Basic knowledge	18
2.	Physical layer	6
3.	Data-link layer	5
4.	Network layer	5
5.	Transport layer	5
6.	TCP/IP fundamentals	16
7.	TCP/IP utilities	11
8.	Remote connectivity	5
9.	Security	6
II.	**Knowledge of Networking Practices**	**23%**
1.	Implementing the installation of the network	6
2.	Maintaining and supporting the network	6
3.	Troubleshooting the network	11

Registering for the Network+ Exam

Anyone can take the Network+ exam. There are no specific requirements or prerequisites, except payment of the fee. However, exam content is targeted to computer technicians with 18 to 24 months of experience in the IT industry. A typical candidate will have CompTIA A+ Certification or equivalent knowledge, but A+ Certification is not required. The Network+ exam consists of 65 questions that must be answered within a maximum allowable time of 90 minutes.

The tests are administered by Sylvan Prometric and NCS/VUE, who have hundreds of authorized testing centers in all 50 states in the United States and in over 150 countries worldwide. To register for the exam, call 1-888-895-6166.

When you call, please have the following information available:

- Social Security number or Sylvan Prometric ID (provided by Sylvan Prometric)
- Mailing address and telephone number
- Employer or organization
- Date on which you want to take the test
- Method of payment (credit card or check)

The test is available to anyone who wants to take it. Payment is made at the time of registration, either by credit card or by requesting that an invoice be sent to you or your employer. Vouchers and coupons are also redeemed at that time.

Preparing for the Network+ Exam

The process of preparing for the Network+ exam is unique to every student, but there are a wide variety of resources to aid you in the process, including the following:

- **Classroom instruction** There are many organizations that offer instructor-led training courses for the Network+ exam. The advantages of this type of training are that you have access to a networking lab in which you can experiment, and a teacher whom you can ask questions. This type of training can be quite expensive, however, often running several hundred dollars per day.

- **Computer-based training (CBT)** CBTs are courses that come on one or more CD-ROMs, and which can contain multimedia training materials such as audio and video, in addition to graphics and text. A typical CBT includes software that you install on your computer that enables you to track the lessons you've completed and the amount of time you've spent on each one, as well as your results for any exercises and practice exams that might be included. The advantage of a CBT is that you can work with it at your own pace and without having to travel to a training center. CBTs can also be expensive, but not as expensive as classroom training.

- **Online Training** Some training companies offer Network+ courses using Web-based training, which is usually similar in format to a CBT, but delivered online instead of from a CD-ROM. One advantage of online training is that usage information and quiz scores can be maintained by the training company on its servers, making it a good solution for corporations looking for an employee training program. Some courses also offer feedback from a live instructor, through online message boards or chat applications, which can place this medium a step above CBTs. Depending on the format of the course, however, online training might not be satisfactory for users limited to relatively low-speed dial-up Internet connections. For corporate customers, however, who usually have high-speed connections, online training could be ideal, and is generally comparable in cost to CBTs.

- **Study guides** Books always provide the most information for your training dollar. A student who is disciplined enough to work through a comprehensive Network+ study guide is likely to absorb more information from books than are even offered by CBTs or online training courses, and for substantially less money. There are many different Network+ books available, many with exercises and practice questions that provide feedback and progress indicators similar to those in the electronic training formats.

- **Practice exams** Practice exams for the Network+ certification are available in book form, on CD-ROM, and on Web sites. The interface used for the examination by the testing centers should not present a challenge to users familiar with computers, so it should make little difference to most people whether their practice tests are in printed or electronic form. What is more important is the content of the practice exams. In addition to providing the correct answers, a good practice exam should also explain why each possible answer to a question is either right or wrong.

- **Braindumps** Although not a commercial product like the other training material listed here, braindumps can be the most valuable resource for information about the Network+ exam, and they're free. A braindump is simply a document, usually posted on a Web site or in a Usenet newsgroup, containing the recollections of a person who has taken the exam. Because no one is permitted to take notes during the test or take them outside the testing room, how much information a braindump provides depends on the person's memory and how long it's been since he or she took the test. Some people are able to recall a great deal of information; some are not. One thing to be careful of when it comes to braindumps, however, is that while a person's memories of the exam might be useful, their networking knowledge might be incomplete or incorrect. Don't rely on braindumps for explanations of right or wrong answers; just note the content of the questions and research them yourself, if necessary.

Taking the Network+ Exam

The Network+ exam is administered by computer, and is completely "closed book." You are not permitted to bring any written materials into the testing room with you, although you are given a pencil and a blank piece of paper or a scratch tablet on which you can write any information you want before the exam begins. Many students memorize a page full of crucial facts and jot them down in the testing room before the exam begins. You can then use your own notes during the exam, but you must turn them in afterward; you cannot take them out with you.

The testing room typically contains a group of computers, with cubicles or dividers to prevent any distraction or communication between students. In most cases, there is a window through which a proctor observes the testing process. You are given time in the testing room to make your own notes. You can then take an orientation exam on the testing computer to familiarize yourself with the format of the software.

The exam is pre-loaded on the computer when you arrive, and you can start the test at any time. The exam consists of 65 questions, chosen at random from a pool, so that the probability of two people taking the exact same exam are very slight. You have 90 minutes to take the exam; a clock on the computer screen keeps you informed of the time remaining. Each question appears on a separate screen, and you can move forward and backward through the questions by clicking the appropriate arrows. Instructions for using the testing software appear on each screen, although most users familiar with graphical user interfaces don't need them.

The questions are all multiple choice. Some questions require you to select a single answer; these questions have radio buttons on the answers so you can make only one choice. Some questions require more than one answer. These questions have check boxes and might also indicate how many selections you can make. Others might instruct you to choose all of the answers that apply. All questions are graded either right or wrong; there is no partial credit. If you do not select the required number of responses to a question, the software flags that question and reminds you that it is incomplete at the end of the exam. In some cases, questions include graphics, such as charts or network diagrams. You are asked a question about the graphic, and you might have to click on a particular part of the graphic to indicate your answer.

As you take the test, you can answer each question as it appears, or you can fill a checkbox that flags an unanswered question to review later. This feature is for user convenience only. You can return to any question at any time in the exam by clicking the forward and backward arrows. The flags only enable you to return to specific questions without having to go through all the questions you have already completed.

Students have different techniques for taking multiple choice exams. Some people read all of the questions first before selecting any responses. This can be beneficial, because later questions might provide a hint or trigger your memory about the subject of an earlier question. However, don't waste too much time doing this, or you might find yourself rushing through the last few questions. Answering 65 questions in 90 minutes works out to 83 seconds each, so you can't afford to spend too much time on any one question.

The key to taking an exam of this type is to read each question extremely well. The language of the questions is chosen very carefully, and sometimes very deviously. In many cases, questions are designed to trick you into thinking that they are easier than they actually are. If an answer seems painfully obvious, read the question over again. Chances are, the obvious answer is not the correct one. In some cases, all of the responses are correct, and you are instructed to select the one that best answers the question, so always be sure to read all of the possible responses, even when the first one seems correct.

Even if you are completely stumped about a question, you should take a guess before the exam is over. Leave yourself a few minutes at the end of the test to make any guesses you need to, so that you don't leave any questions unanswered.

When 90 minutes have elapsed and the exam is over, there is a brief delay as the computer totals your score. You then receive the results on the spot, with a printed report that breaks down your score into several topics. If you fail the test, this report can be an excellent guide to the material that requires further study. If you pass, the report contains the certification number that you can use to prove your status.

The Network+ exam is now graded using a scaled format. Before February 28, 2001, your score was a percentage, with 82 per cent being a passing grade. Now, your score is expressed as a number between 100 and 900, with 752 being a passing grade. The Network+ Certification exam is strictly pass/fail. While you can use your high score for bragging rights among your friends and colleagues, all students passing the exam receive the same certification, which is a certificate that CompTIA mails to you a few weeks after the exam.

CHAPTER 1

Networking Basics

About This Chapter

This chapter introduces the basic principles and architectural structure of network communications. These concepts and structures are referred to repeatedly in the rest of this book as well as in real-life networking situations. Even if you plan to skip other chapters in this book, you must read and fully understand this one. You are certain to need it, both for the Network+ exam and on the job.

Lesson 1: Network Communications

This lesson introduces the basic building blocks of network communications and some of the structures used to construct data networks. There are many different kinds of data networks—from enterprise networks used by large corporations to a simple two-node local area network (LAN) used in a private home. However, many of the same principles apply to all networks, regardless of size or complexity.

After this lesson, you will be able to
- List the services provided by network protocols
- Describe how protocols enable networked computers to communicate
- Distinguish a local area network (LAN) from a wide area network (WAN)
- Understand the difference between baseband and broadband networks
- Identify and distinguish the characteristics of a packet-switched network and a circuit-switched network
- Understand full-duplex and half-duplex communications
- Describe the basic segment and backbone design of an enterprise network
- Distinguish a server-based network from a peer-to-peer network

Estimated lesson time: 30 minutes

When you connect two or more computers so they can communicate with each other, you create a data network. This is true whether you connect the computers using a cable, a wireless technology such as infrared or radio waves, or even modems and telephone lines. The technology that connects the computers together, no matter what form it takes, is called the *network medium*. Copper-based cables are the most common form of network medium, and for this reason the term "network cable" is often used to refer to any kind of network medium.

Signals and Protocols

Computers can communicate over a network in many ways and for many reasons, but a great deal that goes on in the networking process is unconcerned with the nature of the data passing over the network medium. By the time the data generated by the transmitting computer reaches the cable or other medium, it has been reduced to *signals* that are native to that medium. These might be electrical voltages, for a copper cable network; pulses of light, for fiber optic; or infrared or radio waves. These signals form a code that the network interface in each receiving computer converts back into the binary data understood by the software running on that computer. The computer then interprets the binary code into information that it can use in a variety of ways. Of course there is a great deal more complexity to this process than this description indicates, and there is a lot going on in order to make it possible that the e-mail you just sent to your mother gets reduced to electrical voltages, transmitted halfway across the country, and then reconstituted into text.

In some cases, a network consists of identical computers running the same version of the same operating system and using all the same applications, while other networks can consist of many different computing platforms running entirely different software. It may seem as though it would be easier for the identical computers to communicate than it would be for the different ones, and in some ways it is. But no matter what kind of computers the network uses and what software the computers are running, they must have a common language in order to understand each other. These common languages are called *protocols*, and computers use many of them during even the simplest exchanges of network data. Just as two people must speak a common language in order to communicate, two computers must have one or more protocols in common to exchange data.

A network protocol can be relatively simple or highly complex. In some cases, a protocol is simply a code—such as a pattern of electrical voltages—that defines the binary value of a bit of data: zero or one. The concept is the same as that of Morse code, in which a pattern of dots and dashes represents a letter of the alphabet. More complicated networking protocols can provide a variety of services, including the following:

- **Packet acknowledgment** This is the transmission of a return message by the recipient that verifies the receipt of a packet or packets. A packet is the fundamental unit of data transmitted over a LAN.

- **Segmentation** This is the division of a lengthy data stream into segments sufficiently small for transmission over the network.

- **Flow control** This is the generation of messages by a receiving system that instruct the sending system to speed up or slow down its transmissions.

- **Error detection** This is the inclusion of special codes in a packet that the receiving system uses to verify that the content of the packet wasn't damaged in transit.

- **Error correction** This is the generation by a receiving system of messages that inform the sender that specific packets were damaged and must be retransmitted.

- **Data compression** This is a mechanism for reducing the amount of data transmitted over a network by eliminating redundant information.

- **Data encryption** This is a mechanism for protecting the data transmitted over a network by encrypting it using a key already known by the receiving system.

In most cases, protocols are based on public standards developed by an independent committee, and not a single manufacturer or developer. These public standards ensure that different types of systems can use them without incurring any obligation to a particular company. There are still a few protocols, however, that are proprietary, having been developed by a single company and never released into the public domain.

One of the most important things to remember about networking is that every computer on a network uses many different protocols during the communications process. The functions provided by the various protocols are divided into the layers that make up the Open Systems Interconnection (OSI) reference model (which is described in Lesson 2, later in this chapter). You might see references to an Ethernet network in networking books and articles, for example, but Ethernet is not the only protocol running on that network. Ethernet is, however, the only protocol running at one particular layer (called the data-link layer). Some layers, however, can have multiple protocols running on them simultaneously.

Protocols are implemented on a computer in several different ways. Some take the form of hardware, such as the network interface adapter (generally a network interface card, or NIC) installed in the computer. Others are device drivers, such as the driver for a particular network interface adapter supplied by its manufacturer. And there are yet others that are integrated into a computer's operating system.

Protocol Interaction

The protocols operating at the various OSI layers are often referred to as a *protocol stack*. The protocols running on a networked computer work together to provide all of the services required by a particular application. Generally speaking, the services provided by the protocols are not redundant. If, for example, a protocol at one layer provides a particular service, the protocols at the other layers do not provide exactly the same service. Protocols at adjacent layers in the stack provide services to each other, depending on the direction in which the data is flowing. As illustrated in Figure 1.1, on a transmitting system, the data originates in an application at the top of the protocol stack and works its way down through the layers. Each protocol provides a service to a protocol operating at the layer below it. At the bottom of the protocol stack is the network medium itself, which carries the data to another computer on the network.

When the data arrives at its destination, the receiving computer performs the same procedure as did the transmitting computer, except in reverse. The data is passed up through the layers to the receiving application, with each protocol providing an equivalent service to the protocol on the layer above it. For example, if a protocol at layer three on the transmitting computer is responsible for encrypting data, the same protocol at layer three of the receiving system is responsible for decrypting it. In this way, protocols at the various layers in the transmitting system communicate with their equivalent protocols operating at the same layer in the receiving system. This is illustrated in Figure 1.2.

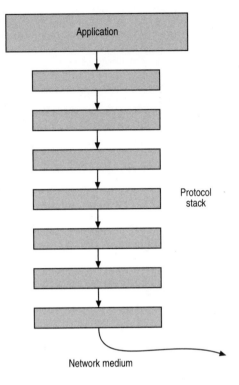

Protocol
stack

Network medium

Figure 1.1   The networking protocols running on a computer form a layered stack,
with each protocol providing services to the protocol operating at the layer above or
below it, depending on the direction of data flow.

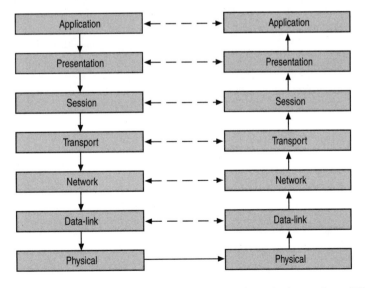

Figure 1.2   Protocols operating at the same layer in the stack on different systems
can be said to communicate indirectly by providing complementary services.

Local Area Networks and Wide Area Networks

A group of computers located in a relatively small area and connected by a common medium is called a *local area network* (LAN). Each of the computers on the LAN is also called a *node*. A LAN is characterized by three primary attributes: its topology, its medium, and its protocols. The *topology* is the pattern used to connect the computers together. With a *bus* topology, a network cable connects each computer to the next one, forming a chain. With a *star* topology, each of the computers is connected to a central nexus called a hub. A *ring* topology is essentially a bus network with the two ends joined together. You will learn more about network topologies in Chapter 2, "Network Hardware."

The network medium, as defined earlier, is the actual physical connection between the networked computers. The topology and the medium used on a particular network are specified by the protocol operating at the data-link layer of the OSI model, such as Ethernet or Token Ring. Ethernet, for example, supports several different topologies and media. When you select one combination of topology and medium for a LAN, such as unshielded twisted pair (UTP) cable in a star topology, you must (in most cases) use the same topology and medium for all of the computers on that LAN. There are some hardware products that enable you to connect computers to the same LAN with different media, but this is only true for closely related technologies. You can't connect a bus Ethernet system to a star Ethernet system and have both systems be part of the same LAN.

In the same way, all of the systems on a LAN must share common protocols. You can't connect an Ethernet system to a Token Ring system on the same LAN, for example. The same is true for the protocols operating at the other layers of the OSI model. If the systems on the LAN don't have common protocols at every layer of the stack, communication among them is not possible.

In most cases, a LAN is confined to a room, a floor, or perhaps a building. To expand the network beyond these limits, you can connect multiple LANs together using devices called routers, forming what is known as an *internetwork*. An internetwork is essentially a network of networks. A computer on one LAN can communicate with the systems on another LAN, because they are all interconnected. By connecting LANs in this way, you can build an internetwork as large as you need. Many sources use the term "network" when describing a LAN, but just as many use the same term when referring to an internetwork.

Note It is important to distinguish between an internetwork, which is any collection of interconnected LANs, and the Internet. While the Internet is an example of an internetwork, not every internetwork involves the Internet.

In many cases, an internetwork is composed of LANs in distant locations. To connect remote LANs, you use a different type of network connection called a *wide area network* (WAN) connection. WAN connections can use telephone lines, radio waves, or any one of many other technologies. WAN connections are usually point-to-point connections, meaning that they connect only two systems. They are unlike LANs, which can connect many systems. An example of a WAN connection would be a company with two offices in distant cities, each with its own LAN and connected by a leased telephone line. This type of WAN is illustrated in Figure 1.3. Each end of the leased line is connected to a router and the routers are connected to individual LANs. Any computer on either of the LANs can communicate with any one of the other computers at the other end of the WAN link or with a computer on its own LAN.

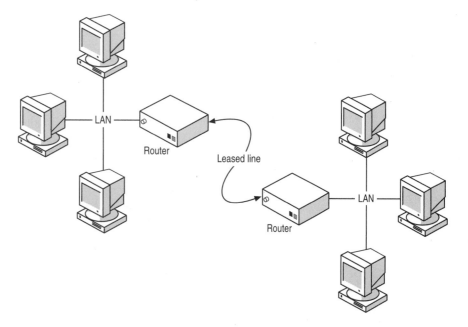

Figure 1.3 WAN connections create internetworks by connecting LANs in distant locations.

Broadband and Baseband

In most cases, LANs use a shared network medium. The cable connecting the computers can carry one signal at a time, and all of the systems take turns using it. This type of network is called a *baseband* network. To make a baseband network practical for many computers to share, the data transmitted by each system is broken up into separate units called *packets*. If you were to tap into the cable of a baseband network and examine the signals as they flow by, you would see a succession of packets generated by various systems and destined for various systems. When your computer transmits an e-mail message, for example, it might be broken up into many packets, and the computer transmits each packet separately. If another computer on the network also wants to transmit, it would also send one packet at a time. When all of the packets constituting a particular transmission reach their destination, the receiving computer reassembles them back into your original e-mail. This is the basis for a *packet-switching* network.

The alternative to a packet-switching network is a circuit-switching network. *Circuit-switching* means that the two systems wanting to communicate establish a circuit before they transmit any information. That circuit remains open throughout the life of the exchange, and is only broken when the two systems are finished communicating. This is an impractical solution for computers on a baseband network, because two systems could conceivably monopolize the network medium for long periods of time, preventing other systems from communicating. Circuit switching is more common in environments like the public switched telephone network (PSTN), in which the connection between your telephone and that of the person you're calling remains open for the entire duration of the call.

To make circuit switching practical, telephone companies use broadband networks. A *broadband* network is the opposite of a baseband network, in that it carries multiple signals in a single cable at the same time. One broadband network that you probably use every day is that operated by your local cable television company. A cable TV (CATV) service runs a single cable into a user's home, but that one cable carries the signals for dozens of TV channels and often provides Internet access as well. Broadband technologies are almost never used for local area networking, but they are becoming an increasingly popular solution for wide area networking.

Half-Duplex and Full-Duplex Communications

When two computers communicate over a LAN, data typically travels in only one direction at a time, because the baseband network used for most LANs supports only a single signal. This is called *half-duplex* communication. By contrast, two systems that can communicate in both directions simultaneously are operating in *full-duplex* mode. These two kinds of communication are illustrated in Figure 1.4. The most common example of a full-duplex network is, once again, the telephone system. Both parties can speak simultaneously during a telephone call and each party can also hear the other at the same time. An example of a half-duplex communication system is a two-way radio like a CB radio, in which only one party can transmit at any one time, and each party must say "over" to signal that he or she has finished talking.

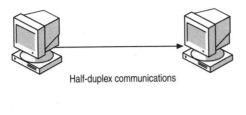

Half-duplex communications

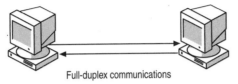

Full-duplex communications

Figure 1.4   Most LANs use half-duplex communications, meaning that only one side of a connection can transmit at a time.

With the right equipment, full-duplex communication is possible on certain types of LANs. The first requirement is a separate channel for traffic running in each direction. Whether this is possible depends on the network medium. Coaxial cable, for example, contains a single conductor and a ground, so there is no physical way that traffic could run in both directions, unless you were to install two cable runs for each connection. Twisted pair cable, on the other hand, contains four separate wire pairs within a single sheath, one of which is dedicated to incoming traffic and one to outgoing. Networks that use this type of cable can therefore theoretically operate in full-duplex mode, and some manufacturers are making Ethernet equipment that makes this possible. Full-duplex Ethernet essentially doubles the throughput of the existing network.

Segments and Backbones

When a small network begins to grow, it is possible to connect LANs together in a haphazard manner for a while. However, building a large enterprise network by connecting many LANs is a complex undertaking that requires careful planning. One of the most common designs for a network of this type is a series of segment LANs connected by a backbone LAN.

The term *segment* is sometimes used synonymously with "LAN" or "network" to refer to any collection of networked computers, but in this context it refers to a LAN composed of user workstations and other end-user devices, such as printers. An enterprise network would consist of many such LANs, all of which are connected to another LAN called a *backbone*. The backbone exists solely as a conduit that enables the segments to communicate with each other. One common configuration for an office building with multiple floors calls for a horizontal segment connecting all of the workstations on each floor and a backbone running vertically from the top of the building to the bottom that connects all of the segments. Such a configuration is illustrated in Figure 1.5.

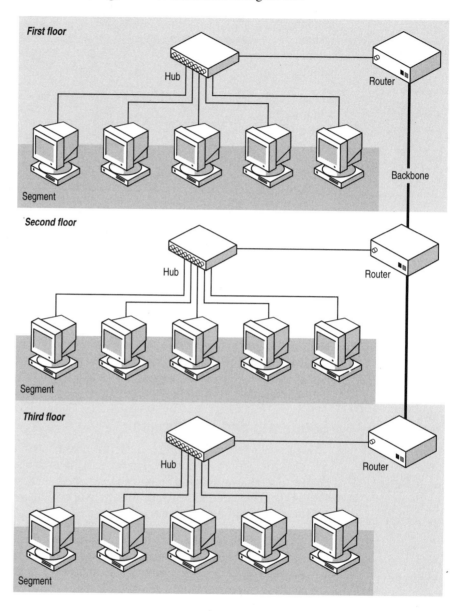

Figure 1.5   An enterprise network spanning an entire building can consist of an individual segment on each floor and a backbone connecting the segments on all of the floors.

This type of configuration increases the efficiency of the network by using the backbone to carry all of the traffic going from one network to another. No packet has to traverse more than three LANs using this model. By contrast, if you were to connect each of the horizontal segments to the adjacent segment, daisy-chain fashion, most of the internetwork packets would have to travel through many more segments to reach their destinations, thus burdening the intermediate segments with through traffic for no good reason.

In many cases, the backbone network runs at a higher speed than the segments, and may also use a different type of network medium. For example, a typical network might use 10BaseT Ethernet, running at 10 megabits per second (Mbps) over copper UTP cable, for the segments, and it might use 100BaseFX Ethernet, running at 100 Mbps over fiber optic cable, for the backbone. There are two reasons for using a different type of network for the backbone. First, the backbone by definition must carry all of the internetwork traffic generated by all of the segments, and a faster protocol can prevent the backbone from becoming a bottleneck. Second, the backbone may have to span a much longer distance than the segments, and a network that uses fiber optic cable can better handle long distances.

Client/Server and Peer-to-Peer Networking

Computers can interact with each other on a network in different ways, and fulfill different roles. There are two primary networking models used to define this interaction, called *client/server* and *peer-to-peer*. On a client/server network, certain computers act as servers while others act as clients. A *server* is simply a computer (or more precisely, an application running on a computer) that provides a service to other computers. The most basic network functions are the sharing of files and the sharing of printers; the machines that do this are called file servers and print servers. There are many other types of servers as well: application servers, e-mail servers, Web servers, database servers, and so on. A client is a computer that avails itself of the services provided by servers.

Note While servers are often thought of as computers, they are actually applications. A single computer can conceivably run several different server applications at the same time and, in most cases, perform client operations as well.

At one time, it was common for computers to be limited to either client or server roles. Novell NetWare, which was the most popular network operating system for many years, consists of a separate server operating system and clients that run on DOS and Microsoft Windows workstations. The server computer functions only as a server and the clients only as clients. The most popular network operating systems today, however, include both client and server functions. All of the current versions of Windows (95, 98, Me, NT, and 2000), for example, can function as both clients and servers. How to utilize each system is up to the network administrator. You will learn more about the networking capabilities of various operating systems in Chapter 4, "Networking Software."

You can construct a client/server network by designating one or more of the networked computers as a server and the rest as clients, even when all of the computers can perform both functions. In most cases, servers are better-equipped systems, and on a large network many administrators connect them to the backbone so that all of the segments have equal access to them. A client/server network typically uses a directory service to store information about the network and its users. Users log on to the directory service instead of logging on to individual computers, and administrators can control access to the entire network using the directory service as a central resource.

On a peer-to-peer network, every computer is an equal, and functions both as a client and as a server. This means that any computer can share its resources with the network and access the shared resources on other computers. You can therefore use any of the Windows versions mentioned earlier for this type of network, but you cannot use a dedicated client/server operating system like NetWare. Peer-to-peer networks are generally limited to 10 or 15 nodes or less on a single LAN, because each system has to maintain its own user accounts and other security settings.

Exercise 1.1: Networking Definitions

Match the concepts in the numbered list with the definitions that follow it.

Concepts

1. Full-duplex
2. Broadband
3. Circuit switching
4. Client/server network
5. Baseband

Definitions

a. A medium that carries multiple signals simultaneously

b. A network in which a connection is established before any data is transmitted

c. A network on which systems perform designated roles

d. A medium that carries traffic in both directions simultaneously

e. A medium that carries only one signal

Lesson 2: The OSI Reference Model

The OSI reference model illustrates the networking process as being divided into seven layers. This theoretical construct makes it easier to learn and understand the concepts involved. At the top of the model is the application that requires access to a resource on the network, and at the bottom is the network medium itself. As data moves down through the layers of the model, the various protocols operating there prepare and package it for transmission over the network. Once the data arrives at its destination, it moves up through the layers on the receiving system, where the same protocols perform the same process in reverse.

Run the **c01dem01** video located in the **Demos** folder on the CD-ROM accompanying this book for a demonstration of the data encapsulation process.

After this lesson, you will be able to

- Identify the layers of the OSI reference model
- Describe the functions associated with each of the layers

Estimated lesson time: 50 minutes

In 1983, the International Organization for Standardization (ISO) and what is now the Telecommunications Standardization Sector of the International Telecommunications Union (ITU-T) published a document called "The Basic Reference Model for Open Systems Interconnection." The model described in that document divides a computer's networking functions into seven layers, as shown in Figure 1.6. Originally, this seven-layer structure was to be the model for a new protocol stack, but this never materialized in a commercial form. Instead, the OSI model has come to be used with the existing network protocols as a teaching and reference tool.

Most of the protocols in common use today pre-date the OSI model, so they don't conform exactly to the seven-layer structure. In most cases, single protocols combine the functions of two or more of the layers in the model, and the boundaries between protocols often don't exactly conform to the layer boundaries of the OSI model. However, the model remains an excellent tool for studying the networking process, and professionals frequently make reference to functions and protocols associated with specific layers.

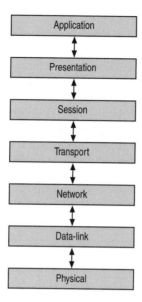

Figure 1.6   The OSI reference model

Data Encapsulation

The interaction between the protocols operating at the various layers of the OSI model takes the form of each protocol adding headers (and in one case, a footer) to the information it receives from the layer above it. For example, when an application generates a request for a network resource, it passes the request down through the protocol stack. When the request reaches the transport layer, the transport layer protocol adds its own header to the request. The *header* consists of fields containing information that is specific to the functions of that protocol, and the original request becomes the data field, or payload, for the transport layer protocol.

The transport layer protocol, after adding its header, passes the request down to the network layer. The network layer protocol then adds its own header in front of the transport layer protocol's header. The original request and the transport layer protocol header thus become the payload for the network layer protocol. This entire construct then becomes the payload for the data-link layer protocol, which typically adds both a header and a footer. The final product, called a *packet,* is then ready for transmission over the network. After the packet reaches its destination, the entire process is repeated in reverse. The protocol at each successive layer of the stack (traveling upwards this time) removes the header applied by its equivalent protocol in the transmitting system. When the process is complete, the original request arrives at the application for which it was destined in the same condition as when it was generated.

The process by which the protocols add their headers and footer to the request generated by the application is called *data encapsulation* (see Figure 1.7). The procedure is functionally similar to the process of preparing a letter for mailing. The application request is the letter itself, and the protocol headers represent the process of putting the letter into an envelope, addressing, stamping, and mailing it.

 Run the **c01dem02**, **c01dem03**, and **c01dem04** videos located in the **Demos** folder on the CD-ROM accompanying this book for a demonstration of the data encapsulation process.

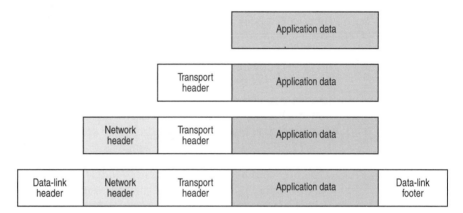

Figure 1.7   As data travels down through the protocol stack, it is encapsulated by the protocols operating at the various layers.

The functions of the OSI model layers are covered in the following sections.

The Physical Layer

The physical layer, at the bottom of the OSI model, is, as the name implies, the layer that defines the nature of the network's hardware elements, such as what medium the network uses, how the network is installed, and the nature of the signals used to transmit binary data over the network. The physical layer also defines what kind of network interface adapter must be installed in each computer and what kind of hubs (if any) to use. Physical layer options include various types of copper or fiber optic cable, as well as many different wireless solutions. In the case of a LAN, the physical layer specifications are directly related to the data-link layer protocol used by the network. When you select a data-link layer protocol, you must use one of the physical layer specifications supported by that protocol.

For example, Ethernet is a data-link layer protocol that supports several differ-ent physical layer options. You can use one of two types of coaxial cable with Ethernet, any one of several types of twisted pair cable, or fiber optic cable. The specifications for each of these options include a great deal of detailed information about the physical layer requirements, such as the exact type of cable and connectors to use, how long the cables can be, how many hubs you can have, and many other factors. These specific conditions are required for the protocol to function properly. A cable segment that is too long, for example, can prevent an Ethernet system from detecting packet collisions. When the system can't detect errors, it can't correct them, and data is lost.

While some aspects of the physical layer are defined in the data-link layer protocol standard, others are defined in separate specifications. One of the most commonly used physical layer specifications is the "Commercial Building Telecommunications Cabling Standard," published jointly by the American National Standards Institute (ANSI), the Electronics Industry Association (EIA), and the Telecommunications Industry Association (TIA) as EIA/TIA 568A. This document includes detailed specifications for installing cables for data networks in a commercial environment, including the required distances from sources of electromagnetic interference and other general cabling policies. Nowadays, in most cases, large network cabling jobs are outsourced to specialized contractors, and any such contractor you hire for a LAN cabling job should be intimately familiar with EIA/TIA 568A and other such documents, including your city's building codes.

The other communications element found at the physical layer is the particular type of signaling that is used to transmit data over the network medium. For copper-based cables, these signals are electrical charges. For fiber optic cables, the signals are pulses of light. Other types of network media can use radio frequencies, infrared pulses, and other types of signals. In addition to the physical nature of the signals, the physical layer dictates the signaling scheme that the computers use. The signaling scheme is the pattern of electrical charges or light pulses used to encode the binary data generated by the upper layers. Ethernet systems use a signaling scheme called Manchester encoding, and Token Ring systems use a scheme called Differential Manchester.

The Data-Link Layer

The protocol at the data-link layer is the conduit between the computer's networking hardware and its networking software. Network layer protocols pass their outgoing data down to the data-link layer protocol, which packages it for transmission over the network. When the other systems on the network receive the transmitted data, their data-link layer protocols process it and pass it up to the network layer.

When it comes to designing and building a LAN, the data-link layer protocol you choose is the single most important factor in determining what hardware you buy and how you install it. To implement a data-link layer protocol, you need the following hardware and software:

- Network interface adapters (When an adapter is a discrete card plugged into a bus slot, it is referred to as a network interface card or NIC.)

- Network adapter drivers
- Network cables (or other media) and ancillary connecting hardware
- Network hubs (in some cases)

Network interface adapters and hubs are both designed for specific data-link layer protocols, and are not interchangeable with products for other protocols. Some network cables are protocol-specific, while others can be used with various protocols.

By far the most popular data-link layer LAN protocol in use today (and throughout the history of the LAN) is Ethernet. Token Ring is a distant second, followed by other protocols such as the Fiber Distributed Data Interface (FDDI). Data-link layer protocol specifications typically include the following three basic elements:

- A format for the frame (that is, the header and footer applied to the network layer data before transmission)
- A mechanism for controlling access to the network medium
- One or more physical layer specifications for use with the protocol

These three components are discussed in the following sections.

Frame Format

The data-link layer protocol encapsulates the data it receives from the network layer protocol by adding a header and footer to it, forming what is called a *frame* (see Figure 1.8). Using the mail analogy given earlier, the header and footer are the equivalent of the envelope that you use to mail a letter. They contain the address of the system sending the packet and the address of its destination system. For LAN protocols like Ethernet and Token Ring, these addresses are 6-byte hexadecimal strings assigned to network interface adapters by their manufacturers. The addresses are referred to as hardware addresses or media access control (MAC) addresses, to distinguish them from addresses used at other layers of the OSI model.

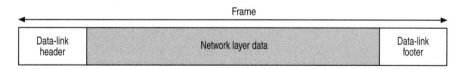

Figure 1.8 A typical data-link layer protocol frame contains source and destination address fields, a network layer protocol identifier, and error detection information.

Note Protocols operating at different layers of the OSI model have different names for the data structures they create by adding a header to the data they receive from the layer above. What the data-link layer protocol calls a frame, for example, the network layer protocol calls a datagram. Packet is a more generic term for the unit of data created at any layer.

It is important to understand that data-link layer protocols are limited to communications with computers on the same LAN. The hardware address in the header always refers to a computer on the same local network, even if the data's ultimate destination is a system on another network.

The other primary functions of the data-link layer frame are to identify the network layer protocol that generated the data in the packet and to provide error detection information. A computer can use multiple protocols at the network layer, and the data-link layer protocol frame usually contains a code that specifies which network layer protocol generated the data in the packet. This is so that the data-link layer protocol on the receiving system can pass the data to the appropriate protocol at its own network layer.

The error detection information takes the form of a *cyclical redundancy check (CRC)* computation performed on the payload data by the transmitting system, the results of which are included in the frame's footer. On receiving the packet, the receiving system performs the same computation and compares its results to those in the footer. If the results match, the data has been transmitted successfully. If they do not, the receiving system assumes that the packet is corrupted and discards it.

Media Access Control

The computers on a LAN usually share a common half-duplex network medium, which means that it is possible for two computers to transmit data at the same time. When this happens, a packet collision is said to occur, and the data in both packets is lost. One of the main functions of the data-link layer protocol on this type of network is to provide a mechanism that regulates access to the network medium. This mechanism, called a *media access control (MAC)* mechanism, provides each computer with an equal opportunity to transmit its data while minimizing the occurrence of packet collisions.

 Run the **c01dem05**, **c01dem06**, and **c01dem07** videos located in the **Demos** folder on the CD-ROM accompanying this book for a demonstration of media access control.

The MAC mechanism is one of the primary defining characteristics of a data-link layer protocol. Ethernet uses a MAC mechanism called Carrier Sense Multiple

Access with Collision Detection (CSMA/CD). Several other protocols, including Token Ring, use a scheme called token passing.

Note For more information on specific MAC mechanisms, see Chapter 5, "Data-Link Layer Protocols."

Physical Layer Specifications

The data-link layer protocols used on LANs often support more than one network medium, and the protocol standard includes one or more physical layer specifications. The data-link layer and physical layer are closely related, because the characteristics of the network medium have a profound effect on the functionality of the protocol's MAC mechanism. For this reason, you can say that the data-link layer protocols used on a LAN also encompass the functions of the physical layer. There are other data-link layer protocols used for WAN links, however, such as the Serial Line Internet Protocol (SLIP) and the Point-to-Point Protocol (PPP), which do not include physical layer information.

The Network Layer

At first glance, the network layer seems to duplicate some of the functions of the data-link layer. This is not so, however, because network layer protocols are responsible for end-to-end communications, while data-link layer protocols function only on the local LAN. To say that network layer protocols are responsible for end-to-end communications means that the network layer protocol is responsible for a packet's complete journey from the system that created it to its final destination. Depending on the nature of the network, the source and destination systems can be on the same LAN, on different LANs in the same building, or on LANs separated by thousands of miles. When you connect to a server on the Internet, for example, the packets your computer creates may pass through dozens of different networks before reaching their destination. The data-link layer protocol may change many times to accommodate those dozens of networks, but the network layer protocol remains intact throughout the trip.

The Internet Protocol (IP) is the cornerstone of the Transmission Control Protocol/Internet Protocol (TCP/IP) suite, and the most commonly used network layer protocol. Novell NetWare has its own network layer protocol, called Inter-network Packet Exchange (IPX), and the NetBIOS Extended User Interface (NetBEUI) protocol is often used on small Microsoft Windows networks. Most of the functions attributed to the network layer are based on the capabilities of IP.

Like the data-link layer protocol, the network layer protocol applies a header to the data it receives from the layer above it, as shown in Figure 1.9 on the following page. The unit of data created by the network layer protocol, which consists of the transport layer data plus the network header, is called a *datagram*.

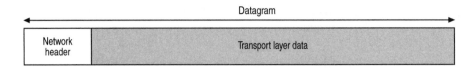

Datagram

| Network header | Transport layer data |

Figure 1.9   The network layer protocol packages transport layer information into a datagram.

The functions associated with the network layer are discussed in the following sections.

Addressing

The network layer protocol header contains source address and destination address fields, just as the data-link layer protocol does. However, in this case, the destination address is the packet's final destination, which may be different from the data-link layer protocol header's destination address. For example, when you type the address of a Web site in your browser, the packet your system generates contains the address of the Web server as its network layer destination, but the data-link layer destination is the address of the router on your LAN that provides you with Internet access.

IP has its own addressing system that is completely separate from the data-link layer addresses. Each computer on an IP network is assigned a 32-bit IP address by an administrator or an automated service. This address identifies both the network on which the computer is located and the computer itself, so that one address can uniquely identify any computer. IPX, on the other hand, uses a separate address to identify the network on which a computer is located and uses the hardware address to identify a computer on the network. NetBEUI identifies computers using a NetBIOS name assigned to each system during its installation.

Fragmenting

Network layer datagrams may have to pass through many different networks on the way to their destinations, and the data-link layer protocols that the datagrams encounter can have different properties and limitations. One of these limitations is the maximum packet size permitted by the protocol. For example, Token Ring frames can be as large as 4,500 bytes, but Ethernet frames are limited to 1,500 bytes. When a large datagram that originated on a Token Ring network is routed to an Ethernet network, the network layer protocol must split it into pieces no larger than 1,500 bytes each. This process is called *fragmentation*.

During the fragmentation process, the network layer protocol splits the datagram into as many pieces as necessary to make them small enough for transmission using the data-link layer protocol. Each fragment becomes a datagram in itself that continues the journey to the network layer destination. The fragments are not reassembled until all of the datagrams that make up the transmission reach the destination system. In some cases, datagrams may be fragmented, and their fragments may be fragmented again repeatedly before reaching their destination.

Routing

Routing is the process of directing a datagram from its source, through an internetwork, and to its ultimate destination using the most efficient path possible. On complex internetworks such as the Internet or a large corporate network, there are often many possible routes to a given destination. The designers of the network deliberately create redundant links so that in the event of a failure of one of the computers on the network, traffic can still find its way to its destination.

The individual LANs that make up an internetwork are connected by routers. The function of a router is to receive incoming traffic from one network and transmit it to a particular destination on another network. There are two types of systems involved in internetwork communications, *end systems* and *intermediate systems*. End systems are the source of individual packets and also their ultimate destination. Routers are the intermediate systems. End systems utilize all seven layers of the OSI model, while packets arriving at intermediate systems rise only as high as the network layer. The router then processes the packet and sends it back down through the stack to be transmitted to its next destination, as shown in Figure 1.10.

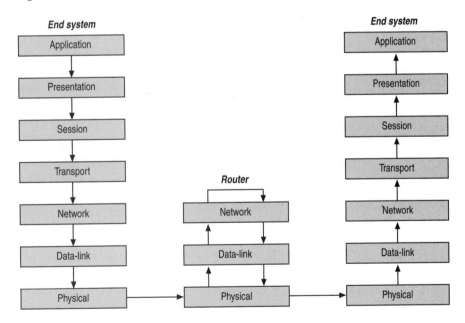

Figure 1.10 The network layer protocol in a router is responsible for accepting incoming packets and transmitting them to the next stop on their journey.

In order to properly direct a packet to its destination, routers maintain information about the network in tables that they store in memory. The information in the tables can be either manually supplied by an administrator or gathered automatically from other routers by using specialized routing protocols. A typical routing table entry specifies the address of another network and the router that packets should use to get to that network. Routing table entries also contain a metric that indicates the comparative efficiency of that particular route. If there are two or more routes to a particular destination, the router selects the more efficient one and passes the datagram down to the data-link layer for transmission to the router specified in the table entry. On large networks, routing can be an extraordinarily complicated process, but most of it is automated and invisible to the average user.

Identifying the Transport Layer Protocol

Just as the data-link layer header specifies the network layer protocol that generates the data that it transports, the network layer header identifies the transport layer protocol from which it receives the data that it carries. With this information, the receiving system can pass the incoming datagrams to the correct transport layer protocol.

The Transport Layer

The transport layer protocols provide services that complement those provided by the network layer. The transport and network layer protocols used to transmit data are often thought of as a matched pair. This is seen in the case of TCP/IP. These protocols include the TCP, which runs at the transport layer, plus the IP, which runs at the network layer. Most protocol suites provide two or more transport layer protocols, which provide different levels of service. The alternative to TCP is the User Datagram Protocol (UDP). The IPX protocol suite also provides a choice between transport layer protocols, including the NetWare Core Protocol (NCP) and Sequenced Packet Exchange (SPX).

The difference between the protocols provided at the transport layer within a particular protocol suite is that some are connection oriented and some are connectionless. A *connection-oriented* protocol is one in which the two communicating systems exchange messages to establish a connection before they transmit any application data. This ensures that the systems are both active and ready to exchange messages. TCP, for example, is a connection-oriented protocol. When you use a Web browser to connect to an Internet server, the browser and the server first perform what is known as a three-way handshake to establish the connection. Only then does the browser transmit the address of the desired Web page to the server. When the data transmission is completed, the systems perform a similar handshake to break down the connection.

Connection-oriented protocols also provide additional services such as packet acknowledgment, data segmentation, flow control, and end-to-end error detection and correction. Systems generally use this type of protocol to transmit relatively large amounts of information that can't tolerate even a single bit error, such as data or program files, and these services ensure the correct transmission of the data. Because of these services, connection-oriented protocols are often said to be *reliable*. Reliable here is a technical term that refers to the fact that each packet transmitted using the protocol has been acknowledged by the recipient and verified as having been transmitted without error. The drawback of this type of protocol is that it greatly increases the amount of control data exchanged by the two systems. In addition to the extra messages needed to establish and terminate the connection, the header applied by a connection-oriented protocol is substantially larger than that of a connectionless one. In the case of the TCP/IP transport layer protocols, TCP uses a 20-byte header and UDP uses only an 8-byte one.

A *connectionless* protocol is one in which there is no preliminary communication between the two systems before the transmission of application data. The sender simply transmits its data to the destination without knowing if the system is ready to receive data, or even if the system exists. Systems generally use connectionless protocols, such as UDP, for brief transactions that consist only of single requests and responses. The response from the recipient functions as a tacit acknowledgment of the transmission.

Note Connection-oriented and connectionless protocols are not limited to the transport layer. Network layer protocols are usually connectionless, for example, because they leave the reliability functions to the transport layer.

Transport layer protocols typically provide a path through the layers above, just as network and data-link layer protocols do. The headers for both TCP and UDP, for example, include port numbers that identify the applications from which the packet originated and for which it is destined.

The Session Layer

The session layer is the point at which the actual protocols used on networks begin to differ substantially from the OSI model. There are no separate session layer protocols as there are at the lower layers. Session layer functions are instead integrated into other protocols that also include presentation and application layer functions. The transport, network, data-link, and physical layers are concerned with the proper transmission of data across the network, but the protocols at the session layer and above are not involved in that part of the communications process. The session layer provides 22 services, many of which are concerned with the ways in which networked systems exchange information. The most important of these services are called dialog control and dialog separation.

The exchange of information between two systems on the network is called a dialog, and *dialog control* is the selection of a mode that the systems will use to exchange messages. When the dialog is begun, the systems can choose one of two modes, two-way alternate (TWA) mode or two-way simultaneous (TWS) mode. In TWA mode, the two systems exchange a data token, and only the computer in possession of the token is permitted to transmit data. This eliminates problems caused by messages that cross in transit. TWS mode is more complex, because there is no token and both systems can transmit at any time, even simultaneously.

Dialog separation is the process of creating checkpoints in a data stream that enable communicating systems to synchronize their functions. The difficulty of the checkpointing process depends on whether the dialog is using TWA or TWS mode. Systems involved in a TWA dialog perform minor synchronizations, which require only a single exchange of checkpointing messages, while systems using a TWS dialog perform a major synchronization using a major/activity token.

The Presentation Layer

There is only one function found at the presentation layer, and that is the translation of syntax between different systems. In some cases, computers communicating over a network use different syntaxes, and the presentation layer enables them to negotiate a common syntax for the network communications. When the communicating systems establish a connection at the presentation layer, they exchange messages containing information about the syntaxes they have in common, and together they choose the syntax they will use during the session.

Both of the systems involved in the connection have an *abstract syntax*, which is their native form of communication. During the negotiation process, the systems choose a *transfer syntax*. The transmitting system converts its abstract syntax to the transfer syntax, and the receiving system converts the transfer syntax to its own abstract syntax. When called for, the systems can select a transfer syntax that provides additional services, such as data compression or encryption.

The Application Layer

The application layer is the entrance point that programs use to access the OSI model and utilize network resources. Most application layer protocols provide services that programs use to access the network, such as the Simple Mail Transfer Protocol (SMTP), which most e-mail programs use to send e-mail messages. In some cases, such as the File Transfer Protocol (FTP), the application layer protocol is a program in itself.

Application layer protocols often include the session and presentation layer functions. As a result, a typical protocol stack consists of four separate protocols, which run at the application, transport, network, and data-link layers.

Exercise 1.2: OSI Model Layers

For each of the protocols, functions, or concepts listed below, specify the OSI model layer with which it is associated.

1. Ethernet

2. Dialog separation

3. Transfer syntax

4. Routing

5. Segmentation

6. SMTP

7. Differential Manchester

Chapter Summary

The key points covered in this chapter are as follows.

Network Communications

- Computer networks use signals to transmit data, and protocols are the languages computers use to communicate.

- Protocols provide a variety of communications services to the computers on the network.

- Local area networks connect computers using a shared, half-duplex, baseband medium, and wide area networks link distant networks.

- Enterprise networks often consist of clients and servers on horizontal segments connected by a common backbone, while peer-to-peer networks consist of a small number of computers on a single LAN.

The OSI Reference Model

- The OSI reference model consists of seven layers: physical, data-link, network, transport, session, presentation, and application.

- The OSI model layers usually do not correspond exactly to the protocol stack running on an actual system.

- The data-link layer protocols often include physical layer specifications.

- The network and transport layer protocols work together to provide a cumulative end-to-end communication service.

- The functions of the session, presentation, and application layers are often combined into a single application layer protocol.

Chapter Review

1. Which layer of the OSI reference model is responsible for controlling access to the network medium?

2. On which type of network does each computer maintain its own permissions and security settings?

3. A language that two computers "speak" while communicating over a network is called _____.

4. A series of LANs connected together by any means is called _____.

5. What kind of network is often used to connect horizontal segments on a large enterprise internetwork?

6. Which layer of the OSI model is responsible for translating different syntaxes?

7. A network in which the medium carries only one signal is called _____.

8. An example of full-duplex communications is _____.

9. The address of a packet's final destination is specified in the _____ layer.

10. TCP is an example of a _____ layer protocol.

11. Electrical voltages, light pulses, and infrared waves are all examples of types of _____.

12. A technology used to connect LANs at distant locations is called _____.

13. The type of network in which data is split into discrete units that are transmitted over the network individually is called _____.

14. The process by which a receiving system sends messages instructing a sending system to slow down its transmission rate is called _____.

15. A protocol that uses a handshake to establish a connection before sending data is called _____.

CHAPTER 2

Network Hardware

About This Chapter

This chapter examines the components used to build a standard local area network (LAN), including network interface adapters, cables, and hubs. There are other hardware devices used on more complex networks, but these are the basic elements found on almost every LAN. The Network+ exam invariably includes questions about these components and the procedures for installing and troubleshooting them.

Lesson 1: Network Cables

Most LANs use some form of cable as their network medium. Although there are many types of wireless media, cables are more reliable and generally provide greater transmission speeds than other media. Data-link layer protocols often provide more than one cable specification to choose from. Each specification includes the type of cable to use, the cable grade, and the basic guidelines for installing it. The type of cable you choose should be based on the requirements of your installation, the nature of the site where your network is to be installed, and, of course, your budget.

After this lesson, you will be able to

- List the cabling topologies used to build networks
- Name the types of cables used to build local area networks
- Understand the grading systems used for the various cable types

Estimated lesson time: 40 minutes

Cable Topologies

As explained in Chapter 1, the topology of a network is the pattern used to connect computers. Network topology is directly related to the type of cable used. You cannot select a particular type of cable and install it using just any toplogy. However, you can create individual LANs using a different topology for each LAN and connect them together using devices such as bridges, switches, and routers.

The three primary topologies used to build LANs are as follows:

- Bus
- Star
- Ring

The Bus Topology

A bus network is one in which the computers are connected in a single line, with each system logically cabled to the next system. Bus networks are illustrated in Figure 2.1. Early Ethernet systems used the bus topology with coaxial cable, a type of network that is rarely seen today. The cabling of a bus network can take two forms: *thick* and *thin*. Thick Ethernet networks use a single length of coaxial cable and connect the computers to it using smaller individual cables called transceiver cables, as shown on the top half of Figure 2.1. Thin Ethernet networks use separate lengths of a narrower type of coaxial cable, and each length of cable connects one computer to the next, as shown in the bottom half of Figure 2.1.

Run the **c02dem01** video located in the **Demos** folder on the CD-ROM accompanying this book for a demonstration of Thin Ethernet bus topology connections.

Note The transceiver is an integral component of the network interface that is responsible for both transmitting and receiving data over the network medium. Thick Ethernet is the only form of Ethernet network that uses a transceiver that's separate from the network interface adapter. The transceiver itself connects to the coaxial cable using a device called a *vampire tap*, named for the metal teeth with which it penetrates the cable sheath to make a connection with the copper conductor inside. The transceiver is then connected to the network interface adapter in the computer using a transceiver cable. All of the other Ethernet physical layer standards have their transceivers integrated into the network interface adapter card, and do not require separate transceiver cables.

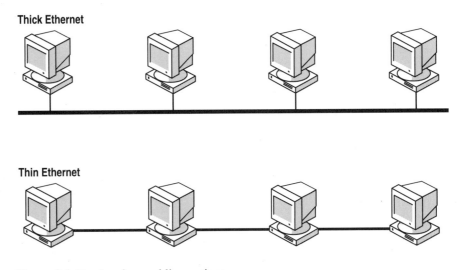

Figure 2.1 Bus topology cabling options

When any one of the computers on the network transmits data, the signals travel down the cable in both directions, reaching all of the other systems. A bus network always has two open ends, which must be terminated. *Termination* is the process of installing a resistor pack at each end of the bus to negate the signals that arrive there. Without terminators, the signals reaching the end of the bus would reflect back in the other direction and interfere with the newer signals being transmitted.

Run the **c02dem02**, **c02dem03**, **c02dem04**, **c02dem05**, and **c02dem06** videos located in the **Demos** folder on the CD-ROM accompanying this book for a demonstration of bus topology communications, signal bounce, and termination.

The main problem with the bus topology is that a single faulty connector, terminator, or break in the cable affects the functionality of the entire network. Signals that cannot pass beyond a certain point fail to reach all of the computers beyond that point. In addition, the break in the cable is also unterminated. On the half of the network that does receive the transmitted signals, the data can be affected by reflected signals. This is one of the primary reasons that bus networks are almost never used nowadays.

 Run the **c02dem07** and **c02dem08** videos located in the **Demos** folder on the CD-ROM accompanying this book for a demonstration of a bus topology failure.

The Star Topology

While the bus topology has the computers in a network logically connected directly to each other, the star topology uses a central cabling nexus called a *hub* or *concentrator*. In a star network, each computer is connected to the hub using a separate cable, as shown in Figure 2.2. Most LANs installed today use the star topology. LANs can use several different cable types, including various twisted pair and fiber optic configurations. The main advantage of the star network is that each computer has its own dedicated connection to the hub. If a single cable or connector should fail, only one computer is affected.

 Run the **c02dem09**, **c02dem10**, and **c02dem11** videos located in the **Demos** folder on the CD-ROM accompanying this book for a demonstration of star topology.

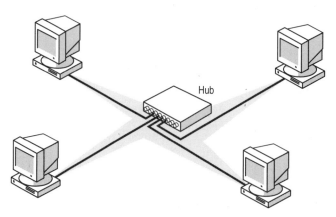

Figure 2.2 The star topology uses an individual connection for each computer to provide a greater measure of fault tolerance than the bus topology.

The disadvantage of the star topology is that an additional piece of hardware, the hub, is required to implement it. If the hub should fail, the entire network goes down. However, this is a relatively rare occurrence, since hubs are usually found in a protected environment, such as a data center or server closet.

The Ring Topology

As far as signal transmissions are concerned, a ring network is like a bus in that each computer is logically connected to the next. The difference is that in a ring network the two ends are connected instead of being terminated. This enables a signal originating on one computer to travel around the ring to all of the other computers and eventually back to its point of origin. Networks such as Token Ring, which use token passing for their media access control (MAC) mechanism (as explained in Lesson 2: The OSI Reference Model, in Chapter 1, "Networking Basics"), are wired using a ring topology. The most important thing to understand about the ring topology, however, is that it is strictly a logical construction, not a physical one. Or, to be more precise, the ring exists in the wiring of the network, but not in the cabling.

Note A *cable* is a device that contains a number of signal conductors, usually in the form of separate wires. A twisted pair cable, for example, contains eight individual wires within a single sheath.

When you look at a network that uses the ring topology, you may be puzzled to see what looks like a star. In fact, the cables for a ring network connect to a hub and take the form of a star. The ring topology is actually implemented logically, using the wiring inside the cables. Ring networks use a special type of hub, called a multistation access unit (MAU), which receives data through one port and transmits it out through the next. This process continues until the MAU has transmitted the signals to each computer on the ring. If you were to remove the wires from the cable sheath, you would have a circuit that runs from the MAU to each computer and back to the MAU, as shown in Figure 2.3.

Run the **c02dem12**, **c02dem13**, **c02dem14**, and **c02dem15** videos located in the **Demos** folder on the CD-ROM accompanying this book for a demonstration of the ring topology.

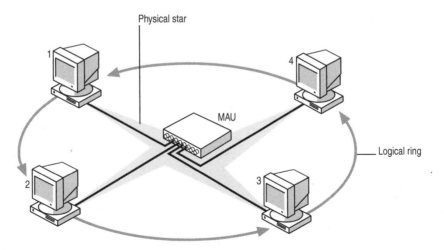

Figure 2.3 A ring network uses a ring topology in a logical sense only. The cables are actually arranged in the form of a star.

The design of the star topology used by the ring makes it possible for the network to function even when a cable or connector fails. The MAU contains special circuitry that removes a malfunctioning workstation from the ring. By comparison, a network that is literally cabled as a ring would have no MAU, but that would cause the network to cease to function in the event of a cable failure.

 Run the **c02dem16** video located in the **Demos** folder on the CD-ROM accompanying this book for a demonstration of a ring topology failure.

Cable Types

There are three primary types of cable used to build LANs: coaxial, twisted pair, and fiber optic. Coaxial and twisted pair cables are copper-based, while fiber optic cables use glass or plastic conductors.

Coaxial Cable

Coaxial cable is so named because it contains two conductors within the sheath. Unlike other two-conductor cables, however, coaxial cable has one conductor inside the other. This is illustrated in Figure 2.4. At the center of the cable is the copper core, which actually carries the electrical signals. The core can be solid copper or composed of braided strands of copper. Surrounding the core is a layer of insulation, and surrounding that is the second conductor, which is typically made of braided copper mesh. This second conductor functions as the cable's ground. Finally, the entire assembly is encased in an insulating sheath made of PVC or Teflon.

Warning The outer sheath—also called a casing—of electrical cables can be made of different types of materials, and the sheath you use should depend on your local building codes and the location of the cables in the network's site. Cables that run through a building's air spaces (called *plenums*) usually must have a sheath made of a material that doesn't generate toxic gases when it burns. Plenum cable costs more than standard PVC-sheathed cable and is somewhat more difficult to install, but it's an important feature that should not be overlooked when you are considering what type of cable to purchase.

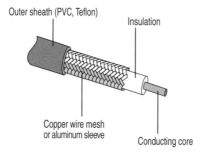

Figure 2.4 Coaxial cable consists of two electrical conductors sharing the same axis, with insulation in between and encased in a protective sheath.

There are two types of coaxial cable that have been used in local area networking: RG8, also known as Thick Ethernet, and RG58, which is known as Thin Ethernet. These two cables are similar in construction but differ primarily in their thickness (0.405 inches for RG8 versus 0.195 inches for RG58) and in the types of connectors they use (N connectors for RG8 and BNC connectors for RG58). Both cable types are wired using a bus topology.

Note Thick Ethernet and Thin Ethernet are also known as *10Base5* and *10Base2*, respectively. These abbreviations indicate that the networks on which they are used run at 10 Mbps, use baseband transmissions, and are limited to maximum cable segment lengths of 500 and 200 (actually 185) meters, respectively.

Coaxial cable is used today for many applications, most noticeably on cable television networks, but it has fallen out of favor as a LAN medium. This is due to the bus topology's fault-tolerance problems and the size and relative inflexibility of the cables, which make them difficult to install and maintain.

Twisted Pair Cable

Twisted pair cable wired in a star topology is the most common type of network medium used in LANs today. Most of the LANs installed today use unshielded twisted pair (UTP) cable, but there is also a shielded twisted pair (STP) variety for use in environments more prone to electromagnetic interference. UTP cable contains eight separate conductors, as opposed to the two used in coaxial cable. Each conductor is a separate insulated wire, and the eight wires are arranged in four pairs of twisted conductors. The twists prevent the signals on the different wire pairs from interfering with each other (called *crosstalk*) and also provide resistance to outside interference. The four wire pairs are then encased in a single sheath, as shown in Figure 2.5. The connectors used for twisted pair cables are called RJ45s; they are the same as the connectors used on standard telephone cables, except that they have eight electrical contacts instead of four.

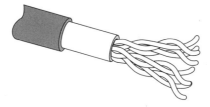

Figure 2.5 UTP cable has four separate wire pairs, each pair individually twisted, enclosed in a protective sheath.

Twisted pair cable has been used for telephone installations for decades; its adaptation to LAN use is relatively recent. Twisted pair cable has replaced coaxial cable in the data networking world, because it has several distinct advantages. First, because it contains eight separate wires, the cable is more flexible than the more solidly constructed coaxial cable. This makes it easier to flex, which simplifies installation. The second major advantage is that there are thousands of qualified telephone cable installers who can easily adapt to installing LAN cables as well. In new construction, telephone and LAN cables are often installed at the same time, by the same contractor.

UTP Cable Grades

UTP cable comes in a variety of different grades, called "categories" by the Electronics Industry Association (EIA) and the Telecommunications Industry Association (TIA), the combination being referred to as EIA/TIA. These categories are listed in Table 2.1. The two most significant UTP grades for LAN use are Category 3 and Category 5. Category 3 cable was designed for voice-grade telephone networks and eventually came to be used for Ethernet. Category 3 cable is sufficient for 10 Mbps Ethernet networks (where it is called 10BaseT), but it is generally not used for Fast Ethernet (except under certain conditions). If you have an existing Category 3 cable installation, you can use it to build a standard Ethernet network, but virtually all new UTP cable installations today use at least Category 5 cable.

Table 2.1   EIA/TIA UTP cable grades

Category 1	Used for voice-grade telephone networks only; not for data transmissions
Category 2	Used for voice-grade telephone networks, as well as IBM dumb-terminal connections to mainframe computers
Category 3	Used for voice-grade telephone networks, 10 Mbps Ethernet, 4 Mbps Token Ring, 100BaseT4 Fast Ethernet, and 100VG AnyLAN
Category 4	Used for 16 Mbps Token Ring networks
Category 5	Used for 100BaseTX Fast Ethernet, SONet, and OC-3 ATM
Category 5e	Used for Gigabit (1000 Mbps) Ethernet protocols

Tip When you install a network with a particular grade of cable, you need to know more than the category of the cable. You must also be sure that all of the connectors, wall plates, and patch panels you use are rated for the same category as the cable. A network connection is only as strong as its weakest link.

Category 5 UTP is suitable for 100BaseTX Fast Ethernet networks running at 100 Mbps, as well as for slower protocols. In addition to the officially ratified EIA/TIA categories, there are other UTP cable grades available that have not yet been standardized. A cable standard called Level 5 by a company called Anixter, Inc. is currently being marketed using names such as Enhanced Category 5. This cable increases the bandwidth of Category 5 from 100 to 350 MHz, making it suitable to run the latest Gigabit Ethernet protocol at 1,000 Mbps (1 Gbps). Level 6 cable increases the bandwidth even further.

Note There is also a Fast Ethernet protocol called 100BaseT4 that is designed to use Category 3 UTP cable and run at 100 Mbps. This is possible because 100BaseT4 uses all four wire pairs in the cable, while 100BaseTX uses only two pairs. See Chapter 5, "Data-Link Layer Protocols," for more information.

STP Cable Grades

Shielded twisted pair cable is similar in construction to UTP, except that it has only two pairs of wires and it also has additional foil or mesh shielding around each pair. The additional shielding in STP cable makes it preferable to UTP in installations where electromagnetic interference is a problem, often due to the proximity of electrical equipment. The various types of STP cable were standardized by IBM, who developed the Token Ring protocol that originally used them. STP networks use Type 1A for longer cable runs and Type 6A for patch cables. Type 1A contains two pairs of 22 gauge solid wires with foil shielding, and Type 6A contains two pairs of 26 gauge stranded wires with foil or mesh shielding. Token Ring STP networks also use large, bulky connectors called IBM data connectors (IDCs). However most Token Ring LANs today use UTP cable.

Note Token Ring networks, both UTP and STP, use the ring topology implemented in a MAU, even though the cable is installed in the form of a star.

Fiber Optic Cable

Fiber optic cable is a completely different type of network medium. Instead of carrying signals over copper conductors in the form of electrical voltages, fiber optic cables transmit pulses of light over a glass or plastic conductor. Fiber optic cable is completely resistant to the electromagnetic interference that so easily affects copper-based cables. Fiber optic cables are also much less subject to attenuation than are copper cables. *Attenuation* is the tendency of a signal to weaken as it travels over a cable. The longer the cable, the weaker the signal gets. On copper cables, signals weaken to the point of unreadability after 100 to 500 meters (depending on the type of cable). Some fiber optic cables, by contrast, can span distances up to 120 kilometers without excessive signal degradation. This makes fiber optic the medium of choice for installations that span long distances or that connect buildings on a campus. Fiber optic cable is also inherently more secure than copper, because it is not possible to tap into a fiber optic link without affecting the normal communication over that link.

A fiber optic cable, as illustrated in Figure 2.6, consists of a clear glass or clear plastic core that actually carries the light pulses, and is surrounded by a reflective layer called the cladding. Around the cladding is a plastic spacer layer, a protective layer of woven Kevlar fibers, and an outer sheath.

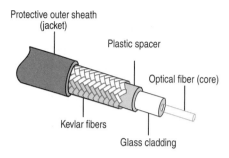

Figure 2.6 Fiber optic cable has a glass or plastic core surrounded by cladding that reflects the light pulses back and forth along the cable's length.

There are two primary types of fiber optic cable, called singlemode and multimode. The difference between the two is in the thickness of the core and the cladding. The measurements are the primary specifications used to identify each type of cable. Singlemode fiber typically has a core diameter of 8.3 microns, and the thickness of the core and cladding together is 125 microns. You will generally see this referred to as 8.3/125 singlemode fiber. Multimode fiber is usually rated as 62.5/125.

Singlemode fiber uses a single-wavelength laser as a light source, and as a result, it can carry signals for extremely long distances. For this reason, singlemode fiber is more commonly found in outdoor installations that span long distances, such as telephone and cable television networks. This type of cable is less suited to LAN installations because it is much more expensive than multimode and has a higher bend radius, meaning that it cannot be bent around corners as tightly. Multimode fiber, by contrast, uses a light emitting diode (LED) as a light source instead of a laser and carries multiple wavelengths. Multimode fiber cannot span distances as long as singlemode, but it bends around corners better and is much cheaper.

Installing fiber optic cable is very different from any copper cable installation. The tools and testing equipment required for installation are different, as are the cabling guidelines. Generally speaking, fiber optic cable is quite a bit more expensive than twisted pair or coaxial in every way, although prices have come down in recent years.

Exercise 2.1: Network Cable Types

Match the applications in the left column with the network cable types in the right column that best suit them.

1. Uses the bus topology	a. UTP
2. Used for the original Token Ring networks	b. Singlemode fiber optic
3. Used for Gigabit Ethernet networks	c. Shielded twisted pair
4. Contains eight wires	d. Coaxial cable
5. Used for LANs that span long distances	e. Category 5e UTP
6. Uses a laser to generate signals	f. Multimode fiber optic

Lesson 2: Network Interface Adapters

The network interface adapter (called the network interface card, or NIC, when installed in a computer's expansion slot) is the component that provides the link between a computer and the network of which it is a part. Every computer must have an adapter that connects to the system's expansion bus and provides a connection to the network medium. Some computers have the network interface adapter integrated into the motherboard, but in the majority of cases the adapter takes the form of an expansion card that plugs into the system's ISA, PCI, or PC Card bus. An ISA-bus network interface card is illustrated in Figure 2.7. The network connection is, in most cases, a cable jack such as an RJ45 for UTP cables, but it can also be a wireless transmitter of some sort.

After this lesson, you will be able to

- Describe the functions of a network interface adapter
- List the various types of network interface cards on the market
- Understand the NIC installation and troubleshooting process

Estimated lesson time: 30 minutes

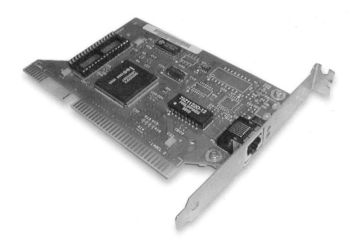

Figure 2.7 Network interface adapters usually take the form of expansion cards.

The network interface adapter, in cooperation with its device driver, is responsible for performing most of the functions of the data-link layer protocol, and those of the physical layer. When you buy a NIC for a computer, you must select one for a particular protocol, such as Ethernet or Token Ring; they are not interchangeable. You must also select a card that plugs into the appropriate type of bus slot in the computer, and that has the proper connector for the network medium. PCI cards are generally preferable, because the slots are self-configuring and the bus is much faster than ISA, but you may use an ISA card if the computer has only ISA slots available. Ensure that the data rate of the card is compatible with the other network components. Some NICs have more than one cable connector, which enables you to connect to different types of network media, but these combo NICs can be much more expensive than those with only one connector.

Tip One of the few scenarios in which combo NICs are practical is when a large number of cards are needed for an internetwork that uses multiple cable types and it is cheaper to buy the NICs in quantity. Many NIC manufacturers sell their products in multi-unit packs that are deeply discounted.

Understanding Network Interface Adapter Functions

Network interface adapters perform a variety of functions that are crucial to getting data to and from the computer over the network. These functions are as follows:

- **Data encapsulation** The network interface adapter and its driver are responsible for building the frame around the data generated by the network layer protocol, in preparation for transmission. The network interface adapter also reads the contents of incoming frames and passes the data to the appropriate network layer protocol.

- **Signal encoding and decoding** The network interface adapter implements the physical layer encoding scheme that converts the binary data generated by the network layer—now encapsulated in the frame—into electrical voltages, light pulses, or whatever other signal type the network medium uses, and converts received signals to binary data for use by the network layer.

- **Data transmission and reception** The primary function of the network interface adapter is to generate and transmit signals of the appropriate type over the network and to receive incoming signals. The nature of the signals depends on the network medium and the data-link layer protocol. On a typical LAN, every computer receives all of the packets transmitted over the network, and the network interface adapter examines the destination address in each packet, to see if it is intended for that computer. If so, the network interface adapter passes the packet to the computer for processing by the next layer in the protocol stack; if not, the network interface adapter discards the packet.

- **Data buffering** Network interface adapters transmit and receive data one frame at a time, so they have built-in buffers that enable them to store data arriving either from the computer or from the network until a frame is complete and ready for processing.

- **Serial/parallel conversion** The communication between the computer and the network interface adapter runs in parallel, that is, either 16 or 32 bits at a time, depending on the bus the adapter uses. Network communications, however, are serial (running one bit at a time), so the network interface adapter is responsible for performing the conversion between the two types of transmissions.

- **Media access control** The network interface adapter also implements the MAC mechanism that the data-link layer protocol uses to regulate access to the network medium. The nature of the MAC mechanism depends on the protocol used.

Installing a NIC

The process of installing a network interface card consists of physically inserting the card into the computer, configuring the card to use appropriate hardware resources, and installing the card's device driver. Depending on the age and capabilities of the computer, these processes can be very simple or quite a chore.

 Run the **c02dem17** and **c02dem18** videos located in the **Demos** folder on the CD-ROM accompanying this book for a demonstration of a NIC installation.

Warning Before touching the internal components of the computer or removing the NIC from its protective bag, be sure to ground yourself by touching the metal frame of the computer's power supply or use a wrist strap or static-dissipative mat to protect the equipment from damage due to electrostatic discharge.

▶ **To physically install the NIC**

1. Turn off the power to the computer. Inserting a NIC in a slot while the computer is powered up can destroy the NIC. Accidentally dropping a screw or slot cover can also cause serious damage if the computer is powered up.

2. Open the computer case. In some instances, this can be the most difficult part of the installation process. You may have to remove several screws in order to loosen the case cover and wrestle with the computer a bit in order to get the cover off. Many newer systems, on the other hand, secure the case cover with thumbscrews and are much easier to open.

3. Locate a free slot. There are both ISA and PCI NICs on the market, and you must check to see what type of slots the computer has free before you select a card. An ISA card is sufficient for average network use, but this bus is gradually being phased out, and PCI is replacing it. The PCI bus is preferable if you are planning to connect the computer to a Fast Ethernet or other 100 Mbps network.

4. Remove the slot cover. Empty slots are protected by a metal cover that prevents them from being exposed through the back of the computer. Loosen the screw securing the slot cover in place, and remove both the screw and slot cover.

5. Insert the card into the slot. Line up the edge connector on the card with the slot and press it down until it is fully seated, as shown in Figure 2.8.

6. Secure the card. Replace the screw that held the slot cover on. This secures the card firmly into the slot. This is a step that network technicians frequently omit, but an important one, as a yank on the network cable can pull the card

partially out of the slot, causing intermittent problems that are difficult to diagnose.

7. Replace the computer case and secure it with the fasteners provided.

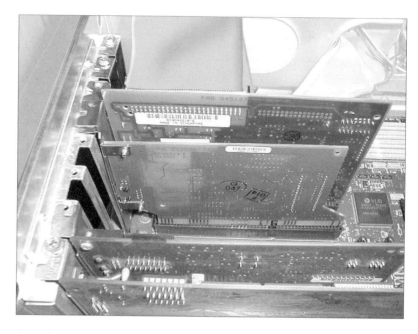

Figure 2.8 Press the NIC down firmly until it is seated all the way into the slot.

Tip It's usually a good idea to fully test the network card before closing up the case and returning the computer to its original location. For some unknown reason, newly installed components are more likely to malfunction if you put the cover on before testing them.

The procedure described above is for installing a NIC into a standard expansion slot on a desktop computer. If you are working with a laptop, the network interface adapter takes the form of a PC Card, which you install simply by inserting it into a PC Card slot from the outside of the computer.

Configuring a Network Interface Adapter

Configuring a network interface adapter is a matter of configuring it to use certain hardware resources, such as the following:

- **Interrupt requests (IRQs)** These are hardware lines that peripheral devices use to send signals to the system processor, requesting its attention.

- **Input/Output (I/O) port addresses** These are locations in memory assigned for use by particular devices to exchange information with the rest of the computer.

- **Memory addresses** These are areas of upper memory used by particular devices, usually for installation of a special-purpose basic input/output system (BIOS).

- **Direct Memory Access (DMA) channels** These are system pathways used by devices to transfer information to and from system memory.

Network interface adapters do not usually use memory addresses or DMA channels, but this is not beyond the realm of possibility. Every network interface adapter requires an IRQ and an I/O port address in order to communicate with the computer.

When you have a computer and a network interface adapter that both support the Plug and Play standard, the resource configuration process is automatic. The computer detects the adapter, identifies it, locates free resources, and configures the adapter to use them. However, it is important for a network support technician to understand more about the configuration process, because you may run into computers or network interface adapters that do not support Plug and Play, or you may encounter situations where Plug and Play doesn't quite work as advertised. Improper network interface adapter configuration is one of the main reasons that a computer fails to communicate with the network, and knowing how to troubleshoot this problem is a useful skill.

In order for a network interface adapter (or any type of adapter) to communicate with the computer in which it is installed, the hardware (that is, the adapter) and the software (the adapter driver) must both be configured to use the same resources. Before the availability of Plug and Play, this meant that you had to configure the network interface adapter itself to use a particular IRQ and I/O port, and then configure the network interface adapter driver to use the same settings. If the settings of the network interface adapter and the driver do not match, it's like dialing the wrong number on a phone; the devices are speaking to someone, but it isn't who they expected. In addition, if the network interface adapter is configured to use the same resources as another device in the computer, then both of the conflicting devices are likely to malfunction.

On older NICs, you configure the hardware resources by installing jumper blocks or setting DIP switches. If you are working with a card like this, you must configure the card before you install it into the computer. In fact, you may have to remove the card from the slot in order to reconfigure it if you find that the settings you've chosen are unavailable. Later model NICs use a proprietary software utility supplied by the manufacturer to set the card's resource settings. This makes it easier to reconfigure the settings in the event of a conflict. The Plug and Play cards available today usually include a configuration utility also, but you won't need to use it unless your computer doesn't properly support Plug and Play.

When you're working with older equipment, determining the right resource settings for the NIC can be a trial-and-error process. Older NICs often have a relatively limited number of available settings, and you may have to try several before you find a configuration that works. Newer cards have more settings to choose from, and when you're working with a newer computer that's running an operating system like Windows 2000, Windows 98, Windows 95, or Windows Me, you have better tools to help you resolve hardware resource conflicts. The Device Manager utility (illustrated in Figure 2.9) lists the resource settings for all of the components in the computer, and can even inform you when a newly installed NIC is experiencing a resource conflict. You can use Device Manager to find out which device the NIC is conflicting with and which resource you need to adjust.

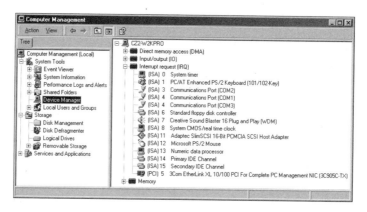

Figure 2.9 The Windows 2000 Device Manager utility

Installing Network Interface Adapter Drivers

The device driver is an integral part of the network interface adapter, as it enables the computer to communicate with the network interface adapter and implements many of the required functions. Virtually all network interface adapters come with a driver disk supporting all of the major operating systems, but in many cases you won't even need the disk, because operating systems like Windows include a collection of drivers for most of the popular network interface adapter models.

In addition to configuring the network interface adapter's hardware resource settings, Plug and Play also installs the appropriate driver, assuming that the operating system includes one. If it doesn't, you'll have to supply the driver disk included with the card. Like any piece of software, network interface adapter drivers are upgraded from time to time, and you can usually obtain the latest driver from the network interface adapter manufacturer's Web site. However, it usually is not necessary to install every new driver release unless you're experiencing problems and the new driver is designed to address those problems. In other words, network interface adapter drivers are usually subject to the "if it's not broken, don't fix it" rule.

Troubleshooting a Network Interface Adapter

When a computer fails to communicate with the network, the network interface adapter can conceivably be at fault, but it's far more likely that some other component is causing the problem. Before addressing the network interface adapter itself, check for the following alternative problems first:

- Make sure the network cable is firmly seated into the connector on the network interface adapter. If you're using a hub, check the cable connection there as well. Loose connections are a common cause of communications problems.

- Try using a different cable that you know works, or if you are using a permanently installed cable run, plug another computer that you know works into it and use different patch cables. It is possible for the cable to be causing the problem, even if there is no visible fault.

- Make sure that you have the proper driver installed on the computer. You may want to check the driver documentation and the network interface adapter manufacturer's Web site for information on possible driver problems on your operating system before you open up the computer.

- Check to see that all of the other software components required for network communications, such as clients and protocols, are properly installed on the computer.

If you can find no problem with the driver, the cable, or the network configuration parameters, it's time to start looking at the NIC itself. Before you open the computer case, check to see if the NIC manufacturer has provided its own diagnostic software. In some cases, the same utility you use to configure the NIC's hardware resources manually also includes diagnostic features that test the functions of the card. If you're using Plug and Play, you might not have even looked at the disk included with the NIC, but this is a time when it can be worth your while to do so. In troubleshooting a hardware component like this, you should exhaust all other options before you actually open the computer.

If the NIC diagnostics indicate that the card is functioning properly, and assuming that the software providing the upper layer protocols is correctly installed and configured, the problem you're experiencing is probably caused by the hardware resource configuration. There is either a resource conflict between the network interface adapter and another device in the computer, or the network interface adapter is not configured to use the same resources as the network interface adapter driver. Use the configuration utility supplied with the adapter to see what resources the network interface adapter is physically configured to use, and then compare this information with the driver configuration. You may have to adjust the settings of the card or the driver, or even those of another device in the computer, to accommodate the card.

If the diagnostics program finds a problem with the card itself, it is time to open up the computer and physically examine the NIC. If the NIC is actually malfunctioning, due to a static discharge or a manufacturer's defect, for example, there is not much you can do except replace it. However, before you do this, you should check to see that the NIC is fully seated in the slot, as this is a prime cause of communication problems. If the card is not secured with a screw, press it down firmly into the slot at both ends and secure it. If the problem persists, try removing the card from the slot, cleaning out the slot with a can of compressed air, and installing the card again. If there is still a problem, you can try using another slot, if one is available. After exhausting all of these avenues, trying installing a different card in the computer, either a new one or one from another computer that you know is working properly. If the replacement card functions, then you know that the card itself is to blame, and you should obtain a replacement.

Exercise 2.2: Network Adapter Functions

1. The two hardware resources used by every network interface adapter are
   _____ and _____.

2. Network interface adapters are associated with the protocol operating at the
   _____ layer.

3. The network interface adapter encapsulates data by enclosing it within a
   _____.

Lesson 3: Network Hubs

A hub or concentrator is a device used to connect all of the computers on a star or ring network. A hub, as shown in Figure 2.10, is nothing more than a box with a series of cable connectors in it. Hubs are available in a variety of sizes, from four- and five-port devices designed for home and small business networks to large rack-mounted units with up to 24 ports or more. Installing a single hub is simply a matter of connecting it to a power source and plugging in cables connected to the network interface adapters in your computers. However, it's important for a network technician to understand what goes on inside a hub.

After this lesson, you will be able to
- Describe the different types of hubs
- Understand the functions of a hub
- Add additional hubs to a network

Estimated lesson time: 30 minutes

Figure 2.10 Hubs have ports into which you plug the cables connected to your computers' network interface adapters.

Like network interface adapters, hubs are associated with specific data-link layer protocols. Ethernet hubs are the most common, because Ethernet is the most popular data-link layer protocol, but Token Ring MAUs are hubs too, and other protocols, such as the Fiber Distributed Data Interface (FDDI) also use hubs.

Understanding Ethernet Hubs

An Ethernet hub is also called a multiport repeater. A *repeater* is a device that amplifies a signal as it passes through it, to counteract the effects of attenuation. If, for example, you have a thin Ethernet network with a cable segment longer than the prescribed maximum of 185 meters, you can install a repeater at some point in the segment to strengthen the signals and increase the maximum segment length. This type of repeater only has two BNC connectors, and is rarely seen these days. The hubs used on UTP Ethernet networks are repeaters as well, but they can have many RJ45 ports instead of just two BNC connectors.

When data enters the hub through any of its ports, the hub amplifies the signal and transmits it out through all of the other ports. This enables a star network to have a shared medium, even though each computer has its own separate cable. The hub relays every packet transmitted by any computer on the network to all of the other computers, and also amplifies the signals. The maximum segment length for a UTP cable on an Ethernet network is 100 meters. A segment is defined as the distance between two communicating computers. However, because the hub also functions as a repeater, each of the cables connecting a computer to a hub port can be up to 100 meters long, allowing a segment length of up to 200 meters when one hub is inserted in the network.

Using Smart Hubs

The hubs used on most Ethernet networks are purely physical-layer devices. This means that the hub works with the signals native to the network medium, such as electrical voltages, but does not interpret the signals or read the data inside packets or even recognize that there is data there. This type of hub is relatively inexpensive. However, there are Ethernet hubs with more intelligence, which can process the data they receive in more elaborate ways.

Some hubs with greater data processing capabilities provide a service called *store and forward,* which means that the hub contains buffers in which it can retain packets in order to retransmit them out through specific ports as needed. This is one step short of a switch, which reads the destination address from each incoming packet and transmits it only to the system for which it is intended.

Some *intelligent hubs* also include management features that enable them to monitor the operation of each of the hub's ports. In most cases, an intelligent hub uses the Simple Network Management Protocol (SNMP) to transmit periodic reports to a centralized network management console. This type of manageability isn't needed on a small LAN, especially because it significantly increases the price of the hardware, but for a large enterprise network that has dozens of hubs, it can be a boon to the network administrator.

Connecting Hubs

You can build a simple Ethernet LAN by plugging a number of computers into a single hub, but what happens when your network outgrows your hub? The solution is to get another hub and connect it to the first one. Large networks can have a great many interconnected hubs forming large LANs, which are in turn connected by routers. Almost every Ethernet hub on the market has an extra port called an *uplink port,* which is used to connect to another hub instead of to a computer. The uplink port differs from the other ports in the hub in how it is wired.

As explained in Lesson 1 of this chapter, UTP cables contain eight wires in four pairs, and each pair consists of a signal wire and a ground. Computers transmit data over one wire pair and receive data over another. In most cases, the other two pairs of wires are left unused. In order for two computers to communicate, the transmit pair on each system must be connected to the receive pair on the other system. In all but exceptional cases, UTP cables are wired *straight through*. This means that each of the eight pins in the connector at one end of the cable is wired to the same pin in the connector at the other end. If you were to use a cable like this to connect two computers, you would have the transmit pins connected to the transmit pins and the receive pins to the receive pins, making communication impossible.

Another function of a hub is to provide the *crossover circuit* that connects the transmit pins to the receive pins for each connection between two computers. The uplink port is the one port in the hub that does not have the crossover circuit. When you connect the uplink port in one hub to a regular port in another, you enable the computers on one hub to connect to those on the other, with only a single crossover between them. Without the uplink port, connecting one hub to another would cause a connection between computers on different hubs to go through two crossover circuits, which would cancel each other out. To avoid such a connection failure, you shouldn't plug an uplink port on one hub into the uplink port on another.

Note On some hubs, the uplink port is switched, meaning that you can choose whether that port uses the crossover circuit or not. This can be an important factor to consider when evaluating hubs, because the switched port might count towards the total number of usable ports in the hub. In other words, a hub advertised as having eight ports might have one that is switchable, while an eight-port hub with a dedicated uplink port might have eight regular ports and one uplink port, for a total of nine. Be sure you know what you're getting before making a purchase.

Tip It is possible to create a simple two-node Ethernet network without using a hub by connecting the network interface adapters of two computers directly, using what is known as a crossover cable. A crossover cable is a UTP cable that has the transmit pins on one end of the cable wired to the receive pins on the other end, thus eliminating the need for the crossover circuit in the hub. Of course you can create this sort of network with two computers, and since you're eliminating the repeater from the network, the crossover cable can be no longer than 100 meters.

Understanding Token Ring MAUs

The MAUs used on Token Ring networks may look similar to Ethernet hubs, but they could not be more different. Unlike Ethernet hubs, Token Ring MAUs are *passive* devices, meaning that they are not repeaters, and they perform certain data-link layer functions that are crucial to the operation of the network. The primary difference in the operation of a MAU is the fact that it does not retransmit all incoming traffic out through the other ports simultaneously. Instead, the MAU transmits a packet arriving through port 5 (for example) out through port 6, and then waits for the packet to return to the MAU through port 6, after which it transmits it through port 7, waits for it to return, and so on. This pattern is shown in Figure 2.11. Once the MAU has transmitted the packet to each of the computers on the network and has received it back, it sends the packet to the system that originated it, and that system removes it from the network. This is the process that enables the computers in a physical star topology to communicate as though they are cabled in a ring topology.

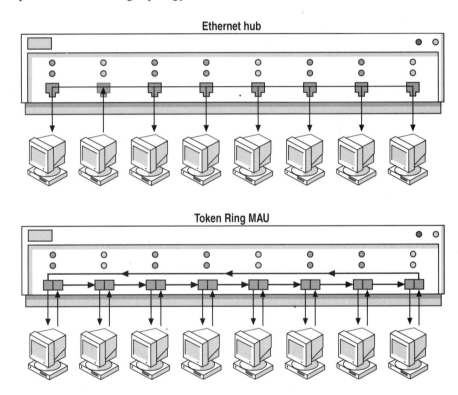

Figure 2.11 Token Ring MAUs relay packets serially, while Ethernet hubs transmit them in parallel.

When forwarding packets in this way, the role of the computer is at least as important as that of the MAU. If a computer is not there to return each packet that was sent to it back to the MAU, that packet can never be forwarded out through the next port. To prevent packets from being lost in this way, Token Ring computers perform an initialization process when starting up that informs the MAU of their presence. Once the MAU receives the proper signals from the NIC in the computer, it figuratively adds the system to the logical ring and begins forwarding packets to it. Ports to which no computer is connected are never added to the ring, and the MAU skips them when forwarding packets. These unused ports are said to be in the *loopback* state. Token Ring MAUs also do not have an uplink port like an Ethernet hub, but they do have dedicated Ring In and Ring Out ports that are used to connect one MAU to another.

Exercise 2.3: Network Hub Functions

Match the concept in the left column with the definition in the right column that best describes it.

1. Token Ring MAU

2. Intelligent hub

3. Uplink port

4. Loopback port

5. Repeater

6. Ring In and Ring Out ports

a. Amplifies signals

b. Used to send reports to a network management console

c. Used to connect MAUs

d. Forwards packets serially

e. Excluded from a Token Ring network

f. Used to connect one Ethernet hub to a standard port on another Ethernet hub

Chapter Summary

The key points covered in this chapter are as follows.

Network Cables

There are three basic topologies used to connect LANs: bus, star, and ring.

- Coaxial cables have two conductors, use the bus topology, and are no longer in common use for LAN installations.

- Unshielded twisted pair (UTP) cable in the star topology is the most common network medium used today.

- Fiber optic cable uses light pulses for signaling instead of electrical voltages, and are resistant to many of the forms of interference that affect copper cables.

Network Interface Adapters

- A network interface adapter—generally a network interface card (NIC)—provides the link between a computer and the network medium.

- The network interface adapter and its driver implement the data-link layer protocol on the computer.

- NIC installation problems are most often caused by hardware resource configuration issues or device conflicts.

Network Hubs

- Ethernet hubs are also called multiport repeaters.

- Ethernet hubs forward incoming traffic out through all other ports simultaneously.

- You connect Ethernet hubs together by cabling the uplink port on one hub to a standard port on the other.

- Token Ring hubs are called multistation access units (MAUs).

- Token Ring MAUs forward packets out through each port in turn and wait for each packet to be returned.

- You connect Token Ring MAUs using the Ring In and Ring Out ports.

Chapter Review

1. What is the name of an Ethernet cable that contains two electrical conductors?

   a. A shielded twisted pair cable

   b. A coaxial cable

   c. A dielectric cable

   d. An unshielded twisted pair cable

2. What are the names of the two most common conditions that degrade the signals on copper-based cables?

3. Which topology requires the use of terminators?

   a. Bus

   b. Star

   c. Ring

   d. None of the above

4. Which of the following topologies is implemented only logically, not physically?

   a. Bus

   b. Star

   c. Ring

   d. All of the above

5. How many wire pairs are actually used on a typical UTP Ethernet network?

   a. One

   b. Two

   c. Three

   d. Four

6. What is the name of the process of building a frame around network layer information?

   a. Data buffering

   b. Signal encoding

   c. Media access control

   d. Data encapsulation

7. Which of the connectors on a network interface adapter transmits data in parallel?

8. Which two of the following hardware resources do network interface adapters always require?

   a. DMA channel

   b. I/O port address

   c. IRQ

   d. Memory address

9. What is the name of the process by which a network interface adapter determines when it should transmit its data over the network?

10. Which bus type is preferred for a NIC that will be connected to a Fast Ethernet network?

11. A passive hub does not do which of the following?

    a. Transmit management information using SNMP

    b. Function as a repeater

    c. Provide a crossover circuit

    d. Store and forward data

12. To connect two Ethernet hubs together, you must do which of the following?

    a. Purchase a special crossover cable

    b. Connect the uplink ports on the two hubs together

    c. Connect any standard port on one hub to a standard port on the other

    d. Connect the uplink port in one hub to a standard port on the other

13. Which term describes a port in a Token Ring MAU that is not part of the ring?

    a. Passive

    b. Loopback

    c. Crossover

    d. Intelligent

14. A hub that functions as a repeater inhibits the effect of _____.

15. You can use which of the following to connect two Ethernet computers together using UTP cable?

    a. An Ethernet hub

    b. A multiport repeater

    c. A crossover cable

    d. All of the above

C H A P T E R   3

Network Connections

About This Chapter

With a hub, some cables, and some network interface adapters (or network interface cards, or NICs), you can turn a group of computers into a network. As networks grow larger, other types of hardware devices are needed. When a network grows beyond a certain point, the computers generate too much traffic for the network medium to handle. This is particularly true on Ethernet networks, which decrease in efficiency as traffic increases. This chapter examines some of the more complex components you can use to connect local area networks (LANs) together at the data-link and network layers. By using these tools, you can increase the network's size without diminishing its efficiency, even though network traffic increases significantly.

Lesson 1: Bridging

Bridging is a technique used to connect networks at the data-link layer. As explained in Chapter 2, "Network Hardware," hubs connect networks at the physical layer, and are unaware of the data structures operating at the higher layers. When you expand your network by adding another hub, the effect is no different than if you substituted a hub with more ports for the old one. Each packet generated by a computer on the network reaches every other computer. A *bridge*, on the other hand, provides packet filtering at the data-link layer, meaning that it only propagates the packets that are destined for the other side of the network. If you have a large LAN that is experiencing excessive collisions or delays due to high traffic levels, you can reduce the traffic by splitting the network in half with a bridge.

After this lesson, you will be able to

- Understand the concept of a collision domain
- Describe the function of a bridge
- List the types of bridges available

Estimated lesson time: 20 minutes

Connecting Local Area Networks with a Bridge

A bridge is a physical unit, typically with two ports, that you use to connect network segments together. You can use a bridge to join two existing LANs or to split one LAN into two segments. Bridges operate in what is called *promiscuous mode*, meaning that they read and process all of the packets transmitted over the network segments. Because a bridge functions at the data-link layer, it is capable of interpreting the information in the data-link layer protocol header. Data packets enter the bridge through either one of the ports, and the bridge then reads the destination address in each packet header and decides how to process that packet. This process is called *packet filtering*. If the destination address is that of a computer on the other network segment, the bridge propagates it out through the other port. If the destination address is that of a computer on the same network segment as the system that generated it, the bridge discards the packet.

Note While bridges can read the contents of a packet's data-link layer protocol header, they cannot go any farther up the protocol stack than that protocol layer. A bridge cannot read the contents of the data field in a data-link layer frame, which contains the information generated by a network layer protocol.

Figure 3.1 shows two LANs connected by a bridge. When a computer on one LAN transmits a packet to a computer on the other, the bridge receives that packet and relays it to the other LAN. In this case, the destination system receives the packet just as if the two computers were on the same LAN. If a computer on one LAN transmits a packet to another computer on the same LAN, the bridge receives the packet and discards it, because there is no reason for the packet to go to the other LAN. The use of the bridge (theoretically) cuts in half the unnecessary traffic passing over each network segment, because packets not needed on the other network segment don't go there.

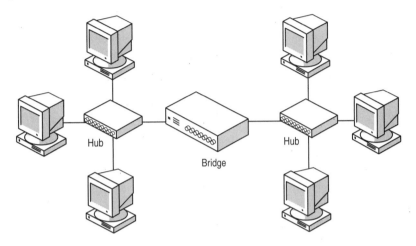

Figure 3.1 A bridge filters the packets passing between two LANs or two LAN segments by reading their data-link layer protocol headers. The bridge relays the packets destined for the other network segment and discards those that are not.

Bridges and Collisions

A *collision domain* is a network (or part of a network) that is constructed so that when two computers transmit packets at precisely the same time, a collision occurs. When you add a new hub to an existing network, the computers connected to that hub become part of the same collision domain as the original network. This is because hubs relay the signals that they receive immediately upon receiving them, without filtering packets.

Bridges, on the other hand, do not relay signals to the other network until they have received the entire packet. For this reason, two computers on different sides of a bridge that transmit at the same time do not cause a conflict. The two network segments connected by the bridge are thus said to be in different collision domains. On an Ethernet network, collisions are a normal and expected part of network operations, but when the number of collisions grows too large, the efficiency of the network goes down, because more packets must be retransmitted. An increase in the number of collisions on a network is a natural result of an increase in the number of computers on that network. The more systems there are sharing the network medium, the more likely it is that two will transmit at the same time. When the network is split into two collision domains with a bridge, the reduction in traffic on the two network segments results in fewer collisions, fewer retransmissions, and an overall increase in efficiency.

Bridges and Broadcasts

Another important concept in bridging technology is that of the broadcast domain. A *broadcast* message is a packet with a special destination address that causes it to be read and processed by every computer that receives it. By contrast, a *unicast* message is a packet addressed to a single computer on the network, and a *multicast* message is addressed to a group of computers on the network (but not necessarily all of them). A *broadcast domain* is a group of computers that will all receive a broadcast message transmitted by any one of the computers in a group.

Broadcasts are a crucial part of the networking process. The most common method computers use to locate a particular system on the local network is to transmit a broadcast that essentially asks, "Does any computer here have this Internet Protocol (IP) address or this NetBIOS name?" and wait for that computer to reply (see Figure 3.2). From that reply message, the broadcaster can determine the desired destination computer's hardware address and send subsequent packets to it as unicasts.

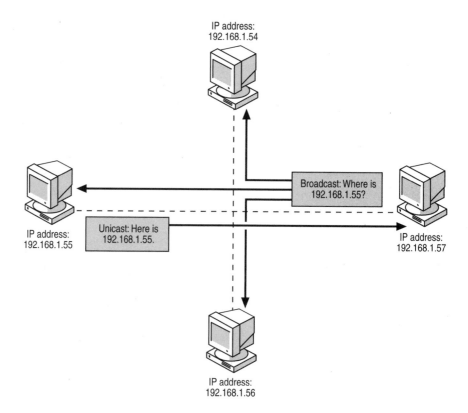

Figure 3.2 Computers use broadcast messages to locate specific systems on the LAN.

Adding a bridge separates a network into two different collision domains, but the segments on either side of the bridge remain part of the same broadcast domain, because the bridge always relays all broadcast messages from both sides. This behavior mitigates the benefit of the bridge somewhat, because a portion of the broadcast traffic being relayed is not utilized by the systems on the other side of the network. However, the retention of a single broadcast domain is what enables the two network segments to remain part of the same LAN. This method is unlike using a router, which completely separates the network into two LANs.

Transparent Bridging

The next logical question to ask when you're learning about how bridges filter packets is, "How do the bridges know which computers are located on each network segment?" The answer is that bridges have this information because they maintain an internal address table that lists the hardware addresses of the computers on both segments. When the bridge receives a packet and reads the destination address in the data-link layer protocol header, it checks that address against its lists. If the address is associated with a segment other than that from which the packet arrived, the bridge relays it to that segment.

Tip One of the specifications that bridge manufacturers often supply is the number of addresses that the device can maintain in its table. In most cases, bridges can maintain address tables that are far larger than required by any network, but it's still a good idea to check this specification before you make a purchase.

The question still remains, however, of where the bridge gets its information about the locations of the computers. Originally, network administrators had to manually create the lists of hardware addresses for each segment connected to the bridge. This was obviously an onerous chore. Today, bridges use a technique called *transparent bridging* to automatically compile their own address lists. When you activate a transparent bridge for the first time, it begins processing packets. For each incoming packet, the bridge reads the source address in the data-link layer protocol header and adds it to the address list for the network segment over which the packet arrived. At first, the bridge doesn't have the information needed to decide whether it should relay the packet or discard it, so the bridge errs on the side of caution and relays the packet to all of the other network segments. When a sufficient number of packets pass through the bridge to enable the compilation of the address tables, the bridge begins using them to selectively forward packets.

It is a common practice for network administrators to install multiple bridges between network segments to provide redundancy in case of an equipment failure. However, this practice can cause data loss when multiple bridges process the same packets and determine that the source computer is on two different network segments. In addition, it's possible for multiple bridges to forward broadcast packets around the network endlessly, in what is called a *bridge loop*. To prevent these problems from occurring, bridges communicate among themselves using a protocol known as the *spanning tree algorithm (SPA)*, which selects one bridge to process the packets. All other bridges on that network segment remain idle until the first one fails.

Source Route Bridging

It is typical for Ethernet networks to use transparent bridging and the SPA, but Token Ring networks use a different system. Instead of the bridges themselves selecting a designated bridge between two segments, Token Ring systems select for themselves which bridge they will use. The technique these systems use is called *source route bridging*, and it works by each system transmitting packets called All Rings Broadcast (ARB) frames over the network. As each bridge processes these packets (by forwarding them to all connected segments, as with any broadcast), it adds a route designator to them, which identifies the bridge and the port through which it received the packet. When the packet arrives at its destination, the receiving system sends it back to the source. Bridges use the route designators to avoid sending packets to the same bridge twice, and the original source system uses them to select the most efficient route through the network to a given destination.

Bridge Types

The standard type of bridge used to connect network segments of the same type and the same location is called a *local bridge*. This is the simplest type of bridge because it doesn't modify the data in the packets; it simply reads the addresses in the data-link layer protocol header and passes the packet on or discards it. There are also two other types of bridges that you can use to handle segments of different types and segments at different locations.

A *translation bridge,* as illustrated in Figure 3.3, is a data-link layer device that connects network segments using different network media or different protocols. This type of bridge is more complicated than a local bridge, because in addition to reading the headers in the packet, the bridge strips the data-link layer frame off the packets to be relayed to other network segments and constructs another frame. This way, the bridge can connect an Ethernet network to a Fiber Distributed Data Interface (FDDI) network or to two different types of Ethernet (such as 100BaseTX and 100BaseT4) while retaining a single broadcast domain. Because of the additional packet manipulations, translation bridging is slower than local bridging, and translation bridges are more expensive as well. Because there are other types of devices that can connect different network types, such as routers, the use of translation bridges is relatively rare.

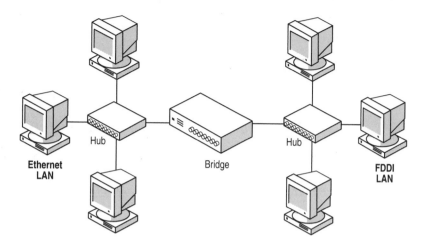

Figure 3.3 Translation bridges enable you to build a single network using multiple protocols or media types.

A *remote bridge* is designed to connect two network segments at distant locations using some form of wide area network (WAN) link. The link can be a modem connection, leased telephone line, or any other type of WAN technology. The advantage of using a bridge in this manner is that you minimize the amount of traffic passing over the WAN link, which is usually far slower and more expensive than the local network.

Exercise 3.1: Bridge Functions

1. At what layer of the Open Systems Interconnection (OSI) reference model does a bridge function?

   a. Physical

   b. Data-link

   c. Network

   d. Transport

2. What does a bridge do when it receives a packet that is destined for a system on the same network segment over which the packet arrived?

   a. Discards it

   b. Relays it

   c. Broadcasts it

   d. Unicasts it

3. What is a bridge called that connects network segments using different types of cable?

   a. Transparent

   b. Remote

   c. Translation

   d. Source route

4. Two network segments connected by a bridge share what type of domain?

   a. Collision

   b. Broadcast

   c. Source route

   d. Unicast

5. What is the technique used to prevent bridge loops called?

   a. Transparent bridging

   b. Packet filtering

   c. Translation bridging

   d. The spanning tree algorithm

Lesson 2: Switching

There is another type of data-link layer connection device, called a switch, which has largely replaced the bridge in the modern network, and which is replacing routers in many instances as well. A *switch* is a box with multiple cable jacks in it that looks a lot like a hub. In fact, some manufacturers have hubs and switches of various sizes that are all but identical in appearance, except for their markings. The difference between a hub and a switch is that while a hub forwards every incoming packet out through all of its ports, a switch forwards each incoming packet only to the port that provides access to the destination system, as shown in Figure 3.4.

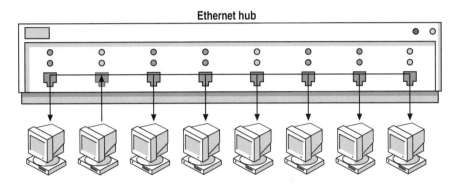

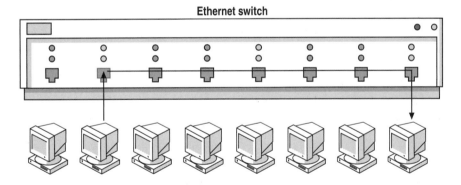

Figure 3.4 A switch forwards incoming packets only to the port that provides access to the destination system.

After this lesson, you will be able to

- Identify the functions of a switch
- Understand how switches can improve network efficiency
- Identify the basic types of switches available

Estimated lesson time: 15 minutes

Because they forward data to a single port only, switches essentially convert the LAN from a shared network medium to a dedicated one. If you have a small network that uses a switch instead of a hub (such a switch is sometimes called a *switching hub*), each packet takes a dedicated path from the source computer to the destination, forming a separate collision domain for those two computers. Switches still forward broadcast messages to all of their ports, but not unicasts and multicasts. No systems receive packets destined for other systems, and no collisions occur during unicast transmissions because every pair of computers on the network has what amounts to a dedicated cable segment connecting them. Thus, while a bridge reduces unnecessary traffic congestion on the network, a switch all but eliminates it.

Another advantage of switching is that each pair of computers has the full bandwidth of the network dedicated to it. A standard Ethernet LAN using a hub might have 20 or more computers sharing the same 10 Mbps of bandwidth. Replace the hub with a switch, and every pair of computers has its own dedicated 10 Mbps channel. This can greatly improve the overall performance of the network without the need for any workstation modifications at all. In addition, some switches provide ports that operate in Full-duplex mode, which means that two computers can send traffic in both directions at the same time using separate wire pairs within the cable. Full-duplex operation can effectively double the throughput of a 10 Mbps network to 20 Mbps.

Note Switches are, in general, more expensive than repeating hubs and less expensive than routers. As with hubs, you can purchase switches that range from small standalone units to large rack-mounted models.

Installing Switches

Switches generally aren't needed on small networks that only use a single hub. They are more often found on larger networks, where they're used instead of bridges or routers. If you take a standard enterprise network consisting of a backbone and a series of segments and replace the routers with switches, the effect is profound. On the routed network, the backbone must carry the internetwork traffic generated by all the segments. This can lead to high traffic conditions on the backbone, even if it uses a faster protocol than the segments. On a switched network, you connect the computers to individual workgroup switches, which are in turn connected to a high-performance backbone switch, as shown in Figure 3.5. The result is that any computer on the network can open a dedicated channel to any other computer, even when the data path runs through several switches.

Note For more information on the backbone/segment internetwork configuration, see Lesson 1: Network Communications, in Chapter 1, "Networking Basics."

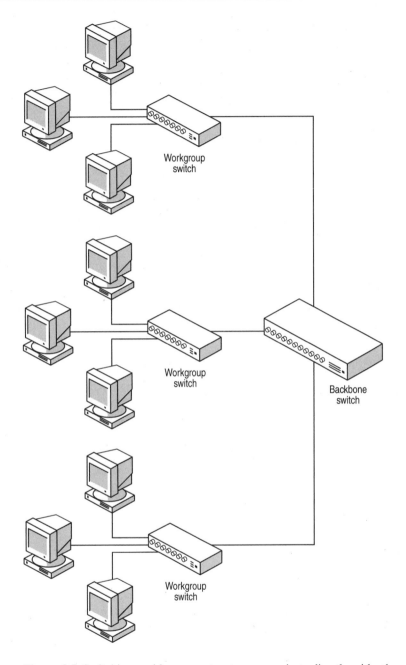

Figure 3.5 Switching enables computers to communicate directly with other computers, without the need for a shared backbone network.

There are many different ways to use switches on a complex internetwork; you don't have to replace all of the hubs and routers with switches at one time. For example, you can continue to use your standard shared network hubs and connect them all to a multiport switch instead of a router. This increases the efficiency of your internetwork traffic. On the other hand, if your network tends to generate more traffic within the individual LANs than between them, you can replace the workgroup hubs with switches to increase the available intranetwork bandwidth for each computer while leaving the backbone network intact.

The problem with replacing all of the routers on a large internetwork with switches is that you create one huge broadcast domain, instead of several small ones. The issue of collision domains is no longer a problem, because there are far fewer collisions. However, switches relay every broadcast generated by a computer anywhere on the network to every other computer, which increases the number of unnecessary packets processed by each system. There are several technologies that address this problem, such as the following:

- **Virtual LANs (VLANs)** With a virtual LAN you can create subnets on a switched network that exist only in the switches themselves. The physical network is still switched, but administrators can specify the addresses of the systems that are to belong to a specific subnet. These systems can be located anywhere, because the subnet is virtual and not constrained by the physical layout of the network. When a computer on a particular subnet transmits a broadcast message, the packet goes only to the computers in that subnet, rather than being propagated throughout the entire network. Communication between subnets can be either routed or switched, but all traffic within a VLAN is switched.

- **Layer 3 Switching** Layer 3 switching is a variation on the VLAN concept that minimizes the amount of routing needed between the VLANs. When communication between systems on different VLANs is required, a router establishes a connection between the systems and then the switches take over. Routing occurs only when absolutely necessary.

Switch Types

There are two basic types of switches: *cut-through* and *store-and-forward*. A cut-through switch forwards packets immediately by reading the destination address from their data-link layer protocol headers as soon as they're received and relaying the packets out through the appropriate port with no additional processing. The switch doesn't even wait for the entire packet to arrive before it begins forwarding it. In most cases, cut-through switches use a hardware-based mechanism that consists of a grid of input/output circuits, which enable data to enter and leave the switch through any port. This is called *matrix switching* or *crossbar switching*.

This type of switch is relatively inexpensive and minimizes the delay incurred during the processing of packets by the switch (which is called *latency*).

A store-and-forward switch waits until an entire packet arrives before forwarding it to its destination. This type of unit can be a *shared-memory switch*, which has a common memory buffer that stores the incoming data from all of the ports, or a *bus architecture switch* with individual buffers for each port, connected by a bus. While the packet is stored in the switch's memory buffers, the switch takes the opportunity to verify the data by performing a cyclical redundancy check (CRC). The switch also checks for other problems, peculiar to the data-link layer protocol involved, which result in malformed frames—commonly (and colorfully) known as runts, giants, and a jabber condition. This checking naturally introduces additional latency into the packet forwarding process, and the additional functions make store-and-forward switches more expensive than cut-through switches.

Exercise 3.2: Switch Functions

1. The functionality of a switch is best described as being a combination of what two devices?

   a. A router and a gateway

   b. A hub and a bridge

   c. A bridge and a router

   d. A repeater and a hub

2. Which of the following effects is a result of replacing the routers in a segment/backbone network with switches?

   a. The speed of the network increases.

   b. The traffic on the backbone increases.

   c. The number of LANs increases.

   d. The bandwidth available to workstations increases.

3. When you use switches instead of routers and hubs, what is the effect on the number of collisions on the network?

   a. Increases

   b. Decreases

   c. Stays the same

4. When you replace the routers with switches on an internetwork consisting of three segments connected by one backbone, how many broadcast domains do you end up with?

   a. None

   b. One

   c. Three

   d. Four

5. What is a switch called that immediately relays signals from the incoming port to the outgoing port?

   a. A cut-through switch

   b. A shared memory switch

   c. A bus architecture switch

   d. A store-and-forward switch

Lesson 3: Routing

A router is a device that connects two networks together, forming an internetwork. Unlike bridges and switches, routers function at the network layer of the OSI reference model. This means that a router can connect LANs that run completely different data-link layer protocols (such as Ethernet and Token Ring), as long as all of the systems are running the same network layer protocol. Transmission Contol Protocol/Internet Protocol (TCP/IP) is the most popular protocol suite in use today, and IP is TCP/IP's network layer protocol, so most of the router information you come across refers to IP routing.

After this lesson, you will be able to

- Understand the functions of a router
- List the various types of routers
- Distinguish between a router and a gateway

Estimated lesson time: 20 minutes

When a computer on a LAN wants to transmit data to a computer on another LAN, the system sends its packets to a router on the local network, and the router forwards them to the destination network. In many cases, the destination system is not located on an adjacent network, so the router has to forward the packets to another router. On a large internetwork, such as the Internet, packets may have to pass through a dozen or more routers on the way to their destination.

Routers and Gateways

The term "router" always refers to a hardware or software device that connects two LANs together at the network layer. In TCP/IP parlance, however, routers are often referred to using the term "gateway." For example, when you configure the TCP/IP client on a Microsoft Windows system, you supply the address of a default gateway, which is actually a router on the local network that the system uses to access other networks. Unfortunately, gateway can also refer to a hardware or software device that operates at the application layer and provides an interface between two programs. For example, an e-mail gateway enables people using one particular e-mail system to send messages to people using another e-mail system. Don't confuse the two.

Because routers operate at the network layer, they transcend the limitations of the data-link layer protocols. Packets arriving at the router travel upwards through the protocol stack to the network layer, and in the process, the data-link layer frame is stripped away. Once the router determines where to send the packet, it passes the data down to a different network interface which encapsulates it within a new frame for transmission. If the two data-link layer protocols involved support different sized packets, the router might have to fragment the network layer data and create multiple frames that are small enough for transmission.

Packet Routing

Routers are more selective than hubs, bridges, and switches in the packets that they forward to other ports. Because they operate at the boundaries of LANs, they do not forward broadcast messages, except in certain highly specific cases. A router forwards a packet based on the destination address in the network layer protocol header, which specifies the packet's ultimate destination, and not the hardware address used at the data-link layer. A router has internal tables (called *routing tables*) that contain information about the networks around it, and it uses these tables to determine where to send each packet. If the packet is destined for a system on one of the networks to which the router is connected, the router transmits the packet directly to that system. If the packet is destined for a system on a distant network, the router transmits the packet across one of the adjacent networks to another router.

As an example, consider a typical corporate internetwork composed of a backbone and several segments connected to the backbone using routers, as shown in Figure 3.6. The computers on each segment use the router connecting it to the backbone as their default gateway. The computers transmit all of the packets they generate either to a specific system on the local network or to the default gateway. The gateway router strips the data-link layer frame from each packet and reads the destination address from its network layer protocol header.

Using the information in its routing tables, the gateway determines which router it must use to access the network on which the destination system is located. The gateway then constructs a new frame for the packet, using the backbone's data-link layer protocol (which can be different from the protocol used on the segment) and specifying the router leading to the destination network as the data-link layer destination address. When the packet reaches the next router, the process repeats itself, except that this router's tables indicate that the destination system is on the segment to which the router is attached. The router can therefore construct a frame that transmits the packet directly to the destination system.

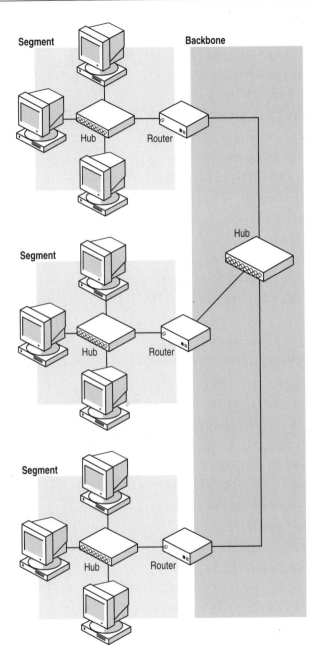

Figure 3.6 On a typical internetwork configuration, the routers are responsible for directing the packets to their next interim destination.

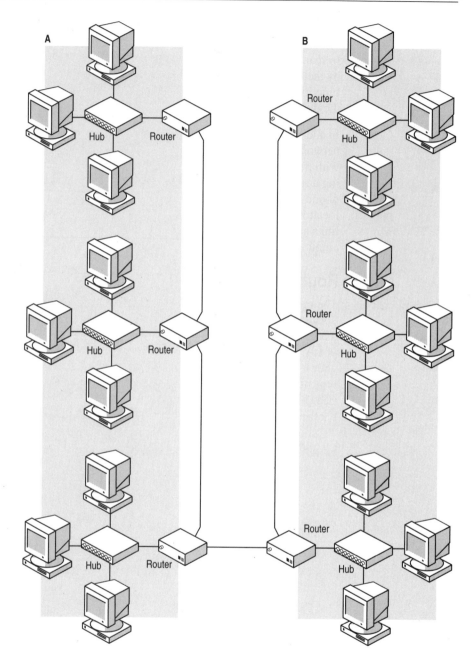

Figure 3.7 The distance between the two end systems in an internetwork connection is often measured by the number of hops (or routers) between them. In this case, system A is six hops away from system B.

When the packet has to pass through multiple networks on the way to its final destination, each router that processes it is referred to as a *hop*, as shown in Figure 3.7. In many cases, routers measure the efficiency of a given path through the network by the number of hops that are required to reach the destination. One of the primary functions of a router is to select the most efficient path to a destination, based on the data in its routing tables.

In addition to connecting networks at a single location, such as a corporate internetwork, routers can also connect distant networks using WAN links. Organizations with multiple branch offices often connect the networks in those offices by installing a router at each location, and connecting the routers together using leased telephone lines, or some other WAN technology, such as frame relay. Because each location has a separate broadcast domain, the only packets that pass over the WAN links are those destined for systems on the other networks. This minimizes the amount of traffic passing over those links, thus minimizing their cost.

Routing to the Internet

The most common use for a WAN router is to connect a network to an Internet Service Provider (ISP), providing the computers on the network with access to the Internet. The Internet is the ultimate example of a routed network; thousands of LANs are connected together using many different kinds of routers. To connect your LAN to the Internet, you install a router that can connect to an ISP using any type of technology, from a dial-up modem to Integrated Services Digital Network (ISDN) to a leased line. The router is configured to forward all traffic not destined for the local network to the ISP, which relays it to the Internet.

Understanding Routing Tables

The routing tables are the heart of a router; without them, there's no way for the router to know where to send the packets it receives. However, the question then arises of where the routing tables come from. Unlike bridges and switches, routers cannot compile routing tables from the information in the data packets they process. This is because the routing table contains more detailed information than is found in a data packet, and also because the router needs the information in the table to process the first packets it receives after being activated. A router can't forward a packet to all possible destinations in the way that a bridge can.

However, the process of building the routing table can still be either manual or automatic. *Static routing* is the process of manually creating routing table entries. A network administrator decides what the router should do when it receives packets addressed to systems on a particular network and adds entries to the routing table that reflect these decisions. This process is possible on a relatively small network with a handful of routers, but on a larger network, the manual configuration process is too much work and the routers are unable to modify their table to accommodate changes in network status.

The alternative to static routing is *dynamic routing*, in which routers use specialized protocols to exchange information about themselves and the networks around them. Routers have direct information about the LANs to which they are connected, and use routing protocols to send that information to other routers. When the routers on an internetwork share the contents of their tables using these protocols, all of the routers can have information about more distant networks as well.

There are many different routing protocols, particularly on the Internet, where routing is one of the most complex and vital parts of the internetwork infrastructure. Dynamic routing requires no direct participation by network administrators, other than to install and run the routing protocols, and it also enables routers to automatically modify the information in their tables when the network changes. For example, should a router malfunction, all of the routers that normally communicate with it remove that router from their tables after a given period of time. Those routers then inform others of the malfunction, and the entire network eventually stops trying to use that router. When the offending router is put back into service, the other routers update their tables and begin to use it again.

Note For more information on routing tables, routing protocols, and specific IP routing practices, see Chapter 9, "TCP/IP Routing."

Routing Metrics

Part of a router's function is to select the most efficient route to each packet's destination. On a relatively small internetwork such as that pictured in Figure 3.6, there is only one possible route to any particular destination. However, on a more complex network, administrators often install more than one router on each network, to provide alternate routes in case of a malfunction. When multiple routes to a particular destination exist, routers include all of them in their routing tables, along with a value called a *metric* that specifies the relative efficiency of each route. The nature of the metric depends on the routing protocol used to generate it. In some cases, the metric is simply the number of hops between the router and the destination network. Other protocols use more complex computations to determine the metric.

Router Types

Most people think of a router as a large, complex device costing tens or hundreds of thousands of dollars, used only on giant enterprise networks. Actually, routers can take many different forms and are far more commonly used than you may think. It is true that many routers are large, powerful, and very expensive. Generally speaking, routers are more expensive than switches, bridges, and hubs. You can indeed find routers on large corporate networks, where they're mounted in racks in data centers and in server closets. These types of routers connect segments to a backbone and provide an entire private internetwork with access to computers in their branch offices and/or the Internet.

However, there are also much smaller and less expensive routers on the market. In fact, if you use the Internet Connection Sharing (ICS) feature in Windows 2000, Windows 98 second edition (SE), or Windows Me to connect your home network to the Internet, you are actually using your computer as a router. Other software-based router products enable you to share dial-up, cable television (CATV) network, and Digital Subscriber Line (DSL) connections with a small network. There are also relatively small hardware routers on the market that you can use for connecting a LAN to the Internet.

For private internetworking, you can use any one of many hardware routers that cover a range of prices, or use a Windows 2000 or Windows NT system with two or more NICs installed in it to route IP traffic between networks. Every computer with a TCP/IP client has a routing table in it, even those that are not strictly functioning as routers. For example, when you use a computer on a LAN to connect to the Internet with a dial-up connection, the system uses its routing table to determine whether requests for network resources should go to the NIC providing the LAN connection or to the modem providing the Internet connection. Even though the system is not providing Internet access to the LAN, it still uses the routing table.

Exercise 3.3: Routing Functions

1. At what layer of the OSI reference model do routers operate?

    a. Physical

    b. Data-link

    c. Network

    d. Transport

2. Multiples of what are created by connecting several LANs with routers?

    a. Collision domains

    b. Broadcast domains

    c. Subnets

    d. All of the above

3. What is the information in a routing table that specifies the relative efficiency of a particular route called?

    a. Metric

    b. Static route

    c. Dynamic route

    d. Hop

4. With which of the following techniques are routing protocols associated?

   a. WAN routing

   b. Static routing

   c. Dynamic routing

   d. All of the above

5. What is the term for a group of LANs in one building connected by routers?

   a. A WAN

   b. A broadcast domain

   c. A collision domain

   d. An internetwork

Chapter Summary

The key points covered in this chapter are as follows.

Lesson 1: Bridging

- Bridges selectively relay packets between network segments, depending on their data-link layer destination addresses.

- Bridges maintain a single broadcast domain while creating separate collision domains.

- Transparent bridging and source route bridging are techniques that bridges use to gather information about the network segments they're servicing.

- Local bridges connect network segments of the same type; translation bridges connect network segments of different types, and remote bridges connect network segments at distant locations.

Lesson 2: Switching

- Switches improve on the function of bridges by forwarding packets only to their destination systems.

- Switches reduce the collisions on a network and increase the bandwidth available to each computer.

- Virtual LANs can help you create multiple broadcast domains on a switched network.

- Several types of switches are available, from relatively simple and inexpensive workgroup units to complex enterprise network switches.

Lesson 3: Routing

- Routers are used to connect networks together at the network layer of the OSI reference model.

- Routers strip away the data-link layer frame of incoming packets and build a new frame using the data-link layer protocol of the outgoing network.

- Routers use internal tables of information about the surrounding networks to forward packets to their destinations.

- Routing tables are created either manually by the network administrator or automatically by a routing protocol. These techniques are called static routing and dynamic routing, respectively.

Chapter Review

1. Which of the following devices are you most likely to use to connect a LAN to the Internet?

   a. A hub

   b. A bridge

   c. A switch

   d. A router

2. Which of the following devices does not read the data-link layer protocol header in incoming packets?

   a. A hub

   b. A bridge

   c. A switch

   d. A router

3. Suppose that you have a 10 Mbps Ethernet LAN that consists of 45 computers connected to three standard repeating hubs. Traffic levels are getting too high, causing excessive collisions and reduced performance. Which of the following courses of action is the most inexpensive way to reduce the overall traffic level on the network?

   a. Split the network into three LANs and connect them using dedicated hardware routers.

   b. Replace the three hubs with switches.

   c. Connect the three hubs to a high-performance switch, instead of to each other.

   d. Install a transparent bridge between two of the hubs.

4. Using the same scenario as in question 3, which of the following courses of action would not increase the bandwidth available to each workstation?

   a. Split the network into three LANs and connect them using dedicated hardware routers.

   b. Replace the three hubs with switches.

    c. Connect the three hubs to a high-performance switch, instead of to each other.

    d. Upgrade the network to 100 Mbps by installing Fast Ethernet NICs and hubs.

5. The spanning tree algorithm is used to prevent which of the following networking problems?

    a. Excessive collisions

    b. Packet filtering

    c. Bridge loops

    d. Static routing

6. Source route bridging is associated with which of the following protocols?

    a. Ethernet

    b. Token Ring

    c. FDDI

    d. TCP/IP

7. On a switched network, virtual LANs are used to create multiples of what?

    a. Collision domains

    b. Broadcast domains

    c. Internetworks

    d. All of the above

8. ICS enables a computer running Windows to function as what?

    a. A hub

    b. A bridge

    c. A switch

    d. A router

9. Which of the following processes requires manual intervention from a network administrator?

    a. Transparent bridging

    b. Source route bridging

    c. Static routing

    d. Dynamic routing

10. Which of the following devices does not have buffers to store data during processing?

    a. A repeating hub

    b. A local bridge

    c. A cut-through switch

    d. All of the above

C H A P T E R   4

Networking Software

About This Chapter

You may need hardware, such as network interface adapters—generally network interface cards (NICs)—and cables, to physically connect your computers together into a network, but software is also an important component. This chapter examines the various software elements that provide network connectivity, including operating systems, clients, and directory services. These components provide the protocols that make up the networking stack, as well as the applications that make use of the network. Although you may be intimately familiar with some of the components discussed in this chapter, there are probably others that you have never used and should become familiar with.

Before You Begin

This chapter assumes a basic knowledge of the networking concepts discussed in Chapter 1, "Networking Basics," and particularly an understanding of the layers of the Open Systems Interconnection (OSI) reference model, as covered in Lesson 2: The OSI Reference Model, in Chapter 1.

Lesson 1: Network Operating Systems

In the past, there was a significant difference between a standalone operating system and a network operating system. The typical operating system provided no networking capabilities, and you had to purchase and install networking software to run on it. Today, virtually all operating systems are network operating systems, because they include, right in the box, the software needed to connect to a network. This lesson is concerned primarily with operating systems that provide server functions, although in some cases you can use the server system as a client or as a member of a peer-to-peer network as well.

Note For more information about the difference between client/server and peer-to-peer networks, see Lesson 1: Network Communications, in Chapter 1, "Networking Basics."

After this lesson, you will be able to

- List the network operating systems used for server systems
- Describe the basic networking capabilities of Microsoft Windows 2000 Server, Windows NT Server, Novell Network, and UNIX

Estimated lesson time: 40 minutes

Windows NT and Windows 2000

All Windows operating systems except Windows NT and Windows 2000 are built on the MS-DOS kernel. Windows NT 3.1, first released in 1993, was a radical departure from the MS-DOS tradition. It was newly designed from the ground up to support an entirely different memory architecture and to integrate networking capabilities into the operating system itself. Windows NT and Windows 2000 also offer *preemptive multitasking,* which enables the system processor to run multiple programs simultaneously without relying on the programs themselves to return control to the processor. In the years since the original release, Microsoft has released several relatively minor Windows NT upgrades, culminating in version 4.0, and then finally released Windows 2000, which was a major upgrade.

Windows NT and Windows 2000 have always existed in versions intended both for servers and for client workstations. Windows NT is available in Server and Workstation versions, and Windows 2000 is available in three Server versions (Server, Advanced Server, and Datacenter Server) for systems with various numbers of processors, and a Professional version for client workstations. The underlying kernels of both server and workstation versions are essentially identical;

the difference between the two is that the server version includes a large collection of additional programs, services, and utilities designed for server use, many of which are concerned with networking. The following sections examine some of these components and how they affect the networking capabilities of the operating systems.

File Systems

Sharing files is one of the main reasons for networking computers, and all network operating systems include a service that makes file sharing possible. One of the most important elements of file sharing is the ability to restrict access to the server files. Windows NT and Windows 2000 both include a file system called NTFS (the NT file system) that is specifically designed for this purpose. The MS-DOS–based versions of Windows use the File Allocation Table (FAT) file system, and Windows NT and Windows 2000 support FAT, too. You can share FAT drives with other users on the network, but the FAT file system's security capabilities are extremely limited. When you create NTFS drives during a Windows NT or Windows 2000 installation, you can specify access permissions for specific files and folders to the users and groups on your network with great precision, using the controls shown in Figure 4.1. NTFS also supports larger amounts of storage than do FAT drives.

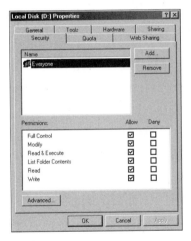

Figure 4.1 The NTFS file system enables a network administrator to control access to files and folders on Windows NT and Windows 2000 drives.

For example, if you store your company's accounting spreadsheets on a Windows NT or Windows 2000 NTFS drive, you can grant the bookkeepers full Read/Write access to the files, grant Read-only access to other company executives, and prevent any other users from even seeing that the files exist. Maintaining these permissions is an important part of the network administrator's job.

Warning NTFS drives can be read only by the Windows NT and Windows 2000 operating systems. If you were to boot a computer with NTFS drives using an MS-DOS boot disk, for example, the drives would be invisible. However, this compatibility issue has nothing to do with access to the drives over the network. Any operating system can access shared NTFS drives, as long as the appropriate permissions are in place.

Services

In Windows NT and Windows 2000 terminology, a *service* is a program that runs continuously in the background while other operations are running at the same time (see Figure 4.2). Most of the networking capabilities in Windows NT and Windows 2000, and particularly the server functions, are provided by services. In most cases, you configure services to load when the system boots, and they remain loaded and running even when users log on and log off the computer.

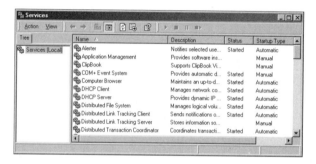

Figure 4.2 Windows NT and Windows 2000 include a variety of services that you can configure to load at boot time.

The following services are the core of the operating system's networking capabilities:

- **Server** Enables the system to share its resources, such as files and printers
- **Workstation** Enables the system to access the shared resources on another computer
- **Computer Browser** Maintains a list of the shared resources on a network from which users can choose
- **Messenger** Enables the system to display pop-up messages about the activities on other network systems
- **Alerter** Works with the Messenger service to notify selected users of administrative alerts that occur on the system

The following services are optional, but provide important networking support:

- **Internet Information Server (IIS)** Provides Internet services, such as World Wide Web and File Transfer Protocol (FTP) servers

- **Windows Internet Naming Service (WINS)** Resolves Windows computer (NetBIOS) names into Internet Protocol (IP) addresses

- **Domain Name System (DNS) Server** Resolves DNS host names into IP addresses

- **Dynamic Host Configuration Protocol (DHCP) Server** Automatically configures Transmission Control Protocol/Internet Protocol (TCP/IP) settings on multiple client systems

- **Routing and Remote Access (RRA) Server** Enables a server to route traffic between two local area networks (LANs) or a wide area network (WAN) and a LAN, and provides support for various routing protocols

- **Distributed File System (DFS)** Enables shared drives on servers all over the network to appear to clients as a single combined share

- **Microsoft Cluster Server** Enables systems running Windows NT 4.0 Enterprise Server or Windows 2000 Advanced Server to operate as part of a cluster—a group of servers that perform the same exact operations in unison, for fault-tolerance purposes

Security

Security is a primary concern on larger networks, and Windows NT and Windows 2000 provide a much more comprehensive security model than do the MS-DOS-based versions of Windows. Windows NT Server and Windows 2000 Server systems have the ability to function as *domain controllers,* which store information about accounts and other network resources, for access by clients anywhere on the network. Using domain controllers instead of individual computers to store security information makes it easier for network administrators to control access to network resources. For more information about domain controllers, see Lesson 3: Directory Services, later in this chapter.

Novell NetWare

Novell NetWare was the first commercially successful network operating system, and while its popularity has largely been eclipsed by Windows NT and Windows 2000, it still remains a viable networking platform. NetWare is strictly a client/server operating system, unlike Windows NT and Windows 2000, which can function as both clients and servers. This means that you cannot use a NetWare server to access shared resources on other computers or run workstation applications. The NetWare operating system is not DOS-based (although it loads from a DOS prompt), and is dedicated solely to server operations. NetWare clients communicate only with NetWare servers, and not with each other. To transfer files from one workstation to another, for example, you must copy them from the first workstation to a server, and then from the server to the other workstation.

NetWare is available in two primary versions, 3.2 and 5.1. Version 3.2 was intended to be the final release of the original NetWare product that stores user account information in a simple flat database called the *bindery*. The bindery was replaced by Novell Directory Services (NDS) in NetWare version 4.0 (released in 1993), but Novell continues to develop and market the 3.*x* version because it has a large installed user base that does not need the more advanced capabilities of NDS, and these users have no plans to upgrade their networks. Version 5.1 is the current release of the NDS-based NetWare product that began with version 4.0.

NetWare is a network operating system that was originally designed primarily to provide clients with access to file and print services, and these remain NetWare's strengths. As a network application platform, NetWare trails behind both Windows and UNIX, and there is currently relatively little application development for NetWare.

Note Novell Directory Services is NetWare's greatest strength. NDS is a full-featured directory service that was released in 1993, and has therefore had a long time to mature. Microsoft's equivalent directory service, called Active Directory, was only released in 2000. For more information about NDS, see Lesson 3: Directory Services, later in this chapter.

Because they do not have to perform workstation operations, NetWare servers have a relatively simple, character-based interface, as shown in Figure 4.3. There is no need for a graphical interface on a server (although the most current versions have an optional Java-based interface called ConsoleOne that you can use), and as a result, the computer can devote less of its resources to maintaining a graphical display and more to performing its server functions.

Figure 4.3 The NetWare server console is character-based, but uses keyboard-driven menus.

Like Windows NT and Windows 2000, NetWare has its own file system that enables you to control access to the server resources with great precision. You can assign access permissions based on either bindery accounts or NDS objects, depending on which version of NetWare you are using. The NetWare file system consists of volumes that you create on server drives. By adding specialized components called name space modules, you can create NetWare volumes that support various client file systems, such as Windows Virtual File Allocation Table (VFAT), Macintosh, and Network File System (NFS). This enables clients to store their files on NetWare servers using their own native formats.

NetWare Protocols

When NetWare was first developed in the mid-1980s, networking was more of a proprietary venture, and interoperability between products made by different manufacturers was less of a concern than it is today. Novell, therefore, developed their own set of networking protocols, which have come to be named after the main network layer protocol, called Internetwork Packet Exchange (IPX). Unlike Windows NT, Windows 2000, and UNIX, which have long since adopted TCP/IP as their native protocols, NetWare still relies heavily on IPX. Fortunately, Microsoft has developed its own protocol, called NWLink, to be compatible with IPX. All of the Windows operating systems can use NWLink to access shared NetWare resources.

Note For more information about the IPX protocols, see Chapter 6, "Network Layer Protocols," and Chapter 7, "Transport Layer Protocols."

NetWare Services

In addition to its core file and print services, which have been present since the early days of NetWare, the latest versions include many other additional services, such as the following:

- **Novell Storage Services (NSS)** This is a 64-bit, indexed storage service that enables administrators to use the storage space on multiple drives to create an unlimited number of logical volumes up to 8 terabytes in size. (A terabyte is 2^{40} bytes, approximately 1 trillion bytes, or precisely 1,099,511,627,776.)

- **Novell Distributed Print Services (NDPS)** This is a new network printing architecture that replaces NetWare's traditional queue-based printing with a single printer object in NDS that provides simplified, centralized administration.

- **NetWare Internet Servers** NetWare includes Web, FTP, News, and Multimedia Servers, as well as a Web Search Server that indexes your Web sites for easier client access.

- **DNS and DHCP Servers** NetWare now supports TCP/IP in addition to IPX, and includes DNS and DHCP servers that can resolve host names into IP addresses and configure TCP/IP clients, all from the NetWare platform.

- **Multiprotocol WAN Router** This service enables a NetWare server to route multiple network-layer protocols between two LANs or between a LAN and a WAN. You can use the router to connect private networks together, or to connect a network to the Internet.

UNIX

UNIX is a network operating system that was originally developed in the 1970s, and is now available in dozens of different versions and variants. Unlike Windows and NetWare, UNIX is not the product of one particular company. A variety of different development teams worked on their own UNIX versions during the ensuing decades, which were released under many different names, including the following:

- **UNIX System V** This is the descendent of the original UNIX development program started by AT&T in the 1970s. The UNIX trademark has changed hands several times over the years, and UNIX System V is now owned by The Santa Cruz Operation, Inc., generally known as SCO.

- **BSD UNIX** Berkeley Software Distribution (BSD) UNIX is one of the first variants to splinter off from the original AT&T development effort, and has become one of the most consistently popular UNIX products. The most popular BSD UNIX versions today are FreeBSD, OpenBSD, and NetBSD, all of which are available for download from the Internet, free of charge.

- **Sun Solaris** Sun Microsystems markets Solaris, one of the most popular and user-friendly commercial UNIX operating systems available. Solaris is essentially a modified version of BSD UNIX with elements of SVR4, one of the progenitors of UNIX System V. Solaris also includes Open Windows, one of the better graphical interfaces for UNIX.

- **Linux** Linux is a UNIX-based subculture unto itself, in that there are many different versions, both free and commercial. Originally developed as a school project by a student named Linus Torvalds, Linux is the quintessential open source operating system, because its development and maintenance was almost totally a noncommercial collaboration until quite recently. There are now some Linux versions being sold as commercial products with documentation and technical support, but others are still available free of charge.

- **Hardware-specific UNIX variants** Several manufacturers of computer hardware have developed their own UNIX variants, which are designed specifically to run on their computers. These include Hewlett Packard's HP-UX and IBM's Advanced Interactive Executive (better known as AIX).

Note While NetWare runs solely on computers with Intel-based processors, and Windows NT and Windows 2000 run on the Intel and Alpha platforms, the various UNIX operating systems run on computers with a wide variety of processors, including Intel, Alpha, Sun Microsystems' proprietary SPARC processor, and others.

The UNIX operating systems are built around the TCP/IP protocols, and while all have certain similarities, they vary greatly in their capabilities. This is due to the variations in the additional software included with the operating system and the commercial (or non-commercial) nature of the various products. Some UNIX variants are commercial products marketed by large software companies, such as Hewlett Packard, Sun Microsystems, and IBM. Others are developed and maintained as part of the open source movement, in which volunteer programmers work on the software in their spare time, usually communicating with their colleagues over the Internet, and freely releasing their work to the public domain. There are many different UNIX operating systems that you can download from the Internet free of charge, such as FreeBSD, NetBSD, and various forms of Linux.

This non-commercial side of UNIX development is based on the fact that many of the development teams freely post the source code for the operating system. Users with programming expertise then modify the code to suit their particular needs and post the revised code for use by others. This is in stark contrast to companies like Microsoft and Novell, who zealously guard the source code for their operating systems.

UNIX is primarily an application server platform, and is typically associated with Internet services, such as Web, FTP, and e-mail servers. As with Windows NT and Windows 2000, UNIX systems can function as both servers and clients at the same time. While you can use UNIX as a general purpose LAN server, it is much more difficult to install and administer than either Windows or NetWare. There are UNIX programs that provide the file and print services needed by LAN users, such as the NFS and the Line Printer Daemon (LPD), but they are far from being as easy to use as their Windows NT, Windows 2000, and NetWare equivalents. NetWare's strength is in file and print services, while the strength of UNIX is in its network application capabilities. Windows NT and Windows 2000 fall somewhere between the two, fulfilling both roles but doing neither as well as the more specialized operating systems.

Note *Daemon* is the UNIX term for an application that runs continuously in the background, like a service in Windows NT or Windows 2000.

UNIX, in general, is a less intuitive operating system than either Windows or NetWare. Although many UNIX variants now include graphical user interfaces (GUIs), UNIX is still primarily a character-based platform, and the command interface requires a good deal of study and practice to use efficiently. While a relatively unsophisticated user can install a Windows NT, Windows 2000, or NetWare server and get it running without too much trouble, the same cannot be said for the typical UNIX operating system.

Exercise 4.1: Network Operating System Products

Match the network operating system in the left column with the phrase in the right column that best describes it.

1. Linux

   a. Uses a bindery to store user accounts

2. Windows NT

   b. Current version of the original AT&T UNIX

3. UNIX System V

   c. Available in Server, Advanced Server, and Datacenter versions

4. NetWare 3.*x*

   d. First version of Windows not based on MS-DOS

5. Windows 2000

   e. Open source UNIX version

Lesson 2: Network Clients

A *client* is a software component that enables a computer to access the resources provided by a server. Clients can take many forms, and can either be included as part of an operating system or distributed as a separate product. In its simplest form, a client can be a standalone program that sends requests to and receives replies from a server. Your Web browser, for example, is a client that communicates with Web servers on your local network or the Internet. In the same way, FTP, e-mail, and news reader programs are all clients. These clients function at the application layer of the OSI reference model and are highly specialized; they only communicate with one type of server. Application-layer clients contain no lower-layer protocols of their own, relying instead on protocols such as TCP/IP and Ethernet, which are already installed on the computer, to provide network communication services.

After this lesson, you will be able to

- Describe the client capabilities of the major operating systems
- Identify the components of the client networking stack on a Windows system
- Distinguish between the Microsoft and the Novell versions of clients for NetWare

Estimated lesson time: 30 minutes

The other main type of client on a workstation is the one that enables you to access shared resources on the local network, such as files and printers. This type of client is more tightly integrated with the operating system; you don't have to launch a special program and you can access files and printers through your regular applications, just as though they were part of your local computer environment. This type of client is specific to the platform used by the server. There are clients for Windows networks, clients for NetWare, and clients for UNIX systems. In some cases, the client is supplied as part of the operating system, while in others you must install a separate client software package. The following sections examine the different LAN client platforms.

Windows Clients

Almost all versions of Windows (including Windows for Workgroups, Windows 95, Windows 98, Windows Me, as well as Windows NT and Windows 2000, in both Server and Workstation versions) include both client and server capabilities with the operating system. This means that you can share the files and printers on any of these Windows systems and also use the client capabilities to access shared files and printers on other systems. Note that Windows 3.1 and earlier ship with no network client at all.

In the case of Windows 95, Windows 98, Windows Me, Windows NT, and Windows 2000, the operating system includes everything you need to connect to a Windows network, including a complete client networking stack. The stack (shown in Figure 4.4) consists of the following major components:

- **Clients** What these operating systems often call a "client" is actually a component called a redirector. A *redirector* is a module that receives requests for file system resources from an application and determines whether the requested resource is located in a local or network drive. It's the redirector that enables you to open a network file in your word processing program as easily as you would open a local file.

- **Protocol drivers** The Windows protocol drivers implement the protocol suites required for network communications, such as TCP/IP, IPX, or NetBEUI. In Windows terminology, the singular word "protocol" is used to refer to components such as TCP/IP and IPX, both of which are actually suites consisting of several different protocols. There are also other software components running on the system (such as Ethernet, for example) that Windows doesn't refer to as protocols, but which actually are.

- **Network interface adapter drivers** The network interface adapter driver is a Windows device driver that provides the connection between the network interface adapter and the rest of the networking stack. The combination of the network interface adapter and its driver implement the data-link layer protocol used by the system, such as Ethernet or Token Ring. Windows supports network interface adapters that conform to the Network Driver Interface Specification (NDIS). The various operating systems use different NDIS driver versions.

- **Services** While they are not essential to client functionality, there are services included in Windows that provide additional networking capabilities. For example, to share resources on a Windows system, you must install the File And Printer Sharing For Microsoft Networks service.

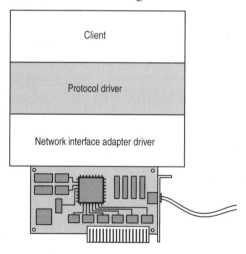

Figure 4.4 The Windows networking stack consists of several components that work together to provide client access to network resources.

Together with the network interface adapter, these software components provide the functions of all seven layers of the OSI model. A system can have more than one of each component installed, providing alternative paths through the networking stack for different applications. Most of the Windows operating systems include two redirectors. For example, there might be one for Windows networking and one for connecting to NetWare servers. The operating systems include multiple protocol drivers for the same purpose. NetWare connectivity traditionally requires the IPX protocol (although the latest versions of NetWare do support TCP/IP), and a Windows network can use TCP/IP or NetBEUI. Windows and NetWare systems usually share the same network medium, but it's also possible to install two network interface adapters, each with its own driver, and connect the computer to two networks, one for Windows and one for NetWare.

Note Although the drivers can take different forms, all of the Windows operating systems contain the same set of basic networking components, with the exception of Windows for Workgroups. Windows for Workgroups was developed in the early days of Microsoft networking, and is rarely used today. That operating system includes a redirector for Windows networking and the NetBEUI and IPX protocols, but no NetWare client is included, nor is the TCP/IP protocol. However, you can add NetWare support by installing a client supplied by Novell, and you can add TCP/IP support by downloading and installing the TCP/IP-32 update, available from Microsoft at *ftp://ftp.microsoft.com/peropsys/windows/public/tcpip/wfwt32.exe*.

The protocols at the various layers specify the path up or down through the OSI model. For example, when a packet arrives at a workstation from the network, the Ethernet frame contains a code that specifies the network layer protocol that it should use. The network layer protocol header then specifies a transport layer protocol, and the transport layer header contains a port number that identifies the application that should receive the data. For packets generated by the workstation, the process works in reverse. The redirector specifies a transport layer protocol, the transport layer specifies the network layer protocol, and the network layer specifies the data-link layer protocol.

Installing Windows Networking Components

While technologies like Plug and Play now automate the installation of the Windows networking components in most cases, you may still find yourself having to install a client or a protocol manually. The process of installing a protocol module on a Windows 2000 Professional system is described below. The procedure is virtually identical in Windows 95, Windows 98, and Windows Me. Windows NT uses a slightly different user interface, but the networking architecture is essentially the same.

▶   **To install a protocol module**

1. From the Start menu's Settings group, select Network And Dial-up Connections.

2. Right-click the Local Area Connection icon and select Properties from the shortcut menu to display the Local Area Connection Properties dialog box shown in Figure 4.5.

3. Click the Install button to display the Select Network Component Type dialog box.

4. Highlight the Protocol entry in the components list and click the Add button to display the Select Network Protocol dialog box. To install a different component, such as a client, make a different selection in the Select Network Component Type dialog box.

5. Highlight an entry (such as NetBEUI Protocol) in the list of protocols and click the OK button.

6. Click the Close button in the Local Area Connection Properties dialog box to complete the component installation. You might need to supply the Windows 2000 installation CD-ROM so that the program can copy the required files. When the process is complete, you are prompted to restart the computer.

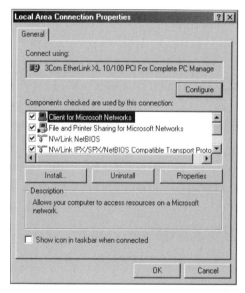

Figure 4.5 The Local Area Connection Properties dialog box lists all of the networking components installed on the system.

Note The only networking component that you do not install from the Network And Dial-up Connections dialog box is the network interface adapter driver, because this module is associated with the network interface adapter in the system. To install a network interface adapter driver manually, use the Add/Remove Hardware facility found in Control Panel.

NetWare Clients

When Microsoft first introduced its own network operating systems (Windows for Workgroups and Windows NT) in 1993, Novell NetWare ruled the local area networking industry. In order to successfully compete with Novell, Microsoft knew that their operating systems had to be able to access NetWare resources, but early attempts to have Novell supply a NetWare client for the Windows operating systems failed. As a result, Microsoft developed the NetWare clients for Windows, and Novell subsequently released clients of their own. Both have continued to update their software, and to this day you can choose between the Microsoft client for NetWare that ships with Windows or download Novell's client from their Web site.

Microsoft Clients for NetWare

The NetWare clients provided in the Windows operating systems by Microsoft fit into the same networking architecture as the client for Microsoft networking. In order to access NetWare resources in Windows 2000 Professional, you must install the Client Service for NetWare (CSNW) and the NWLink IPX/SPX/NetBIOS Compatible Transport Protocol modules using the same procedure described earlier in this lesson under "Installing Windows Networking Components." In Windows 95, Windows 98, or Windows Me, the names of the modules are slightly different; you must install the Client for NetWare Networks and the IPX/SPX-compatible Protocol.

The CSNW module is a second redirector that you can use along with—or instead of—the Microsoft networking client. When an application requests access to a network resource, the system determines whether the request is for a Windows or NetWare file and sends it to the appropriate redirector. The NWLink protocol module is a reverse-engineered version of Novell's IPX protocols. In most cases, Windows systems use the IPX protocols only to access NetWare servers. The NetWare redirector is connected to the NWLink protocol module, while the Microsoft redirector uses TCP/IP or NetBEUI. Both protocols' modules are then connected to the same network interface adapter driver, as shown in Figure 4.6.

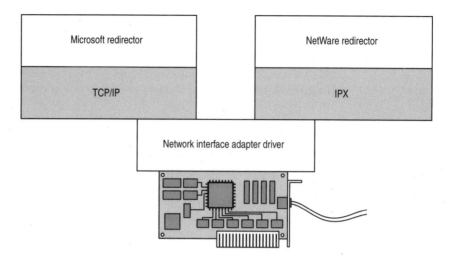

Figure 4.6 Microsoft's NetWare client functions as a second redirector within the networking architecture, using its own version of the IPX protocols.

Using the Gateway Service for NetWare

The CSNW included with Windows 2000 Professional and Windows NT Workstation provides basic NetWare connectivity, but Windows 2000 Server and Windows NT Server include the Gateway Service for NetWare (GSNW), which expands this functionality. In addition to providing client access to NetWare servers, GSNW also enables Windows systems without a NetWare client installed to access NetWare resources. Once you've installed GSNW, the service's client capabilities enable it to connect to NetWare servers. You can then configure GSNW to share those NetWare resources using the system's Microsoft networking capabilities. When a Windows client accesses the share on the Windows NT or Windows 2000 server, the server accesses the files on the NetWare server and relays them to the client.

Novell Clients for NetWare

Novell continues to maintain its own client software packages for NetWare, which you can use instead of those included with the Windows operating systems. The Microsoft and Novell clients both provide the same basic functionality, such as access to NetWare volumes and printers and access to Novell Directory Services, but Novell's clients also provide additional capabilities that are helpful to administrators and power users.

The primary difference between the Microsoft and Novell clients is that the Novell clients include the NetWare Administrator application, which is the tool that administrators use to create and maintain objects in the NDS database. This is a critical part of NetWare administration, and it's the main reason for using Novell clients instead of Microsoft clients. Apart from including NetWare Administrator, Novell clients provide additional file management functions and utilities accessible from shortcut menus and the Taskbar tray, but they also tend to be noticeably slower than Microsoft clients.

Novell maintains the following three NetWare clients for Windows:

- Novell Client for DOS and Windows 3.1*x*
- Novell Client for Windows 95 and Windows 98
- Novell Client for Windows NT and Windows 2000

The Windows 95, Windows 98, Windows NT, and Windows 2000 clients all consist of modules that fit into the existing Windows networking architecture. Each client includes its own redirector—which is a genuine Novell IPX protocol module, rather than Microsoft's compatible version—and network interface adapter drivers that conform to the Open Data-Link Interface (ODI) standard used by Novell. However, the client can use the NDIS drivers supplied with Windows, if one is already installed.

Though Novell has not added Windows Me to the list of supported clients, they claim that the client for Windows 95 and Windows 98 will fully support Windows Me, as well.

The client for DOS and Windows 3.1*x* is different, because these operating systems don't have their own networking capabilities. The client provides a complete networking architecture in itself, which can also work alongside the Windows client included in Windows for Workgroups.

Exercise 4.2: Network Client Concepts

1. What is the protocol traditionally associated with NetWare networking?
    a. NetBEUI
    b. IPX
    c. TCP/IP
    d. Ethernet

2. What is the Windows component that enables an application to access a network resource in the same way as a local one?
    a. A redirector
    b. A protocol
    c. A client
    d. A service

3. Which of the following Windows network components is not required for client functionality?

   a. A redirector

   b. A service

   c. A protocol

   d. A network interface adapter driver

4. What is the most important reason for a network administrator to use a Novell client for NetWare rather than Microsoft's NetWare?

   a. Novell's client includes a genuine version of the IPX protocols.

   b. Novell's client is faster than Microsoft's.

   c. Novell's client is less expensive than Microsoft's.

   d. Novell's client includes the NetWare Administrator application.

5. Which of the following Windows 2000 networking modules do you not install from the Network And Dial-up Connections dialog box?

   a. Services

   b. Clients

   c. Protocols

   d. Network interface adapter drivers

Lesson 3: Directory Services

A *directory service* is a database of user accounts and other information that network administrators use to control access to shared network resources. When users connect to a network, they have to be authenticated before they can access network resources. Authentication is the process of checking the user's credentials (usually a user name and a password) against the directory. Users that supply the proper credentials are permitted access according to the permissions specified by the network administrator.

As explained in Lesson 1: Network Communications, in Chapter 1, "Networking Basics," on a peer-to-peer network, each computer maintains its own user accounts and security settings, while client/server networks rely on a centralized security database or directory service. Directory services range from simple flat file databases containing a list of accounts to complex hierarchical databases that store information about a network's many different resources: hardware, software, and human.

Flat file directory services are suitable for relatively small installations, but for large enterprise networks, they are difficult to maintain. For this reason, both Novell and Microsoft have developed hierarchical directory services that can support networks of virtually any size, and that have the fault tolerance and security capabilities needed for large installations.

After this lesson, you will be able to

- Identify the directory services provided with the Windows NT Server, Windows 2000 Server, and Novell NetWare operating systems
- Describe the difference between a flat file directory and a hierarchical directory
- List the fault tolerance and security features of the major directory services

Estimated lesson time: 20 minutes

The NetWare Bindery

The bindery—included in all versions of NetWare up to and including 3.2—is a simple database that contains a list of user and group accounts, information about those accounts, and little else. The bindery even stretches the definition of a directory service, since it is not a centralized storehouse of information for an entire network. Every NetWare bindery server maintains its own list of accounts, which it uses to authenticate users trying to access its resources. If network users need to access files or printers on more than one NetWare server, they must have an account on each server, and each server performs its own user authentication.

In the early days of NetWare, LANs were relatively small and users generally required access to only one or two servers, so the bindery was all they needed. In fact, there is still a substantial user base of NetWare shops that don't feel the need for an enterprise directory service like NDS, which is why there is a bindery-based version of NetWare (version 3.2) still on the market, years after the release of the newer NDS versions.

Novell Directory Services

NetWare 4.0, released in 1993, was the first version to include NDS, which at that time stood for NetWare Directory Services, but is now Novell Directory Services. NDS was the first hierarchical directory service to be a commercial success, and in the years since its initial release, it has matured into a robust enterprise network solution.

A hierarchical directory service is composed of *objects*, which are arranged in tree-like structure, much like a directory tree (see Figure 4.7). There are two basic kinds of objects, called containers and leaves. *Containers* are the equivalent of directories in a file system; they hold other objects. *Leaves* represent network resources, such as users, groups, computers, and applications. All objects are composed of attributes (which NDS calls properties), the nature of which depend on the object's type. For example, the properties of a user object can specify the user's name, password, telephone number, e-mail address, and other pertinent information.

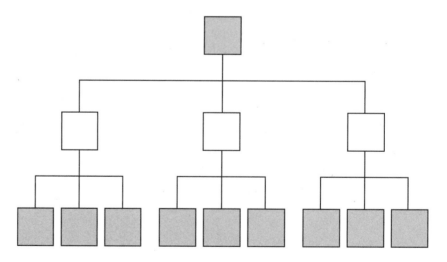

Figure 4.7 NDS and other hierarchical directory services consist of objects arranged in a tree structure.

Note The basic components of the hierarchical directory services in NetWare and Windows 2000, such as the use of objects and attributes, containers and leaves, and the tree structure, are derived from the X.500 directory service standard, which was developed by the International Telecommunications Union (ITU) and the International Organization for Standardization (ISO). X.500 is not a commercial directory services product. Rather, it is a model for a global directory that is designed to enable users to search for people and objects by providing an object naming standard and a hierarchical tree structure.

The types of objects that you can create in the NDS tree, and the properties of those object types are determined by the directory schema. Network applications can modify the schema to create their own specialized object types or to add new properties to existing object types. This makes the directory service a flexible tool for application developers. For example, a network backup program can create an object type used to represent a job queue, which contains backup jobs waiting to be executed.

Deploying the directory service is a matter of designing and building an NDS tree, which involves the creation of a hierarchy of containers into which administrators put the various leaf objects. The tree design can be based on the geographical layout of the network, with containers representing buildings, floors, and rooms, or it can be based on the structure of the organization using the network, with containers representing divisions, departments, and workgroups. An NDS tree can also use a combination of the two, or any other organizational paradigm the administrator chooses. The important part of the design process is grouping together users with similar network access requirements, to simplify the process of assigning them permissions. Like a file system, permissions flow down through the NDS tree and are inherited by the objects beneath. Granting a container object permission to access a particular resource means that all of the objects in that container receive the same permission.

Unlike the NetWare bindery, which is server-specific, there is usually only one NDS database for the entire network. When a user logs in, he or she logs into NDS, not into a specific server, and one authentication can grant the user access to resources located anywhere on the network. This means that administrators need only create and maintain one account for each user, instead of one for each server the user accesses, as in bindery-based NetWare.

Because the entire NetWare network relies on NDS, the directory is designed with features that ensure its availability at all times. You can split the NDS database into *partitions*, which are stored on different servers, to make it easy for a user to log in using a nearby server. In addition, you can create replicas of the partitions, and store those on different servers as well. This way, if a server containing all or part of the NDS tree should fail, users can still access the directory from another server.

Windows NT Domains

Windows NT uses a directory service that is more capable and more complex than the NetWare bindery, but is still not suitable for a large enterprise network. Windows NT networks are organized into *domains*, which contain accounts that represent the users, groups, and computers on the network. A domain is a flat file database like a bindery, but it is not server-specific. The domain directory is stored on Windows NT servers that have been designated as domain controllers during the operating system installation.

Warning A Windows NT domain is not the same as an Internet domain, such as those used by the DNS. Windows NT domains are named using a single word, while DNS domains have names that are at least two words long and are separated by periods (such as *microsoft.com*). Be sure not to confuse the two.

A server can be a Primary Domain Controller (PDC) or a Backup Domain Controller (BDC). Most domains have at least two domain controllers, for fault tolerance purposes. Each domain has one PDC, which contains the main copy of the domain directory, and can have any number of BDCs, each of which contains a replica of the domain. Whenever network administrators modify the directory by adding, deleting, or modifying accounts, they are making changes to the files on the PDC, which holds the master copy of the data. At periodic intervals, the PDC replicates the directory database to the BDCs (as shown in Figure 4.8), which keeps them updated with the latest information. This process is called *single master replication*.

Note You can only designate a Windows NT server as a domain controller during the installation of the operating system. Once Windows NT is installed, you can promote a BDC to a PDC or demote a PDC to a BDC, but you can't convert a regular server into a domain controller, nor can you convert a domain controller into a regular server.

It's common for larger Windows NT networks to have multiple domains, and the domains can communicate with each other. To have this happen, administrators must create trust relationships between the domains, using a utility called the Server Manager. Trust relationships operate in one direction only. If Domain A trusts Domain B, users from Domain B can access resources in Domain A (assuming they have the appropriate permissions). In order for Domain A users to access Domain B resources, an administrator must create a trust running in that direction.

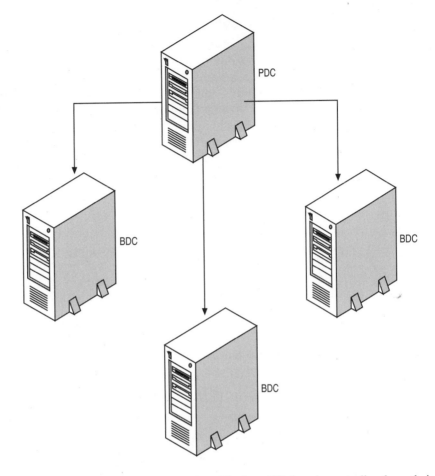

Figure 4.8 Single master replication: Windows NT domain controllers keep their information updated by replicating in one direction, from the PDC to the BDCs.

Because you have to create trust relationships manually, managing a large enterprise Windows NT network with many domains can be labor intensive. Users that have to access resources in multiple domains must have a separate account in each domain, just as users of bindery-based NetWare need a separate account on each server.

Run the **c04dem01**, **c04dem02**, **c04dem03**, **c04dem04**, and **c04dem05** videos located in the **Demos** folder on the CD-ROM accompanying this book for a demonstration of Windows NT domains.

Active Directory

After many years of anticipation, Microsoft introduced an enterprise directory service in the Windows 2000 Server product line, called Active Directory. This directory service is similar in structure to NDS, in that it uses a hierarchical tree design comprised of container and leaf objects. The fundamental unit of organization in Active Directory directory service is still the domain, but now you can group domains together into a *tree*, and even group multiple trees together into a *forest*. Domains that are in the same tree automatically have bidirectional trust relationships established between them, which eliminates the need for administrators to create them manually. The trust relationships are also *transitive*, meaning that if Domain A trusts Domain B and Domain B trusts Domain C, then Domain A trusts Domain C.

In Windows NT, the domain structure is completely separate from the concept of DNS domains, but in Active Directory architecture, the two are more similar. Domains in the same tree are named using multiword domain names (as in DNS), which reflect the tree structure of the directory. If the root domain in a tree is called *abccorp.com*, the other domains beneath the root would have names like *sales.abccorp.com* and *engineering.abccorp.com*.

Active Directory architecture still uses domain controllers like Windows NT, but you have a great deal more flexibility in their configuration. In Windows 2000, you can promote any server to a domain controller at any time or demote it back to a standard server, using a Windows wizard. In addition, there are no more PDCs and BDCs; all domain controllers on an Active Directory network function as peers. Administrators can make changes to the Active Directory data on any domain controller, and the servers propagate those changes to the other domain controllers throughout the network, as shown in Figure 4.9. This is called *multiple master replication*.

With these features, Active Directory can support networks of virtually any size, including corporate networks with sites located anywhere in the world. You can configure the replication of data between domain controllers to occur only at specific times (in order to minimize the traffic on expensive WAN links), create a directory hierarchy that reflects the locations of the branch offices, and even create links between separate trees or forests built by different companies, in the event of a merger.

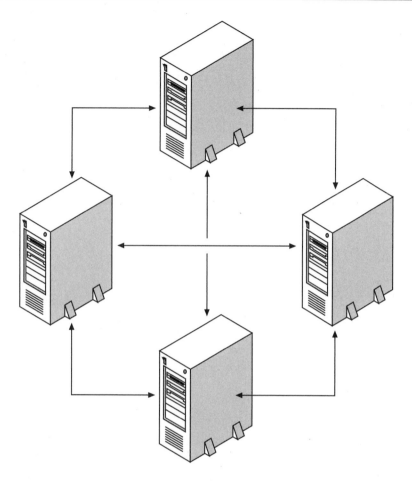

Figure 4.9 Active Directory architecture uses multiple master replication to keep all its domain controllers updated.

Exercise 4.3: Directory Service Concepts

1. Which directory service requires users to have a separate account for each server?

   a. Windows NT Domains

   b. Active Directory

   c. NetWare bindery

   d. Novell Directory Services

2. What provides communication between Windows NT domains?

   a. Trust relationships

   b. Single master replication

   c. Multiple master replication

   d. Partitioning

3. On an Active Directory network, a tree is composed of multiples of what?

   a. Servers

   b. Partitions

   c. Forests

   d. Domains

4. The types of objects you can create in an NDS tree are determined by what?

   a. Number of partitions

   b. Directory schema

   c. Number of containers

   d. X.500 directory service

5. Which of the following terms does not describe the trust relationships between Active Directory domains in the same tree?

   a. Transitive

   b. Bi-directional

   c. Automatic

   d. Single master

Chapter Summary

The key points covered in this chapter are as follows.

Network Operating Systems

- The Windows NT, Windows 2000, and UNIX operating systems all include both server and client functionality.
- NTFS is a file system that enables network administrators to control access to shared files and folders.
- Many of the Windows NT and Windows 2000 networking functions are performed by services.
- Novell NetWare is strictly a client/server network operating system.
- Early versions of NetWare used a bindery to store user accounts, while later versions use Novell Directory Services.
- UNIX is available in many different versions produced by different companies.
- UNIX systems excel in running network applications; NetWare's strength is file and print services; Windows NT and Windows 2000 can fulfill both roles.

Network Clients

- The Windows networking stack consists of components called clients, protocols, network interface adapter drivers, and services.
- You install most of the Windows 2000 networking components from the Network And Dial-up Connections dialog box.
- Most Windows versions include a client for NetWare networks created by Microsoft, but you can also use a client supplied by Novell.

Directory Services

- The NetWare bindery is a simple list of user and group accounts maintained on each server.
- NDS was the first hierarchical directory service to achieve commercial success.
- Windows NT stores user account information in domains that are stored on servers called domain controllers.
- Active Directory directory service expands on the domain concept by adding administrative units called trees and forests.
- Directory services such as Active Directory and NDS provide fault tolerance by replicating their information to multiple servers.

Chapter Review

1. Which of the following ITU standards is the basis for NDS and Active Directory?

    a. X.25

    b. X.400

    c. X.500

    d. X.5

2. Which types of network clients are included in Windows 2000 Professional?

    a. Client Service for NetWare

    b. Gateway Service for NetWare

    c. Client for Microsoft Networks

    d. Client Service for UNIX

3. What is the Windows NT and Windows 2000 file system called that enables administrators to assign permissions to individual files?

    a. Active Directory

    b. NDS

    c. FAT

    d. NTFS

4. Which of the following services on a Windows NT or Windows 2000 network is responsible for configuring TCP/IP clients?

    a. DNS

    b. WINS

    c. IIS

    d. DHCP

5. Which of the following network operating systems is generally considered to be the best application server platform?

    a. Windows NT

    b. Windows 2000

    c. Novell NetWare

    d. UNIX

6. What is a program called that runs in the background on a UNIX system?

   a. A service

   b. A daemon

   c. An application

   d. A domain

7. Which of the following directory services uses multiword names for its domains?

   a. NetWare bindery

   b. NDS

   c. Windows NT Domains

   d. Active Directory

8. What is splitting an NDS tree into pieces and storing those pieces on different servers called?

   a. Replication

   b. Partitioning

   c. Establishing trust relationships

   d. Creating a tree

9. What is the Windows NT and Windows 2000 service that maintains a list of shared resources on the network called?

   a. Server

   b. Client

   c. Computer Browser

   d. Messenger

10. Which of the following is not a true statement?

   a. Containers are composed of objects.

   b. Trees are composed of domains.

   c. Objects are composed of attributes.

   d. Forests are composed of trees.

C H A P T E R   5

Data-Link Layer Protocols

About This Chapter

The protocol operating at the data-link layer of the Open Systems Interconnection (OSI) reference model describes the nature of the network medium and performs the final preparation of outgoing data before it is transmitted. This protocol also receives incoming data, evaluates it, and, if necessary, passes it on to the appropriate network layer protocol. This chapter examines the protocols most commonly found at the data-link layer and how they affect the performance of the network. These protocols are vital to any study of computer networking, as they determine how the network is constructed and how computers actually transmit and receive data.

Before You Begin

This chapter requires a basic understanding of the OSI reference model, as described in Chapter 1, "Networking Basics," as well as familiarity with the hardware components of the network as examined in Chapter 2, "Network Hardware."

Lesson 1: Ethernet

Ethernet is the most popular local area network (LAN) protocol operating at the data-link layer, and has been for decades. In most cases, when people talk about a LAN, they are referring to an Ethernet LAN. The Ethernet protocol was developed in the 1970s and has since been upgraded repeatedly to satisfy the changing requirements of networks and network users. Today's Ethernet networks run at speeds of 10, 100, and 1,000 Mbps (1 Gbps), which enables them to fulfill roles ranging from home and small business networks to high-capacity backbones.

After this lesson, you will be able to

- List the Ethernet physical layer standards
- Describe the functions of the Ethernet frame
- Understand the CSMA/CD MAC mechanism

Estimated lesson time: 50 minutes

Ethernet Standards

There have been two sets of Ethernet standards in place over the years. The first was the original Ethernet protocol, as developed by Digital Equipment Corporation (DEC), Intel, and Xerox, and which came to be known as DIX Ethernet. The DIX Ethernet standard was first published in 1980 and defined a network running at 10 Mbps using RG8 coaxial cable in a bus topology. This standard is known as thick Ethernet, Thicknet, or 10Base5. The DIX Ethernet II standard, published in 1982, added a second physical layer option to the protocol using RG58 coaxial cable. This standard is called thin Ethernet, Thinnet, Cheapernet, or 10Base2.

Around the same time that these standards were published, an international standards-making body called the Institute of Electrical and Electronic Engineers (IEEE) set about creating an international standard defining this type of network, which would not be held in private hands as was the DIX Ethernet standard. In 1980, the IEEE assembled what they called a working group with the designation IEEE 802.3, which began the development of an Ethernet-like network standard. They couldn't call their network Ethernet because Xerox had trademarked the name, but in 1985, they published a document called the "IEEE 802.3 Carrier Sense Multiple Access with Collision Detection (CSMA/CD) Access Method and Physical Layer Specifications." This document included specifications of the same two coaxial cable options as DIX Ethernet and, after further development, added a specification of the unshielded twisted pair (UTP) cable option known as 10BaseT. Additional documents published by the IEEE 802.3 group in later years include IEEE 802.3u in 1995, which includes the 100 Mbps Fast Ethernet specifications, and IEEE 802.3z and IEEE 802.3ab, which are the 1,000 Mbps Gigabit Ethernet standards.

The IEEE 802.3 standard differs only slightly from the DIX Ethernet standard. The IEEE standard contains additional physical layer options, as already noted, and some differences in the frame format. Despite the continued use of the name Ethernet in the marketplace, however, the protocol that networks use today is actually IEEE 802.3, because this version provides the additional physical layer options and the Fast Ethernet and Gigabit Ethernet standards. Development of the DIX Ethernet standards ceased after Ethernet II, and when people use the term Ethernet today, it is understood that they actually mean IEEE 802.3. The only element of the DIX Ethernet standard still in common use is the Ethernet II frame format, which contains the Ethertype field that is used to identify the network layer protocol that generates the data in each packet.

Both the IEEE 802.3 and DIX Ethernet standards consist of the following three basic components:

- Physical layer specifications
- Frame format
- CSMA/CD media access control (MAC) mechanism

Physical Layer Specifications

The physical layer specifications included in the Ethernet standards describe the types of cables you can use to build the network, define the topology, and provide other crucial guidelines such as the maximum cable lengths and the number of repeaters you can use. The basic specifications for the Ethernet physical layer guidelines are listed in Table 5.1. Observing these guidelines is an important part of building a reliable Ethernet network, because they limit the effect of problems like attenuation and crosstalk, which are common to all networks and can inhibit the functionality of the CSMA/CD mechanism. The precise timing involved in Ethernet's collision detection mechanism makes the length of the network cables and the number of repeaters used highly significant to the network's smooth operation.

Table 5.1 Ethernet physical layer specifications

Designation	Cable Type	Topology	Speed	Maximum Segment Length
10Base5	RG8 Coaxial	Bus	10 Mbps	500 meters
10Base2	RG58 Coaxial	Bus	10 Mbps	185 meters
10BaseT	Category 3 UTP	Star	10 Mbps	100 meters
FOIRL	62.5/125 Multimode Fiber Optic	Star	10Mbps	1,000 meters
10BaseFL	62.5/125 Multimode Fiber Optic	Star	10 Mbps	2,000 meters
10BaseFB	62.5/125 Multimode Fiber Optic	Star	10 Mbps	2,000 meters
10BaseFP	62.5/125 Multimode Fiber Optic	Star	10 Mbps	500 meters
100BaseTX	Category 5 UTP	Star	100 Mbps	100 meters
100BaseT4	Category 3 UTP	Star	100 Mbps	100 meters
100BaseFX	62.5/125 Multimode Fiber Optic	Star	100 Mbps	412 meters
1000BaseLX	9/125 Singlemode Fiber Optic	Star	1,000 Mbps	5,000 meters
1000BaseLX	50/125 or 62.5/125 Multimode Fiber Optic	Star	1,000 Mbps	550 meters
1000BaseSX	50/125 Multimode Fiber Optic (400 MHz)	Star	1,000 Mbps	500 meters
1000BaseSX	50/125 Multimode Fiber Optic (500 MHz)	Star	1,000 Mbps	550 meters
1000BaseSX	62.5/125 Multimode Fiber Optic (160 MHz)	Star	1,000 Mbps	220 meters
1000BaseSX	62.5/125 Multimode Fiber Optic (200 MHz)	Star	1,000 Mbps	275 meters
1000BaseLH	9/125 Singlemode Fiber Optic	Star	1,000 Mbps	10 km
1000BaseZX	9/125 Singlemode Fiber Optic	Star	1,000 Mbps	100 km
1000BaseCX	150-ohm Shielded Copper Cable	Star	1,000 Mbps	25 meters
1000BaseT	Category 5 (or 5E) UTP	Star	1,000 Mbps	100 meters

Note For more information about the actual cables used to build Ethernet networks, see Lesson 1: Network Cables, in Chapter 2, "Network Hardware."

Coaxial Ethernet

The coaxial Ethernet standards (10Base5 and 10Base2) are the only standards that call for a bus topology. The maximum segment length indicates the length of the entire bus, from one terminator to the other, with all of the computers in between, as shown in Figure 5.1. A cable segment that connects more than two computers is called a *mixing segment*. The coaxial standards are no longer in use today, except on a few older networks, because they are more difficult to install and maintain than UTP and because they are limited to a maximum speed of 10 Mbps.

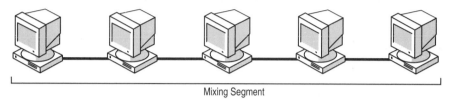

Mixing Segment

Figure 5.1 Ethernet's coaxial cable specifications use a mixing segment to connect multiple computers to the network.

UTP Ethernet

All of the other Ethernet physical layer specifications use the star topology, in which a separate cable segment connects each computer to a hub. A cable segment that connects only two devices is called a *link segment*. Unshielded twisted pair (UTP) is the most popular type of cable used on Ethernet networks today, because it is easy to install and it is upgradeable from 10 Mbps to 100 or even 1,000 Mbps. 10BaseT Ethernet uses link segments up to 100 meters long to connect computers to a repeating hub, which enables the incoming signals to go out to a computer another 100 meters away, as shown in Figure 5.2. 10BaseT uses only two of the four wire pairs in the cable, one pair for transmitting data and one pair for receiving it.

Warning Even though there are two pairs of wires left unused on many UTP networks, do not be tempted to run voice telephone or other signals over those other two pairs while the network is in use. This practice can lead to excessive amounts of signal interference due to crosstalk between the wires.

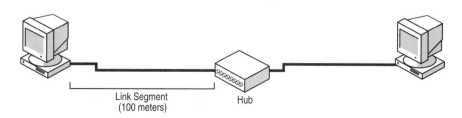

Link Segment
(100 meters)   Hub

Figure 5.2 UTP cables can connect Ethernet systems to a hub 100 meters away, and the hub repeats the signal to another hub or computer.

The Fast Ethernet standard (IEEE 802.3u) includes two UTP cable specifications, both of which retain the 100-meter maximum segment length. 100BaseTX does this by requiring a higher grade of cable, Category 5, which provides better signal transmission capabilities. 100BaseT4, however, provides the increased speed using the same Category 3 cable as older Ethernet and telephone networks. The difference between the two is that 100BaseTX uses only two pairs of wires, just like 10BaseT, while 100BaseT4 uses all four wire pairs. In addition to the transmit and receive pairs, 100BaseT4 uses the other two pairs for bi-directional communications.

Most of the physical layer specifications for Gigabit Ethernet use fiber optic cable, but there is one UTP option, defined in a separate document called IEEE 802.3ab, that does not. The 1000BaseT standard, designed specifically as an upgrade for existing UTP networks with 100-meter cable segments, calls for Category 5 cable, but is better serviced by the higher performance cables now being marketed as Enhanced Category 5 or Category 5E. The Category 5E cable rating has been officially ratified by the Electronics Industry Association and Telecommunications Industry Association (EIA/TIA). It doubles the bandwidth provided by Category 5 cable and is much less prone to signal interference resulting from crosstalk. 1000BaseT achieves its great speed by using all four wire pairs like 100BaseT4, and by using a different signaling scheme called Pulse Amplitude Modulation-5 (PAM-5).

Fiber Optic Ethernet

The use of fiber optic cable has been an Ethernet physical layer option since its early days. The Fiber Optic Inter-Repeater Link (FOIRL) was part of the DIX Ethernet II standard, and the IEEE 802.3 standards later included the 10BaseFL, 10BaseFB, and 10BaseFP specifications, which were intended for various types of networks. None of these fiber solutions were extremely popular, because running a fiber optic network at 10 Mbps is a terrible waste of potential. Fiber Distributed Data Interface (which is not a form of Ethernet), running at 100 Mbps, soon became the fiber optic backbone protocol of choice. Later, Fast Ethernet arrived with its own 100 Mbps fiber optic option, 100BaseFX. 100BaseFX uses the same hardware as 10BaseFL, but limits the length of a cable segment to 412 meters.

Gigabit Ethernet is the newest form of Ethernet, and raises the network transmission speed to 1,000 Mbps. Gigabit Ethernet relies heavily on fiber optic cabling, and provides a variety of physical layer options using different types of cable to achieve different segment lengths. Singlemode fiber cable is designed to span extremely long distances, which makes Gigabit Ethernet suitable for connecting distant networks or large campus backbones.

Cabling Guidelines

Repeating is an essential part of most Ethernet networks, and the standards include rules regarding the number of repeaters that you can use on a single LAN. For the original 10 Mbps Ethernet, the use of repeaters is governed by the *5-4-3 rule*, which states that you can have up to five cable segments, connected by four repeaters, with no more than three of these segments being mixing segments. In the days of coaxial cable networks, this meant that you could have up to three mixing segments of 500 or 185 meters each (for 10Base5 and 10Base2, respectively) populated with multiple computers and connected by two repeaters. You could also add two additional repeaters to extend the network with another two cable segments of 500 or 185 meters each, as long as these were link segments connected directly to the next repeater in line, with no intervening computers, as shown in Figure 5.3. A 10Base2 network could therefore span up to 925 meters and a 10Base5 network up to 2,500 meters.

Note For information about repeaters and their functions, see Lesson 3: Network Hubs, in Chapter 2, "Network Hardware."

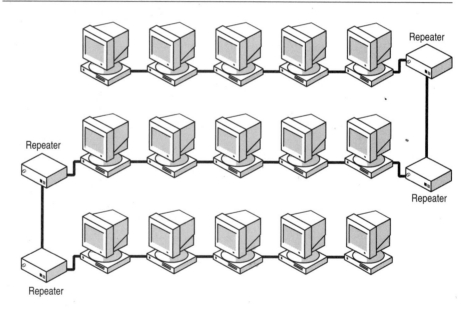

Figure 5.3 Coaxial Ethernet networks consist of up to three mixing segments and two link segments,which are all connected by repeaters.

On networks using the star topology, all of the segments are link segments, so this means that you can connect up to four repeating hubs together using their uplink ports and still adhere to the 5-4-3 rule (see Figure 5.4). As long as the traffic between the two most distant computers doesn't pass through more than four hubs, the network is configured properly. Because the hubs function as repeaters, each 10BaseT cable segment can be up to 100 meters long, for a maximum network span of 500 meters.

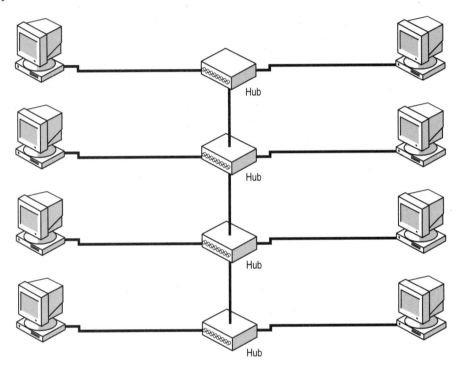

Figure 5.4 10BaseT Ethernet networks can have up to four repeating hubs connected together.

Because Fast Ethernet networks run at higher speeds, they can't support as many hubs as 10 Mbps Ethernet. The Fast Ethernet standard defines two types of hubs, Class I and Class II, which must be marked with the appropriate Roman numeral in a circle. Class I hubs connect Fast Ethernet cable segments of different types, such as 100BaseTX to 100BaseT4 or UTP to fiber optic, while Class II hubs connect segments of the same type. You can have as many as two Class II hubs on a network, with a total cable length (for all three segments) of 205 meters when using UTP cable and 228 meters using fiber optic. Since Class I hubs must perform an additional signal translation, which slows down the transmission process, you can have only one hub on the network, with maximum cable lengths of 200 and 272 meters for UTP and fiber optic, respectively.

Note The hub configuration rules for standard and Fast Ethernet given here are general guidelines that in most cases result in a network that functions properly. A certain amount of leeway in real world configuration practices is understood to exist. For example, if all of your cable segments in a 10BaseT network are substantially shorter than 100 meters (and they usually are), you can probably get away with adding a fifth hub. To ensure that your network conforms to the specifications, it is possible to achieve greater accuracy by calculating the precise round-trip delay time for your network. The round-trip delay time is the time it takes for a packet to travel between the two most distant systems on the network, and you calculate it by using specific values for each meter of cable and each type of hub.

The Ethernet Frame

One of the primary functions of the Ethernet protocol is to encapsulate the data it receives from the network layer protocol in a frame, in preparation for its transmission across the network. The frame consists of a header and a footer that are divided into fields containing specific information needed to get each packet to its destination. The format of the Ethernet frame is shown in Figure 5.5.

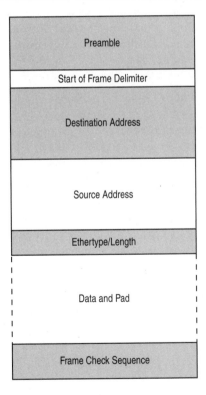

Figure 5.5 The Ethernet/IEEE 802.3 frame

The functions of the fields are as follows:

- **Preamble (7 bytes)** This field contains 7 bytes of alternating 0s and 1s, which the communicating systems use to synchronize their clock signals.

- **Start of Frame Delimiter (1 byte)** This field contains 6 bits of alternating 0s and 1s, followed by two consecutive 1s, which is a signal to the receiver that the transmission of the actual frame is about to begin.

- **Destination Address (6 bytes)** This field contains the 6-byte hexadecimal address of the network interface adapter on the local network to which the packet will be transmitted.

- **Source Address (6 bytes)** This field contains the 6-byte hexadecimal address of the network interface adapter in the system generating the packet.

- **Ethertype/Length (2 bytes)** In the DIX Ethernet frame, this field contains a code identifying the network layer protocol for which the data in the packet is intended. In the IEEE 802.3 frame, this field specifies the length of the data field (excluding the pad).

- **Data and Pad (46 to 1,500 bytes)** This field contains the data received from the network layer protocol on the transmitting system, which will be sent to the same protocol on the destination system. Ethernet frames (including the header and footer, except for the Preamble and Start of Frame Delimiter) must be at least 64 bytes long, so if the data received from the network layer protocol is less than 46 bytes, the system adds padding bytes to bring it up to its minimum length.

- **Frame Check Sequence (4 bytes)** The frame's footer is a single field that comes after the network layer protocol data and which contains a 4-byte checksum value for the entire packet. The sending computer computes this value and places it into the field. The receiving system performs the same computation and compares it to the field to verify that the packet was transmitted without error.

Ethernet Addressing

The Destination Address and Source Address fields use the 6-byte hardware addresses coded into network interface adapters to identify systems on the network. Every network interface adapter has a unique hardware address (also called a MAC address), which consists of a 3-byte value called an *organizationally unique identifier* (OUI), which is assigned to the adapter's manufacturer by the IEEE, plus another 3-byte value assigned by the manufacturer itself.

Ethernet, like all data-link layer protocols, is concerned only with transmitting packets to another system on the local network. If the packet's final destination is another system on the LAN, the Destination Address field contains the address of that system's network adapter. If the packet is destined for a system on another network, the Destination Address field contains the address of a router on the local network that provides access to the destination network. It is then up to the network layer protocol to supply a different kind of address (such as an Internet Protocol [IP] address) for the system that is the packet's ultimate destination.

Ethertypes

The 2-byte field after the Source Address field is the primary difference between the DIX Ethernet and IEEE 802.3 standards. For any network that uses multiple protocols at the network layer, it is essential for the Ethernet frame to somehow identify which network layer protocol has generated the data in a particular packet. The DIX Ethernet frame does this very simply by specifying an Ethertype in this field, using values like those shown in Table 5.2. The IEEE 802.3 standard uses this field to specify the length of the data field.

Table 5.2 Common Ethertype values, in hexadecimal

Network Layer Protocol	Ethertype
Internet Protocol (IP)	0800
X.25	0805
Address Resolution Protocol (ARP)	0806
Reverse ARP	8035
AppleTalk on Ethernet	809B
NetWare IPX	8137

The IEEE 802.3 takes a different approach. In this frame, the field after the Source Address specifies the length of the data in the packet. How then does the frame identify the network layer protocol? The answer is by using an additional frame component called Logical Link Control (LLC). The IEEE's 802 working group is not devoted solely to the development of Ethernet-like protocols. In fact, there are other protocols that fit into the IEEE 802 architecture, the most prominent of which (aside from IEEE 802.3) is IEEE 802.5, which is a Token Ring–like protocol. To make the IEEE 802 architecture adaptable to these various protocols, the data-link layer is split into two sublayers, as shown in Figure 5.6.

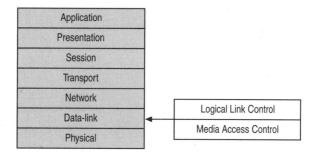

Figure 5.6 The IEEE 802 protocols split the data-link layer into two sublayers, the MAC layer and the LLC layer.

The MAC sublayer is the part that contains the elements particular to the IEEE 802.3 specification, such as the Ethernet physical layer options, the frame, and the CSMA/CD MAC mechanism. The functions of the LLC sublayer are defined in a separate document, published as IEEE 802.2. This same LLC sublayer is also used with the MAC sublayers of other IEEE 802 protocols, such as 802.5.

The LLC standard defines an additional 3-byte or 4-byte subheader that is carried within the Data field, which contains Service Access Points (SAPs) for the source and destination systems. These SAPs identify locations in memory where the source and destination systems store the packet data. To provide the same function as the Ethertype field, the LLC subheader can use a SAP value of 170, which indicates that the Data field also contains a second subheader called the Subnetwork Access Protocol (SNAP). The SNAP subheader is 5 bytes long and contains a 2-byte Local Code that performs the same function as the Ethertype field in the Ethernet II header.

It is typical for computers on a Transmission Control Protocol/Internet Protocol (TCP/IP) network to use the Ethernet II frame, because the Ethertype field performs the same function as the LLC and SNAP subheaders, and saves 8 to 9 bytes per packet. Windows servers and clients automatically negotiate a common frame type when communicating, and when you install a NetWare server, you can select the frame type you want to use. There are two crucial factors to be aware of when it comes to Ethernet frame types. The first is that computers must use the same frame type in order to communicate. The second is that if you are using multiple network layer protocols on your network, such as TCP/IP for Windows networking and Internetwork Packet Exchange (IPX) for NetWare, you must use a frame type that contains an Ethertype or its functional equivalent, such as Ethernet II or Ethernet SNAP.

CSMA/CD

The MAC mechanism is the single most defining element of the Ethernet standard. A protocol that is very similar to Ethernet in other ways, such as 100VG AnyLAN, is placed in a separate category because it uses a different MAC mechanism. Carrier Sense Multiple Access with Collision Detection may be a confusing name, but the basic concept is simple. It's only when you get into the details that things become complicated.

 Run the **c05dem01** and **c05dem02** videos located in the **Demos** folder on the CD-ROM accompanying this book for a demonstration of 100VG AnyLAN's demand priority mechanism.

When an Ethernet system has data to transmit, it first listens to the network to see if it is in use by another system. This is the *carrier sense* phase. If the network is busy, the system does nothing for a given period and then checks again. If the network is free, the system transmits the data packet. This is the *multiple access* phase, because all of the systems on the network are contending for access to the same network medium.

Run the **c05dem03** video located in the **Demos** folder on the CD-ROM accompanying this book for a demonstration of the carrier sense and multiple access phases.

Even though an initial check is performed during the carrier sense phase, it is still possible for two systems on the network to transmit at the same time, causing a *collision*. For example, when a system performs the carrier sense, another computer may have already begun transmitting, but its signal has not yet reached the sensing system. The second computer then transmits and the two packets collide somewhere on the cable. When a collision occurs, both packets are discarded and the systems must retransmit them. These collisions are a normal and expected part of Ethernet networking, and they are not a problem unless there are too many of them or the computers are unable to detect them.

Run the **c05dem04** video located in the **Demos** folder on the CD-ROM accompanying this book for a demonstration of a collision.

Note Although the term *collision* is commonly used, the IEEE 802.3 standard refers to the condition as a *signal quality error (SQE)*. This is a common practice for these standards, which often use convoluted terminology when a simple phrase will do.

What Is 100VG AnyLAN?

100VG AnyLAN is a data-link layer protocol that was developed by Hewlett Packard and AT&T in the early 1990s as a rival to the emerging Fast Ethernet standard. Like Fast Ethernet, 100VG AnyLAN runs at 100 Mbps over UTP cable. When using Category 3 cable, the maximum segment length is 100 meters, but Category 5 cable extends the maximum length to 200 meters. The protocol uses all four pairs of wires in the cable (like 100BaseT4), with a technique called *quartet signaling*. The primary element that differentiates 100VG AnyLAN from Ethernet is *demand priority*, a new MAC mechanism in which the hub determines which system on the network can transmit at any given time. 100VG AnyLAN never achieved the popularity that Fast Ethernet did, and today it remains a marginal technology with few advocates.

The *collision detection* phase of the transmission process is the most important part of the operation. If the systems can't tell when their packets collide, corrupted data may reach the destination system and be treated as valid data. Ethernet networks are designed so that packets are large enough to fill the entire network cable with signals before the last bit leaves the transmitting computer. This is why Ethernet packets must be at least 64 bytes long, why systems pad out short packets to 64 bytes before transmission, and why the Ethernet physical layer guidelines impose strict limitations on the lengths of cable segments.

As long as a computer is still in the process of transmitting, it is capable of detecting a collision on the network. On a UTP or fiber optic network, a system assumes that a collision has occurred if it detects signals on both its transmit and receive wires at the same time. On a coaxial network, a voltage spike indicates the occurrence of a collision. If the network cable is too long or if the packet is too short, a system might finish transmitting before the collision occurs.

Warning It is conceivable that collisions might occur after the last bit of data has left the transmitting system. This is called a *late collision,* and it is not a normal occurrence. Late collisions are an indication of a serious problem, such as a malfunctioning NIC, and must be corrected as soon as possible.

When a system detects a collision, it immediately stops transmitting data and starts sending a jam pattern instead. The jam pattern serves as a signal to every system on the network that a collision has taken place, that it should discard any partial packets it may have received, and that it should not attempt to transmit any data until the network has cleared. After transmitting the jam pattern, the system waits a specific period of time before attempting to transmit again. This is called the *backoff period*, and both of the systems involved in a collision compute the length of their own backoff periods using a randomized algorithm called *truncated binary exponential backoff*. They do this to try to avoid causing another collision by backing off for the same period of time.

Because of the way that CSMA/CD works, the more systems you have on a network or the more data the systems transmit over the network, the more collisions there are. Collisions are a normal part of Ethernet operation, but they still cause delays, because systems have to retransmit packets. When the number of collisions is nominal, the delays aren't noticeable, but when network traffic increases, the number of collisions increases, and the accumulated delays can begin to have a palpable effect on network performance. For this reason, it is not a good idea to run an Ethernet network at high traffic levels. You can reduce the traffic on the network by installing a bridge or switch, or by splitting it into two LANs and connecting the LANs with a router.

Using CSMA/CD may seem to be an inefficient way of controlling access to the network medium, but the process by which the systems contend for access to the network and recover from collision occurs many times a second, so rapidly that the delays caused by a moderate number of collisions are negligible.

Run the **c05dem05** video located in the **Demos** folder on the CD-ROM accompanying this book for a demonstration of how Ethernet systems contend for access to the network.

Exercise 5.1: CSMA/CD Procedures

Place the following steps of the CSMA/CD transmission process in the proper order.

1. System begins transmitting data.
2. System retransmits data.
3. System detects incoming signal on receive wires.
4. System backs off.
5. System listens to the network.
6. System stops transmitting data.
7. System transmits jam pattern.
8. System detects no network traffic.

Lesson 2: Token Ring

Token Ring is a protocol that contains the same basic elements as Ethernet: physical layer options, a frame format, and a MAC mechanism. However, it approaches the tasks of transmitting and receiving data on a shared network medium in a completely different manner. Token Ring was originally designed by IBM, but since it was standardized in the IEEE 802.5 document, there are many manufacturers now producing Token Ring hardware. Token Ring networks were originally designed to run at 4 Mbps, but later implementations increased the speed to 16 Mbps, which is faster than standard Ethernet, but nowhere near the 100 Mbps speed of Fast Ethernet. However, it's important to note that Token Ring networks experience no collisions (under normal circumstances) like Ethernet, which improves the network's overall efficiency.

After this lesson, you will be able to

- List the physical layer options for Token Ring networks
- Diagram the Token Ring frames
- Understand the token-passing MAC mechanism

Estimated lesson time: 30 minutes

Token Ring is far less commonly used than Ethernet, and one of the major reasons is the price of Token Ring hardware, which is substantially higher than that of Ethernet. You can build a simple Ethernet network by purchasing NICs for as little as $20 and a hub for less than $75. Token Ring multistation access units (MAUs) are considerably more complex than Ethernet hubs, however, and start at around $250, while Token Ring NICs generally run $120 and more.

Physical Layer Specifications

As described in Lesson 1: Network Cables, in Chapter 2, "Network Hardware," Token Ring networks use a ring topology, which is implemented logically inside the MAU, the Token Ring equivalent of a hub. The network cables take the form of a star topology, but the MAU forwards incoming data to the next port only, not to all of the ports at the same time as in an Ethernet hub. This topology enables data packets to travel around the network from one workstation to the next, until they arrive back at the system that originally generated them.

Token Ring networks still use a shared medium, however, meaning that every packet is circulated to every computer on the network. When a system receives a packet from the MAU, it reads the destination address from the Token Ring header to determine if it should pass the packet up through that computer's networking stack, but no matter what the address, the system returns the packet to the MAU, so that it can be forwarded to the next computer on the ring.

The physical layer specifications for Token Ring networks are not as numerous as are those for Ethernet, and they are not as precisely standardized. The IEEE 802.5 document contains no physical layer specifications at all. Cabling guidelines are derived from practices established by IBM and may very well differ when you are working with products made by other manufacturers.

Originally, the medium for Token Ring networks was a cable known as IBM Type 1, also called the IBM Cabling System. Type 1 is a heavy, shielded cable that is sold in various lengths, generally with connectors attached. The connector at the MAU end of the cable is a large, proprietary jack called an IBM Data Connector (IDC) or a Universal Data Connector (UDC), as shown in Figure 5.7. The NICs in the computers use standard DB9 connectors. Cables with one IDC and one DB9 connector, which are used to connect a computer to a MAU, are called a *lobe cable*. Cables with IDC connectors at both ends, used for connecting MAUs together, are called *patch cables*.

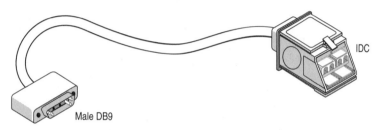

Figure 5.7 A Type 1 cable with an IBM Data Connector attached

Type 1 cable is thick, relatively inflexible, and difficult to install in walls and ceilings because of its large, pre-attached connectors. Type 1 MAUs also require a special IDC "key," which is a separate device that you plug into each MAU port and remove to initialize the port before connecting it to a lobe cable. Today, most Token Ring networks use Category 5 UTP cable with standard RJ45 connectors at both ends, which is known in the Token Ring world as Type 3 cabling. Type 3 networks use the same connectors for both computers and MAUs, so only one type of cable is needed. In addition, it's possible to install the network inside walls and ceilings using bulk cable and attach the connectors afterward. Type 3 MAUs also don't require a separate key, as the ports are self-initializing.

The only advantages of Type 1 networks over Type 3 is that they can span longer distances and connect more workstations. A Type 1 lobe cable can be up to 300 meters long, while Type 3 cables are limited to 150 meters. Type 1 networks can have up to 260 connected workstations, while Type 3 networks can have only 72.

Token Passing

The MAC mechanism of a Token Ring LAN, called token passing, is the single most defining element of the network, just as CSMA/CD is for Ethernet. Token passing is an inherently more efficient MAC mechanism than CSMA/CD, because it provides each system on the network with an equal opportunity to transmit its data without generating any collisions and without diminished performance at high traffic levels. Other data-link layer protocols, like Fiber Distributed Data Interface (FDDI), also use token passing as their MAC mechanism.

Token passing works by circulating a special packet called a *token* around the network. The token is only 3 bytes long and contains no useful data. Its only purpose is to designate which system on the network is allowed to transmit its data. In their idle state, computers on a Token Ring network are in what is known as *repeat* mode. While in this state, the computer systems receive packets from the network and immediately forward them back to the MAU for transmission to the next port. If a system doesn't return the packet, the ring is effectively broken and network communication ceases. After a designated system (called the *active monitor*) generates it, the token circulates around the ring from system to system. When a computer has data to transmit, it must wait for the token to arrive before it can send its data. No system can transmit without being in possession of the token, and since there is only one token, only one system on the network can transmit at any one time. This means that there can be no collisions on a Token Ring network unless something is seriously wrong.

 Run the **c05dem06** video located in the **Demos** folder on the CD-ROM accompanying this book for a demonstration of how token passing works.

When a system takes possession of the token, it changes the value of one bit (called the *monitor setting bit*) and forwards the packet back to the MAU for transmission to the next system on the ring. At this point, the system enters *transmit* mode. The new value of the monitor setting bit informs the other systems that the network is in use and that they can't take possession of the token themselves. Immediately after the system transmits the "network busy" token, it transmits its data packet.

As with the token frame transmitted immediately before it, the MAU forwards the data packet to each computer on the ring in turn. Eventually, the packet arrives back at the computer that generated it. At the same time that the sending computer goes into transmit mode, its receive-wire pair goes into *stripping* mode. When the data packet traverses the entire ring and returns to its source, it is the responsibility of the sending computer that generated the packet to strip it from the network. This prevents the packet from circulating endlessly around the ring.

 Run the **c05dem07**, **c05dem08**, **c05dem09**, and **c05dem10** videos located in the **Demos** folder on the CD-ROM accompanying this book for a step-by-step illustration of the path that packets take on a Token Ring network.

The original Token Ring network design calls for the system transmitting its data packet to wait for the last bit of data to arrive back at its source before it modifies the monitor setting bit in the token frame back to its original value and then transmits it. Today, most 16 Mbps Token Ring networks have a feature called *early token release*, which enables them to transmit the "network free" token immediately after the data packet. This way, another system on the network can receive a data packet, take possession of the token, and begin transmitting its own data frame before all of the data from the first packet has returned to its source. There are parts of two data frames on the network at the same time, but there is never more than one "network free" token.

Token Ring Frames

Unlike Ethernet, which uses one frame format for all communications, Token Ring uses four different frames: the data frame, the token frame, the command frame, and the abort delimiter frame. The largest and most complex of the Token Ring frames is the data frame, shown in Figure 5.8. This is the frame that is most comparable to the Ethernet frame, because it encapsulates the data received from the network layer protocol using a header and a footer. The other three frames are strictly for control functions, such as ring maintenance and error notification.

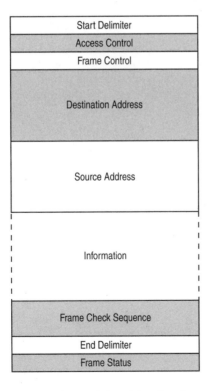

Figure 5.8 The Token Ring data frame

The functions of the fields in the data frame are as follows:

- **Start Delimiter (1 byte)** This field contains a bit pattern that signals the beginning of the frame to the receiving system.

- **Access Control (1 byte)** This field contains bits that can be used to prioritize Token Ring transmissions, enabling certain systems to have priority access to the token frame and the network.

- **Frame Control (1 byte)** This field contains bits that specify whether the frame is a data or a command frame.

- **Destination Address (6 bytes)** This field contains the 6-byte hexadecimal address of the network interface adapter on the local network to which the packet will be transmitted.

- **Source Address (6 bytes)** This field contains the 6-byte hexadecimal address of the network interface adapter in the system generating the packet.

- **Information (up to 4,500 bytes)** This field contains the data generated by the network layer protocol, including a standard LLC header, as defined in IEEE 802.2.

- **Frame Check Sequence (4 bytes)** This field contains a 4-byte checksum value for the packet (excluding the Start Delimiter, End Delimiter, and Frame Status fields), which the receiving system will use to verify that the packet was transmitted without error.

- **End Delimiter (1 byte)** This field contains a bit pattern that signals the end of the frame, including a bit that specifies if there are further packets in the sequence yet to be transmitted, and a bit that indicates that the packet has failed the error check.

- **Frame Status (1 byte)** This field contains bits that indicate whether the destination system has received the frame and copied it into its buffers.

The token frame is 3 bytes long (as shown in Figure 5.9), and contains only the Start Delimiter, Access Control, and End Delimiter fields. The Start Delimiter and End Delimiter fields use the same format as in the data frame, and the token bit in the Access Control field is set to a value of 1.

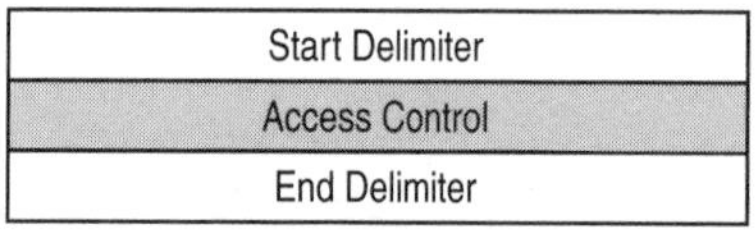

Start Delimiter
Access Control
End Delimiter

Figure 5.9 The Token Ring token frame

The command frame (also called a MAC frame because it operates at the MAC sublayer, while the data frame operates at the LLC sublayer) uses the same basic format as the data frame, differing only in the value of the Frame Control field and the contents of the Information field. The Information field, instead of containing network layer protocol data, contains a 2-byte *major vector ID*, which specifies the control function the packet is performing, followed by the actual control data itself, which can vary in length. Some of the most common control functions performed by these packets are indicated by the following major vector IDs:

- **0010—Beacon** Beaconing is a process by which systems on a Token Ring network indicate that they are not receiving data from their nearest active upstream neighbor, presumably because a network error has occurred.

- **0011—Claim Token** This vector ID is used by the active monitor system to generate a new token frame on the ring.

- **0100—Ring Purge** This vector ID is used by the active monitor system in the event of an error to clear the ring of unstripped data and to return all of the systems to repeat mode.

The abort delimiter frame consists of only 2 bytes, the same Start Delimiter and End Delimiter fields, and uses the same values for those fields as the data and command frames. When a problem occurs, such as an incomplete packet transmission, the active monitor system generates an abort delimiter frame to flush all existing data from the ring.

Exercise 5.2: Ethernet Standards and Technologies

Match the standard in the left column with the most suitable technology in the right column.

1.	IEEE 802.2	a.	Gigabit Ethernet
2.	IEEE 802.3	b.	Fast Ethernet
3.	IEEE 802.3u	c.	Thick Ethernet
4.	IEEE 802.3z	d.	Logical Link Control
5.	IEEE 802.3ab	e.	10BaseT
6.	IEEE 802.5	f.	Thin Ethernet
7.	DIX Ethernet	g.	1000BaseT
8.	DIX Ethernet II	h.	Token Ring

Exercise 5.3: Selecting a Data-Link Layer Protocol

For each of the following scenarios, specify which data-link layer protocol you think is preferable, Ethernet or Token Ring, and give reasons why. In some cases, either protocol would be suitable; the reasons you provide are more significant than the protocol you select.

1. A family with two computers in the home wants to network them in order to share a printer and an Internet connection.

2. A small graphics design firm wants to build a 10-node network to handle the extremely large image files that they must transfer between systems and to a print server.

3. A company with a 50-node LAN used by their order entry staff will be going public in the near future and is expected to grow enormously over the next year.

Lesson 3: SLIP and PPP

The Serial Line Internet Protocol (SLIP) and the Point-to-Point Protocol (PPP) are also data-link layer protocols, but they are very different from Ethernet and Token Ring. SLIP and PPP, which are part of the TCP/IP protocol suite, are not designed to connect systems to a LAN that uses a shared network medium. Instead, they connect one system to another using a dedicated connection, such as a telephone line. For this reason, they are called *end-to-end protocols*. Because the medium isn't shared, there is no need for a MAC mechanism, and because there are only two systems involved, there is no need to address the packets. The result is that these protocols are far simpler than Ethernet and Token Ring protocols. SLIP and PPP also do not include physical layer specifications; they operate strictly at the data-link layer. The physical layer is provided by another standard, such as the RS-232 specification, which defines the nature of the serial port that you use to connect a modem to your computer.

After this lesson, you will be able to

- Describe the SLIP and PPP frame formats
- Diagram the PPP connection establishment process

Estimated lesson time: 20 minutes

SLIP

SLIP is so simple, it hardly deserves to be called a protocol. It is designed to transmit signals over a serial connection (which in most cases means a modem and a telephone line) and has very low control overhead, meaning that it doesn't add much information to the network layer data that it is transmitting. Compared to the 18 bytes that Ethernet adds to every packet, for example, SLIP adds only 1 byte. Of course, with only 1 byte, SLIP can't provide functions like error detection, network layer protocol identification, security, or anything else.

SLIP works by transmitting an IP datagram received from the network layer and following it with a single framing byte called an End Delimiter (see Figure 5.10). This byte informs the receiving system when it has finished receiving the data portion of the packet. In some cases, the system surrounds the datagram with two End Delimiter fields, which makes it possible for the receiving system to easily ignore any line noise that occurs outside of the frame. Because of its limited capabilities, SLIP is rarely used today, having been replaced by PPP.

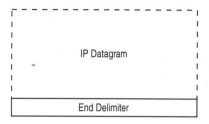

Figure 5.10 SLIP uses an End Delimiter to mark the end of each data packet.

PPP

PPP is, in most cases, the protocol you use when you access the Internet by establishing a dial-up connection to an Internet Service Provider (ISP). PPP is more complex than SLIP and is designed to provide a number of services that SLIP lacks. These include the abililily of the systems to exchange IP addresses, carry data generated by multiple network layer protocols (which is called multiplexing), and support different authentication protocols. Still, PPP does all this using only a 5-byte header, larger than SLIP but still less than half the size of the Ethernet frame.

The PPP Frame

The PPP frame is illustrated in Figure 5.11.

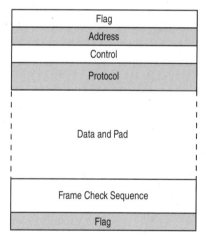

Figure 5.11 The PPP frame

It consists of the following fields:

- **Flag (1 byte)** This field indicates the transmission of a packet is about to begin.

- **Address (1 byte)** This field contains a value indicating that the packet is addressed to all recipients.

- **Control (1 byte)** This field contains a code indicating the packet contains an unnumbered information packet.

- **Protocol (2 bytes)** This field identifies the protocol that generated the information found in the Data field.

- **Data and Pad (up to 1,500 bytes)** This field contains information generated by the protocol identified in the Protocol field, plus padding if necessary.

- **Frame Check Sequence (2 or 4 bytes)** This field contains a checksum value that the receiving system will use for error detection.

- **Flag (1 byte)** This field indicates the transmission of the packet has been completed.

Establishing a PPP Connection

As small as it is, the PPP frame can't possibly provide all of the functions listed earlier. Instead, the protocol performs many of these functions by performing an elaborate connection establishment procedure when the two systems first communicate. This method is more efficient than increasing the size of the PPP header, because there's no need to include this additional information in every packet. For example, it's beneficial for the two communicating systems to know each other's IP addresses, but there's no need to include address fields in every packet header, as in Ethernet, because there are only two computers involved, and they only have to identify themselves once. The same is true for functions like user authentication.

The PPP connection establishment procedure consists of the following phases, which occur before the systems exchange any application data.

1. **Link Dead** The two systems begin with no communication, until one of the two initiates a physical layer connection, such as by running a program that causes the modem to dial.

2. **Link Establishment** Once the physical layer connection is established, one system generates a PPP frame containing a Link Control Protocol (LCP) Request message. The systems use the LCP to negotiate the parameters they will use during the rest of the PPP session. The message contains a list of options, such as the use of a specific authentication protocol, header compression, network layer protocols, and so on. The receiving system can then acknowledge the use of these options or deny them and propose a list of its

own. Eventually, the two systems agree on a list of options they have in common.

3. **Authentication** If the two systems have agreed to the use of a particular authentication protocol during the link establishment phase, they then exchange PPP frames containing messages peculiar to that protocol in the Data field. Systems commonly use the Password Authentication Protocol (PAP) or the Challenge Handshake Authentication Protocol (CHAP), but there are other authentication protocols as well.

4. **Link Quality Monitoring** If the two systems have negotiated the use of a link quality monitoring protocol during the link establishment phase, the exchange of messages for that protocol occurs here.

5. **Network Layer Protocol Configuration** For each of the network layer protocols that the systems have agreed to use, a separate exchange of Network Control Protocol (NCP) messages occurs at this point.

6. **Link Open** Once the NCP negotiations are complete, the PPP connection is fully established, and the exchange of packets containing network layer application data can commence.

7. **Link Termination** When the two systems have finished communicating, they sever the PPP connection by exchanging LCP termination messages, after which the systems return to the Link Dead state.

Exercise 5.4: PPP Connection Establishment

Place the following steps of the PPP connection establishment process in the correct order.

1. Link Open
2. Link Termination
3. Network Layer Protocol Configuration
4. Authentication
5. Link Quality Monitoring
6. Link Establishment
7. Link Dead

Chapter Summary

The key points covered in this chapter are as follows.

Ethernet

- There are two sets of Ethernet standards: DIX Ethernet and IEEE 802.3, which differ primarily in their frame formats.

- Ethernet supports many different physical layer configurations, using various types of cables: coaxial, twisted pair, and fiber optic.

- Ethernet uses the CSMA/CD media access control mechanism, which relies on the ability of the computers to detect packet collisions when they occur.

Token Ring

- Token Ring supports two physical layer options, called Type 1 cables and Type 3 cables.

- Token Ring uses the token passing MAC mechanism, in which only the system in possession of a special token frame is permitted to transmit data.

- Token Ring uses four different types of frames, while Ethernet uses only one.

SLIP and PPP

- SLIP is a simple protocol that enables two systems connected through their serial ports to exchange messages with very little control overhead.

- PPP is a more complicated end-to-end protocol that enables two systems to negotiate the use of optional features such as authentication protocols and multiple network layer protocols.

Chapter Review

1. What is the name of the protocol that systems use to negotiate options during the PPP connection establishment procedure?

   a. CHAP

   b. LCP

   c. PAP

   d. NCP

2. What does an Ethernet system generate when it detects a collision?

   a. A beacon frame

   b. An error message

   c. A jam signal

   d. None of the above

3. Which of the following is not a required component of a 10BaseT Ethernet network?

   a. Network interface adapters or NICs

   b. Cables

   c. A hub

   d. Computers

4. To achieve 100 Mbps speed over Category 3 cable, 100BaseT4 Ethernet uses which of the following?

   a. PAM-5 signaling

   b. Quartet signaling

   c. CSMA/CD

   d. All four wire pairs

5. In which of the following standards is Gigabit Ethernet defined?

   a. IEEE 802.2

   b. IEEE 802.3

   c. IEEE 802.3u

   d. IEEE 802.3z

6. The Frame Check Sequence field in a data-link layer protocol header is used for _____.

7. List the hardware components that you have to replace when upgrading a ten-year-old 10BaseT network to 100BaseTX.

8. How could you upgrade a ten-year-old 10BaseT network to Fast Ethernet without replacing the cables?

9. Which data-link layer protocol is preferred on a network with high levels of traffic, Ethernet or Token Ring? Why?

10. Which Fast Ethernet physical layer option is best suited for a connection between two campus buildings 200 meters apart? Why?

C H A P T E R   6

Network Layer Protocols

About This Chapter

The protocols operating at the network layer of the Open Systems Interconnection (OSI) reference model are responsible for the end-to-end transmission of data across an internetwork. This is in contrast to data-link layer protocols, which are concerned only with transmitting packets to other systems on the local area network (LAN). This chapter examines the three most commonly used network layer protocols: Internet Protocol (IP) from the Transmission Control Protocol/Internet Protocol (TCP/IP) suite; Novell NetWare's Internetwork Packet Exchange (IPX); and Microsoft Windows' NetBIOS Enhanced User Interface (NetBEUI).

Before You Begin

This chapter requires a basic understanding of the OSI reference model, as described in Chapter 1, "Networking Basics," as well as familiarity with the data-link layer protocols discussed in Chapter 5, "Data-Link Layer Protocols."

Lesson 1: IP

The Internet Protocol (IP) is the cornerstone of the TCP/IP protocol suite. TCP/IP refers to a combination of two protocols, IP and the Transmission Control Protocol (TCP), which together provide one of the most common network transport services used today. TCP data is encapsulated within IP, as are most of the other protocols in the TCP/IP suite. IP essentially functions as the envelope that delivers TCP/IP data to its destination.

After this lesson, you will be able to

- Describe the functions of the IP protocol
- Describe the functions of the various IP header fields
- Understand the basics of IP routing and fragmentation

Estimated lesson time: 40 minutes

On a TCP/IP internetwork, IP is the protocol responsible for transmitting data from its source to its final destination. IP is a connectionless protocol, meaning that it transmits messages to a destination without first establishing a connection to the receiving system. IP is connectionless because it carries data generated by many other protocols, only some of which require connection-oriented service. TCP/IP supports both connection-oriented and connectionless services at the transport layer, which makes it possible to keep the network layer connectionless, thus reducing the amount of control overhead generated by the protocol stack.

A transport layer protocol like TCP or the User Datagram Protocol (UDP) passes data down to the network layer, and IP encapsulates it by adding a header, creating what's known as a *datagram*, as shown in Figure 6.1. The datagram is addressed to the computer that will ultimately make use of the data, whether that computer is on the local network or on another network far away. Except for a few minor modifications, the datagram remains intact throughout the packet's journey to its destination. Once it has created the datagram, IP passes it down to a data-link layer protocol for transmission over the network.

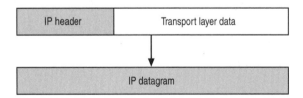

Figure 6.1 IP encapsulates transport layer data into units called datagrams.

Note Protocols operating at different layers of the OSI reference model use different names for the protocol data units (PDUs) they create. Network layer protocols create datagrams, for example, while data-link layer protocols create frames. The term "packet" is generic and can refer to the PDU created by any protocol.

During the transportation process, various systems might encapsulate the datagram in different data-link layer protocol headers, but the datagram itself remains intact. The process is similar to the delivery of a letter by the post office, with IP functioning as the envelope. The letter might be placed into different mailbags and transported by various trucks and planes during the course of its journey, but the envelope remains sealed. Only the addressee is permitted to open it and make use of the contents.

The IP Standard

The TCP/IP protocols are defined in documents called Requests For Comments (RFCs), which are published by a body called the Internet Engineering Task Force (IETF). Unlike most networking standards, TCP/IP specifications are released to the public domain and are freely available on the Internet at many different sites, including the IETF's home page at *www.ietf.org*. The "Internet Protocol" specification was published as RFC 791 in September 1981, and was later ratified as Internet Standard 5.

IP Functions

IP performs several functions that are essential to the internetworking process, including the following:

- **Encapsulation** The packaging of the transport layer data into a datagram
- **Addressing** The identification of systems in the network using IP addresses
- **Routing** The identification of the most efficient path to the destination system through the internetwork
- **Fragmentation** The division of data into fragments of the appropriate size for transmission over the network
- **Protocol Identification** The specification of the transport layer protocol that generated the data in the datagram

These functions are discussed in the following sections.

IP Encapsulation

The header that IP applies to the data it receives from the transport layer protocol is typically 20 bytes long. The datagram format is shown in Figure 6.2.

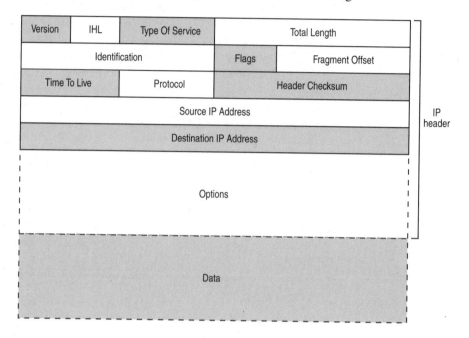

Figure 6.2 The IP datagram format.

The datagram fields perform the following functions:

- **Version (4 bits)** This field specifies the version of the IP protocol used to create the datagram. The version in current use is 4, but IP version 6 is currently in development.

- **Internet Header Length (IHL)(4 bits)** This field specifies the length of the datagram's header, in 32-bit (4-byte) words. The typical length of a datagram header is five words (20 bytes), but if the datagram includes additional options, it can be longer, which is the reason for having this field.

- **Type Of Service (1 byte)** This field contains a code that specifies the service priority for the datagram. This is a rarely used feature that enables a system to assign a priority to a datagram that routers observe while forwarding it through an internetwork. The values provide a trade-off between delay, throughput, and reliability.

- **Total Length (2 bytes)** This field specifies the length of the datagram, including that of the Data field and all of the header fields, in bytes.

- **Identification (2 bytes)** This field contains a value that uniquely identifies the datagram. The destination system uses this value to reassemble datagrams that have been fragmented during transmission.

- **Flags (3 bits)** This field contains bits used to regulate the datagram fragmentation process.

- **Fragment Offset (13 bits)** When a datagram is fragmented, the system inserts a value in this field that identifies this fragment's place in the datagram.

- **Time To Live (1 byte)** This field specifies the number of networks that the datagram should be permitted to travel through on the way to its destination. Each router that forwards the datagram reduces the value of this field by one. If the value reaches zero, the datagram is discarded.

- **Protocol (1 byte)** This field contains a code that identifies the protocol that generated the information found in the Data field.

- **Header Checksum (2 bytes)** This field contains a checksum value computed on the IP header fields only (and not the contents of the Data field), for the purpose of error detection.

- **Source IP Address (4 bytes)** This field specifies the IP address of the system that generated the datagram.

- **Destination IP Address (4 bytes)** This field specifies the IP address of the system for which the datagram is destined.

- **Options (variable)** This field is present only when the datagram contains one or more of the 16 available IP options. The size and content of the field depends on the number and the nature of the options.

- **Data (variable)** This field contains the information generated by the protocol specified in the Protocol field. The size of the field depends on the data-link layer protocol used by the network over which the system will transmit the datagram.

IP Addressing

The IP protocol is unique among network layer protocols in that it has its own self-contained addressing system that it uses to identify computers on an internetwork of almost any size. Other network layer protocols (such as IPX) use hardware addresses to identify computers on a LAN, with a separate address for the network, while NetBEUI assigns a name to each computer on the LAN and has no network address. IP addresses are 32 bits long and contain both a network identifier and a host identifier. In TCP/IP parlance, the term "host" refers to a network interface adapter found in a computer or other device. In most cases, each computer on a network has one IP address, but it is actually the network interface adapter (generally a network interface card, or NIC) that the address represents. A computer with two adapters (such as a router) or one adapter and a modem connection to a network will actually have two IP addresses, one for each interface.

Note For more information about the structure of IP addresses, see Lesson 2: IP Addressing, in Chapter 8, "TCP/IP Fundamentals."

The IP addresses that a system inserts into the Source IP Address and Destination IP Address fields of the IP header identify, respectively, the system that created the packet and the system that will eventually receive it. If the packet is intended for a system on the local network, the Destination IP Address refers to the same system as the Destination Address in the data-link protocol header. However, if the packet's destination is a system on another network, the Destination IP Address refers to a different system because IP is an end-to-end protocol that deals with the entire journey of the data to its ultimate destination, not just with a single network hop, as is the case with the data-link layer protocol.

Data-link layer protocols cannot work with IP addresses, however, so in order to actually transmit the datagram, IP has to supply the data-link layer protocol with a hardware address of a system on the local network. To do this, IP uses another TCP/IP protocol called the Address Resolution Protocol (ARP). ARP works by generating broadcast messages that contain an IP address on the local network. The system using that IP address must respond to the broadcast, and the data-link layer protocol header of the reply message contains the system's hardware address. If the datagram's destination system is on the local network, the IP protocol generates an ARP message containing the IP address of that system. If the destination system is located on another network, IP generates an ARP message containing the address of a router on the local network. Once it has received the ARP reply, the IP protocol on the original system can pass the datagram down to the data-link layer protocol and provide it with the hardware address it needs to build the frame.

IP Routing

Routing is the most important and the most complex function of the IP protocol. When a TCP/IP system has to transmit data to a computer on another network, the packets must travel through the routers that connect the networks together. As explained in Chapter 1, "Networking Basics," the source and final destination computers in a case like this are called *end systems* and the routers are called *intermediate systems* (see Figure 6.3). When the packets pass through an intermediate system, they only travel up through the protocol stack as high as the network layer, where IP is responsible for deciding where to send the packet next. If the router is connected to the network where the destination system is located, it can transmit the packet there, and the packet's journey is over. If the destination system is located on another network, the router sends the packet to another router, which brings the packet one hop closer to its destination. Depending on the complexity of the internetwork, a packet might pass through dozens of routers on the way to its destination.

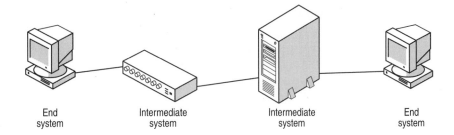

End
system

Intermediate
system

Intermediate
system

End
system

Figure 6.3 Packets can travel through multiple intermediate systems to reach an end system.

Note Intermediate systems use their own internal routing tables to determine where to send each packet they receive, and it is the compiling of the routing tables that is the most complicated part of the routing process. For more information about routing tables and the other complexities of IP routing, see Chapter 9, "TCP/IP Routing."

Because packets only reach as high as the network layer in an intermediate system, the datagrams are not opened and used. The router strips off the data-link layer frame and later builds a new one, but the datagram "envelope" remains sealed until it reaches its destination. However, each intermediate system does make some changes to the IP header. The most important of these is the Time To Live (TTL) field, which is set with a predetermined value by the computer that generates the packet. Each router, as it processes the packet, reduces this value by one. If the TTL value reaches zero, the router discards the packet. This mechanism prevents packets from circulating endlessly around an internetwork, in the event of a routing problem.

When a router discards a packet with a TTL value of zero, it generates an error message called a Time To Live Exceeded In Transit message using the Internet Control Message Protocol (ICMP) and sends it to the system where the packet originated. This informs the system that the packet has not reached its destination. There is a utility program called Traceroute included with most TCP/IP implementations that uses the TTL field to display a list of the routers that packets are using to reach a particular destination system. By generating a series of packets with successively larger TTL values, each router in turn generates an ICMP error message identifying the router that discarded the packet. The Traceroute program assembles the router addresses from the error messages and displays the entire route to the destination. For more information about Traceroute, see Lesson 2: TCP/IP Utilities, in Chapter 10, "TCP/IP Applications."

IP Fragmentation

Routers can connect networks that use different media types and different data-link layer protocols, but in order to forward packets from one network to another, routers must often repackage the datagrams into different data-link layer frames. In some cases, this is simply a matter of stripping off the old frame and adding a new one, but at other times the data-link layer protocols are different enough to require more extensive repackaging. For example, when a router connects a Token Ring network to an Ethernet network, datagrams arriving from the Token Ring network can be up to 4,500 bytes long, while the datagrams in Ethernet packets can only be as large as 1,500 bytes.

To overcome this problem, the router splits the datagram arriving from the Token Ring network into multiple fragments, as shown in Figure 6.4. Each fragment has its own IP header and is transmitted in a separate data-link layer frame. The size of each fragment is based on the *maximum transfer unit (MTU)* size for the outgoing network. If they encounter a network with an even smaller MTU, fragments can themselves be split into smaller fragments. Once fragmented, the individual parts of a datagram are not reassembled until they reach the end system, which is their final destination.

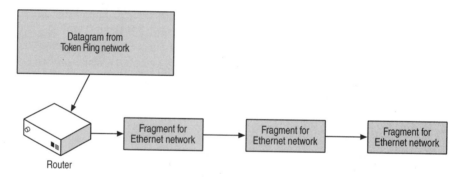

Figure 6.4 Routers can split datagrams into fragments for transmission over networks with smaller MTUs.

When it fragments a datagram, IP attaches an IP header to each fragment. The Identification field in each fragment's header contains the same value as the datagram's original header, which enables the destination system to associate the fragments of a particular datagram. The router modifies the value of the Total Length fields to reflect the length of each fragment, and also changes the value of the More Fragments bit in the Flags field from 0 to 1 in all of the fragments except the last one. The value of 1 in this bit indicates that there are more fragments coming for that datagram. The destination system uses this bit to determine when it has received all of the fragments and can begin to assemble them back into the whole datagram.

The Fragment Offset field contains a value that specifies each fragment's place in the datagram. The first fragment has a value of 0 in this field, while the value in the second fragment is the size (in bytes) of the first fragment. The third fragment's offset value is the size of the first two fragments, and so forth. The destination system uses these values to reassemble the fragments in the proper order. Another bit in the Flags field, called the Don't Fragment bit, instructs routers to discard a datagram rather than fragment it. The router returns an ICMP error message to the source system when it discards a packet for this reason.

Protocol Identification

In order for the destination system to process the incoming datagram properly, it must know which protocol generated the information carried in the Data field. The Protocol field in the IP header provides this information, using codes that are defined in RFC 1700, called "Assigned Numbers," which contains lists of the many codes used by the TCP/IP protocols. "Assigned Numbers" contains dozens of protocol codes, most of which are for obsolete or seldom-used protocols. The most commonly used values for the Protocol field are as follows:

- **0** Internet Protocol (IP)
- **1** Internet Control Message Protocol (ICMP)
- **3** Gateway-to-Gateway Protocol (GGP)
- **6** Transmission Control Protocol (TCP)
- **8** Exterior Gateway Protocol (EGP)
- **17** User Datagram Protocol (UDP)

Tip Every TCP/IP system has a text file called PROTOCOL that also contains a partial list of the protocol codes expected to be recognized or used by that system. Should you need to look up a protocol code, you may find it easier to look at this file than to find a copy of the "Assigned Numbers" RFC.

The protocols that you most expect to see in the list are TCP and UDP, which are the transport layer protocols that account for much of the IP traffic on a TCP/IP network. However, IP also carries other types of information in its datagrams, including ICMP messages, which notify systems of errors and other network conditions, and messages generated by routing protocols like GGP and EGP, which TCP/IP systems use to automatically update their routing tables.

IP Options

IP options are additional header fields that enable datagrams to carry extra information and, in some cases, accumulate information as they travel through an internetwork on the way to their destinations. Some of the options defined in the IP standard are as follows:

- **Loose Source Route** This option contains a list of router addresses that the datagram must use as it travels through the internetwork. The datagram can use other routers in addition to those listed.

- **Strict Source Route** This option contains a complete list of the router addresses that the datagram must use as it travels through the internetwork. The datagram cannot use any routers other than those listed.

- **Record Route** This option provides an area in which routers can add their IP addresses when they process the datagram.

- **Timestamp** This option provides an area in which routers can add timestamps indicating when they processed the datagram. The source system can supply a list of router addresses that are to add timestamps, or the routers can be allowed to add their own IP addresses along with the timestamps.

Exercise 6.1: IP Header Properties

1. What does the IP header's protocol field identify?

    a. The physical layer specification of the network that will carry the datagram

    b. The data-link layer protocol that will carry the datagram

    c. The transport layer protocol that generated the information in the Data field

    d. The application that generated the message carried in the datagram

2. Which of the following IP header elements is never modified during the IP fragmentation process?

    a. The Identification field

    b. The More Fragments bit

    c. The Fragment Offset field

    d. The Time To Live field

3. What does an IP address identify?

    a. A network

    b. A computer

    c. A network interface adapter

    d. A network and a network interface adapter

Lesson 2: IPX

When Novell created NetWare, the company designed its own suite of protocols, which is generally referred to by the name of the network layer protocol: Internetwork Packet Exchange, or IPX. The IPX protocols have never been published in public standards like TCP/IP and Ethernet. These protocols remain the property of Novell, and NetWare's core file and print services used them exclusively until 1998, when Novell belatedly incorporated TCP/IP into its native communications architecture. Independently, Microsoft engineered its own version of IPX to provide NetWare connectivity for their Windows operating systems.

Note Novell added support for TCP/IP to NetWare many years ago, but the TCP/IP protocols could only be used with applications designed for them. It was not possible to share NetWare files and printers using TCP/IP without using a process called tunneling, in which IPX packets were carried inside IP datagrams. It was only with the release of NetWare version 5 in 1998 that a NetWare network could function without using the IPX protocols at all. The IPX protocols are now being gradually phased out, even in NetWare, in favor of TCP/IP.

After this lesson, you will be able to

- Describe the functions of the IPX protocol
- Describe the functions of the various IPX header fields

Estimated lesson time: 20 minutes

IPX is based on a protocol called Internetwork Datagram Packet (IDP), which was designed for an early networking system called Xerox Networking Services (XNS). IPX is a connectionless protocol that is similar to IP in that it functions at the network layer of the OSI reference model and carries the data generated by several other protocols across the network. However, IPX and the other protocols in the IPX suite are designed for use on LANs, while the TCP/IP protocols were designed for what is now the Internet. This means that IPX does not have its own self-contained addressing system like IP, but it does perform some of the same functions as IP, such as routing traffic between different types of networks and identifying the protocol that generated the data it is carrying.

The IPX Header

Like IP, IPX creates datagrams by adding a header to the data it receives from transport layer protocols. The IPX header is longer than that of IP—30 bytes as opposed to 20. The format of the IPX header is shown in Figure 6.5.

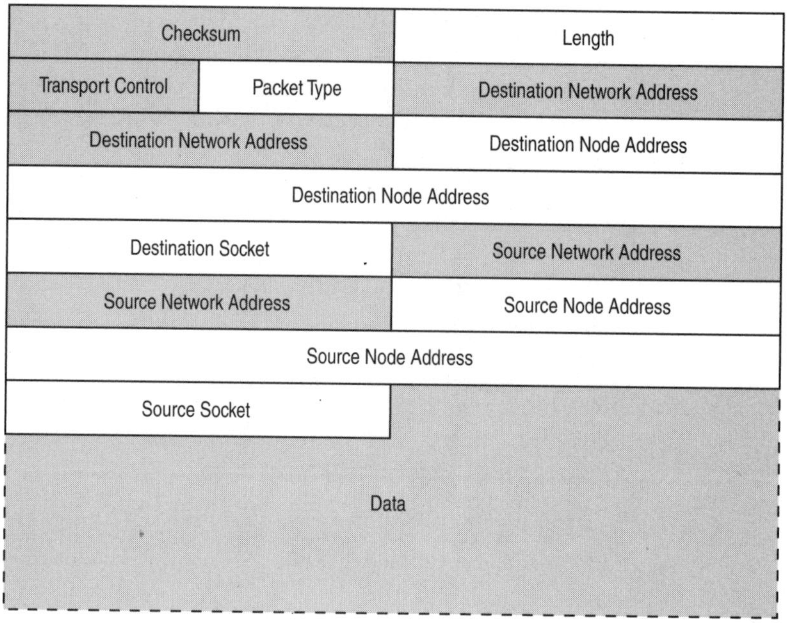

Checksum		Length
Transport Control	Packet Type	Destination Network Address
Destination Network Address		Destination Node Address
Destination Node Address		
Destination Socket		Source Network Address
Source Network Address		Source Node Address
Source Node Address		
Source Socket		
Data		

Figure 6.5 The IPX header format

The fields have the following functions:

- **Checksum (2 bytes)** This field always contains the hexadecimal value *FFFF*. Originally, this field contained a CRC value used for error detection in the IDP protocol, but IPX relies on the transport layer protocol for error detection, so the field is now unused.

- **Length (2 bytes)** This field specifies the length (in bytes) of the entire datagram, including all of the header fields and the data.

- **Transport Control (1 byte)** This field specifies the number of routers that the datagram has passed through on the way to its destination.

- **Packet Type (1 byte)** This field specifies which protocol generated the information found in the Data field.

- **Destination Network Address (4 bytes)** This field identifies the network on which the destination system is located.

- **Destination Node Address (6 bytes)** This field specifies the hardware address of the destination system.

- **Destination Socket (2 bytes)** This field specifies the process or application on the destination system for which the datagram is intended.

- **Source Network Address (4 bytes)** This field identifies the network on which the source system is located.

- **Source Node Address (6 bytes)** This field specifies the hardware address of the source system.

- **Source Socket (2 bytes)** This field specifies the process or application on the source system that generated the datagram.

- **Data (variable)** This field contains the information generated by the protocol specified in the Packet Type field.

The IPX header's Transport Control field is similar to the TTL field in the IP header, except that the Transport Control field starts at a value of 0 and is incremented by each router that forwards the datagram. If the value of the field reaches 16, the packet is discarded. The IP TTL field, by contrast, starts at a value specified by the system generating the datagram and is decremented by each router. The difference in the functionality of these two fields is indicative of the differences between IPX and IP in general. IP has almost unlimited scalability, as demonstrated by the fact that a system can be configured with a relatively large TTL value. Windows-based systems, for example, use a default value of 128 for this field. IPX, which is designed for use on private networks, is limited to 16 hops, more than enough for most corporate networks, but not sufficient for Internet communications.

The Packet Type field uses codes to specify the protocol that generated the information stored in the datagram. There are codes for NetWare's transport layer protocols, such as the NetWare Core Protocol (NCP), as well as codes for NetWare's Routing Information Protocol (RIP) and Service Advertising Protocol (SAP). NetWare servers use RIP to exchange routing data and SAP to advertise their existence on the network.

IPX Addressing

As mentioned earlier, IPX, unlike IP, does not have its own addressing system. Instead, IPX uses the same hardware addresses that data-link layer protocols use to identify the computers on the network. This is possible with NetWare because the operating system is intended for use with LAN-based computers, while IP has to accommodate all of the different types of computers found on the Internet. The Destination Node Address and Source Node Address fields are each 6 bytes long, to hold the hardware addresses coded into the network interface adapters installed in the computers.

Another important difference between the hardware address and an IP address is that IP addresses identify both a network and a host on that network, while hardware addresses identify a network interface adapter only. In order for a router on a NetWare network to forward packets properly, it must know which network the destination system is on, and this requires some means to identify particular networks.

NetWare uses separate network addresses that administrators assign to the networks when they install the NetWare servers. Because NetWare is designed for private LANs, there's no reason why network addresses must be registered, as they are with IP. The network administrators only need to be sure to assign a unique address to each network. The network addresses are 4 bytes long, and the IPX header provides them in the Destination Network Address and Source Network Address fields. The combination of the network address and the node (or hardware) address provides a specific location for a computer on an internetwork.

In addition to getting the data to the correct computer, IPX must also deliver the data to the correct process on that computer. To do this, it also includes 2-byte codes in the Destination Socket and Source Socket fields to identify the function of the datagram.

Exercise 6.2: IPX Properties

1. In the IP header, the IPX equivalent to the TTL field is called what?

    a. Packet Type

    b. Transport Control

    c. Checksum

    d. Source Socket

2. Which of the following statements about IPX is untrue?

    a. IPX routes datagrams between different types of networks.

    b. IPX has its own network addressing system.

    c. IPX uses a checksum to verify the proper transmission of data.

    d. The IPX header is larger than the IP header.

3. How many bytes long is the information that IPX uses to identify the datagram's destination computer on a particular network?

    a. 2

    b. 4

    c. 6

    d. 10

Lesson 3: NetBEUI

The default protocol for the Microsoft Windows operating systems today is TCP/IP, but the early versions of Windows NT and Windows for Workgroups relied on another protocol called the NetBIOS Extended User Interface, or NetBEUI. NetBEUI support is still included in all of the Windows operating systems, and certain elements of it are an integral part of Windows networking, whether you use the NetBEUI protocol or not.

After this lesson, you will be able to

- Understand the function of NetBIOS in the Windows operating systems
- Describe the NetBEUI Frame format
- Understand the functions of the four protocols that use NetBEUI Frames

Estimated lesson time: 30 minutes

NetBEUI differs substantially from IP and IPX. The primary difference is that NetBEUI does not route packets between networks. This means that the protocol is not suitable for use on large internetworks.

NetBEUI was adopted by Microsoft for use with Windows at a time when the company was first adding networking capabilities to the operating system. Like NetWare, the initial market was for small LANs, and it is in this environment that NetBEUI excels. For a small standalone network, NetBEUI provides excellent performance, is self-adjusting, and is self-configuring. There's no need to supply the client with an address and other configuration parameters, as with TCP/IP. NetBEUI, however, does not support Internet communications. This requires TCP/IP; if you will be connecting your network to a shared Internet connection, you must run TCP/IP.

Tip If you're having problems getting a Windows-based system to communicate with the other systems on the network, installing NetBEUI on the systems involved is a good way of isolating the problem. If the systems can communicate using NetBEUI, you know that the networking hardware and the network interface adapter driver are all functioning properly, and that the problem most likely lies with the TCP/IP configuration on one or both systems.

NetBIOS Naming

The Network Basic Input/Output System (NetBIOS) is a programming interface that applications use to communicate with the networking hardware in the computer and, through that, with the network. NetBIOS includes its own name space, which NetBEUI uses to identify computers on the network, just as IP uses its own IP addresses and IPX uses hardware addresses. The computer name that you assign to a system during the Windows installation is in reality a NetBIOS name, which must be unique on the network.

A NetBIOS name is 16 characters long. Windows reserves the sixteenth character for a code that identifies the type of resource using the name, leaving 15 user-assigned alphanumeric characters. Different codes can identify NetBIOS names as representing computers, domain controllers, users, groups, and other resources. If you assign a name of fewer than 15 characters to a computer, the system pads it out to 15, so that the identification code always falls on the sixteenth character.

Note Windows 2000 departs from previous Windows practices by storing its computer and user names using the Domain Name System (DNS) name space instead of NetBIOS. However, Active Directory, Windows 2000's directory service, maintains NetBIOS functionality, for purposes of backward compatibility. A previous version of Windows can see and interact with Windows 2000 systems using NetBIOS equivalents of the DNS names, and in the same way, Windows 2000 can work with the NetBIOS name of systems running earlier versions of Windows.

NetBIOS names are stored in a flat file database; there is no hierarchy among the names. IP and IPX both use a hierarchical system of addressing in which one value identifies the computer, and another value identifies the network on which the computer is located. NetBIOS names have no network identifier, which is why NetBEUI is not routable; it has no means of addressing packets to specific networks or maintaining routing tables containing information about networks. NetBEUI deals solely with computer identifiers, which means that all of the computers must be accessible from the one network.

The NetBEUI Frame

The NetBEUI Frame (NBF) protocol is a multipurpose protocol that Windows-based systems use for a variety of purposes, including the registration and resolution of NetBIOS names, the establishment of sessions between computers on the network, and the transport of file and print data using Windows' Server Message Blocks (SMB) protocol. All of these functions use a single frame format, as diagrammed in Figure 6.6.

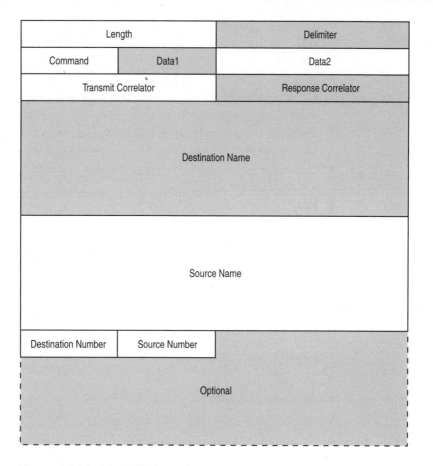

Figure 6.6 The NetBEUI frame format

The following are the functions of the frame fields.

- **Length (2 bytes)** This field specifies the length of the NBF header (in bytes).
- **Delimiter (2 bytes)** This field signals the receiving system that the message should be delivered to the NetBIOS interface.
- **Command (1 byte)** This field identifies the function of the NBF message.
- **Data1 (1 byte)** This field is used to carry optional data specific to the message type specified by the Command field.
- **Data2 (2 bytes)** This field is used to carry optional data specific to the message type specified by the Command field.

- **Transmit Correlator (2 bytes)** This field contains a value that the receiving system will duplicate in the same field in its reply messages, enabling the sending system to associate the requests and replies.
- **Response Correlator (2 bytes)** This field contains the value that the sending system expects to receive in the Transmit Correlator field of the reply to this message.
- **Destination Name (16 bytes)** This field contains the NetBIOS name of the system that will receive the packet.
- **Source Name (16 bytes)** This field contains the NetBIOS name of the system sending the packet.
- **Destination Number (1 byte)** This field contains the number assigned to the session by the destination system.
- **Source Number (1 byte)** This field contains the number assigned to the session by the source system.
- **Optional (variable)** This field contains the actual data payload of the packet.

The value in the Command field dictates the type of message contained in the packet, using the following values:

- **00** Add Group Name Query
- **01** Add Name Query
- **02** Name in Conflict
- **03** Status Query
- **07** Terminate Trace (remote)
- **08** Datagram
- **09** Datagram Broadcast
- **0A** Name Query
- **0D** Add Name Response
- **0E** Name Recognized
- **0F** Status Response
- **13** Terminate Trace (local and remote)
- **14** Data Ack
- **15** Data First Middle
- **16** Data Only Last
- **17** Session Confirm
- **18** Session End
- **19** Session Initialize

- **1A** No Receive
- **1B** Receive Outstanding
- **1C** Receive Continue
- **1F** Session Alive

There are four separate protocols that make use of the NBF frame: the Name Management Protocol (NMP), the Session Management Protocol (SMP), the User Datagram Protocol (UDP), and the Diagnostic and Monitoring Protocol (DMP).

NMP

Name Management Protocol (NMP) is the protocol that systems use to register and resolve NetBIOS names on the network. When a system first starts up, it generates an Add Name Query message containing its NetBIOS name and transmits it to the other NetBIOS systems on the network. The function of this message is to ensure that no other system is using that same name. If there is a duplication, the system already using the name must reply with an Add Name Response message, and the querying system displays an error message. If the system receives no response, the name is considered to be registered to that system.

Name resolution is the process of converting a NetBIOS name into the hardware address needed for a system to transmit data-link layer frames to it. When a NetBEUI system has data to transmit to a particular system or wants to establish a session with another system, it begins by generating a Name Query message containing the name of the target system in the Destination Name field and sending it to all of the NetBIOS systems on the network. All of the systems on the network with registered NetBIOS names are required to respond to Name Query messages containing their name. The system with the requested name responds by transmitting a Name Recognized message back to the sender as a unicast message. The sender, on receiving this message, extracts the hardware address of the system holding the requested name and can then transmit subsequent packets to it as unicasts.

One of the drawbacks of NetBEUI, and one of the reasons why it is only suitable for relatively small networks, is the large number of broadcast packets it generates. These Name Query requests are actually transmitted to a special NetBIOS address, but on a Windows-based network, this is the functional equivalent of a broadcast. On a large network or one with high traffic levels, systems must process a large number of these name resolution broadcasts for no reason, because they are intended for other systems.

SMP

The NBF messages used by NMP use NetBEUI's connectionless service. These messages are part of brief request and response transactions that don't require additional services like packet acknowledgement. For more extensive data transfers, however, a connection-oriented, reliable service is required, and to do this, the two communicating systems must first create a session between them. The systems use NBF's Session Management Protocol (SMP) messages to establish a session, transmit data, and then break down the session afterward.

The session establishment process begins with a standard name resolution exchange, followed by the establishment of a session at the Logical Link Control (LLC) layer. Then the client system initiating the session transmits a Session Initialize to the server system, which responds with a Session Confirm message. At this point, the session is established, and the systems can begin to transmit application data using Data First Middle and Data Only Last messages. These messages may contain data generated by other protocols, such as SMBs. The system receiving the data replies with Receive Continue or Data Ack messages that serve as acknowledgments of successful transmissions.

During the session, when no activity is taking place, the systems transmit periodic Session Alive messages, which prevent the session from timing out. When the exchange of data packets is completed, the client generates a Session End message, which terminates the session.

UDP

To exchange small amounts of data, systems can also use the same connectionless service as NMP. This is sometimes referred to as the User Datagram Protocol (UDP), but it is important not to confuse this protocol with the TCP/IP transport layer protocol of the same name. The UDP is the simplest of the NBF protocols, consisting only of two message types, the Datagram message and the Datagram Broadcast message. Systems can transmit various kinds of information using these messages, including SMB data.

DMP

NetBEUI systems use the Diagnostic and Monitoring Protocol (DMP) to gather status information about systems on the network. A NetBEUI system generates a Status Query message and transmits it to all of the NetBIOS systems on the network. The systems reply with Status Response messages containing the requested information.

Exercise 6.3: NBF Protocols

For each of the NBF message types listed below, specify which of the four NBF protocols—NMP, SMP, UDP, or DMP— is primarily associated with it.

1. Datagram Broadcast
2. Data First Middle
3. Name Query
4. Status Response
5. Add Name Response

Chapter Summary

The key points covered in this chapter are as follows.

IP

- IP is a connectionless protocol in the TCP/IP suite that is used to carry information generated by several other protocols in units called datagrams.

- The primary functions of IP are data encapsulation, packet addressing, packet routing, datagram fragmentation, and transport layer protocol identification.

- IP has its own addressing system that it uses to identify networks and the hosts on those networks.

- IP routes packets by repackaging them to use different data-link layer frames.

- When data-link layer protocols have different maximum transfer units (MTUs), IP can split datagrams into smaller fragments to facilitate transmission.

IPX

- IPX is the NetWare equivalent to IP.

- To identify systems, IPX uses the hardware addresses coded into network interface adapters.

- To identify networks, IPX uses network addresses assigned during the NetWare installation.

- IPX uses socket numbers to identify the processes that generate datagrams.

NetBEUI

- NetBEUI is a network layer protocol used by small Windows networks for LAN networking services.

- NetBEUI differs from IP and IPX primarily in that it has no network identifiers and is therefore not routable.

- The NetBEUI frame provides transport services for four protocols: the Name Management Protocol (NMP), the Session Management Protocol (SMP), the User Datagram Protocol (UDP), and the Diagnostic and Monitoring Protocol (DMP).

Chapter Review

1. Specify which network layer protocol you would use on each of the following networks, and explain why.

   a. A private internetwork with mixed Windows and NetWare systems

   b. A two-node home Windows-based network with individual dial-up Internet connections

   c. A ten-node Windows-based network with a router connecting it to the Internet

2. How does a NetBEUI network prevent two systems from using the same NetBIOS name?

3. Which IP header field makes the Traceroute utility possible?

   a. Version

   b. Type of Service

   c. Identification

   d. Time To Live

4. Which two protocols carried within IP datagrams operate at the transport layer of the OSI model?

   a. IMCP

   b. TCP

   c. UDP

   d. IGMP

5. Give two reasons why NetBEUI is not suitable for use on a large internetwork.

6. Place the following phases of a NetBEUI Frame session in the proper order:

   a. Session Alive

   b. Session Initialize

   c. LLC session establishment

   d. Name resolution

   e. Session End

   f. Session Confirm

7. What is the maximum number of routers that an IPX datagram can pass through on the way to its destination?

   a. 0

   b. 16

   c. 128

   d. 256

8. Which of the following protocols is capable of providing connection-oriented service?

   a. IP

   b. IPX

   c. NetBEUI

   d. None of the above

C H A P T E R 7

Transport Layer Protocols

About This Chapter

The protocols that operate at the transport layer of the Open Systems Interconnection (OSI) reference model work with the network layer protocols to provide a unified quality of service that is suitable for the applications using them. Both the Transmission Control Protocol/Internet Protocol (TCP/IP) and the Internetwork Packet Exchange (IPX) suites have multiple protocols at the transport layer, which provide various levels of service. This chapter examines the options available to applications at this layer and describes the mechanisms used by the protocols to provide the services they supply.

Before You Begin

This chapter requires a basic understanding of the OSI reference model, as described in Chapter 1, "Networking Basics," as well as familiarity with the network layer protocols discussed in Chapter 5, "Network Layer Protocols."

Lesson 1: TCP and UDP

The TCP/IP protocol suite has two protocols at the transport layer; the Transmission Control Protocol (TCP) and the User Datagram Protocol (UDP). TCP is a connection-oriented protocol that provides reliable service with guaranteed delivery, packet acknowledgment, flow control, and error correction and detection. TCP is designed for the transmission of large amounts of data that require perfect bit-accuracy, such as program and data files. UDP is a connectionless protocol that provides unreliable service, and is used primarily for short request or reply transactions. Not surprisingly, TCP generates much more control traffic as it provides all of these services, while UDP's overhead is quite low.

Note The term "reliable," in the context of a protocol's service, refers to the protocol's ability to provide guaranteed delivery of data with acknowledgment from the recipient. It is not a reflection of the protocol's relative value. In fact, unreliable protocols can usually be counted on to deliver their messages to the destination without error.

After this lesson, you will be able to
- Describe the services provided by TCP and UDP
- Understand the functions of the various TCP and UDP header fields

Estimated lesson time: 50 minutes

The TCP/IP suite uses two protocols at the transport layer to provide different levels of service for applications. Both TCP and UDP generate protocol data units (PDUs) that are carried inside Internet Protocol (IP) datagrams. TCP provides a variety of services that IP lacks, so the two protocols complement each other without duplicating functions. The combination of UDP and IP provides a minimal transport service that keeps overhead low.

TCP

The TCP/IP protocol suite gets its name from the combination of the TCP and IP protocols, which together provide the service that accounts for the majority of traffic on a TCP/IP network. Internet applications such as Web browsers, File Transfer Protocol (FTP) clients, and e-mail readers all depend on the TCP protocol to retrieve, without error, large amounts of data from servers. TCP is defined in the Request For Comments (RFC) 793 document published in 1981 by the Internet Engineering Task Force (IETF).

The TCP Header

Transport layer protocols encapsulate data that they receive from those application layer protocols operating above them by applying a header, just as the protocols at the lower layers do. In many cases, the application layer protocol passes to the TCP more data than can fit into a single packet, so the TCP splits the data into smaller pieces. Each piece is called a *segment*, and segments are known collectively as a *sequence*. Each segment receives its own TCP header, as illustrated in Figure 7.1, and is passed down to the network layer for transmission in a separate datagram.

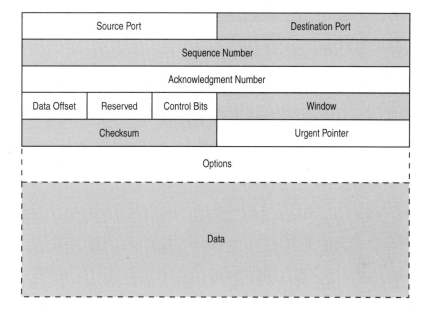

Figure 7.1 The TCP message format

The functions of the TCP message fields are as follows:

- **Source Port (2 bytes)** This field identifies the process on the transmitting system that generated the information carried in the Data field.

- **Destination Port (2 bytes)** This field identifies the process on the receiving system for which the information in the Data field is intended.

- **Sequence Number (4 bytes)** This field identifies the location of the data in this segment in relation to the entire sequence.

- **Acknowledgment Number (4 bytes)** In acknowledgment (ACK) messages, this field specifies the sequence number of the next segment expected by the receiving system.

- **Data Offset (4 bits)** This field specifies the number of 4-byte words in the TCP header.

- **Reserved (6 bits)** This field is unused.

- **Control Bits (6 bits)** This field contains 6 flag bits that identify the functions of the message.

- **Window (2 bytes)** This field specifies how many bytes the computer is capable of accepting from the connected system.

- **Checksum (2 bytes)** This field contains the results of a cyclical redundancy check (CRC) computation performed by the transmitting system, and is used by the receiving system to detect errors in the TCP header, data, and parts of the IP header.

- **Urgent Pointer (2 bytes)** When the urgent (URG) control bit is present, this field indicates which part of the data in the segment the receiver should treat as urgent.

- **Options (variable)** This field may contain information related to optional TCP connection configuration features.

- **Data (variable)** This field may contain one segment of an information sequence generated by an application layer protocol.

Ports and Sockets

As with data-link and network layer protocols, one of the important functions of a transport layer protocol is to identify the protocol or process that generated the data it carries. Both TCP and UDP do this by specifying the number of a port that has been assigned to a particular process by the Internet Assigned Numbers Authority (IANA). These port numbers are published in RFC 1700—the "Assigned Numbers" RFC—and a list of the most common ports is included with every TCP/IP client in a text file called SERVICES. When a TCP/IP packet arrives at its destination, the transport layer protocol receiving the IP datagram reads the value in the Destination Port field and delivers the information in the Data field to the program or protocol associated with that port.

All of the common Internet applications have particular port numbers associated with them, which are called *well-known ports*. For example, Web servers use port 80, and Domain Name System (DNS) servers use port 53. TCP and UDP both maintain their own separate lists of well-known port numbers. FTP uses TCP ports 20 and 21. Because FTP uses only TCP (and not UDP) at the transport layer, it is also possible for a different application layer protocol to use the same ports (20 and 21) with the UDP protocol. However, in some cases, a protocol can use either transport layer protocol. DNS, for example, is associated with both TCP port 53 and UDP port 53.

When one TCP/IP system addresses traffic to another, it uses a combination of an IP address and a port number. The combination of an IP address and a port is called a *socket*. To specify a socket in a Uniform Resource Locator (URL), you enter the IP address first and then follow it with a colon and then the port number. So then the socket 192.168.2.10:21, for example, addresses port 21 on the system with the address 192.168.2.10. Since 21 is the port number for FTP, this socket addresses the FTP server running on that computer.

You usually don't have to specify the port number when you're typing a URL, because the program you use assumes that you want to connect to the well-known port. Your Web browser, for example, addresses all the URLs you enter to port 80, the Hypertext Transfer Protocol (HTTP) Web server port, unless you specify otherwise. The IANA port numbers are recommendations, not ironclad rules, however. You can configure a Web server to use a port number other than 80, and in fact, many Web servers assign alternate ports to their administrative controls, so that only users who know the correct port number can access them. You can create a semi-secret Web site of your own by configuring your server to use port 81 (for example) instead of 80. Users would then have to type a URL like *http://www.myserver.com:81* into their browsers instead of just *http://www.myserver.com*.

The well-known ports published in the "Assigned Numbers" RFC refer to servers. Since it is the client that initiates communication with the server (and not the other way around), clients don't need permanently assigned port numbers. Instead, a client program typically selects a port number at random to use while communicating with a particular server. This is called an *ephemeral port number*. The IANA only controls the port numbers from 1 to 1,023, so ephemeral port numbers always have values of 1,024 or higher. A server receiving a packet from a client uses the value in the TCP header's Source Port field to address its reply to the correct ephemeral port in the client system.

Control Bits

The Control Bits field of the TCP header contains six flags that signify particular message functions. In most cases, systems activate the various flags to make a TCP message perform a control function; for example, to participate in the connection establishment process or to acknowledge the proper receipt of a data segment. The functions of the six flags are as follows:

- **URG** This flag indicates that the segment contains urgent data. When this flag is present, the receiving system reads the contents of the Urgent Pointer field to determine which part of the Data field contains the urgent information.

- **ACK** This flag indicates that the message is an acknowledgment of a previous transmitted segment. When this flag is present, the system receiving the message reads the contents of the Acknowledgment Number field to determine what part of the sequence it should transmit next.

- **PSH** This flag indicates that the receiving system should forward the data it has received in the current sequence to the process identified in the Destination Port field immediately, rather than wait for the rest of the sequence to arrive.

- **RST** This flag causes the receiving system to reset the TCP connection and discard all of the segments of the sequence it has received thus far.

- **SYN** This flag is used to synchronize the systems' respective Sequence Number values during the establishment of a TCP connection.

- **FIN** This flag is used to terminate a TCP connection.

Establishing a Connection

TCP is a connection-oriented protocol, which means that before two systems can exchange application layer data, they must first establish a connection between them. This connection ensures that both computers are present, operating properly, and ready to receive data. The TCP connection remains alive during the entire exchange of data, after which the systems close it in an orderly manner.

In most cases, a TCP connection exists for the duration of a single file transmission. For example, when a Web browser connects to a server on the Internet, it first establishes a connection and then receives the file specified in the requested URL. Once the file is transferred, the systems terminate the connection. As the browser processes the downloaded file, it may detect links to graphic images, audio clips, or other files needed to display the Web page. The browser then establishes a connection to the server for each of the linked files, retrieves them, and displays them as part of the downloaded page. Thus, a single Web page may require the browser to create dozens of separate TCP connections to the server to download the individual files.

The TCP connection establishment process is known as a *three-way handshake*. The process consists of an exchange of three messages (as shown in Figure 7.2), none of which contain any application layer data. The purpose of these messages, apart from ascertaining that the other computer actually exists and is ready to receive data, is to exchange the sequence numbers that the computers will use to number the messages they will transmit. At the start of the connection establishment process, each computer selects an *initial sequence number (ISN)* for the first TCP message it transmits. The systems then increment the sequence numbers for each subsequent message. The computers select an ISN using an incrementing algorithm that makes it highly unlikely for connections between the same two sockets to use identical sequence numbers at the same time. Each system maintains its own sequence numbers, and, during the handshake, each informs the other of the numbers it will be using.

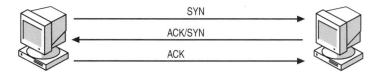

Figure 7.2 TCP uses a three-way handshake to establish a connection between two systems.

The messages that contain the ISN for each system have the synchronize (SYN) flag set in the Control Bits field. In a typical TCP transaction, a client system generates its SYN message, with its ISN in the Sequence Number field. The server, on receiving this message, generates a response that performs two functions. First, the ACK flag is set, so that the message functions as an acknowledgment of the client's SYN message. Second, the server's response has the SYN flag set as well, and includes its own ISN in the Sequence Number field. When the client system receives the server's SYN message, it generates a response of its own, which contains the ACK flag. Once the server receives the client's acknowledgment, the connection is established, and the systems are ready to exchange messages containing application data. Thus, a TCP connection is actually two separate connections, running in opposite directions. TCP is therefore known as a full-duplex protocol, because the systems establish each connection separately, and later terminate each one separately.

Note It is important to remember that the connection established by two TCP systems is only a logical connection. The individual TCP messages are still carried within IP datagrams, using IP's connectionless service. The messages may take different routes to the destination and may even arrive in a different order from that in which they were transmitted. TCP is designed to account for all of these possibilities, and it rearranges the data segments into the proper sequence.

Another function of the SYN messages generated by the two computers during the three-way handshake is for each system to inform the other of its *maximum segment size (MSS)*. Each system uses the other system's MSS to determine how much data it should include in its upcoming messages. The MSS value for each system depends on which data-link layer protocol is used by the network on which each system resides. The MSS is included as an option in the two SYN packets. This option takes the form of 4 additional bytes in the TCP header's Options field, using the following subfields:

- **Kind (1 byte)** This subfield specifies the option type. The MSS option uses a value of 2.

- **Length (1 byte)** This subfield specifies the length of the option, in bytes. For MSS, the value is 4.

- **Maximum Segment Size (2 bytes)** This subfield specifies the MSS for the system, in bytes.

Transmitting Data

After the connection has been established, each computer has all of the information it needs for TCP to begin transmitting application data, as follows.

- **Port number** The client is already aware of the well-known port number for the server, which it needed to initiate the connection. The messages from the client to the server contain the ephemeral port number (in the Source Port field) that the server must use in its replies.

- **Sequence number** Each system uses the other system's sequence numbers in the Acknowledgment Number field of its own messages.

- **MSS** Using the information in the MSS option, the systems know how large to make the segments of each sequence.

Whether the client or the server first transmits data depends on the nature of the application. A transaction between a Web browser client and a Web server begins with the client sending a particular URL to a server, typically requesting a site's home page. Other client/server transactions may begin with the server sending data to the client.

Acknowledging Packets

The Sequence Number and Acknowledgment Number fields are the key to TCP's packet acknowledgment and error correction systems. During the handshake, when the server replies to the client's SYN message, the SYN/ACK message that the server generates contains its own ISN in the Sequence Number field, and it also contains a value in its Acknowledgment Number field. This Acknowledgment Number value is the equivalent of the client's ISN plus one. The function of the Acknowledgment Number field is to inform the other system what value is expected in the next message's Sequence Number field, so if the client's ISN is 1000000, the server's SYN/ACK message contains the value 1000001 in its Acknowledgment Number field. When the client sends its first data message to the server, that message will have the value 1000001 in its Sequence Number field, which is what the server expects.

Note You may wonder why the client's first data message has the Sequence Number value 1000001 when it previously had to send an ACK message in response to the server's SYN. It may seem that the ACK message should have used Sequence Number 1000001, but in fact, messages that function solely as acknowledgments do not increment the sequence number counter. The server's SYN/ACK message does increment the counter, because of the inclusion of the SYN flag.

When the systems begin to send data, they increment their Sequence Number values for each byte of data they transmit. When a Web browser sends its URL request to a Web server, for example, its Sequence Number value is its ISN plus one (1000001), as expected by the server. Assuming that the actual file or Web page requested by the client is 500 bytes (not including the IP or TCP headers), the server will respond to the request message with an ACK message that contains the value 1000501 in its Acknowledgment Number field. This indicates that the server has received 500 bytes of data successfully, and is expecting the client's next data packet to have the Sequence Number 1000501. Because the client has transmitted 500 bytes to the server, it increments its Sequence Number value by that amount, and the next data message it sends will use the value that the server expects (assuming there are no transmission errors).

The same message numbering process also occurs simultaneously in the other direction. The server has transmitted no data yet, except for its SYN/ACK message, so the ACK generated by the client during the handshake contains the server's ISN plus one. The server's acknowledgment of the client's request contained no data, so the Sequence Number field was not incremented. Thus, when the server responds to the client's URL request, its first data message will use the same ISN-plus-one value in its Sequence Number field, which is what the client expects (see Figure 7.3).

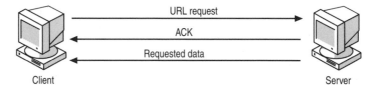

Figure 7.3 After the Web browser client transmits its URL request message, the server responds with an ACK message, which is followed by a data message containing the requested Web page.

In the case described here the client's URL request is small and so requires only one TCP message, but in most cases, the Web server responds by transmitting a Web page, which is likely to require multiple segments. The server divides the Web page (which becomes the sequence it is transmitting) into segments no larger than the client's MSS value. As the server begins to transmit the segments, it increments its Sequence Number value according to the amount of data in each message. If the server's ISN is 20000, the Sequence Number of its first data message will be 20001. Assuming that the client's MSS is 1000, the server's second data message will have a Sequence Number of 21001, the third will be 22001, and so on.

Once the client begins receiving data from the server, the client is responsible for acknowledging the data. TCP uses a system called *delayed acknowledgments*, which means that the systems do not have to generate a separate acknowledgment message for every data message they receive. The intervals at which the systems generate their acknowledgments is left up to the individual TCP implementation. Each acknowledgment message that the client sends in response to the server's data messages has the ACK flag, of course, and the value of its Acknowledgment Number field reflects the number of bytes in the sequence that the client has successfully received.

If the client receives messages that fail the CRC check or fails to receive messages containing some of the segments in the sequence, it signals these failures to the server using the Acknowledgment Number field in the ACK messages. The Acknowledgment Number value always reflects the number of bytes from the beginning of the sequence that the destination system has received correctly. If, for example, a sequence consists of ten segments, and all are received correctly except segment number seven, the recipient's acknowledgment message will contain an Acknowledgment Number value that reflects the number of bytes in the first six segments only. Segments eight through ten, even though they were received correctly, are discarded and must be retransmitted along with segment seven. This system is called *positive acknowledgment with retransmission*, because the destination system only acknowledges the messages that were sent correctly. A protocol that uses *negative acknowledgement* would assume that all messages have been received correctly, except for those that the destination system explicitly lists as having errors.

The source system maintains a queue of the messages that it has transmitted, and deletes those messages for which acknowledgments have arrived. Messages that remain in the source system's queue for a predetermined period of time are assumed to have been lost or discarded, and the system automatically retransmits them.

Once the server has transmitted all of the segments in the sequence that contains the requested Web page, and the client acknowledges that it has received all of the segments correctly, the systems terminate the connection. This termination procedure is described in "Terminating the Connection," later in this lesson. If the segments have arrived at their destination out of sequence, the receiving system uses the Sequence Number values to reassemble them into the proper order. The client system then processes the data it has received in order to display the Web page. In all likelihood, the page will contain links to images or other elements, and the client will have to initiate additional connections to the server to download more data. This is the nature of the Web client/server process. However, other types of applications might maintain a single TCP connection for a much longer period of time and perform repeated exchanges of data in both directions. In a case like this, both systems can exchange data messages and acknowledgments, with the error detection and correction processes occurring on both sides.

Detecting Errors

There are basically two things that can go wrong during a TCP transaction: either messages arrive in a corrupted state or they fail to arrive at all. When messages fail to arrive, the lack of acknowledgments from the destination system causes the sender to retransmit the missing messages. If a serious network problem arises that prevents the two systems from exchanging any messages, the TCP connection will eventually time out, and the entire process must start again.

When messages do arrive at their destination, the receiving system checks them for accuracy by performing the same checksum computation that the sender performed before transmitting the data, and comparing the results to the value in the Checksum field. If the values don't match, the system discards the message. This is a crucial element of the TCP protocol, because it is the only end-to-end checksum performed on the actual application layer data. IP includes an end-to-end checksum, but only on its header data, and data-link layer protocols like Ethernet and Token Ring contain a checksum, but only for one hop at a time. If the packets pass through a network that doesn't provide a checksum, such as a Point-to-Point Protocol (PPP) link, there is a potential for errors to be introduced that can't be detected at the data-link or network layer.

The checksum performed by TCP is unusual because it is calculated not only on the entire TCP header and the application data, but also on a *pseudo-header*. The pseudo-header consists of the IP header's Source IP Address, Destination IP Address, Protocol, and Length fields, plus 1 byte of padding, to bring the total number of bytes to an even 12 (three 4-byte words), as shown in Figure 7.4. The inclusion of the pseudo-header ensures that the datagrams are delivered to the correct computer and the correct transport layer protocol on that computer.

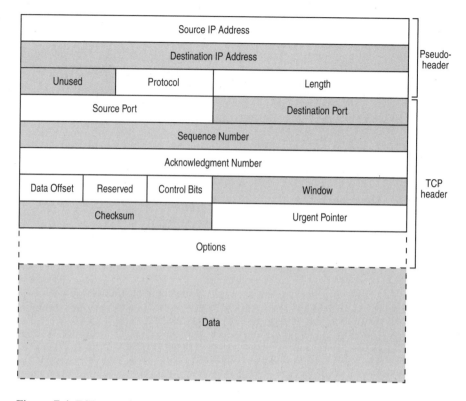

Figure 7.4 TCP computes its checksum on the header, data, and a pseudo-header derived from the IP header.

Flow Control

Flow control is the process by which the destination system in a TCP connection provides information to the source system that enables that source system to regulate the speed at which it transmits data. Each system has a limited amount of buffer space in which to store incoming data. The data remains in the buffer until the system generates messages acknowledging that data. If the system transmitting the data sends too much information too quickly, the receiver's buffers could fill up, forcing it to discard data messages. The system receiving the data uses the Window field in its acknowledgment messages to inform the sender of how much buffer space it has available at that time. The transmitting system uses the Window value along with the Acknowledgment Number value to determine what data in the sequence the system is permitted to transmit. For example, if an acknowledgment message contains an Acknowledgment Number value of 150000 and a Window value of 500, the sending system knows that all of the data in the sequence through byte 150000 has been received correctly at the destination, and that it can now transmit bytes 150001 through 150500. If, by the time the sender transmits those 500 bytes, it has received no additional acknowledgments, it must stop transmitting until the next acknowledgment arrives.

This type of flow control is called a *sliding window* technique. The *offered window* (shown in Figure 7.5) is the series of bytes that the receiving system has permitted the transmitting system to send. As the receiving system acknowledges the incoming bytes, the left side of the window moves to the right, and as the system passes the acknowledged bytes up to the application layer process indicated by the Destination Port number, the right side of the window moves to the right. Thus the window can be said to be sliding along the incoming byte stream, from left to right.

Figure 7.5 TCP uses a sliding window technique to provide flow control.

Terminating the Connection

Once the systems involved in a TCP connection have finished their exchange of data, they terminate the connection using control messages, much like those used in the three-way handshake that established the connection. As with the establishment of the connection, which system initiates the termination sequence depends on the application generating the data. In the case of the Web client/server transaction used as an example in this lesson, the server begins the termination process by setting the FIN flag in the Control Bits field of its last data message. In other cases, the system initiating the termination process might use a separate message containing the FIN flag and no data.

The system receiving the FIN flag transmits an acknowledgment message, and it then generates its own message containing a FIN flag, to which the other system must respond with an ACK message. This is necessary because, as was shown in the establishment process, the connection runs in both directions, and it is necessary for both systems to terminate their respective connections using a total of four messages (see Figure 7.6). Unlike the connection establishment procedure, the computers can't combine the FIN and ACK flags in the same message, which is why four messages are needed instead of three. There are some occasions when only one of the two connections is terminated and the other is left open. This is called a *half close*.

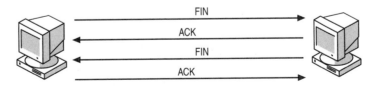

Figure 7.6 The TCP connection termination process

UDP

UDP is defined in RFC 768, "User Datagram Protocol." Unlike TCP, UDP is a connectionless protocol and provides no packet acknowledgment, flow control, segmentation, or guaranteed delivery. As a result, UDP is far simpler than TCP, and generates far less overhead. Not only is the UDP header much smaller than that of TCP—8 bytes as opposed to 20 or more—there are no separate control messages, such as those used to establish and terminate connections. UDP transactions consist of only two messages, a request and a reply, with the reply functioning as a tacit acknowledgment. For this reason, the applications that use UDP must transport small amounts of data, small enough to fit into a single message. DNS and the Dynamic Host Configuration Protocol (DHCP) are two of the most commonly used application layer protocols that use UDP.

The format of a UDP message is shown in Figure 7.7.

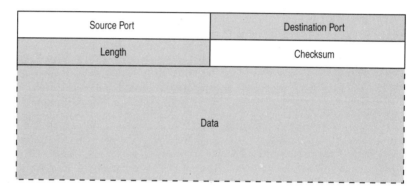

Figure 7.7 The UDP message format

The functions of the UDP message fields are as follows:

- **Source Port (2 bytes)** This field identifies the process on the transmitting system that generated the information carried in the Data field.

- **Destination Port (2 bytes)** This field identifies the process on the receiving system for which the information in the Data field is intended.

- **Length (2 bytes)** This field specifies the length of the UDP header and data, in bytes.

- **Checksum (2 bytes)** This field contains the results of a CRC computation performed by the transmitting system, and is used by the receiving system to detect errors in the UDP header, data, and parts of the IP header.

- **Data (variable)** This field contains the information generated by the application layer process specified in the Source Port field.

The Source Port and Destination Port fields in a UDP header perform the same function as in the TCP header. The Length field specifies how much data is included in the UDP message, and the Checksum is computed using the message header, data, and the IP pseudo-header, just as in TCP. The UDP standard specifies that the use of the checksum is optional. When it isn't used, the transmitting system fills the Checksum field with zeroes. There has been a great deal of debate about whether UDP messages should include checksums. RFC 768 requires all UDP systems to be capable of checking for errors using checksums, and most implementations these days do include the checksum computations.

Exercise 7.1: TCP Header Fields

Match the TCP header field in the left column with the correct description in the right column.

1. Source Port
2. Sequence Number
3. Checksum
4. Window
5. Urgent Pointer
6. Data Offset
7. Destination Port
8. Acknowledgment Number
9. Control Bits
10. Data

a. Specifies how many bytes the sender can transmit
b. Specifies the number of bytes in the sequence that have been successfully transmitted
c. Specifies the functions of messages used to initiate and terminate connections
d. Contains information for the application layer
e. Specifies which of the bytes in the message should receive special treatment from the receiving system
f. Identifies the application or protocol that generated the data carried in the TCP message
g. Used to reassemble segments that arrive at the destination out of order
h. Specifies the length of the TCP header
i. Contains error detection information
j. Specifies the application that will make use of the data in the message

Lesson 2: SPX and NCP

Like TCP/IP, NetWare's IPX protocol suite includes multiple protocols at the transport layer, which provide varying levels of service. Interestingly, the transport layer protocol most frequently associated with IPX, called the Sequenced Packet Exchange (SPX) protocol, is actually far less frequently used than the NetWare Core Protocol (NCP).

After this lesson, you will be able to

- Describe the services provided by the SPX and NCP protocols
- Identify the functions of the SPX and NCP header fields

Estimated lesson time: 15 minutes

SPX

SPX is NetWare's connection-oriented protocol. It provides many of the same services as TCP, including packet acknowledgment and flow control. Compared to TCP, however, SPX is rarely used. NetWare servers use SPX for communication between print queues, print servers, and printers; and for specialized applications that require its services, such as Rconsole.

SPX messages are carried within IPX datagrams using the message format illustrated in Figure 7.8.

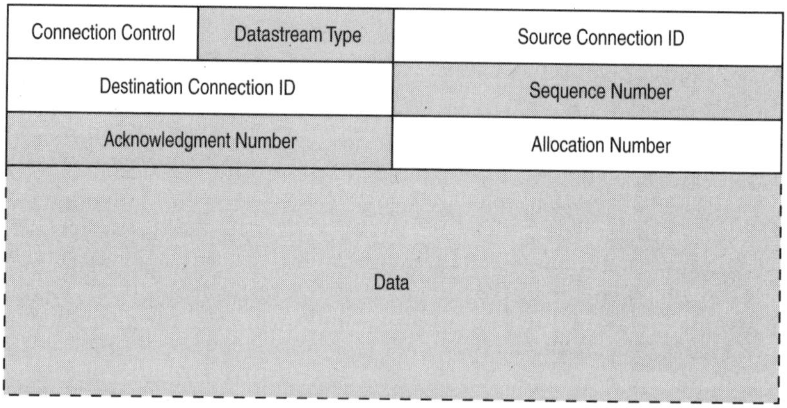

Connection Control	Datastream Type	Source Connection ID
Destination Connection ID		Sequence Number
Acknowledgment Number		Allocation Number
Data		

Figure 7.8 The SPX message format

The functions of the SPX message fields are as follows.

- **Connection Control (1 byte)** This field contains a code that identifies the message as performing a certain control function, such as End of Message or Acknowledgment Required.

- **Datastream Type (1 byte)** This field identifies the type of information found in the Data field or contains a code used during the connection termination sequence.

- **Source Connection ID (2 bytes)** This field contains the number used by the transmitting system to identify the current connection.

- **Destination Connection ID (2 bytes)** This field contains the number used by the receiving system to identify the current connection.

- **Sequence Number (2 bytes)** This field specifies the location of this message in the sequence.

- **Acknowledgment Number (2 bytes)** This field contains the Sequence Number value that the system expects to find in the next packet it receives, thus acknowledging the successful receipt of all of the previous packets.

- **Allocation Number (2 bytes)** This field specifies the number of packet receive buffers that are available on the transmitting system.

- **Data (variable)** This field contains the information generated by an application or upper layer protocol.

NCP

NCP is responsible for all of the file-sharing traffic generated by NetWare clients and servers, and also has a number of other functions. As a result, NCP is far more commonly used than is SPX. The large number of network functions that use NCP make it difficult to pinpoint the protocol's place in the OSI reference model. File transfers between clients and servers place the protocol firmly in the transport layer, but NetWare clients also use NCP messages to log in to the Novell Directory Services (NDS) tree, which is a session layer function. In addition, there are other presentation and application layer services that NCP provides. However, for all of these services, NCP messages are carried within IPX datagrams, which affirms its dominant presence at the transport layer.

Unlike SPX and the TCP/IP transport layer protocols, NCP uses different formats for client request and server reply messages. In addition, there is another form of NCP message called the NetWare Core Packet Burst (NCPB) protocol, which enables systems to transmit multiple messages with only a single acknowledgment. NCPB was developed relatively recently to address a shortcoming of NCP, which requires an individual acknowledgment message for each data packet.

The NCP request message format is illustrated in Figure 7.9.

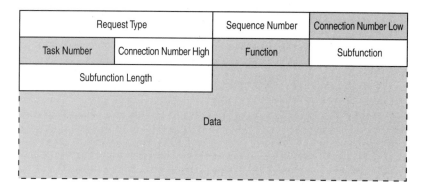

Figure 7.9 The NCP Request message format

The NCP Request message fields perform the following functions:

- **Request Type (2 bytes)** This field specifies the basic type of request performed by the message, using codes that represent the following functions: Create a Service Connection, File Server Request, Connection Destroy, and Burst Mode Protocol Packet.

- **Sequence Number (1 byte)** This field contains a value that indicates this message's place in the current NCP sequence.

- **Connection Number Low (1 byte)** This field contains the number of the client's connection to the NetWare server.

- **Task Number (1 byte)** This field contains a unique value that the connected systems use to associate requests with replies.

- **Connection Number High (1 byte)** This field is unused.

- **Function (1 byte)** This field specifies the exact function of the message.

- **Subfunction (1 byte)** This field further describes the function of the message.

- **Subfunction Length (2 bytes)** This field specifies the length of the Data field.

- **Data (variable)** This field contains information that the server will need to process the request, such as a file location.

Note The NCP request format has three fields that describe the function of the message, which may seem redundant, but there are over 200 combinations of function and subfunction codes, covering virtually all of the services provided by NetWare servers.

The NCP message reply format is illustrated in Figure 7.10.

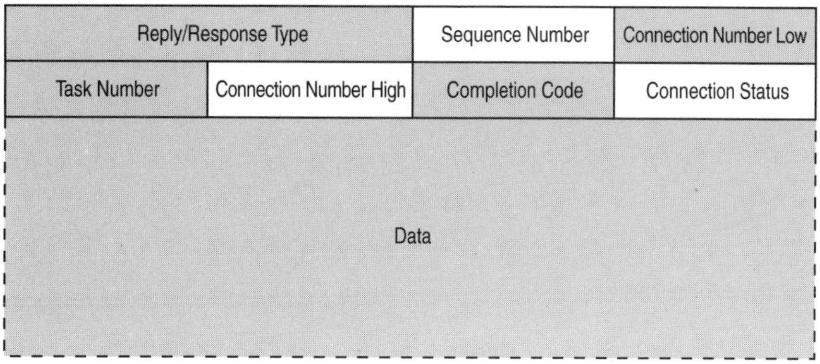

Reply/Response Type		Sequence Number	Connection Number Low
Task Number	Connection Number High	Completion Code	Connection Status
Data			

Figure 7.10 The NCP Reply message format

The functions of the NCP Reply message fields are as follows:

- **Reply/Response Type (2 bytes)** This field specifies the type of reply in the message, using codes that represent the following functions: File Server Reply, Burst Mode Protocol, and Positive Acknowledgment.

- **Sequence Number (1 byte)** This field contains a value that indicates this message's place in the current NCP sequence.

- **Connection Number Low (1 byte)** This field contains the number of the client's connection to the NetWare server.

- **Task Number (1 byte)** This field contains a unique value that the connected systems use to associate requests with replies.

- **Connection Number High (1 byte)** This field is unused.

- **Completion Code (1 byte)** This field indicates whether or not the request associated with this reply has been successfully completed.

- **Connection Status (1 byte)** This field indicates whether the connection between the client and the server is still active.

- **Data (variable)** This field contains information sent by the server in response to the request.

Chapter Summary

The key points covered in this chapter are as follows.

TCP and UDP

- TCP is a connection-oriented protocol that provides services such as packet acknowledgment, flow control, error detection and correction, and segmentation.

- Establishing a TCP connection between two systems requires a three-way handshake, during which each computer supplies the other with the sequence number it will assign to its messages, plus its maximum segment size.

- To transmit large amounts of data over a TCP connection, a system divides a byte stream into multiple segments, each of which is transmitted in a separate message.

- The system receiving the data segments acknowledges them with occasional messages used for that purpose. Unacknowledged messages are eventually retransmitted.

- Acknowledgment messages inform the other system how much data it can transmit. This is called flow control.

- TCP messages contain a checksum that the receiving system uses to detect transmission errors.

- Closing a TCP connection requires the systems to exchange termination (FIN) messages and acknowledgments.

- UDP is a connectionless protocol that provides error detection through checksums, but it provides none of the other services found in TCP.

SPX and NCP

- SPX is NetWare's connection-oriented protocol, which includes most of the same features as TCP, but is used far less often than NCP.

- NCP is the transport layer protocol most often used by NetWare systems, because it supports a great many functions, including client/server file sharing and NDS communications.

Chapter Review

1. In TCP, what does "delayed acknowledgment" mean?

    a. A predetermined time interval must pass before the receiving system can acknowledge a data packet.

    b. Data segments are not acknowledged until the entire sequence has been transmitted.

    c. The receiving system doesn't have to generate a separate acknowledgment message for every segment.

    d. A data segment must be acknowledged before the next segment is transmitted.

2. What does the Data Offset field in the TCP header specify?

    a. The length of the TCP header

    b. The location of the current segment in the sequence

    c. The length of the Data field

    d. The checksum value used for error detection

3. Specify whether each of the following statements describes TCP, UDP, or both.

    a. It provides flow control.

    b. It is used for DNS communications.

    c. It detects transmission errors.

    d. It is used to carry DHCP messages.

    e. It divides data to be transmitted into segments.

    f. It acknowledges transmitted messages.

    g. It is used for Web client/server communications.

    h. It requires a connection establishment procedure.

    i. It contains a Length field. `

    j. It uses a pseudo-header in its checksums.

4. What is the combination of an IP address and a port number called?

    a. A sequence number

    b. A checksum

    c. A data offset

    d. A socket

5. Which of the following is not true of the SPX protocol?

    a. It is connection-oriented.

    b. It operates at the transport layer only.

    c. Clients use it to access server files.

    d. It provides flow control.

6. Which of the following TCP/IP systems uses an ephemeral port number?

    a. The client

    b. The server

    c. The system initiating the TCP connection

    d. The system terminating the TCP connection

7. What flag does the first message transmitted in any TCP connection contain?

    a. ACK

    b. SYN

    c. FIN

    d. PSH

8. At which layers of the OSI reference model does the NCP provide functions?

9. What TCP header field provides flow control?

    a. Window

    b. Data Offset

    c. Acknowledgment

    d. Sequence Number

10. Which of the following services does the UDP protocol provide?

    a. Flow control

    b. Guaranteed delivery

    c. Error detection

    d. None of the above

C H A P T E R   8

TCP/IP Fundamentals

About This Chapter

Because of the explosive growth of the Internet in recent years, Transmission Control Protocol/Internet Protocol (TCP/IP) is now used on more networks than any other suite of protocols. This chapter describes the functions of the most commonly used protocols in the TCP/IP suite and examines in detail TCP/IP's self-contained addressing system, one of its most important and unique features.

Before You Begin

This chapter requires that you have a basic knowledge of the Open Systems Interconnection (OSI) reference model, as described in Chapter 1, "Networking Basics," in order to understand the roles of the various TCP/IP protocols in the networking protocol stack. The IP, TCP, and User Datagram Protocol (UDP) protocols referred to in this chapter are introduced in Chapter 6, "Network Layer Protocols," and Chapter 7, "Transport Layer Protocols."

Lesson 1: TCP/IP Protocols

The TCP/IP protocols were developed in the 1970s specifically for use on a packet-switching network built by the United States Department of Defense. Their network was then known as the ARPANET but is now the Internet. The TCP/IP protocols have also been associated with the UNIX operating systems since early in their inception. Thus, these protocols pre-date the personal computer, the OSI reference model, the Ethernet protocol, and most other elements that today are considered the foundations of computer networking. Unlike the other protocols that perform some of the same functions, such as Novell's Internetwork Packet Exchange (IPX), TCP/IP was never the product of a single company, but rather has been a collaborative effort from the very beginning.

After this lesson, you will be able to

- List the layers of the TCP/IP protocol stack and locate the TCP/IP protocols in the OSI reference model
- Understand the function of the Address Resolution Protocol (ARP)
- Describe the various functions of the Internet Control Message Protocol (ICMP)
- Describe the properties of TCP/IP's various application layer protocols

Estimated lesson time: 45 minutes

In addition to not being restrained in any way by copyrights, trademarks, or other publishing restrictions, the non-proprietary nature of the TCP/IP standards also means that the protocols are not limited to any particular computing platform, operating system, or hardware implementation. This platform independence was the chief guiding principle of the TCP/IP development effort, and many of the protocol features are designed to make it possible for any computer with networking capabilities to communicate with any other networked computer using TCP/IP.

The TCP/IP standards are published in documents called Requests for Comments (RFCs) by the Internet Engineering Task Force (IETF). The list of RFCs contains documents that define protocol standards in various stages of development, but also contains informational, experimental, and historical documents that range from the fascinating to the downright silly. These documents are in the public domain and are accessible from many Internet Web and FTP sites. For links to the standards, see the IETF home page at *www.ietf.org*.

Note Once a document is published by the IETF as an RFC and assigned a number, that document never changes. If the IETF publishes a revised version of an RFC at a later time, it assigns the document a new number. The RFC-INDEX file, which contains the complete listing of the published documents, contains cross-references that indicate when RFCs make other documents obsolete or when they have been made obsolete by other documents.

TCP/IP Layers

The TCP/IP protocols were developed long before the OSI reference model was, but they operate using layers in much the same way. Splitting the networking functionality of a computer into a stack of separate protocols, rather than creating a single monolithic protocol, has several advantages, including the following:

- **Platform independence** Separate protocols make it easier to support a variety of computing platforms. Creating or modifying protocols to support new physical layer standards or networking application programming interfaces (APIs) doesn't require modification of the entire protocol stack.

- **Quality of service** Having multiple protocols operating at the same layer makes it possible for applications to select the protocol that provides only the level of service they require.

- **Simultaneous development** Because the stack is split into layers, the development of the various protocols can proceed simultaneously, using personnel that are uniquely qualified in the operations of the particular layers.

Note For more information on the OSI model and the functions of its various layers, see Lesson 2: The OSI Reference Model, in Chapter 1, "Networking Basics."

TCP/IP has its own four-layer networking model, which is defined in RFC 1122, "Requirements for Internet Hosts—Communication Layers." The layers are roughly analogous to the OSI model, as shown in Figure 8.1.

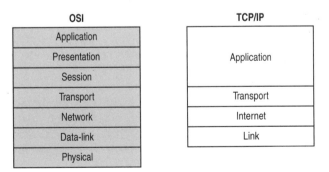

Figure 8.1 The seven-layer OSI reference model versus the four TCP/IP protocol layers

The four TCP/IP layers are as follows:

- **Link** The TCP/IP protocol suite includes rudimentary link layer protocols, such as the Serial Line Internet Protocol (SLIP) and the Point-to-Point Protocol (PPP). However, TCP/IP does not include physical layer specifications or complex local area network (LAN) protocols such as Ethernet and Token Ring. Therefore, while TCP/IP does maintain a layer that is comparable to the OSI data-link layer, in most cases the protocol operating at that layer is not part of the TCP/IP suite. TCP/IP does, however, include the Address Resolution Protocol (ARP), which can be said to function at least partially at the link layer, because it provides services to the internet layer above it.

- **Internet** The internet layer is exactly equivalent to the network layer of the OSI model. IP is the primary protocol operating at this layer, and provides data encapsulation, routing, addressing, and fragmentation services to the protocols at the transport layer above it. Two additional protocols, called the Internet Control Message Protocol (ICMP) and the Internet Group Message Protocol (IGMP), also operate at this layer.

  Remember, the word *internet,* in this instance, is a generic reference to an internetwork, not to the Internet. Be careful not to confuse the two.

- **Transport** The transport layer is equivalent to the layer of the same name in the OSI model. The TCP/IP suite includes two protocols at this layer, the Transmission Control Protocol (TCP) and the User Datagram Protocol (UDP), which provide connection-oriented and connectionless data transfer services, respectively.

- **Application** The TCP/IP protocols at the application layer can take several different forms. Some protocols, such as the File Transfer Protocol (FTP), are applications in themselves, while others, such as the Hypertext Transfer Protocol (HTTP), provide services to applications.

The following sections examine some of the protocols that operate at the various layers of the TCP/IP protocol stack.

SLIP and PPP

SLIP and PPP are link layer protocols that systems use for wide area connections using telephone lines and other types of physical connections. SLIP is defined in RFC 1055, "A Nonstandard for Transmission of IP Datagrams over Serial Lines." PPP is more complex than SLIP, and uses additional protocols to establish a connection between two systems. These protocols are defined in separate documents, including RFC 1661, "The Point-to-Point Protocol," and RFC 1662, "PPP in HDLC-like Framing." For more information about SLIP and PPP, see Lesson 3: SLIP and PPP, in Chapter 5, "Data-Link Layer Protocols."

ARP

ARP, as defined in RFC 826, "Ethernet Address Resolution Protocol," occupies an unusual place in the TCP/IP suite. ARP provides a service to IP, which seems to place it in the link layer (or the data-link layer of the OSI model). However, its messages are carried directly by data-link layer protocols and are not encapsulated within IP datagrams, which is a good reason for calling it an internet (or network) layer protocol. Whichever layer you assign it to, ARP provides an essential service when TCP/IP is running on a LAN.

The TCP/IP protocols rely on IP addresses to identify networks and hosts, but when the computers are connected to an Ethernet or Token Ring LAN, they must eventually transmit the IP datagrams using the destination system's hardware address. ARP provides the interface between the IP addressing system used by IP and the hardware addresses used by the data-link layer protocols.

When IP constructs a datagram, it knows the IP address of the system that is the packet's ultimate destination. That address may identify a computer connected to the local network or a system on another network. In either case, IP must determine the hardware address of the system on the local network that will receive the datagram next. To do this, IP generates an ARP message and broadcasts it over the LAN. The format of the ARP message is shown in Figure 8.2.

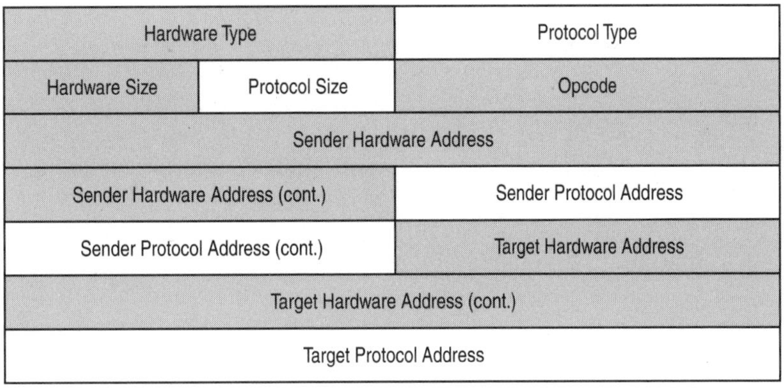

Hardware Type		Protocol Type	
Hardware Size	Protocol Size	Opcode	
Sender Hardware Address			
Sender Hardware Address (cont.)		Sender Protocol Address	
Sender Protocol Address (cont.)		Target Hardware Address	
Target Hardware Address (cont.)			
Target Protocol Address			

Figure 8.2 The ARP message format

The functions of the ARP message fields are as follows:

- **Hardware Type (2 bytes)** This field identifies the type of hardware addresses in the Sender Hardware Address and Target Hardware Address fields. For Ethernet and Token Ring networks, the value is 1.

- **Protocol Type (2 bytes)** This field identifies the type of addresses in the Sender Protocol Address and Target Protocol Address fields. The hexadecimal value for IP addresses is 0800 (the same as the Ethertype code for IP).

- **Hardware Size (1 byte)** This field specifies the size of the addresses in the Sender Hardware Address and Target Hardware Address fields, in bytes. For Ethernet and Token Ring networks, the value is 6.

- **Protocol Size (1 byte)** This field specifies the size of the addresses in the Sender Protocol Address and Target Protocol Address fields, in bytes. For IP addresses, the value is 4.

- **Opcode (2 bytes)** This field specifies the function of the packet: ARP Request, ARP Reply, RARP Request, or RARP Reply.

- **Sender Hardware Address (6 bytes)** This field contains the hardware address of the system generating the message.

- **Sender Protocol Address (4 bytes)** This field contains the IP address of the system generating the message.

- **Target Hardware Address (6 bytes)** This field contains the hardware address of the system for which the message is destined. In ARP Request messages, this field is left blank.

- **Target Protocol Address (4 bytes)** This field contains the IP address of the system for which the message is intended.

Note The Reverse Address Resolution Protocol (RARP) performs the opposite function of ARP. RARP was once used by diskless workstations because it enables a system to discover its IP address by transmitting its hardware address to a RARP server. RARP is a progenitor of the Bootstrap Protocol (BOOTP) and the Dynamic Host Configuration Protocol (DHCP), which are used to automatically configure TCP/IP clients. It is rarely used today.

The process by which IP uses ARP to discover the hardware address of the destination system is as follows:

1. IP packages transport layer information into a datagram, inserting the IP address of the destination system into the Destination IP Address field of the IP header.

2. IP compares the network identifier in the destination IP address to its own network identifier and determines whether to send the datagram directly to the destination host or to a router on the local network.

3. IP generates an ARP Request packet containing its own hardware address and IP address in the Sender Hardware Address and Sender Protocol Address fields. The Target Protocol Address field contains the IP address of the datagram's next destination (host or router), as determined in Step 2. The Target Hardware Address Field is left blank.

4. The system passes the ARP Request message down to the data-link layer protocol, which encapsulates it in a frame and transmits it as a broadcast to the entire local network.

5. The systems on the LAN receive the ARP Request message and read the contents of the Target Protocol Address field. If the Target Protocol Address value does not match the system's own IP address, it silently discards the message and takes no further action.

6. If the system receiving the ARP Request message recognizes its own IP address in the Target Protocol Address field, it generates an ARP Reply message. The system copies the two sender address values from the ARP Request message into the respective target address values in the ARP Reply and copies the Target Protocol Address value from the request into the Sender Protocol Address field in the reply. The system then inserts its own hardware address into the Sender Hardware Address field.

7. The system transmits the ARP Reply message as a unicast message back to the computer that generated the request, using the hardware address in the Target Hardware Address field.

8. The system that originally generated the ARP Request message receives the ARP Reply and uses the newly supplied value in the Sender Hardware Address field to encapsulate the datagram in a data-link layer frame and transmit it to the desired destination as a unicast message.

The ARP specification requires TCP/IP systems to maintain a cache of hardware addresses that the system has recently discovered using the protocol. This prevents systems from flooding the network with separate ARP Request broadcasts for each datagram transmitted. When a system transmits a file in multiple TCP segments, for example, only one ARP transaction is usually required, because IP checks the ARP cache for a hardware address before generating a new ARP request. The interval during which unused ARP information remains in the cache is left up to the individual implementation, but it is usually relatively short, so as to prevent the system from using outdated address information.

Tip The TCP/IP protocol stack in the Windows-based operating systems includes a utility called Arp.exe, which you can use to manipulate the contents of the ARP cache. When you manually add a hardware address into the cache this way, it remains there permanently, which can help to reduce the broadcast traffic on your network. For more information about Arp.exe, see Lesson 2: TCP/IP Utilities, in Chapter 10, "TCP/IP Applications."

IP

IP is the protocol that is responsible for carrying the data generated by nearly all of the other TCP/IP protocols from the source system to its ultimate destination. For detailed information about IP and its functions, see Lesson 1: IP, in Chapter 6, "Network Layer Protocols."

ICMP

The Internet Control Message Protocol (ICMP), as defined in RFC 792, is another protocol that IP uses to perform network administration tasks. ICMP is considered to be an internet (or network) layer protocol, despite the fact that it carries no application data and its messages are carried within IP datagrams. Although it uses only one message format, ICMP performs many different functions, which are generally divided into errors and queries.

The ICMP message format is illustrated in Figure 8.3.

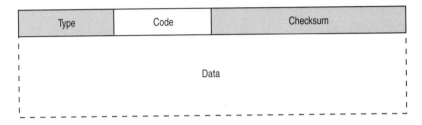

Figure 8.3 The ICMP message format

The functions of the ICMP message fields are as follows:

- **Type (1 byte)** This field contains a code that specifies the basic function of the message.

- **Code (1 byte)** This field contains a code that indicates the specific function of the message.

- **Checksum (2 bytes)** This field contains a checksum computed on the entire ICMP message; it is used for error detection.

- **Data (variable)** This field may contain information related to the specific function of the message.

ICMP Error Message Types

Reporting errors of various types is the primary function of ICMP. IP is a connectionless protocol, so there are no internet/network layer acknowledgments returned to the sending system, and even the transport layer acknowledgments returned by TCP are generated only by the destination end system. ICMP functions as a monitor of internet layer communications, enabling intermediate or end systems to return error messages to the sender. For example, when a router has a problem processing a datagram during the journey to its destination, it generates an ICMP message and transmits it back to the source system. The source system may then take action to alleviate the problem in response to the ICMP message. The Data field in an ICMP error message contains the entire 20-byte IP header of the datagram that caused the problem, plus the first 8 bytes of the datagram's own Data field. The following sections examine the various types of ICMP error messages.

Destination Unreachable Messages

When an intermediate or end system attempts to forward a datagram to a resource that is inaccessible, it can generate an ICMP Destination Unreachable message and transmit it back to the source system. Destination Unreachable messages all have a Type value of 3; the Code value specifies exactly what resource is unavailable, using values shown in Table 8.1. For example, when a router fails to transmit a datagram to the destination system on a local network, it returns a Host Unreachable message to the sender. If the router can't transmit the datagram to another router, it generates a Net Unreachable message. If the datagram reaches the destination system but the designated transport layer or application layer protocol is unavailable, the system returns a Protocol Unreachable or Port Unreachable message.

Table 8.1 ICMP Destination Unreachable error messages

Code	Description
0	Net Unreachable
1	Host Unreachable
2	Protocol Unreachable
3	Port Unreachable
4	Fragmentation Needed And Don't Fragment Was Set
5	Source Route Failed
6	Destination Network Unknown
7	Destination Host Unknown
8	Source Host Isolated
9	Communication With Destination Network Is Administratively Prohibited
10	Communication With Destination Host Is Administratively Prohibited
11	Destination Network Unreachable For Type Of Service
12	Destination Host Unreachable For Type Of Service

Source Quench Messages

Source Quench messages have a Type value of 4 and function as a rudimentary flow control mechanism for the internet layer. When a router's memory buffers are nearly full, it can send a Source Quench message to the source system, which instructs it to slow down its transmission rate. When the Source Quench messages cease, the sending system can gradually increase the rate again.

Redirect Messages

Routers generate ICMP Redirect messages to inform a host or another router that there is a more efficient route to a particular destination. Many internetworks have a matrix of routers that enables packets to take different paths to a single destination, as shown in Figure 8.4. If System 1 sends a packet to Router A in an attempt to get it to System 2, Router A forwards the packet to Router B, but it also transmits an ICMP Redirect message back to System 1, informing it that it can send packets destined for System 2 directly to Router B.

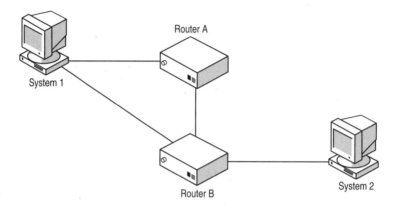

Figure 8.4 ICMP Redirect messages enable routers to inform other systems of more efficient routes.

The ICMP Redirect message's Data field contains the usual 28 bytes from the datagram in question (the 20-byte IP header plus eight bytes of IP data) plus an additional 4-byte Gateway Internet Address field, which contains the IP address of the router that the system should use from now on when transmitting datagrams to that particular destination. By altering its practices, the source system saves a hop on the packet's path through the internetwork and lessens the processing burden on Router A.

Time Exceeded Messages

When a TCP/IP system creates an IP datagram, it inserts a value in the IP header's Time To Live (TTL) field that each router processing the datagram reduces by one during the packet's journey through the internetwork. Should the TTL value reach zero during the journey, the last router to receive the packet discards it and transmits an ICMP Time Exceeded (Type 11, Code 0) message back to the sender, informing it that the packet has not reached its destination and telling it why. This is called a Time To Live Exceeded In Transit message.

Note The Time To Live Exceeded In Transit message is the basis for the functionality of the Traceroute program included in most TCP/IP implementations. For more information about Traceroute, see Lesson 2: TCP/IP Utilities, in Chapter 10, "TCP/IP Applications."

Another type of Time Exceeded message is used when a destination system is attempting to reassemble datagram fragments and one or more fragments fail to arrive in a timely manner. The system then generates a Fragment Reassembly Time Exceeded (Type 11, Code 1) message and sends it back to the source system.

ICMP Query Message Types

The other function of ICMP messages is to carry requests to another system for some type of information and also to return the replies containing that information. These are called ICMP query messages. ICMP query messages are not reactions to an outside process, as error messages are. However, external programs, such as the TCP/IP utility Ping, can generate query messages as part of their functionality.

Because query messages aren't generated in response to an external problem, their Data fields do not contain the IP header information from another datagram. Instead, the various types of query messages include more divergent information in the Data field, according to their functions. The following sections examine the most important query message types.

Echo Request and Echo Reply Messages

The Echo Request (Type 8, Code 0) and Echo Reply (Type 0, Code 0) messages form the basis for the TCP/IP Ping utility, and are essentially a means to test whether another system on the network is up and running. Both messages contain two-byte Identifier and two-byte Sequence Number subfields in the Data field, which are used to associate requests and replies, plus a certain amount of padding, as dictated by the Ping program. Ping functions by generating a series of Echo Request messages and transmitting them to a destination system specified by the user. The destination system, on receiving the messages, reverses the values of the Source IP Address and Destination IP Address fields, changes the Type value from 8 to 0, recalculates the checksum, and transmits the messages back to the sender. When Ping receives the Echo Reply messages, it assumes that the destination system is functioning properly.

Note For more information about the Ping program, see Lesson 2: TCP/IP Utilities, in Chapter 10, "TCP/IP Applications."

Router Solicitation and Router Advertisement Messages

Router Solicitation (Type 10, Code 0) and Router Advertisement (Type 9, Code 0) messages cannot truly constitute a routing protocol, because they don't provide information about the efficiency of particular routes, but they do enable a TCP/IP system to discover the address of a default gateway on the local network. The process begins with a workstation broadcasting a Router Solicitation message to the local network. The routers on the network respond with unicast Router Advertisement messages, which contain the router's IP address and other information. The workstation can then use the information in these replies to configure the default gateway entry in its routing table.

TCP and UDP

TCP and UDP are the TCP/IP transport layer protocols. All application layer protocols use either TCP or UDP to transmit data across the network, depending on the services they require. For more information about these two protocols, see Lesson 1: TCP and UDP, in Chapter 7, "Transport Layer Protocols."

Application Layer Protocols

The protocols that operate at the application layer are no longer concerned with the network communication issues addressed by the link, internet, and transport layer protocols. These protocols are designed to provide communications between client and server services on different computers, and are not concerned with how the messages get to the other system.

Application layer protocols use different combinations of protocols at the lower layers to achieve the level of service they require. For example, servers use HTTP and FTP to transmit entire files to client systems, and it is essential that those files be received without error. These protocols, therefore, use a combination of TCP and IP to achieve connection-oriented, reliable communications. DHCP and Domain Name System (DNS), on the other hand, exchange small messages between clients and servers that can easily be retransmitted if necessary, so they use the connectionless service provided by UDP and IP.

Some of the most commonly used TCP/IP application layer protocols are as follows.

- **Hypertext Transfer Protocol (HTTP)** HTTP is the protocol used by Web clients and servers to exchange file requests and the files themselves. A client browser opens a TCP connection to a server and requests a particular file, and the server replies by sending that file, which the browser displays as a home page. HTTP messages also contain a variety of fields containing information about the communicating systems.

- **File Transfer Protocol (FTP)** FTP is a protocol used to transfer files between TCP/IP systems. An FTP client can browse through the directory structure of a connected server and select files to download or upload. FTP is unique in that it uses two separate ports for its communications. When an FTP client connects to a server, it uses TCP port 21 to establish a control connection. When the user initiates a file download, the program opens a second connection using port 20 for the data transfer. This data connection is closed when the file transfer is complete, but the control connection remains open until the client terminates it. FTP is also unusual in that on most TCP/IP systems, FTP is a self-contained application, rather than a protocol used by other applications.

- **Simple Mail Transport Protocol (SMTP)** SMTP is the protocol that e-mail servers use to transmit messages to each other across the Internet.

- **Post Office Protocol (POP3)** POP3 is one of the protocols that e-mail clients use to retrieve their messages from an e-mail server.

- **Domain Name System (DNS)** TCP/IP systems use DNS to resolve Internet host names into the IP addresses they need to communicate.

- **Dynamic Host Configuration Protocol (DHCP)** DHCP is a protocol that workstations use to request TCP/IP configuration parameter settings from a server.

- **Simple Network Management Protocol (SNMP)** SNMP is a network management protocol used by network administrators to gather information about various network components. Remote programs—called agents—gather information and transmit it to a central network management console using SNMP messages.

Note For more information about TCP/IP services such as DNS and DHCP, see Lesson 1: TCP/IP Services, in Chapter 10, "TCP/IP Applications."

Exercise 8.1: TCP/IP Layers and Protocols

Specify the layer of the TCP/IP protocol stack at which each of the following protocols operates.

1. DHCP
2. ARP
3. IP
4. UDP
5. POP3
6. ICMP
7. SMTP
8. TCP
9. DNS
10. SLIP

Lesson 2: IP Addressing

The self-contained IP addressing system is one of the most important elements of the TCP/IP protocol suite. IP addresses enable systems running any operating system on any platform to communicate by providing unique identifiers for the system itself and for the network on which it is located. Understanding how IP addresses are constructed and how they should be assigned is an essential part of the TCP/IP network administration process.

After this lesson, you will be able to

- Understand the elements of an IP address
- List the IP address classes and their properties
- Understand the function of a subnet mask
- Describe how to create subnets on a network

Estimated lesson time: 20 minutes

An IP address is a 32-bit value that contains both a network identifier and a host identifier. The address is notated using four decimal numbers ranging from 0 to 255, separated by periods, as in 192.168.1.44. This is known as *dotted decimal notation*. Each of the four values is the decimal equivalent of an 8-bit binary value. For example, the binary value 10101010 is equal to the decimal value 170. To properly understand some of the concepts of IP addressing, it is important to remember that the familiar decimal numbers have binary equivalents.

Note In TCP/IP terminology, each of the 8-bit values that make up an IP address is often called an *octet* (or sometimes even a *quad*), and the combination of four octets is called a *word*. The more traditional term *byte* was avoided because some computing platforms use a 7-bit rather than an 8-bit byte. Today, either octet or byte is appropriate.

IP addresses represent network interface adapters, of which there can be more than one in a computer. A router, for example, has interfaces to at least two networks, and must therefore have an IP address for each of those network interface adapters. Workstations typically have only a single LAN interface, but in some cases, they use a modem to connect to another network, such as the Internet. When this is the case, the modem interface has its own separate IP address (usually assigned by the server at the other end of the connection) as well as that of the LAN connection. If other systems on the LAN access the Internet through that computer's modem, that system is actually functioning as a router.

IP Address Assignments

Unlike hardware addresses, which are hardcoded into network interface adapters at the factory, network administrators must assign IP addresses to the systems on their networks. It is essential for each network interface adapter to have its own unique IP address; when two systems have the same IP address, they cannot communicate with the network properly.

As mentioned earlier, IP addresses consist of two parts: a network identifier and a host identifier. All of the network interface adapters on a particular subnet have the same network identifier, but a different host identifier. For systems that are on the Internet, the network identifiers are assigned by a body called the Internet Assigned Numbers Authority (IANA). This is to ensure that there is no address duplication on the Internet. When an organization registers its network, it is assigned a network identifier, and it is then up to the network administrators to assign unique host identifiers to each of the systems on that network. This two-tier system of administration is one of the basic principles of the Internet. Domain names are assigned in the same way.

Note While the IANA is responsible for maintaining the network address assignments, virtually all of the IP addresses available using the current addressing scheme have already been assigned to Internet Service Providers (ISPs). When you are building a new network and want to obtain a registered network address, you now get one from an ISP, not directly from the IANA.

IP Address Classes

The most complicated aspect of an IP address is that the division between the network identifier and the host identifier is not always in the same place. A hardware address, for example, consists of 3 bytes assigned to the manufacturer of the network adapter and 3 bytes which the manufacturer itself assigns to each card. IP addresses can have various numbers of bits assigned to the network identifier, depending on the size of the network.

The IANA defines several different classes of IP addresses, which provide support for networks of different sizes, as shown in Figure 8.5. The configurations of the three basic IP address classes are listed in Table 8.2.

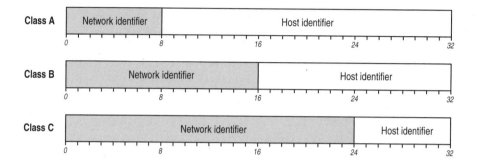

Figure 8.5 The three classes of IP addresses have different sized network and host identifiers.

Table 8.2 IP address classes and parameters

Class	First Bits	First Byte Values	Network ID Bits	Host ID Bits	Number of Networks	Number of Hosts
A	0	1 through 127	8	24	126	16,777,214
B	10	128 through 191	16	16	16, 384	65,534
C	110	192 through 223	24	8	2,097,152	254

Note In addition to Classes A, B, and C, there are two more classes: Class D and Class E. Class D addresses begin with the bit values 1110 and are reserved for use as multicast addresses. A multicast transmission is one that addresses a specific group of systems on a network. Class E addresses begin with bits 11110 and are as yet unused.

To the mathematically adept, the numbers for supported networks and hosts might appear low. However, there are a few rules that exclude some possible values.

- All the bits in the network identifier cannot be set to zeros.
- All the bits in the network identifier cannot be set to ones.
- All the bits in the host identifier cannot be set to zeros.
- All the bits in the host identifier cannot be set to ones.

The binary values of the first bits of each address class determine the possible decimal values for the first byte of the address. For example, because the first bit of Class A addresses must be 0, the binary values of the first byte range from 00000001 to 01111111, which in decimal form is 1 to 127. Thus, when you see an IP address in which the first byte is a number from 1 to 127, you know that this is a Class A address. In a Class A address, the network identifier is the first 8 bits and the host identifier is the remaining 24 bits. This means that there are only 126 possible Class A networks (network identifier 127 is reserved for diagnostic purposes), but each network can have up to 16,777,214 network interface adapters on it. Class B and Class C addresses devote more bits to the network identifier, which means that they support a greater number of networks, but at the cost of having fewer host identifier bits, which reduces the number of hosts on each network.

Subnet Masking

It may at first seem odd that IP address classes are assigned in this way. After all, there aren't any private networks that have 16 million hosts on them, so it makes little sense even to have Class A addresses. However, it's possible to subdivide IP addresses even further by creating subnets on them. A *subnet* is simply a subdivision of a network address that can be used to represent one LAN on an internetwork or the network of one of the ISP's clients. Thus, a large ISP might have a Class A address registered to it, and it might farm out pieces of the address to its clients in the form of subnets. In many cases, a large ISP's clients are smaller ISPs, which in turn supply addresses to their own clients.

To understand the process of creating subnets, you must understand the function of the *subnet mask*. When you configure a TCP/IP system, you assign it an IP address and a subnet mask, but many people don't know what the function of the mask is. Simply put, the subnet mask specifies which bits of the IP address are the network identifier and which bits are the host identifier. For a Class A address, for example, the correct subnet mask value is 255.0.0.0. When expressed as a binary number, a subnet mask's 1 bits indicate the network identifier, and its 0 bits indicate the host identifier. A mask of 255.0.0.0 in binary form is as follows:

```
11111111 00000000 00000000 00000000
```

Thus, this mask indicates that the first 8 bits of a Class A IP address are the network identifier bits and the remaining 24 bits are the host identifier. The subnet masks for the three main address classes are listed in Table 8.3.

Table 8.3 Subnet masks for IP address classes

Class	Subnet Mask
A	255.0.0.0
B	255.255.0.0
C	255.255.255.0

If all addresses of a particular class used the same number of bits for the network and host identifiers, there would be no need for a subnet mask. The value of the address's first byte would indicate its class. However, you can create multiple subnets within a given address class by using a different mask. If, for example, you have a Class B address, using a subnet mask of 255.255.0.0 would allocate the first 16 bits for the network identifier and the last 16 bits for the host identifier. If you use a mask of 255.255.255.0, you allocate an additional 8 bits to the network identifier. The third byte of the address thus becomes a subnet identifier, as shown in Figure 8.6. You can create up to 254 subnets using that one Class B address, with up to 254 network interface adapters on each subnet. An IP address of 131.24.67.98 would therefore indicate that the network is using the Class B address 131.24.0.0, and that the interface is host number 98 on subnet 67. A large corporate network might do this to create a separate subnet for each of its LANs.

Figure 8.6 Changing the subnet mask enables you to create multiple subnets out of one network address.

To complicate matters further, however, the boundary between the network identifier and the host identifier does not have to fall in between two bytes. An IP address can use any number of bits for its network address, and more complex subnet masks are needed in this type of environment. Suppose, for example, you have a Class C address of 199.24.65.0 that you want to subnet. There are already 24 bits devoted to the network address, and you obviously can't allocate the entire fourth byte as a subnet identifier, or there would be no bits left for the host identifier. You can, however, allocate part of the fourth byte. If you use 4 bits of the last byte for the subnet identifier, you have 4 bits left for your host identifier. To do this, the binary form of your subnet mask must appear as follows:

```
11111111 11111111 11111111 11110000
```

The decimal equivalent of this binary value is 255.255.255.240, because 240 is the decimal equivalent of 11110000. This leaves you with a 4-bit subnet identifier and a 4-bit host identifier, which means that you can create up to 14 subnets (subnet identifiers have the same *not all ones* and *not all zeros* rules as do network IDs and host IDs) with 14 hosts on each one. Figuring out the correct subnet mask for this type of configuration is relatively easy. Figuring out the IP addresses you must assign to your workstations is harder. To do this, you have to increment the 4 subnet bits separately from the 4 host bits. Once again, this is easier to understand when you look at the binary values. The 4-bit subnet identifier can have any one of the following fourteen values:

```
0001 0010 0011 0100 0101 0110 0111 1000 1001 1010 1011 1100 1101 1110
```

Tip The Calculator program included with Windows has a scientific mode that easily converts numbers between binary and decimal values. After launching the program, choose Scientific from the View menu, and then select either the Dec or the Bin radio button. You can then enter a value and click the other radio button to convert it.

Each one of these subnets can have up to 14 workstations, with each host identifier having one of the values from that same set of 14 values. Thus, to calculate the value of the IP address's fourth byte, you must combine the binary values of the subnet and host identifiers and convert them to decimal form. For example, the first host (0001) on the first subnet (0001) would have a fourth byte binary value of 00010001, which in decimal form is 17. Thus, the IP address for this system would be 199.24.65.17, and its subnet mask would be 255.255.255.240.

Tip Fortunately, there are utilities available that simplify the process of calculating these addresses, so that you don't have to do them manually. One of the best of these is a freeware program from Net3 Group called IP Subnet Calculator, which is available for download at *www.net3group.com/ipcalc.asp.*

Registered and Unregistered Addresses

Registered IP addresses are required for computers that are accessible from the Internet, but not by every computer that is connected to the Internet. For security reasons, networks typically use a firewall or some other technology to protect their systems from intrusion by outside computers. These firewalls use various techniques that provide workstations with access to Internet resources without making them accessible to other systems on the Internet.

These workstations typically use unregistered private IP addresses, which the network administrator can freely assign without the necessity of obtaining them from an ISP or the IANA. There are special network addresses in each class (as shown in Table 8.4) that are intended for use on private networks and are not registered to anyone. When building your own private network, you should use these addresses rather than simply choose an address at random.

Table 8.4 IP addresses for private networks

Class	Network Address
A	10.0.0.0 through 10.255.255.255
B	172.16.0.0 through 172.31.255.255
C	192.168.0.0 through 192.168.255.255

Exercise 8.2: Variable-Length Subnetting

Specify the subnet mask value you would use for each of the following network configurations:

1. A Class C network address with a 2-bit subnet identifier

2. A Class A network address with a 16-bit host identifier

3. A Class B network address with a 6-bit subnet identifier

4. A Class A network address with a 21-bit host identifier

5. A Class B network with a 9-bit host identifier

Chapter Summary

The key points covered in this chapter are as follows.

TCP/IP Protocols

- The TCP/IP protocols were developed for use on the fledgling Internet, and are designed to support systems using any computing platform or operating system.

- The TCP/IP protocol stack consists of four layers: link, internet, transport, and application.

- The ARP protocol is used by IP to resolve IP addresses into the hardware addresses needed for data-link layer protocol communications.

- The ICMP protocol performs numerous functions at the internet layer, including reporting errors and querying systems for information.

- Application layer protocols are not involved in the data transfer processes performed by the lower layers, but instead they enable specific programs and services running on TCP/IP computers to exchange messages.

IP Addressing

- IP addresses are 32 bits long, are expressed as four decimal numbers separated by periods, and consist of a network identifier and a host identifier.

- Every network interface adapter on a TCP/IP network must have its own unique IP address.

- The Internet Assigned Numbers Authority (IANA) assigns IP network addresses in three classes, and network administrators assign the host addresses to each individual system.

- The subnet mask specifies which bits of an IP address identify the network and which bits identify the host.

- Modifying the subnet mask for an address in a particular class enables you to create subnets by "borrowing" some of the host bits to create a subnet identifier.

Chapter Review

1. Match the protocols in the left column with the appropriate descriptions in the right column.

    a. DHCP   1.   Transmits e-mail messages between servers

    b. ARP   2.   Routes datagrams to their final destination

    c. IP   3.   Provides connection-oriented service at the transport layer

    d. POP3   4.   Resolves host names into IP addresses

    e. SNMP   5.   Connects two systems at the link layer

    f. ICMP   6.   Converts IP addresses into hardware addresses

    g. TCP   7.   Automatically configures TCP/IP clients

    h. DNS   8.   Provides communications between e-mail clients and servers

    i. PPP   9.   Carries network management data to a central console

    j. SMTP   10.   Carries error messages from routers to end systems

2. Which of the following fields is blank in an ARP Request message?

    a. Sender Hardware Address

    b. Sender Protocol Address

    c. Target Hardware Address

    d. Target Protocol Address

3. Which ICMP message type is the basis for the Traceroute utility?

    a. Echo Request

    b. Time To Live Exceeded In Transit

    c. Host Unreachable

    d. Fragment Reassembly Time Exceeded

4. Why are ARP Request messages transmitted as broadcasts?

5. Which ICMP message type performs a rudimentary form of flow control?

    a. Source Quench

    b. Router Solicitation

    c. Redirect

    d. Echo Request

6. Which of the following fields in an ARP Reply message contains a value supplied by the system transmitting the message?

   a. Sender Hardware Address

   b. Sender Protocol Address

   c. Target Hardware Address

   d. Target Protocol Address

7. How does ARP minimize the number of broadcasts it generates?

8. Which application layer protocol uses two port numbers at the server?

   a. SMTP

   b. HTTP

   c. DHCP

   d. FTP

9. Which IP address class provides for the largest number of hosts?

   a. Class A

   b. Class B

   c. Class C

   d. All three classes provide the same number of hosts.

10. What kind of IP address must a system have to be visible from the Internet?

   a. Subnetted

   b. Registered

   c. Class A

   d. Binary

C H A P T E R   9

TCP/IP Routing

About This Chapter

This chapter examines the routing capabilities of the Internet Protocol (IP), the principles by which Transmission Control Protocol/Internet Protocol (TCP/IP) systems route packets to their destinations, and the methods by which computers gather, compile, and share routing information.

Before You Begin

This chapter requires an understanding of the Open Systems Interconnection (OSI) reference model, as described in Chapter 1, "Networking Basics"; the functions of the IP, as covered in Chapter 6, "Network Layer Protocols"; and the basics of router hardware, as discussed in Chapter 3, "Network Connections."

Lesson 1: Routing Principles

Routing is one of the most important and most complex operations performed by TCP/IP. The protocols were designed with scalability in mind, but no one in the 1970s could have predicted the massive growth of the Internet that would occur two decades later. While packets might pass through a handful of routers on a private internetwork, Internet packets routinely pass through a dozen or more routers on the way to their destinations. Some of the routers on the Internet have to maintain information about a great many networks, and the process of compiling and maintaining this information makes routing very complicated.

After this lesson, you will be able to

- Understand the functions of a router
- Describe the information in a routing table
- Understand the process by which a TCP/IP system selects a routing table entry

Estimated lesson time: 30 minutes

Understanding Routing

A router is a system that is connected to two or more networks and that forwards packets from one network to another. Routers operate at the network layer of the OSI reference model, so they can connect networks running different data-link layer protocols and different network media. On a small network, a router's job can be quite simple. When you have two LANs connected by one router, for example, the router needs simply to receive packets from one network and forward those destined for the other network. On a large internetwork, however, routers connect many different networks together, and in many cases, networks have more than one router connected to them, as shown in Figure 9.1. This enables packets to take different paths to a given destination. If one router on the network should fail, packets can bypass it and still reach their destinations.

On a complex internetwork, an important part of a router's job is to select the most efficient route to a packet's destination. Usually, this is the path that enables a packet to reach the destination with the fewest number of hops, that is, by passing through the smallest number of routers. Routers share information about the networks to which they are attached with other routers in the immediate vicinity. As a result, a composite picture of the internetwork eventually develops, but no single router possesses the entire image. Instead, the routers work together by passing each packet from router to router, one hop at a time.

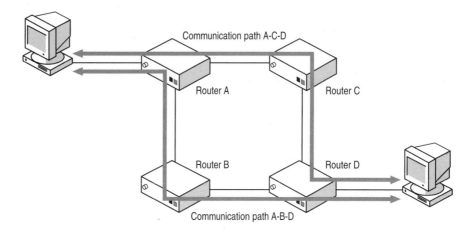

Figure 9.1 Internetworks with redundant routers provide multiple paths between two end systems.

Note See Lesson 3: Routing, in Chapter 3, "Network Connections," for more information about the packet-routing process.

Routers and Brouters

A router can be a standalone hardware device or a regular computer. Operating systems like Microsoft Windows 2000, Windows NT, and Novell NetWare have the ability to route IP traffic, so creating a router out of a computer is simply a matter of installing two network interface adapters, connecting the system to two different networks, and configuring it to route traffic between those networks. A computer with two or more network interfaces is called a *multihomed* system. Windows 95, Windows 98, and Windows Me can't route IP between two network interface adapters, but you can use these operating systems as a dial-in server that enables you to access a network from a remote location using NetBIOS Enhanced User Interface (NetBEUI) or Internetwork Packet Exchange (IPX).

Windows 98 Second Edition and Windows Me also include an Internet Connection Sharing (ICS) feature, which enables other systems on the local area network (LAN) to access the Internet through one computer's dial-up connection to an Internet Service Provider (ISP). There are also third-party software products that provide Internet connection sharing. In essence, these products are software routers that enable your computer to forward packets between the local network and the network run by your ISP.

When you use a computer as an IP router, each of the network interface adapters must have its own IP address that is appropriate for the network to which it is attached. When one of the two networks is an ISP connection, the ISP's server typically supplies the address for that interface. The other IP address is the one that you assign to your network interface adapter when you install it.

A standalone router is a hardware device that is essentially a special-purpose computer. The unit has multiple built-in network interface adapters, a processor, and memory in which it stores its routing information and temporary packet buffers. Routers are now available in a wide range of prices and with a variety of capabilities. You can purchase an inexpensive router for a few hundred dollars that enables you to share an Internet connection with a small network, or you can move up to enormously expensive models that connect the LANs of a large inter-network or provide wide area connectivity to remote offices or ISPs. Another hardware device, rarely used these days, is a combination of a bridge and a router called a brouter. A *brouter* is a device that forwards some packets based on data-link layer information and others based on network layer information, depending on the unit's configuration.

Routing Tables

The routing table is the heart of any router; without it, all that's left is mechanics. The routing table holds the information that the router uses to forward packets to the proper destinations. However, it is not only routers that have routing tables; every TCP/IP system has one, which it uses to determine where to send its packets. Routing is essentially the process of determining what data-link layer protocol address the system should use to reach a particular IP address. If a system wants to transmit a packet to a computer on the local network, for example, the routing table instructs it to address the packet to that system. This is called a *direct route*. In this case, the Destination IP Address field in the IP header and the Destination Address field in the data-link layer protocol header refer to the same computer.

If a packet's destination is on another network, the routing table contains the address of the router that the system should use to reach that destination. In this case, the Destination IP Address and Destination Address fields specify different systems because the data-link layer address has to refer to a system on the local network, and in order for the packet to reach a computer on a different network, that local system must be a router. Because the two addresses refer to different systems, this is called an *indirect route*.

The Routing Table Format

A routing table is essentially a list of networks (and possibly hosts) and addresses of routers that the system can use to reach them. The arrangement of the information in the routing table can differ depending on the operating system, but it generally appears in something like the following format, which is the routing table from a Windows 2000 system.

Network Address	Netmask	Gateway Address	Interface	Metric
0.0.0.0	0.0.0.0	192.168.2.99	192.168.2.2	1
127.0.0.0	255.0.0.0	127.0.0.1	127.0.0.1	1
192.168.2.0	255.255.255.0	192.168.2.2	192.168.2.2	1
192.168.2.2	255.255.255.255	127.0.0.1	127.0.0.1	1
192.168.2.255	255.255.255.255	192.168.2.2	192.168.2.2	1
224.0.0.0	224.0.0.0	192.168.2.2	192.168.2.2	1
255.255.255.255	255.255.255.255	192.168.2.2	192.168.2.2	1

The functions of the various columns in the table are as follows:

- **Network Address** This column specifies the address of the network or host for which routing information is provided in the other columns.

- **Netmask** This column specifies the subnet mask for the value in the Network Address column. As with any subnet mask, the system uses the Netmask to determine which parts of the Network Address value are the network identifier, the subnet identifier (if any), and the host identifier.

- **Gateway Address** This column specifies the address of the router that the system should use to send datagrams to the network or host identified in the Network Address column. The hardware address for the system identified by the Gateway Address value will become the Destination Address value in the packet's data-link layer protocol header.

- **Interface** This column specifies the address of the network interface adapter that the computer should use to transmit packets to the system identified in the Gateway Address column.

- **Metric** This column contains a value that enables the system to compare the relative efficiency of routes to the same destination.

Routing Table Entries

The sample routing table shown earlier contains the typical entries for a workstation that is not functioning as a router. The value 0.0.0.0 in the Network Address column, found in the first entry in the table, identifies the default gateway entry. The *default gateway* is the router on the LAN that the system uses when there are no routing table entries that match the Destination IP Address of an outgoing packet. Even if there are multiple routers available on the local network, a routing table can have only one default gateway entry. On a typical workstation that is not a router, the majority of packets go to the default gateway; only packets destined for systems on the local network do not use this router. The Gateway Address column in the default gateway entry contains the IP address of a router on the local network, and the Interface column contains the IP address of the network interface adapter that connects the system to the network.

Note In TCP/IP terminology, the term *gateway* is synonymous with the term *router*. However, this is not the case in other networking disciplines, in which a gateway can refer to a different device that connects networks at the application layer instead of at the network layer.

The second entry in the sample routing table contains a special IP address that is designated as the TCP/IP loopback address. IP automatically routes all packets destined for any address on the 127.0.0.0 network right back to the incoming packet queue on the same computer. The packets never reach the data-link layer or leave the computer. The entry ensures this by specifying that the system should use its own loopback address (127.0.0.1) as the "router" to the destination.

The IP address of the network interface adapter in the computer to which this routing table belongs is 192.168.2.2. Therefore, the third entry in the sample routing table contains the address of the local network on which the computer is located. The Network Address and Netmask values indicate that it is a Class C network with the address 192.168.2.0. This is the entry that the system uses for direct routes when it transmits packets to other systems on the local network. The Gateway Address and Interface columns both contain the IP address of the computer, indicating that the computer should use itself as the gateway. In other words, the computer should transmit the data-link layer frames to the same computer identified by the Destination IP Address value in the datagrams.

The fourth entry in the sample routing table contains the host address of the computer itself, and instructs the system to transmit data addressed to itself to the loopback address. IP always searches the routing table for host address entries before network address entries, so when processing any packets addressed to the computer's own address (192.168.2.2), IP would select this entry before the entry above it, which specifies the system's network address.

The fifth and seventh entries in the sample routing table contain broadcast addresses, both the generic IP broadcast address (255.255.255.255) and the local network's broadcast address (192.168.2.255). In both of these cases, packets are transmitted to the computers on the local network, so the system again uses itself as a gateway. The sixth entry in the sample routing table contains the network address for the multicast addresses that the Internet Assigned Numbers Authority (IANA) has designated for specific purposes.

The routing table on a router is considerably more complex because it contains entries for all of the networks to which it's attached, as well as entries provided manually by administrators and dynamically by routing protocols. A router also makes more use of the Interface and Metric columns. On a system with one network interface adapter, there is only one interface to use, so the Interface column is actually superfluous. Routers have at least two network interfaces, so the value in the Interface column is a crucial part of transmitting a packet correctly. In the same way, a singlehomed system has no information about routes more distant than those on the local network, so the Metric value for all of the entries is 1.

Selecting a Table Entry

When a TCP/IP system has data to transmit, the IP protocol selects a route for each packet using the procedure shown in Figure 9.2.

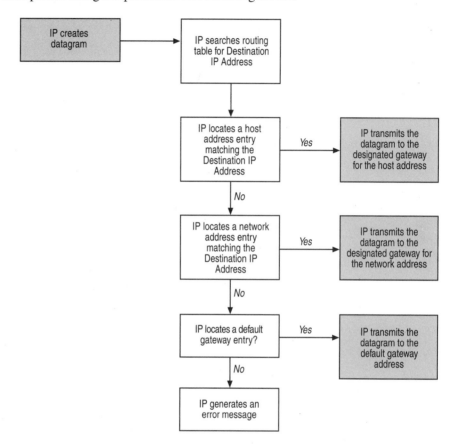

Figure 9.2 TCP/IP systems search the routing table for an address that matches the Destination IP Address value found in the header of each datagram.

The steps of the procedure are as follows:

1. After packaging the transport layer information into a datagram, IP compares the Destination IP Address for the packet with the routing table, looking for a host address with the same value. A host address entry in the table has a full IP address in the Network Address column and the value 255.255.255.255 in the Netmask column.

2. If there is no host address entry that exactly matches the Destination IP Address value, the system then scans the routing table's Network Address and Netmask columns for an entry that matches the address's network and subnet identifiers. If there is more than one entry in the routing table that contains the desired

network and subnet identifiers, IP uses the entry with the lower value in the Metric column.

3. If there are no table entries that match the network and subnet identifiers of the Destination IP Address value, the system searches for a default gateway entry which has a value of 0.0.0.0 in the Network Address and Netmask columns.

4. If there is no default gateway entry, the system generates an error message. If the system transmitting the datagram is a router, it transmits an Internet Control Message Protocol (ICMP) Destination Unreachable message back to the end system that originated the datagram. If the system transmitting the datagram is itself an end system, the error message gets passed back up to the application that generated the data.

5. When the system locates a viable routing table entry, IP prepares to transmit the datagram to the router identified in the Gateway Address column. The system consults the Address Resolution Protocol (ARP) cache or performs an ARP procedure to obtain the hardware address of the router.

6. Once it has the router's hardware address, IP passes it and the datagram down to the data-link layer protocol associated with the address specified in the Interface column. The data-link layer protocol constructs a frame using the router's hardware address in its Destination Address field and transmits it out over the designated interface.

Exercise 9.1: Routing Tables

1. What type of routing is used by a packet in which the Destination IP Address and the data-link layer Destination Address values refer to different computers?

   a. The default gateway

   b. A direct route

   c. The default route

   d. An indirect route

2. Place the following steps of the routing table search process in the proper order.

   a. Default gateway search

   b. Host address search

   c. Network address search

3. What is a TCP/IP system with interfaces to two different networks called?

   a. A gateway

   b. Multihomed

   c. A router

   d. All of the above

Lesson 2: Building Routing Tables

Now that you have learned how TCP/IP systems use the routing table to determine the destination for a packet, the next thing to consider is how the information gets into the routing table. The sample routing table in Lesson 1 contains only the default entries created automatically by a Windows-based workstation. This is known as *minimal routing*. Routers can have a great many more entries, depending on the size of the internetwork and the method used to create the table.

After this lesson, you will be able to

- Distinguish between static and dynamic routing
- Create a static route in a routing table
- Understand the operation of routing protocols

Estimated lesson time: 30 minutes

Static and Dynamic Routing

There are two techniques for updating the routing table—static routing and dynamic routing. *Static routing* is the process by which a network administrator manually creates routing table entries, using a program designed for this purpose. *Dynamic routing* is the process by which routing table entries are automatically created by specialized routing protocols that run on the router systems. Some of these protocols include the Routing Information Protocol (RIP) and the Open Shortest Path First (OSPF) protocol. Routers use these protocols to exchange messages containing routing information with other nearby routers. Each router is, in essence, sharing its routing table with other routers.

It should be obvious that, while static routing can be an effective routing solution on a small internetwork, it isn't a suitable solution for a large installation. If you have a network whose configuration never changes, or one in which there is only one possible route to each destination, running a routing protocol would be a waste of energy and bandwidth. The advantage of dynamic routing, in addition to reducing the network administrator's workload, is that it automatically compensates for changes in the network infrastructure. If a particular router goes down, for example, its failure to communicate with the other routers nearby means that it will eventually be deleted from their routing tables and packets will take different routes to their destinations. If and when that router comes back online, it resumes communications with the other routers and is again added to their tables. On an internetwork as large as the Internet, for which the IP routing system was designed, it would be all but impossible for administrators to keep up with the constant changes occurring on the network.

Creating a Static Route

Creating static routes is a matter of using a utility supplied with the TCP/IP protocol stack to create (or delete) entries in the routing table. In most cases, the utility runs from the command line. UNIX systems use a program called *route*, and the various Windows operating systems use a similar program called Route.exe. Both of these utilities use roughly the same syntax. The samples that follow are for Windows 2000's Route.exe program. Standalone routers run their own proprietary software that uses a command set created by the manufacturer.

The syntax for Route.exe is as follows:

```
ROUTE [-f] [-p] [command [destination] [MASK netmask] [gateway] [METRIC
metric] [IF interface]]
```

- **–f** This parameter deletes all of the entries from the routing table. When used with the ADD command, it deletes the entire table before adding the new entry.

- **–p** When used with the ADD command, this parameter creates a persistent route entry in the table. A persistent route is one that remains in the table permanently, even after the system is restarted. When used with the PRINT command, only persistent routes are displayed.

- *command* This variable contains a keyword that specifies the function of the command.

- *destination* This variable specifies the network or host address of the table entry being managed.

- **MASK** *netmask* The variable *netmask* specifies the subnet mask to be applied to the address specified by the *destination* variable.

- *gateway* This variable specifies the address of the router that the system should use to reach the host or network specified by the *destination* variable.

- **METRIC** *metric* The variable *metric* specifies a value that indicates the relative efficiency of the route in the table entry.

- **IF** *interface* The variable *interface* specifies the address of the network interface adapter that the system should use to reach the router specified by the *gateway* variable.

Route.exe's *command* variable takes one of four values, which are as follows:

- **PRINT** This value displays the contents of the routing table. When used with the –p parameter, it displays only the persistent routes in the routing table.
- **ADD** This value creates a new entry in the routing table.
- **DELETE** This value deletes an existing entry from the routing table.
- **CHANGE** This value modifies the parameters of an entry in the routing table.

The ROUTE PRINT command displays the current contents of the routing table. To delete an entry, you use the ROUTE DELETE command with a *destination* parameter to identify the entry you want to remove. To create a new entry in the table, you use the ROUTE ADD command with parameters that specify the values for the entry. The ROUTE CHANGE command works in the same way, except that it modifies the table entry specified by the *destination* variable. The *destination* variable is the address of the network or host for which you are providing routing information. The other parameters contain the subnet mask, gateway, interface, and metric information, as described in Lesson 1 of this chapter. For example, using the network configuration shown in Figure 9.3, to create an entry that informs the Windows 2000 system labeled Router A of the existence of Router B on the same LAN, you would execute a Route.exe command like the following at the Router A system's command line:

```
ROUTE ADD 192.168.5.0 MASK 255.255.255.0 192.168.2.7 IF 192.168.2.2
METRIC 1
```

The functions of the Route.exe parameters are as follows:

- **ADD** Indicates that the program should create a new entry in the existing routing table
- **192.168.5.0** The address of the other network to which Router B provides access
- **MASK 255.255.255.0** The subnet mask to be applied to the destination address, which in this case indicates that the address represents an unsubnetted Class C network
- **192.168.2.7** The address of the network interface adapter with which Router B is connected to the same network as Router A
- **IF 192.168.2.2** The address of the network interface adapter in Router A that provides access to the network it shares with Router B
- **METRIC 1** Indicates that the destination network is one hop away

This new routing table entry essentially tells Router A that when it has traffic to send to any computer on the network with the address 192.168.5.0, it should send the traffic to the router with the address 192.168.2.7, using the Router A network interface adapter with the address 192.168.2.2.

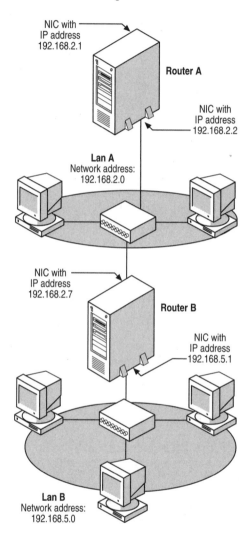

Figure 9.3 By adding a static route to the routing table in the Router A system, Router A can forward packets to Router B.

Routing And Remote Access

In addition to their normal routing capabilities, Windows 2000 Server and Windows NT Server 4.0 include an additional service called Routing And Remote Access, which expands their routing capabilities. Among other things, Routing And Remote Access provides support for the RIP version 2 and OSPF routing protocols, ICMP router discovery, demand dialing, and the Point-to-Point Tunneling Protocol (PPTP) for virtual private network (VPN) connections, all in a single service with a graphical interface (see Figure 9.4). With Routing And Remote Access, you can view the server's routing table as well as those of other systems running the service, and you can create static routes using a standard Windows dialog box rather than the command line.

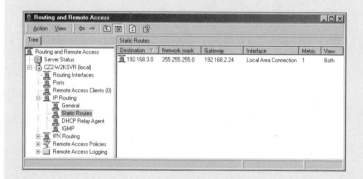

Figure 9.4 The Windows 2000 Routing And Remote Access console

Dynamic Routing

A router only has direct knowledge of the networks to which it is connected. When a network has two or more routers connected to it, dynamic routing enables each of the routers to know about the others and creates routing table entries that specify the networks to which the other routers are connected. For example, as seen in Figure 9.5, Router A can have direct knowledge of Router B from routing protocol broadcasts, because both are connected to the same network. Router B has knowledge of Router A for the same reason, but it also has knowledge of Router C, because Router C is on another network to which Router B is connected. Router A has no direct knowledge of Router C, because they are in different broadcast domains, but by using a dynamic routing protocol, Router B can share its knowledge of Router C with Router A, enabling A to add C to its routing table. By sharing the information in their routing tables using a routing protocol, routers obtain information about distant networks and can route packets more efficiently as a result.

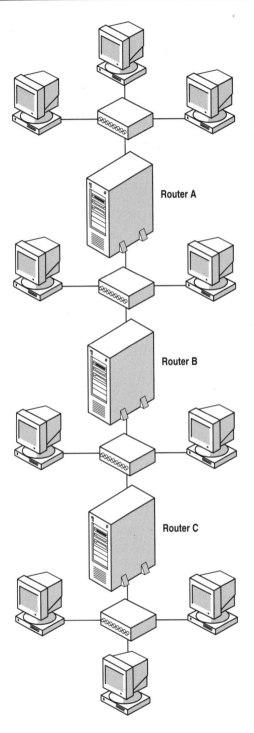

Figure 9.5 Dynamic routing enables routers to share their routing tables and disseminate their routing information throughout the network.

There are many different routing protocols in the TCP/IP suite. On a private inter-network, running a single routing protocol like RIP is usually sufficient to keep all of the routers updated with the latest network information. On the Internet, however, routers use various protocols, depending on their place in the network hierarchy. Routing protocols are generally divided into two categories: *interior gateway protocols (IGPs)* and *exterior gateway protocols (EGPs)*. On the Internet, a collection of networks that all fall within the same administrative domain is called an *autonomous system (AS)*. The routers within an autonomous system all communicate using an IGP selected by the administrators, while EGPs are used for communications between autonomous systems, as shown in Figure 9.6.

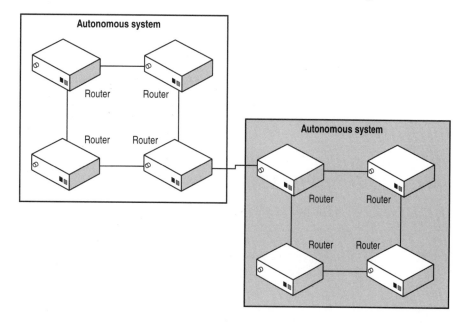

Figure 9.6 Interior gateway protocols are used for communications between routers within an autonomous system, while exterior gateway protocols are used for communications between routers in different autonomous systems.

The following sections examine some of the most common routing protocols.

RIP

The Routing Information Protocol (RIP) is the most commonly used interior gate-way protocol in the TCP/IP suite and on networks around the world. Originally designed for UNIX systems in the form of a daemon called *routed* (pronounced *route-dee*), RIP was eventually ported to many other platforms and standardized in the Request for Comments (RFC) 1058 document by the Internet Engineering Task Force (IETF). Some years later, RIP was updated to a version 2, which was published as RFC 2453.

Most RIP exchanges are based on two message types, requests and replies, both of which are packaged in User Datagram Protocol (UDP) packets addressed to the IANA-assigned well-known port number 520. When a RIP router starts, it generates a RIP request and transmits it as a broadcast over all of its network interfaces. On receiving the broadcast, every other router on either network that supports RIP generates a reply message that contains its routing table information. A reply message can contain up to 25 routes, each of which is 20 bytes long as shown in Figure 9.7. If the routing table contains more than 25 entries, the router generates multiple reply messages until it has transmitted the entire table. When it receives the replies, the router integrates the information in them into its own routing table.

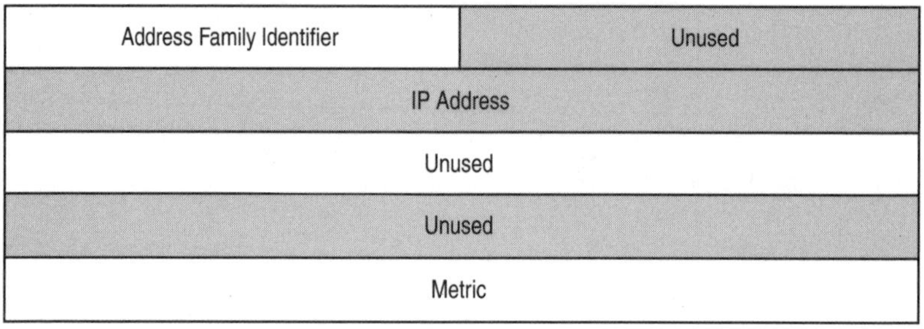

Address Family Identifier	Unused
IP Address	
Unused	
Unused	
Metric	

Figure 9.7 A RIP version 1 route

The metric value included with each table entry determines the efficiency of the route, based on the number of hops required to reach the destination. When routers receive routing table entries from other routers using RIP, they increment the value of the metric for each route to reflect the additional hop required to reach the destination. The maximum value for a metric in a RIP message is 15. Routing that uses metrics based on the number of hops to the destination is called *distance vector routing*.

After their initial exchange of RIP messages, routers transmit updates every 30 seconds to ensure that all of the other routers on the networks to which they are connected have current information. If a RIP-supplied routing table entry is not refreshed every 3 minutes, the router assumes that the entry is no longer viable, increases its metric to 16 (an illegal value), and eventually removes it from the table altogether.

The frequent retransmission of routing data is the main reason that RIP is criticized. The protocol generates a large amount of redundant broadcast traffic. In addition, the message format does not support the inclusion of a subnet mask for each route. Instead, RIP applies the subnet mask of the interface over which it receives each route, which may not always be accurate. RIP version 2 is designed to address these problems.

The primary difference between RIP 1 and RIP 2 is the format of the routes included in the reply messages. The RIP 2 message is no larger than that of RIP 1, but it utilizes the unused fields from RIP 1 to include additional information about each route. The format of a RIP version 2 route is shown in Figure 9.8.

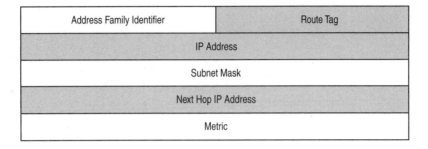

Figure 9.8 A RIP version 2 route

The functions of the RIP version 2 route fields are as follows:

- **Address Family Identifier (2 bytes)** This field contains a code that identifies the protocol for which routing information is being provided. The code for IP is 2. (RIP supports other protocols besides IP.)

- **Route Tag (2 bytes)** This field contains an autonomous system number that enables RIP to communicate with exterior gateway protocols.

- **IP Address (4 bytes)** This field specifies the address of the network or host for which routing information is being provided.

- **Subnet Mask (4 bytes)** This field contains the subnet mask that the router should apply to the IP Address value.

- **Next Hop IP Address (4 bytes)** This field specifies the address of the gateway that the router should use to forward traffic to the network or host specified in the IP Address field.

- **Metric (4 bytes)** This field contains a value that specifies the relative efficiency of the route.

The other main difference between RIP version 1 and RIP version 2 is that the latter supports the use of multicast transmissions. A multicast address is a single address that represents a group of computers. By using a multicast address that represents all of the routers on the network instead of broadcasts, the amount of extraneous traffic processed by the other computers is greatly reduced.

OSPF

Judging routes by the number of hops required to reach a destination is not always very efficient. A hop can refer to anything from a Gigabit Ethernet connection to a dial-up line, so it is entirely possible for a route with a smaller number of hops to take longer than one with more hops. There is another type of routing called *link-state routing* that measures the actual properties of each connection and stores the information in a database which is shared among the routers on the network. The most common IGP that uses this method is called the Open Shortest Path First (OSPF) protocol, as defined in RFC 2328. OSPF has many other advantages over RIP as well, including the ability to update routing tables more quickly when changes occur on the network (called *convergence*), the ability to balance the network load by splitting traffic between routes with equal metrics, and authentication of routing protocol messages.

Exercise 9.2: Static and Dynamic Routing

Specify whether each of the following terms is associated with static routing, dynamic routing, both, or neither.

1. *Routed*
2. Default gateway
3. Convergence
4. Route.exe
5. Link-state routing
6. Routing And Remote Access
7. Distance vector routing
8. ROUTE ADD
9. Autonomous system
10. Metric

Chapter Summary

The key points covered in this chapter are as follows.

Routing Principles

- Routing is one of the complicated functions of IP. Routers receive packets and forward them on toward their destinations.

- Complex internetworks can have redundant routers that provide multiple paths to the same destination. The job of a router is to forward packets using the most efficient path.

- A router can be a standalone hardware device, an operating system, or a separate software product.

- Routers store information about the network in a routing table. When forwarding a packet, the router searches the table for a route to each destination and transmits the packet to the appropriate destination.

- When a router fails to locate a route to a particular destination in the table, it sends the packet to the designated default gateway.

Building Routing Tables

- Information gets into the routing table in two ways: using either static routing, which is the manual creation and maintenance of table entries, or dynamic routing, which uses specialized routing protocols to update the table.

- The Windows 2000 Route.exe and other such programs provide direct access to the routing table, usually from the command line. Administrators can use these tools to display, add, delete, and change routing table entries.

- Dynamic routing enables routers to share the information in their tables with the other routers on the network.

- RIP is the most common routing protocol used today; it relies predominantly on broadcast transmissions to share routing table information and uses the number of hops to the destination as its metric.

- OSPF is a more advanced routing protocol that uses link-state routing, which measures the actual efficiency of a route rather than simply counting the number of hops.

Chapter Review

1. Which of the following is not a dynamic routing protocol?

    a. OSPF

    b. RIP

    c. ICMP

    d. EGP

2. What is the name for the use of metrics based on the number of hops between a source and a destination?

    a. Distance vector routing

    b. Loose source routing

    c. Link-state routing

    d. Open shortest path first routing

3. What is the primary difference between OSPF and RIP?

4. Which of the following fields is not included in a RIP version 1 route?

    a. Metric

    b. Subnet mask

    c. IP address

    d. Address Family Identifier

5. What is the primary criticism leveled at RIP?

6. In a Windows routing table, what column contains the address of the router that should be used to reach a particular network or host?

    a. Network Destination

    b. Netmask

    c. Gateway

    d. Interface

7. What is the name of the process of updating routing tables to reflect changes in the network?

   a. Divergence

   b. Link-state routing

   c. Minimal routing

   d. Convergence

8. What does a router do when it fails to find a routing table entry for a particular network or host?

9. On a Windows system, what command do you use to display the contents of the routing table?

10. The Next Hop IP Address in a RIP version 2 route ends up in which column of a Windows routing table?

    a. Network Destination

    b. Netmask

    c. Gateway

    d. Interface

11. In a Windows routing table, what is the Network Destination value for the default gateway entry?

    a. 0.0.0.0

    b. The address of the network to which the router is connected

    c. 255.255.255.255

    d. The address of the router's network interface

C H A P T E R   1 0

TCP/IP Applications

About This Chapter

In addition to its communication capabilities, the Transmission Control Protocol/Internet Protocol (TCP/IP) suite includes a number of applications that range from helpful tools to essential services. This chapter examines some of the most important of these services as well as some of the tools that network administrators use to maintain and troubleshoot TCP/IP systems.

Before You Begin

This chapter requires knowledge of the TCP/IP concepts discussed in Chapter 6, "Network Layer Protocols"; Chapter 7, "Transport Layer Protocols"; Chapter 8, "TCP/IP Fundamentals"; and Chapter 9, "TCP/IP Routing." It also requires an understanding of the structure of the networking protocol stack, as discussed in Lesson 2: The OSI Reference Model, in Chapter 1, "Networking Basics."

Lesson 1: TCP/IP Services

The core protocols that TCP/IP uses to provide communication between computers—the Internet Protocol (IP), the Transmission Control Protocol (TCP), and the User Datagram Protocol (UDP)—rely on several other services in order to perform their functions. Some of these services take the form of independent protocols, such as the Address Resolution Protocol (ARP), which runs on every TCP/IP computer and enables IP to discover the hardware address of a computer using a particular IP address. Other services, such as the Dynamic Host Configuration Protocol (DHCP) and the Domain Name System (DNS), are both protocols and applications that run on their own servers.

After this lesson, you will be able to

- Explain how DHCP assigns TCP/IP configuration settings to workstations
- Understand the history of name resolution on the Internet
- Understand the functions of DNS and the Windows Internet Name Service (WINS)

Estimated lesson time: 60 minutes

DHCP

In Chapter 6, "Network Layer Protocols," and Chapter 8, "TCP/IP Fundamentals," you learned about the advantages of TCP/IP's self-contained addressing system and about the nature of IP addresses themselves. While there are many advantages of IP addressing, there are several significant problems with it, including that every computer on the network must have a unique IP address. This requirement complicates the process of configuring the TCP/IP client. The administrators of a TCP/IP network must be sure that every computer is configured properly, which means keeping track of the IP address assignments so that no duplication occurs. On a small network, configuring the individual TCP/IP workstations and keeping track of their IP addresses is relatively painless, but on a large corporate internetwork, it can be a monumental task.

DHCP Origins

Over the years, the developers of the TCP/IP protocols have worked out several solutions that address the problem of configuring the TCP/IP settings for large fleets of workstations. The first of these was the Reverse Address Resolution Protocol (RARP), which was designed for diskless workstations that had no means of permanently storing their TCP/IP settings. RARP is essentially the opposite of the Address Resolution Protocol (ARP). While ARP broadcasts an IP address in an effort to discover its equivalent hardware address, RARP broadcasts the hardware address; as shown in Figure 10.1. A RARP server then responds by transmitting the IP address assigned to that client computer. While RARP was suitable for use with diskless workstations on early TCP/IP networks, it isn't sufficient for today's needs, because it supplies the computer with an IP address only. It provides none of the other settings needed by a typical workstation today, such as a subnet mask and a default gateway.

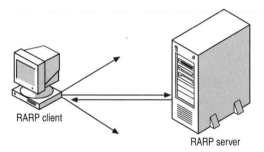

Figure 10.1 A workstation that uses RARP receives an IP address from a RARP server in response to a broadcast message containing the client's hardware address.

Note For more information about ARP, including its message format, which is the same as that used by RARP, see Lesson 1: TCP/IP Protocols, in Chapter 8, "TCP/IP Fundamentals."

The next attempt at an automatic TCP/IP configuration was called the Bootstrap Protocol (BOOTP). BOOTP does more than RARP, which is why it is still used today, while RARP is not. BOOTP enables a TCP/IP workstation to retrieve settings for all of the configuration parameters it needs to run, including an IP address, subnet mask, default gateway, and DNS server addresses. A workstation can also download an executable boot file from a BOOTP server, using the Trivial File Transfer Protocol (TFTP), which makes it clear that BOOTP, like RARP, was designed for diskless workstations. The drawback of BOOTP is that while it is capable of performing all of the TCP/IP client communication tasks required by today's computers, an administrator must still specify the settings for each workstation on the BOOTP server. There is no mechanism for automatically assigning a unique IP address to each computer, nor is there any means of preventing two computers from receiving the same IP address due to administrator error.

The Dynamic Host Configuration Protocol (DHCP) was developed by Microsoft for the express purpose of addressing the shortcomings in RARP and BOOTP. DHCP is based on BOOTP to a great extent, but instead of simply feeding predetermined configuration parameters to TCP/IP clients, DHCP can dynamically allocate IP addresses from a pool and reclaim them when they are no longer in use. This prevents workstations from ever being assigned duplicate IP addresses and enables administrators to move computers around between subnets without having to manually reconfigure them. In addition, DHCP can deliver a wide range of configuration parameters to TCP/IP clients, including platform-specific parameters added by third-party developers.

DHCP Architecture

DHCP consists of three components: a client, a server, and the protocol that they use to communicate with each other. Most TCP/IP implementations these days have DHCP integrated into the networking client, even if the operating system doesn't specifically refer to it as such. On a Microsoft Windows 98 system, for example, when you select the Obtain An IP Address Automatically radio button in the TCP/IP Properties dialog box, you are actually activating the DHCP client. The DHCP server is an application that runs on a computer and exists to service requests from DHCP clients. The Windows 2000 Server and Windows NT Server operating systems both include the DHCP server application, but there are many other implementations available for other platforms as well. DHCP is widely used on UNIX, Novell NetWare, and Microsoft networks. Any DHCP client can retrieve configuration settings from a DHCP server running on any platform. Despite having been developed largely by Microsoft, DHCP is based on public BOOTP standards, and is itself published as an open TCP/IP standard.

Note The basic components of DHCP are defined in the Request For Comments (RFC) 2131 document, published by the Internet Engineering Task Force (IETF). RFC 2132 defines additional DHCP options and vendor extensions that can supply other types of information to client computers.

The core function of DHCP is to assign IP addresses. This is the most complicated part of the service, because an IP address must be unique for each client computer. The DHCP standard defines three types of IP address allocation, which are as follows:

- **Manual allocation** An administrator assigns a specific IP address to a computer in the DHCP server and the server provides that address to the computer when it is requested.

- **Automatic allocation** The DHCP server supplies clients with IP addresses taken from a common pool of addresses, and the clients retain the assigned addresses permanently.

- **Dynamic allocation** The DHCP server supplies IP addresses to clients from a pool on a leased basis. The client must periodically renew the lease or the address returns to the pool for reallocation.

Manual allocation is the functional equivalent of BOOTP address assignment. This option saves the least amount of administrative labor, but it is necessary for systems that require permanently assigned IP addresses, such as Internet servers that have DNS names associated with specific addresses. Administrators could conceivably configure the TCP/IP clients of these computers directly, but using the DHCP server for the assignment prevents IP addresses from being accidentally duplicated.

Automatic allocation is a fitting solution for networks on which administrators rarely move workstations around between subnets. Assigning IP addresses from a pool (called a *scope*) eliminates the need to furnish a specific address for each computer and prevents address duplication. Permanently assigning those addresses minimizes the network traffic generated by DHCP client/server communications.

Once the server is configured, dynamic allocation completely automates the TCP/IP client configuration process, and enables administrators to add, remove, and relocate computers as needed. When a computer boots, the server leases an address to the computer for a given period of time, renews the lease if the computer remains active, reclaims the address when it is no longer in use, and returns the address to the pool.

DHCP Message Format

Communications between DHCP clients and servers use a single message format, which is illustrated in Figure 10.2. All DHCP messages are carried within UDP datagrams, using the IANA-established well-known port numbers 67 at the server and 68 at the client.

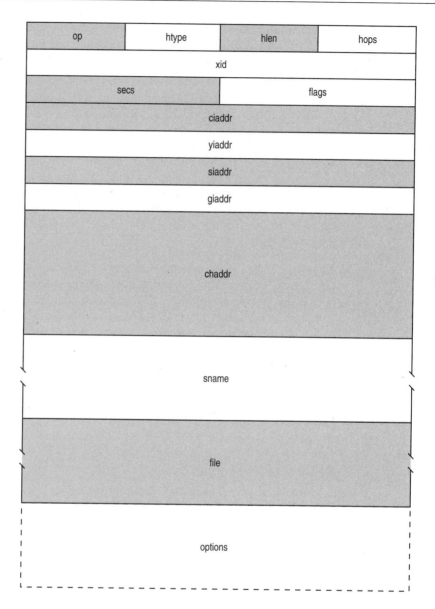

Figure 10.2 The DHCP message format

The functions of the fields in the DHCP message are as follows:

- **op (1 byte)** Specifies whether the message has originated at a client or a server
- **htype (1 byte)** Specifies the type of hardware address in the chaddr field
- **hlen (1 byte)** Specifies the length of the hardware address in the chaddr field, in bytes

- **hops (1 byte)** Specifies the number of routers in the path between the client and the server

- **xid (4 bytes)** Contains a transaction ID used to associate requests and replies

- **secs (2 bytes)** Specifies the elapsed time (in seconds) since the beginning of an address allocation or lease renewal process

- **flags (2 bytes)** Indicates whether or not DHCP servers and relay agents should use broadcast transmissions to communicate with a client instead of unicast transmissions

- **ciaddr (4 bytes)** Contains the client computer's IP address when it is in the bound, renewal, or rebinding state

- **yiaddr (4 bytes)** Contains the IP address being offered to a client by a server

- **siaddr (4 bytes)** Specifies the IP address of the next server in a bootstrap sequence; used only when the DHCP server supplies an executable boot file to a diskless workstation

- **giaddr (4 bytes)** Contains the IP address of a DHCP relay agent located on a different network, when necessary

- **chaddr (16 bytes)** Contains the hardware address of the client system, using the type and length specified in the htype and hlen fields

- **sname (64 bytes)** Contains either the host name of the DHCP server or over-flow data from the options field

- **file (128 bytes)** Contains the name and path to an executable boot file for diskless workstations

- **options (variable)** Contains a series of DHCP options, which specify the configuration parameters for the client computer

The options field is where the DHCP message carries all of the TCP/IP parameters assigned to a client, except for the IP address. Each option consists of three subfields, as shown in Figure 10.3.

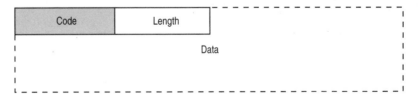

Figure 10.3 The DHCP option format

The functions of the option subfields are as follows:

- **Code (1 byte)** Specifies the function of the option

- **Length (1 byte)** Specifies the length of the data field

- **Data (variable)** Contains information specific to the option type

Although it sounds like a contradiction in terms, there is one DHCP option which is, in fact, required. This is the DHCP Message Type option, which contains a code that specifies the function of each message. There are eight possible values for this option, as follows:

- **1—DHCPDISCOVER** Used by clients to request configuration parameters from a DHCP server
- **2—DHCPOFFER** Used by servers to offer IP addresses to requesting clients
- **3—DHCPREQUEST** Used by clients to accept or renew an IP address assignment
- **4—DHCPDECLINE** Used by clients to reject an offered IP address
- **5—DHCPACK** Used by servers to acknowledge a client's acceptance of an offered IP address
- **6—DHCPNAK** Used by servers to reject a client's acceptance of an offered IP address
- **7—DHCPRELEASE** Used by clients to terminate an IP address lease
- **8—DHCPINFORM** Used by clients to obtain additional TCP/IP configuration parameters from a server

DHCP Communications

DHCP clients initiate communication with servers when they boot for the first time. This initial exchange of messages is illustrated in Figure 10.4. The client generates a series of DHCPDISCOVER messages, which it transmits as broadcasts. At this point, the client has no IP address, and is said to be in the *init* state. Like all broadcasts, these transmissions are limited to the client's local network, but administrators can install a DHCP Relay Agent service on a computer on the local area network (LAN), which relays the messages to DHCP servers on other networks. This enables a single DHCP server to service clients on multiple LANs.

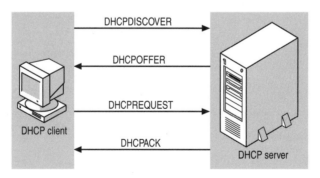

Figure 10.4 DHCP client/server communications

When a DHCP server receives a DHCPDISCOVER message from a client, it generates a DHCPOFFER message containing an IP address and whatever other optional parameters the server is configured to supply. In most cases, the server transmits this as a unicast message directly to the client. Because the client broadcasted its DHCPDISCOVER messages, it may receive DHCPOFFER responses from multiple servers. After a specified period of time, the client stops its broadcasting and accepts one of the offered IP addresses. To signal its acceptance, the client generates a DHCPREQUEST message containing the address of the server whose offer it is accepting along with the offered IP address. Because the client has not yet configured itself with the offered parameters, it transmits the DHCPREQUEST message as a broadcast. This broadcast notifies the server that the client is accepting the offered address and also notifies the other servers on the network that the client is rejecting their offers.

Upon receipt of the DHCPREQUEST message, the server commits the offered IP address and other settings to its database, using a combination of the client's hardware address and the offered IP address as a unique identifier for the assignment. This is known as the *lease identification cookie*. To conclude its part of the transaction, the server sends a DHCPACK message to the client, acknowledging the completion of the process. If the server cannot complete the assignment (because it has already assigned the offered IP address to another system, for example), it transmits a DHCPNAK message to the client, and the whole process begins again.

As a final test, the client performs an ARP test, to ensure that no other system on the network is using the assigned IP address. After broadcasting an ARP message containing its new IP address, the client hopes not to receive any response. If no response is received, the DHCP transaction is completed and the client enters what is known as the *bound* state. If another system does respond, the client can't use the IP address and transmits a DHCPDECLINE message to the server, nullifying the transaction. The client can then reissue a series of DHCPDISCOVER messages, restarting the whole process.

DHCP Leasing

The process by which a DHCP server assigns configuration parameters to a client is the same whether the server uses manual, automatic, or dynamic allocation. With manual and automatic allocation, this one process is the end of the DHCP client/server communications. The client retains the settings assigned to it by the server until someone explicitly changes them or forces a reassignment. However, when the server dynamically allocates settings, the client leases its IP address for a certain period of time (configured at the server) and must renew the lease in order to continue using it.

The length of an IP address lease is typically measured in days, and is generally based on whether computers are frequently moved around the network or whether IP addresses are in short supply. Shorter leases generate more network traffic but enable servers to reclaim unused addresses faster. For a relatively stable network, longer leases reduce the amount of traffic that DHCP generates.

The lease renewal process (as illustrated in Figure 10.5) begins when a bound client reaches what is known as the *renewal time value,* or *T1 value,* of its lease. By default, the renewal time value is 50 percent of the lease period. When a client reaches this point, it enters the *renewing* state and begins generating DHCPREQUEST messages. The client transmits the messages to the server that holds the lease as unicasts, unlike the broadcast DHCPREQUEST messages the client generates while in the *init* state. If the server is available to receive the message, it responds with either a DHCPACK message, which renews the lease and restarts the lease time clock, or a DHCPNAK message, which terminates the lease and forces the client to begin the address assignment process again from the beginning.

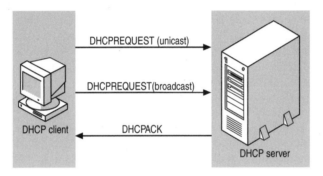

Figure 10.5 The DHCP lease renewal process

If the server does not respond to the DHCPREQUEST unicast message, the client continues to send them until it reaches the *rebinding time value* or *T2 value*, which defaults to 87.5 percent of the lease period. At this point, the client enters the *rebinding* state and begins transmitting DHCPREQUEST messages as broadcasts, soliciting an address assignment from any DHCP server on the network. Again, a server can respond with either a DHCPACK or DHCPNAK message. If the lease time expires with no response from any DHCP server, the client's IP address is released and all of its TCP/IP communication ceases, except for the transmission of DHCPDISCOVER broadcasts.

Releasing an IP Address

It is also possible for a client to terminate an IP address lease at any time, by transmitting a DHCPRELEASE message containing the lease identification cookie to the server. On a Microsoft Windows system, for example, you can do this manually, using the Ipconfig.exe utility in Windows 2000 and Windows NT or the Winipcfg.exe utility in Windows Me, Windows 98, or Windows 95. For more information about these utilities, see Lesson 2: TCP/IP Utilities, later in this chapter.

Exercise 10.1: DHCP Message Types

1. Place the following DHCP message types in the order in which a successful IP address assignment procedure uses them.

   a. DHCPACK

   b. DHCPOFFER

   c. DHCPREQUEST

   d. DHCPDISCOVER

2. Place the following DHCP message types in the proper order for an unsuccessful attempt to renew an IP address lease.

   a. DHCPDISCOVER

   b. DHCPREQUEST (broadcast)

   c. DHCPREQUEST (unicast)

   d. DHCPNAK

Host Files

IP addresses may be an excellent way for computers to recognize and communicate with each other, but they are not exactly user-friendly. Imagine having to remember the IP address for every site that you visit while surfing the Web, or for every computer on the local network whose drives or printers you want to access. To make TCP/IP more user-friendly, the TCP/IP developers created host names, which enable administrators to assign friendly names to the computers on a network and resolve them into IP addresses as needed.

A host name is simply a name used to represent a computer. The names of the hosts on a network are stored in a text file called HOSTS on each computer. The HOSTS file also contains the IP address of the computer associated with each of those names. In order to communicate with another computer on the network by specifying its host name, your computer must first resolve that name into its IP address by looking it up in the HOSTS file. *Name resolution* is the process of converting a name into its equivalent IP address. The name resolution process is essential, because an IP datagram must use an IP address, and not a name, to identify its destination.

Every computer must have its own HOSTS file, which is why this name resolution method is not widely used today. In the early days of the Internet, when the entire network consisted of a few dozen computers, administrators regularly downloaded updated HOSTS files containing entries for all of the computers on the Internet. Today a HOSTS file for the entire Internet would be enormous, even if you could compile one, and requiring every computer to download it would bring the entire network to its knees. However, if there are computers on the network that you visit frequently, you can put them in a HOSTS file on your computer in order to bypass the more elaborate name resolution methods used today.

DNS

When the Internet outgrew the HOSTS file, it also outgrew the flat name space the file used. There were too many systems to assign them each a unique single name. To address these problems, the TCP/IP developers created the Domain Name System (DNS), which enables administrators to assign hierarchical names to the computers on a network and resolve them into IP addresses as needed. The DNS is defined in two primary IETF documents: RFC 1034, "Domain Names: Concepts and Facilities," and RFC 1035, "Domain Names: Implementation and Specification." There are many additional RFCs that provide updates and augmentations to the DNS.

Whenever you use a DNS name to refer to a TCP/IP computer, such as when you type *www.microsoft.com* into your Web browser, your workstation performs a name resolution process before it sends any traffic to the destination server. If you look quickly, you might see your browser display a status message for a fraction of a second, indicating that it is resolving the name. To perform a name resolution, the client computer transmits a message containing the name to a DNS server, the address of which is specified as part of its TCP/IP client configuration. The DNS client implementation found in every computer running TCP/IP is called a *resolver*. The DNS server determines the IP address associated with the name requested by the resolver and returns it to the client. Then, the client can send its original message to the desired destination using its IP address.

Understanding how your local DNS server obtains the IP addresses for the names sent to it by your computer can be complicated, however, and requires you to understand how DNS names are structured and assigned. The primary element of the DNS is its hierarchical name space, which identifies computers using names composed of three or more words, separated by periods. The DNS name of a computer consists of a *host name* and a *domain name*. The domain name, which consists of two or more words, identifies a network or organization, and the host name identifies a specific computer on that network or in that organization. In the name *www.microsoft.com*, for example, *www* is the name of a particular computer in the domain *microsoft.com*.

Domain names on the Internet must be registered with an organization that is responsible for making sure that there is no duplication of names. DNS names are read from right to left, with the word furthest to the right representing the top of the domain hierarchy. Therefore, the *com* in *www.microsoft.com* is known as a *top-level domain*. The original DNS standards defined eight top-level domains: com, edu, gov, mil, net, org, int, and arpa. All of these top-level domains are intended to be used for computers belonging to different types of organizations, with *edu* being for educational institutions, *mil* for the military, and so on. The term *arpa* is a special case used for reverse—that is, address-to-name—mapping.

Today, in addition to these eight, there are numerous other top-level domains that represent various countries around the world. These international top-level domain names have only two letters, and are often abbreviations for the country name, in its own language. For example, *de* is the top-level domain for Germany (Deutschland) and *fr* for France. There has also been talk about the introduction of other, special-purpose top-level domains for years, but these have yet to appear in popular use.

By contacting a registrar who is responsible for one or more top-level domains, any individual or organization can register a second-level domain within that top-level domain, for a nominal fee. Top-level domains like *gov* and *mil* are restricted to the government and military organizations they describe, but the registrars of the *com*, *org*, and *net* top-level domains allow anyone to register names in those domains, as do many of the international domain registrars.

Once an individual or organization has registered a domain name, the owner is free to create as many hosts or subdomains in that domain as they wish. The word furthest to the left in a full DNS name is the host, and any names to the right of the host identify the domain. Thus, as shown in Figure 10.6, the owner of the microsoft.com domain can create any number of subdomains, such as *msn.microsoft.com*, and any number of hosts in each of those subdomains, such as *www.msn.microsoft.com*. This two-tiered administrative arrangement is the same as that for IP addresses. An administrative body is responsible for registering the network addresses assigned to various organizations, and the administrators of the organizations themselves then create the host address assignments.

Domain Name Registration and Big Business

With the increasing commercialization of the Internet, domain name registration has become a lucrative business, and a point of legal contention as well. In some cases, popular domain names are being sold for millions of dollars, either by failed companies that no longer need them or by forward-thinking entrepreneurs who registered them before the Internet boom. In other cases, large corporations have filed legal suits to have certain domain names stripped from their legal registrants, simply because they have the same name as the corporation. Creative domain registration is also being used for unscrupulous business practices, as well. For example, the owners of a corporation might register domains using the names of its competitors, so that potential customers are directed to the corporation's Web site when they look for a Web site using a competitor's name. At this time, the courts are still mulling over the legal issues pertaining to Internet rights.

Note Although they use the same basic administrative model, IP address registrations and domain name registrations are completely separate. You can have computers on many different IP networks using the same domain name, or you can have multiple domain names used by computers on the same network.

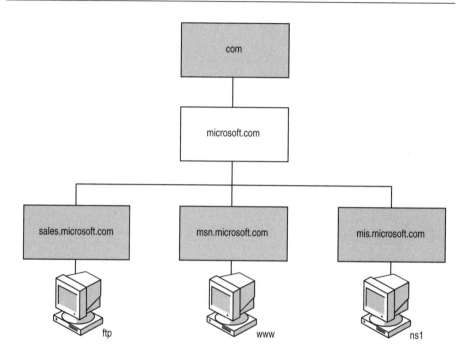

Figure 10.6 A DNS name can include several domain levels, or as few as two, plus a host name.

Splitting the administrative chores between a central body and the individual registrant is part of what makes it possible to keep the DNS name space up to date. There are thousands of domains on the Internet today, and millions of hosts in those domains. To try and create a central registry for all of this information would require enormous resources of manpower and technology. Instead, the responsibility for maintaining the DNS name space is distributed among servers and administrators all over the Internet. It's remarkable that a system designed when the Internet wasn't a hundredth of its current size still functions well, even though it has grown far beyond the wildest dreams of its conceivers.

DNS Communications

The relationship of the various domain levels becomes apparent when you examine the process by which DNS servers resolve names into IP addresses. Because of the distributed nature of the DNS name space, there is no single server that contains a complete listing of all the domains on the Internet and all of the hosts on those domains. Therefore, when a client system sends a name to its DNS server for resolution, the server must have some means of locating the information it needs. The server does this by parsing the DNS name it receives from the client and working with one domain level at a time.

Every DNS server has the IP addresses of several *root-name servers*. These servers are responsible for maintaining a list of the top-level domains and the IP addresses of the DNS servers that are authoritative for those domains. An *authoritative server* is the computer that is the final source of information about a particular domain. Usually this is a server run by the administrators of the domain, on which they make changes when they modify their network configuration. The root-name servers are, in fact, the authoritative servers for most of the original eight top-level domains, but they also contain the addresses of the authoritative servers for the many international domains. These servers handle only a small part of the name resolution process, but they still must process hundreds of requests per second.

A DNS server trying to resolve a name sends a message to one of the root-name servers, requesting the address of the authoritative server for the top-level domain in the name (see Figure 10.7). Thus, a server trying to resolve the name *www.microsoft.com* sends a request to a root-name server, asking for the address of the authoritative server for the *com* domain. Since that server is authoritative for the *com* domain, it skips a step and supplies the address for the *microsoft.com* domain's authoritative server. Otherwise, the root-name server would respond with the address of the top-level domain server, and the original server would send a new request to the top-level domain server for the address of the second-level domain's authoritative server. Once the original server knows the address of the *microsoft.com* domain's authoritative server, it generates a request for the IP address of the host *www*. The *microsoft.com* server responds with the requested IP address, and the original server passes that address to the client.

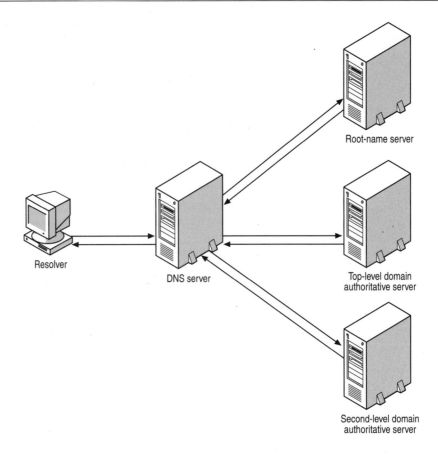

Figure 10.7 The DNS name resolution process

In this way, any DNS server on the Internet can locate the IP address for a computer in any domain. However, in many cases, the servers can bypass part of this process, because they can usually cache information about the names they resolve. For a popular DNS name like *www.microsoft.com*, for example, it is very possible that the client's DNS server already has the required IP address in its cache, and can furnish it directly to the client without communicating with other servers.

Reverse Name Resolution

DNS is designed to resolve names into IP addresses, but there are cases in which TCP/IP computers require the opposite service, the conversion of an IP address into a name. Because the DNS name space is distributed based on the domain names, however, this task is almost impossible when using the system's standard capabilities. Finding a specific IP address in the name space would require a search of all of the authoritative DNS servers on the Internet, which obviously is not practical.

To address this problem, the DNS name space includes a special domain called *in-addr.arpa*, which reverses the name/address relationship by containing domains that are named using IP addresses. In other words, *in-addr* is a second-level domain beneath *arpa*, and beneath *in-addr* there are 256 possible third-level domains, which are named using the numbers 0 to 255. These third-level domains represent the first byte of an IP address. Each of the third-level domains has 256 possible fourth level domains, representing the second byte of an IP address. The fifth- and sixth-level domains work in the same way, enabling you to search in the DNS name space for any possible IP address. For example, the IP address 192.168.2.6 would be found in the domain name *6.2.168.192.in-addr.arpa*. This domain would contain a resource record that specifies the DNS name of the computer using this IP address. The bytes of the IP address are reversed in the domain name because in an IP address, the most significant identifier is first, while in a domain name, the top-level domain comes last.

DNS Resource Records

Despite the complexity of the distributed name space, DNS servers themselves are actually relatively simple. DNS servers store their information in units called *resource records*, which administrators of authoritative servers must create manually, in most cases. In response to a request from a resolver or another server, the DNS server transmits a message containing the resource record for the requested name. There are many different types of resource records, the most important of which are as follows:

- **Start of Authority (SOA)** Indicates that the name server is the authoritative source for the domain

- **Name Server (NS)** Identifies the DNS servers in the domain

- **Address (A)** Contains a name-to-address mapping for a computer in the domain

- **Canonical Name (CNAME)** Used to create an alternative (or alias) name for a computer already represented by an Address record

- **Pointer (PTR)** Contains an address-to-name mapping in *in-addr.arpa* for a computer in the domain

- **Mail Exchange (MX)** Identifies a computer that is responsible for processing e-mail traffic addressed to the domain

---

Note The need to manually create resource records is one of the long-standing shortcomings of DNS. Now that Windows 2000 relies heavily on DNS for its Active Directory directory service, the IETF has published additional documents that define new server features, such as RFC 2136, "Dynamic Updates in the Domain Name System," which specifies a method for automatically creating and updating DNS resource records.

WINS

Windows Internet Naming Service (WINS) is similar to DNS, in that it is designed to resolve computer names into IP addresses. However, WINS is designed specifically for Windows networks, and resolves the NetBIOS names used by Windows systems, rather than the DNS names used on the Internet. The NetBIOS name space that Windows uses to provide friendly names for computers is not hierarchical like that of the DNS, but the problem of using TCP/IP with these names is the same. A computer must resolve the name of the computer it wants to communicate with into an IP address before it can send IP datagrams to it.

Note The WINS service is included with the Windows NT Server and Windows 2000 Server operating systems. However, the Active Directory technology in Windows 2000 uses DNS instead of NetBIOS names, so the WINS server is included only to service downlevel clients, that is, workstations running earlier versions of Windows.

Windows has several ways of resolving NetBIOS names into IP addresses, so WINS is not an essential part of a Windows network. Without WINS, a computer resolves NetBIOS names either by looking them up in a text file similar to HOSTS, called LMHOSTS, or by transmitting broadcast messages containing the desired name on the LAN, and then waiting for the computer using that name to respond with its IP address. WINS is designed to increase the efficiency of the network by reducing the amount of broadcast traffic. Instead of broadcasting a request, a WINS client transmits a request to its designated WINS server as a unicast message, and the server responds with the IP address associated with the requested name.

Note For more information about NetBIOS names, see Lesson 3: NetBEUI, in Chapter 6, "Network Layer Protocols."

Unlike DNS, which requires administrators to create resource records manually, WINS automatically registers clients as they boot, then adds their names and IP addresses to its database. WINS is also designed for use on large internetworks. You can run multiple WINS servers to provide fault tolerance and service thousands of clients. WINS servers can also communicate with each other to replicate their database information, enabling you to maintain a composite picture of the entire network on all of your servers.

Lesson 2: TCP/IP Utilities

Virtually every operating system with networking capabilities includes support for the TCP/IP protocols, and in most cases the TCP/IP stack includes an assortment of utilities that enable you to gather information about the various protocols and about the network. Traditionally, these utilities run from the command line, although graphical versions are sometimes supplied. In many cases, a program uses the same syntax, even on different operating systems. This lesson examines some of the most common TCP/IP utilities and the purposes for which they are used.

After this lesson, you will be able to

- Understand the functions of the primary TCP/IP utilities

Estimated lesson time: 20 minutes

Ping

Ping is the most basic of the TCP/IP utilities. Virtually every TCP/IP implementation includes a version of Ping; on UNIX systems, the program is called *ping*, on Microsoft Windows, it is Ping.exe. NetWare even includes a server-based version called Ping.nlm. Ping is a program that can tell you if the TCP/IP stack of another system on the network is functioning normally. The Ping program generates a series of Echo Request messages using the Internet Control Message Protocol (ICMP) and transmits them to the computer whose name or IP address you specify on the command line. The basic syntax of the Ping program is as follows:

```
ping target
```

The *target* variable contains the IP address or name of a computer on the network. You can use either DNS names or NetBIOS names in Ping commands. The program resolves the name into an IP address before sending the Echo Request messages, and it then displays the address in its readout. Most Ping implementations also have command-line switches that enable you to modify the operational parameters of the program, such as the number of Echo Request messages it generates and the amount of data in each message.

All TCP/IP computers must respond to any Echo Request messages they receive by generating Echo Reply messages and transmitting them back to the sender.

When the pinging computer receives the Echo Reply messages, it produces a display like the following:

```
Pinging cz1 [192.168.2.10] with 32 bytes of data:

Reply from 192.168.2.10: bytes=32 time<10ms TTL=128
Reply from 192.168.2.10: bytes=32 time<10ms TTL=128
Reply from 192.168.2.10: bytes=32 time<10ms TTL=128
Reply from 192.168.2.10: bytes=32 time<10ms TTL=128

Ping statistics for 192.168.2.10:
    Packets: Sent = 4, Received = 4, Lost = 0 (0% loss),
Approximate round trip times in milli-seconds:
    Minimum = 0ms, Maximum =  0ms, Average =  0ms
```

In the case of this Ping implementation (from Windows 2000), the display shows the IP address of the computer receiving the Echo Requests, the number of bytes of data included with each request, the elapsed time between the transmission of each request and the receipt of each reply, and the value of the Time To Live (TTL) field in the IP header. In this particular example, the target computer was on the same LAN, so the time measurement is very short—less than 10 milliseconds. When pinging a computer on the Internet, the interval is likely to be longer. A successful use of Ping like this one indicates that the target computer's networking hardware is functioning properly, as are the protocols, at least as high as the network layer of the OSI model. If the Ping test fails, one or both of the computers is experiencing a problem with its networking hardware or software.

Traceroute

Traceroute is a variant of the Ping program that displays the path that packets take to their destination. Because of the nature of IP routing, paths through an internetwork can change from minute to minute, and Traceroute displays a list of the routers that are currently forwarding packets to a particular destination. The program is called *traceroute* on UNIX systems, Tracert.exe by Windows, and Iptrace.nlm by NetWare.

Traceroute uses ICMP Echo Request and Echo Reply messages just like Ping, but it modifies the messages by changing the value of the TTL field in the IP header. The TTL field is designed to prevent packets from getting caught in router loops that keep them circulating endlessly around the network. The computer generating the packet normally sets a relatively high value for the TTL field; on Windows systems, the default value is 128. Each router that processes the packet reduces the TTL value by one. If the value reaches zero, the last router discards the packet and transmits an ICMP error message back to the original sender.

When you start the Traceroute program with the name or IP address of a target computer, the program generates its first set of Echo Request messages with TTL values of one. When the messages arrive at the first router on their path, the router decrements their TTL values to zero, discards the packets, and reports the errors to the sender. The error messages contain the router's address, which the Traceroute program displays as the first hop in the path to the destination. Traceroute's second set of Echo Request messages use a TTL value of two, causing the second router on the path to discard the packets and generate error messages. The third set of Echo Request messages have a TTL value of three, and so on. Each set of packets travels one hop farther than the previous set before causing a router to return error messages to the source. The list of routers displayed by Traceroute as the path to the destination is the result of these error messages. The following is an example of a Traceroute display:

```
Tracing route to www.abccorp.co.uk [173.146.1.1]
over a maximum of 30 hops:
  1    <10 ms     1 ms    <10 ms   192.168.2.99
  2    105 ms    92 ms     98 ms   qrvl-67terminal01.epoch.net [199.24.67.3]
  3    101 ms   110 ms     98 ms   qrvl.epoch.net [199.24.67.1]
  4    123 ms   109 ms    118 ms   svcr03-7b.epoch.net [199.24.103.125]
  5    123 ms   112 ms    114 ms   clsm02-2.epoch.net [199.24.88.26]
  6    136 ms   130 ms    133 ms   sl-gw19-pen-6-1-0-T3.sprintlink.net [144.228.116.5]
  7    143 ms   126 ms    138 ms   sl-bb10-pen-4-3.sprintlink.net [144.232.5.117]
  8    146 ms   129 ms    133 ms   sl-bb20-pen-12-0.sprintlink.net [144.232.5.1]
  9    131 ms   128 ms    139 ms   sl-bb20-nyc-13-0.sprintlink.net [144.232.18.38]
 10    130 ms   134 ms    134 ms   sl-gw9-nyc-8-0.sprintlink.net [144.232.7.94]
 11    147 ms   149 ms    152 ms   sl-demon-1-0.sprintlink.net [144.232.173.10]
 12    154 ms   146 ms    145 ms   ny2-backbone-1-ge021.router.demon.net [195.173.173.121]
 13    230 ms   225 ms    226 ms   tele-backbone-1-ge023.router.demon.net [195.173.173.12]
 14    233 ms   220 ms    226 ms   tele-core-3-fxp1.router.demon.net [194.159.252.56]
 15    223 ms   224 ms    224 ms   tele-access-1-14.router.demon.net [194.159.254.245]
 16    236 ms   221 ms    226 ms   tele-service-2-165.router.demon.net [194.159.36.149]
 17    220 ms   224 ms    210 ms   www.abccorp.co.uk [173.146.1.1]
Trace complete.
```

In this example, Traceroute is displaying the path between a computer in Pennsylvania and one in the United Kingdom. Each of the hops contains the elapsed times between the transmission and reception of three sets of Echo Request and Echo Reply packets. In this trace, you can clearly see the point at which the packets begin traveling across the Atlantic Ocean. At hop 13, the elapsed times increase from approximately 150 to 230 milliseconds (ms) and stay in that area for the subsequent hops. This additional delay of only 80 ms is the time it takes the packets to travel the thousands of miles across the ocean.

Traceroute can be a handy tool for isolating the location of a network communications problem. Ping simply tells you whether or not a problem exists; it can't tell you where. A failure to contact a remote computer could be due to a problem in your workstation, in the remote computer, or in any of the routers in between. Traceroute can tell you how far your packets are going before they run into the problem.

Ifconfig and Ipconfig.exe

UNIX systems have a program called *ifconfig* (the name is derived from *interface configuration*) that you use to assign TCP/IP configuration parameters to a particular network interface. Running *ifconfig* with just the name of an interface displays the current configuration of that interface. Windows 2000 and Windows NT have a version of this program that omits the configuration capabilities, retains the configuration display, and goes by the name Ipconfig.exe. Windows Me, Windows 98, and Windows 95 include a graphical version of the utility, called Winipcfg.exe.

When you run Ipconfig.exe with the /all parameter at the Windows 2000 command line, you see a display like the following:

```
Windows 2000 IP Configuration
        Host Name . . . . . . . . . . . . : cz2-w2ksvr
        Primary DNS Suffix  . . . . . . . : zacker2.com
        Node Type . . . . . . . . . . . . : Hybrid
        IP Routing Enabled. . . . . . . . : Yes
        WINS Proxy Enabled. . . . . . . . : No
        DNS Suffix Search List. . . . . . : zacker2.com
Ethernet adapter Local Area Connection:
        Connection-specific DNS Suffix  . :
        Description . . . . . . . . . . . : 3Com EtherLink XL 10/100 PCI
For Complete PC Management NIC (3C905C-TX)
        Physical Address. . . . . . . . . : 00-01-02-68-24-DD
        DHCP Enabled. . . . . . . . . . . : No
        IP Address. . . . . . . . . . . . : 192.168.2.2
        Subnet Mask . . . . . . . . . . . : 255.255.255.0
        Default Gateway . . . . . . . . . : 192.168.2.99
        DNS Servers . . . . . . . . . . . : 199.224.86.15
                                            199.224.86.16
```

Running the program with no parameters displays a limited list of configuration data. Running Winipcfg.exe (which you must do by finding the file in the \Windows directory and executing it, since there is no shortcut on the Start menu) produces a display like that shown in Figure 10.8.

Figure 10.8 The Windows 98 Winipcfg.exe utility

Both Ipconfig.exe and Winipcfg.exe have another function as well. These utilities are often associated with DHCP, because there is no easier way on a Windows system to see what IP address and other parameters the DHCP server has assigned to your computer. However, these programs also enable you to manually release IP addresses obtained through DHCP and renew existing leases. By running Ipconfig.exe with the /release and /renew command-line parameters or by using the Release, Renew, Release All, or Renew All buttons in Winipcfg.exe, you can release or renew the IP address assignment of one of the network interfaces in the computer or for all of the interfaces at once.

ARP

The Address Resolution Protocol (ARP) enables a TCP/IP computer to convert IP addresses to the hardware addresses that data-link layer protocols need to transmit frames. IP uses ARP to discover the hardware address to which each of its datagrams will be transmitted. To minimize the amount of network traffic ARP generates, the computer stores the resolved hardware addresses in a cache in system memory. The information remains in the cache for a short period of time (usually 2 to 10 minutes), in case the computer has additional packets to send to the same address.

Note For more information about ARP and its function, see Lesson 1: TCP/IP Protocols, in Chapter 8, "TCP/IP Fundamentals."

Windows systems include a command-line utility called Arp.exe that you can use to manipulate the contents of the ARP cache. For example, you can use Arp.exe to add to the cache the hardware addresses of computers you contact frequently, thus saving a little time and network traffic during the connection process. Addresses that you add to the cache manually are static, meaning that they are not deleted after the usual expiration period. The cache is stored in memory only, however, so it is erased when you reboot the computer. If you want to pre-load the cache whenever you boot your system, you can create a batch file containing Arp.exe commands and execute it from the Windows Startup group.

Arp.exe uses the following syntax:

```
ARP [-a {ipaddress}] [-n ipaddress] [-s ipaddress hwaddress
{interface}] [-d ipaddress {interface}]
```

- **-a** *{ipaddress}* This parameter displays the contents of the ARP cache. The optional *ipaddress* variable specifies the address of a particular cache entry to be displayed.

- **-n** *ipaddress* This parameter displays the contents of the ARP cache, where *ipaddress* identifies the network interface whose cache you want to display.

- **-s** *ipaddress hwaddress* **{interface}** This parameter adds a new entry to the ARP cache, where the *ipaddress* variable contains the IP address of the computer, the *hwaddress* variable contains the hardware address of the same computer, and the *interface* variable contains the IP address of the network interface in the local system whose cache you want to modify.

- **-d** *ipaddress* **{interface}** This parameter deletes the entry in the ARP cache that is associated with the computer represented by the *ipaddress* variable. The optional *interface* variable specifies the cache from which the entry should be deleted.

Netstat

Netstat is a command-line program that displays information about a TCP/IP computer's current network connections and about the traffic generated by the various TCP/IP protocols. On UNIX computers, the program is simply called *netstat*, and on Windows computers, it's called Netstat.exe. The command-line parameters differ for the various implementations of Netstat, but the information they display is roughly the same. The syntax for the Windows version of Netstat.exe is as follows:

```
NETSTAT [interval] [-a] [-p protocol] [-n] [-e] [-r] [-s]
```

- *interval* Refreshes the display every *interval* seconds until the user aborts the command

- **-a** Displays the current network connections and the ports that are currently listening for incoming network connections

- **-p** *protocol* Displays the currently active connections for the protocol specified by the *protocol* variable

- **-n** When combined with other parameters, causes the program to identify computers using IP addresses instead of names

- **-e** Displays incoming and outgoing traffic statistics for the network interface, broken down into bytes, unicast packets, non-unicast packets, discards, errors, and unknown protocols

- **-r** Displays the routing table, plus the current active connections

- **-s** Displays detailed network traffic statistics for the IP, ICMP, TCP, and UDP protocols

Nbtstat.exe

Nbtstat.exe is a Windows command-line program that displays information about the NetBIOS over TCP/IP connections that Windows uses when communicating with other Windows computers on the TCP/IP LAN. The syntax for Nbtstat.exe is as follows:

```
NBTSTAT [-a name] [-A ipaddress] [-c] [-n] [-r] [-R] [-s] [-S] [-RR]
```

- **-a** *name* Displays the NetBIOS names registered on the computer identified by the *name* variable

- **-A** *ipaddress* Displays the NetBIOS names registered on the computer identified by the *ipaddress* variable

- **-c** Displays the contents of the local computer's NetBIOS name cache

- **-n** Displays the NetBIOS names registered on the local computer

- **-r** Displays the number of NetBIOS names registered and resolved by the local computer, using both broadcasts and WINS

- **-R** Purges the local computer's NetBIOS name cache of all entries and reloads the LMHOSTS file

- **-s** Displays a list of the computer's currently active NetBIOS settings (identifying remote computers by name), their current status, and the amount of data transmitted to and received from each system

- **-S** Displays a list of the computer's currently active NetBIOS settings (identifying remote computers by IP address), their current status, and the amount of data transmitted to and received from each system

- **-RR** Sends Name Release requests to WINS, then starts Refresh

Warning Unlike the other utilities discussed in this section, the command-line parameters for Nbtstat.exe are case-sensitive.

Telnet

The Telecommunications Network Protocol (Telnet) is a command-line client/ server program that essentially provides remote control capabilities for computers on a network. A user on one computer can run a Telnet client program and connect to the Telnet server on another computer. Once connected, the user can execute commands on the other system and view the results. It's important to distinguish this type of remote control access from simple access to the remote file system. When you use a Telnet connection to execute a program on a remote computer, the program actually runs on the remote computer. By contrast, if you use Windows to connect to a shared drive on another computer and execute a program, the program runs on your computer.

Telnet was originally designed for use on UNIX systems, and is still an extremely important tool for UNIX network administrators. The various Windows operating systems all include a Telnet client. Windows 2000 and Windows NT have strictly command-line clients, but Windows Me, Windows 98, and Windows 95 have a semi-graphical client that still provides command-line access to servers, as shown in Figure 10.9. Only Windows 2000 has a Telnet server. This is because Windows is primarily a graphical operating system, and there isn't much that you can do on a Windows server when you are connected to it with a character-based client like Telnet.

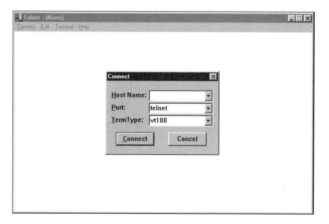

Figure 10.9 Windows 98 has a graphical Telnet client.

FTP

The File Transfer Protocol (FTP) is similar to Telnet, but it is designed for performing file transfers instead of executing remote commands. FTP includes basic file management commands, which can create and remove directories, rename and delete files, and manage access permissions. FTP has become a mainstay of Internet communications in recent years, but it also performs a vital role in communications between UNIX computers, all of which have both FTP client and server capabilities. All Windows computers have a character-based FTP client, but FTP server capabilities are built into the Internet Information Server (IIS) application that is included with Windows 2000 Servers and Windows NT Servers. Generally speaking, Windows computers don't need FTP for communications on the LAN because they can access the shared files on other computers directly. On many UNIX networks, however, FTP is an important tool for transferring files to and from remote computers.

Exercise 10.2: TCP/IP Utilities

Match the utilities in the left column with the functions in the right column.

1.	FTP	a.	Provides remote control access to a UNIX system
2.	Ipconfig.exe	b.	Displays TCP/IP configuration on a Windows 98 system
3.	Tracert.exe	c.	Creates cache entries containing IP and hardware addresses
4.	Ping	d.	Configures the network interface on a UNIX system
5.	Telnet	e.	Tests communications between two computers
6.	Netstat	f.	Transfers files between two computers
7.	Winipcfg.exe	g.	Displays network traffic statistics
8.	Nbtstat.exe	h.	Lists the routers forwarding packets to a particular destination
9.	Arp.exe	i.	Releases and renews IP address assignments on Windows 2000
10.	*Ifconfig*	j.	Displays NetBIOS connection information

Chapter Summary

The key points covered in this chapter are as follows.

TCP/IP Services

- DHCP is a combination of a client, a server, and a protocol that can automatically configure the TCP/IP clients on computers all over the network.

- DHCP is capable of leasing IP addresses from a common pool to client computers, reclaiming them when they are no longer in use and then returning them to the pool for reassignment.

- DNS enables users to identify computers on a network using friendly names instead of IP addresses. DNS servers resolve the names into the IP addresses that computers need to communicate using TCP/IP.

- The DNS name space is hierarchical; a computer's DNS name consists of a host name followed by two or more domain names, separated by periods.

- DNS servers store information in the form of resource records, which contain name-to-address mappings and other information.

- WINS is a Microsoft Windows service that converts NetBIOS names into IP addresses.

TCP/IP Utilities

- Ping is a utility that tests whether one TCP/IP computer can communicate with another one.

- Traceroute is a program that displays the path that packets take through a network to reach their destinations.

- Ipconfig.exe and Winipcfg.exe are Windows programs that display information about the computer's TCP/IP configuration and manipulate DHCP IP address assignments.

- Arp.exe enables you to view and modify the contents of the ARP cache maintained by a TCP/IP system.

- Netstat displays information about a computer's TCP/IP connections and the traffic passing over them.

- Nbtstat.exe displays information about NetBIOS connections and their traffic.

- Telnet is a character-based terminal emulation program that provides remote control access to another computer on the network.

- FTP is a file transfer utility that enables you to manage files and transfer them to and from a remote computer.

Chapter Review

1. Which TCP/IP utility should you use to most easily identify which router on your internetwork is malfunctioning?

   a. Ipconfig.exe

   b. Ping

   c. Traceroute

   d. Netstat

2. What does the first word in a full DNS name identify?

   a. The top-level domain

   b. The second-level domain

   c. The DNS server

   d. The host

3. What happens to a DHCP client when its attempts to renew its IP address lease fail and the lease expires?

4. Which of the following message types is not used during the DHCP lease assignment process?

   a. DHCPDISCOVER

   b. DHCPRELEASE

   c. DHCPOFFER

   d. DHCPREQUEST

5. What is the DNS resource record type that contains the basic name-to-address mapping used for name resolution?

   a. Address

   b. Pointer

   c. Canonical Name

   d. Start of Authority

6. What is the name of the DNS domain that contains address-to-name mappings?

7. Which of the following protocols does the Ping program never use to carry its messages?

    a. Ethernet

    b. ICMP

    c. IP

    d. UDP

8. Name one method other than WINS that computers running Windows can use to resolve NetBIOS names into IP addresses.

9. What is the name of the time during the lease renewal process when a DHCP client begins broadcasting DHCPREQUEST messages?

    a. Lease identification cookie

    b. Rebinding time value

    c. Renewal time value

    d. Init value

10. What is the function of a WINS server?

    a. To convert IP addresses into hardware addresses

    b. To convert host names into IP addresses

    c. To convert IP addresses into host names

    d. To convert NetBIOS names into IP addresses

C H A P T E R   1 1

TCP/IP Configuration

About This Chapter

Understanding the theory behind Transmission Control Protocol/Internet Protocol (TCP/IP) is an important part of the network administrator's education, but that theory must eventually be put into practice. This chapter examines the procedures for installing and configuring the TCP/IP protocols on a computer running Microsoft Windows 2000. The procedures used for installation on the other Windows operating systems are similar to those in Windows 2000, although the user interface is slightly different. Operating systems such as UNIX and Novell NetWare generally rely on a text file to hold the configuration settings for the TCP/IP client. In some cases, these operating systems include a graphical or menu-driven utility that facilitates the creation or modification of this file.

Before You Begin

No previous knowledge other than a basic familiarity with Windows 2000 controls is needed to perform the procedures in this chapter. However, understanding the place of the TCP/IP protocols in the operating system's protocol stack, as explained in Lesson 1: Network Operating Systems, in Chapter 4, "Networking Software," is important for gaining an overall picture of data networking. More detailed explanations of the various TCP/IP configuration parameters can be found in the following chapters:

- Chapter 6, "Network Layer Protocols" See Lesson 1: IP.

- Chapter 8, "TCP/IP Fundamentals" See Lesson 2: IP Addressing.

- Chapter 9, "TCP/IP Routing"

- Chapter 10, "TCP/IP Applications" See Lesson 1: TCP/IP Services.

Lesson 1: Installing the TCP/IP Protocols

Windows 2000, like most other Windows operating systems, provides support for the TCP/IP protocol suite in the form of a single component that you can install from the Windows Control Panel. This one component installs all of the basic protocols needed to transmit data across the network, including the Internet Protocol (IP), the Transmission Control Protocol (TCP), and the User Datagram Protocol (UDP). Microsoft's TCP/IP client also provides support for ancillary protocols, such as the Internet Control Message Protocol (ICMP) and the Address Resolution Protocol (ARP), and includes Dynamic Host Configuration Protocol (DHCP), Domain Name System (DNS), and Windows Internet Name Service (WINS) clients. In addition, the Microsoft TCP/IP client includes utilities such as Arp.exe, Route.exe, Ping.exe, and Tracert.exe as well as File Transfer Protocol (FTP) and Telnet client programs.

Note For more information about the protocols that make up the TCP/IP suite, see Lesson 1: TCP/IP Protocols, in Chapter 8, "TCP/IP Fundamentals." For more information about the various TCP/IP client services and utilities, see Chapter 10, "TCP/IP Applications."

After this lesson, you will be able to

- Install TCP/IP protocol support on a computer running Windows 2000 Server or Windows 2000 Professional

Estimated lesson time: 15 minutes

Windows 2000 uses the TCP/IP protocols by default. If the operating system's Setup program detects a network interface adapter in the computer, Plug and Play identifies it, installs the appropriate network adapter driver, and installs the Internet Protocol (TCP/IP), Client For Microsoft Networks, and File And Printer Sharing For Microsoft Networks modules, as shown in Figure 11.1. However, sometimes it is necessary to install the TCP/IP protocols manually.

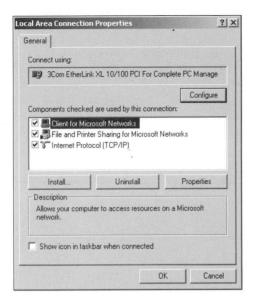

Figure 11.1 The Local Area Connection Properties dialog box

▶ To manually install the TCP/IP protocols

1. From the Start menu's Settings group, select Network And Dial-up Connections to display the Network And Dial-up Connections window, as shown in Figure 11.2.

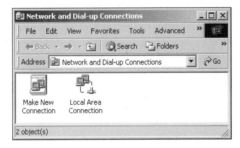

Figure 11.2 The Network And Dial-up Connections window

2. Right-click the Local Area Connection icon in the Network And Dial-up Connections window and select Properties from the shortcut menu to display the Local Area Connection Properties dialog box.

Note If the Network And Dial-up Connections window does not have a Local Area Connections icon in it, your computer does not have a network adapter driver installed. Use the Add/Remove Hardware window, accessed from the Control Panel, to install the appropriate driver for your network adapter.

3. In the Local Area Connection Properties dialog box, click the Install button to display the Select Network Component Type dialog box, shown in Figure 11.3.

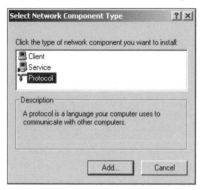

Figure 11.3 The Select Network Component Type dialog box

4. In the component list, highlight Protocol and click the Add button to display the Select Network Protocol dialog box, as shown in Figure 11.4.

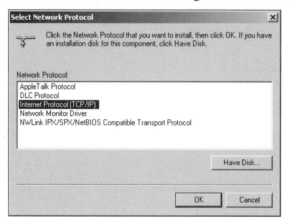

Figure 11.4 The Select Network Protocol dialog box

5. In the protocol listing, highlight Internet Protocol (TCP/IP) and click the OK button. This adds the protocol module to the component list on the Local Area Connection Properties dialog box, as shown in Figure 11.5.

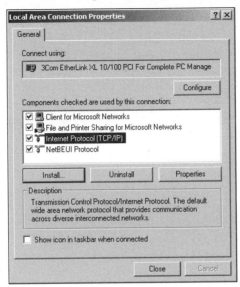

Figure 11.5 The Local Area Connection Properties dialog box with the Internet Protocol (TCP/IP) module added

6. Click the Close button to install the TCP/IP protocols, bind them to the client and adapter driver already installed on the computer, and copy the TCP/IP utilities to the \Winnt\System32 folder. You may have to insert your Windows 2000 distribution CD-ROM into the drive so that the operating system can copy essential files to the computer.

7. After the installation procedure is completed, you must reboot the computer before the new protocols are activated.

Exercise 11.1: Microsoft TCP/IP Client Components

Specify whether each of the following is installed as part of the Microsoft TCP/IP client.

1. The DHCP client
2. Route.exe
3. The WINS server
4. The ICMP protocol
5. The DNS resolver
6. The SNMP Protocol
7. The DNS server
8. The WINS client
9. Tracert.exe
10. The Telnet server

Lesson 2: Configuring TCP/IP

By default, Windows 2000 (like the other Windows operating systems) configures the Microsoft TCP/IP client to use its DHCP client capabilities to request configuration settings from a DHCP server on the network. However, if no DHCP server is available, someone has to configure the TCP/IP client manually. This lesson examines the process of configuring the various TCP/IP client parameters and the functions of each parameter on the computer and the network. As in the previous lesson, the procedure that follows uses the Microsoft Windows 2000 operating system as an example. The other Windows operating systems have most of the same parameters, although the user interface might be slightly different.

After this lesson, you will be able to

- Manually configure the TCP/IP client in a computer running Windows 2000 and understand the functions of the various parameters

Estimated lesson time: 30 minutes

Configuring Basic TCP/IP Properties

The Local Area Connection Properties dialog box that you used to install the TCP/IP protocols in Lesson 1 of this chapter is also where you configure the TCP/IP client. Use the following procedure to access the TCP/IP client's configuration interface and supply values for its various operational parameters.

Warning If you plan to experiment with this TCP/IP configuration procedure on a live network, be sure that the values you supply for the TCP/IP parameters, and particularly the IP address, are correct for your computer and your network. Some TCP/IP parameters, when incorrectly set, can prevent your computer from communicating with the network, while others can cause conflicts with other computers on the network, preventing them from communicating. If you want to avoid explaining to your boss why she couldn't retrieve her e-mail this morning, check with your network's administrator before you begin experimenting.

▶ **To access the TCP/IP client's configuration interface**

1. From the Start menu's Settings group, select Network And Dial-up Connections to display the Network And Dial-up Connections window.

2. Right-click the Local Area Connection icon in the Network And Dial-up Connections window and select Properties from the shortcut menu to display the Local Area Connection Properties dialog box.

3. Highlight the Internet Protocol (TCP/IP) module in the components list and click the Properties button to display the Internet Protocol (TCP/IP) Properties dialog box, shown in Figure 11.6.

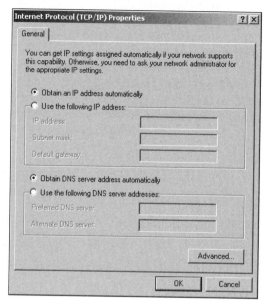

Figure 11.6 The Internet Protocol (TCP/IP) Properties dialog box

4. Click the Use The Following IP Address radio button to activate the IP Address, Subnet Mask, and Default Gateway fields, which provide the dialog box's manual configuration capability. Although its label does not indicate this, the Obtain An IP Address Automatically radio button activates the DHCP client.

5. In the IP Address field, enter a valid IP address using the standard dotted decimal notation, as shown in Figure 11.7. The address you supply must be unique on the network, and it must conform to the subnet configuration used on your network. If you don't know anything about the addresses used on your network, ask an administrator to supply you with an IP address you can use. Do not simply select one at random or change the last number of the address used by the computer next to yours.

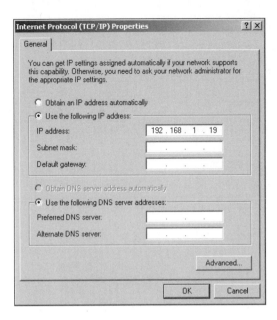

Figure 11.7 Entering a unique IP address into the appropriate field

---

Note The IP address and the subnet mask are the only two TCP/IP configuration parameters that are absolutely required for the computer to communicate with the network. Others might be required for convenience or for certain types of communication, but they are not essential.

---

6. In the Subnet Mask field, enter an appropriate mask for the IP address you supplied, as shown in Figure 11.8. Windows 2000 supplies a subnet mask based on your IP address's first byte value. However, if your network is subnetted, the subnet mask value supplied by Windows 2000 might not be correct.

Note Windows 2000 determines its value for the Subnet Mask field by examining the first three bits of the 32-bit IP address you have supplied. If the first bit of the address is a 0, Windows 2000 supplies the subnet mask for a Class A address (255.0.0.0). If the first two bits are 10, Windows assumes the use of a Class B address and supplies a subnet mask of 255.255.0.0. If the first three bits are 110, the subnet mask value is for a Class C address (255.255.255.0). For more information about the nature of IP addresses and subnet masking, see Lesson 2: IP Addressing, in Chapter 8, "TCP/IP Fundamentals."

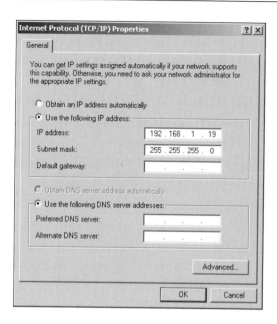

Figure 11.8 Windows 2000 supplies a value for the Subnet Mask field, but you may have to change it to conform with your network's subnet configuration.

7. The Default Gateway field should contain the IP address of the router on the local network that the computer should use to send TCP/IP traffic to destinations on other networks. On a private internetwork, the default gateway is a router that provides access to the other networks. On a standalone local area network (LAN) connected to the Internet, the default gateway refers to the system that provides the shared Internet connection. If the computer is connected to a LAN that is not part of an internetwork and not connected to the Internet, leave this field blank.

Note The address that you enter into the Default Gateway field becomes an entry in the computer's routing table with a Network Destination value of 0.0.0.0. You can also create, delete, or modify the default gateway (or any other routing table entry) manually by using the Route.exe utility, as explained in Lesson 2: Building Routing Tables, in Chapter 9, "TCP/IP Routing."

8. When you select the Use The Following IP Address option in the Internet Protocol (TCP/IP) Properties dialog box, Windows 2000 deactivates the DHCP client completely, and as a result, the Obtain DNS Server Address Automatically option becomes unavailable. In the Preferred DNS Server and Alternate DNS Server fields, enter the IP addresses of the DNS servers that your computer will use to resolve DNS names into IP addresses. The Microsoft TCP/IP

client only uses the Alternate DNS Server address if the primary DNS server is unreachable. If your network is connected to the Internet, you must supply at least one DNS server address in order to convert the DNS names in your Uniform Resource Locators (URLs) into IP addresses. If your computer is part of a Windows 2000 Active Directory domain, you must supply the address of a Windows 2000 DNS server on your internetwork. If you are not using Active Directory services, the DNS server can be either on your internetwork or that of your Internet Service Provider (ISP).

9. Click the OK button to close the Internet Protocol (TCP/IP) Properties dialog box and click OK again to close the Local Area Connection Properties dialog box. You must reboot your computer before the configuration parameters that you have specified will become active.

Configuring Advanced TCP/IP Properties

In many cases, a Windows 2000 system needs only the TCP/IP parameters configured in the preceding procedure. However, the Internet Protocol (TCP/IP) Properties dialog box also has an Advanced button that provides access to a tabbed dialog box called Advanced TCP/IP Settings, in which you can configure a more complete set of TCP/IP parameters. These parameters are discussed in the following sections.

The IP Settings Page

The IP Settings page of the Advanced TCP/IP Settings dialog box (shown in Figure 11.9) enables you to specify multiple IP addresses and subnet masks for the network interface adapter in your computer, as well as multiple default gateway addresses. Most computers with multiple IP addresses have multiple network interface adapters as well, and use one address per network interface adapter. However, there are situations in which a computer can use more than one IP address for a single network interface adapter, such as when a single physical network hosts multiple TCP/IP subnets. In such cases, a computer needs an IP address on each of the two subnets in order to participate on both subnets.

When you open the Advanced TCP/IP Settings dialog box, the parameters you have already configured elsewhere in the Internet Protocol (TCP/IP) Properties dialog box appear in the listings. You can add to the existing settings, modify them, or delete them altogether. To add a new IP address and subnet mask, click the Add button, enter the desired address and mask values in the TCP/IP Address dialog box, and then click the Add button to add your entries to the IP Addresses list. Windows 2000 supports an unlimited number of IP address/subnet mask combinations for each network interface adapter in the computer.

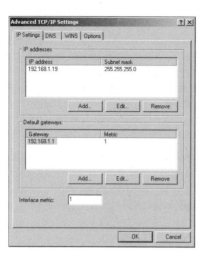

Figure 11.9 The IP Settings page on the Advanced TCP/IP Settings dialog box enables you to specify multiple IP addresses and default gateways.

The procedure for creating additional default gateways is the same as that for adding IP addresses. A computer can use only one default gateway at a time, however, so the ability to specify multiple default gateways in the Advanced TCP/IP Settings dialog box is simply a fault-tolerance mechanism. If the first default gateway in the list is unavailable for any reason, Windows 2000 sends packets to the second address listed. This practice assumes that the computer is connected to a LAN that has multiple routers on it, each of which provides access to the rest of the internetwork.

The DNS Page

The DNS page of the Advanced TCP/IP Settings dialog box, shown in Figure 11.10, also provides a fault-tolerance mechanism for Windows 2000's DNS client. You can specify more than the two DNS server addresses provided in the main Internet Protocol (TCP/IP) Properties dialog box, and you can modify the order in which the computer uses them if one or more of the servers should be unavailable.

Note Unlike the IP address, subnet mask, and default gateway settings, which apply only to a specific network interface adapter, the DNS server addresses apply to the entire Microsoft TCP/IP client. You cannot specify different DNS server addresses for each network interface adapter.

The other controls on the DNS page control how the TCP/IP client resolves unqualified names. An *unqualified name* is an incomplete DNS name, one that does not specify the domain in which the host resides. The Windows 2000 TCP/IP client can still resolve these names by appending a suffix to the unqualified name before sending it to the DNS server for resolution. For example, with a properly configured TCP/IP client, you can supply only the name *www* as a URL in your Web browser, and the client will append your company's domain name (for example, *adatum.com*) to the URL as a suffix, resulting in the fully qualified DNS name *www.adatum.com*, which is presumably the name of your network's intranet Web server.

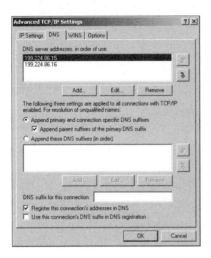

Figure 11.10 The DNS page of the Advanced TCP/IP Settings dialog box

The DNS controls enable you to configure the client to append the primary and connection-specific DNS suffixes to unqualified names, or you can create a list of suffixes that the client will append to unqualified names, one after the other, until the name resolution process succeeds. The primary DNS suffix is the domain name you specify for the computer on the Network Identification page of the System dialog box, accessed from the Control Panel. This suffix applies to all of the computer's network interface adapters. You can create a connection-specific suffix by entering a domain name in the DNS Suffix For This Connection field on the DNS page. To create a list of suffixes, click the Append These DNS Suffixes (In Order) radio button, click the Add button, enter the suffix you want to add to the list, and click the Add button.

The two check boxes at the bottom of the DNS page enable you to specify whether the computer should register its DNS name with its designated DNS server. This option requires a DNS server that supports dynamic updates, such as the DNS server service supplied with Windows 2000 Server. The Register This Connection's Addresses In DNS check box causes Windows 2000 to use the system's primary DNS suffix to register the addresses, while the Use This Connection's DNS Suffix In DNS Registration check box causes the computer to use the connection-specific suffix you've entered in the DNS Suffix For This Connection field.

The WINS Page

Windows 2000 includes a WINS client for NetBIOS name resolution, but on a Windows 2000 network that uses the Active Directory service, WINS is not needed. This is because the Active Directory service uses DNS names for the computers on the network and relies on DNS for its name resolution services. However, if you run Windows 2000 systems that use Windows NT domains or no directory service at all, you can use the Advanced TCP/IP Settings dialog box's WINS page, as shown in Figure 11.11, to configure the Microsoft TCP/IP client to use WINS.

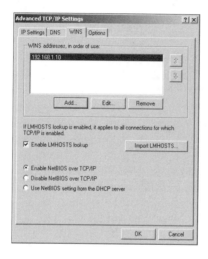

Figure 11.11 The WINS page of the Advanced TCP/IP Settings dialog box

Click the Add button on the WINS page to open a TCP/IP WINS Server dialog box in which you can specify the address of a WINS server on your network. You can create a list of WINS servers and specify the order in which Windows 2000 should use them. As with the default gateway and DNS server settings, supplying multiple WINS server addresses is a fault-tolerance feature.

The Enable LMHOSTS Lookup check box forces the computer to use a file called LMHOSTS to resolve NetBIOS names before contacting the designated WINS server. LMHOSTS is a text file found, by default, in the \Winnt\System32\ Drivers\Etc folder on the computer's local drive, which contains a list of NetBIOS names and their equivalent IP addresses. LMHOSTS functions in much the same way as the HOSTS file, which was used for host name resolution before the advent of DNS. Because each computer must have its own LMHOSTS file, Windows 2000 enables you to import a file from a network drive to the local computer. To do this, click the Import LMHOSTS button and browse to the desired file.

Using the radio buttons at the bottom of the WINS page, you can specify whether the computer should or should not use NetBIOS over TCP/IP, or whether the computer should rely on a DHCP server to specify the NetBIOS setting. Once again, on a Windows 2000 network that uses the Active Directory service, you can disable NetBIOS over TCP/IP, because the computers use DNS names instead of NetBIOS names.

Note For more information about NetBIOS naming and WINS, see Lesson 3: NetBEUI, in Chapter 6, "Network Layer Protocols."

The Options Page

The Options page in the Advanced TCP/IP Settings dialog box (as shown in Figure 11.12) contains a list of additional features included with the Microsoft TCP/IP client. You can select any item in the list and click the Properties button to open a dialog box that enables you to configure that option. Windows 2000 includes two TCP/IP options, IP Security and TCP/IP Filtering. These options are discussed in the following sections.

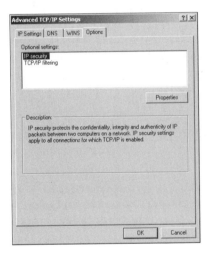

Figure 11.12 The Options page of the Advanced TCP/IP Settings dialog box

Using the IPSec Protocol

The IP Security option controls whether the Microsoft TCP/IP client uses the IPSec protocol when communicating with other computers on the network. IPSec is a security protocol that provides end-to-end encryption of data transmitted over the network. By default, IPSec is disabled in Windows 2000, but you can activate it. To open the IP Security dialog box (see Figure 11.13), highlight the IP Security option and click the Properties button. When IPSec is enabled, computers perform an IPSec negotiation before they begin transmitting data to each other. This negotiation enables each computer to determine if the other computer supports IPSec and what policies are in place to govern its use.

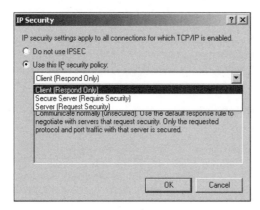

Figure 11.13 The IP Security dialog box

When you click the Use This IP Security Policy radio button on the IP Security dialog box, you can select one of the following policies, which govern when the computer should use the IPSec protocol:

- **Client (Respond Only)** This option causes the computer to use the IPSec protocol only when another computer requests it.

- **Secure Server (Require Security)** This option causes the computer to require IPSec for all communications. Connections requested by other computers that are not configured to use IPSec are refused.

- **Server (Request Security)** This option causes the computer to request the use of IPSec for all communications, but not to require it. If the other computer does not support IPSec, communications proceed without it.

Using TCP/IP Filtering

The TCP/IP Filtering option is essentially a rudimentary form of firewall that you can use to control what kinds of network and transport layer traffic can pass over the computer's network interface adapters. By selecting the TCP/IP Filtering option on the Options page and clicking the Properties button, you open the TCP/IP Filtering dialog box, shown in Figure 11.14. In this dialog box, you can specify which protocols and which ports the computer can use. Clicking the Enable TCP/IP Filtering (All Adapters) check box activates three separate selectors, one for TCP ports, one for UDP ports, and one for IP protocols. By default, all three selectors permit all traffic to pass through the filters, but clicking the Permit Only radio button on any selector enables you to build a list of permitted ports or protocols. The filters prevent traffic generated by all unlisted ports and protocols from passing through any of the computer's network interface adapters.

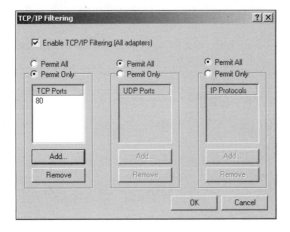

Figure 11.14 The TCP/IP Filtering dialog box

Exercise 11.2: TCP/IP Configuration Requirements

For each of the network scenarios 1 through 5 listed below, specify which of the following TCP/IP parameters (a, b, c, d, and/or e) you must configure to provide a computer running Windows 2000 with full communications capabilities.

    a. IP address

    b. Subnet mask

    c. Default Gateway

    d. DNS server address

    e. WINS server address

1. A private internetwork using Windows NT domains

2. A single peer-to-peer LAN

3. A corporate internetwork using Active Directory service

4. A peer-to-peer LAN using a shared Internet connection

5. A Windows NT internetwork with a router connected to the Internet

Chapter Summary

The key points covered in this chapter are as follows.

Installing the TCP/IP Protocols

- The Windows operating systems implement the TCP/IP protocol suite as a single module.

- You install support for the TCP/IP protocols in Windows 2000 using the Local Area Connections dialog box.

Configuring TCP/IP

- If you don't have DHCP servers on your network, you must configure the Microsoft TCP/IP client manually.

- Every computer on the network must have a unique IP address and an appropriate subnet mask.

- A default gateway address instructs the computer where to send packets that are destined for other networks.

- The DNS server parameters instruct the computer where to send DNS names for resolution into IP addresses.

- The Advanced TCP/IP Settings dialog box provides access to the complete set of TCP/IP configuration options, including WINS, IPSec, and TCP/IP filtering.

Chapter Review

1. Which of the following IP security policies does not request the use of IPSec?

   a. Client

   b. Server

   c. Secure Server

   d. All of the above

2. Which of the following services is not used on a Windows 2000 Active Directory network?

   a. DHCP

   b. WINS

   c. DNS

   d. IPSec

3. What is the function of a DNS suffix?

4. Which utility can you use to specify a default gateway address?

   a. Tracert.exe

   b. Arp.exe

   c. Ipconfig.exe

   d. Route.exe

5. Which of the Windows 2000 Control Panel selections do you use to install the Microsoft TCP/IP client?

6. Which of the following is a valid reason for assigning more than one IP address to a single network interface adapter?

   a. To balance the network traffic load between the addresses

   b. To support multiple subnets on one network

   c. To provide fault tolerance

   d. To support both TCP and UDP traffic

7. How many default gateway addresses does a computer need to function on a LAN?

   a. 0

   b. 1

   c. 2

   d. 3

8. At which of the following layers does the TCP/IP filtering option operate?

   a. Physical and data-link

   b. Application and session

   c. Data-link and network

   d. Network and transport

9. How does Windows 2000 supply a subnet mask for the IP address you specify?

   a. By performing a reverse DNS name resolution on the address

   b. By checking the values of the first three address bits

   c. By checking the HOSTS file

   d. By querying the directory service

10. What is the function of an LMHOSTS file?

C H A P T E R   1 2

Remote Network Access

About This Chapter

While most people associate the phrase "computer networking" with local area networks (LANs), other types of computer connections are networks as well. For example, when you use a dial-up modem to connect to the Internet, you are actually connecting to a remote network. In this case, the serial port or bus slot on your computer is the network interface and the telephone system is the network medium. Your computer gains access to the Internet by connecting to a network run by your Internet Service Provider (ISP). Using the same type of dial-up connection, you can connect to other networks as well, such as the LAN in your office when you are at home or traveling. This chapter examines the hardware and software tools that you use to connect to a network at a remote location.

Before You Begin

While remote network connections use many of the same protocols and services as LAN connections, detailed knowledge of these concepts is not required to understand the material in this chapter. However, a general understanding of data networking concepts, such as that gained from Chapter 1, "Networking Basics," is helpful.

Lesson 1: Using Remote Connections

There are several different technologies that you can use to connect a computer to a network at a remote location. From the network layer up, a remote connection is no different than a direct LAN connection, but the data-link and physical layers can take several different forms. This lesson examines some of the connection types most commonly used for remote networking and discusses the issues involved in installing and configuring them.

After this lesson, you will be able to

- Describe the various types of technologies used to connect remote computers to networks
- Understand how to configure a modem
- List additional requirements for a remote network connection

Estimated lesson time: 30 minutes

Connection Types

The following sections examine the physical layer options that you can use for remote network connections. The interface to the computer can vary from a serial port to a bus slot to a standard network interface adapter, but the actual network medium is the service that carries the signals for most of their journey.

PSTN

The Public Switched Telephone Network (PSTN) is just a technical name for the Plain Old Telephone Service, or POTS. This is the standard voice telephone system, found all over the world, which you can use with asynchronous modems to transmit data between computers at virtually any location. The PSTN service in your home or office uses copper-based twisted pair cable, as do most LANs, and RJ11 jacks, which are the same as the RJ45 jacks used on twisted pair LANs, except that RJ11 jacks have four electrical contacts instead of eight. The PSTN connection leads to a central office belonging to the telephone company, which can route calls from there to any other telephone in the world. Unlike a LAN, which is digital and uses packet switching, the PSTN is an analog, circuit-switched network.

Note For more information about packet switching and circuit switching, see Lesson 1: Network Communications, in Chapter 1, "Networking Basics."

To transmit computer data over the PSTN, the digital signals generated by your computer must be converted to analog signals that the telephone network can carry. This conversion is performed by a device called a modulator/demodulator, more commonly known as a *modem*. A modem takes the digital signals fed to it through a serial port or the system bus, converts them to analog signals, and transmits them over the PSTN (see Figure 12.1). At the other end of the PSTN connection, another modem performs the same process in reverse, converting the analog data back into its digital form and sending it to another computer. The combination of the interface to the computer, the two modems, and the PSTN connection form the physical layer of the networking stack.

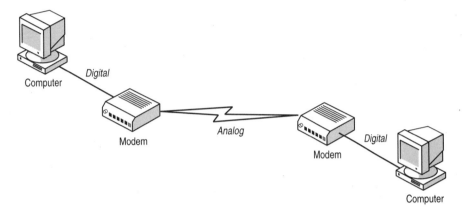

Figure 12.1 Modems convert digital signals to analog signals that the PSTN can carry, and then convert analog signals back to digital signals.

Note At the data-link layer, remote network connections that use modems and the PSTN typically use the Point-to-Point Protocol (PPP) to communicate. In a few cases, computers still use the Serial Line Internet Protocol (SLIP) at the data-link layer. For more information about these protocols, see Lesson 3: SLIP and PPP, in Chapter 5, "Data-Link Layer Protocols."

The first modems used proprietary protocols for the digital/analog conversions, but this meant that users had to use the same manufacturer's modems at each end of the PSTN connection. To standardize modem communications, organizations like the Comité Consultatif International Téléphonique et Télégraphique (CCITT), now known as the International Telecommunications Union (ITU), began developing specifications for the communication, compression, and error detection protocols that modems use when generating and interpreting their analog signals. Today, virtually all of the modems on the market support a long list of protocols that can serve as a history of modem communications. The current industry standard modem communication protocol is V.90, which defines the 56 kilobytes per second (Kbps) data transfers that most modem connections use today.

The PSTN was designed for voice transmissions, not data transmissions. As a result, PSTN connections are relatively slow, with a maximum speed of only 56 Kbps. The quality of the connections can also vary widely, depending on the location of the modems and the state of the cables connecting the modems to their respective central offices. When modems detect errors while transmitting data, they revert to a slower transmission speed. This is one reason that the quality of modem connections can vary from minute to minute. Dedicated, permanent PSTN connections between two locations, called leased lines, are also available and provide a more consistent quality of service, but they lack the flexibility of dial-up connections, and they are quite expensive.

Configuring a Modem

As with most computer peripherals these days, most of the modems on the market support the Plug and Play standard, which enables operating systems to detect the modem's presence, identify its manufacturer and model, and install and configure the appropriate driver for it. As with most hardware peripherals, modems use an interrupt request (IRQ) line and an input/output (I/O) port address to send signals to the computer. With external modems, the IRQ and I/O address are assigned to the serial port that you use to connect the modem to the computer. Most computers are equipped with two serial ports, which are assigned to two of the computer's four default communications (COM) ports, COM1 and COM2. Each COM port has its own I/O port address, but COM1 and COM3 share IRQ4, while COM2 and COM4 share IRQ3.

Internal modems plug into a bus slot instead of a serial port, so you must configure the modem itself to use a particular COM port, which specifies the IRQ and I/O address assignments. If you have other devices plugged into any of the computer's serial ports, you must be sure that the modem is not configured to use the same IRQ as the ports in use.

The other configuration parameter you should be familiar with is the maximum port speed. Serial ports use a chip called a *universal asynchronous receiver-transmitter (UART)* to manage the communications of the device connected to the port. Most computers today have 16550 UART chips for both of their serial ports, which can run as fast as 256 Kbps. Older computers might have slower UART chips, such as the 16450, which runs at a maximum of 115.2 Kbps. Some computers even have a 16550 UART on one port and a slower chip on the other. For today's high-speed modems, you always want to be using a 16550 UART. Internal modems have their own UART chips built onto the card, which are nearly always 16550 UART chips.

VPNs

One of the advantages of using the PSTN to connect a computer to a distant network is that no special service installation is required and the only hardware you need is a modem and a telephone jack. This means that users with portable computers can dial into their office networks wherever they happen to be. However, dialing into a network a long distance away using the PSTN can be an expensive proposition, especially when a company has a large number of network users traveling to distant places. One way to minimize these long distance telephone charges is to use what is known as a *virtual private network (VPN)* connection.

A VPN is a connection between a remote computer and a server on a private network that uses the Internet as its network medium. The network is permanently connected to the Internet and has a server that is configured to receive incoming connections through the Internet. The remote user connects to the Internet by using a modem to dial in to an ISP located nearby. There are many ISPs that offer national and even international service, so the user can connect to the Internet with a local telephone call. The remote computer and the network server then establish a secured connection that protects the data exchanged between them as it travels over the Internet. This technique is called *tunneling*, because the connection runs across the Internet inside a secure conduit, protecting the data in the way that a tunnel under a river protects cars from the water above it.

The primary protocol that makes this tunneling possible is called the *Point-to-Point Tunneling Protocol (PPTP)*. PPTP works with PPP to establish a connection between the client computer and a server on the target network, both of which are connected to the Internet. The connection process begins with the client computer dialing up and connecting to a local ISP, using the standard PPP connection establishment process. When the computer is connected to the Internet, it establishes a *control connection* to the server using the TCP protocol. This control connection is the PPTP tunnel through which the computers will transmit and receive all subsequent data.

Note For more information about PPP communications, see Lesson 1: SLIP and PPP, in Chapter 5, "Data-Link Layer Protocols."

When the tunnel is in place, the computers send their data through it by encapsulating the PPP data that they would normally transmit over a dial-up connection within IP datagrams. The computer then sends the datagrams through the tunnel to the other computer. Although it violates the rules of the Open Systems Interconnection (OSI) model, you actually have a data-link layer frame being carried within a network layer datagram. The PPP frames are encapsulated by IP, and yet at the same time, they can also contain other IP datagrams, which contain the actual user data that one computer is sending to the other. Thus, the messages transmitted through the TCP connection that forms the tunnel are IP datagrams that contain PPP frames, and the PPP frames can contain messages generated by any network layer protocol. In other words, because the PPP user data is secured within the IP datagrams, that user data can be another IP datagram or an Inter-network Packet Exchange (IPX) or NetBIOS Enhanced User Interface (NetBEUI) message, as shown in Figure12.2. Because the tunnel is encrypted and secured using an authentication protocol, the data is protected from interception. After the IP datagrams pass through the tunnel to the other computer, the PPP frames are extracted and processed by the receiver in the normal manner.

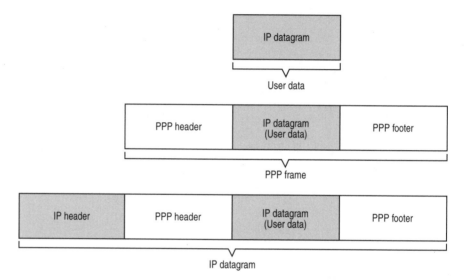

Figure 12.2 The PPTP violates data encapsulation rules by carrying PPP frames within IP datagrams.

ISDN

Although it has only recently achieved a modest popularity in the United States, the Integrated Services Digital Network (ISDN) has been around for several decades, and is especially popular in Europe, where leased telephone lines are prohibitively expensive. ISDN is a digital communications service that uses the same network infrastructure as the PSTN. ISDN was designed as a complete digital replacement for the analog telephone system, but it had few supporters in the United States until relatively recently, when the need for faster Internet connections led people to explore its capabilities. However, other high-speed Internet access solutions, such as Digital Subscriber Line (DSL) and cable television (CATV) services, have also become available in recent years. These other solutions are generally faster and cheaper than ISDN, and have largely eclipsed it in popularity.

ISDN is a dial-up service, like the PSTN, but its connections are digital, so no modems are required. While ISDN can support specially made telephones, fax machines, and other devices, most ISDN installations in the United States are used only for data transmissions. Because it's a dial-up service, ISDN can be used to connect to various different sites. For example, if you have an ISDN connection to the Internet, you can change ISPs simply by dialing a different number. No intervention from the telephone company is required. However, because ISDN needs special equipment, it cannot be used in mobile devices.

ISDN also delivers greater transmission speeds than PSTN connections. The ISDN *Basic Rate Interface (BRI)* service consists of two 64 Kbps channels (called *B channels*) that carry the actual user data, plus one 16 Kbps channel (called a *D channel*), which carries only control traffic. Because of these channel names, the BRI service is sometimes called *2B+D*. The B channels can function separately or be combined into a single 128 Kbps connection. A higher grade of service, called *Primary Rate Interface (PRI)*, consists of 23 B channels and one 64 Kbps D channel. The total bandwidth is the same as that of a T1 leased line. PRI is not often used in the United States.

ISDN uses the same wiring as the PSTN, but additional equipment is required at the terminal locations. The telephone company provides what is called a *U interface*, which connects to a device called an *NT1*; NT stands for network termination. The NT1 can provide a four-wire connection, called an *S/T interface*, for up to seven devices, called *terminal equipment (TE)*. Digital devices designed for use with ISDN connect directly to the S/T interface and are called TE1 devices. A device that can't connect directly to the S/T interface is called a TE2 device, and requires a *terminal adapter*, which connects to the S/T interface and provides a jack for the TE2 device (see Figure 12.3).

Note Because of the increased speed at which ISDN operates, the length of the connection is limited. Your home or office must be within 18,000 feet of the telephone company's nearest central office. For longer distances, an expensive repeater is required, which makes the service impractical for most users.

When you plan to connect multiple devices to the ISDN service, you purchase an NT1 as a separate unit. However, most ISDN installations in the United States use the service solely for Internet access, so there are many products on the market that combine an NT1 and a terminal adapter into a single unit. These combined ISDN solutions can take the form of expansion cards that plug into a bus slot, or separate units that connect to the computer's serial port.

ISDN has never become hugely popular in the United States, partly because of its reputation for being expensive and for installation and reliability problems. Most telephone companies that provide ISDN service charge both a monthly subscription fee and a per-minute rate (usually about 1 cent per minute). If you will be connecting to the Internet using ISDN, you must also pay a monthly fee to an ISP for the Internet access. All together, this can be quite expensive when compared to services like DSL and CATV.

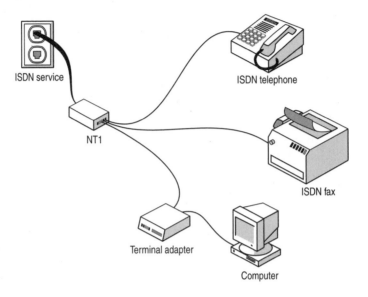

Figure 12.3 The NT1 provides connectors for the terminal equipment that will use the ISDN service.

Many ISDN users can tell you stories of difficult ISDN installations, service outages, and repeated technical support calls. To some extent, ISDN's reputation for technical difficulties is justified, but the whole installation process has become more user-friendly in recent years. Some ISPs now offer a complete ISDN service in which they arrange for the service installation by the telephone company and provide Internet access using that service.

DSL

Digital Subscriber Line (DSL) is a blanket term for a variety of digital communication services that use standard telephone lines, and also provide data transfer speeds much greater than the PSTN or even ISDN. The various DSL service types each have a different descriptive word added to the name, which is why some sources use the generic abbreviation xDSL. Some of the many DSL services are shown in Table 12.1.

Table 12.1 DSL services and their properties

Service	Transmission Rate	Link Length	Applications
High-bit-rate Digital Subscriber Line (HDSL)	1.544 Mbps full-duplex (using two wire pairs) or 2.048 Mbps full-duplex (using three wire pairs)	12,000 to 15,000 feet	Used by large networks as a substitute for T1 leased line connections, LAN and and PBX interconnections, or frame relay traffic aggregation
Symmetrical Digital Subscriber Line (SDSL)	1.544 Mbps full-duplex or 2.048 Mbps full-duplex (one wire pair)	10,000 feet	Same as HDSL
Asymmetrical Digital Subscriber Line (ADSL)	1.544 to 8.448 Mbps downstream; 16 Kbps to 640 Kbps upstream	10,000 to 18,000 feet	Internet/intranet access, remote LAN access, virtual private networking, video-on-demand, voice-over-IP
Rate-Adaptive Digital Subscriber Line (RADSL)	640 Kbps to 2.2 Mbps downstream; 272 Kbps to 1.088 Mbps upstream	10,000 to 18,000 feet	Same as ADSL, except that the transmission speed is dynamically adjusted to accommodate the link length and signal quality
ADSL Lite	Up to 1 Mbps downstream; up to 512 Kbps upstream	18,000 feet	Internet/intranet access, remote LAN access, IP telephony, videoconferencing
Very-high-bit-rate Digital Subscriber Line (VDSL)	12.96 to 51.84 Mbps downstream; 1.6 to 2.3 Mbps upstream	1,000 to 4,500 feet	Multimedia Internet access, high-definition television delivery
ISDN Digital Subscriber Line (IDSL)	Up to 144 Kbps full-duplex	18,000 feet	Internet/intranet access, remote LAN access, IP telephony, videoconferencing

As seen in the transmission rates listed in Table 12.1, many DSL services run at different upstream and downstream speeds. These are called *asymmetrical* services. This is because the nature of the DSL signals causes greater levels of crosstalk in the data traveling from the customer site to the central office than in the other direction. For end-user Internet access, this is usually not a problem, because Web surfing and other common activities generate far more downstream than upstream traffic. However, if you plan to use DSL to connect your own servers to the Internet, make sure that you obtain a service that is either symmetrical or that offers sufficient upstream bandwidth for your needs. DSL services are also subject to distance restrictions, just like ISDN.

DSL provides higher transmission rates by utilizing high frequencies that the standard telephone services don't use, and by employing special signaling schemes. This is why, in many cases, you can use your existing telephone lines for a DSL connection and still support voice traffic at the same time. The most common DSL services are HDSL, used by phone companies and large corporations for wide area network (WAN) links, and ADSL, which is the service that ISPs use to provide Internet access to end users. DSL is an excellent Internet access solution, and it can be suitable for connecting a home user to the office LAN, as long as the upstream bandwidth is suitable for your needs.

The additional hardware needed for an ADSL connection is an *ADSL Termination Unit-Remote (ATU-R)*, sometimes called a DSL transceiver or a DSL modem, plus a line splitter if you will be using the line for voice traffic as well. A DSL modem is not really a modem, since it does not convert signals between digital and analog formats; all DSL communications are digital. The ATU-R connects to your computer using either a standard Ethernet network interface adapter or a Universal Serial Bus (USB) port. At the other end of the link at the ISP's site is a more complicated device called a *Digital Subscriber Line Access Multiplexer (DSLAM)*, as shown in Figure 12.4. Unlike ISDN, DSL connections are direct, permanent links between two sites that remain connected at all times. This means that if you use DSL to connect to the Internet, you have to have your telephone company install the DSL connection between your home or office and the ISP's site. If you want to change your ISP, the phone company must install a new link. In many cases, however, telephone companies are themselves offering DSL Internet access, which eliminates one party from the negotiation.

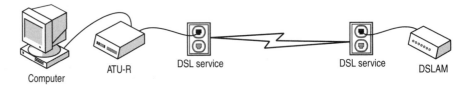

Figure 12.4 An ADSL connection is a direct link between your home or office and an ISP or other network site.

CATV

All of the remote connection technologies described up to this point rely on the cables installed and maintained by telephone companies. However, the cable television (CATV) industry has also been installing a vast network infrastructure throughout most of the United States over the past few decades. In recent years, many cable television systems have begun taking advantage of their networks to provide Internet access to their customers through the same cable as the TV service. CATV Internet access is very fast, sometimes as fast as 512 Kbps, and usually quite inexpensive. CATV networks use broadband transmissions, meaning that the one network medium carries many discrete signals at the same time.

Each of the TV channels you receive over the cable is a separate signal, and all of the signals arrive over the cable simultaneously. By devoting some of this bandwidth to data transmissions, CATV providers can deliver Internet data at the same time as the television signals. If you already have cable TV, installing the Internet service is simply a matter of connecting a splitter to the cable and running it to a device called (again, erroneously) a cable modem, which is connected to an Ethernet card in your computer, as shown in Figure 12.5.

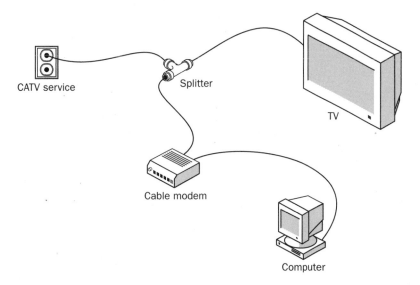

Figure 12.5 CATV data connections use the same cable that delivers television signals to carry Internet data.

CATV data connections are different from both ISDN and DSL in that they are not dedicated links. In effect, you are connecting to a metropolitan area network (MAN) run by your cable company. If you run Windows on your computer and attempt to browse the network, you will see your neighbors' computers on the same network as yours. This arrangement has the potential to cause two major problems. One is that you are sharing your Internet bandwidth with all of the other users in your area. During peak usage periods, you might notice a significant slowdown in your Internet downloads. ISDN and DSL, by contrast, are not shared connections, so you have the same bandwidth available at all times. The second potential problem is one of security. If you share the drive on your computer without specifying a password, anyone else on the network can access your files, modify them, or even delete them. The installers from the cable company are usually careful to disable file sharing on your computer, however, and there are personal firewall products that you can use to provide yourself with additional protection.

Like most DSL services, CATV data connections are asymmetrical. CATV networks are designed to carry data primarily in one direction, from the provider to the customer. There is a small amount of upstream bandwidth, which some systems use for purposes such as ordering Pay-Per-View movies from your remote control, and part of this upstream bandwidth is allocated for Internet traffic. In most cases, the upstream speed of a CATV connection is far less than the downstream speed, making the service unsuitable for hosting your own Internet servers, but it is still faster than a PSTN connection.

CATV connections are an excellent Internet access solution, inexpensive and fast, but you can't use them to connect your home computer to your office LAN, unless you do so by using a VPN connection through the Internet, as described earlier in this chapter. If you plan to implement VPNs, be sure that the cable modem you select supports them.

Remote Connection Requirements

In addition to a physical layer connection, there are other elements you need to establish a remote network connection, such as the following:

- **Common protocols** The two computers to be connected must share common protocols at the data-link layer and above. This means that you must configure both computers to use a data-link layer protocol suitable for point-to-point connections, such as PPP or SLIP, and that there must also be network and transport layer protocols in common, such as TCP/IP, IPX, or NetBEUI.

- **TCP/IP configuration** If your remote computer will be using the TCP/IP protocols to communicate with the host network, the computer must be assigned an IP address and other configuration parameters appropriate for that network. You can configure the TCP/IP settings if someone familiar with the host network supplies them to you, but most remote networking solutions enable the network server to assign configuration parameters automatically using DHCP or some other mechanism.

- **Host and remote software** Each of the computers to be connected must be running an application appropriate to its role. The remote (or client) computer needs a client program that can use the physical layer medium to establish a connection, by instructing the modem to dial a number, for example. The host (or server) computer must have a program that can respond to a connection request from the remote computer and provide access to the network.

- **Security** The host computer and the other systems on the network to which it is attached must have security mechanisms in place that control access to the network resources. These mechanisms must ensure that only authorized users are permitted access and restrict the access of the authorized users to the resources they need.

Exercise 12.1: Remote Connection Technologies

Specify which of the remote connection technologies (PSTN, ISDN, DSL, and/or CATV) discussed in this lesson are associated with each of the following concepts.

1. Asymmetrical transfer rates

2. Uses standard telephone lines

3. Slowest of the connection types discussed

4. Uses an NT1

5. Also called POTS

6. Uses an ATU-R

7. Uses analog signals

8. Shares bandwidth with other users

9. Uses dial-up connections

10. Requires the nearest central office to be relatively close by

Chapter Summary

The key points covered in this chapter are as follows.

Using Remote Connections

- Standalone computers become remote clients when they connect to a distant network, using any one of several different technologies.

- PSTN connections use modems and standard telephone lines to transmit data. They are relatively slow, but also flexible and universal.

- VPNs are secure tunnels through the Internet that enable remote computers to communicate with their networks without using long-distance telephone connections.

- ISDN is a digital dial-up service provided by telephone companies that offers greater speeds and dial-up flexibility than PSTN, but is also more expensive.

- DSL is a point-to-point connection that also uses standard telephone lines to carry digital signals at much higher speeds than PSTN connections.

- CATV networks use cable television technology to provide users with economical high-speed Internet access. However, CATV is a shared service, which can mean that bandwidth diminishes as more local users concurrently access the Internet.

Chapter Review

1. To communicate with its host computer, a modem does not always need which of the following system resources?

   a. A serial port

   b. An IRQ

   c. A COM port

   d. An I/O port address

2. Why are "cable modems" and "DSL modems" not really modems?

3. Which of the DSL types is most commonly used to provide Internet access to end users?

   a. HDSL

   b. ADSL

   c. SDSL

   d. VDSL

4. An ISDN installation in the United States provides you with a connection using which interface?

   a. The Basic Rate Interface

   b. The S/T interface

   c. The U interface

   d. The Primary Rate Interface

5. Which of the following protocols can be transmitted through a PPTP tunnel?

   a. IP only

   b. IP and NetBEUI

   c. IP and IPX

   d. IP, IPX, and NetBEUI

6. Which of the following is not the name of an ISDN service?

   a. BRI

   b. 2B+D

   c. PRI

   d. IDSL

7. What three new hardware components are required to install CATV Internet access on the computer of an existing cable TV customer?

8. Name one of the data-link layer protocols that computers can use with a PSTN connection.

9. Which of the following UART chips enables a modem to achieve the best possible performance?

   a. 8250

   b. 16450

   c. 16550

   d. 16650

10. Which device enables you to use a computer with an ISDN connection?

   a. A terminal adapter

   b. An NT1

   c. Terminal equipment

   d. A U interface

CHAPTER 13

Network Security

About This Chapter

Security is a part of every network administrator's job, whether there is confidential data stored on computers that must be protected, or there are users who need to be prevented from deleting vital operating system and application files. There are various mechanisms used to provide security on a network because different types of protection are needed. Network security is a huge and complex subject. This chapter examines some of the most basic tools and techniques that you can use to protect your network from accidental or deliberate damage.

Before You Begin

This chapter assumes a basic knowledge of the Microsoft Windows operating systems and of network communications processes. The study of firewalls requires an understanding of TCP/IP communications, as discussed in Lesson 1: TCP/IP Protocols, in Chapter 8, "TCP/IP Fundamentals," and Lesson 1: IP, in Chapter 6, "Network Layer Protocols."

Lesson 1: Password Protection

No matter what operating systems you use on your networked computers, you probably use passwords to control user access to specific resources. There are some quite sophisticated identification tools available for those networks that require extraordinary amounts of security. For example, the Smart Card, a credit card–like device with a magnetic strip, must be run through a card reader connected to a computer for a user to gain access to the network. There are also biometric devices on the market that can identify users by scanning unique physical characteristics, such as thumbprints or retinas. However, most networks don't require such elaborate security measures. Instead, most network administrators require users to supply passwords to access network drives, server applications, and other resources.

After this lesson, you will be able to

- Understand what types of passwords are most secure
- Describe the most common password enforcement policies used by Microsoft Windows 2000 and other operating systems

Estimated lesson time: 20 minutes

Using passwords can be an excellent method of securing network resources, or it can be worse than useless. The usefulness of password protection is largely determined by the policies that the network's administrators establish to govern the creation of the passwords. When administrators give users too much freedom to create their own passwords, the users' tendency is to specify short, simple passwords that are easy to remember, and to rarely, if ever, change their passwords. For example, some users create passwords that are the same as their user names, or that consist of letters or numbers that are easy to guess, such as their initials or their birthday, while others use no password at all. This defeats the purpose of having a password in the first place because these are the first things that a potential intruder will try to guess.

Of course, it is also possible to carry password assignment to the opposite extreme. Some administrators assign passwords to their users, which ensures the selection of better passwords, but this can backfire as well. If a security-conscious administrator decides to assign passwords that consist of random sequences of letters and numbers, the users are likely to have trouble remembering them. The result is that the users will undoubtedly write down their passwords and probably leave them in obvious places, such as taped to their monitors. This solution is no better than creating a bad password in the first place, and it also adds to the administrator's workload.

There is a middle ground between these two extremes, however. Most operating systems provide network administrators with tools they can use to impose password policies on their users, such as forcing them to choose passwords of a specific length and change them at regular intervals. This enables users to select their own passwords within parameters established by the administrator. The result is a password that the user can remember more easily and is less work for the network administrator. Setting effective password policies requires psychological as well as technological insight. The idea is to set policies that are strict enough to maintain adequate security, but that don't incite open revolt from users. Some of these password policy tools are discussed in the following sections.

Note Password policies are typically available in network operating systems that use some kind of directory service to authenticate users and grant them access to network resources. For example, you can set password policies on Windows 2000 and Windows NT domain controllers and Novell NetWare servers, but you won't find them in Windows Me, Windows 98, or Windows 95.

User Account Password Settings

When you create a new user account in Windows 2000 or Windows NT, you are presented with a series of check boxes that you can use to control the most basic elements of the password policies for the account, as shown in Figure 13.1.

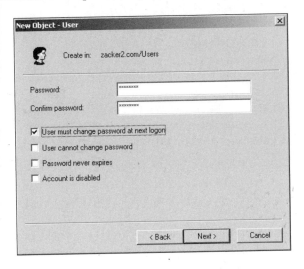

Figure 13.1 The Windows 2000 New Object - User dialog box

The checkboxes for controlling the account's password policies are as follows:

- **User Must Change Password At Next Logon** This option enables an administrator to assign the same password to each new user account created and forces the user to change that password during the first logon. This way, the administrator can password-protect the new accounts without having to track individual password assignments.

- **User Cannot Change Password** This option prevents users from changing the password assigned to the account during its creation. If an administrator elects to assign passwords to users, activating this option on all accounts ensures that he or she retains control over the password assignments.

- **Password Never Expires** This option overrides other policies that cause passwords to expire after a specified length of time. Users can still change their passwords at will, but are not required to do so.

- **Account Is Disabled** This option allows the administrator to temporarily prevent access to an account, eliminating the need to delete and recreate the account.

Specifying Password Lengths

When given free rein to choose any passwords they like, many users opt for a short password, because it's easier to remember and type, or even elect to use no password at all. Because short passwords are easier to remember, they are also easier to guess. One of the most basic password policies provided in most network operating systems is the ability to specify a minimum password length. A longer password is mathematically more difficult to penetrate. The Windows 2000 directory service, Active Directory, supports passwords up to 104 characters, although passwords this long would hardly be practical. Windows NT supports passwords of up to 14 characters. Generally speaking, a minimum password length of five or six characters is suitable for most networks. Some organizations requiring greater security might force users to specify passwords of eight characters or more.

As with all password policies, length requirements are implemented by operating systems in various ways. In Windows 2000, you set password restrictions using the Group Policies feature. You can apply policies to particular domains or organizational units, as needed, using the interface shown in Figure 13.2. When you activate the Minimum Password Length policy, you specify the minimum number of password characters using the Security Policy Setting dialog box shown in Figure 13.3.

Note All of the policies listed in the Domain Security Policy dialog box have their own Security Policy Setting dialog boxes, which you use to enable and configure the individual policies. These dialog boxes can have different types of controls, depending on the function of the policy.

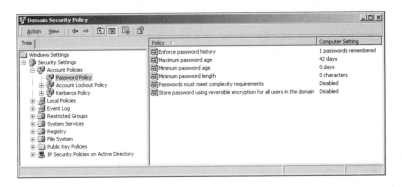

Figure 13.2 The Domain Security Policy dialog box is one of the places where you can implement group policies.

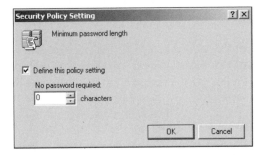

Figure 13.3 This Security Policy Setting dialog box controls the Minimum Password Length policy.

Setting Password Change Intervals

Another important factor in password security is the regular changing of passwords. In many cases, users give out their passwords to other users, for the sake of convenience, and rarely remember to change them afterward. By requiring changes at regular intervals, you prevent passwords from becoming common knowledge. In a typical implementation of this feature, the user sees a special dialog box when logging on after the change interval has expired. The dialog box forces the user to specify a new password before being granted access to the network or other resources.

As explained earlier in this lesson, some administrators assign an initial password to an account to keep it secure, and then force users to change that password during their first logon. Along those lines, in Windows 2000 you can configure a group policy called Maximum Password Age, which forces users to change their passwords at intervals of a specified number of days, as shown in Figure 13.4. A typical setting for this policy can range anywhere from a week to a month, depending on your security needs.

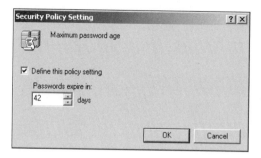

Figure 13.4 This Security Policy Setting dialog box controls the Maximum Password Age policy.

Some users become attached to a particular password, however, and resent having to change it. As a result, these users might change their passwords as directed, and then immediately try to change it back to its original value. Windows 2000 anticipates this behavior, however, and includes two additional policies that help to reinforce your intentions. The Enforce Password History policy enables you to specify a number of previous passwords that the operating system is to remember for each user. When users change their passwords as required by the Maximum Password Age policy, they cannot reuse any of the previous passwords stored in the history. This can prevent users from switching back and forth between two passwords, as they make the required changes. The Minimum Password Age policy forces users to wait for a specified number of days after changing their passwords before they can change them again. This prevents users from rapidly changing their passwords several times in a few minutes in an attempt to defeat the history feature.

Enforcing Password Complexity

When intruders try to penetrate passwords, they often begin by making a series of guesses based on what they can find out about the person whose account they are trying to access. Names of spouses and children, birthdays, initials, and other bits of common knowledge make bad passwords, because it usually isn't too difficult for someone to find them out. Less obvious items, such as the name of the rabbit you had at age nine, make better passwords, but better still is to make your passwords more complex by mixing up the characters in them. For example, most operating systems use passwords that are case sensitive, so mixing uppercase and lowercase letters (in a pattern that isn't too obvious) can make a simple password much harder to guess. *FluFFy* is much better than *fluffy*, for example.

Tip It is also important to remember that mixed case letters also make a password harder to type, so don't overdo it.

Passwords can usually use numbers and certain symbols as well as uppercase and lowercase characters. Adding these elements to your passwords can make them much more difficult to penetrate. *FluFFy_9* is an even better password than *FluFFy*. Another technique is to take a sentence that's easy to remember, and use the first letter of each word to form a password, converting some words to numbers in the process. For example, the sentence "I eat fish for dinner every Friday" can become *Ief4deF*, a password that is difficult to guess.

A policy that forces users to specify complex passwords like these is not as common a feature as the others discussed thus far. You can configure both Windows 2000 and Windows NT to require complex passwords, although in the case of Windows NT, you have to install the password filter module (Passfilt.dll) yourself. When you enable the Passwords Must Meet Complexity Requirements policy in the dialog box shown in Figure 13.5, the passwords that users supply for their accounts must meet the following criteria:

- The password must contain at least six characters.

- The password cannot contain any part of the account's user name. For example, the password for an account with the name *abaldwin* cannot be *abaldwin* or contain *baldwin*, *bald*, and so forth.

- The password must include three of the following four character types: uppercase letters, lowercase letters, numerals, and symbols.

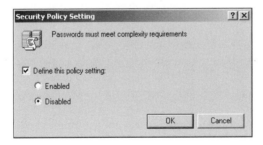

Figure 13.5 This Security Policy Setting dialog box controls the Passwords Must Meet Complexity Requirements policy.

Controlling Password Encryption

Most operating systems store user passwords in encrypted form so that a potential intruder can't discover them by using a disk editing program to read the contents of the drive on which they are stored. The encryption algorithm used on the pass-words in a Windows 2000 system is not reversable; this is the default. However, if necessary, you can enable a policy called Store Password Using Reversible Encryption For All Users In The Domain to use an encryption method that can be reversed to recover forgotten passwords.

Setting Account Lockout Policies

Given a sufficient number of guesses, a motivated intruder can penetrate any password. This is known as the brute force method. Most operating systems include an account lockout feature that prevents anyone from repeatedly trying to guess the password to a given account. In Windows 2000, there are three policies that control the lockout features, as shown in Figure 13.6.

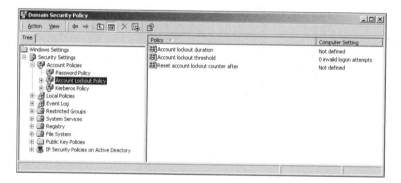

Figure 13.6 The Account Lockout Policy security settings

The policies that control the lockout features are as follows:

- **Account Lockout Duration** This policy specifies how long accounts should remain locked (in minutes) when the user exceeds the account lockout threshold. Setting the value of this policy to zero causes accounts to remain locked out until an administrator manually releases them (by clearing the Account Is Locked Out check box on the Account page of the user's Properties dialog box in the Active Directory Users and Computers console).

- **Account Lockout Threshold** This policy specifies the number of logon attempts that users are allowed before their account is locked. When the account is locked, no future logon attempts are permitted until the account is reset. Occasional failed logon attempts, due to typographic errors, improper case, or forgotten passwords, are common, so you should generally permit users at least three tries before locking the account. A value of zero disables the lockout function.

- **Reset Account Lockout Counter After** This policy causes the failed logon counter to reset after a specified amount of time (in minutes). When a user logs on successfully, the failed logon counter is reset. However, if the user does not log on successfully, the counter that registers the number of times the user tried to logon and failed remains in place until it is reset by this policy.

Exercise 13.1: Password Policies

For each of the characteristics in the left column, specify which of the policies in the right column best applies to it.

1. Specifies the number of logon attempts a user is permitted

2. Requires passwords to contain at least six characters

3. Prevents users from reusing the same passwords

4. Prevents users from defeating the Enforce Password History policy

5. Enables passwords to be recovered

a. Enforce Password History

b. Maximum Password Age

c. Minimum Password Age

d. Minimum Password Length

e. Passwords Must Meet Complexity Requirements

f. Store Password Using Reversible Encryption

g. Account Lockout Threshold

h. Account Lockout Duration

i. Reset Account Lockout Counter After

Lesson 2: Security Models

In Chapter 1, "Networking Basics," you learned about the difference between a client/server network and a peer-to-peer network. The primary difference between these two network types is in the security models they use. This lesson examines the nature of these security models and how they are implemented in the various Windows operating systems.

After this lesson, you will be able to

- Understand how the client/server and peer-to-peer networking models affect security
- Distinguish between user-level and share-level security

Estimated lesson time: 10 minutes

On a client/server network, the user accounts are stored in a central location. A user logs on to the network from a computer that transmits the user name and password to a server, which either grants or denies access to the network. Depending on the operating system, the account information can be stored in a centralized directory service or on individual servers. A directory service, such as Microsoft's Active Directory or Novell Directory Services, provides authentication services for an entire network. A user logs on once and the directory service grants access to shared resources anywhere on the network.

On a peer-to-peer network, each computer maintains its own security information and performs its own authentications. Computers can function as both clients and servers on this type of network. When a computer functioning as a client attempts to use resources (called shares) on another computer that is functioning as a server, the server itself authenticates the client before granting it access.

The two basic security models used by Windows and most other operating systems are called *user-level security* and *share-level security*. These models are examined in the following sections.

User-Level Security

The user-level security model is based on individual accounts created for specific users. When you want to grant users permission to access resources on a specific computer, you select them from a list of user accounts and specify the permissions you want to grant them, as shown in Figure 13.7. Windows 2000 and Windows NT always use user-level security, whether they are operating in client/server or peer-to-peer mode. In peer-to-peer mode, each computer has its own user accounts. When users log on to their computers, they are authenticated against an account on that system. If several people use the same computer, they must each have their own user account (or share a single account). When users elsewhere on the network attempt to access server resources on that computer, they are also authenticated using the accounts on the computer that hosts the resources.

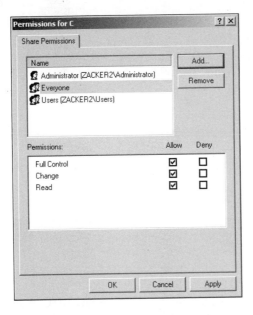

Figure 13.7 A Windows 2000 Permissions dialog box

For example, the user Mark Lee must have an account (*mlee*) on his own computer in order to log on to it. However, to access other network resources, there must be an *mlee* account on each computer that the user wants to access. If Mark Lee attempts to access a network-attached computer on which there is no *mlee* account, he will be prompted to supply the name and password of an account on that computer. In the same way, if there is an *mlee* account on the network-attached computer, but with a different password, the user is prompted to supply the correct password for that account.

This user-level, peer-to-peer security model is suitable only for relatively small networks, because users must have separate accounts on every computer they want to access. If users want to change their account passwords, they must change them on every computer on which they have an account. In many cases, users maintain the accounts on their computers themselves, because it would be impractical for an administrator to travel to each computer and create a new account whenever a new user is added.

User-level security on a client/server network is easier to administer and can support networks of almost any size. In the user-level, client/server security model, administrators create user accounts in a directory service, such as Active Directory in Windows 2000 or a Windows NT domain. When users log on to their computers, they are actually being authenticated by the directory service. Their computer sends the account name and password supplied by the user to a domain controller where the directory service information is stored. The domain controller then checks the credentials and indicates to the computer whether the authentication has succeeded or failed. In the same way, when you want to grant other network users access to resources on your computer, you select their user accounts from a list provided by the domain controller, and when they try to connect to your computer, the domain controller authenticates them and either grants or denies them access.

With only a single set of user accounts stored in a centralized directory service, administrators and users can make changes more easily. Changing a password, for example, is simply a matter of making the change in one directory service record, and the modification is automatically replicated throughout the network.

Share-Level Security

Windows Me, Windows 98, and Windows 95 cannot maintain their own user accounts. These operating systems can employ user-level security when they are participating in an Active Directory or Windows NT domain, using a list of accounts supplied by a domain controller. But in peer-to-peer mode, they operate using share-level security. In share-level security, users assign passwords to the individual shares they create on their computers. When network users want to access a share on another computer, they must supply the appropriate password. The share passwords are stored on the individual computers, and in the case of shared drives, users can specify two different passwords to provide both Read-only access and full control of the share, using the interface shown in Figure 13.8.

Share-level security is not as flexible as user-level security, and it does not provide as much protection. Because everyone uses the same password to access a shared resource, it is difficult to keep the passwords secure. Changing a password means informing everyone who might have to use that resource. In addition, the access control provided by this security model is not as granular as that of user-level control, which you can use to grant users highly specific sets of access permissions to network resources. The advantage of share-level security is that even unsophisticated users can learn to set up and maintain their own share passwords, eliminating the need for constant attention from a network administrator.

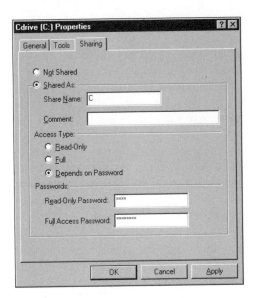

Figure 13.8 The Sharing page of a drive's Properties dialog box on a Windows 98 computer using share-level security

Exercise 13.2: Security Levels

Specify whether each of the following statements applies to user-level security, share-level security, both, or neither.

1. Requires a directory service

2. Uses the same password for all users

3. Provides variable degrees of access to shared network resources

4. Stores passwords on individual computers

5. Requires separate accounts

Lesson 3: Firewalls

The security mechanisms covered thus far in this chapter are primarily concerned with internal network security, that is, with preventing users on the same local area network (LAN) or internetwork from accessing files and other resources that they do not need. This type of security is important, but routine. There is a whole world of other potential security hazards outside the private internetwork, however, and the Internet connection that most networks have today is the door through which these hazards can enter. A *firewall* is a hardware or software product that is designed to protect a network from unauthorized access by outside parties. If your network is connected to the Internet, you must have some sort of firewall to protect it, because intruders can wreak havoc on the network that you have so carefully designed and constructed.

Tip Firewalls are usually deployed to protect a private network or internetwork from unauthorized access via the Internet. However, you can also use a firewall internally, to protect one section of the network from the rest of it. For example, you can use a firewall to isolate the LAN used by your company's Accounting department to prevent other users from accessing confidential financial records.

After this lesson, you will be able to

- Describe how you can use packet filtering to protect a network from unauthorized access

- Understand how Network Address Translation (NAT) enables networked computers to use unregistered Internet Protocol (IP) addresses and still participate on the Internet

- Understand how proxy servers protect networked computers at the application layer and how administrators can use them to restrict users' Internet access

Estimated lesson time: 20 minutes

A firewall is essentially a barrier between two networks that evaluates all incoming traffic to determine whether or not it should be permitted to pass over to the other network. A firewall can take many different forms and use different criteria to evaluate the network traffic it receives. Some firewalls are dedicated hardware devices, essentially routers with additional software that monitors the incoming and outgoing traffic. In other cases, firewalls are software products that run on a standard computer. At one time, all firewalls were complex, hugely expensive, and used only in professional network installations. These high-end products still exist, but today you can also purchase inexpensive firewall software products designed to protect a small network or even an individual computer from unauthorized access through an Internet connection.

There are several methods that firewalls can use to examine network traffic and detect potential threats. Most firewall products use more than one of these methods, and often provide other services as well. For example, one firewall product—a proxy server—not only enables users to access Web pages with complete safety, but also can cache frequently used pages for quicker retrieval by other systems. Some of the most common firewall technologies are covered in the following sections.

Packet Filtering

A packet filter is the most basic type of firewall, one that examines packets arriving over its interfaces and decides whether to allow them access to the other network based on the information found in the various protocol headers used to construct the packets. Packet filtering can occur at any one of several layers of the Open Systems Interconnection (OSI) reference model. A firewall can filter packets based on any of the following characteristics:

- **Hardware addresses** Packet filtering based on hardware addresses enables only certain computers to transmit data to the other network. This type of filtering isn't often used to protect networks from unauthorized Internet access, but you can use this technique in an internal firewall to permit only specific computers to access a particular network.

- **IP addresses** You can use IP address filtering to permit only traffic destined or originating from specific addresses to pass through to the other network. If, for example, you have a public Web server on your network, you can configure a firewall to admit only the Internet traffic that is destined for that server's IP address. This can prevent Internet users from accessing any of the other computers on the network.

- **Protocol identifiers** Firewalls can filter packets based on the protocol that generated the information carried within an IP datagram, such as the Transmission Control Protocol (TCP), the User Datagram Protocol (UDP), or the Internet Control Message Protocol (ICMP).

- **Port numbers** Firewalls can filter packets based on the source or destination port number specified in a packet's transport layer protocol header. This is called service-dependent filtering. These port numbers identify the application or service that generated the packet or for which the packet is destined. For example, you can configure a firewall to permit network users to access the Internet using ports 110 and 25 (the well-known port numbers used for incoming and outgoing e-mail) but deny them Internet access using port 80 (the port number used to access Web servers).

The strength of the protection provided by packet filtering is its ability to combine the various types of filters. For example, you might want to permit Telnet traffic into your network from the Internet, so that network support personnel can remotely administer certain computers. However, leaving port 23 (the Telnet port) open to all Internet users is a potentially disastrous security breach. Therefore, you can combine the port number filter with an IP address filter to permit only certain computers (those of the network administrators) to access the network using the Telnet port.

Packet filtering capabilities are usually provided with a standard router. In Lesson 2: Configuring TCP/IP, in Chapter 11, "TCP/IP Configuration," it was explained that Windows 2000 includes its own basic packet filtering mechanism. This means that you can implement packet filters to protect your network without incurring massive additional expenses. Packet filtering usually does not have a major effect on the router's throughput, unless you create a large number of filtering rules. Remember that the router must process each packet individually against the filtering rules you create, and a very complex system of filters can conceivably slow the network down.

The main drawback of packet filtering is that it requires a detailed understanding of TCP/IP communications and the ways of the criminal mind. Using packet filters to protect your network means participating in an ongoing battle of wits with those who would infiltrate your network. Potential intruders are constantly inventing new techniques to defeat standard packet filter configurations, and you must be ready to modify your filters to counteract these techniques.

NAT

Network Address Translation (NAT) is a network layer technique that protects the computers on your network from Internet intruders by masking their IP addresses. If you connect a network to the Internet without firewall protection of any kind, you must use registered IP addresses for your computers so that they can communicate with other computers on the Internet. However, registered IP addresses are, by definition, visible from the Internet. This means that any user on the Internet can conceivably access your network's computers and, with a little ingenuity, gain access to any resource they wish. The results can be disastrous. NAT prevents this from happening by enabling you to assign unregistered IP addresses to your computers. Unregistered addresses are those that fall into a range of addresses specifically designated as being for use on private networks. These addresses are not registered to any Internet user, so you can safely deploy them on your network without limiting your users' access to Internet sites.

Note For more information about registered and unregistered IP addresses, see Lesson 2: IP Addressing, in Chapter 8, "TCP/IP Fundamentals."

After you assign these private IP addresses to the computers on your network, outside users can't see your computers from the Internet. However, this also means that an Internet server can't send packets to your network, which means that your users can send traffic to the Internet, but not receive it.

To make normal Internet communications possible again, the router that provides Internet access can use NAT. For example, when one of the computers on your network attempts to access an Internet server using a Web browser, the Hypertext Transfer Protocol (HTTP) request packet it generates contains its own private IP address in the IP header's Source IP Address field. When this packet reaches the router, the NAT software substitutes its own registered IP address for the client computer's private address and sends the packet on to the designated server. When the server responds, it addresses its reply to the NAT router's IP address. The router then inserts the original client's private address into the Destination IP Address field and sends the packet on to the client system. All of the packets to and from the computers on the private network are processed in this manner, using the NAT router as a middleman between the private network and the Internet. Because only the router's registered IP address is visible to the Internet, it is the only computer that is vulnerable to attack.

NAT is a popular security solution that is implemented in a great many firewall products, ranging from high-end systems used on large corporate networks to inexpensive Internet connection-sharing solutions designed for home and small business networks.

Proxy Servers

Proxy servers are software products that are similar to NAT routers, except that they function at the application layer of the OSI reference model. Like a NAT router, a proxy server acts as a middleman between the clients on a private network and the Internet resources they want to access. The clients send their requests to the proxy server and the proxy server sends a duplicate request to the desired Internet server. The Internet server replies to the proxy and the proxy relays the response to the client. This effectively renders the private network invisible to the Internet and provides other features as well.

As mentioned earlier, proxy servers can cache the information they receive from the Internet, so that if another client requests the same information, the proxy can supply it immediately from its cache instead of issuing another request to the Internet server. Administrators can also configure proxy servers to filter the traffic they receive, blocking users on the private network from accessing certain services. For example, you can configure most Web proxy servers to permit user access only to specific Web sites.

The main problem with proxy servers is that you have to configure applications to use them, using an interface like that shown in Figure 13.9. A NAT router provides protection to the network computers while remaining essentially invisible to them, but the process of configuring a client computer to use proxies for a variety of applications can be time-consuming. However, some proxy clients and servers now have automatic detection capabilities that enable a client application to discover the proxy servers on the network and use them.

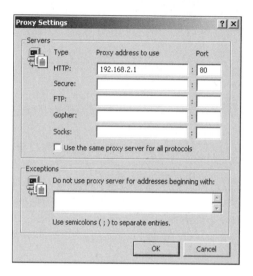

Figure 13.9 The Internet Explorer Proxy Settings dialog box

Generally speaking, proxy servers are the preferred solution when you want to impose greater restrictions on your users' Internet access, such as limiting the applications they can use to access the Internet and the sites that they are permitted to visit. NAT provides more general Internet access without any unusual client configuration, and still provides a similar degree of protection.

Chapter Summary

The key points covered in this chapter are as follows.

Password Protection

- For passwords to be an effective means of protecting network resources, users and administrators must select suitable passwords.

- Most network operating systems enable administrators to implement policies that govern how and when users should create new passwords.

- Effective passwords should be at least five or six characters long and use a combination of uppercase and lowercase letters, numbers, and symbols.

- Users should be compelled to change their passwords at regular intervals, and should not be allowed to repeatedly use the same few passwords.

- User accounts should be automatically locked out after a specified number of failed logon attempts.

Security Models

- Client/server networks store authentication data in a central database, while each computer on a peer-to-peer network maintains its own security information.

- User-level security is based on individual accounts created for each user on the network. To grant users access to network resources, you select their account names from the user list.

- Share-level security assigns passwords to specific network resources. Every-one on the network uses the same password to access a resource.

Firewalls

- Firewalls protect networks from outside interference by using a variety of techniques to limit the traffic passing between the internal network and the Internet.

- Packet filtering is a technique in which a router determines whether to allow network access to each packet, based on the contents of its protocol headers.

- NAT enables the computers on a private network to use unregistered IP addresses and still access the Internet normally, through a special router that modifies the contents of the IP header in each packet.

- Proxy servers are application-layer products that act as intermediaries between network clients and Internet servers. Client applications must be configured to use proxy servers and administrators can configure the servers to limit users' access to specific Internet resources.

Chapter Review

1. Where does a peer-to-peer network that uses user-level security store its security information?

    a. On a domain controller

    b. In a directory service

    c. On each individual computer on the network

    d. On a central server

2. Service-dependent packet filtering bases its decision to allow or deny access to a network based on what criterion?

    a. Port numbers

    b. IP addresses

    c. Hardware addresses

    d. Protocol identifiers

3. Which type of firewall operates at the application layer?

4. Which of the following is not a password characteristic enforced by the Passwords Must Meet Complexity Requirements policy?

    a. Passwords cannot contain all or part of the account's user name.

    b. Passwords must be changed weekly.

    c. Passwords must be at least six characters long.

    d. Passwords must include numerals or symbols, or both.

5. What is the maximum length of an Active Directory password?

    a. 8 characters

    b. 14 characters

    c. 24 characters

    d. 104 characters

6. NAT operates at which layer of the OSI model?

    a. The data-link layer

    b. The network layer

    c. The transport layer

    d. The application layer

7. Why does share-level security provide less protection than user-level security?

8. What does setting the Account Lock Threshold policy prevent intruders from using to penetrate your network security?

    a. Stolen passwords

    b. Illegal software

    c. The brute force method

    d. Unencrypted passwords

9. What is the main drawback to using proxy servers?

10. Where is a firewall typically located?

    a. At the boundary between your ISP's network and the Internet

    b. On your private network

    c. On the Internet

    d. At the boundary between your private network and your ISP's network

C H A P T E R   1 4

Planning the Network

About This Chapter

Planning is an essential part of any network installation or upgrade. Before you install or even select new hardware, you must think about issues such as hardware compatibility, business requirements, and ergonomics. This chapter examines some of the factors you should consider during the network planning stage and discusses how your decisions can affect your future actions.

Before You Begin

This chapter requires an understanding of a network's hardware components, as discussed in Chapter 2, "Network Hardware," and Chapter 3, "Network Connections," as well as the basics of Transmission Control Protocol/Internet Protocol (TCP/IP) communications, as covered in Chapter 8, "TCP/IP Fundamentals."

Lesson 1: Determining Network Needs

The first step in developing a network plan is to understand the requirements of the organization that will run the network and the needs of the people who will use it. After you have determined the company's requirements and the users' needs, you can set about developing a technical configuration that satisfies those requirements and needs.

After this lesson, you will be able to

- Ascertain what type of network a particular organization needs
- Evaluate the physical installation site for a network and understand how environmental conditions can affect the network planning process
- Select appropriate hardware for a network installation

Estimated lesson time: 15 minutes

Evaluating Business Requirements

The first order of business is to determine why the organization wants a new network installed. You might be providing a network for a brand new installation that has no existing equipment, or you might be asked to network a group of existing standalone computers. A third possibility is that the organization has an existing network, but it wants to upgrade it to a new or different technology. Each of these situations presents a different set of user and administrator requirements.

An organization with an existing network (or a group of computers that it wants to connect to a network) probably has some idea of what services it wants the network to provide; an organization wanting new installations might have less of an idea about what it needs. At the most basic level, businesses usually want their users to be able to access shared drives and printers and connect to the Internet. These factors alone allow the administrator to make some basic decisions. Sharing drives and printers is a fundamental networking task that almost any network technology can provide, but you know that the computers will have to run the TCP/IP protocols to access the Internet, and that you will need a router of some kind to connect the network to an Internet Service Provider (ISP).

Some organizations might have more elaborate requirements. It is also important to remember that when it comes to computers, businesspeople often know what they want but have no idea what's involved in getting it. For example, some organizations might need to maintain elaborate databases, which requires that they have powerful servers with fast processors, a lot of memory, and large hard drives. Other companies might need to work with huge graphic images or full-motion video, which requires enormous amounts of network bandwidth and a lot of storage. A financial company might want to provide its users with real-time data feeds from multiple stock markets around the world, which requires large amounts of internal bandwidth and high-speed Internet access. You need to determine what the organization wants and what they can afford, and then try to find a solution that satisfies both requirements.

In addition to talking to the heads of organizations about their network needs, it's also a good idea to spend some time in the trenches with the people who will actually be using the network. You might find out things that can affect what equipment you select for the network, where components are located, and what ergonomic factors you should consider. For example, the owner of a company might decide that three laser printers are sufficient to service all of the network's users, but it is the users who will be able to point out the best locations for the printers and explain that a printer with an envelope feeder would save a lot of time otherwise spent manually feeding envelopes.

Evaluating the Installation Site

The next step in developing a network plan is to examine the site where you plan to install the network and assess the conditions in which the equipment will operate. This site evaluation helps you to determine which basic network type you should choose, which network medium you should use, and how you should install it. With this information, you can begin to consider the requirements of your users and start to choose appropriate hardware products. Some factors that you should consider when evaluating the site are covered in the following sections.

Distances Between Components

One of the most crucial elements of the site evaluation is understanding where the various computers and other network components must be located in relation to each other. On a typical 10BaseT or 100BaseTX Ethernet network, computers can be up to 100 meters away from the hub, which is far more than is needed in the average office networking environment. However, you should be sure to consider the actual route that your cables will take, not just the distance between the components. Cables must often snake up through a wall, through ceilings, around lighting fixtures, around doorways and other obstacles, and back down through another wall to complete a connection. The final length of the cable can be much longer than just the walking distance from a computer to the hub. You'll need this information in order to know how much cable you'll need. Or, if you're going to use prefabricated cables, you'll need to know how long they have to be. In other cases, you might find yourself having to connect computers that are great distances apart, on different floors, or even in different buildings. In these circumstances, you might need to consider a fiber optic networking solution, which can span longer distances and run safely outdoors.

Another consideration is what obstacles there are between the computers that are to be connected to the network. This factor can determine what kind of cabling job is needed for the site. For example, if the network will consist of computers that are all located in a single room, you might be able to network them using prefabricated cables running loose around the perimeter of the room. This is a relatively simple project that requires no special equipment. However, if the network will be a large one; if the computers are located in many different rooms; or if the site requires the most professional appearance possible, you have to plan on an internal cable installation. This type of installation uses bulk cable, installed into ceilings and walls and connected to a central patch panel at one end and connected to individual wall plates at each of the computer locations. Internal installations require additional planning, more equipment, and greater expertise. They also add significantly to the cost of the job.

All network plans require an evaluation of the areas where the workstations and other client components will go, but on more elaborate network installations you must also consider where to put the "back end" components, such as hubs, servers, routers, and so on. In all but the smallest installation, it is important to secure this type of equipment physically, such as in a locked room or closet, so that it's protected from damage, either accidental or malicious. It's not uncommon for expensive tower servers located in public areas to be turned into stands for potted plants or targets for refrigerator magnets, or even to disappear entirely. Depending on the size of the installation, you might need several lockable closets in which to put servers, hubs, and patch panels; you might even need a full-fledged data center that contains all of these things and functions as the cabling nexus for an entire building or campus.

Ergonomics

The science of ergonomics involves more than the development of strangely shaped keyboards. Part of the job of planning a network includes selecting equipment designs that are suitable for the working environment and placing them in locations where they will provide the most utility and cause the least distraction. For example, you might be able to make one user very happy by moving the departmental laser printer off her desk and onto a printer stand in a more central location. This might mean spending a few extra dollars on an external print server device that enables you to connect the printer directly to the network cable, but if more people have more convenient access to the printer, it's probably worth it.

Another factor to consider is the selection and placement of client workstations themselves. Many of the computers designed for office use have small-footprint cases, which are either desktops or mini-towers. Even these smaller cases can occupy a lot of space on the average user's desk, and you might want to avoid this by purchasing computers that can easily be placed on the floor or that fit under or beside desks.

Environmental Conditions

In addition to the physical locations of the network components, you must also be aware of the physical environment in which they will run. This might seem unnecessary in an office building that maintains constant levels of temperature and humidity, but there are several important factors to consider. One of these factors is whether the comfortable climate you feel during working hours is maintained around the clock. Some buildings shut off the heat and air conditioning at night, and any computer equipment that is left running could easily overheat on a hot summer night in a sealed building. Excessively cold temperatures can affect the performance of computer equipment as well.

Consider also that the equipment closets in which you plan to locate your servers and other components might not be climate controlled. If you plan to create a data center containing a large number of computers, routers, and other heat-producing devices, you will probably need an independent climate control system to keep the room cool enough. A source of clean, consistent electrical power is also important. A data center might require its own electrical circuits to support a lot of equipment in a single location. If this is the case, you might also want to consider adding surge protection and even a backup power supply for the entire installation. This could include standard uninterruptible power supply (UPS) units, or even a backup generator with a fail-over switch.

Of course not every network installation is located in a comfortable office building. You might find yourself having to plan for a network that is exposed to extreme environments, such as outdoors or in industrial areas that expose the equipment to abnormal amounts of heat or cold, humidity, dust, electromagnetic interference, chemical vapors, and so forth. There are a variety of products available that enable computer networks to operate in these conditions, including waterproof keyboards, computers with air filtering systems that keep out dust and other contaminants, and networking technologies to suit a variety of conditions, such as fiber optic and wireless media.

Sources of Interference

If you will be performing an internal cable installation, you need to examine the places where the cables will run for possible obstructions and sources of interference. Copper-based cables are highly susceptible to electromagnetic fields caused by fluorescent light fixtures, electric motors, and other types of electrical equipment. Even seemingly benign factors like the locations of television sets, radios, and electric heaters can affect network performance. If you will be upgrading a network that already exists, you might find that these environmental factors are the cause of error messages or other problems the network is experiencing.

To ensure that your network is reliable, check to see that there are cable routes you can use that avoid these sources of interference. Otherwise, you might have to use cable with additional shielding, or even fiber optic cable, which is not affected by electromagnetic interference. Also, you must be aware of the fire and building codes in your area that govern the cabling process. You might need to purchase cables with a special plenum-rated sheath in order to run them through the building's ventilation spaces (which are called plenums).

> **Note** Even if you are planning to outsource the cable installation, you should be aware of conditions that can affect its cost.

Selecting Hardware

After you have determined the organization's networking needs, you can start to design the network and begin selecting the products you'll need to construct it. For a brand new network, you might be responsible for the computers themselves, and you must be careful to select models that can fully support the networking tasks expected of them. If you will be networking existing computers, consider their age and whether you need to upgrade them by adding memory or disk space. It doesn't make sense to install a state-of-the-art, high-speed network to connect a bunch of old 486 computers. Depending on the users' needs and the budget, you may have to settle for a more modest network or purchase new computers.

Hardware compatibility is always a major issue when you're planning a network, but if you will be working with existing equipment—either an existing network or a group of standalone computers—compatibility becomes even more crucial. Many of the purchasing decisions you make for network equipment will be based on the protocols you choose to run, especially at the data-link layer.

Most Ethernet products work well together, even when they're made by different manufacturers, but you still want to be sure that the products you select all support the same type of Ethernet. For example, if you're expanding an existing network, you might want to use Fast Ethernet on the new computers and upgrade the existing computers from regular Ethernet at a later time. You might purchase dual-speed network interface cards (NICs) for the new computers, but leave the 10 Mbps NICs in the older ones. In such a case, you must purchase a dual-speed hub as well because, while a Fast Ethernet hub will support the new computers at 100 Mbps, it won't support the old computers at 10 Mbps. You can't connect a 10 Mbps hub to a 100 Mbps hub, so the old and the new computers won't be able to communicate with each other. A dual-speed hub with ports that can support either Fast or regular Ethernet enables you to connect all of the computers to one network.

In addition to major compatibility issues like these, there are many small decisions you must make to ensure that all of the components of your network work together properly. For example, you must make sure that you purchase NICs that use the appropriate bus type for the computers and the correct connector for the network medium you've chosen. Also, make sure that there are NIC drivers available for the operating system you want to use. When you decide to use a particular grade of cable (such as Category 5), you must be sure that all of the cabling components that carry network signals, including connectors, wall plates, patch panels, and patch cables, are of the same grade.

Lesson 2: Providing Fault Tolerance

Many organizations rely heavily on their computers, and once the computers are networked, they come to rely on those network communications as well. Depending on the type of organization using the network, an equipment failure or other service interruption can mean lost productivity, lost revenue, and, in some cases, even lost lives. This is why many networks have some fault-tolerance mechanisms built into them. When the functions of a network are absolutely critical, such as in hospitals or airport control towers, the fault-tolerance mechanisms can be incredibly elaborate. In most cases, however, only a few key components are protected from outages due to hardware or software faults. This lesson examines some of the systems that you can use to protect a network from such disasters.

After this lesson, you will be able to

- Understand the various mechanisms used to make network data continuously available

- Describe how clustering ensures the constant availability of vital network servers

- Understand how to use redundant equipment to provide fault-tolerant network communications

Estimated lesson time: 15 minutes

Data Availability

Many organizations must have their data available all the time in order to function. If a drive on a server fails, the data should be restorable from a backup, but the time lost replacing the drive and restoring the data can mean lost productivity that costs the company dearly. To provide a higher degree of data availability, there are a variety of hardware technologies that work in different ways to ensure that network data is continuously accessible. Some of these technologies are as follows:

- **Mirroring** Disk mirroring is an arrangement by which two identical hard disk drives connected to a single host adapter always contain identical data. The two drives appear to users as one logical drive, and whenever anyone saves data to the mirror set, the computer writes it to both drives simultaneously. If one hard drive unit should fail, the other can take over immediately until the malfunctioning drive is replaced. Many operating systems, including Microsoft Windows 2000, Windows NT, and Novell NetWare, support disk mirroring. The two main drawbacks of this technique are that the server provides only half of its available disk space to users, and that while mirroring protects against a drive failure, a failure of the host adapter or the computer can still render the data unavailable.

- **Duplexing** Disk duplexing is a technique that provides a higher degree of data availability by using duplicate host adapters as well as disk drives. Identical disk drives on separate host adapters maintain exact copies of the same data, creating a single logical drive, just as in disk mirroring, but in this case, the server can survive either a disk failure or a host adapter failure and still make its data available to users.

- **Volumes** A volume is a fixed amount of data storage space on a hard disk or other storage device. On a typical computer, the hard disk drive may be broken up into multiple volumes to separate data into discrete storage units. For example, if you have a C: and a D: drive on your computer, these two letters can refer to two different hard drives or to two volumes on a single drive. Network servers function in the same way, but with greater flexibility. You can create multiple volumes on a single drive or create a single volume out of multiple drives. This latter technique is called *drive spanning*. You can use drive spanning to make all the storage space on multiple drives in a server appear to users as a single entity. The drawback of this technique is that if one of the hard drives containing part of the volume fails, the whole volume is lost.

- **Striping** Disk striping is a method by which you create a single volume by combining the storage on two or more drives and writing data alternately to each one. Normally, a spanned volume stores whole files on each disk. When you use disk striping, the computer splits each file into multiple segments and writes alternate segments to each disk. This speeds up data access by enabling one drive to read a segment while the other drive's heads are moving to the next segment. When you consider that network servers might need to process dozens of file access requests at once (from various users), the speed improvement provided by disk striping can be significant. However, striped volumes are subject to the same problem as volumes that are merely spanned. If one drive in the stripe set fails, the entire volume is lost.

- **Redundant Array of Independent Disks (RAID)** RAID is a comprehensive data availability technology with various levels that provide all of the functions described in the technologies listed earlier. For example, RAID Level 0 provides disk striping and RAID Level 1 is disk mirroring. Higher RAID levels store error correction information along with the data, so that even if a drive in a RAID array fails, its data still remains available from the other drives. RAID is available as a software product that works with standard disk drives, but many high-end servers use dedicated RAID drive arrays, which consist of multiple hard drive units in a single housing, often with hot swap capability. Hot swapping is when you can remove and replace a malfunctioning drive without shutting off the other drives in the array. This enables the data to remain continuously available to network users, even when the support staff is dealing with a drive failure.

Note None of the data availability techniques described here is intended to be a replacement for regular backups using a device such as a tape drive. For more information about backing up network data, see Lesson 1: Backups, in Chapter 16, "Network Maintenance."

Server Availability

Data availability techniques are useful, but they do no good if the server running the disks malfunctions for some other reason. In addition to specialized data availability techniques, there are similar technologies designed to make servers more reliable. For example, some servers take the concept of hot swapping to the next level by providing redundant components, such as fan assemblies and various types of drives, which you can remove and replace without shutting down the entire computer. Of course the ultimate solution for server fault tolerance is to have more than one server, and there are various solutions available that enable multiple computers to operate as one, so that if one server should fail, another can immediately take its place.

One of the first commercially successful server duplication technologies was Novell NetWare SFT III. NetWare SFT III is a version of NetWare that consists of two copies of the network operating system, plus a proprietary hardware connection that is used to link the two separate server computers, as shown in Figure 14.1. The servers run an application that synchronizes their activities. When a user saves data to one server volume, for example, the data is written to both servers at the same time. If one of the servers should malfunction for any reason, the other server instantaneously takes its place.

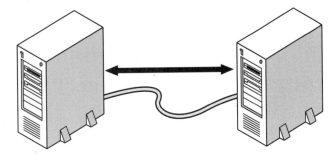

Figure 14.1 NetWare SFT III connects two servers, using one as a failover backup to the other.

SFT III was designed solely to provide fault tolerance, but the next generation of this technology does more. *Clustering* is a technique for interconnecting multiple computers to form a unified computing resource (see Figure 14.2). In addition to providing fault tolerance, a cluster can also distribute the processing load for specific tasks among the various computers or balance the processing load by allocating client requests to different computers in turn. To increase the speed and efficiency of the cluster, administrators can simply connect another computer to the group, which adds its capabilities to those of the others. Both Microsoft and Novell support clustering, Microsoft with Windows 2000 and Novell with NetWare Cluster Services for NetWare 5.1.

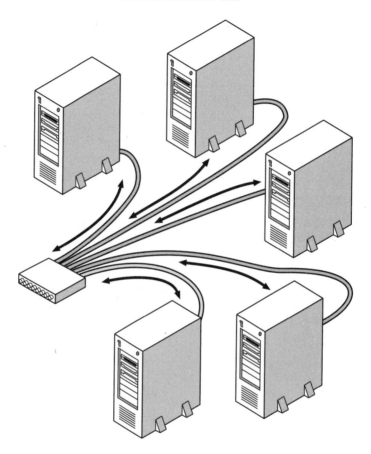

Figure 14.2 A server cluster provides fault tolerance, load balancing, and process distribution services.

Network Redundancy

Service interruptions on a network are not always the result of a computer or drive failure. Sometimes the network itself is to blame. For this reason, many larger internetworks are designed with redundant components that enable traffic to reach a given destination in more than one way. If a network cable is cut or broken, or if a router or switch fails, redundant equipment enables data to take another path to its destination. There are several ways to provide redundant paths. Typically, you have at least two routers or switches connected to each network, so that the computers can use either one as a gateway to the other segments. For example, you can build an internetwork with two backbones, as shown in Figure 14.3. Each workstation can use either of the routers on its local segment as a gateway. You can also use this arrangement to balance the traffic on the two backbones by configuring half of the computers on each local area network (LAN) to use one of the routers as its default gateway and the other half to use the other router.

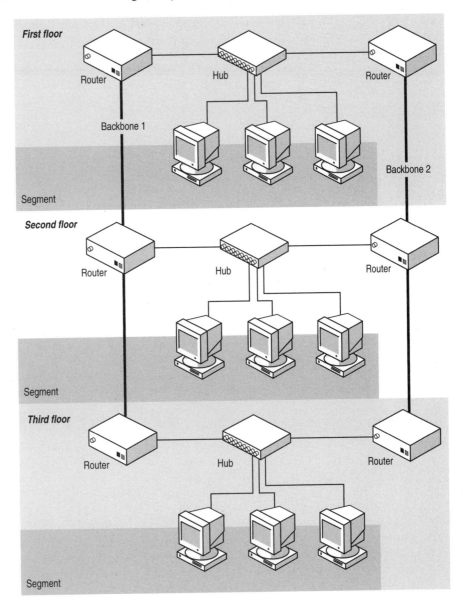

Figure 14.3 Building a network with two backbones provides both fault tolerance and load balancing.

Exercise 14.1: Data Availability Technologies

Which of the disk technologies (mirroring, duplexing, spanning, or striping) applies to each of the following statements?

1. Enables a server to survive a drive failure
2. Uses multiple hard drives to create a single logical hard drive
3. Enables a server to survive a disk host adapter failure
4. Stores a single file on multiple drives
5. Causes an entire volume to be lost when one drive fails

Lesson 3: Collecting Essential Information

When you have determined the needs of the network you intend to build and have selected the hardware components you will use to build it, it's time to begin assembling the information you'll need during the installation and documenting the administration policies for the network. Many network administrators create a great deal of additional work for themselves by letting the configuration of the network evolve on its own. To facilitate the support process throughout the life of the network, the best course of action is to set policies and create workstation configurations now, before everyone gets used to doing things in certain ways. This lesson examines some of the information you'll need to gather to perform the network installation and some of the standard policies you should establish and document.

After this lesson, you will be able to

- List the elements of a standardized workstation configuration
- Understand the TCP/IP configuration decisions you have to make before installing a network
- Develop a plan for the creation of computer names, as well as user and group accounts

Estimated lesson time: 10 minutes

Standardizing Workstation Configurations

Allowing individual users to install and configure their own software might make them happy at first, but when something goes wrong later on, it will be you, the network administrator, who will be responsible for fixing it. If you don't know anything about the configuration of the user's workstation, your job will be that much harder. That's why it is a good idea to create a standard workstation configuration for your users, so that all of their computers are functionally the same. A workstation configuration can include any or all of the following elements:

- Which applications are installed
- Where the applications are installed
- Where the user will store data files
- Drive letter mappings for shared network drives
- Local drive sharing parameters
- Printer connections

The ideal situation when deploying new network workstations is to make them completely identical, except for obvious parameters such as computer names and IP addresses, which must be unique. Many administrators use a disk imaging program to build new workstations, which creates bit-for-bit copies of a drive's contents, which makes it possible to create identically configured computers with a minimum of effort. Of course, you might have users with different requirements, which means that you might need to create several different workstation configurations. The point is, you need to know exactly how a computer should be configured, so that when a problem arises as a result of a hardware failure or user error, you can easily correct it and, in the worst-case scenario, completely restore the computer to its base configuration.

Selecting TCP/IP Parameters

Configuring TCP/IP clients is one of the most problematic aspects of building a new network, because you can't create the exact same configuration for every workstation. Every computer on the network must have its own unique IP address, and other parameters, such as the default gateway, can vary depending on the location of the computer.

The first part of developing a TCP/IP configuration for your network is to determine what IP addresses you intend to use. The IP addresses you assign to your computers depend on many factors, including the following:

- How many computers there are
- How many network segments there are
- Whether you will be connecting the network to the Internet
- How you will connect the network to the Internet
- Whether your new computers must interact with existing ones

In most cases, it's a good idea to use private, unregistered network addresses for your computers, such as those listed in Lesson 2: IP Addressing, in Chapter 8, "TCP/IP Fundamentals." This is especially true when you will connect the network to the Internet, because using these addresses protects the computers from unauthorized access. To use private addresses on an Internet-connected network, you must have some mechanism that enables the users to access Internet services, such as Network Address Translation (NAT) or a proxy server. If, on the other hand, you want to use registered IP addresses (thus making your computers visible from the Internet), you must obtain a range of addresses from your ISP.

In addition to deciding which IP addresses should be assigned, you must also decide what routers your workstations should use as their default gateways, which Domain Name System (DNS) servers they should use, and whether you should run Windows Internet Naming Service (WINS). After you have determined what parameters you will be assigning to each workstation, you must create individual address assignments for each computer and devise a means to keep track of them. You will probably be adding more computers to the network someday, and you will need to know then which addresses are available.

The most convenient method for assigning and tracking TCP/IP configuration parameters is to use the Dynamic Host Configuration Protocol (DHCP). Even if you want to assign a specific address to each computer permanently, DHCP is an excellent tool for keeping track of the assignments and determining which computer is using which address.

Note For more information about configuring TCP/IP clients, see Chapter 11, "TCP/IP Configuration." For more information about securing your network using NAT and proxy servers, see Lesson 3: Firewalls, in Chapter 13, "Network Security."

Creating Accounts

Other important elements of network configuration that you should plan in advance are the computer names, user account names, and passwords you intend to use. The best way to assign computer names and account names is to develop a formula and stick to it. For example, you can create computer names using codes to represent the subnet on which the computer is located or the physical location of the computer in the building. For example, 3FLRNW9 might represent computer number nine in the northwest corner of the building's third floor. It's usually not a good idea to assign computer names based on the names of their users, because people have a way of coming and going, and you don't want to have to change the name of the computer whenever someone new uses it.

For user account names, some combination of the user's initials and several letters of the first and last name is appropriate. For example, using the first initial and the first five letters of the surname makes David Jaffe's user name DJAFFE. In smaller companies, you might want to use the first name and last initial, as in DAVIDJ, but that can tend to cause conflicts when you have David Jaffe and David Johnson working in the same department.

You also have to set a policy regarding the administrative accounts for your network and their passwords. Depending on the network operating system you intend to use and the network configuration, you might need to create individual administrative accounts on many different computers (or possibly all of them). It's a good idea to use the same password for these accounts, so that you don't find yourself locked out while you look up one of a hundred passwords.

In addition to creating individual user accounts, you must also decide what groups or organizational units you want to create to administer the accounts most efficiently. If you will be using a hierarchical directory service, such as the Microsoft Active Directory directory service or Novell Directory Services (NDS), planning the directory tree is a complex undertaking (see Lesson 3: Directory Services, in Chapter 4, "Networking Software," for more information).

Note Passwords are another issue to consider at this stage of the planning process. If you intend to allow your users to select their own passwords, you might want to set policies to enforce suitable selections. For more information about password protection, see Lesson 1: Password Protection, in Chapter 13, "Network Security."

Chapter Summary

The key points covered in this chapter are as follows.

Determining Network Needs

- Consult with both management and staff to determine what network services are required.

- Examine the site where the network is to be located to determine which technologies are most suitable for the installation.

- Check distances between network components, environmental conditions, local building codes, and possible sources of structural and electromagnetic interference; all these factors can affect how you install the network.

- Select network hardware carefully, ensuring that all of the products are compatible.

Providing Fault Tolerance

- Networks often use data storage techniques such as mirroring, duplexing, spanning, striping, and RAID to increase the efficiency and fault tolerance of the network storage subsystem.

- Redundant servers, possibly configured in clusters, enable a network to survive even a major server failure without interrupting user productivity.

- Creating redundant paths through the network enable communications to continue, even in the event of a cable break or a router failure.

Collecting Essential Information

- Before installing the network, you must decide what IP addresses you will use, and how you will assign them.

- Devising a formula for the creation of computer names and user accounts is a good way to prevent difficulties later.

Chapter Review

1. Name three physical characteristics you should evaluate during your inspection of the network installation site.

2. Name one method you can use to connect a network that uses private, unregistered IP addresses to the Internet.

3. List five environmental factors that you should check while inspecting a network site.

4. Which is the most practical network medium to use when connecting computers that are all fewer than 100 meters apart, but located in two buildings?

   a. Unshielded twisted pair cable

   b. Shielded twisted pair cable

   c. Fiber optic cable

   d. Wireless

5. Which of the following storage services is not provided by RAID?

   a. Data striping

   b. Tape backup

   c. Disk mirroring

   d. Error correction

6. Which service do you use to assign IP addresses to your network workstations?

   a. DHCP

   b. DNS

   c. WINS

   d. NAT

7. What is the primary reason for developing standardized workstation configurations?

8. What services does a cluster of servers provide that Novell's NetWare SFT III does not?

9. Name two applications that can cause a network to require larger than normal amounts of bandwidth.

10. What additional hardware can you install to create redundant paths through the network?

    a. NICs

    b. Hubs

    c. Servers

    d. Routers

C H A P T E R   1 5

Installing a Network

About This Chapter

Once you have designed the network and selected the hardware you'll need, it's time to proceed with the installation. This chapter discusses how to install network cables and use them to connect your computers with other components to form a local area network (LAN).

Before You Begin

This chapter requires an understanding of the cable types and topologies used in LANs, as explained in Lesson 1: Network Cables, in Chapter 2, "Network Hardware," as well as the basic functions of network interface adapters and hubs, as discussed in Lesson 2 and Lesson 3 of that chapter.

Lesson 1: Pulling Cable

Installing network cables is often called "pulling cable," because the process can involve threading one end of a cable through a wall or ceiling and then pulling the rest of the cable through from the other end. Depending on the type of cable involved and the nature of the site, installing cable can be very simple or extraordinarily complex. This lesson concentrates primarily on the installation of unshielded twisted pair (UTP) cable, which is by far the most popular network medium used today.

After this lesson, you will be able to

- Describe how to install cables externally, secure them in place, and run them around common obstacles
- Explain the steps involved in an internal cable installation
- List the different techniques used when installing different types of cables

Estimated lesson time: 30 minutes

External Installations

An external installation is one in which you use prefabricated UTP cables and run them from each computer to the hub, inside the room where the equipment is located. You don't have to run cables through walls or ceilings, attach connectors, or purchase additional hardware, such as wall plates and patch panels. External installations are also portable; you can coil up the cables and take them with you if you have to move the network. The drawbacks of an external installation are that the cables are often left visible, and the obstacles lying between the various pieces of network equipment can make running the cable difficult. However, there are steps you can take that help to minimize these drawbacks.

The fundamental parts of an external cable installation are as follows. (More detailed information about the individual steps of the procedure is provided later in this lesson.)

1. Select the locations for your computers (and other network-connected devices, such as printers) and your hub. The hub should be in a central location relative to the computers, both to keep your cable lengths to a minimum and to avoid having too many cables running along the same route.

2. Plan the exact route for each of your cables from the computer (or other device) to the hub. Examine all of the obstacles, such as furniture, doorways, and walls, found on each route and plan how you are going to run your cables around them or through them.

3. Measure each of your routes from the computer to the hub, taking the entire path of the cable into account, including vertical runs around doorways, paths through walls, and other obstacles. Leave at least a few extra yards of slack to compensate for unforeseen obstacles and adjustments in the location of the computer or hub.

4. Purchase prefabricated cables of the appropriate lengths (and possibly colors) for each of your runs. If you're installing UTP cable, make sure that all of the cables you purchase are rated at least Category 5. It is a good idea to use molded boots on the cable connectors to protect them from damage.

5. Lay out the cable loosely for each of your cable runs, without connecting them to the equipment or securing them to the walls. Be sure to leave enough slack to reach around doorways or other obstacles and at each end, so that the connectors can reach the computer and the hub comfortably.

6. Starting at one end of each cable run, secure the cable to the walls, floor, or woodwork, working your way to the other end. Make sure that none of the cables is compressed or kinked anywhere along its length, and that all cables are protected from damage caused by foot traffic or furniture.

7. When the cables are secured, plug one end of each cable run into the hub and the other end into the computer or other device. When the hub is connected to a power source and the computer is turned on, the link pulse lights in the hub and the computer's network interface adapter (if any) should light up, indicating a proper connection.

The network that is most obviously suitable for an external cable installation is one in which all of the computers and other devices are located in the same room. A one-room network eliminates the single biggest problem of external cable installations, which is having to run cables between rooms, or worse, between floors. For a small, one-room network, you can generally run the cables around the room next to the walls, securing them to the baseboard or running them behind furniture, as shown in Figure 15.1. You can purchase prefabricated UTP cables in a variety of colors, to match your décor and keep the installation as discreet as possible.

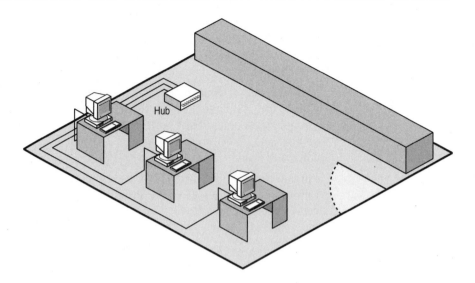

Figure 15.1 A simple external installation runs cables around the perimeter of the room.

Caution One thing you want to avoid in any cable installation is a loose cable running across a floor. Not only is this a hazard to foot traffic, but stepping on cables can eventually damage them, generating intermittent network outages that are difficult to troubleshoot.

Problems arise if you have to run cables to computers or other devices that are located in the center of the room, and not next to a wall. There are several solutions to this, depending on your environment. You can buy rubber cable protectors that run across the floor; a cross-section of two cable protectors is shown in Figure 15.2. These provide a safe conduit for the cable and prevent people from tripping over it. You can also run prefabricated cables through a drop ceiling and down through a ceiling tile to the appropriate location on the floor. This can look odd, although it is possible to purchase thin floor-to-ceiling service poles that provide a safe cable conduit and a neater appearance. When you begin thinking about running cables through the ceiling, however, you should consider whether an internal installation might be a better idea.

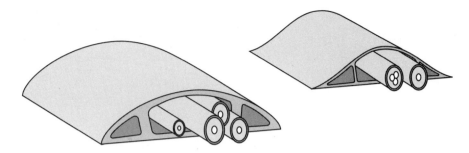

Figure 15.2 Rubber cable protectors might be unsightly, but in situations where you must run cables across the floor, they provide effective protection.

Securing External Cables

Although it's possible to run your cables around a room and leave them loose, it's a good idea to secure them in place. Securing the cables ensures that they won't move into a high-traffic area where they can be trodden on or otherwise damaged. It also prevents people from accidentally yanking on the cable, which can damage the connectors. There are a number of hardware solutions you can use to secure your cables in place. However, you should first lay out your cables in the exact route from one connection to the other. Don't fasten the cables as you run them or you run the risk of falling short of the destination and starting over.

Stapling cables to walls or baseboards is the simplest—and usually the least expensive—solution. However, do not use the standard square staples shot out of most staple guns because they can crush the cable and damage the wires within it. Instead, buy individual staples. An individual staple either has a cap at the top that simplifies the task of hammering it into the wall, or it has a cable holder that consists of a semicircular plastic sleeve with a wire brad through it. Hammering the brad into the wall anchors the sleeve with the open end into the wall, as shown in Figure 15.3.

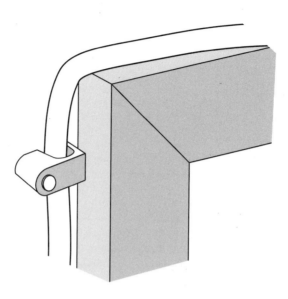

Figure 15.3 Individual staples hold cables securely to a surface without squeezing the sheath.

If you have a sufficient amount of cable to install, it might be worth the expense to buy a staple gun designed specifically for cable installations, like the one shown in Figure 15.4. This type of staple gun shoots round-headed staples and has an adjustable depth setting. The idea is for the staples to be well secured in the wall while the cable can be pulled through them freely. If the cable cannot move laterally through the staple, the staple is secured too tightly. Also, if you accidentally pierce the cable sheath with a staple, you should start over with a new cable. While this type of stapler might not be available at your local home center, computer dealers that carry bulk cable and other network cabling supplies often have them. A good stapler of this type can use square as well as round-topped staples, so it's not completely useless for doing other jobs.

Figure 15.4 A cable stapler shoots round-headed staples and has an adjustable depth setting.

Another option for securing cables in place is to use cable ties, which are loops of plastic or fabric that secure to a surface. They can hold one or more cables. Some of these products use a nylon hook-and-ratchet design (much like the flexible handcuffs that police use) and often come with an eyelet for nailing the tie to a wall. Others consist of a wider loop of cloth or plastic whose ends are attached using a hook and loop fastener, such as Velcro. An example of a cable tie is shown in Figure 15.5. Such ties are more visible than staples, and they are more often used to secure bundles of cables in place. An advantage of the Velcro ties is that they can be opened so you can add more cables as your network grows.

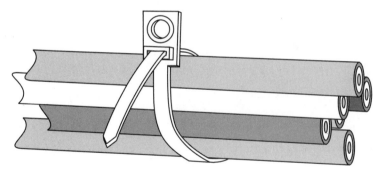

Figure 15.5 A cable tie

Tip Both staples and cable ties are excellent solutions for securing cables to a wall or other surface, but they don't provide any protection from objects that might bump into the wall and squeeze the cable. If at all possible, you should secure the cables in such a way as to make it difficult for furniture or other objects to come into contact with the cables.

Another option for securing cables that also provides better protection than staples or cable ties is called a raceway. A *raceway* is a small enclosed conduit, usually made of plastic, that holds cables inside and is designed to run along walls. Some raceways screw to the wall, while others have an adhesive backing; the screw-in models are definitely more secure. Because the raceway completely encloses the cables within a rigid housing, they are protected from bumps and abrasions.

Raceways are more expensive and more difficult to install than staples or cable ties. Because raceways are rigid, you have to purchase fittings of exactly the right size and shape, but they allow you to run the cables up and down walls or around corners or doorways while completely enclosing them. The products are usually modular, meaning that you can buy straight runs, corners, and other components separately, all of which fit together, as shown in Figure 15.6. Raceway products usually come in a limited range of colors; most are a neutral putty color, which, depending on your décor, may or may not be very noticeable.

Tip In some cases, you can also get surface-mounted connection boxes that attach to the raceway, enabling you to run bulk cable and connect it directly to the jacks in the boxes. This is the functional equivalent of an internal installation without having to run cables inside walls or ceilings. If you are installing a network in a building with cinderblock walls, for example, this could be your only option for a bulk cable installation.

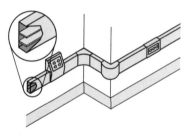

Figure 15.6 Raceways completely enclose cables and protect them from damage.

Running Cables Around Doors

One of the most common obstacles encountered during a one-room external cable installation is a doorway. Generally speaking, if you can avoid doorways by running your cables the long way around the room, you should do so, even if it means using a longer cable. However, sometimes you have no choice other than to run the cable past a doorway, and this leaves you two options. You can run the cable up and around the door or you can run it on the floor along the doorway's threshold.

In most cases, you should avoid the latter option. Even if you secure the cable to the floor very well, you expose it to repeated compressions from foot traffic that can eventually damage the wires inside. It is better to run the cable underneath the threshold. If there is a threshold in the doorway that you can remove temporarily, you can route the cable underneath it, as long as there are no sharp edges exposed that might cut the cable sheath.

Most of the time, however, you will have to run your cable up and over the doorway, using staples to hold it in place, as shown in Figure 15.7. This is usually not a difficult task, especially if there is a wooden molding around the doorway, but it can be unsightly because it brings the cables up to eye level. You might want to try to find cabling in a color that closely matches the walls, or even paint over the cable after it's installed.

Running multiple cables over a single doorway can be even more problematic. You might want to consider adding an additional hub to your network so that you can get by with only one cable over the doorway, or you might use a raceway large enough to hold multiple cables.

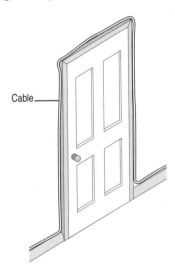

Cable

Figure 15.7 Staple cables securely around a doorway rather than routing the cable on the floor across the doorway.

Warning Running cable around a doorway adds significantly to its length, so be sure to factor doorways into your cable length estimations.

Running Cables to Other Rooms

When you have computers in different rooms, even an external installation can become complicated. There are generally two ways to get a cable from one room to another: through the door or through the wall. While running cable on the floor across a doorway causes problems, running cable through a doorway is often an acceptable solution. To run cable through a doorway, there must be sufficient space between the bottom of the door and the floor for the cable to pass through, even when the door is closed.

Running a cable through a wall is also an acceptable solution, even if it isn't strictly an external installation. The best course of action is to select a spot on the wall that's covered by furniture in both rooms and drill a hole from one room to the other that is large enough to pass the cable through. When you're running a prefabricated cable through a wall, drill holes that are large enough for the connector to pass through. Taping one end of the cable to a length of straightened wire coat hanger makes it easier to thread the cable through the wall to the other side.

Warning When drilling through walls, be sure to avoid any cables or pipes that might be inside the wall. While it might be tempting to use a very long drill bit to go through both sides of the wall at once, it is usually safer to drill a hole in one side, and use a long screwdriver to probe around inside the wall and poke a hole through the far wall on the other side. Using this method, you won't accidentally drill through a vital service connection. This also ensures that the holes in both sides of the wall line up properly.

Running Cables Between Floors

In many cases, the most difficult type of internal installation is one that has to span two or more floors of the same building. It can be difficult to find an appropriate place to run the cables, and the installation might require special tools. In a wooden structure, drilling a hole in the floor is relatively easy, but you must carefully plan the location of the hole from both above and below, so that you don't end up with a cable hanging down through the middle of a ceiling. If both floors have walls in the same places, you can sometimes drill through the floor inside a wall, using your wall plate holes for access to the interior of the wall. This might require a special drill with a right-angle chuck and a long bit, or you might be able to drill up through the floor from below. One method of finding the proper location for the hole is to drill a one–eighth-inch-diameter hole down through the floor next to the wall and push a bent coat hanger through to mark the location. From the floor below, find the protruding coat hanger, measure about 2 inches from your first hole in the direction of the wall, and drill a three–quarter-inch hole upward, as shown in Figure 15.8. You should then be able to push your cable up through the floor and grab it from above. As always, make sure that you don't disturb any of the building's service connections in the process.

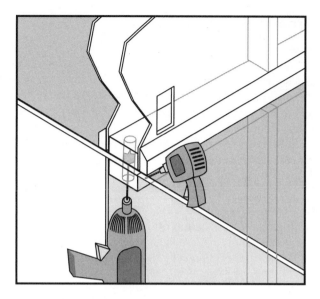

Figure 15.8 Running cables up through a floor into the interior of a wall can be tricky, but it makes for a neater installation.

In an office building, you are more likely to find some sort of conduit between floors that you can use to run your cables. In some cases, this conduit can also be an air space that is part of the building's ventilation system. If this is so, be sure you use the proper cable for the installation. Your local building codes might require a plenum-rated cable, and failure to use the correct cable can result in penalties and a forced reinstallation. If no such conduit exists, however, you might have a difficult time because the floors in commercial office buildings are often made of concrete that is several inches thick. Drilling through it might require heavy tools and a consultation with an engineer and building inspector.

Note For more information about plenum cables, see Lesson 1: Network Cables, in Chapter 2, "Network Hardware."

Internal Installations

Most professional cable installations are internal, meaning that all of the cables are run inside walls, ceilings, or floors. Unlike an external installation, which typically uses a single prefabricated cable to run from each computer all the way to the hub, an internal cable installation splits the connection into three parts, as shown in Figure 15.9. The main part of the connection is a length of bulk cable that runs from a wall plate in the vicinity of each computer's location to a patch panel at the location of the hub. The other two elements are relatively short, prefabricated cables called *patch cables*, which connect the computer to the wall plate and the patch panel jack to a hub port.

Note This lesson deals with the process of pulling the cable from the location of the wall plate to the location of the patch panel. For more information about wall plates, patch panels, and connecting cables to them, see Lesson 2: Making Connections, later in this chapter.

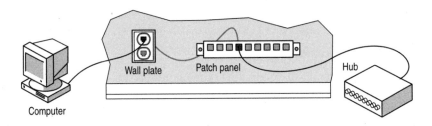

Figure 15.9 Each internal cable connection consists of three parts: a bulk cable connection inside the walls and two patch cables.

Internal installations use bulk cable, which is a long, unbroken length of cable, usually stored on a large spool, with no connectors attached, as shown in Figure 15.10. The installer pulls off as much as is needed for a particular run, cuts it off the spool, and attaches the ends to the wall plate jacks and the patch panel jacks. Prefabricated, or patch, cables are relatively short in length and already have the RJ45 connectors attached. You can also purchase modular RJ45 connectors and attach them to lengths of bulk cable yourself, to make your own patch cables. This enables you to use only as much cable as you actually need, which is often considerably less than when you use prefabricated cables.

To use bulk cable, you must have the appropriate tools and fittings to attach connectors to both ends. The advantages of bulk cabling are that it is easier to pull the cable without the connectors attached to it, you have greater flexibility in the types of connectors you use, and you save money by purchasing cable in large quantities.

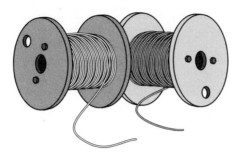

Figure 15.10 Bulk cable on spools

Cable intended for use as a patch cable or an external cable is generally made from stranded wire, which allows the cable to be more flexible, but makes it difficult to use for internal cable installations, which rely on punchdown connections (described below). Cable for internal installations generally uses solid wire conductors, which work well with the punchdown connectors. Solid wire cable is a bit less expensive than stranded wire cable, and is more resistant to attenuation, enabling you to have longer cable runs.

Note Although the Ethernet guidelines specify that you can have cable runs of up to 100 meters between a computer and a hub, you rarely if ever see a prefabricated cable that long. One reason for this is because stranded wire is used in prefabricated cables. For cable runs longer than 30 meters, you should always use a solid wire cable. It is also possible to purchase prefabricated solid wire cables from some specialty vendors.

Most internal cabling jobs are performed by professionals who specialize in data and telephone cabling. As mentioned earlier, in new construction, both data and telephone cable systems are often installed simultaneously. Pulling cable for this type of installation is not especially difficult, but it helps to have the proper tools and a strong sense of organization. When installing a large network, all those cables running through the same ceiling system tend to look alike, so it's important to proceed systematically and label each cable run carefully. That way you don't have to retrace your steps later.

The basic steps involved in installing internal cable runs are as follows:

1. Select the locations for your computers and other network-connected devices and a central, protected location for your hubs and patch panel. One end of all your cable runs will terminate at the patch panel, so be sure to select a location with sufficient access to the entire site, away from possible sources of electromagnetic interference, and with room to work easily.

2. Plan the routes for your cables from the patch panel to the location of each wall plate or other connector, taking into account all obstacles, such as barrier walls, light fixtures, and plenums.

3. With your spool of bulk cable located at the patch panel site, label the lead end of the cable with its intended location.

4. Feed the lead end of the bulk cable into the ceiling, wall, or floor into which you will install it and pull the cable to the location of the wall plate. Do not cut the cable off the spool until you have pulled it all the way to the wall plate. Leave several yards of slack inside the ceiling, wall, or floor, to avoid problems making the connections or locating the equipment.

5. Secure the cables in place along their routes, so that they can't shift their locations or be damaged by other people working in the same area.

6. Label the end of the cable with the name of the wall plate location and cut the cable from the spool. Never cut an unlabeled cable from the spool.

7. Proceed with the cable connection process, as detailed in the next lesson.

To a large extent, how difficult an internal cabling job is depends on the construction of the site. The typical office building, with plasterboard walls and drop ceilings, is an ideal environment for cable installation. You can usually run the cables freely through the ceiling to any room on the floor, and then drop them down inside the walls to a wall plate at almost any location. Of course, these projects rarely come off without a hitch, and there are a variety of barriers that the cable installer might encounter. These barriers can include sources of electromagnetic interference that can disturb data signals, fire breaks that prevent you from running cable down from the ceiling, asbestos insulation, service components such as ventilation ducts and light fixtures, and structural components, such as concrete pilings and steel girders. All of these obstructions should have been detected during the planning stage, however, and you should have established a proper route around or through them for each cable run.

Warning You should never cut, drill through, or in any way disturb a structural member of a building without consulting someone with full knowledge of the consequences. Apart from engineering concerns, there are local fire laws and building codes to consider. Violating them means that you, the installer, might be held responsible, not only for making the job right later, but for any fines and penalties that may apply.

In other types of buildings, you might run into conditions that make an internal cable installation difficult, if not impossible. If there is no access to the interiors of ceilings or walls, consider other solutions, such as an under floor cable installation or the surface-mounted raceways described earlier in this lesson.

Installing a Cable Run

When installing multiple cable runs, you typically start at the location of the patch panel, which is where one end of all the cable runs will terminate. The other ends can be spread out all over the floor, but one end of all these cables come together at this one point. With your spool of bulk cable at the patch panel location, you typically proceed by stripping a few yards of cable off the spool, threading it through the ceiling to the proper location, leaving sufficient extra cable to reach the locations of the connectors, and only then cutting it off the spool. Be sure to label each end with a piece of tape or some other type of tag, so that you can tell which cable is which. It is essential that you have a master diagram of the space with all of the cable runs and their names. This is important not only for installation, but for troubleshooting afterward.

Tip It's a good idea to leave some extra slack in your cable runs, which can be hidden inside a wall or ceiling, in case someone wants to move the location of the wall plate or patch panel later.

The process of pulling the cable through the ceiling space is the actual work of installing cable. The process goes much more smoothly when there are at least two people working together, so that one person can pass the cable inside the drop ceiling to the other person. The tools involved in this process are simple but essential. Several ladders are a must, of course, but beyond that you might be surprised to see what other tools professional installers use to pull cable.

A simple ball of string is often the cable installer's most valuable tool. If you have multiple cable runs going to destinations that are close together, you can tape one end of a length of string to the leading end of your cable. After you get the cable to its destination, you can tape the other end of the string to another cable and pull it through the ceiling to the same destination. There are also pre-fabricated cable pullers that you can buy, as shown in Figure 15.11, which might make the job a little bit easier.

For moving the cable through the ceiling, you can stick to the basic "coil and throw" technique: a person on one ladder coils up a length of cable and throws it to a person on another ladder some distance away. Throwing the cable inside a small ceiling space can be difficult, however, and installers have come up with other methods, some of which are quite ingenious.

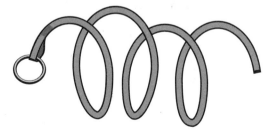

Figure 15.11 A cable puller allows you to attach multiple cables, and pull them all through a ceiling, wall, or floor at once.

The "official" tool for extending cable through ceiling spaces is called a telepole. A *telepole* is a telescoping pole, rather like a collapsible fishing rod, with a hook at one end to which you connect a cable (see Figure 15.12). You carry the collapsed telepole with the attached cable into the ceiling; you then extend the pole and hand off the cable end to the next person down the line. This is a brilliant idea, but the telepole is a specialized piece of equipment that many installers find they don't really need. Many installers use yardsticks or flexible nylon rods that they push through the ceiling. With a little practice, even a tennis ball with one end of a length of string taped to it makes an effective cabling tool. Simply throw the ball through the ceiling and use the string to pull a cable through along the same route.

Figure 15.12 By connecting one end of a cable to the hook on a telepole, you can easily push it through wall or ceiling spaces.

Securing Cables

It's just as important to secure internally installed cables as it is to secure external ones. The object here is not so much cosmetic as it is to prevent the cables from being moved. Remember that you might not be the only person that goes poking around inside the drop ceiling. Maintenance people have access to light fixtures, ventilation ducts, or other components, and securing your cables makes sure that they don't get moved closer to possible sources of damage or interference. Another advantage of a drop ceiling is that the framework used to suspend the ceiling panels provides many places to secure cables. Nylon cable ties are good for this purpose, as are the plastic ties that sometimes come with trash bags.

Dropping Cables

After you have pulled the cable to the approximate location of the computer or other device it will connect to, drop it down inside the wall where you want to affix the wall plate. Most commercial office buildings use metal studs and do not have horizontal cross members inside the walls, which makes it relatively easy to drop cables to wall plate locations down near the floor. In most cases, vertical cable drops are easily accomplished. Cut a hole in the wall where you will install the wall plate, thread the cable down inside the wall from the ceiling, and pull the cable out through the hole. Later, you attach the cable to the connector in the wall plate, push the excess cable back into the wall, and plug the hole by mounting the wall plate over it.

If you encounter a horizontal barrier inside a wall that prevents the cable from dropping down to the location of the wall plate, you have several options. One option is to cut another hole in the wall to drill through the barrier. This is more feasible if the barrier is wood and not metal, but in any case, you will have to patch the wall afterward. Another option is to move the wall plate to the left or right and hope you find a passage in the wall that isn't blocked. As a last resort, you can entirely avoid dropping the cable inside the wall by installing a raceway from the ceiling down to a surface-mounted connection box. This is not as neat as a true internal cable run, but it's better than leaving a loose cable hanging from the ceiling.

As with horizontal cable runs, there are special tools that can make the process of dropping a cable easier. A *fish tape* is a flexible band of metal or fiberglass that winds up on a reel and has a hook on the end, much like a plumber's snake. You push the tape up to the ceiling through the hole in the wall, attach the cable to the hook, and pull it down and out through the hole. You can also run the tape down and out through the hole to pull a cable up to the ceiling, or through the ceiling to the floor above, as shown in Figure 15.13. Many professional installers have devised their own tools for catching hold of cables inside walls. You can probably make do with a bent coat hanger most of the time.

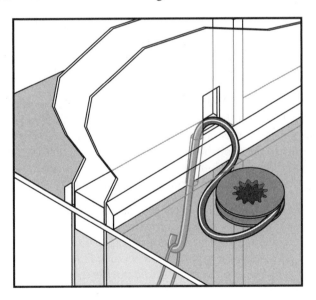

Figure 15.13 You can use a fish tape to pull cables up and down inside walls.

Depending on where and how you will be installing your patch panel, you might have to drop the other end of your cable runs down through a wall as well. Smaller networks often use patch panels that mount on a wall, and you can drop the cables down to a hole that will eventually be located behind the mounted panel. Larger networks might use rack-mounted equipment, in which case the cables can drop down from an open ceiling into the back of the rack assembly.

Pulling Other Cable Types

UTP cable is easy to install because it is thin and quite flexible. Other types of cable have different properties, however, that can make the process of pulling cable more difficult. The RG58 coaxial cable used for Thin Ethernet networks is roughly the same diameter as UTP, but it is heavier and much less flexible. Therefore, while it is possible to install this type of cable internally, it tends not to bend around corners as tightly.

The biggest problem with an internal coaxial installation is the fact that Thin Ethernet networks use a bus topology. This means that you must pull one length of cable to each computer and then pull another length of cable from that computer to the next one. Two cables must protrude from the wall to a T-connector mounted on the computer's network interface adapter in order to connect it to the network properly.

Note For more information about coaxial cable and the bus topology, see Lesson 1: Network Cables, in Chapter 2, "Network Hardware."

Thick Ethernet networks use RG8 coaxial cable, which is nearly half an inch thick and very inflexible. This type of cable is hardly ever used today, but even in its heyday it was rarely installed internally. The main advantage of Thick Ethernet to the cable installer is that each computer uses a separate cable that connects the network interface card (NIC) to the main RG8 trunk. Therefore, only one cable has to protrude through the wall.

Pulling fiber optic cable is roughly similar to pulling UTP. The multimode fiber used for most LAN connections is reasonably flexible, but because of the nature of the medium, the placement of the cable must be more precise with respect to the bend radius as it turns around corners. One advantage of fiber optic cable is that it is immune to electromagnetic interference, so many of the obstacles around which you must normally route copper-based cables, such as fluorescent light fixtures, are of no consequence in a fiber optic installation.

Moving On

It's a good idea to pull all of your cable runs before you begin making connections to wall plates and patch panels. This enables you to move cables as needed and bundle them together before they are permanently affixed. When you perform an installation this way, however, you must be extra careful to label all your cables at both ends, so that when you make your connections, you're certain which cable you're holding.

After all the cables are pulled, you're ready to begin making the connections. This process is discussed in the next lesson.

Exercise 15.1: Internal and External Cabling

For each of the following network scenarios, state whether you would perform an internal or external cable installation, and give a reason why.

1. A 10-node UTP network installed in a temporary office space by a seasonal business

2. A 100-node corporate UTP network being installed in a newly constructed office building

3. A 50-node Thick Ethernet network being moved to a new location

Lesson 2: Making Connections

After you have all your cable runs in place, you're ready to make the connections so that the computers can communicate with each other through the hubs. Depending on the type of cable installation you've performed—internal or external—the connection process can be extremely simple or quite complex. In come cases, you must be familiar with the function of each wire inside the UTP cable, while in others you never have to see the wires at all.

After this lesson, you will be able to

- Describe the wiring of a crossover cable
- Complete external cable connections
- Connect bulk cables to jacks using a punchdown block tool
- Attach RJ45 connectors to make patch cables

Estimated lesson time: 30 minutes

Two-Computer Networking

The simplest possible LAN consists of two computers, with network interface adapters installed, connected together by a single cable. If the two computers are located in the same room, the cable installation should be very simple. However, if the computers are far away from each other, and especially if they're located in different rooms or on different floors, the cable installation might require special attention.

Back in the days when an Ethernet network meant coaxial cable, it was possible to connect the NICs in two computers with a Thin Ethernet cable to set up a simple network. Today, however, the standard for Ethernet networking is UTP cable, and this generally requires the use of a hub.

In Lesson 3: Network Hubs, in Chapter 2, "Network Hardware," you learned how the hub on an Ethernet network provides a vital service by crossing over the signals between the transmit and receive wires. This enables the signals sent over the transmit wires by each computer to arrive at the receive connections at the other computers. When you connect two Ethernet network interface adapters directly using a UTP cable, there is no hub and this crossover is absent. For these two computers to be able to communicate, you must supply a special cable called a crossover cable, which wires the transmit contacts in each connector to the receive contacts in the other connector.

Note One limitation of a UTP Ethernet network without a hub is that the two computers can be no more than 100 meters apart. On a standard UTP network, the Ethernet hub functions as a repeater, which enables each cable connecting a computer to the hub to be 100 meters long, for a total span between computers of 200 meters, when separated by a single hub.

If you are connecting two computers in the same room, you can purchase a pre-fabricated crossover cable and simply plug the ends into the network interface adapters in the two computers. Be aware, however, that you might have trouble finding a crossover cable in your local computer store. Virtually all computer stores these days stock basic networking equipment, such as NICs, hubs, and prefabricated UTP cables. Larger stores might have crossover cables as well, but you might find it easier to order one from an online or catalog dealer, particularly if you need a relatively long one.

If you want to connect two computers in different rooms or on different floors using a crossover cable, you might have to perform an internal installation by running cable through the building's walls, ceilings, or floors. If this is the case, the cable that you use for a crossover connection is the same as that for a hub-based network, and the procedures for pulling the cable are the same as those detailed in Lesson 1: Pulling Cable. The difference between a crossover installation and a standard installation is in the attachment of the wires to the connectors at each end of the cable.

As explained in Chapter 2, a UTP cable contains eight separate wires, which are joined together in four twisted pairs. The RJ45 connector at each end of the cable (whether it is male, as on a patch cable, or female, as part of a wall plate or patch panel) has eight conductive contacts, to which the eight wires are attached. When you plug a male connector into a female one, the corresponding contacts touch, creating electrical circuits. Figure 15.14 shows the functions of the eight contacts on a standard 10BaseT or 100BaseTX Ethernet network.

Note While 10BaseT and 100BaseTX networks use only four of the eight wires in a UTP cable, a 100BaseT4 network uses all eight. The four that are designated as unused in the figure can carry signals in either direction on a 100BaseT4 network.

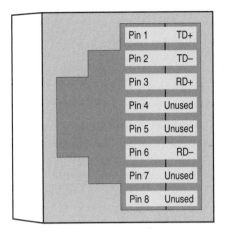

Figure 15.14 RJ45 connector contact assignments for 10BaseT and 100BaseTX networks

Standard network cable runs and prefabricated cables use straight-through connections. In a *straight-through connection*, each wire is attached to the same contact in both connectors, as shown in Figure 15.15. The transmit contacts at one end are connected to the transmit contacts at the other end, and the receive contacts are connected in the same way. This is possible because the crossover circuit is supplied in the hub, which makes the job much easier for the cable installer.

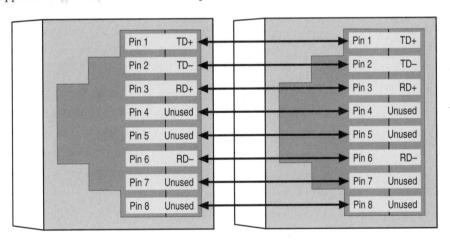

Figure 15.15 Straight-through connections use the eight wires in a UTP cable to connect the corresponding contacts in the connectors at each end.

To create a crossover connection in the cable, you must connect the two transmit contacts to their corresponding receive contacts, as shown in Figure 15.16. The positive transmit data (TD+) contact at each end is connected to the positive receive data (RD+) contact at the other end. Likewise, the two negative transmit data (TD-) contacts are connected to the two negative receive data (RD-) contacts. When you install a cable using a crossover connection like this, you cannot use the cable run with a hub, because the crossover circuit in the hub would cancel out the crossover circuit in the cable. In other words, the TD+ contact that is crossed to the RD+ contact in the cable would be crossed again, back to the TD+ contact, inside the hub. The only way you could use this connection with a hub (in the event that you had to expand the network, for example) would be to plug the cable into the hub's uplink port, which does not have a crossover circuit.

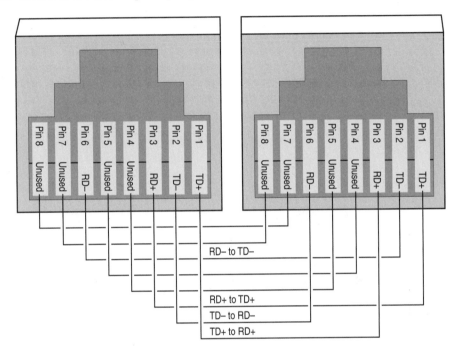

Figure 15.16 A crossover cable connection attaches the TD contacts in one connector to the RD contacts in the other, eliminating the need for a hub.

Connecting External Cables

If you've installed prefabricated cables externally, making your final connections is simply a matter of plugging them in to the hub and the computers. Set up the hub in a central location, preferably where it is protected from traffic or vibrations that can pull on or loosen the cable connections, and connect it to a power source. Plug the connector for each of your cables into one of the hub's ports. Push it firmly into the socket until it clicks. Do not use the hub's uplink port for a computer connection, unless the port has a switch that allows the crossover circuit to be disabled. Most hubs have light emitting diodes (LEDs) that correspond to the ports; these will not be lit until you connect the other end of the cables to the computers and turn them on.

At the other end of each cable, you should have a computer that is set up and ready to go. Shut the computer down, and plug the network cable into the jack provided by the computer's network interface adapter. Again, make sure that it clicks into place. If the jack does not fit in the socket, you're probably trying to plug the cable into a modem jack, which won't work.

Most Ethernet NICs have an LED next to the RJ45 connector; most network interface adapters built into the motherboard do not show this LED. The LED lights up when the NIC is connected to an operating hub. When you turn on the computer, the NIC generates a signal called a *link pulse* and transmits it over the cable. When the hub receives the signal, it responds with a signal of its own. If either the NIC or the hub is a Fast Ethernet device, the devices use these link pulse signals to negotiate the fastest speed they have in common. For example, when you plug a dual speed NIC into a Fast Ethernet hub, the link pulse signals enable the two devices to determine that they are both capable of operating at 100 Mbps, and they configure themselves to use that speed.

If you connect a dual speed NIC to a standard Ethernet hub, the NIC determines that it must run at 10 Mbps in order to use the hub, and it adjusts itself accordingly. When this negotiation is complete, the LEDs on both the hub and the NIC should light up, even if you haven't yet installed the network interface adapter driver on the computer. Some dual speed NICs have two LEDs, one of which specifies the speed at which the card is operating. If the LEDs don't light up, there might be a problem with your cable connection, or possibly with the NIC or hub. See Chapter 17, "Network Troubleshooting Procedures," for more information about what to do next.

Assuming that the LEDs on both the NIC and the hub do light, your hardware installation is complete. If you haven't done so already, you must install the networking software components on your computers, after which your network should be operational.

Connecting Internal Cables

If you have installed bulk cable internally, the process of making your final connections is more complicated. The essential steps for making each cable connection are as follows:

1. Connect one end of the cable run to a port in a patch panel.
2. Connect the patch panel port to a hub port using a patch cable.
3. Connect the other end of the cable run to a port in a wall plate.
4. Mount the wall plate in the wall.
5. Connect the port in the wall plate to the network interface adapter in a computer using a patch cable.

Connector Components

When you install bulk cable, you must purchase the connectors you need and the tools for attaching the connectors separately. Most internal installations use wall plates for the computer end of each cable run and one or more patch panels for the hub end. A wall plate is a metal or plastic face plate that screws into a hole in a wall, much like an electrical outlet, except that the wall plate contains female RJ45 connectors (jacks) instead of electrical outlets. A connector on the back of the wall plate jack contains the contacts to which you attach the wires inside the UTP cable. For each of your cable runs, you must connect the eight wires to a jack at each end of the cable. When the cable is connected and the wall plate installed, the cable is hidden in the wall, and the only part visible is the front of the wall plate. You can then plug a patch cable into the jack, just as you would a telephone cable.

As shown in Figure 15.17, some wall plates have integrated jacks, while others are modular. You can buy wall plates that hold one, two, four, or more jacks, and you can insert different types of jacks to support various cable connections. For example, in new construction, it's possible to install telephone and data network cables simultaneously and to use a single wall plate as the terminus for both networks. If you do this, be sure to label the jacks carefully so that users don't confuse them.

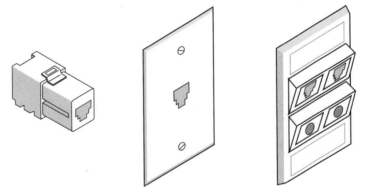

Figure 15.17 Wall plates and jacks

Warning While it's perfectly acceptable to use one wall plate for both telephone and data network connections, these two services must use separate cables. Some people assume that because two wire pairs are left unused in the typical UTP Ethernet network, it's all right to use those wires for voice traffic. This is most assuredly not the case, as the voice signals can cause crosstalk that interferes with the data signals on the other wires.

A patch panel, sometimes called a *punchdown block*, is similar in function to a wall plate, except that it supports many more ports. A patch panel is essentially a face plate or box with a number of RJ45 jacks mounted in it. It provides a row of ports on its front, as shown in Figure 15.18. A patch panel is not a hub; it is nothing more than a nexus that is a convenient place to terminate the hub-end of all your cable runs. You plug patch cables into the patch panel's ports to connect them to hub ports, thus completing the connection at that end. Patch panels are available in a variety of sizes and configurations, and are either mounted on a wall or integrated into a rack-mount system.

Warning Make sure that all the jacks you use on your network conform to the same rating as your cables. If you are installing Category 5 cable, you must use jacks that are rated for Category 5 as well.

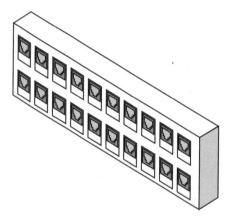

Figure 15.18 A patch panel

Punching Down

The process of connecting the ends of your bulk cable runs to the jacks in your wall plates and patch panels is called punching down. Each jack contains eight sets of contacts that correspond to the eight wires in the cable. Punching down a cable consists of the following steps:

1. Strip some of the insulating sheath off the cable end to expose the wires.

2. Separate the twisted wire pairs at the ends.

3. Strip a small amount of insulation off each wire.

4. Insert the wires into the appropriate contacts in the jack.

5. Press the bare wire down between the two metal contacts that hold it in place.

6. Cut off the excess wire that protrudes past the contacts.

Remember that you must repeat this process at both ends for each of your internal cable runs. This can be a lot of work but, fortunately, there are tools that simplify the process. A *punchdown block tool* is a handheld device (shown in Figure 15.19) that you use to insert each wire between its set of contacts. The tool strips the insulation off the wire, presses it into place between the contacts, and cuts off the excess wire. This is the one tool that is all but essential to an internal UTP cable installation. Without it, the process of stripping, installing, and cutting each wire is very laborious.

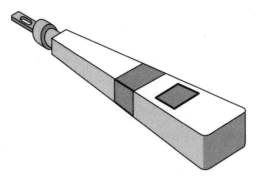

Figure 15.19 A punchdown block tool

The punchdown block tool you purchase must be the same type as your jacks. The types usually refer to the configuration of the blade that cuts off the wire ends. The jacks (or blocks) most often used today are called *110-style*. You can purchase a tool designed specifically for this type of block, or a modular one with interchangeable parts that supports multiple block types.

The most important part of the punchdown process is matching up the wires with the correct contacts. The wires inside the UTP cable are color-coded orange, green, blue, and brown. The positive wire in each pair is solid-colored, and the negative wire has a white stripe. You can buy jacks that have corresponding colors on the contacts, so that you simply have to match up the wires with the same-colored contacts when punching down.

Wiring Standards

There are two standards used today that specify which color wire in a UTP connection should be associated with each contact on the connector. These standards are called 568A and 568B. They are actually the configurations found in two versions of the Electronics Industry Association/Telecommunications Industry Association (EIA/TIA) 568 "Commercial Building Telecommunication Cabling Standard" document. The colors and the corresponding contacts for each of the standards are shown in the following illustration.

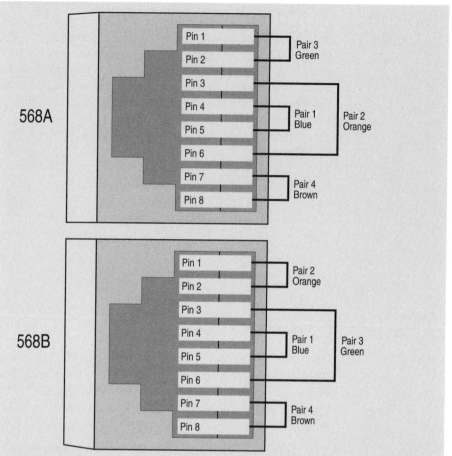

Which standard you choose when wiring your connectors is not important. The two are functionally identical, and you could even make up your own color code if you want to. What is important (indeed, crucial) is that you select a wiring configuration and use it consistently throughout the entire cabling project. A cable wired per the 568A standard on one end and the 568B standard on the other will not function. If there are several people working together to install the cable, make sure that they are all using the same wiring standard. You need not be concerned about the wiring standard used to construct prefabricated cables. As long as each contact in one connector is wired to the corresponding contact in the other connector, the cable will function properly.

To punch down a cable, begin by stripping about 2 inches of sheathing off the end, and then untwist each of the four wire pairs. You then lay down the cable in the center of the jack and spread out the wires so that they lay out between the appropriate sets of contacts, as shown in Figure 15.20. To protect the wires, the beginning of the cable sheath should be no more than one eighth of an inch from the jack. You should also be careful to untwist each wire pair only as much as is necessary for the wire to fit between the contacts. The twisted wire pairs are not simply used for organizational purposes. The twists provide an essential function by preventing the signals on the various wire pairs from interfering with each other. Each pair uses a different number of twists per foot, and you want to preserve this configuration as much as possible.

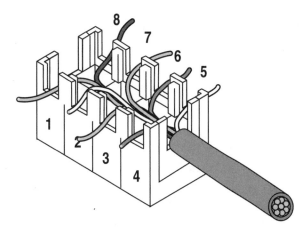

Figure 15.20 Lay out the wires between the appropriate contacts and use the tool to punch them down.

When you have the wires laid out on their respective contacts, take the punchdown tool and place it over the first set of contacts with the blade on the outside of the jack and the handle of the tool tilted slightly outward. Press down firmly on the tool and it presses the wire into place, stripping off the insulation as it goes, and cutting off the loose wire end. Repeat this process for the remaining seven wires and be sure to remove the cut off wire ends. This is a process that takes a bit of getting used to, so it's a good idea to buy some extra jacks for practice before you start working with your actual cables. This is also another good reason to allow some extra slack in your cable runs. If you make a mistake, you can simply cut off the end of the cable and start again with a new jack.

After you have punched down all eight wires, you can insert the jack into the wall plate or patch panel (if necessary). You can then mount the wall plate into the hole you cut previously, pushing all of the excess cable inside the wall. Mount the patch panel on the wall or rack after you've punched down all of your cables.

Installing Patch Cables

A patch cable is simply a shorter length of cable with standard male RJ45 connectors on both ends, which you use to connect a wall plate to a computer's network interface adapter or to connect a patch panel port to a hub port. You can purchase prefabricated cables for this purpose, or you can build them yourself. Making the final connections is no different than the process for an external cable installation, as described earlier in this chapter. When you have an unbroken connection between a NIC and a hub, and both devices are switched on, the link pulse LEDs at both ends should light up, indicating that communication is possible. If the LEDs don't light up, the troubleshooting process is a bit more involved than for an external cable installation, because there are more components that can go wrong. See Chapter 17, "Network Troubleshooting Procedures," for more information.

Attaching Connectors

While wall plates and patch panels make for the neatest installation, you don't have to go this route if you don't want to. You can also attach male RJ45 connectors to the ends of your cables and plug them directly into your hubs and computers, just as you would with prefabricated cables. You can also attach these connectors to shorter lengths of cable, if you want to build your own patch cables.

Male RJ45 connectors for UTP come in three configurations; ensure that your RJ45 connectors are compatible with the selected cable.

- Round cable with stranded wire
- Round cable with solid wire
- Flat cable (commonly referred to as "silver satin") with stranded wire

---

Warning "Silver satin" cables are designed for telephone network connections, and should not be used for data networking.

Attaching male RJ45 connectors to UTP cable requires another special tool, called a crimper, which is illustrated in Figure 15.21. A *crimper* is a jawed device that looks like a pair of pliers. It has a set of dies in it that enables you to squeeze the two halves of an RJ45 connector together with the wires inside. As with the punch down process, you strip some of the sheath off a cable and lay the wires out in the bottom half of the connector, making sure you use the same wiring standard at both ends. You then lay the other half of the connector on top of the wires and squeeze the handles of the crimper to lock the two halves together. This process is more tricky than using a punchdown tool, because you have to get all eight wires in place at the same time. Some practice is necessary to get the hang of it. When you consider the price of the crimper and the dies (about $50), plus the bulk cable and the connectors you'll ruin while learning how to crimp, not to mention your valuable time, buying prefabricated patch cables might be a more economical alternative.

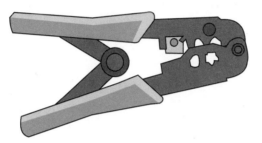

Figure 15.21 A crimper

Note Testing is an essential part of every cable installation. While you test your cable runs by simply connecting up your computers and hubs to see if they work, professional cable installers use a special cable testing device to check for problematic conditions that might not be immediately apparent in a real-world test. For more information about testing cable runs, see Lesson 3: Network Testing and Monitoring Tools, in Chapter 18, "Network Troubleshooting Tools."

Exercise 15.2: Cable Installation Tools

Match the tools in the left column with the proper functions in the right column.

1. Telepole
2. Punchdown block tool
3. Fish tape
4. Raceway
5. Crimper

a. Used to attach male RJ45 connectors to UTP cables
b. Pulls cables up through walls
c. Used to attach UTP cables to jacks
d. Used to pull cable through drop ceilings
e. Secures and protects external cable runs

Chapter Summary

The key points covered in this chapter are as follows.

Pulling Cable

- External UTP cable installations use prefabricated cables to connect computers directly to hubs.

- You typically install external cables along the walls of a room, and you secure them in place using staples, cable ties, or raceways.

- Internal cable installations use bulk cable, which you pull through walls, ceilings, or floors.

- Cables other than UTP have their own unique properties, which can complicate the installation process.

Making Connections

- To connect two computers without a hub, you must use a crossover cable connection, which reverses the transmit and receive signals.

- External cables have the connectors attached, and you simply plug them into your computers and hubs to make the final connections.

- For internal cables, you must manually attach a jack at each end, which becomes part of the wall plate or patch panel.

- The process of attaching a jack is called punching down; it requires a specialized punchdown block tool.

- Patch cables connect wall plates to computers and connect patch panel ports to hub ports.

- You can build your own patch cables using a tool called a crimper for attaching RJ45 connectors.

Chapter Review

1. Which of the following components is not required for an internal cable installation?

    a. A raceway

    b. A wall plate

    c. A patch panel

    d. A punchdown block tool

2. What is the primary function of the twists in a twisted pair cable?

    a. They bundle the positive and negative wires together.

    b. They prevent the cables from catching fire.

    c. They protect the signals against crosstalk.

    d. They separate the wire pairs.

3. In a crossover cable, the TD- contact at one end is connected to which contact at the other end?

    a. TD+

    b. TD-

    c. RD+

    d. RD-

4. Which of the following is not a function of the punchdown block tool?

    a. To cut off the wire ends

    b. To strip the sheath off the cable

    c. To strip the insulation off the wires

    d. To push the wires down between the contacts

5. What components of an internal cable network do patch cables connect?

    a. Hubs to computers

    b. Computers to patch panels

    c. Wall plates to patch panels

    d. Patch panels to hubs

6. What is the name of the signal that a NIC exchanges with a hub?

   a. Link pulse

   b. Test wave

   c. Crossover circuit

   d. Punchdown block

7. Why should all your cable runs use the same wiring standard?

   a. Because Ethernet can only transmit signals over wires of a certain color

   b. Because the wires in a UTP cable are different gauges and carry signals differently

   c. To ensure that all of the connections are wired straight through

   d. To prevent crosstalk

8. Which tool do you use to make a patch cable?

   a. A pair of pliers

   b. A punchdown block tool

   c. A fish tape

   d. A crimper

9. Why has Thick Ethernet cable rarely been installed internally?

10. What is the style of most jacks used today?

   a. 110

   b. 568A

   c. 568B

   d. RG58

CHAPTER 16

Network Maintenance

About This Chapter

This chapter discusses the three most important preventive maintenance areas that every network administrator must know about. Performing regular backups, and guarding against virus infections and other damaging programs are essential for protecting your data. Likewise, knowing when and if to apply software updates is essential for maintaining the health of a network and its applications. This chapter discusses the basic principles of these three network maintenance tasks and the tools involved in performing them.

Before You Begin

This chapter requires some background knowledge about network operating systems, which is found in Chapter 4, "Networking Software."

Lesson 1: Backups

It might not happen today or tomorrow, but someday you will lose a hard drive containing essential network data. The drive might be stolen along with the computer, destroyed in a fire or other catastrophe, or simply fail. Whatever happens, the data is gone and it's up to you, as the network administrator, to get it back. The day this occurs is the day you will thank yourself for all the effort you took to set up a network backup strategy. If you don't have a backup strategy in place, this might be the day you start working on your resume.

After this lesson, you will be able to

- Describe the various types of hardware used to perform backups
- Understand the capabilities of software backup products
- Distinguish between full, incremental, and differential backups

Estimated lesson time: 45 minutes

Backups are simply copies of your data that you make on a regular basis, so that if a storage device fails or is damaged and the data stored there is lost, you can restore it in a timely manner. Networks both complicate and simplify the process of making regular backups. The process is more complicated because you have data stored on multiple devices that must be protected, and it is simpler because you can use the network to gain access to those devices. A network backup strategy specifies what data you back up, how often you back it up, and what medium you use to store the backups. The decisions you make regarding the backup hardware, software, and administrative policies you will use depend on how much data you have to back up, how much time you have to back it up, and how much protection you want to provide.

Backup Hardware

You can perform backups using any type of storage device. One objective in developing an effective backup strategy, however, is to automate as much of the process as possible. While you can back up a gigabyte of data onto 1.44-MB floppy disks, you probably don't want to be the person sitting around feeding 695 disks into a floppy drive. Therefore, you usually want to select a device that is capable of storing all of your data without frequent media changes. This enables you to schedule backup jobs to run unattended. This doesn't mean, however, that you have to purchase a drive that can hold all of the data stored on all of your network's computers. You can be selective about which data you want to back up, so it's important to determine just how much of your data needs protecting before you decide on the capacity of your backup device.

Another important criterion to use when selecting a backup device is the speed at which the drive writes data to the medium. Backup drives are available in many different speeds, and, not surprisingly, the faster ones are generally more expensive. It is typical for backup jobs to run during periods when the network is not otherwise in use. This ensures that all of the data on the network is available for backup. The amount of time that you have to perform your backups is sometimes called the *backup window*. The backup device that you choose should depend in part on the amount of data you have to protect and the amount of time that you have to back it up. If, for example, you have 10 gigabytes (GB) of data to back up and your company closes down from 5 o'clock each night until 9 o'clock the next morning, you have a 16-hour backup window—plenty of time to copy your data, using a medium-speed backup device. However, if your company operates three shifts and only leaves you one hour, from 7:00 A.M. to 8:00 A.M., to back up 100 GB of data, you will have to use a much faster device, or in this case, several devices.

Cost is always a factor in selecting a hardware product. When you evaluate backup devices, you must be aware of the product's extended costs as well. Backup devices nearly always use a removable medium, such as a tape or disk cartridge. This enables you to store copies of your data off site, such as in a bank's safe deposit vault. If the building where your network is located is destroyed by a fire or other disaster, you still have your data, which you can use to restart operations elsewhere. Therefore, in addition to purchasing the drive, you should purchase storage media as well. Some products might seem at first to be economical because the drive is inexpensive, but in the long run they are not, because the media are so expensive. One of the most common methods of evaluating various backup devices is to determine the cost per megabyte of the storage it provides. Divide the price of the medium by the number of megabytes it can store, and use this figure to compare the relative cost of various devices. Of course, in some cases you might need to sacrifice economy for speed or for capacity.

Magnetic Tape Drives

The most common hardware device used to back up data is a magnetic tape drive, like that shown in Figure 16.1. Unlike hard disk, floppy disk, and CD-ROM drives, tape drives are not random access devices. This means that you can't simply move the drive heads to a particular file on a backup tape without spooling through all of the files before it. As with other types of tape drives, such as audio and video, the drive unwinds the tape from a spool and pulls it across the heads. As a result, you can't mount a tape drive in a computer's file system, assign it a drive letter, and copy files to it, as you can with a hard disk drive. A special software program is required to address the drive and send the data you select to it for storage. This also means that tape drives are useless for anything other than backups, while other media, such as writable CD-ROMs, can be used for other things.

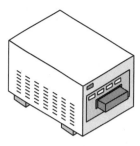

Figure 16.1 An external magnetic tape drive

Magnetic tape drives are well suited for backups; they're fast, they can hold a lot of data, and their media cost per megabyte is low, often less than one-half cent per megabyte. There are many different types of magnetic tape drives, which differ greatly in speed, capacity, and price. At the low end are quarter-inch cartridge (QIC) drives, which can cost as little as US $200. A QIC tape cartridge can hold anywhere from 150 MB to 20 GB on a tape. At the high end are Digital Linear Tape (DLT) and Linear Tape-Open (LTO) drives, which can cost many thousands of U.S. dollars and store as much as 100 GB on a single tape. The most common magnetic tape technologies used for backups are listed in Table 16.1.

Table 16.1 Magnetic tape technologies

Type	Tape Width	Cartridge Size	Capacity (uncompressed)	Speed
Quarter-inch cartridge (QIC)	.25 inch	4 x 6 x 0.625 inches (data cartridge); 3.25 x 2.5 x 0.6 inches (minicartridge)	Up to 20 GB	2 to 120 MB/min
Digital Audio Tape (DAT)	4mm	2.875 x 2.0625 x 0.375 inches	Up to 20 GB	3 to 144 MB/min
8mm	8mm	3.7 x 2.44 x 0.59 inches	Up to 60 GB	Up to 180 MB/min
Digital Linear Tape (DLT)	.50 inch	4.16 x 4.15 x 1 inches	Up to 40 GB	Up to 360 MB/min
Linear Tape-Open (LTO), Ultrium media	.50 inch	4.0 x 4.16 x 0.87 inches	Up to 100 GB	Up to 1920 MB/min

Note The capacities of magnetic tape drives are generally specified using two figures, such as 40 GB to 80 GB. These numbers refer to the capacity of a tape without compression and with compression. Most tape drives have hardware-based data compression capabilities built into them, but the additional capacity that you achieve when using compression is based on the type of data you are storing. The capacity figures assume an average compression ratio of 2:1. Some types of files, such as image files using uncompressed BMP or TIF formats, can compress at much higher ratios, as high as 8:1. Files that are already compressed, such as GIF or JPG image files or ZIP archives, cannot be compressed further and are stored at a 1:1 compression ratio.

Selecting a Drive Interface

Backup devices can use any of the standard computer interfaces, such as Integrated Drive Electronics (IDE), the universal serial bus (USB), and the small computer systems interface (SCSI). Some backup drives even connect to the computer's parallel port, although this is just a form of SCSI that uses a different interface. The most common interface used in high-end network backup solutions, however, is SCSI.

SCSI devices operate more independently than those using IDE, which means that the backup process, which often entails reading from one device while writing to another on the same interface, is more efficient. When multiple IDE devices share a channel, only one operates at a time. Each drive must receive, execute, and complete a command before the other drive can receive its next command. SCSI devices, on the other hand, can maintain a queue of commands that they have received from the host adapter and execute them sequentially and independently.

Magnetic tape drives, in particular, require a consistent stream of data in order to write to the tape with maximum effectiveness. If there are constant interruptions in the data stream, as can be the case with the IDE interface, the tape drive must repeatedly stop and start the tape, which reduces its speed and lessens its overall storage capacity. A SCSI drive can often operate continuously, without pausing to wait for the other devices on the channel.

A SCSI backup device is always more expensive than a comparable IDE alternative, because the drive requires additional electronics and because you must have a SCSI host adapter installed in the computer. SCSI devices are available as internal or external units, the latter of which have their own power supplies, which also adds to the cost. However, the additional expense is worth it for a reliable network backup solution.

CD-ROM Drives

The popularity of writable CD-ROM drives, such as CD-Rs and CD-RWs, has led to their increasing use as backup devices. Although the capacity of a CD is limited to approximately 650 MB, the low cost of the media makes CDs an economical solution, even if the disks can only be used once, as is the case with CD-Rs. The biggest factor in favor of CD-ROMs for backup is that many computers already have CD-ROM drives installed for other purposes, which eliminates the need to purchase a dedicated backup drive.

For network backups, CD-ROMs are usually inadequate, however. Most networks have multiple gigabytes worth of data to back up, which would require many disk changes. In addition, CD-R and CD-RW drives are usually not recognized by network backup software products. Although these drives often come with software that provides its own backup capabilities (intended for relatively small, single-system backups), this software usually does not provide the features needed for backing up a network effectively.

Cartridge Drives

Another storage device that is commonly found in computers these days, and which can easily be used for backups, is the removable cartridge drive. Products like Iomega's Zip and Jaz drives provide performance that approaches that of a hard disk drive, but they use removable cartridges. These drives mount into a computer's file system, meaning that you can assign them a drive letter and copy files to them just as with a hard drive.

Zip cartridges hold only 100 or 250 MB, which makes them less practical than CDs for backups. However, Jaz drives are available in 1-GB and 2-GB versions, which is sufficient for a backup device. The drawback of using this type of drive for backup purposes is the extremely high cost of the media. A 2-GB Jaz cartridge can cost US $125 or more, which is more than 6 cents per megabyte, far more than virtually any other storage device.

Autochangers

In some cases, even the highest capacity drive isn't sufficient to back up a large network with constantly changing data. To create an automated backup solution with a greater capacity than that provided by a single drive, you can purchase a device called an autochanger. An *autochanger,* shown in Figure 16.2, is a unit that contains one or more drives (usually tape drives, but optical disk and CD-ROM autochangers are available also) and a robotic mechanism that swaps the media in and out of the drives. Sometimes these devices are called jukeboxes or tape libraries. When a backup job fills one tape (or other storage medium), the mechanism extracts it from the drive and inserts another, after which the job continues.

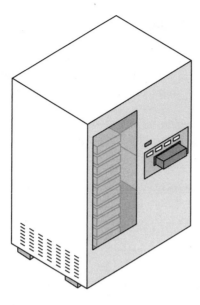

Figure 16.2 A tape autochanger

Some autochangers are small devices with a single drive and an array that holds four or five tapes, while others are enormous, with four or more drives and an array of 100 tapes or more. If you purchase a large enough autochanger, you can create a longterm backup strategy that enables backups to run completely unattended for weeks at a time. However, before you solidify your plans to get a refrigerator-sized autochanger and never load a tape into a drive again, be aware that the cost of these devices can be astonishingly high, reaching as much as six figures in some cases.

Backup Software

Apart from the hardware, the other primary component in a network backup solution is the software that you use to perform the backups. Storage devices designed for use as backup solutions are not treated like the other storage subsystems in a computer; a specialized software product is required to package the data that you want to back up and to then send it to the drive. Depending on the operating system you're using, you might already have a backup program that you can use with your drive, but in many cases an operating system's own backup program provides only basic functionality and lacks features that can be especially useful in a network environment.

The primary functions of a good backup software product are examined in the following sections.

Target Selection and Filtering

The most basic function of a backup software program is to let you select what you want to back up, which is sometimes called the target. A good backup program enables you to do this in many ways. You can select entire computers to back up, specific drives on those computers, specific directories on the drives, or specific files in specific directories. Most backup programs provide a directory tree display that you can use to select the targets for a backup job. Figure 16.3 shows the interface that the Microsoft Windows 2000 Backup program uses to select backup targets.

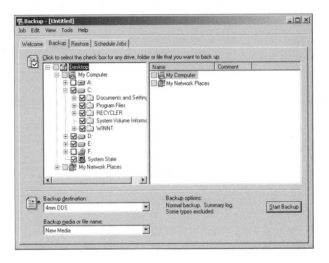

Figure 16.3 The Backup dialog box in the Windows 2000 Backup program

In most cases, it isn't necessary to back up all of the data on a computer's drives. If a hard drive is completely erased or destroyed, you are likely to have to reinstall the operating system before you can restore files from a backup tape, so it might not be worthwhile to back up all of the operating system files each time you run a backup job. The same is true for applications. You can reinstall an application from the original distribution media, so you might want to back up only your data files and configuration settings for that application. In addition, most operating systems today create temporary files as they run, which you do not need to back up. Windows, for example, creates a temporary file for memory paging that can be several hundred megabytes in size. Because this file is recreated each time you start the computer, you can save space on your backup tapes by omitting files like this from your backup jobs. Judicious selection of backup targets can mean the difference between fitting an entire backup job onto one tape or staying late after work to insert a second tape into the drive.

Individually selecting the files, directories, and drives that you want to back up can be quite tedious, though, so many backup programs provide other ways to specify targets. One common method is to use filters that enable the software to evaluate each file and directory on a drive and decide whether to back it up. A good backup program provides a variety of filters that allow you to select targets based on file and directory names, extensions, sizes, dates, and attributes. For example, you can configure the software to back up a computer running Windows 2000 and use filters to exclude Pagefile.sys, which is the memory paging file; the \Temporary Internet Files directories, which contain Microsoft Internet Explorer's browser cache; and all files with a .tmp extension, which are temporary files created by various applications. None of these files are needed during the restoration of a backup tape, so it's worthless to save them in the first place, and they can add up to a significant amount of storage space.

You can also use filters to limit your backups only to files that have changed recently, by using either date or attribute filters. The most common type of filter used by backup programs is the one for the Archive attribute, which enables the software to back up only the files that have changed since the last backup. This filter is the basis for incremental and differential backups.

Incremental and Differential Backups

The most basic type of backup job is a full backup, which copies the entire contents of a computer's drives either to tape or to another medium. You can perform a full backup every day, if you want to, or each time that you back up that particular computer. However, this practice can be wasteful, both in terms of time and tape. When you perform a full backup every day, the majority of the files you are writing to the tape are exactly the same as they were yesterday. The program files that make up the operating system and your applications do not change. Only your data files and perhaps the files that store configuration data change on a regular basis, along with special resources like the Windows registry and directory service databases.

To save on tape and shorten the backup time, many network administrators perform full backups only once a week, or even less frequently. In between the full backups, they perform special types of filtered jobs that back up only the files that have recently been modified. These types of jobs are called incremental backups and differential backups.

An *incremental backup* is a job that backs up only the files changed since the last backup job of any kind. A *differential backup* is a job that backs up only the files that have changed since the last full backup. The backup software filters the files for these jobs using a special file attribute called the *Archive bit*, which every file on the computer possesses. File attributes are 1-bit flags stored with each file on a drive, which perform various functions. For example, the Read-only bit, when activated, prevents any application from modifying that particular file, and the Hidden bit prevents most applications from displaying that file in a directory listing. The Archive bit for a file is activated by any application that modifies that file. When the backup program scans the target drive during an incremental or differential job, it selects for backup only the files with active Archive bits.

During a full backup, the software backs up the entire contents of a computer's drives, and also resets the Archive bit on all of the files. Immediately after the job is completed, you have a complete copy of the drives on tape, and none of the files on the target drive has an active Archive bit. As work on the computer proceeds after the backup job is completed, applications and operating system processes modify various files on the computer, and when they do, they activate the Archive bits for those files. The next day, you can run an incremental or differential backup job, which is also configured to back up the entire computer, except that it filters out all files that do not have an active Archive bit. This means that all of the program files that make up the operating system and the applications are skipped, along with all data files that have not changed. When compared to a full backup, an incremental or differential backup job is usually much smaller, so it takes less time and less tape.

The difference between an incremental and a differential job lies in the behavior of the backup software when it either resets or does not reset the Archive bits of the files it copies to tape. Incremental jobs reset the Archive bits; differential jobs don't. This means that when you run an incremental job, you're only backing up the files that have changed since the last backup, whether it was a full backup or an incremental backup. This uses the least amount of tape, but it also lengthens the restore process. If you should have to restore an entire computer, you must first perform a restore from the last full backup tape, and you must then restore each of the incremental jobs performed since the last full backup. For example, suppose that you run a full backup job on a particular computer every Monday evening and incremental jobs every evening from Tuesday through Friday. If the computer's hard drive fails on a Friday morning, you must restore the previous Monday's full backup, and you must then restore the incremental jobs from Tuesday, Wednesday, and Thursday, in that order. The order of the restore jobs is essential if you want the computer to have the latest version of every file.

Differential jobs do not reset the Archive bit on the files they back up. This means that every differential job backs up all of the files that have changed since the last full backup. If you perform a full backup on Monday evening, Tuesday evening's differential job will back up all files changed on Tuesday, Wednesday evening's differential job will back up all files changed on Tuesday and Wednesday, and Thursday evening's differential will back up all files changed on Tuesday, Wednesday, and Thursday. Differential backups use more tape, because some of the same files are backed up each day, but differential backups also simplify the restore process. To completely restore the computer that failed on a Friday morning, you only have to restore Monday's full backup tape and the most recent differential, which was performed Thursday evening. Because the Thursday tape includes all of the files modified on Tuesday, Wednesday, and Thursday, no other tapes are needed. The Archive bits for these changed files are not reset until the next full backup job is performed.

Running incremental or differential jobs is often what makes it possible to automate your backup regimen without spending too much on hardware. If your full backup job totals 50 GB, for example, you might be able to purchase a 20-GB drive. You'll have to manually insert two additional tapes during your full backup jobs, once a week, but you should be able to run incremental or differential jobs the rest of the week using only one tape, which means that the jobs can run unattended.

Drive Manipulation

When you have selected what you want to back up, the next step is to specify where to send the selected data. The backup software typically enables you to select a backup device (if you have more than one) and prepare to run the job by configuring the drive and the storage medium. For backup to a tape drive, this part of the process can include any of the following tasks:

- Formatting a tape
- Supplying a name for the tape you're creating
- Specifying whether you want to append the backed up files to the tape or overwrite the tape
- Turning on the drive's compression feature

Scheduling

All backup products enable you to create a backup job and execute it immediately, but the key to automating a backup routine is being able to schedule jobs to execute unattended. This way, you can configure your backup jobs to run when the company is closed and the network is idle, so that all resources are available for backup and users are not disturbed by a sudden surge of network traffic. Not all of the backup programs supplied with operating systems or designed for standalone computers support scheduling, but all network backup software products do.

Backup programs use various methods to automatically execute backup jobs. The Windows 2000 Backup program uses the operating system's Task Scheduler application, while other programs supply their own program or service that runs continuously and triggers the jobs at the appropriate times. Some of the higher-end network backup products can use a directory service, such as Microsoft's Active Directory or Novell Directory Services (NDS). These programs modify the directory schema (the code that specifies the types of objects that can exist in the directory) to create an object representing a queue of jobs waiting to be executed.

Note For more information about enterprise directory services such as Active Directory and NDS, see Lesson 3: Directory Services in Chapter 4, "Networking Software."

No matter which mechanism the backup software uses to launch jobs, the process of scheduling them is usually the same. You specify whether you want to execute the job once, or repeatedly at a specified time each day, week, or month, using an interface like that shown in Figure 16.4. The idea of the scheduling feature is for the network administrator to create a logical sequence of backup jobs that execute by themselves at regular intervals. After this is done, the only thing that remains to be done is to change the tape in the drive each day. If you have an autochanger, you can even eliminate this part of the job and create a backup job sequence that runs for weeks or months without any attention at all.

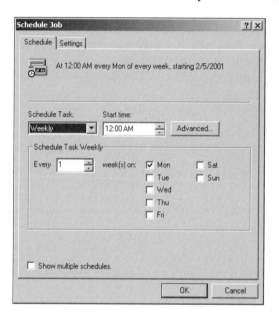

Figure 16.4 The Windows 2000 Backup program's Schedule Job dialog box

Logging and Cataloging

When a backup job runs, the software accesses the specified targets and feeds the data to the backup drive in the appropriate manner. Because of the nature of the media typically used for backups, it is important for the data to arrive at the storage device in a consistent manner and at the proper rate of speed. The software, therefore, must be designed to address specific drives in the manner appropriate for that device.

While the software feeds the data to the drive, it is also keeps track of the software's activities. Most backup software products can maintain a log of the backup process as it occurs. You can often specify a level of detail for the log, such as whether it should contain a complete list of every file backed up or just record the major events that occur during the job. Periodically checking the logs is an essential part of administering a network backup program. The logs tell you when selected files are skipped for any reason, for example if the files are locked open by an application or if the computers where they are stored are turned off. The logs also let you know when errors occur, on either the backup drive or one of the computers involved in the backup process. Some software products can generate alerts when errors occur, notifying you by sending a status message to a network management console, by sending you an e-mail message, or by other methods.

Tip It is also important to keep an eye on the size of your log files, particularly when you configure them to maintain a high level of detail. These files can grow huge very quickly, and can consume all of the available disk space on the drive on which they are stored.

In addition to logging their activities, backup software programs also catalog the files they back up, thus facilitating the process of restoring files later. The catalog is essentially a list of every file that the software has backed up during each job. To restore files from the backup medium, you browse through the catalog and select the files, directories, or drives that you want to restore. Different backup software products store the catalog in different ways. The Windows 2000 Backup program, for example, stores the catalog for each tape on the tape itself. The problem with this method is that you have to insert a tape into the drive to read the catalog and browse the files on that tape.

More elaborate network backup software programs take a different approach by maintaining a database of the catalogs for all of your backup tapes on the computer where the backup device is installed. This database enables you to browse through the catalogs for all of your tapes and select any version of any file or directory for restoration. In some cases, you can view the contents of the database in several different ways, such as by the computer, drive, and directory where the files were originally located; by the backup job; or by the tape or other media name. After you make your selection, the program specifies which tape contains the file or directory. The database feature can use a lot of the computer's disk space and processor cycles, but it greatly enhances the usability of the software, particularly in a network environment.

Note Backup software products that rely on a database store a copy of the database on your tapes as well as on the computer's hard drive. This is done so that if the computer you use to run the backups should suffer a drive failure, you can restore the database later.

Media Rotation

Some network administrators use new tapes for every backup job and store them all permanently. However, this can become extremely expensive. It's more common for administrators to reuse their backup tapes but, to do this properly, you must have a carefully wrought media rotation scheme, so that you don't inadvertently reuse a tape you'll need later. While you can always create such a scheme yourself, some backup software products do it for you. One of the most common media rotation schemes is called Grandfather-Father-Son, which refers to backup jobs that run monthly, weekly, and daily. You have one set of tapes for your daily jobs, which you reuse every week; a set of weekly tapes, which you reuse every month; and a set of monthly tapes, which you reuse each year. There are other schemes, which vary in complexity and utility, depending on the software product.

When the software program implements the rotation scheme, it provides a basic schedule for the jobs (which you can modify to have the jobs execute at specific times of the day), tells you what name to write on each tape as you use it, and once you begin to reuse tapes, tells you which tape to put in the drive for each job. The end result in that you maintain a perpetual record of your data while using the minimum number of tapes, without fear of overwriting a tape you need.

Restoring

Restoring data from your backups is, of course, the sole reason for making them in the first place. The ease with which you can locate the files you need to restore is an important feature of any backup software product. It is absolutely essential that you perform periodic test restores from your backup tapes or other media, to ensure that you can get back any data that is lost. Even if all your jobs complete successfully and your log files show that all of your data has been backed up, there is no truer test of a backup system than an actual restore. There are plenty of horror stories of network administrators who dutifully perform their backups every day for a year, only to find out when disaster strikes that all their carefully labeled tapes are blank, due to a malfunctioning drive.

While making regular backups is usually thought of as protection against a disaster that causes you to lose an entire hard drive, the majority of the restore jobs you will perform in a network environment are of one or a few files that a user has inadvertently deleted. As mentioned earlier, the program's cataloging capability is a critical part of the restoration process. If a user needs to have one particular file restored and you have to insert tape after tape into the drive to locate it, everyone's time is wasted. A backup program with a database that lets you search for that particular file makes your job much easier and enables you to restore any file in minutes.

Restore jobs are similar to backup jobs, in that you typically select the files or directories that you want to restore, using an interface like that shown in Figure 16.5. You then specify whether you want to restore the files to the locations they originally came from or to another location. If you restore them to a different location, you can usually configure the software to place all of the restored files into one directory or recreate the directory structure from which the files were backed up.

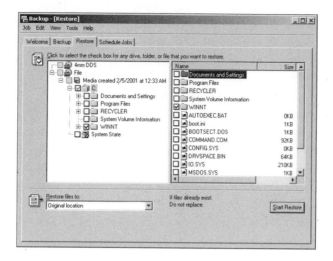

Figure 16.5 The Windows 2000 Backup program's Restore dialog box

Network Backup Functions

It is particularly important that you choose a backup software product that is designed for network use. The primary difference between network backup software and an application designed for standalone systems is that the former can back up other computers on the network. This means you can purchase one backup drive and use it to protect your entire network. Many standalone backup products can access drives on networked computers that you have mapped to a drive letter, but a fully functional network backup product can also back up important operating system features on other computers, such as the Windows registry and directory service databases. This type of remote backup may require you to install a software component on the target computer, as well as on the computer where the backup drive is located.

In many cases, network backup products also have optional add-on components that enable you to perform specialized backup tasks, such as backing up live databases or computers running other operating systems. These can be a critical part of your network backup solution. If, for example, you have database or e-mail servers that run around the clock, you might not be able to fully back them up using a standard software product because the database files are locked open. The result would be that your backup job protects the program files for the database engine (the part that's easily replaceable) while leaving your actual data unprotected. To back up a database of this type, you either have to close it by shutting it down or use a specialized piece of software that creates temporary database files (called *delta files*) that the server can use while the database itself is closed for the duration of the backup process.

Exercise 16.1: Incremental and Differential Backups

1. If you back up your network by performing a full backup every Wednesday at 6:00 P.M. and differential backups in the evening of the other six days of the week, how many jobs would be needed to completely restore a computer with a hard drive that failed on a Tuesday at noon?

2. If you back up your network by performing a full backup every Wednesday at 6:00 P.M., how many jobs would be needed if you performed incremental backups in the evening of the other six days of the week?

3. For a complete restore of a computer that failed at noon on Tuesday, how many jobs would be needed if you performed full backups at 6:00 A.M. every Wednesday and Saturday and incremental backups at 6:00 A.M. every other day?

Lesson 2: Anti-Virus Policies

Most business networks provide their users with access to the Internet, and while there might be a firewall in place to prevent outside users from breaking in, this doesn't mean that the network is completely protected. Potentially damaging programs such as viruses, trojans, and worms can still find their way onto the network, through file downloads, e-mails, or even floppy disks. While it's possible to screen out and eliminate most of these hazards using any one of many anti-virus software products intended for standalone systems, network administrators often use products that centralize the virus-scanning process, so that every file transmitted over the network is checked.

After this lesson, you will be able to

- Understand how viruses work
- List the major types of viruses
- Describe the functions of anti-virus software

Estimated lesson time: 15 minutes

A virus is a software routine that is deliberately designed to attach itself to another piece of software on a computer and perform some preprogrammed activity. The worst types of viruses are engineered to irretrievably destroy all or part of the data stored on the computer by wiping out hard drives. However, there are many viruses whose effects are not so catastrophic. Some viruses can cause intermittent problems on the computer, such as system lockups or specific feature failures, while others do nothing but display a message programmed by its author. Viruses are deliberately created by unethical individuals who think that tampering with other people's property is an amusing way to spend their time. Anti-virus software products must be continually updated to cope with the constantly evolving techniques used by the creators of viruses.

Like biological viruses, computer viruses are designed to replicate themselves by infecting other software. If you insert a virus-infected floppy disk into your computer, the virus can migrate from the floppy disk to the computer's hard drive, infecting the code that it finds there in one of several ways. In some cases, viruses are designed to remain dormant until the computer's clock registers a particular date and time. There have been, at various times, well-publicized scares about "time bomb" viruses that are due to trigger on a particular date. There is usually a rush to purchase anti-virus software on these occasions, but the danger is always overrated, as few cases of the virus in question are found.

When a virus-infected computer is connected to a network, you have the functional equivalent of one sick child sharing a room with a group of healthy children. When one gets sick, the others are likely to get sick also. Files transferred from the infected computer to the other systems on the network can spread the infection, as shown in Figure 16.6. Depending on the design of the virus, the effect can range from a nuisance to a catastrophe. Once the network is infected, it can be very difficult to completely remove the virus. If you miss one infected file on one computer, the virus can reassert itself and start spreading all over again.

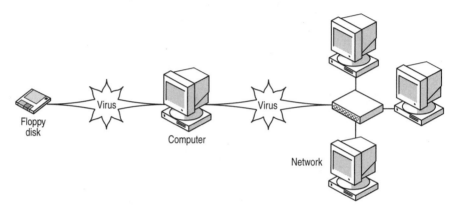

Figure 16.6 A virus can spread from a floppy disk to one computer, and then through the network to other computers.

Viruses can attach themselves to various parts of a computer's software, and are often classified by the area of the disk in which they reside. The most common types of viruses are as follows:

- **Boot sector viruses** A boot sector virus can come from a floppy disk or an executable file. It infects your computer by inhabiting the master boot record (MBR) of your hard drive. Because the MBR executes whenever you start the computer, the virus is always loaded into memory, and is therefore very dangerous. Unlike a virus that infects files (which you can remove by deleting the file), to remove a boot sector virus, you must either delete and recreate the MBR (which causes the data on the disk to be lost) or use an anti-virus program.

- **Executable file viruses** An executable file virus attaches itself to .exe or .com files, or less often, to other types of application modules, such as .dll and .bin files. The virus is loaded into memory when you run the infected program, and can then spread to other software that you execute. You can receive executable file viruses in e-mail attachments and downloads, but they can only infect your computer if you run the infected program.

- **Polymorphic viruses** A polymorphic virus can reside in both the MBR and in executable files, and is designed to change its signature periodically to fool virus-scanning routines that search for the code associated with particular viruses. The virus modifies itself and uses encryption to hide the majority of its code. This type of virus is a direct result of the ongoing competition between the people who design viruses and those who design the tools to protect against them.

- **Stealth viruses** Many virus-scanning products function by detecting changes in the sizes of files stored on a computer's hard drive. Normal viruses add code to executable files, so the files grow in size by a small amount. This is why installing an updated version of an application can sometimes trigger false positive results from a virus scanner. Stealth viruses attach themselves to executable files in the normal way, but they disguise their appearance by subtracting the same number of bytes from the infected file's directory entry that their code added to the file. The end result is that the file appears not to have changed in size, even though virus code has been added to it.

- **Macro viruses** A fairly recent innovation in the world of technological delinquency is the virus that can infect data files. It used to be that viruses were only able to infect executables, but data file viruses attach themselves to documents and spread themselves using the application's macro capability. Microsoft Word documents in particular were the original targets for this type of virus. When a user opens an infected document file, the macro code executes, enabling the virus to enter into memory and spread to the template file (Normal.dot) that Word uses for all open documents. Once in the template file, the virus is read into memory whenever the application is launched, and spreads to all of the documents the user loads afterward. Macro viruses don't usually cause severe damage, but because many businesses frequently exchange document files using e-mail and other methods, they spread very rapidly and are difficult to eradicate. Applications with macro capabilities now usually have a switch that lets you disable any macro code found in a document. If you don't use macros, you can protect yourself from virus infections by using this feature.

- **Worms** A worm is not really a virus, because although it is a program that replicates itself, it does not infect other files. Worms are separate programs that can insinuate themselves into a computer in various ways, such as by inserting an entry in the Run registry key that causes them to execute whenever the computer starts. Once in memory, worms can create copies of themselves on the same computer or replicate to other computers over a network connection.

- **Trojans** A trojan (or trojan horse) is not a virus either, because it neither replicates nor infects other files. Trojans are programs that masquerade as other, innocuous programs, so that the user doesn't suspect that they are running. Once loaded into memory, trojans can perform any number of tasks that can be dangerous to the computer or to the network. Some trojans are essentially remote control server programs that open up a "back door" into the computer where they are running. A user elsewhere on the network or on the Internet can run the client half of the program and gain access to the remote computer through the back door. Other types of trojans can gather information on the remote system, such as passwords or data files, and transmit it to a host program running on another computer.

Preventing Virus Infections

To protect your network against virus infections, you should implement a series of policies that affect both the behavior of your users and the configuration of their computers. All users should be wary of floppy disks from outside sources and particularly of files attached to e-mail messages. One of the most common techniques for disseminating viruses these days is code that causes the victim's computer to send an e-mail message with an infected attachment to all of the people in the user's address book. Because the recipients recognize the name of the sender, they often open the e-mail and launch the attachment without thinking, thus infecting themselves and beginning the same e-mail generation process on their own computers.

Anti-virus software products can protect individual computers from infection by viruses and other malicious programs arriving on floppy disks, through Internet downloads, and in e-mail attachments. A typical anti-virus program consists of a scanner that examines the computer's MBR when the computer starts and that checks each file as the computer accesses it. A full-featured program also checks e-mail attachments and Internet downloads by intercepting the files as they arrive from the e-mail or Internet server and by scanning them for viruses before passing them to the client application.

A virus scanner works by examining files and searching for specific code signatures that are peculiar to certain viruses. The scanner has a library of virus definitions that it uses to identify viruses. To keep your computers fully protected, you must update the virus signatures for your program on a regular basis. In many cases, anti-virus programs have a feature that automatically connects to a server on the Internet and downloads the latest signatures when they become available. The product you select should update its virus signatures at least once a month. In addition, be sure to check on the software manufacturer's policies for virus signature updates. Some products include perpetual updates in the price of the software, while others include updates only for a limited period of time before you must purchase a subscription.

In a network environment, all of the computers, both servers and workstations, should run an anti-virus program so that the entire network is protected. Anti-virus programs designed for use on networks do not provide greater protection against viruses; they simplify the process of implementing the protection. The centralized management and monitoring capabilities in network-enabled anti-virus products typically allow you to create policies for the computers on the network that force them to run the virus-scanning mechanisms you specify. They also simplify the process of deploying virus signature updates to all of the computers on the network.

Exercise 16.2: Virus Types

Match the virus types in the left column with the characteristics in the right column.

1. Executable file viruses
2. Trojans
3. Stealth viruses
4. Boot sector viruses
5. Macro viruses
6. Worms
7. Polymorphic viruses

a. Modify a file's directory entry size
b. Replicate themselves, but do not infect other files
c. Load into memory when the computer starts
d. Infect document files
e. Periodically change their signatures
f. Do not replicate or infect other files
g. Load into memory when you run a specific program

Lesson 3: Patches and Updates

Another important part of the network administrator's job is to keep up to date the software running on the network's computers. All manufacturers of operating systems and applications periodically release patches or updates that correct problems with the software, enhance or modify existing features, or add new capabilities. In most cases, the process of updating a computer involves downloading an update program from the manufacturer's Web site and running it on the computer in question. However, keeping your network software updated is not simply a matter of blindly downloading and installing every patch you can find. The process includes researching the various updates that the manufacturers release, determining if they apply to your environment, and, in some cases, testing them before deployment.

After this lesson, you will be able to

- Understand how software manufacturers release product updates
- Install a Microsoft Service Pack
- Describe how to determine when or if you should install a particular update release

Estimated lesson time: 10 minutes

Major Updates

Even a computer with a relatively simple configuration can have many different software components that are regularly updated. The operating system is the chief element you should keep up to date, but applications and device drivers should also be updated periodically. Years ago, manufacturers of operating systems would release many different software patches, each addressing a specific issue. This tended to cause problems for both users and developers, because users sometimes had to download and apply a dozen or more patches to keep current, and because it was difficult for developers to know exactly how a particular installation was configured. If there are 10 patches available for a particular operating system version, people trying to support the product will have a difficult time keeping up with whether all of the patches have been applied and in what order they were applied.

To address this problem, operating system manufacturers started releasing groups of updates in a single package. This practice was pioneered by Microsoft with its Service Pack releases for the Windows NT operating system. Each Service Pack release for a particular product contains a collection of patches and updates, all of which are applied by one installation program. Because the various patches have all been tested together, the operating system environment is consistent. Now all Microsoft products are updated using Service Packs, and most other operating system and application manufacturers have followed suit (although they might use different names for their releases).

When Microsoft releases multiple Service Packs for a product, the later releases are cumulative, meaning that they contain all of the updates from the previous Service Packs. This way, a user does not have to apply multiple Service Packs to bring a newly installed computer up to speed. The only problem with this method of updating an operating system is that the Service Pack releases tend to become extremely large after a time. Windows NT 4.0 Service Packs are now more than 30 MB in size, and the full version of Windows 2000 Service Pack 1 is over 80 MB. Because of their size, Microsoft also makes Service Packs available on CD-ROM for a nominal fee.

The downloadable versions of Microsoft's Service Packs take the form of a single compressed executable file that contains a large number of operating system components. To install the Service Pack, you run the file. The program then expands the components and installs them to the proper locations. The CD version of a Service Pack is the now-typical self-starting CD with a menu of options, one of which is installing the update. Figure 16.7 shows the update in progress for Windows 2000. Deploying a Service Pack on a network, however, can be a lengthy process. Depending on the capabilities of your users, you might need to travel to every computer to install the Service Pack, or you might be able to e-mail the Service Pack file to your users with instructions on how to install it. There are also network management software products available that can automate the process of installing Service Packs and other updates on all of the computers on the network.

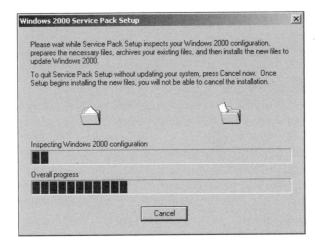

Figure 16.7 The Windows 2000 Service Pack Setup dialog box

> **Tip** Operating system updates can include upgraded components for features you have not installed on a particular computer. If at any time you go back to the original distribution disk for the operating system to install new components, be sure to reinstall the latest update afterward, so that you are certain that the new components you've installed are properly upgraded as well.

Operating system update releases go through a testing period, just like the operating system itself, but this does not necessarily mean that they are perfect. It's a good idea to check an operating system update before you install it, either by running it yourself in a lab environment or by monitoring Web sites and trade publications for news on problems with the latest release. You should also familiarize yourself with the release notes for the update, which list all of the specific changes that have been made to the operating system. There have been several occasions when major operating system updates have been modified to correct problems with the initial release of an update, and where your network is concerned, it pays to be cautious.

Patches

Between the releases of Service Packs or other major software updates, manufacturers may also make individual patches available. A patch is usually a small fix that is designed to address a highly specific problem. While you can be fairly confident that you should install major updates (after they are tested), you should carefully read about any patches that become available, to determine whether you even need to install them. In some cases, manufacturers recommend that you install a patch only under certain conditions, such as when you are using a particular combination of components or when you are experiencing a specific error. If your environment does not qualify, do not assume that you should install the patch anyway, just to keep your software current. Read all of the documentation accompanying the release and carefully follow the manufacturer's instructions.

Driver Updates

The device driver is another type of software component that is regularly updated, and you want to be even more judicious with your deployment of updates to this component than with operating system updates. If your hardware devices are functioning properly, there is probably no reason to update their device drivers with every new release that comes out. Many network administrators become over-zealous in this respect and start to assume that the latest release is automatically the greatest. In fact, this is often not the case. Unless you have a specific reason for applying a device driver update (for example, if you are experiencing the exact problem the update is documented to address), you are generally better off leaving your installations alone.

Software Upgrades

In addition to patches and updates, software manufacturers typically release periodic upgrades as well. Although the definitions differ depending on the manufacturer, an update is usually a relatively minor release that addresses specific issues or provides modest enhancements. An upgrade, by contrast, is a major release that provides new features and capabilities. In most cases, patches and updates are free, while you have to purchase an upgrade.

Deciding whether to upgrade your software can be difficult. In a network environment, a major software upgrade, whether you are talking about an operating system or an application, can be a complex and expensive undertaking. In addition to purchasing the software itself, you might need to upgrade the hardware in your computers (by adding memory, for example), pay people to install the new software on all of the computers, and even retrain your users to bring them up to speed on the new version. The cumulative cost of the process can be enormous.

Many applications today have gotten to the point where the developers are inventing new features just for the purpose of releasing an upgrade. If you don't have a need for these new features, it might not be worth upgrading. However, it's also important to not allow your software to get too out of date. If you stay with an older version of a software product because it does everything you want it to and because all of your users are familiar with it, you may eventually get to the point where the manufacturer no longer supports the product, and the cost of upgrading is much higher than it would have been earlier.

Chapter Summary

The key points covered in this chapter are as follows.

Backups

- Magnetic tape is the most popular storage medium for backups, because it is fast, inexpensive, and holds a lot of data.

- Tape drives are available in a variety of speeds and capacities to suit the needs of different installations.

- Backup software enables you to select the data you want to back up and sends it to the tape drive or other device.

- Daily backup jobs can be full backups, which copy all of the data on a computer, or incremental or differential backups, which only copy the data that has recently changed.

- A good backup software program enables you to schedule jobs to execute at any time, and it maintains both a tape version and a hard disk version of a catalog of all of the files that have been backed up.

- Network backup software enables you to back up data from computers anywhere on the network, and may also provide optional features such as live database backups.

Anti-Virus Policies

- Viruses are dangerous programs that can damage the data on a computer and spread to the other computers on a network.

- There are many different types of viruses that are constantly being modified to make them even more destructive than their predecessors.

- To protect your network against viruses, you must run anti-virus software on every computer.

Patches and Updates

- Obtaining, evaluating, and deploying software patches and updates is an important part of the network administrator's job.

- Device driver updates are frequently unnecessary, unless you are experiencing a specific problem that the upgrade is designed to fix.

- Software upgrades are major undertakings that can be extremely expensive and time-consuming.

Chapter Review

1. Which of the following types of backup jobs does not reset the Archive bits of the files it backs up?

   a. Full

   b. Incremental

   c. Differential

   d. Supplemental

2. Which of the following is the criterion most commonly used to filter files for backup jobs?

   a. File name

   b. File extension

   c. File attributes

   d. File size

3. Why is a worm not considered to be a true virus?

4. Name three reasons why a software upgrade can be an expensive proposition.

5. How does an autochanger increase the overall storage capacity of a backup solution?

6. How does a stealth virus disguise its presence?

   a. By masquerading as an innocuous file

   b. By changing the size of the infected file's directory entry

   c. By encrypting its signature

   d. By infecting the disk's master boot record

7. What are the three elements in the Grandfather-Father-Son media rotation system?

   a. Hard disk drives, CD-ROM drives, and magnetic tape drives

   b. Incremental, differential, and full backup jobs

   c. Monthly, weekly, and daily backup jobs

   d. QIC, DAT, and DLT tape drives

8. Which of the following software releases is a fix designed to address one specific issue?

   a. A patch

   b. An update

   c. An upgrade

   d. A Service Pack

9. How does a macro virus differ from the other major types of viruses?

   a. It doesn't replicate.

   b. It infects data files.

   c. It doesn't infect other files.

   d. It hides itself using encryption.

10. What drive interface is most commonly used by network backup devices?

   a. IDE

   b. SCSI

   c. USB

   d. Parallel port

CHAPTER 17

Network Troubleshooting Procedures

About This Chapter

One of the primary functions of the network administrator is to be there when something goes wrong. Troubleshooting a network is, by definition, more complex than troubleshooting a single computer, because the problem can be caused by one of several computers or other devices, or by any of the connections that join them together. Troubleshooting skills are a combination of common sense and knowledge about the hardware and software that make up the network. This chapter examines some of the basic aspects of the troubleshooting process and how to proceed from the investigation of a problem to its resolution.

Before You Begin

This chapter requires a basic knowledge of networking components, as discussed in Chapter 2, "Network Hardware," and Chapter 3, "Network Connections," as well as an understanding of the fundamental networking concepts covered in Chapter 1, "Networking Basics."

Lesson 1: Identifying Network Components

Network technicians are often charged with troubleshooting a problem on a network with which they are not familiar. A technician may work for an organization with a large network and be summoned to a remote location, or he or she may work for a consulting company and regularly travel to various client sites. As a technician, when you are faced with an unfamiliar network installation, your first order of business should be to determine the network's basic hardware configuration. In a perfect world, the network would be meticulously documented by the people who designed and built it, and you would have access to schematic diagrams of the cabling and an inventory of the network hardware. This is rarely the case, however, and often you must approach a problem with no information about the network infrastructure and the equipment used to build it. When this happens, you must be able to examine the equipment yourself to find out what's what. This lesson is designed to help you recognize the various types of network components when you see them.

After this lesson, you will be able to

- Recognize the functions of the various ports on the back of a computer
- Distinguish between the various types of network and small computer system interface (SCSI) connectors
- Recognize network components by their appearance

Estimated lesson time: 20 minutes

Recognizing Computer Ports

Computers have many different ports on them, and although most of the ports on computers manufactured today are labeled, you might come across units that have no markings. When this occurs, you must be able to discern the functions of the various ports so that, when you are working with the computer, you connect it properly to external devices.

The ports on a typical computer are located either on the motherboard or on expansion cards that plug into the system bus. In a few cases where the same type of port can have more than one function, you can sometimes tell what a port does by where it is located. The location of the motherboard ports can vary depending on the design of the computer. Figure 17.1 shows the back of an older computer, which has the motherboard ports grouped in a separate area away from the motherboard itself. In this type of computer, the motherboard ports are separate modules that are bolted to the back of the computer case and connected to the motherboard with cables. The computer's expansion slots are grouped in a different area, where you find the ports provided by the expansion cards installed in the system.

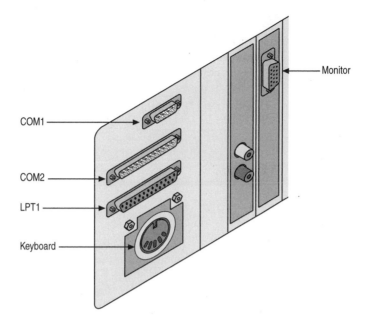

Figure 17.1 The back panel of an older computer

Figure 17.2 shows a newer computer with all of the motherboard ports lined up in a row. On this computer, the ports are actually part of the motherboard which, in this figure, runs horizontally along the bottom of the computer. All ports on this computer are located on the motherboard, including the video port, which in most cases is provided by an expansion card.

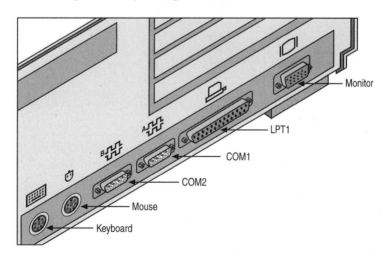

Figure 17.2 The back panel of a newer computer

Serial Ports

Serial ports are nearly always used by modems, but there are a few proprietary networking systems that use standard unshielded twisted pair (UTP) cable that plugs into an adapter connected to a serial port. The computers manufactured today typically have two serial ports on the motherboard, both of which use male DB-9 connectors, as shown in Figure 17.3.

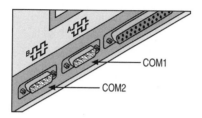

Figure 17.3 Today's computers have two DB-9 serial ports.

Older computers may also use DB-25 connectors for serial ports. Because nine pins more than satisfy the requirements for serial communications, a computer can use either type of connector. The typical configuration used to be one DB-9 and one DB-25, as shown in Figure 17.4. Serial connections can run at speeds that range from 110 to 115,200 bits per second (bps).

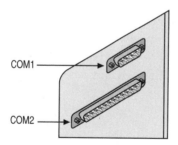

Figure 17.4 Older computers use both DB-9 and DB-25 connectors for serial ports.

Warning D-type connectors are not used exclusively for serial ports. Parallel ports also use DB-25 connectors (although they are female instead of male), and, in rare cases SCSI adapters use DB-25 connectors as well. In addition, DB-9 connectors were at one time used as video ports for connections to monitors, although they were female instead of male. Be sure not to confuse them, because their functions are not interchangeable.

Parallel Ports

Parallel ports were designed for use by printers, and in recent years they have been enhanced to provide more efficient bidirectional communications between the computer and the attached device. Parallel ports always use a female DB-25 connector, and the average computer today is only furnished with one (see Figure 17.5). In addition to printers, there is also a select group of SCSI devices that plug into a computer's parallel port. These devices use the same basic principles of communication as standard SCSI devices, but they use a different interface to the computer. The parallel port interface is slower than that of a dedicated SCSI host adapter but, for many users, the ability to move a device from computer to computer without installing an adapter card is worth the sacrifice in speed.

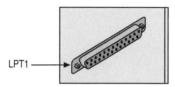

Figure 17.5 The female DB-25 connector used by parallel ports

---

Note Although nearly all computers today have two serial ports and one parallel port, it is still possible to add additional ports using an input/output (I/O) expansion card. However, because of the rise in popularity of the universal serial bus (USB) and the gradual elimination of the Industry Standard Architecture (ISA) slots that most of the I/O cards plug into, it is rarely necessary to add more serial and parallel ports.

Video Ports

The video connector on computers today cannot be mistaken for any other port because no other devices use the same female 15-pin D-shell connector with three rows of five pins each (shown in Figure 17.6). Before the introduction of the Video Graphics Array (VGA) standard in 1987, which eventually gave its name to the 15-pin connector, computers used digital monitors that connected to a female DB-9 port in the video adapter.

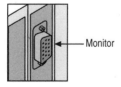

Figure 17.6 The 15-pin VGA connector used for connecting a monitor to the computer

Keyboard and Mouse Ports

A keyboard and mouse (or other type of pointing device) always require ports, which are typically on the computer's motherboard. On today's computers, both devices use the same type of port, which has a round, female, six-pin connector called a mini-DIN (DIN stands for *Deutsche Industrie Norm*, which is the German organization that developed the standard for the connector), as shown in Figure 17.7. This connector has also come to be known as a PS/2 connector, which comes from the name of the IBM computer model that first used it. Although it took far too many years to become standard practice, the mini-DIN connectors on computers are now usually labeled with pictograms that indicate which one is for the keyboard and which is for the mouse, as shown here. Accidentally cross-connecting the keyboard and the mouse does not cause any damage to the hardware, but the two ports are not interchangeable.

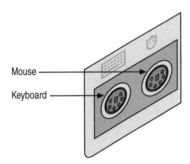

Figure 17.7 The six-pin mini-DIN connectors used for the keyboard and mouse today

Before the mini-DIN connector became standard equipment, a keyboard used a larger, female five-pin DIN connector, illustrated in Figure 17.8. Mice and other pointing devices used either DB-9 serial ports or a port on a dedicated "bus mouse" card.

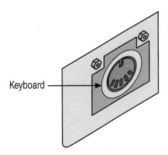

Figure 17.8 The five-pin DIN connector formerly used for keyboard connections

Warning In a few cases, there have been computers and other peripherals that use the older five-pin DIN connector to carry electrical power from a transformer to the device. Plugging a power connector into a keyboard port can severely damage a computer. However, because few computers today use the five-pin DIN keyboard connector, the danger of this happening is remote.

USB Ports

The universal serial bus (USB) is a relatively recent innovation that is rapidly replacing many of the ports commonly included on personal computers, such as the serial, parallel, keyboard, and mouse ports. USB is a multipurpose bus that runs at up to 12 megabits per second (Mbps) and supports a wide range of devices from keyboards and mice to cameras and disk drives, all using the same interface. Computers today typically have two USB ports, which use rectangular, female, four-conductor connectors (shown in Figure 17.9) that are totally unlike any other port in the computer. This port is called an A-connector; USB devices have B-connectors on them, which are more square-shaped.

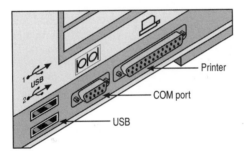

Figure 17.9 USB A-connectors

SCSI Ports

The small computer systems interface (SCSI) is a mass storage interface that supports many different internal and external devices at speeds up to 160 MBps. Network servers often use SCSI for internal hard drives and other storage media, but they can also have external SCSI connections using any one of several different cable connectors. Since its inception in the early 1980s, the interface has undergone several revisions to increase its speed and capabilities. These revisions have necessitated the use of different cables and, consequently, different connectors.

SCSI implementations typically involve a host adapter card that plugs into the computer's expansion bus. Occasionally, you might encounter a computer with a SCSI adapter integrated into the motherboard. The host adapter usually has both internal and external connectors. Internally, SCSI uses ribbon connectors that attach to hard drives and other devices. External SCSI cables are thick and relatively inflexible because of their heavy shielding and the tight bundling of wires contained inside. The earliest SCSI implementations used a 50-pin Centronics connector for external connections, which was identical in design to the Centronics connector used on most printers, except it was larger. This SCSI bus is 8 bits wide and runs at 5 MBps. Sometimes this same bus also used a standard DB-25, such as on early IBM, Apple Macintosh, and Sun Microsystems computers.

Later SCSI implementations use unique 50-pin High-Density or 68-pin High-Density connectors on their cables. These connectors have two rows containing equal numbers of pins that are smaller than those in a DB-25 connector. The 50-pin version has clips on the connector that connect it to the port on the computer, while the 68-pin version has thumbscrews instead. The 50-pin connectors are used primarily on Fast SCSI implementations, running at 10 MBps, while the 68-pin connector is used for Fast/Wide SCSI, running at 20 MBps.

Another type of SCSI used by some drives today is called *Single Connector Attachment (SCA)* SCSI, which uses a special 80-pin connector that supplies both the power and the data connections to the drive. The connector is similar in appearance to a Centronics connector, although a bit wider, and in many cases people use an adapter to attach SCA drives to a standard power connector and a 50- or 68-pin High-Density SCSI connector. Figure 17.10 illustrates the various types of external SCSI connectors you might find on a computer.

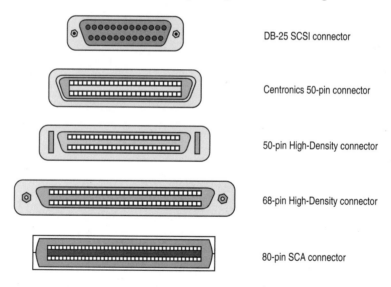

Figure 17.10 SCSI host adapter connectors: DB-25, 50-pin Centronics, 50-pin High-Density, 68-pin High-Density, and 80-pin SCA

Network Cable Connectors

Network interface cards (NICs) can often have several different types of connectors on them, but you can only use one of the connectors at a time. This type of adapter is called a combination NIC (or "combo NIC"). Additional connectors often add substantially to the cost of the NIC. The type of connector you use to attach your computer to a network depends on the data-link layer protocol and the type of cable your network uses. Ethernet NICs often have three network connectors on them: an Attachment Unit Interface (AUI) connector, a Bayonet-Neill-Concelman (BNC) connector, and an RJ45 connector. These network connectors are shown in Figure 17.11.

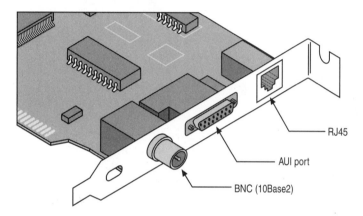

Figure 17.11 A combination Ethernet NIC with RJ45, AUI, and BNC connectors

---

Note For more information about NICs and network cables, see Chapter 2, "Network Hardware."

The AUI connector, the oldest of the Ethernet cable connectors, is a 15-pin female D-shell connector with two rows of pins. You use the AUI connector to attach an AUI cable to the NIC in your computer. The other end of the AUI cable connects to a Thick Ethernet network. While it's still common to see Ethernet NICs with an AUI connector (in addition to others), it's rare to see the connector actually being used. The BNC connector is for attaching a computer to a Thin Ethernet network. You must attach a special T fitting to the connector on the NIC, and you then attach the Ethernet cables to the arms of the T, as shown in Figure 17.12. This enables you to run the cable from computer to computer, forming a bus topology. In some cases, the T connector is included with the NIC; in other cases, you must purchase it separately.

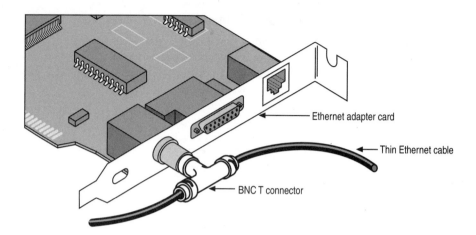

Ethernet adapter card

Thin Ethernet cable

BNC T connector

Figure 17.12 Thin Ethernet connections require a T connector, which you must attach directly to the BNC connector on the NIC.

The connector used on most Ethernet networks installed today is called the RJ45. Because the vast majority of Ethernet networks today use UTP cable, purchasing NICs with just a single RJ45 connector, like that shown in Figure 17.13, is usually the most economical course of action. RJ45 connectors are similar in appearance to telephone jacks, except that the RJ11 telephone connector has four contacts and the RJ45 has eight. An RJ11 plug is slightly narrower than an RJ45, but it's easy to mistake the two. You can insert an RJ11 plug into an RJ45 jack, but you can't plug an RJ45 into an RJ11.

Many computers have internal modems, so it's quite common to see two expansion cards in one computer, and RJ11 and RJ45 jacks that look similar. Obviously, confusing the two connectors can lead to problems. Plugging a telephone cable into a NIC's RJ45 connector won't cause any damage, but neither will any network communication take place. (This is unlike other situations where confusing this type of connector can be more serious; plugging a standard analog modem into a digital telephone jack connected to a switchboard, for example, can ruin the modem.) In most cases, the easiest way to tell modem connectors from NIC connectors on an installed expansion card is by the number of connectors. Most modems have two RJ11 connectors, one for the connection to the telephone line and one for a telephone, while NICs only have one RJ45 connector.

Figure 17.13 An Ethernet NIC that uses an RJ45 jack

Token Ring networks can use UTP cables, just like Ethernet, so the connector you see on the NIC is the same female RJ45. Token Ring networks that use IBM Type 1 cabling have female DB-9 connectors on their NICs, however. This type of Token Ring cable uses a male DB-9 connector on one end to connect to the NIC, and an IBM Data Connector on the other end to connect the computer to its multistation access unit (MAU). In some cases, however, administrators trying to avoid the expense of the Type 1 cabling use devices called *Token Ring media filters* to connect their Type 1 NICs to a UTP network. The media filter is essentially an adapter with a male DB-9 connector and a female RJ45 connector on it, as shown in Figure 17.14. You plug the DB-9 into the NIC and connect a standard UTP network cable to the RJ45 connector.

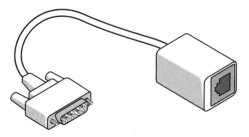

Figure 17.14 A Token Ring media filter

Recognizing Network Components

In addition to being knowledgeable about the ports used to connect computers to the network and to other devices, a network technician must also be familiar with the other types of equipment found at a network location.

Network Interface Adapters

NICs are similar in appearance to other types of expansion cards. NICs are manufactured for each of the bus types commonly found in computers, although the most commonly seen today are Peripheral Component Interconnect (PCI) and ISA NICs. The primary way to distinguish a NIC from another type of card (apart from examining the chips, which often have the name of the manufacturer printed on them) is by looking at the connectors, which can be any one of the types mentioned in the previous section, "Network Cable Connectors."

Motherboard-resident network interface adapters don't require a bus slot, and the electronics can easily be lost in the maze of motherboard circuitry. However, the presence of an RJ45 jack on the back of the computer indicates support for UTP Ethernet.

Note See Lesson 2: Network Interface Adapters, in Chapter 2, "Network Hardware," for more information about NICs.

Hubs and Switches

A hub can be either a standalone box or a unit that mounts into a standard 19-inch-wide rack used for large network installations. Whatever the form, the basic identifying feature of a hub is one or more rows of female connectors, as shown in Figure 17.15. Most of the hubs you'll encounter have rows of RJ45 connectors for Ethernet or Token Ring cables, but there are also hubs that have straight tip (ST) fiber optic connectors, which are bayonet-style connectors; Type 1 Token Ring connectors, which are IBM data connectors (IDCs); and others. A hub can have as few as four ports in it, or as many as 24. When you connect a cable between a computer and a hub port, other computers on an externally wired network segment are directly accessible, while computers on an internally wired network segment are accessible through their connections to patch panel ports.

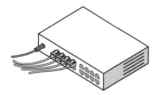

Figure 17.15 The back of a 10BaseT/100BaseTX Ethernet hub

In most cases, a hub has rows of light emitting diode (LED) lamps that correspond to the network cable ports, as shown in Figure 17.16. These LEDs are activated by the link pulse signal generated by a network interface adapter when it is active and functioning properly. An LED that is not lit indicates a malfunction in either the hub or the network interface adapter, a broken or disconnected cable, or a computer that is turned off or missing.

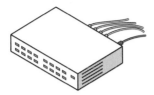

Figure 17.16 The LED display on the same 10BaseT/100BaseTX Ethernet hub

Hubs can support any one of several data-link layer protocols. The most common is Ethernet, but you can also find hubs that support the Fiber Distributed Data Interface (FDDI), Token Ring, or other protocols. These hubs may be called by different names (a Token Ring hub is called a MAU, for example) and use different types of connectors, but their general appearance is the same.

Note See Lesson 3: Network Hubs, in Chapter 2, "Network Hardware," for more information about hubs.

Switches are very similar in appearance to hubs, and units made by the same manufacturer can indeed look identical. The difference between a hub and a switch is in the internal manipulation of incoming data. A hub forwards all incoming traffic out through all the other ports, while a switch forwards traffic only to the device for which it is destined. Switches are available in most of the same configurations as hubs, and they range from small units intended for home or small business networks to large rack-mounted devices.

Some switches have an additional nine-pin serial port on them, which you use to connect the device to a computer using a null modem cable. This interface enables you to perform the initial configuration of the unit before it's connected to the network. After the initial configuration is complete, you can access the switch's management functions by using a Telnet session from a computer on the network.

Patch Panels

Patch panels have rows of female RJ45 jacks or other connectors, just like hubs, but they don't perform any function other than providing connections between internal cable installations and patch cables. Patch panels, also called punchdown blocks, are typically mounted either on a wall or in a rack; they are not standalone units. In many cases, patch panels are modular, and consist of a framework and interchangeable connectors, as shown in Figure 17.17.

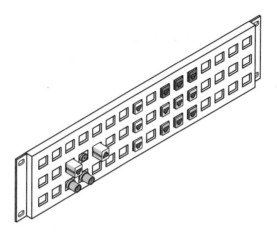

Figure 17.17 A modular patch panel

Bridges and Routers

As with hubs and switches, bridges and routers can be standalone or rack-mounted units. Because bridges and routers only connect two network segments together, they don't have as many ports as hubs do, and are often more difficult to recognize as a result. A standalone bridge or router can take the form of any type of box with two or more ports in it. It sometimes has a few LED lamps for status displays, as shown in Figure 17.18.

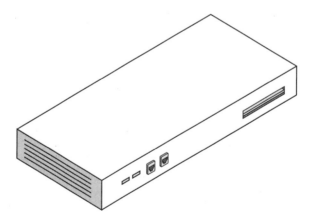

Figure 17.18 A typical standalone router

Bridges and routers can connect local area networks (LANs) of the same type or different types, or they can connect a LAN to a remote network using a leased telephone line or other wide area network (WAN) connection. For a router connected to a WAN link, the identifying element of the unit is a serial port that is connected to a Channel Service Unit/Data Service Unit (CSU/DSU). The

CSU/DSU provides the interface to the leased line, much like a modem provides the interface to a standard telephone line, except that the CSU/DSU is a digital device. In addition to the serial port, the bridge or router also has one or more ports for connecting to the LAN and uses any of the standard cable connectors, such as female RJ45s.

A bridge or router used to connect two internal network segments can have two ports of the same type, such as two RJ45 jacks, or two different ports, which connect to different types of networks. In most cases, bridges used internally are transparent bridges, which connect the same type of network, so they have two identical ports. A device with two different ports, such as an RJ45 jack and a BNC connector, is more likely to be a router. However, routers can also have two identical ports, either because they connect two LANs of the same type or because they connect two different types of LANs that use the same cable, such as 10BaseT and UTP Token Ring. Larger routers can be modular, consisting of a frame with multiple slots into which you plug separate modules supporting a specific type of network, as shown in Figure 17.19. This enables you to custom-build a router configuration to suit virtually any combination of network technologies. Bridge/routers, or brouters, which are combination devices that operate at both the data-link and network layers of the Open Systems Interconnection (OSI) model, can have the characteristics of both bridges and routers, and are often all but identical in appearance to separate bridges or routers.

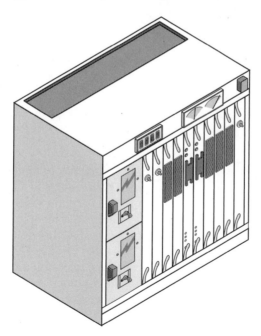

Figure 17.19 A router frame with modules installed

Print Servers

A print server is a device that receives print jobs from clients on a network and feeds them to the printer at the appropriate rate. The print server sometimes spools the print jobs, meaning that it stores them on a hard drive while waiting for the printer to be ready to receive them. This enables network users to share a printer without experiencing delays in their applications while they wait for the printer to become available.

In some cases, a print server is a computer. You can connect a printer directly to a computer and share it with other users on the network. However, there are also standalone print servers, which take the form of either an expansion card that you install in the printer itself or a small box with one or more ports for connecting to the printer (or printers) and another for connecting to a network hub, as shown in Figure 17.20. The device has an IP address of its own, and computers on the network send their print jobs to the print server, which relays them to the appropriate printer. This enables users to locate a printer anywhere on the network.

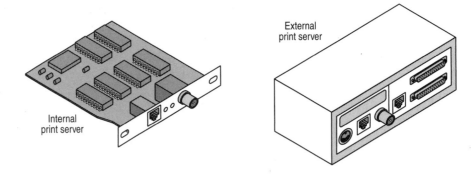

Figure 17.20 External and printer-internal print server devices

UPS Devices

An uninterruptible power supply (UPS) provides equipment with a temporary supply of electrical power in the event of an outage in the building's main power supply. A UPS is essentially a battery that is continuously charged when the main power is on. You plug computers or other equipment into the UPS, and if the power fails, the battery supplies power for a short period of time, long enough to safely turn off a computer without damaging its data. UPS devices are available in models ranging from small units designed to protect a single computer, to larger devices that can protect several computers at once, as shown in Figure 17.21. It's even possible to install a huge UPS that can protect an entire data center or building.

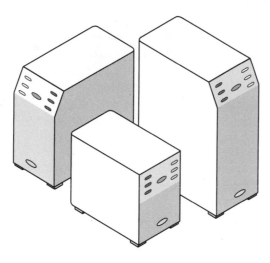

Figure 17.21 Uninterruptible power supplies

A UPS (see Figure 17.22) is a heavy box with a series of power outlets for your equipment (typically on the back) and a standard electrical plug that connects to the building's power source. Larger devices might require special power connections. In many cases, a group of LEDs displays the amount of power left in the battery and the load generated by the connected equipment. Every network server containing important data should be connected to a UPS.

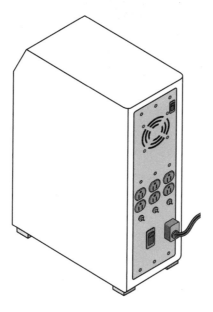

Figure 17.22 The back panel of a UPS

The best UPS units are those whose connected devices run off the battery at all times. This way, when the building power fails, the equipment experiences no interruption at all. Lower-priced units run the equipment from the building's power supply until it fails, at which time it switches over to battery power. This brief interruption can sometimes be enough to interrupt a disk writing process, causing data corruption. High-quality units also have one or more serial ports that you can use to connect the UPS to a computer. A program or service running on the computer receives a signal from the UPS when building power is cut off, and after a specified interval the computer shuts itself down in a controlled fashion. This is so that the UPS continues to provide protection against data loss, even when no one is present to shut down the computer.

Exercise 17.1: Ports and Connectors

Match the ports listed in the left column with the connector descriptions in the right column.

1.	VGA video port	a.	Rectangular four-conductor connector
2.	Serial port	b.	Combined power and data connector
3.	SCA SCSI port	c.	Mini-DIN connector
4.	10BaseT Ethernet port	d.	Three-row, 15-pin D-shell connector
5.	USB port	e.	Female DB-25 connector
6.	AUI port	f.	50-pin Centronics connector
7.	Keyboard/mouse port	g.	Thick Ethernet connector
8.	Parallel port	h.	Male DB-9 connector
9.	5 MBps SCSI port	i.	BNC connector
10.	Thin Ethernet port	j.	RJ45 connector

Lesson 2: Troubleshooting a Network

One of the key elements of troubleshooting a network problem is having a plan of action. Many of the trouble calls you will receive are likely to be user issues involving things like the improper use of software. When you're faced with what appears to be a real problem, you should follow a set troubleshooting procedure. The procedure should consist of a series of steps like the following:

1. Identify the exact problem.
2. Duplicate the problem.
3. Isolate the cause of the problem.
4. Formulate and implement a solution.
5. Test the solution.
6. Document the problem and the solution.
7. Give feedback to the user.

The steps you follow can be slightly different, or you can perform the steps in a slightly different order, but the overall process should be similar. The following sections examine each of these steps.

After this lesson, you will be able to

- Understand the steps involved in troubleshooting a network problem
- List the rules for prioritizing problem calls
- Describe the process of isolating the source of a network problem

Estimated lesson time: 15 minutes

Identifying the Problem

The first step in troubleshooting a network problem is to determine exactly what is going wrong, and to note the effect of the problem on the network. This is so that you can assign a priority to a problem. In a large network environment, it is often the case that there are many more calls for support than the network support staff can handle at one particular time. Therefore, it is essential to establish a system of priorities that dictate which calls get addressed first. As in the emergency department of a hospital, the priorities should not necessarily be based on who is first in line. More often, it is the severity of the problem that determines who gets attention first, although it is usually not wise to ignore the political reality that senior management problems get addressed before those of the rank and file.

The following rules can help you to establish priorities:

- **Shared resources take precedence over individual resources.** A problem with a server or other network component that prevents many users from working must take precedence over one that affects only a single user.

- **Network-wide problems take precedence over workgroup or departmental problems.** Resources that provide services to the entire network, such as e-mail servers, should be considered before departmental resources, such as file and print servers.

- **Rate departmental issues according to the function of the department.** Problems with resources belonging to a department that is critical to the organization, such as order entry or customer service call centers, should take precedence over departments that can better tolerate a period of down time, such as Research and Development.

- **System-wide problems take precedence over application problems.** A problem that puts an entire computer out of commission, preventing a user from getting any work done, should take precedence over a problem a user is experiencing with a single application.

Sometimes it's difficult to determine the exact nature of the problem from the story told by a relatively inexperienced user, but part of the process of narrowing down the cause of a particular problem involves obtaining accurate information about what has occurred. Users can often be vague about what they were doing when they experienced the problem, or even what the indications of the problem were. For example, in many cases, users call the help desk because they received an error message, but neglect to write down the wording of the message. Gentle training of the user in the proper procedures for documenting and reporting problems is part of the network technician's job as well. It might not be any help to you now, but it can help you the next time that user receives an error.

For now, you can begin by asking questions like the following:

- What exactly were you doing when the problem occurred?
- Have you had any other problems?
- Was the computer behaving normally just before the problem occurred?
- Has any hardware or software been installed, removed, or reconfigured recently?
- Did you (or anyone else) do anything to try to resolve the problem?

Duplicating the Problem

The next step in assessing the nature of the problem is to see if it can be duplicated. Network problems that you can easily duplicate are far easier to fix, primarily because you can easily test to see if your solution was successful. However, there are many types of network problems that are intermittent, or that might occur for only a short period of time. In these cases, you might have to leave the incident open until the problem occurs again. In some instances, having the user reproduce the problem can lead to the solution. User error is a common cause of problems that can seem to be hardware or network related to the inexperienced eye.

Isolating the Problem

When you've determined that the problem can be duplicated, you can set about determining the actual source of the difficulty. If, for example, a user has trouble opening a file in a word processing application, the difficulty can lie in the application, in the user's computer, in the file server where the file is stored, or in any of the networking components in between. The process of isolating the location of the problem consists of eliminating the elements that are not the cause, in a logical and methodical manner.

There's an old medical school axiom that says when you hear hoofbeats, think horses, not zebras. In the context of network troubleshooting, this means that when you look for possible causes of a problem, start with the obvious first. For example, if a workstation is unable to communicate with a file server, don't start by checking the routers in between the two systems; check the simple things on the workstation first, such as whether the network cable is plugged into the computer. The other important part of the process is to work methodically and document everything you check, so that you don't duplicate your efforts.

If it's possible to duplicate the problem, you can begin to isolate the cause by reproducing the conditions under which the problem occurred, using a procedure like the following:

1. Have the user reproduce the problem on the computer repeatedly, so that you can determine whether the user's actions are triggering the error.

2. Sit at the computer yourself and perform the same task. If the problem does not occur, the cause might be in how the user is performing a particular task. Check the user's procedures carefully to see if he or she is doing something wrong. It's entirely possible, however, that you and the user perform the same task in different ways, and that the user's method is exposing a problem that yours doesn't.

3. If the problem reoccurs when you perform the task, log off from the user's account, log in using an account with administrative privileges, and repeat the task. If the problem does not reoccur, it is probably the result of the user not having the rights or permissions needed to perform the task.

4. If the problem reoccurs, try to perform the same task on another, similarly equipped computer connected to the same network. If you can't reproduce the problem on another computer, you know that the cause lies in the user's computer or its connection to the network. If the problem does reoccur on another computer, you know that you're dealing with a network problem, either in the server that the computer was communicating with or the hardware that connects the two.

If you determine that the problem lies somewhere in the network and not in the user's computer, you can then begin the process of isolating the area of the network that is the source of the problem. For example, if you are able to reproduce the problem on another nearby computer, you can then begin performing the same task on computers located elsewhere on the network. Again, proceed methodically and document your results. For example, you can proceed by trying to reproduce the problem on another computer connected to the same hub, and then on a computer connected to a different hub on the same LAN. If the problem occurs throughout the LAN, try a computer on a different LAN. Eventually, you should be able to narrow down the source of the problem to a particular component, such as a server, router, hub, or cable.

Note For more information about error messages and other indicators used to troubleshoot network problems, see Lesson 2: Logs and Indicators, in Chapter 18, "Network Troubleshooting Tools."

After you have isolated the problem to a particular piece of equipment, you can proceed in the same way to try and determine if it is caused by hardware or software. If it's a hardware problem, you might then proceed by replacing the unit that is at fault or by using an alternate. Communication problems, for example, might force you to try replacing network cables until you find one that is faulty. If the problem is in a server, you might need to replace components, such as hard drives, until you find the culprit. If you determine that the problem is caused by software, you might want to try running an application or storing data on a different computer, or reinstall the software on the offending system.

Resolving the Problem

In some cases, the process of isolating the source of a problem includes the resolution of the problem. If, for example, you end up replacing network patch cables until you find the one that is faulty, replacing the bad cable is the resolution of the problem. In other cases, however, the resolution might be more involved, such as having to reinstall a server application or operating system. Because other users might need to access that server, you might have to defer the resolution of the problem until a later time, when the network is not in use and after you've backed up the data stored on the server. In some cases, you might even have to bring in outside help, such as a contractor to pull new cables. This can require careful scheduling to avoid having the contractor's work conflict with the activities of you and your users. Sometimes, you might want to provide an interim solution, such as a substitute workstation or server, until you can definitively resolve the problem.

Testing the Solution

When you have implemented your resolution to the problem, you should return to the very beginning of the process and repeat the task that originally caused the problem. If the problem no longer occurs, you should test the other functions related to the changes you've made. This is to ensure that in fixing one problem, you haven't created another.

Documenting the Problem

Although it is presented here as a separate step, documenting your actions is a process that should begin as soon as the user calls for help. A well-organized network support organization should have a system in place in which each problem call is registered as a trouble ticket that eventually contains a complete record of the problem and the steps taken to isolate and resolve it. In many cases, a technical support organization operates using "tiers," which are groups of technicians of different skill levels. Calls come in to the first tier, and if the problem is sufficiently complex or the first-tier technician is unable to resolve it, the call is escalated to the second tier, which is composed of senior technicians. As long as everyone involved in the process documents his or her activities, there should be no problem when one technician hands off the ticket to another. In addition, keeping careful notes prevents people from duplicating each other's efforts.

Giving Feedback

The final phase of the troubleshooting process is to explain to the user what happened and why. Of course, the average network user is probably not interested in hearing all the technical details, but it's a good idea to let users know whether their actions caused the problem, exacerbated it, or made it more difficult to resolve. This gradual education of the network's users can lead to a quicker resolution next time, or even prevent a problem from occurring altogether.

Exercise 17.2: Network Troubleshooting

Place the following steps of the problem isolation process in the proper logical order.

1. Reproduce the problem using a different computer.

2. Reproduce the problem yourself.

3. Have the user reproduce the problem.

4. Reproduce the problem using a different user account.

Chapter Summary

The key points covered in this chapter are as follows.

Identifying Network Components

- Computers have a variety of ports, some of which are implemented by the motherboard, and others by expansion cards.

- Computers use many different types of connectors for their various interfaces, and in some cases the same connector type can provide different functions.

- SCSI host adapters can use any one of several types of connectors, which are not interchangeable.

Troubleshooting a Network

- The process of troubleshooting a network should proceed through several steps, including identifying, duplicating, isolating, resolving, and documenting the problem.

- Isolating a network problem is a matter of eliminating hardware and software components that are not possible causes.

- Maintaining a carefully documented and methodically applied troubleshooting process is an essential part of maintaining a network.

Chapter Review

1. What is the device called that enables you to connect a Type 1 Token Ring NIC to a UTP network?

2. Which of the following ports never uses a DB-25 connector?

   a. Parallel ports

   b. Serial ports

   c. Video ports

   d. SCSI ports

3. Which type of SCSI connector supplies power as well as data signals?

   a. 50-pin Centronics

   b. SCA

   c. 50-pin High-Density

   d. 68-pin High-Density

4. Which of the following problems would you assign the highest priority for your network support team? Explain why.

   a. The printer in the Order Entry department isn't working.

   b. The corporate e-mail server is down.

   c. A hub is malfunctioning in the Sales department.

   d. The president of the company's workstation is locked up.

5. Which type of connector has been used both for keyboards and for power connections?

   a. PS/2

   b. Five-pin DIN

   c. USB

   d. Six-pin mini-DIN

6. In a two-tiered network support system, what do the tiers refer to?

   a. File servers storing network documentation

   b. Priorities for trouble tickets

   c. Problem call databases

   d. Technicians of different skill levels

7. Which of the following devices does not typically contain a row of at least four ports?

   a. A router

   b. A patch panel

   c. A switch

   d. A hub

8. What is the name of the device that provides the interface between a router and a leased telephone line?

9. Which type of Ethernet connector has 15 pins?

   a. RJ45

   b. BNC

   c. AUI

   d. VGA

10. How does a UPS protect a network?

C H A P T E R   1 8

Network Troubleshooting Tools

About This Chapter

A key aspect of network troubleshooting is having the proper tools at your command. While you certainly may need basic hand tools, such as screwdrivers, and some more specialized tools, such as the cabling tools discussed in Chapter 15, "Installing a Network," the primary network troubleshooting tool is information. Being able to find information, gather it, interpret it, and use it properly are all essential skills for the network troubleshooter. This chapter explains how to find information about the products you use on your network, the current condition of your hardware, and the status of your software.

Before You Begin

This chapter builds on the troubleshooting procedures described in Chapter 17, "Network Troubleshooting Procedures," and on the information about operating systems and applications found in Chapter 4, "Networking Software," and Chapter 10, "TCP/IP Applications." Knowledge of the Transmission Control Protocol/ Internet Protocol (TCP/IP) communications covered in Lesson 1: IP, in Chapter 6, "Network Layer Protocols," and Chapter 8, "TCP/IP Fundamentals," as well as an understanding of the Open Systems Interconnection (OSI) model layers, as covered in Lesson 2: The OSI Reference Model, in Chapter 1, "Networking Basics," are also helpful.

Lesson 1: Documentation and Resources

Many people who work with computers and networks don't read the documentation that comes with the products they purchase. Some are even quite smug about it. In addition, as a cost-cutting measure, most hardware and software manufacturers have greatly reduced the amount of printed documentation they include with their products. However, to properly administer and troubleshoot a network, you must have information about the products you are using, and in many cases, you must turn to resources other than the product manufacturer to get it. This lesson investigates some of the many sources of information that are now available to the network administrator.

After this lesson, you will be able to

- List the basic formats used to distribute product documentation
- Understand manufacturers' technical support policies
- Describe the various informational resources available to network administrators on the Internet
- List the various types of books, periodicals, and CD-ROMs useful to network troubleshooters

Estimated lesson time: 25 minutes

Product Documentation

If the hardware and software products you purchase do not come with thick volumes of printed manuals as they used to, there is often documentation included in some form. Even if you don't need to read the manual to install or configure the product, you should always keep all the documentation that comes with it on file, because you might need it later when you're reinstalling, upgrading, or troubleshooting the network.

Although you may be working with devices or software products that you think you know very well, you might still need the documentation some day. Suppose, for example, you're faced with a network that was first installed several years ago. You want to upgrade the computers to a new operating system, but you know that you will have to install additional memory into all the computers first. Even if you know these computers well, if you haven't upgraded them before, you might not know exactly what type of memory modules you need, what combinations of modules the computers support, or how much memory they are capable of using. To complicate things further, suppose that the company that manufactured those computers was acquired by another company and no longer makes or supports that particular model. If whoever bought those computers filed away the documentation that came with them, you'll easily be able to find the information you need. If not, you'll have to determine by trial and error what memory configurations the computers can use, which could take a lot of time and money.

Because of the high costs associated with printing, many products now include their documentation in other forms. CD-ROMs can contain documents in various formats, which are discussed in the following sections.

Text Files

Many manufacturers use plain ASCII text files to provide late-breaking information about problems, revisions, and compatibility issues related to their products. The traditional name for this type of file is Readme.1st or something similar. It's always a good idea to check the software distribution CD-ROMs that accompany the products you buy for files with this type of name or with a .txt extension. To view text files, you can use a simple program like Notepad.exe, which is included with all current versions of Microsoft Windows, or you can simply copy them to a printer, typing a command like **copy readme.1st lpt1** at the MS-DOS command prompt.

Adobe Acrobat PDF files

Acrobat is an application created by Adobe Systems Inc. that creates and displays documents in a proprietary format called the Portable Document Format (PDF). These files preserve all the original design elements, layout, and formatting characteristics of the original documents they are created from, including fonts and full color illustrations. You create .pdf files by using a special printer driver supplied with Acrobat, which compiles the document you've created in another application into a single file.

To view a .pdf file, you must have Acrobat Reader, which is available free of charge from the Adobe Web site at *www.adobe.com/products/acrobat/ readstep2.html*. There are versions supporting over a dozen different hardware platforms. Acrobat Reader displays the documents in fully laid-out pages, just as they would appear when printed, as shown in Figure 18.1. You can print out a .pdf document, if you wish, enabling you to create a facsimile of a printed manual. Acrobat Reader also includes a plug-in for your Web browser, so that you can click on links to .pdf files on Web sites and display them. When the publisher has created the .pdf files in a particular way, the Web browser plug-in can display a document as it's downloading, one page at a time, so that you don't have to wait for the entire file to download before any of it is displayed.

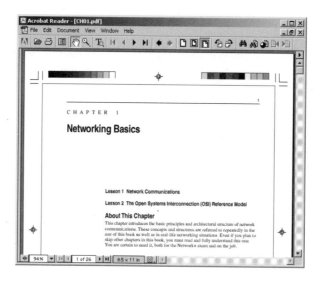

Figure 18.1 Adobe Acrobat creates .pdf files that you can view and print using the free Acrobat Reader program.

The ease with which Acrobat can create .pdf files has made it a very attractive solution for manufacturers seeking to publish their documentation, marketing collateral, and technical documents more inexpensively. Despite being a proprietary format, .pdf has become a de facto standard in the computing industry. These files can be quite large, making them better suited for CD-ROM distribution than over the Web. Adobe allows third parties to include Acrobat Reader on their CD-ROMs, so that if you find that a product includes documentation in .pdf format and you don't already have the reader, you can usually install it from the CD. Another advantage of .pdf files is that they are searchable. Publishers can also choose to create an index of key terms in a collection of .pdf files, which speeds up the searching process.

HTML Files

Although intended for use on Web sites, some manufacturers also use the Hypertext Markup Language (HTML) to create their documentation and include it with the product on a CD-ROM. Viewing the documents on the CD-ROM is the same as viewing them on a Web site once you have pointed your browser to the home page file on the disk. Depending on how the HTML files are organized, searching them may or may not be possible.

Telephone Support

In addition to including printed manuals with their products, virtually every hardware and software company at one time maintained a free technical support line for their products. Whenever you had a problem, you called what was often a toll-free number and usually got the help you needed. Alas, the days of free telephone support are now gone as well. The cost of hiring, training, and maintaining an effective technical support staff has risen so high that manufacturers have had to either limit the support they offer or charge a fee for it. Today, some products include free technical support for a limited period of time or a limited number of incidents, but after that you usually have to pay for help from the manufacturer's technicians. Depending on the company involved, the fee for technical support can be based on an hourly rate or a per incident charge, but it usually isn't cheap.

Because calling for technical support can now be a significant expense or an expenditure of limited company resources, the question of when to pick up the telephone and ask for help is more difficult than it used to be. When support was free, many users called frequently for problems they could easily have solved themselves, simply to avoid the bother of reading the manual. This abuse of the manufacturer's generosity is one of the main reasons that free telephone support is largely a thing of the past. Today, people are more likely to seek out alternative avenues of support before paying for help.

There are times, however, when calling for technical support is proper and, indeed, necessary. Some manufacturers might have known issues with a product that have not yet made it into their documentation, their Web site, or even their Readme files. You could spend hours attempting to research a problem when the whole issue could be solved with a 5-minute telephone call. Generally speaking, the best course of action when you're stuck for information about a product is to check the Web and Usenet (which is discussed later in this lesson) first, and only call technical support as a last resort.

Online Resources

In recent years, the Internet has come to be the single most valuable source of information about computer networking and the products used on networks. Virtually every manufacturer of computer products maintains a Web site, and the information resources that you find there can often be extremely valuable. Some of the features commonly found on manufacturers' Web sites are as follows:

- **Marketing collateral** Although more useful for pre-sales product evaluation than for technical support, product information documents are available on the Web sites of most manufacturers of computer hardware and software. These documents might include datasheets, features and benefits lists, product comparisons, product reviews (at least the favorable ones), and other sales literature. It's common for documents like these to be posted in .pdf format, although they might also be in plain HTML.

- **Product manuals** Online product manuals are a common feature on manufacturers' Web sites. If the manufacturer is already distributing their documentation in .pdf or HTML format, it's a simple matter to post the same files on their Web site. Even if you already have a printed manual for a product, an online version can be of additional value if the site has a search engine that enables you to find the information you need more easily.

- **Technical documents** White papers and other documents often provide technical background information that can help you to evaluate networking products, to understand how they work, and to troubleshoot them when a problem occurs. This type of document, which is often posted in .pdf format, is frequently more concerned with the theoretical aspects of the product than with day-to-day operations.

- **Frequently asked questions** Lists of frequently asked questions, commonly known as FAQs, are one of the best resources for information about common problems that a product is experiencing. When something goes wrong with a manufacturer's product, it isn't likely that you are the first person to have experienced that problem. When enough people report the same problem to the manufacturer, they often address it by adding it to an FAQ, hoping to avoid repetitive support calls. The FAQ should be one of the first resources that you turn to for help, and can be an excellent product evaluation resource as well. Finding out what kind of problems a product is having and how the manufacturer deals with them can help you decide whether a particular product is worth purchasing.

- **Technical support databases** Many manufacturers maintain an online database of technical support articles. Sometimes, it's the same one that the company's technical support representatives use. This type of resource typically works by letting you search for keywords or error messages, and provides information on a solution or workaround, and possibly a link to a software patch. The amount of information available depends on the simplicity or complexity of the product. Microsoft's Knowledge Base (available at *search.support.microsoft.com*), for example, is an enormous compendium of thousands of articles about the company's many products. You can search by keywords, by article ID number, or for a downloadable file. The Microsoft Knowledge Base, like many other sites, also supports plain language queries, which enables you to search for information online just as you would ask a person for it. For example, you can ask, "How do I back up the Active Directory database?" instead of putting together a search string like active+directory+backup.

- **File downloads** Being able to download drivers, software updates, patches, and other files is, of course, a major benefit of using a manufacturer's Web site over its technical support telephone line. Checking to see how many patches have been issued for a particular product is also a good way of evaluating it before buying. If you find that a software product has had a large number of bug fixes in a short time, it's probably a good idea to look elsewhere. Downloadable files on Web sites are typically supplied as compressed ZIP archives that are either self-extracting or require a decompression program like PKUNZIP or Winzip. UNIX downloads are usually supplied in the gzip format.

- **Online messaging** In addition to static information, many manufacturers now have messaging capabilities on their Web sites. Online messaging is the Web equivalent of the old bulletin board systems, where you can leave a text message and receive a reply from a technical support representative. Because these systems are public, you might find that the solution to your problem has already been posted in a response to another user. In addition, you might find helpful information from other users as well as from the manufacturer's representatives. One way of checking the value of a service like this is to see how long it takes for the company to respond to questions from users. In some cases, companies are quick to set up a messaging site of this type, but they fail to realize how much time it takes to maintain it properly. If you notice that several days pass between user questions and the company's replies, or if the replies seem less than helpful in a lot of cases, you should probably look elsewhere for prompt support.

- **Live support** A few companies in the computer industry now offer live sales information and/or technical support over the Web. This usually takes the form of a chat application that uses Sun Microsystem's Java or some other technology to provide a live text-messaging link between users and company representatives. In most cases, the hours during which this type of support is offered are limited, and you should test out the interface carefully on your computer before relying on it as a primary technical support medium. In some cases, difficulties in communication make this type of support connection impractical.

- **Contact information** If all else fails, manufacturers' Web sites nearly always provide the e-mail addresses that you can use and the telephone numbers that you can call for technical support, as well as other contact information, such as mailing addresses and procedures for returning defective products.

Third-Party Web Sites

There are a great many other Web sites containing useful networking information besides those run by product manufacturers. There are hundreds, if not thousands, of sites devoted to each of the popular operating systems in use today, as well as sites devoted to major applications, computer hardware, and networking principles. However, when dealing with information from what is essentially an unknown source, you must be careful to verify anything that seems unlikely or potentially dangerous. You can sometimes tell from the nature of the site whether the information there can be trusted, but the Web has a way of making even the most egregious misinformation seem convincing.

Usenet

Usenet is a worldwide, text-based Internet bulletin board system that consists of tens of thousands of newsgroups devoted to every topic you could possibly imagine. Usenet is not as user-friendly as the Web, but it provides an enormous amount of valuable technical information. To access Usenet newsgroups, you must have a client program called a news reader and access to a news server. The clients and servers communicate with each other using a specialized TCP/IP protocol called the Network News Transfer Protocol (NNTP). News readers are available as standalone programs or they can be incorporated into other applications, such as the Outlook Express client included with Microsoft Internet Explorer.

Most Internet Service Providers (ISPs) include access to a news server as part of a standard Internet access subscription, but the quality of the service that individual ISPs provide can vary greatly. The thousands of Usenet newsgroups generate several gigabytes of information every day, and news servers can only keep a limited amount of information available. Depending on the amount of storage a news server has, it might only be able to keep a few days' worth of messages available at a time. In addition, some servers have incomplete news feeds, which means that you won't see all the messages that have been posted to a particular group. When you're trying to carry on a dialog with someone, this can be a problem, as you might not see all the responses to your questions. If you require more complete and comprehensive Usenet access, you can subscribe to any one of several commercial news services for a small monthly fee, which guarantee full access to all the Usenet newsgroups and usually retain messages for a longer period of time.

To access Usenet, configure your news reader with the name or Internet Protocol (IP) address of a news server and download a list of the newsgroups, as shown in Figure 18.2. The list is alphabetical and the newsgroup names consist of several cryptic abbreviations separated by periods, such as the following:

- comp.infosystems.www.authoring.html

- alt.comp.software.tools

- microsoft.public.win2000.networking

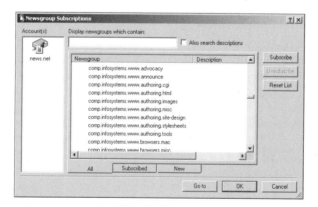

Figure 18.2 The Usenet newsgroup list

In most cases, you can work out the subject of a newsgroup from its name, but you might find yourself stumped with some of them, such as sfnet.tietoliikenne. yhteydentarjoajat. This is due in part to Usenet being an international service, and some of the newsgroups are in languages other than English. As you become accustomed to Usenet jargon, you'll learn where to go to find the newsgroups concerning a particular subject. Because Usenet is a computer-based medium, there are a large number of newsgroups devoted to the technical issues involved in computing, such as networking, programming, applications, and the like. You'll find that there are newsgroups devoted to individual networking protocols, operating systems, programming languages, and many other related topics. For example, there are hundreds of newsgroups beginning with the word "comp," which are all computer-related.

Note Usenet is primarily a text-based service, and "netiquette" dictates that you do not post anything other than text messages on most newsgroups. This is because many news server administrators try to conserve storage space by maintaining only the groups that are text-only. Newsgroups that have the word "binaries" in their name, however, are groups that permit the posting of binary files, such as program and image files. These files are posted to news servers in a format called *uuencode*, which is a series of algorithms for converting files into a series of 7-bit ASCII characters. Most newsreaders today automatically encode and decode binary files as needed, but you might in some cases see that a binary file appears as page after page of seemingly random ASCII characters.

When you have found a newsgroup that you want to access, the news reader enables you to "subscribe" to it. Subscribing means only that the reader adds the selected newsgroup to the list of groups that you want to access regularly. After you've selected a number of groups, you can work with your list of subscribed groups, rather than dealing with the gigantic full list. When you've subscribed to the newsgroups that you want to read, you have the reader download the message headers for them. The message headers contain the subject of each message, the name of the person who posted it, and the date and time it was posted, as shown in Figure 18.3. By scrolling the display, the size of the message is also shown.

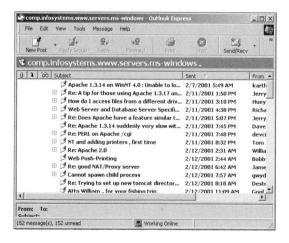

Figure 18.3 Usenet newsgroup message headers

News readers typically can display the headers in several different ways: chronologically, alphabetically by subject or author, by size, or by thread. A *thread* is a series of messages with the same subject. One person posts a message containing a question or comment, and other people reply to that message. This is usually the easiest way to read a newsgroup. By studying the message headers, you can determine which messages you want to read. Most news readers enable you to mark the messages or threads you want to read, so that you can download them all at once. When you instruct the reader to do so, it downloads the text of all the messages you checked. For text-only messages, this is usually a rapid process. If you're downloading messages that contain binary files, it can take quite a while. When the download is complete, you can select a message, and the news reader displays the text, as shown in Figure 18.4.

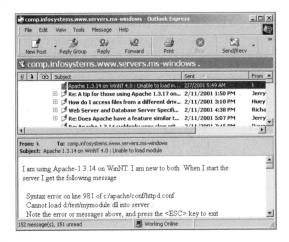

Figure 18.4 A Usenet newsgroup message

After reading the message, you can compose a reply and send it to the newsgroup, or send an e-mail directly to the author. Your message goes to your news server, which eventually uploads it to other servers. Within a matter of hours, your message has been propagated to news servers all over the world.

It's a little more difficult to separate the signals from the noise in Usenet than it is on the Web because anyone can participate. In addition, what used to be a medium frequented primarily by technical people has been invaded by many other types of users. Unfortunately, off-topic material ("spam") is a major problem on Usenet, as it is with e-mail. You might have to wade through any number of get-rich-quick schemes and other advertisements to find what you want. Some newsgroups are moderated to keep out the spam, and some news server administrators run software that filters out a good part of it.

Tip When you configure a news reader, you have to supply your e-mail address in order to post messages to Usenet newsgroups. However, many unscrupulous advertisers use automated programs that strip e-mail addresses out of newsgroup messages to build mailing lists that they use to send spam. It's a good idea to insert an extra word into the e-mail address you supply to prevent yourself from being victimized in this way. For example, if your e-mail address is *marklee@myisp.com*, you might want to change it to *marklee@stopspam.myisp.com*. This is a common practice, and most Usenet users will know to remove the "stopspam" if they have reason to send you legitimate e-mail.

When you evade the spam and other nonsense, Usenet is an extraordinary resource for information of all types. In many cases, you can post a question about a product and get several responses in a few hours, sometimes from the people who designed or invented it.

CD-ROM Resources

The CD-ROM products released by several major manufacturers are another good source of information about computer and networking products. Sometimes the disks are free, but in most cases you must purchase a subscription for CD releases that come out monthly or quarterly. Microsoft's TechNet is one of the most popular CD-ROM subscription products. Each month, you get several CDs that update your library of information about all Microsoft products. The disks include the manuals and Resource Kits for Microsoft products, marketing collateral, the complete Knowledge Base, audio and video training materials, and hundreds of other articles and book excerpts, plus data disks that have the latest Service Packs, patches, and evaluation copies of new products. TechNet includes its own searchable viewer application, which makes it easy to locate the information you need, as shown in Figure 18.5.

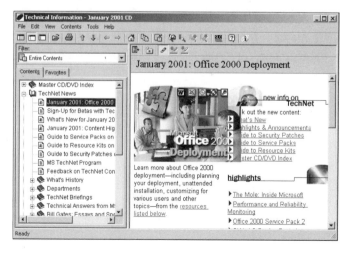

Figure 18.5 The Microsoft TechNet interface

In addition to TechNet, there is also the Microsoft Developers Network (MSDN), which is a subscription-based CD-ROM service intended for software and hardware developers. The disks include software developers' kits (SDKs) and driver developers' kits (DDKs) for all Microsoft products, as well as copies of all the operating systems, a developer Knowledge Base, and an enormous amount of other information. There are three subscription levels with different prices and different levels of access. Other companies produce informational CD-ROMs as well, though few are as comprehensive as those produced by Microsoft.

Books and Periodicals

As you are no doubt aware if you're reading this, there are a great many books available on networking and computer-related topics. Books tend to cover a fairly limited range of specific networking products. You won't find dozens of books on every product you use, but major products, such as operating systems, are covered in depth. However, there is no better resource for background information and networking theory than many of the books currently available on the market. One of the more useful practices in the computer book publishing industry today is that of including a searchable electronic version on a CD-ROM, like the one in this book. Not only does this make the book more portable, it also enables you to search for information with greater speed and precision than if you were looking it up in a printed index.

Magazines and trade newspapers are good places to look for current technical information and news of the industry. However, be aware that the information in a typical monthly magazine is written at least three to four months before you see the issue. Weeklies are more current, and tend to provide more timely information. Many weekly trade newspapers are now available online, which can make paper subscriptions unnecessary.

Exercise 18.1: Technical Resources

Match the resources in the left column with the appropriate descriptions in the right column.

1. PDF
2. TechNet
3. NNTP
4. Readme.1st
5. Newsgroup

a. ASCII text file containing recent product information
b. Internet conference containing messages on a given subject
c. Document format used by Adobe Acrobat
d. A Microsoft CD-ROM subscription service
e. Protocol used by Usenet news clients and servers

Lesson 2: Logs and Indicators

One of the first and most important factors in maintaining a network is knowing when there is something wrong. Networks perform many important processes automatically and in the background, and it's the job of the network administrator to make sure that what is supposed to have been done has been done, without error and without problems. This lesson examines some of the tools that network administrators routinely use to check on the performance of network components and provide indications of trouble.

After this lesson, you will be able to

- Understand the function of Ethernet link pulse LEDs
- List the various types of error messages and event logs used by networking equipment
- Monitor the status of a computer running Windows 2000 by using the Performance console
- Examine network traffic using a protocol analyzer

Estimated lesson time: 40 minutes

Power and Drive Lights

One of the most basic signs that something has gone wrong on your network is when the lights signalling that a piece of equipment is switched on and operational are not lit. This could be caused by a power failure, a tripped circuit breaker, or something as mundane as the electrical plug having fallen out of the socket. However, it is also possible for the device to have experienced a power supply failure, or for a drive light to be out because a drive inside the computer has failed or become disconnected. It's a good idea to become familiar with the light emitting diode (LED) displays of your equipment during normal operation, so that you can quickly determine when something is not as it should be.

Link Pulse Lights

As mentioned in Chapter 15, "Installing a Network," most of the Ethernet network interface adapters designed to use unshielded twisted pair (UTP) cable have an LED on them, as shown in Figure 18.6, that is lit when the adapter is connected to a functioning hub. The hub usually has an LED for each port as well (see Figure 18.7), which enables you to tell from either end of the patch cable whether the devices are connected. However, while these link pulse lights can tell you whether a computer is wired to the hub properly, it's also important to know what these lights do not do.

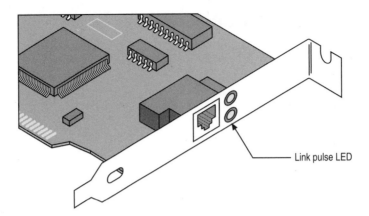

Figure 18.6 The link pulse LED on an Ethernet network interface adapter

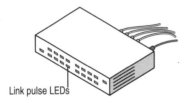

Figure 18.7 The link pulse LEDs on an Ethernet hub

When you connect a UTP network interface adapter to a hub, you should find that the link pulse lights on both devices are lit, as long as both are switched on. Note that the network interface adapter must be installed in the computer and the computer must be turned on, but you don't need to have the network interface adapter driver installed or be logged on to the network to activate the LED.

When an Ethernet adapter and a hub are properly connected, they exchange signals to test the connection. On 10BaseT and 10BaseFL equipment, the signal is called a Normal Link Pulse (NLP). The NLP signals last for two milliseconds and are repeated at intervals of 16.8 milliseconds. These signals occur only when the network is not busy transmitting data, so they do not interfere with normal operations. When the LEDs at both ends of the connection are lit, this indicates that the NLP signals generated by each device are reaching the other device.

If you accidentally use a crossover cable to connect a computer to a hub, the signals sent over the transmit wires do not reach the receive contacts in the other device, and the LEDs will not light. For the same reason, if you connect two network interface adapters together using a straight-through cable and no hub, the LEDs will not light. If the LED lights on one device, but not on the other, then there is a fault in the cable connection. It could be that the cable itself is faulty, one of the devices' connectors is broken, or the cable is not properly seated into the jack at one or both ends. Try reseating the cable connectors into the jacks, or replace the cable with one that you know is functioning properly, and then see if both link pulse lights come on.

Note For more information about straight-through connections and crossover connections, see Lesson 2: Making Connections, in Chapter 15, "Installing a Network."

Fast Ethernet equipment that supports multiple speeds uses Fast Link Pulse (FLP) signals, which differ from NLP signals in that they include a 16-bit data packet that the devices use to auto-negotiate their connection speed. The data packet contains a *link code word* that consists of a selector field and a technology ability field. The devices use these fields to advertise their capabilities, including the speeds they can run at and whether they support full-duplex (that is, simultaneous bi-directional) communications. By examining the link code word supplied by the other device, the network interface adapter and the hub both configure them-selves to use the best transmission mode that they have in common according to the following priorities:

1. 100BaseTX Full Duplex

2. 100BaseT4

3. 100BaseTX

4. 10BaseT Full Duplex

5. 10BaseT

Note Some dual speed devices also have LEDs that light up to indicate the speed at which the device has configured itself to run. Do not confuse this with the link pulse LED.

FLP signals are fully compatible with the NLP signals that are used by devices that cannot operate at multiple speeds. If, for example, you connect a computer with a 10/100 dual speed Fast Ethernet adapter to a standard 10BaseT hub, the adapter receives the NLP signal from the hub and determines that 10 Mbps half duplex is the fastest speed they have in common, and configures itself accord-ingly. The 10BaseT hub, receiving the FLP signal from the adapter, cannot inter-pret the link code word and sees the signal only as a normal NLP link test. No auto-negotiation occurs at the hub because none is possible.

It's important to understand that the link pulse LEDs are only an indication that the network connection is wired properly. Just because the LEDs are lit does not necessarily mean that the connection is capable of carrying actual Ethernet traffic. Link pulse signals run far more slowly than Ethernet data signals, and are not affected by electromagnetic interference, such as crosstalk, the way that actual Ethernet data signals are. For example, if you use a "silver satin"–type telephone cable to connect a network interface adapter to a hub, the link pulse LEDs will usually light. However, in this type of cable, the wire pairs are not twisted, which results in high levels of crosstalk. When Ethernet signals are transmitted over this type of cable, crosstalk causes the signals to bleed over from one wire pair to the others, causing the network interface adapters to receive signals over both the transmit and receive wire pairs simultaneously.

UTP Ethernet adapters interpret simultaneous signals on both wire pairs as an indication that a collision has occurred. In fact, even though there has been no real collision, the adapters behave as though there has been one. They discard the supposedly damaged packets and begin the data retransmission process. This is called a phantom collision, and if it occurs frequently enough, it can seriously degrade the efficiency of the network. Thus, you can use the link pulse LEDs as an indication that you have wired your network correctly, but don't mistake them for a true diagnostic test of the network's transmission capabilities.

Error Displays

The most obvious indications that a problem has occurred on a computer is an error message that appears on the screen. Error messages are generated primarily by applications and operating systems. They can inform you when something has gone wrong with a computer or the software running on it. In most cases, error messages can't give you specific information about a problem with the network itself because there is usually no way for the computer to test or communicate with other network components. For example, an error message generated by an operating system might tell you that the computer was unable to communicate with another computer on the network, but it usually can't tell you why unless the problem is with the computer generating the message.

Error messages can be helpful or they can just add to your confusion, depending on the information they provide. Many operating systems and applications have error messages that are ambiguous or misleading, so you might need help interpreting them, either from the product documentation or from the manufacturer. The most important thing to do if you are faced with an error message you don't understand is to write down the exact message, including all number and letter codes, memory addresses, and other types of information, even if you don't know what they mean. What might appear to be nonsense to you can, when reported to the manufacturer's technical support department, make the difference between successfully resolving the problem or not. You should also inform all network users to do the same thing for any error messages they receive.

Tip One of the easiest ways to preserve a complex error message is to save an image of the entire screen. On a Windows system, pressing the Print Screen (PrtSc) key copies the current screen image to the clipboard. If you open the Windows Paint program and select Paste from the Edit menu, the image is pasted into the program, and you can print it or save it to a bitmap file.

When you're faced with error messages that you don't understand, having the documentation for the products involved on a searchable medium, such as a CD-ROM or a Web site, comes in handy. You can search for the entire message or for key words or phrases much more easily than you could do by poring through a printed manual.

Event Logs

An event log is a running record of processes that functions as an operational history of the product involved. Many applications, operating systems, and networking components are capable of maintaining logs of their activities, and as a network administrator, part of your job is to check the logs on a regular basis for problems or even just for informational messages. Some products keep logs as text files, and may or may not supply the means for you to view them. You might have to open the log file in a separate application to read the contents. In many cases, log files can grow very large, and to read them, you might have to find a text editor that can handle large files.

Logging Options

In some cases, applications enable you to specify whether you want them to log their activities and, if so, how much detail you want in the logs. When you're working with a newly installed or reconfigured application or device, it's always a good idea to keep logs for a while. However, how much detail you want in the logs can be an important consideration. You want to have an accurate picture of the product's activities, but you also don't want to spend hours poring through log files, so selecting the full detail option might not always be recommended. For example, most backup programs have a full detail logging option, which means that the log contains a complete listing of every file that the program has backed up. This might be useful in some instances, but it makes for an enormously large log file that is difficult to scan for basic information, such as whether a backup job has completed successfully. In a case like this, you're better off selecting a less detailed log unless you detect a problem that requires more specific information.

Highly detailed log files can also take up a lot of disk space, and you have to be careful that you don't let them grow unchecked. Many applications that keep logs enable you to set parameters that limit the size to which the files grow. For example, the Internet Information Services (IIS) included with Windows 2000 Server enable you to specify when each service should create a new log file—hourly, daily, weekly, or monthly—using the dialog box shown in Figure 18.8. You can also specify a maximum size for the log file or leave it with no limitations. By clicking the Extended Properties tab, you can select what information the service should include in the log, as shown in Figure 18.9.

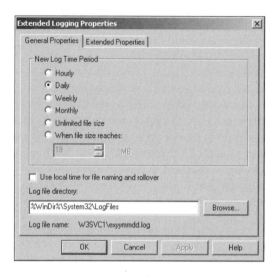

Figure 18.8 The IIS Extended Logging Properties dialog box

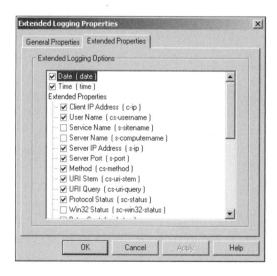

Figure 18.9 The IIS Extended Logging Options

Event Viewer

In some cases, logs are maintained and displayed by a separate application, such as the Event Viewer included in Windows 2000 and Windows NT. To launch Event Viewer in Windows 2000, select Event Viewer from the Start menu's Programs/ Administrative Tools group. By default, the application displays the logs for the current system, but you can also view the logs of another computer running Windows 2000 by selecting Event Viewer in the left window, then selecting Connect To Another Computer from the Action menu.

Event Viewer maintains lists of messages generated by various elements of the operating system. Each log entry is listed as a separate item with the date and time that it was generated, the process that generated it, the Event ID, and other important information, as shown in Figure 18.10. By default, Windows 2000 Professional contains three different logs—an Application Log, a Security Log, and a System Log—all of which are maintained independently. The Windows 2000 Server products include these three logs, plus others, depending on the services installed. An Active Directory domain controller, for example, also has Directory Service, DNS Server, and File Replication Service logs.

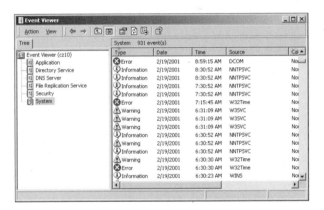

Figure 18.10 The Windows 2000 Event Viewer

Each event in each log is assigned one of the following classifications and marked with a corresponding icon.

- **Information** This indicates the successful completion of an event, such as the launching of a server application or the loading of a device driver. Information messages are a normal byproduct of the computer's operations and are not to be considered problematic.

- **Warning** This indicates a condition that is not necessarily a problem now, but which might become one in the future, such as when available memory or disk space drops below a certain level.

- **Error** This indicates the occurrence of a significant problem that has caused a loss of system functionality or a loss of data, and which requires immediate attention, such as when a service fails to load or a drive goes offline.

When you double-click one of the log entries in Event Viewer's main display, you see an Event Properties dialog box, like that shown in Figure 18.11. This dialog box contains more detailed information about the entry, including a description and any data generated by the event. Using the arrow buttons in the upper right of the dialog box, you can scroll up and down through the events in the log. The entries stored in Event Viewer are sometimes also displayed as pop-up error messages. One of the advantages of using the Event Viewer application is that you don't have to write down most error messages, because you can always view or print them later. Clicking the third button in the upper right corner copies the contents of the entry to the Windows clipboard. You can then paste it into Notepad or another application for printing or faxing to a technical support representative.

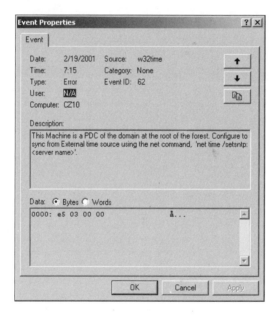

Figure 18.11 An Event Properties dialog box

Network Management Products

Error messages generated by operating systems and applications are usually easy to monitor, but receiving error messages from other network components, such as routers or computers at remote locations, can be more difficult. A standalone router doesn't have a screen on which it can display error messages, but it is possible to arrange for many networking devices to supply you with information about their status. Network management products, such as Hewlett Packard's OpenView, are designed to provide network administrators with a comprehensive view of network systems and processes, using a distributed architecture based on a specialized management protocol, such as the Simple Network Management Protocol (SNMP) or the Remote Monitoring (RMON) protocol.

SNMP is a TCP/IP application layer protocol and query language that specially equipped networking devices use to communicate with a central console. Many networking hardware and software products on the market, including routers, switches, hubs, operating systems, and applications, are equipped with SNMP agents. An *SNMP agent* is a software module that is responsible for gathering information about the product and delivering it to one computer that has been designated as the network management console. The agents gather specific information about the network devices and store them as managed objects in a management information base (MIB). At regular intervals, the agents transmit their MIBs to the console using SNMP messages, which are carried inside User Datagram Protocol (UDP) datagrams.

The console processes the information that it receives from the agents and provides the administrator with a composite picture of the network and its processes. The console software can usually create a map of the interconnections between network devices, as well as display detailed log information for each device. In the event of a serious problem, an agent can generate a special message called a trap, which it transmits immediately to the console, causing it to alert the administrator of a potentially dangerous condition. In many cases, you can configure the console software to send alerts to administrators in a variety of ways, including pop-up messages, e-mails, faxes, and even pager signals.

In addition to network reporting capabilities, network management products often include a large collection of other functions as well, including the following:

- Software distribution and metering
- Network diagnostics
- Network traffic monitoring
- Report generation

Network management products are not designed for small networks, and they are certainly not cheap. Deploying a network management system is a complex undertaking that is intended for administrators of large networks who can't possibly monitor all their network devices individually. To use a product like this effectively, you must be sure that, when designing and building your network, all the equipment you purchase supports the network management protocol you intend to use. However, products like these can greatly simplify the tasks of network administrators and can often bring significant problems to their attention before they cause serious outages.

Performance Monitors

Error messages, logs, and network management products generally inform you about what has already happened on your network. However, there are also products that can help you to know what is currently happening on your network. Network monitoring tools, like the Windows 2000 Performance console, display activities as they are occurring. The Performance console is designed to display ongoing information about the processes running on that individual computer, but many of these processes can involve network activities. Other operating systems have their own monitoring applications. The Novell NetWare Monitor.nlm (shown in Figure 18.12) is one such application, and there are also third-party products that enable you to continually observe the status of your network.

Figure 18.12 The Novell NetWare Monitor.nlm application enables you to view network statistics, such as the number of packets transmitted over a particular interface.

The Windows 2000 Performance console is a graphical application that displays real-time statistics about a computer's activities, and can also maintain logs of those statistics and generate alerts when their values reach certain levels. The System Monitor component of the Performance console, shown in Figure 18.13, is where you can select the statistics you want to monitor and view them in a dynamic display.

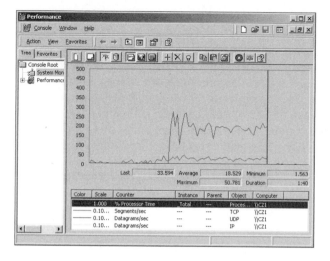

Figure 18.13 The Windows 2000 System Monitor

The various elements that the program can monitor are called *counters*. Windows 2000 includes dozens of counters for many different hardware and software components, such as the processor, the memory, and the network interface, as well as individual services and applications running on the computer. Third-party software products can also add their own counters to System Monitor, enabling you to track their specific activities. To add counters to the display, click the Add button on the toolbar to display the dialog box shown in Figure 18.14. You can select as many counters as you want from each of the categories in the Performance Object list, and for any computer on the network. The Explain button provides a brief definition of what the highlighted counter is designed to measure. However, selecting too many counters at once makes for a confusing display that's difficult to read.

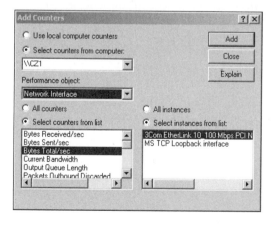

Figure 18.14 System Monitor enables you to add as many counters to the graphical display as you want.

After you've selected all the counters that you want to display, click the Close button in the Add Counters dialog box. The main System Monitor screen immediately begins graphing the values of the counters you selected. By clicking the Properties button, you can change the nature of the display from a line graph to a histogram or to a numerical report, as shown in Figure 18.15. To display information in a graph effectively, you might also have to modify the scale used in the Y axis, so that all of your counters are not piled on top of each other at the bottom of the graph. You can also change the colors used in the graph, the interval at which the information is updated, and other display characteristics.

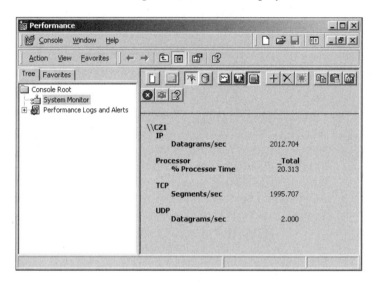

Figure 18.15 System Monitor can also display statistics numerically.

The System Monitor console is a useful tool, as long as you are sitting there looking at the display. You can also use the Performance Logs and Alerts feature of the Performance console to create log files containing the statistics of particular counters over a period of time. You can create alerts that are triggered when the value of a particular counter reaches a level that you specify, using the dialog box shown in Figure 18.16. You can then configure the alert to notify you of the situation by adding an entry to the event log, sending a network message, starting a performance data log, and/or executing a program that you specify. The Performance console, and other tools like it, can provide you with a wealth of information that you can use to monitor and diagnose problems on your network.

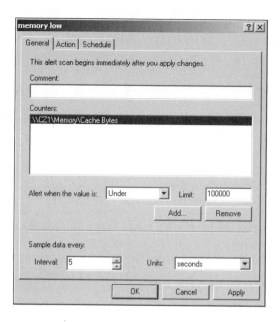

Figure 18.16 Creating alerts enables the Windows 2000 Performance console to notify you when specified conditions are met.

Protocol Analyzers

A protocol analyzer is one of the most powerful tools for learning about, understanding, and monitoring network communications. A protocol analyzer is a tool that captures a sample of the traffic passing over the network, decodes the packets into the language of the individual protocols they contain, and lets you examine them in minute detail. Protocol analyzers also often compile network traffic statistics, such as the number of packets utilizing each protocol and the number of collisions that are occurring on the network. Using the protocol analyzer to capture and display network traffic is relatively easy, but interpreting the information that the analyzer presents and using it to troubleshoot your installation requires a detailed understanding of the protocols running on the network. However, there is no better way to acquire this type of knowledge than to examine the actual data transmitted over a live network.

Warning Protocol analyzers are useful tools in the hands of an experienced network administrator, but they can also be used for malicious purposes. In addition to displaying the information in the captured packets' protocol headers, the analyzer can also display the data carried inside the packets. This can sometimes include confidential information, such as unencrypted passwords and personal correspondence. If you can avoid it, do not permit your users to run protocol analyzers unsupervised.

A protocol analyzer can be a hardware or a software product, either a device with a proprietary interface that you connect to a network to capture traffic, or a software program that runs on a computer that is already connected to the network. Some network consultants who frequently work at different sites install a software-based protocol analyzer on a portable computer and, by changing PC Card network interface adapters, are ready to connect to virtually any network. Protocol analyzers typically work by switching the network interface adapter they use to access the network into *promiscuous mode*. When in promiscuous mode, a network interface adapter reads and processes all the traffic that is transmitted over the network, not just the packets that are addressed to it. This means that you can examine all the traffic on the network from one computer.

The most commonly found protocol analyzer today is the Microsoft Network Monitor application, mostly because it's included with all the Windows 2000 Server and Windows NT Server products. The application is also included with the Microsoft Systems Management Server (SMS) product, but with an important difference. The version of Network Monitor in SMS supports promiscuous mode, but the version in Windows 2000 Server and Windows NT Server does not. This means that, with the server version, you can only capture traffic addressed to or transmitted by the server on which Network Monitor is running.

Note Running a protocol analyzer in promiscuous mode also requires a network interface adapter that is capable of being switched into that mode. Most adapters can run in promiscuous mode, but not all of them can.

Capturing Traffic

The first step of a protocol analysis is to capture a sample of the network traffic. Network Monitor uses the window shown in Figure 18.17 to control the sampling process. Starting a packet capture is a matter of selecting the network interface that you want to use (if there is more than one) and starting the capture process by clicking the Start Capture button on the toolbar. The program reads the packets that arrive over the network interface and stores them in a buffer for later examination. If necessary, you can increase the size of the buffer to capture a larger traffic sampling.

Protocol analyzers, like detailed log files and performance monitors, offer a huge amount of information, and often the trick in using the tool effectively is in zeroing in on what you actually need. On a busy network, a packet capture of only a few seconds can consist of thousands of packets, generated by dozens of different systems. Protocol analyzers have filters that enable you to select the packets that you want to capture, using a number of different criteria, such as the source computer address, the destination computer address, the protocols used to build the packets, and the information found in the packets. For example, if you are having a problem establishing Hypertext Transfer Protocol (HTTP) connections to your Web server, you can use the Capture Filter SAPs and ETYPEs dialog box, shown in Figure 18.18, to enable the capture of IP packets only, because IP is the protocol used for HTTP connections. You can then use the Address Expression dialog box (shown in Figure 18.19) to specify that you only want to capture the traffic arriving at your server from the other computers on the network.

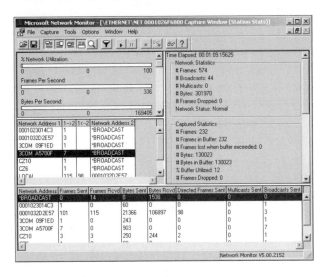

Figure 18.17 The Windows 2000 Server Network Monitor Capture Window

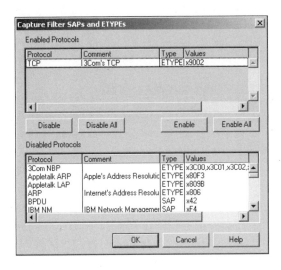

Figure 18.18 The Network Monitor Capture Filter SAPs and ETYPEs dialog box

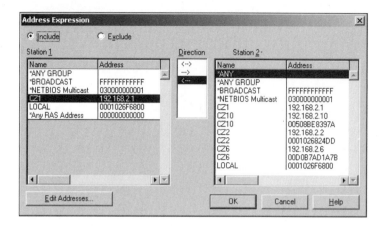

Figure 18.19 The Network Monitor Address Expression dialog box

The result of specifying capture filters is that you have a much smaller traffic sample that contains less of the extraneous information generated by other network processes. If you want to learn how much network traffic is generated by Address Resolution Protocol (ARP) transactions, for example, you can create a filter configuration that captures only ARP traffic for a specific period of time, and work out the number of megabits per hour devoted to ARP from the size of your captured sample. The Capture Filter dialog box, shown in Figure 18.20, displays the combination of filters you've chosen, and enables you to save capture filter configurations to re-use later.

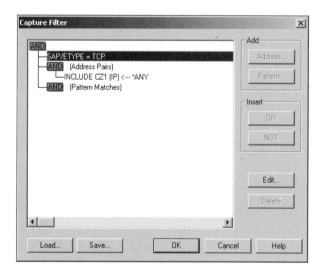

Figure 18.20 The Network Monitor Capture Filter dialog box

Other protocol analyzers offer more comprehensive capture filtering capabilities, such as being able to select specific application layer protocols. When you start the capture, the software displays the number of packets passing over the network and the number that are being captured by the filter. When you have a sample of sufficient size, click the Stop Capture button.

Displaying Captured Traffic

When you've captured a network traffic sample, click the Display Captured Data button to show your sample in the Capture Summary window, as shown in Figure 18.21.

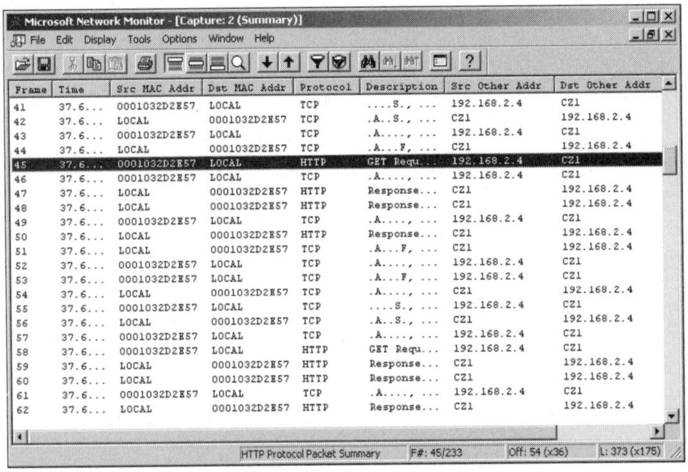

Figure 18.21 The Network Monitor Capture Summary window

This window displays a chronological list of the packets in your sample, including the following information:

- **Frame** This field shows the number of the frame (or packet) in the sample.

- **Time** This field indicates the time (in seconds) that the packet was captured, measured since the beginning of the sample.

- **Src MAC Addr** This field gives the hardware address of the network interface in the computer that transmitted the packet. For computers that the analyzer recognizes by a friendly name, such as a NetBIOS name, this field contains that name instead of the address. The computer on which the analyzer is running is identified as LOCAL.

- **Dst MAC Addr** This field gives the hardware address of the network interface in the computer that received the packet. Friendly names are substituted if available. By building up an address book of the computers on your network, you can eventually have captures that use only friendly names.

- **Protocol** This field shows the dominant protocol in the packet. Each packet contains information generated by protocols running at several different layers of the OSI reference model. The protocol specified here indicates the primary function of the packet. For example, an HTTP packet also uses the TCP, IP, and Ethernet protocols, but the reason for the packet's existence is to deliver an HTTP message.

- **Description** This field indicates the function of the packet, using information specific to the protocol referenced in the Protocol field. For an HTTP packet, for example, this field indicates whether the packet contains an HTTP GET Request or a Response message.

- **Src Other Addr** This field specifies another address used to identify the computer that transmitted the packet. In the case of the TCP/IP protocols, this field contains the IP address.

- **Dst Other Addr** This field specifies another address (such as an IP address) used to identify the computer that received the packet.

- **Type Other Addr** This field specifies the type of address used in the Src Other Addr and Dst Other Addr fields.

From this main display, you can track the progress of transactions between specific pairs of computers on your network. For example, you can see that an exchange of messages between a Web browser and a Web server begins with the exchange of TCP messages that forms a three-way handshake and establishes a connection between the two computers. The browser then transmits an HTTP GET Request message, and the server replies with a series of responses. To zero in on a particular message exchange, Network Monitor enables you to apply filters to already-captured samples as well as during the capture. The interface you use to create the filters is the same as you use to select the desired capture filters. When you apply a filter, you see only the packets that conform to the parameters you've chosen. The other packets are still there in the sample; they're just not being displayed. You can modify the filter at any time to display more or less data.

When you double-click one of the packets listed in the main Capture Summary window, the display splits into three parts, as shown in Figure 18.22. The top section contains the original capture summary, with the selected packet highlighted. The middle section contains the contents of the selected packet, in a fully interpreted, expandable display, and the bottom section contains the raw, uninterpreted contents of the packet, in hexadecimal and alphanumeric form.

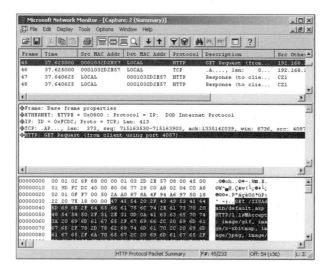

Figure 18.22 Network Monitor can display detailed information about each packet in both raw and interpreted forms.

The center section of the display is where you can learn the most about the contents of each packet. The analyzer interprets the data in the packet and separates it into the headers for the protocols operating at the various layers. Clicking the plus sign next to a protocol expands it to display the contents of the various header fields. Figure 18.23, for example, shows the expanded TCP Header of an HTTP GET Request packet. The header fields display the Source Port and Destination Port numbers, the latter of which contains the protocol code for HTTP, plus the Sequence Number and Acknowledgment Number values used to implement TCP's packet acknowledgment and error detection mechanisms, and the other header fields.

Note For more information about the structure of the TCP header and the functions of its fields, see Lesson 1: TCP and UDP, in Chapter 7, "Transport Layer Protocols."

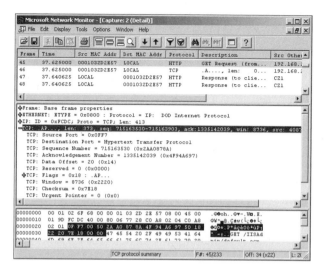

Figure 18.23 Network Monitor interprets the data in a packet and displays the contents of the header fields in each protocol.

The raw data display at the bottom of the window is used primarily to view the application layer data carried as the payload inside a packet. For example, when you look at an HTTP Response packet transmitted by a Web server to a browser, you see the HTML code of the Web page the server is sending to the browser, as shown in Figure 18.24.

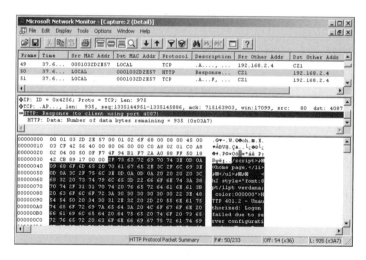

Figure 18.24 Network Monitor's raw data display shows the actual contents of a packet.

Exercise 18.2: Network Indicators

Define each of the following terms in relation to the concepts discussed in this lesson.

1. SNMP

2. NLP

3. Trap

4. Link code word

5. MIB

Lesson 3: Network Testing and Monitoring Tools

Not all of the tools used by network administrators are purely informational. There are also physical tools (beyond the standard screwdrivers and pliers) that can come in handy. Most of these specialized tools are used to install and troubleshoot cables, primarily because this is one component of the network that has no means of displaying error messages.

After this lesson, you will be able to

- Describe the troubleshooting functions of crossover cables and loopback connectors

- Understand the uses of a tone generator and locator

- List the capabilities of more elaborate cable testing equipment

Estimated lesson time: 20 minutes

Crossover Cables

A crossover cable, which is used to connect UTP Ethernet computers without a hub, is also a good tool for eliminating the hub and the cables as a possible source of a network communications problem. If you have two computers that seem to be properly connected using a hub and prefabricated cables (or an internal cable run and patch cables), and they are not communicating, try connecting the computers with a crossover cable that you know works properly. If the computers are able to communicate using the crossover cable, you know that you have a problem in either your hub or the cables connecting the computer to the hub. If the computers fail to communicate using the crossover cable, the problem lies in one or both of the computers or network interface adapters.

Note A crossover cable is a UTP cable in which the transmit contacts in each of the RJ45 connectors is connected to the receive contacts in the other connector, eliminating the need for a hub, which normally supplies the crossover circuit. For more information, see Lesson 2: Making Connections, in Chapter 15, "Installing a Network."

Hardware Loopback Connectors

A loopback connector is an inexpensive device that you plug into a jack, which redirects the outgoing signals from the device right back into it. You can purchase loopback connectors for parallel and serial ports, for example, that work in conjunction with diagnostic software to check the transmission and receive capabilities of the ports. In the same way, you can purchase a loopback connector that plugs into a UTP network interface adapter's RJ45 port. Many adapters have a diagnostic utility built into their configuration programs. After plugging the loopback connector into the adapter port, you run the diagnostic program and it transmits a series of signals out through the adapter. If the adapter receives the signals back in exactly the same format as they were sent, the adapter passes the test.

Be aware that running a test using a loopback connector is completely different from transmitting packets to the TCP/IP loopback address (127.0.0.1). Even though using that address causes all transmitted traffic to return to the incoming buffers of the same computer, the signals never actually reach the network interface adapter. The loopback address is a feature of the IP protocol, and packets sent to it never travel down below the network layer of the OSI reference model. In a loopback connector test, the packets travel all the way down to the physical layer and out of the computer, only to be routed immediately back in by the loopback connector.

Tone Generators and Tone Locators

When you install UTP cable internally, testing each of your connections should be an absolute requirement. The last thing you will want to do—after you've pulled all of your cables, secured them all in the walls and ceilings, punched them all down, installed all the wall plates, and cleaned everything up—is tear everything apart again because of an improperly wired connection.

One of the most basic ways to identify and test a cable connection is to use a tone generator and locator (see Figure 18.25), also known as a "fox and hound" cable tester. The tone generator is a device that you connect to a cable at one end, and which transmits a signal over the cable. The tone locator is a separate device that has a probe capable of detecting the generator's signal, either by touching it to the conductor in the cable, or simply by touching it to the insulation on the outside of the cable. When the locator detects the generator's signal, it emits an audible tone. You can use this type of device to test an entire cable, or to test the individual wire connections inside a UTP cable.

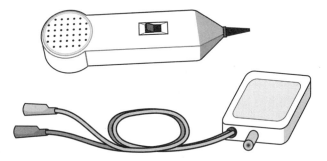

Figure 18.25 A tone generator and locator

Tone generators and locators are most commonly used to identify the cable belonging to a particular connection. For example, if you're performing an internal cable installation, and you forget to label one of your cables, you can connect the tone generator at the wall plate end and touch the probe to each of the cables at the patch panel end until you find the one that produces a tone. Some cable installers omit the labeling process entirely and rely completely on this method for identifying their cable runs. This is not a recommended practice. The tool is also valuable for identifying one particular cable in a bundle in the middle of the connection.

You can also use a tone generator and locator to test the individual wire connections inside a UTP cable. You connect the generator to a single wire or connector contact using alligator clips, and then touch the locator to each wire or contact at the other end of the cable. Using this method, you can test for any major wiring faults that affect internal UTP cable installations. For example, if you fail to detect a signal on the contact to which you have the generator connected at the other end, you have an open circuit. If you detect a signal on the wrong contact, you have punched down the wires to the wrong contacts. If you detect a signal on two or more wires, you have a short.

The tone generator and locator is the simplest and most inexpensive type of cable tester (at approximately $100), but this method of testing UTP cable connections is relatively unreliable and incredibly time-consuming. Testing each of the wires in a UTP cable individually is a slow process, and one that is as prone to error as was connecting them in the first place. You also must have two people to use the equipment, one at the generator end and one at the locator end, who are in constant contact. Or you can do this by yourself if you don't mind running back and forth from one end of your cable connections to the other. For troubleshooting a single cable connection, it's a useful tool. For testing a large number of newly installed cable runs, you can purchase a wire map tester instead that detects all the same faults by testing all of the wire connections in the cable at once.

Wire Map Testers

A wire map tester is a device that is similar in principle to the tone generator and locator, except that it tests all the wire connections in a UTP cable at once. This device also consists of two parts, which you connect to the opposite ends of a cable. The unit at one end transmits signals over all the wires, which are detected by the unit at the other end. A wire map tester can detect transposed wires, opens, and shorts, just as a tone generator and locater can, but it does all the tests simultaneously and provides you with a simple readout telling you what's wrong (if anything). The one common cable fault that a typical standalone wire map tester can't detect is a split pair.

A *split pair* is a wiring fault in which the wires are connected to the wrong contacts at both ends of the cable in exactly the same way. Each of the contacts is wired straight through to its corresponding contact at the other end, yielding a connection that appears to be correct to a normal wire map test. However, the wires that are actually carrying the signals are improperly paired. Normally, a UTP cable has one transmit wire and one receive wire, each of which is twisted into a separate pair with its corresponding ground wire. In a split pair situation, the transmit and receive wires can be twisted into one pair and their two ground wires into another pair. Having the two signal wires twisted into the same pair will generate an excessive amount of crosstalk, which negatively affects communications. A wire map tester knows only that the signals it has transmitted over each wire have reached the other end of the cable at the correct contact. You need a device that can measure crosstalk, such as a multifunction cable tester, to detect split pairs.

Wire map testers are available as standalone devices that are relatively inexpensive ($200 to $300). You can also find the same functions as part of a multifunction cable tester, which costs a great deal more. For a small to medium-sized internal cable installation, a wire map tester is a good investment, both for the installation and for troubleshooting purposes later. You can use the tester to check your prefabricated cables for faults as well. For large installations or professional cable installers, a multifunction cable tester is a better idea.

Multifunction Cable Testers

Multifunction cable testers are handheld devices, like the one shown in Figure 18.26, that perform a variety of tests on a cable connection and compare the results to standard values that have been programmed into the unit. The result is that these are devices that anyone can use. You simply connect the unit to the cable, press a button, and the device comes up with a list of pass or fail ratings for the individual tests.

Figure 18.26 A multifunction cable tester

In addition to the basic wire mapping tests described earlier, multifunction cable testers can also test any of the following:

- **Length** The most common method for determining the length of a cable is called *time domain reflectometry (TDR)*, in which the tester transmits a signal over the cable and measures how long it takes for the signal's reflection to return. Using the *nominal velocity of propagation (NVP)* for the cable, which is the speed at which signals travel through the cable (supplied by the manufacturer) you can compute the length of the cable. This function also enables you to determine the location of a break in a cable.

- **Attenuation** By comparing the strength of a signal at the far end of a cable to its strength when transmitted, the tester determines the cable's attenuation (measured in decibels).

- **Near end crosstalk (NEXT)** Testing for near end crosstalk is a matter of transmitting a signal over one of a cable's wires and then detecting the strength of the signal that bleeds over into the other wires near the end of the cable where the transmitter is located.

- **Power sum NEXT (PSNEXT)** This is a measurement of the crosstalk generated when three of the four wire pairs are carrying signals at one time. This test is intended for networks using technologies like Gigabit Ethernet, which transmit signals over several wire pairs simultaneously.

- **Equal level far end crosstalk (ELFEXT)** This is a measurement of the crosstalk at the opposite end of the cable from the transmitter, corrected to account for the amount of attenuation in the connection.

- **Power sum ELFEXT (PSELFEXT)** This is a measurement of the crosstalk generated at the far end of the cable by three signal-carrying wire pairs, corrected for attenuation.

- **Propagation delay** This indicates the amount of time required for a signal to travel from one end of a cable to the other.

- **Delay skew** This is the difference between the lowest and the highest propagation delay measurements for the wires in a cable. Because the wire pairs inside a UTP cable are twisted at different rates, their relative lengths can differ, and the delay skew measurement quantifies that difference.

- **Return loss** This is a measurement of the accumulated signal reflection caused by variations in the cable's impedance along its length. These impedance variations are typically caused by untwisting too much of the wire pairs when making connections.

Note The tests listed here are those typically found in copper cable testers. Fiber optic cables require completely different testing methodologies and usually require a different type of tester unit.

Not all of these tests are required for every cable installation, but knowing the lengths of your cables and other measurements can help you ensure that your cable installation is within the guidelines established for the protocol you will be using. Measuring elements such as attenuation and delay skew are also useful for testing cables before you install them, so that you can be sure that you've gotten what you've paid for.

Multifunction cable testers can, in some ways, be dangerous because of the very strengths they advertise. The implication in much of the marketing material for these devices is that you don't really have to know what all of these measurements mean; you can just plug your cables in and rely on the device to tell you if they're installed correctly. This is true, as long as the tester is calibrated to the proper standards. If you don't know what the various tests represent, you're relying on the manufacturer of the device to set it to the proper standards, and in some cases, official standards for certain cable types have not yet been ratified.

It's also possible to reprogram the device with your own baseline standards, which can be a problem if you're relying on someone else's tester to tell you that your installation has been performed properly. For example, an unscrupulous cable installer could make a few simple changes to the tester's settings, such as changing the NVP rating for the cable, and cause a network that would previously have failed certain tests to pass them. The bottom line for using these devices is that you should not trust the tester of an untrustworthy person, and that if you purchase a tester of your own, you should familiarize yourself with all of its tests and the standards against which it compares its results.

The other drawback of multifunction cable testers is that most of them carry extremely high price tags. Prices running to several thousand dollars are common, with top-of-the-line units (such as those that combine copper and fiber optic testing capabilities) costing $5,000 or more.

Exercise 18.3: Network Testing Equipment

For each of the devices listed in the left column, specify which of the faults in the right column it is capable of detecting.

1. Crossover cable	a. Cable short
2. RJ45 loopback connector	b. Split pair
3. Tone generator and locator	c. Malfunctioning hub
4. Wire map tester	d. Excessive crosstalk
5. Multifunction cable tester	e. Transposed wires
	f. Faulty network interface adapter
	g. Untwisted cables
	h. Broken cable

Chapter Summary

The key points covered in this chapter are as follows.

Documentation and Resources

- Product documentation can be a valuable network troubleshooting tool. You should always keep all the documentation that comes with your hardware and software.

- Web sites for many hardware and software manufacturers offer a variety of resources for the network administrator, including technical documents, FAQs, online messaging, and technical support databases.

- Usenet is a giant worldwide Internet bulletin board service that consists of tens of thousands of newsgroups for discussions of every topic you can imagine.

- Some manufacturers produce CD-ROMs containing technical information on their products. These are usually available on a subscription basis.

Logs and Indicators

- LEDs and other lights are frequently useful indicators of a piece of equipment's current status.

- The link pulse LEDs on Ethernet hubs and network interface adapters indicate when these devices are connected together properly.

- Checking error messages and event logs should be a routine activity for the network administrator.

- Network management products provide a centralized, comprehensive resource for information about the devices connected to a large enterprise network.

- Tools like the Windows 2000 Performance console enable you to monitor ongoing computer and network operations in real time.

- Protocol analyzers capture network traffic and decode it for further study.

Network Testing and Monitoring Tools

- Crossover cables can eliminate cable runs and hubs as possible sources of communication problems.

- A loopback connector tests the functionality of a network interface adapter by redirecting its outgoing signals back into it.

- A tone generator and locator is a simple cable testing device that determines whether a cable is carrying a signal.

- Wire map testers test all four of the wire pairs in a UTP cable at the same time.

- Multifunction cable testers perform a comprehensive battery of tests on a cable connection and compare the results to established standards.

Chapter Review

1. How does the FLP signal used by Fast Ethernet equipment differ from the NLP signal used by standard Ethernet?

2. A fox and hound tester is another term for what device?

   a. A crossover cable

   b. A tone generator and locator

   c. A wire map tester

   d. A multifunction cable tester

3. Which of the following products do you need to open a .pdf file?

   a. A news reader

   b. NNTP

   c. Adobe Acrobat Reader

   d. A multifunction cable tester

4. How does the performance of a network interface adapter differ while in promiscuous mode?

5. What protocol do Usenet news readers and news servers use to communicate?

   a. HTTP

   b. FTP

   c. SNMP

   d. NNTP

6. Which of the following cabling faults can a wire map tester not detect?

   a. Open pairs

   b. Split pairs

   c. Transposed pairs

   d. Shorts

7. Arrange the following Ethernet technologies in the order of priority established by the FLP signal.

   a. 100BaseT4

   b. 10BaseT Full Duplex

   c. 100BaseTX

   d. 10BaseT

   e. 100BaseTX Full Duplex

8. What are the individual elements measured by the Windows 2000 Performance console called?

    a. Counters

    b. Statistics

    c. Alerts

    d. Traps

9. Which of the following types of cable tester is most expensive?

    a. Fox and hound

    b. Wire map

    c. Multifunction

    d. Loopback

10. Where do agents used by network management products store their information?

    a. SNMP

    b. MIB

    c. NNTP

    d. Console

C H A P T E R   1 9

Network Troubleshooting Scenarios

About This Chapter

The process of troubleshooting network problems varies depending on the size of the organization and the people involved. In medium- to large-sized organizations, there is usually a set procedure that determines how technical support calls are registered, addressed, and escalated. In smaller organizations, the process might be much more informal. This chapter describes the procedures followed for typical technical support calls. In some cases, the cause of the problem might be banal, such as simple user error, but the procedures described illustrate how technical staff can handle even minor problems to everyone's satisfaction. In other cases, the problem itself might seem minor, but is actually a sign of a serious problem that affects the whole network.

Before You Begin

This chapter draws on all of the material presented in this book, and particularly the discussion of troubleshooting tools and techniques presented in Chapter 17, "Network Troubleshooting Procedures," and Chapter 18, "Network Trouble-shooting Tools."

Lesson 1: "I Can't Access a Web Site"

A network user named Alice calls the network help desk and reports that she has been trying to access a particular Web site for several hours and is consistently receiving an error message.

This is a common occurrence for all Internet users, because all Internet resources are prone to occasional and sometimes frequent outages. However, it's also possible that this is an indication of a problem with the caller's computer or with the internal network. Based on the information provided in the scenario, and knowing nothing about Alice's level of expertise, the help desk technician has no way of knowing whether the problem is being caused by user error, a computer configuration problem, a faulty network connection, a malfunction of the router providing the Internet access, or even some issue with the Internet or the specific Web site itself—either of which is beyond the local network's sphere of influence.

After this lesson, you will be able to

- Understand the progression of a technical support help call
- Troubleshoot Internet access problems
- Distinguish between network problems, computer problems, and user problems

Estimated lesson time: 50 minutes

Incident Administration

The first step for any technical support call is for the help desk staff to begin to document the incident. Help desks for many organizations use a software product that enables technicians to document calls and store them in a database. Help desk software typically makes it possible to assign a priority to each call; escalate calls to senior technicians, if necessary; list all of the information obtained from the caller; and document the steps taken to solve the problem.

Prioritizing Calls

Because the technician has only the most rudimentary information about Alice's problem at this point, it isn't possible for him to accurately assign a priority to her call. If the problem turns out to be with the router or the network and a large number of users are affected, it could be very serious indeed, especially if the organization relies on its Internet access for vital business communications. If, for example, the organization is a company that sells products over the Web, and the Web servers are located on-site, an Internet connection failure means that the Web site is down and that no orders are coming in. In a case like this, the call might be assigned the highest possible priority. If, on the other hand, revenue-producing work can go on without Internet access, the priority of the call would be somewhat lower. If the problem lies in Alice's computer or in her procedures, the priority of the call would be much lower, unless of course Alice is the company president. It might seem as though political considerations should not affect the priority assigned to a technical support call, but they invariably do, so you had better learn to live with it.

Escalating Calls

Many technical support operations separate their technicians into two or more tiers, depending on their expertise and experience. Help desk calls are typically taken by first-tier technicians, and if the problem is determined to be serious or complex enough, the first-tier technician escalates the call to the second tier. In a well-organized technical support team, the circumstances in which calls are escalated are explicitly documented. For example, problems involving user error and individual workstations might remain in the first tier, while network outages and problems affecting multiple users might be immediately escalated. Escalation should also occur when a technician in the first tier makes several earnest attempts to resolve the problem, and is unable to do so. Of course, the escalation process is also likely to be affected by political concerns, just like the assignment of priorities. The purpose of this multitiered arrangement is to prevent the organization's more experienced (and presumably more highly paid) technicians from spending their time fielding calls about elementary problems.

Gathering Information

In this particular scenario (and in most others as well), the next step in the troubleshooting process is for the technician to ask the caller about the exact circumstances under which the problem occurred. Until more information is available, it's impossible to assign a priority to the call or determine if it should be escalated.

When asked to describe what she was doing when the error occurred, Alice says that she has been trying to open a Web site in Microsoft Internet Explorer, one that had always worked before, and after a few seconds received an error message. She tried again several times over the course of an hour, and received the same error message every time. Alice had not written down the error message at the time, but she was able to recreate the error at will by trying again to access the site. The error message was the familiar "The Page Cannot Be Displayed" screen, shown in Figure 19.1, which also says "Cannot Find Server or DNS Error."

Figure 19.1 A common Internet Explorer error message

This error message is a common one that every user of Internet Explorer has seen at one time or another. This message can appear for many reasons: because the Web server the browser is trying to contact is down, because the client computer's Internet connection is broken, or because the client's Domain Name System (DNS) server fails to resolve the DNS name in the requested Uniform Resource Locator (URL). Determining the cause of the problem is a matter of isolating the component or components that are malfunctioning, which you do by eliminating all of the properly functioning components until you are left with the problematic ones.

Possible Cause: Internet Router Problem

Difficulty in accessing the Internet is one of the most common problems handled by the help desk in almost any organization with a network that provides routed access to the Internet. For an organization with more than a handful of users, setting up a router that connects to an Internet Service Provider (ISP), as shown in Figure 19.2, is the easiest and most economical way of providing users with Internet access. The alternative is to equip all users with their own modems, telephone lines, and Internet access accounts, which is not only expensive, but requires the network support staff to install the modem and configure the operating system's dial-out capability with the right parameters on each computer. Depending on the size of the organization and the needs of the users, the router could be a standalone unit connected to an ISP using a leased telephone line, such as a T1; a computer with a modem that connects to the ISP using a standard dial-up connection and is configured to share that connection with network users; or any one of many solutions falling between these two extremes.

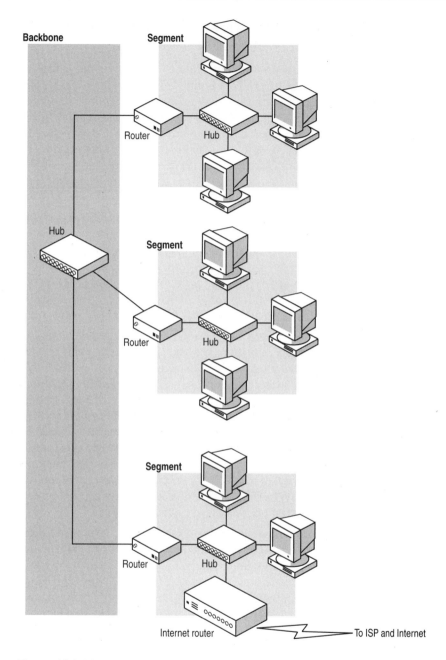

Figure 19.2 Most networks provide users with Internet access by sharing a router's connection to an ISP.

There are a number of things that can go wrong with this type of routed Internet access solution, including the following:

- **The router's connection to the ISP or the ISP's connection to the Internet could be malfunctioning**. Whether the router's connection to the ISP uses a standard dial-up modem, a leased telephone line like a T1, or another service such as the Integrated Services Digital Network (ISDN), it's entirely possible for outages to occur. In addition, the ISP providing Internet access is just as likely to suffer from network problems as you are. These problems can affect all of the service's or ISP's customers, and there's nothing that the user's technical support staff can do about them, except report them to the service's or ISP's own technical support staff.

- **The router device or computer could be experiencing a hardware or power failure**. If the router is not functioning, the Internet access requests generated by the client applications running on the users' computers have no-where to go. When no response from the requested Internet resource is forth-coming, the client application eventually times out and displays the error message shown earlier. This condition would affect all of the users that access the Internet through that router.

- **There could be a problem with the network that prevents access to the router**. A broken network cable, a faulty cable connector, or a malfunctioning hub or other network connection device are all problems that can prevent a user's Internet access requests from reaching the router, even if the router is functioning properly and connected to the Internet. The number of users affected by this type of problem depends on the location of the fault and the function of the component that has malfunctioned. For example, if the cable connecting the user's computer to the hub has been severed, only that one computer is affected. If the hub itself is malfunctioning, all of the computers connected to it will experience the same problem. If a central component is faulty, such as a backbone cable or switch, the problem could extend to a large number of users, or even all of them.

- **The client computer could be misconfigured and is not sending Internet access requests to the router**. The computer running the Web browser or other client application could be experiencing a problem in its networking hardware, in its software, or in its network configuration. These conditions affect only that one computer, and are among the most common causes of error messages like the one experienced by Alice.

Generally speaking, a router problem like this is one of the least likely causes of the problem Alice is experiencing. In addition, if the router was malfunctioning, the help desk would probably be receiving calls from many different users with the same problem. However, router problems are one of the easiest causes to check for, and the potential seriousness of a router problem makes it a high priority for the technical support staff. Therefore, it does no harm for the technician to eliminate the router as a possible source of the problem at the very beginning of the troubleshooting process.

The easiest way for the technician to test the router is to try to access an Internet site himself using a computer that shares the same routed Internet connection. In Alice's organization, all of the users on the network share a single Internet connection, so the technician simply has to launch his own Web browser and connect to an Internet site to determine that the connection and the router are indeed functioning properly. This narrows down the source of the problem to Alice's procedures, her computer, or her computer's connection to the router.

If the technician's computer also fails to access the Internet, the problem could lie in any one of three areas of the network:

- **In a component that both the technician and the user employ to access the router, such as a hub, switch, local area network (LAN) router, or backbone network** The next step would be to see exactly which other users on the network are suffering from the same problem. You should then be able to isolate the problem to a particular hub, cable, or other piece of equipment, depending on how widespread the problem is.

- **In the router itself** To provide the network with Internet access, the router must perform two basic tasks. The router must access the Internet itself (through an ISP), and it must forward packets back and forth between the internal network and the ISP's Internet-connected network. If either one of these two functions fails, users can't access Internet services. If the router is a computer, testing the connection to the ISP is simply a matter of running a Web browser on that computer and trying to connect to an Internet site. If that succeeds, you have to check the router configuration to see if it is communicating with both networks properly and forwarding packets. If the router itself can't connect to the Internet, the problem might lie in the technology used to connect the router to the ISP.

- **In the connection between the router and the ISP** All of the wide area network (WAN) technologies used to connect networks to ISPs require hardware at both sides of the connection and a service that provides the communications link between the hardware devices. If the router uses a simple dial-up connection to the ISP, the problem could lie in either one of the two modems involved, or in the telephone line that provides the connection between them. You can test your line and modem by substituting them with others that you know work properly. With other technologies, the principles are the same, but testing is likely to be more difficult. It's unlikely for even a large organization to have an extra T1 line sitting around idle.

Note In some cases, network users access Internet Web sites through a proxy server or other device that functions as a "middleman" between the client and the Web server. This introduces another possible source of the problem the user is experiencing. However, if the technician or other users can access the Internet through the same server, you know that it, along with the router and the ISP connection, is functioning properly.

If none of these is the cause of the problem, the difficulty lies in the ISP's network or in the Internet itself. The problem might clear up by itself in a few minutes or hours, but if Internet access is essential to the business, the ISP should be contacted. Dealing with the ISP might be the responsibility of a senior technical support representative, so it's likely that the call would be escalated, if this was found to be the problem.

In Alice's case, the technician determines that the router is functioning normally because he can connect to an Internet site using his own browser.

Possible Cause: Internet Communication Problem

The next step in narrowing down the cause of Alice's problem is to determine exactly what kinds of network communications are affected. This procedure should methodically test the entire data connection from Alice's computer to the Internet and, when a failure occurs, should trace backward component by component until the source of the problem is detected.

As a help desk technician, you should begin this process while you are still on the telephone with the user. First, ask the user to try connecting to a different Web site. Using one of the default links supplied with the browser is a good idea because these sites are nearly always in operation, and you minimize the possibility of user error. If you must have the user type in a Web site address, dictate the exact URL to the user, and keep it simple, such as *www.microsoft.com*. If the browser can connect to other Internet Web sites, you know that the network, the router, and the Internet connection are functioning properly. When this is the case, the problem can nearly always be traced to either a Web site that is down or to user error. If the user's Web browser is not able to connect to any other Internet sites, you should then determine if any other network communications are possible.

Next, ask the user to open a different client application and try to connect to the Internet. The application you select doesn't matter, as long as it connects directly to an Internet site. For example, an e-mail client or a news reader is a good choice, as long as the user would not be connecting to a mail or news server on the local network. As a last resort, you can always have the user launch the File Transfer Protocol (FTP) client from the command line. Virtually every operating system that supports Transmission Control Protocol/Internet Protocol (TCP/IP) includes an FTP client, but you might have to walk the user carefully through the process of connecting to an FTP server.

If the user cannot use a Web browser to access Internet sites but can connect to the Internet using a different client application, you know that the problem lies in the browser software running on the user's computer. If the user can't connect to the Internet at all using any client application (and other users can), the next step is to determine which part of the computer's Internet access architecture is failing.

Possible Cause: DNS Failure

One of the most common causes of Internet access problems (and of the error message that Alice received) is the failure of the user's computer to resolve DNS names into the Internet Protocol (IP) addresses that client applications need to communicate with Internet servers. DNS servers are a vital part of any Internet communication that uses a name to refer to an Internet server. IP communications are based solely on IP addresses, not names, so the first thing that a client application does when given a name of a computer, such as *www.microsoft.com*, is send the name to a DNS server for resolution. When you type the name of a server into your Web browser, part of the brief delay that you experience before the Web page starts loading is the result of the time it takes for the client application to generate a DNS Request message containing the server name, send it to a DNS server, and wait for a reply from the DNS server containing the IP addresses associated with the name. Only then can the client transmit its first Hypertext Transfer Protocol (HTTP) message to the Web server.

Checking the TCP/IP Client's DNS Configuration

The address of the DNS server that a computer uses to resolve names is supplied as part of the system's TCP/IP client configuration. On a computer running Windows 2000, for example, the DNS server address is found in the Internet Protocol (TCP/IP) Properties dialog box, shown in Figure 19.3. If the addresses in the Preferred DNS Server and Alternate DNS Server fields in this dialog box do not point to DNS servers that are up and running, the name resolution process will fail when the user attempts to connect to a Web server, resulting in the error message shown earlier.

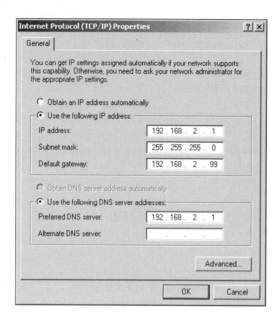

Figure 19.3 The Windows 2000 Internet Protocol (TCP/IP) Properties dialog box

Tip To configure the DNS server addresses on a computer running Windows 2000, open the Network And Dial-up Connections window from the Start menu's Settings group, right-click the Local Area Connection icon, and select Properties from the shortcut menu. Highlight the Internet Protocol (TCP/IP) entry in the components list and click the Properties button to display the Internet Protocol (TCP/IP) Properties dialog box. The other Windows operating systems use a similar arrangement of dialog boxes, although the access procedures are slightly different.

The easiest way to test for a DNS name resolution problem is to use an IP address instead of a server name in the URL you supply to the Web browser. For example, when the user's browser fails to connect to a Web server using its name, but other computers are able to access the Internet, use the Ping program to resolve the name of the desired server into an IP address, using a command like the following:

```
ping servername
```

This command first displays the server's name followed by the server's IP address, then displays the results of the attempt to communicate with that server. When the attempt is successful, the program lists each of the replies received from the server, with information such as the number of data bytes included in the message, the time elapsed between the transmission of the request and the receipt of the reply, and the Time To Live value for the transmission. On a computer running Windows 2000, the Ping output appears as follows:

```
Pinging www.microsoft.com [38.144.95.172] with 32 bytes of data:

Reply from 38.144.95.172: bytes=32 time=320ms TTL=238
Reply from 38.144.95.172: bytes=32 time=280ms TTL=238
Reply from 38.144.95.172: bytes=32 time=381ms TTL=238
Reply from 38.144.95.172: bytes=32 time=280ms TTL=238

Ping statistics for 38.144.95.172:
    Packets: Sent = 4, Received = 4, Lost = 0 (0% loss),
Approximate round trip times in milli-seconds:
    Minimum = 280ms, Maximum =  381ms, Average =  315ms
```

Have the user replace the server name in the browser's URL with the IP address you've discovered. If the browser succeeds in connecting to the server using an IP address when using a server name failed, there is definitely a problem with the DNS name resolution process.

DNS name resolution problems have two major causes: either the computer's TCP/IP client is configured with incorrect DNS server addresses or the DNS servers themselves are not functioning properly. One easy way to check the addresses of the DNS servers on a computer running a Windows operating system is to use the Ipconfig.exe program (for Windows 2000 or Windows NT) or the Winipcfg.exe program (for Windows 95, Windows 98, and Windows Me) to display the TCP/IP configuration. For more information about using these programs, see Lesson 2: TCP/IP Utilities, in Chapter 10, "TCP/IP Applications." If the addresses are incorrect, they must be changed, using the Internet Protocol (TCP/IP) Properties dialog box shown earlier.

Note All of the tests described thus far can conceivably be performed by the user, with instruction from the help desk technician over the telephone. However, modifying the computer's TCP/IP configuration might be a task that the technician should perform in person. Depending on the user's location and computing skills, and on the organization's technical support policies, the technician might decide to travel to the user's site and personally perform the tests on the computer.

How the DNS server addresses got changed, if the computer was previously functioning properly, might remain a mystery. When users are asked if they've changed anything in their computer's configuration recently, those who have been messing around with settings they don't understand invariably answer no. However, if your network uses Dynamic Host Configuration Protocol (DHCP) servers to configure its TCP/IP clients automatically, you should definitely check the DHCP server configuration to see if it is supplying incorrect addresses to the network clients. If this is the case, do not manually change the DNS server configuration in the user's computer, but rather correct the DHCP server's configuration instead. After you have done this, you can repair the user's computer by renewing the DHCP lease using the Ipconfig.exe or Winipcfg.exe program.

Checking the DNS Server

If the DNS server addresses in the user's TCP/IP client configuration are correct, the problem might lie in the DNS servers themselves or in the computer's network connection to the DNS servers. The DNS servers that a network uses for Internet name resolution might be supplied by the organization's ISP, or they might be located on-site. If the DNS servers belong to the ISP, all you can do is test to see if they are available. If you can contact the DNS servers using the Ping command with an IP address, you know that they are at least up and running. However, this does not necessarily mean that they are capable of processing DNS Request messages. Nonetheless, if you can execute a Ping command using a server name successfully, you've proven that the DNS server can resolve the server's name into its IP address.

If the DNS servers belong to your organization, you can check them more thoroughly. However, this is another area in which the first-tier technician might be obligated to escalate the call to a senior technician. A Ping test can determine that the DNS server is functioning, but checking the status of the DNS server software itself depends on the operating system and the application software running on the computer. On a Windows 2000 Server computer running Microsoft DNS Server, for example, you can start by opening the Services console from the Start menu's Administrative Tools group and checking to see that the DNS Server service is running, as shown in Figure 19.4.

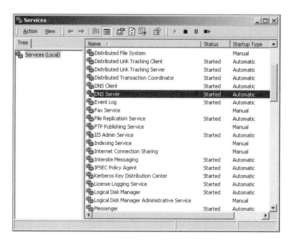

Figure 19.4 The Windows 2000 Services console

If the service isn't running, you must find out why. The Startup Type field for the DNS Server service should be set to Automatic, indicating that the service loads when the computer starts. If the Startup Type field is set to Manual or Disabled, this is why the service isn't running. However, before you manually start the service or change the Startup Type to Automatic, check with your colleagues to see if someone hasn't configured it this way for a good reason. If the Startup Type says Automatic but the service isn't running, someone manually stopped it, the service failed to start, or the service shut itself down.

Check the computer's Event Viewer (also accessible from the Administrative Tools group) for log entries that might explain why the service isn't running. A failure of the service to start during boot time should generate a log entry indicating why. Various types of environmental problems could cause the service to shut down, including a memory shortage or a configuration problem. Troubleshooting issues like these requires knowledge of the operating system and the DNS server software.

If the DNS server service is running but names are still not being resolved, it's time to look at the server software and the DNS communications process in more detail. Examining the DNS server's configuration files is a good place to start. For example, if the server's list containing the names and addresses of the DNS root name servers has somehow been modified or erased, this would prevent names from being resolved, despite everything else functioning correctly. The DNS server's own network connection and Internet access are also vital to the name resolution process. The server itself might be functioning properly, but if network conditions prevent it from receiving DNS Request messages from the client, or if it can't access the Internet to relay the requests to other DNS servers, the name resolution process stops.

If the DNS server's configuration files show no obvious problems, you might have to go so far as to use a protocol analyzer to determine if the DNS server is communicating with the network and the Internet properly, by examining the network traffic running to and from the DNS server computer. A protocol analyzer is a hardware or software program that captures network traffic and displays it for study, as described in Lesson 2: Logs and Indicators, in Chapter 18, "Network Troubleshooting Tools."

Using the protocol analyzer, you should be able to see the DNS Request packets arriving at the server, and the server's own DNS Requests being transmitted to other DNS servers on the Internet, as shown in Figure 19.5. Analyzing network traffic in this way requires familiarity with what is known as a "baseline." In other words, you have to know what the network traffic pattern is supposed to look like before you can determine what's wrong. By analyzing the traffic traveling to and from the server, you might be able to isolate the problem as being in the server's communications with the local network or in its communications with the Internet.

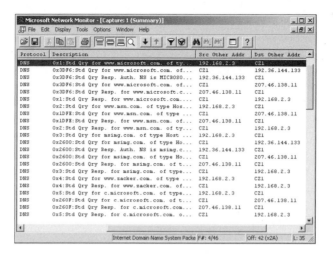

Figure 19.5 A captured DNS traffic exchange, as displayed in a protocol analyzer

Note The procedures for diagnosing and repairing DNS name resolution problems described here are also useful in other scenarios. Computers running the Windows operating system, for example, might use the Windows Internet Name Service (WINS) to resolve NetBIOS names into IP addresses, just as they use DNS servers to resolve DNS names. The same type of client and server configuration problems affecting DNS name resolution can also affect the WINS name resolution process. You can check the addresses of the WINS servers in the client computer's TCP/IP configuration and the functionality of the WINS servers in much the same way as you check the equivalent DNS resources.

Possible Cause: LAN Communication Problem

If the user's problem is not being caused by an Internet communications problem or by a DNS name resolution problem, it's time to start examining the computer's general network communication capabilities. The technician begins by having the user try to access resources on the local network. Local network resources can include shared server drives, internal network applications (such as e-mail or database servers), and browsing the network using a tool like Windows Explorer. The best way to proceed is to start by having the user try to access nearby resources.

Testing the Local Hub

The first test might be for the user to open My Network Places in Windows Explorer and see if the computers belonging to other nearby users are visible. The assumption here is that other computers nearby are connected to the same network hub as the user experiencing the problem. If there is an internal network communications difficulty, the object is to narrow down where it might be.

Information about which computers are connected to specific hubs and LANs should be available to the help desk technician, preferably in the form of a map or diagram that shows the cables and connection devices that make up the network. This is a resource that should be developed during the initial planning stages of the network, and it should be maintained consistently throughout its life. Relying on someone's memory of the network installation makes the technical support process far more difficult, especially as people tend to leave the company or move on to other jobs. It's also important for the technician to remember that users probably do not have access to this type of network information, and wouldn't know what to do with it if they did.

Windows Explorer displays the computers on the network in terms of domains and workgroups, which probably don't correspond to the hubs and LANs that form the network's physical configuration. If the user and the technician are still working together over the telephone at this point, many of the instructions the user is receiving won't make much sense, so it's important for the technician to explain carefully what must be done, without bothering the user with unnecessary technical details. This is another case where the technician might consider traveling to the user's site, if it is at all practical to do so.

Testing the Computer Connection

Using My Network Places, if the user can't see the other computers connected to the same hub, the problem is likely to be in the user's connection to the hub, in the computer hardware or software, or in the user's procedures. In some cases, testing the computer's connection to the hub can be quite easy. If the computer is connected to the hub using a prefabricated network cable, you can try replacing the cable with one that you know is functioning properly. If the computer is connected to the hub using an internal cable run, begin by switching the network cable plugged into the user's computer with a cable from a nearby computer that is working properly. If the user's computer can now access the network, you know that the problem is somewhere in the original cable run, and you can start trying to narrow down exactly where the problem is.

Note Internal cable installations use three lengths of cable per connection: a patch cable connecting the computer to the wall plate, the cable inside the walls or ceilings running from the wall plate to the patch panel, and another patch cable connecting the patch panel port to a hub port. Because the patch cables are exposed, it's easy to test them first by replacing them. For more information about internal cable installations, see Chapter 15, "Installing a Network."

Begin by swapping out the patch cables at both ends of the connection with replacements that you know are working properly. If the patch cables are not the cause of the problem, you can proceed to test the internal cable run. If you have the proper cable testing equipment handy, you can test the cable run that way. A multifunction cable tester, a wire map tester, or even an inexpensive tone generator and locator can tell you if the cable is wired properly and signals are getting through.

If there is a break in the cable, the multifunction tester can also tell you where it is in relation to the end you're testing from. If you don't have cable testing equipment, you can plug the patch cables at both ends into a different cable run that you know is working properly. Swapping out equipment wherever possible is one of the most basic troubleshooting techniques, and one of the most effective.

Note For more information about cable testing equipment, see Lesson 3: Network Testing and Monitoring Tools, in Chapter 18, "Network Troubleshooting Tools."

Problems with internal cable runs don't usually happen by themselves. Usually they're the result of someone working in the spaces where the cables are located and accidentally damaging one of the cables. In fact, just moving a cable that is running inside a drop ceiling closer to a fluorescent light fixture can be enough to induce communication problems on that connection. This is why it is strongly recommended that you secure your cables well when installing them, even when they're running through relatively inaccessible areas, such as walls and ceilings.

Testing Hub Connections

If the user's computer can see and access other computers connected to the same hub, the next step is to try to access other computers on the same LAN that are connected to different hubs. If the user can access computers attached to the same hub, but can't access the other computers on the LAN connected to different hubs, the problem might be in the connection between the user's hub and the rest of the network. What to check next depends on the physical configuration of the network. If, for example, the user's hub is connected to another hub, that connection might not be functioning properly for several reasons, such as one of those described below. The same problems can affect a switch.

- **The cable run connecting the two hubs could be faulty**. As with any network communications problem, the network medium itself could be at fault. If the hubs are connected by a prefabricated cable, it could have a damaged connector or a kink that caused a break in one or more of the wires. If the hubs are connected by an internally installed cable run, the cable connectors could be wired incorrectly or one of the path cables could be damaged. Use the cable testing procedures described earlier to check the connection.

- **The connection between the hubs might not have a crossover circuit in it**. When you connect one Ethernet hub to another hub, you must plug one end of the cable into the uplink port on one (and only one) of the hubs. This reverses the crossover circuit in the connection, so that the crossovers in the two connected hubs don't cancel each other out. The problem could be that neither end of the cable is plugged into an uplink port or that both ends are plugged into an uplink port. Some hubs have a switch that you use to specify whether one of the ports functions as an uplink port. If this switch is set incorrectly, the result is the same as plugging the cable into the wrong port.

- **One or both of the hub ports might be damaged**. The hub unit itself might not be functioning properly because of a damaged connector in one of the ports, or for other reasons. Check the link pulse LEDs for the ports used to connect the two hubs together. If both LEDs are not lit when the hubs are connected, the two hubs are not communicating properly.

Testing Router Connections

If the user can access other computers on other segments of the LAN, it's time to test connections to other LANs. This assumes that the organization's network is really an internetwork that consists of multiple LANs connected by routers. Once again, a technician can test the computer's connectivity simply by using Windows Explorer to access computers that are located on other networks. If the user's computer can access resources in all of the LANs that make up the organization's internetwork, the problem is not one of network connectivity, and it's time to look at the computer itself.

If the user's computer can access resources in some LANs but not others, the problem might be in one of the routers that connect the networks together. The difficulty of locating the malfunction depends on how complicated the internetwork configuration is. If the network consists of 30 LANs interconnected by dozens of routers with redundant access paths, finding one malfunctioning router can be a complicated process, one that almost certainly has to be attended to by the technicians at the top of the organization's technical support hierarchy.

One method for isolating the router causing the user's problem is to use the Traceroute program to see exactly where the packets generated by the computer are going. Traceroute is a TCP/IP command-line utility that transmits packets to a given destination and displays a list of the routers that the packets pass through on the way to that destination. Most TCP/IP implementations include a version of Traceroute; on computers running the Windows operating system, the program is called Tracert.exe. Run Traceroute with the name of the Web server the user is trying to reach. A display similar to the one below will show you exactly how far the packets are going through the local internetwork.

```
Tracing route to www.abccorp.co.uk [173.146.1.1]
over a maximum of 30 hops:
  1   <10 ms    1 ms   <10 ms  192.168.6.1
  2    1  ms    1 ms   <10 ms  192.168.10.1
  3    1  ms   <10 ms  <10 ms  192.168.17.1
```

When the packets reach a router that is malfunctioning, the program should stop displaying information. In other words, the last router listed in the Traceroute display should be that of the last properly functioning router in the path to the destination. With knowledge of your network's configuration, you should be able to figure out which router the packets are trying to go to next. This is the router that either isn't receiving the packets or isn't forwarding them properly, causing the user's communication failure.

Suppose, for example, that your network consists of a number of LANs containing user computers, all of which are connected to a single backbone LAN, as shown in Figure 19.6. One of the user LANs also contains the router that connects the network to the Internet. Any of the following scenarios could cause the problem that Alice is experiencing. All of these scenarios are likely to cause more than one call to the help desk, with the last one probably causing a flood of complaints.

- If the router connecting Alice's LAN to the backbone (Router A) should fail, this would enable Alice to communicate with the computers on her own LAN, but prevent her traffic from reaching the backbone and being forwarded to any of the other LANs, including the LAN containing the router that is connected to the Internet. This problem would also affect all of the other computers on the same LAN as Alice's.

- If the router connecting the backbone to the LAN containing the Internet router (Router B) should fail, all of the users on the LANs other than the one containing the Internet router would be able to communicate among themselves, but not with users on the Internet router LAN. Also, no one would be able to access the Internet except for the users on the LAN containing the Internet router.

- If the problem is a hub failure on the backbone LAN, the result would be the same for the user, but would also affect all of the traffic between LANs on the entire internetwork. In this case, the internetwork would be reduced to a collection of unconnected LANs, because the backbone is unavailable to carry traffic between them. A cable break on the backbone LAN isolates the LAN served by that cable from the rest of the network.

Sometimes router failure is a less likely cause of communication problems because of the configuration of the internetwork. The internetwork in this example has only one path between each pair of LANs. To guard against the outages caused by router failures, many internetworks are designed with redundant routers and backbones, in which case there would have to be two major failures at the same time to cause any of the three preceding problem scenarios.

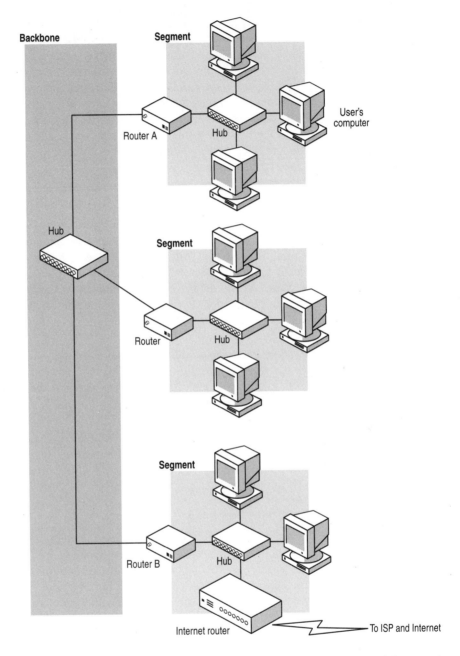

Figure 19.6 Routers provide communications between LANs; a router failure can be inconvenient or catastrophic.

For a single user help call like Alice's, a diagnosis of router failure is comparatively rare. It's far more likely for a problem like Alice's to be caused by a procedural error, a configuration error in her own computer, or possibly a minor network problem. A router failure would probably result in a more general network failure that would cause a large number of simultaneous complaints, which would immediately be brought to the attention of the network's senior support staff, and not left to the help desk. When the network administrators are aware of the problem, the role of the first-tier technician is to inform users that they know of the problem and that a fix is forthcoming. There is no need to troubleshoot each call when they have the same cause.

Possible Cause: Computer Configuration

If the user's computer can't access the network in any way, and troubleshooting has determined that neither the network nor the computer's cable connecting it to the network is at fault, it's time to look at the computer itself. Although it might seem as though it has been a long journey to this point, a problem that prevents any network access would eliminate the hub and router troubleshooting processes described in the previous sections. The technician might even proceed to this point as soon as he determines that no network communication is possible.

Note Unless the user is familiar with the configuration interface of the operating system, it's generally preferable for the technician to troubleshoot the computer in person, to eliminate the difficulties than can arise from giving instructions over the telephone.

If the user's problem is determined to be in the computer, the difficulty can exist at almost any level, and it's a good idea to use the Open Systems Interconnection (OSI) reference model to list the various possible causes, as explained in the following sections.

Physical Layer Problems

If it has been determined that the cable used to connect the computer to the network is functioning properly, the problem could be in the computer's network interface adapter itself. One common cause of communication problems is the network interface card (NIC) being loose in its bus slot. If the card is not installed firmly into the slot and secured in place with a screw or other device, a tug on the network cable can loosen the card and break the connection between the NIC and the computer. If the NIC is completely disconnected, most operating systems will report that the device is not functioning. The Device Manager application in most versions of the Windows operating system can report when a device is or is not functioning properly, for example, as shown in Figure 19.7. However, if the NIC is only slightly loosened and not pulled completely out of the slot, the problem could be intermittent and infuriatingly difficult to detect.

Figure 19.7 The Windows 2000 Device Manager displays information about the network interface adapter and other hardware devices.

The network interface adapter could also be physically damaged by a power surge, static electricity, or a manufacturing defect. If the adapter's cable connector is damaged, the contacts in the cable plug might not connect properly to the contacts in the adapter's jack. Cases like this are difficult to detect, except by ruling out all other possible causes of the problem. The solution is nearly always to replace the network interface adapter, but technicians rarely do this until they have checked the configuration of the computer's networking software. If the network interface adapter comes with a diagnostic program, however, and you have a loopback connector available, you can test the adapter without having to open up the computer.

Note For more information about network adapter loopback testing, see Lesson 3: Network Testing and Monitoring Tools, in Chapter 18, "Network Troubleshooting Tools."

Data-Link Layer Problems

Apart from the network interface adapter itself, the data-link layer protocol is implemented in the computer by the network interface adapter device driver. The driver must be configured with the same hardware settings as the network interface adapter, so that the two can communicate. Incorrect configuration settings are a common reason why a computer cannot communicate with the network, but this generally does not occur in a computer that has been functioning properly unless someone manually changes the configuration settings, or a device installation affects them.

When something used to work but now doesn't work, the technician should ask the user, "What has changed on the computer?" Has the user installed any new hardware or software? Has the user changed any configuration settings? The answer from the user is usually no, however, even when it becomes increasingly obvious that something has changed.

In most cases, the hardware settings of both the network interface adapter and the network interface adapter driver are configurable. You generally configure the adapter driver using an interface provided by the operating system, like that shown in Figure 19.8.

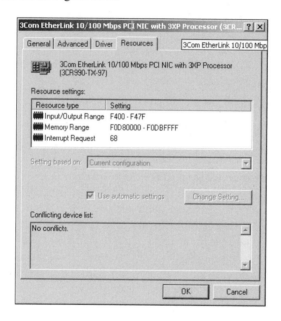

Figure 19.8 The Properties dialog box for a network interface adapter driver

To manually configure the adapter, you typically have to use a special utility that the manufacturer supplies. Today, most network interface adapters are installed using Plug and Play, which automatically configures both the adapter and its driver to use the same settings. The settings chosen are based on an evaluation of the hardware requirements for all of the devices in the computer, so installing a new piece of hardware into the computer can cause Plug and Play to alter the settings of existing devices. It isn't common, but it is possible for Plug and Play to select hardware settings that cause either the adapter or its driver to malfunction. If you determine that some new hardware device has been installed, you might have to disable it or remove it to determine if it is the cause of the network adapter's configuration problem. If this is the case, you might have to manually configure the new device to use it in the computer.

If the configuration of the adapter or driver parameters have been manually changed (presumably accidentally), the best course of action is to delete the device from the system configuration (again using Device Manager in Windows 2000), restart the computer, and let Plug and Play detect the adapter and reinstall it, reconfiguring both the adapter and the driver in the process.

Network/Transport Layer Problems

Although it spans other layers as well, the primary functions of the TCP/IP protocols are at the network and transport layers, and the TCP/IP client configuration is one of the chief causes of network communication problems. As mentioned earlier, improperly configured DNS server addresses can prevent the computer from resolving server names into addresses and, as a result, prevent the user from accessing the Internet. WINS servers perform the same type of name resolution process for NetBIOS names, and incorrect WINS server addresses can prevent the computer from accessing some of the other computers on the network. A computer running the Windows operating system that is not configured with WINS server addresses can still resolve the name of other computers on its own LAN, using broadcast messages. However, broadcasts cannot reach the computers on other LANs, so WINS is needed to resolve these names.

Note WINS support is included in Windows 2000 only to enable the computer to communicate with other computers using NetBIOS names, such as Windows NT and Windows 98 systems. Windows 2000 uses its directory service, Active Directory, which relies on DNS servers to resolve names.

While incorrect DNS and WINS server addresses can prevent a computer from accessing other computers by name, other TCP/IP configuration parameters can have an even greater effect on network communications. An incorrect IP address or subnet mask can completely prevent all network communications, and what's worse, an IP address duplicated on a second computer can prevent both from accessing the network. Therefore, an interruption can occur if the IP address on the user's computer has been changed or if a computer somewhere else on the network has been configured to use the same IP address as the user.

To test for a duplicate IP address, shut down the user's computer and ping that computer's IP address using another workstation. If you receive a response to the Ping command, there is another computer using that same IP address.

An incorrect or missing default gateway parameter can also be the cause of the user's problem. As with the router failures described earlier, a computer that is not configured with a correct default gateway address can access the other computers on its own LAN, but not any of the other LANs on the internetwork. Without a default gateway address, the computer does not know where to send packets that are destined for other networks. This would prevent the user's Web browser from connecting to any sites on the Internet. In Windows 2000, to modify any of the TCP/IP configuration parameters listed here, use the Internet Protocol (TCP/IP) Properties dialog box as described earlier in this chapter.

If the network has DHCP servers that configure the network's TCP/IP clients, none of the fields in the Internet Protocol (TCP/IP) Properties dialog box should have values in them. Manually configured TCP/IP parameters take precedence over those supplied by DHCP. If someone has been "experimenting" by supplying their own TCP/IP values, remove them before reactivating the DHCP client.

It's also important for the technician to know what allocation mode the DHCP servers are using. If they're using automatic allocation, which assigns the IP address to clients permanently, moving the computer to a different subnet requires that you manually release the assigned IP address and renew it so that the DHCP server can assign one from the proper subnet. This is another way for the computer to have an incorrect IP address. If you move computers around on the network frequently, consider using dynamic allocation, which leases addresses to computers for a short period of time and renews them each time the computer starts.

Application Layer Problems

Application layer networking protocols are generally not configurable, but there can be problems at the application level that affect network communications. One issue that is best to get out of the way early is the possibility of a virus infection. It isn't likely that a virus could be the cause of the user's failure to access a Web site, but new viruses are constantly being invented that can have unpredictable effects on a computer. If you do not already have anti-virus software installed on the computer, you should install it, make sure the virus signatures are updated, and run a complete system scan, just to be safe.

Although it doesn't affect Internet access directly, network communication problems can also be caused by having the incorrect network client installed on the computer. In computers running the Windows operating system, the Client for Microsoft Networks module provides the redirector that enables the computer to send resource access requests to other computers running the Windows operating system. If this component is removed, there is a break in the protocol stack and network communication ceases.

Applications themselves can be damaged or improperly configured as well, interfering with network communications. If, for example, Alice was to modify the configuration of her browser, causing it to access the Internet by dialing out to an ISP instead of using the LAN, she would be unable to access any Web sites if a modem was not installed or a dial-up account was not properly configured. This problem would be specific to the browser, however, and would be caught when the technician had her try to use another application to access the Internet.

Possible Cause: User Error

Errors in user procedures are one of the most common causes of help desk calls, and listing this possible cause last does not imply that you should go through all of the testing procedures described thus far before addressing the possibility of user error. In fact, it is often possible to quickly determine that the user's equipment and the network are functioning properly, and that the problem must be in something the user did. However, in the interests of diplomacy, it's often a good idea to be certain that a procedural error is the problem before you broach the subject with the user. Some people are perfectly willing to admit that they might be at fault, while others can be very sensitive about it. Part of the help desk technician's job is to resolve callers' problems without making them feel foolish, and this is a skill that is becoming increasingly rare in the technical support industry.

User error can easily be the reason for a failure to access a Web site, and it can sometimes be difficult for the technician to detect when working with the user over the telephone. Many common Internet access problems are caused by the incorrect entry of URLs into the browser. This is why, when the technician is having the user test the system by trying to access other sites, it is best to use existing shortcuts or favorites whenever possible. It might seem as though the user is experiencing a severe Internet connectivity problem, and the technician might be compelled to perform all sorts of network and hardware tests like those described earlier, when the problem is actually that the user is typing URLs with backslashes instead of forward slashes, or is inserting three forward slashes after the *http:* prefix instead of two.

This latter error is, in fact, what was causing Alice's problem. She had somehow gotten the impression that three forward slashes were correct, and was using them even when the technician was dictating the URLs of other sites she should try over the telephone to test her Internet connectivity. He started his dictation with *www*, knowing that typing the *http://* prefix isn't necessary in most cases, but Alice added it to each URL on her own, assuming that it had to be there, but with three forward slashes instead of two. Thus, this particular problem could have been solved almost immediately if the technician had gone to Alice's site and watched her type in the URLs. This is not to say that every call to the help desk should be immediately followed by a trip to the user's site. In many cases, that would be impractical, but this particular case demonstrates how important the communication between the technician and the user is in a situation like this.

There are many other common procedural errors that can interfere with a user's network connectivity, and many of these can be very difficult to catch over the telephone. Sometimes there is no substitute for actually watching what the user is doing. User logons, for example, are a common source of difficulties. Users often call the help desk because they are unable to log on to the network. If they have been trying to log on repeatedly and are failing every time, the technician should first check to see if the user has been locked out of the account. Many networks are configured to disable accounts after a certain number of failed logon attempts, to prevent brute force attempts by intruders. If the account is not locked, password policies might also be to blame. Users might ignore a message telling them that a periodic password change is required, or attempt to reuse an old password when policy dictates against it. Another common occurrence for Windows 2000 and Windows NT users is for them to be trying to log on to the wrong domain or onto the local system, using the wrong account. The domain selector in the logon dialog box might have been changed somehow, which is something that a technician is not likely to realize without actually watching the user try to log on.

Exercise 19.1: Network Hardware Problems

On an internetwork consisting of several user segments connected by a backbone, with an Internet router connected directly to the backbone, specify whether the following network conditions would normally cause Internet access problems for one user only, for all of the users connected to one hub, for all of the users on one LAN, or for the entire internetwork.

1. Both ends of a cable connecting two hubs are plugged into uplink ports.
2. The router connecting the network to the ISP is down.
3. The cable connecting a user's computer to the hub is cut.
4. The ISP's connection to the Internet fails.
5. The router connecting a user LAN to the backbone malfunctions.

Chapter Summary

The key points covered in this chapter are as follows.

"I Can't Access a Web Site"

- Administrative tasks, such as record keeping, call prioritizing, and call escalation, are essential activities in a professional technical support organization.

- The first step in troubleshooting any networking problem is to gather information from the user experiencing the problem.

- In an Internet access problem, checking the router that connects the network to the ISP is fast, easy, and always a good idea.

- DNS name resolution problems are a common cause of Internet access failures.

- Solving a network communications problem is a matter of isolating the component that is malfunctioning.

- If the network is functioning properly, you should start looking to the user's computer for the problem.

- User error is also a common cause of Internet access difficulties, but this is a subject that should be presented to the user delicately.

Chapter Review

1. Without a DNS server, a user can still access the Internet using which of the following techniques?

   a. By using links saved as Favorites instead of typing URLs

   b. By using NetBIOS names instead of DNS names

   c. By using hardware addresses instead of DNS names

   d. By using IP addresses instead of DNS names

2. A user is unable to access the shared server drive that he uses every day, where his working files are stored. Which of the following questions would you ask the user first? State your reason why.

   a. "Are you able to access any other network resources?"

   b. "Did you have any problems logging on to the network?"

   c. "Can you access the Internet?"

   d. "Is your network cable connected to the computer?"

3. Which of the following is not a possible cause of Internet access failure?

   a. Missing WINS server address

   b. DNS server failure

   c. ISP connection failure

   d. Mistyped URLs

4. Which of the following network/transport layer problems can be caused by another computer on the network?

   a. Missing DNS server address

   b. Incorrect subnet mask

   c. Duplicate IP address

   d. Incorrect default gateway address

5. A computer running the Windows operating system without a WINS server address cannot access which of the following resources?

   a. Internet Web sites

   b. Computers running the Windows operating system that are connected to the same hub

   c. Computers not running the Windows operating system that are connected to the same LAN

   d. Computers running the Windows operating system that are connected to other LANs

6. Which of the following is the best solution for a case in which a user has changed the network interface adapter configuration and can no longer access the network?

   a. Replace the adapter with a new one.

   b. Delete the adapter driver and let Plug and Play reinstall it.

   c. Modify the adapter's configuration parameters using the utility supplied by the manufacturer.

   d. Modify the adapter driver's configuration parameters using the operating system interface.

7. Which of the following is the easiest way to test a patch cable for a fault?

   a. Replace it with one that you know is working properly.

   b. Connect it to a multifunction cable tester.

   c. Plug the computer end of the cable into the wall plate and the wall plate end into the computer.

   d. Connect it to a computer that you know is functioning properly.

8. Which of the following tools can pinpoint the exact location of a cable break?

   a. A tone generator and locator

   b. A protocol analyzer

   c. A multifunction cable tester

   d. A wire map tester

9. When a computer lacks a correct default gateway address, how far do packets destined for other networks travel?

   a. As far as the Internet access router

   b. As far as the backbone

   c. As far as the hub

   d. As far as the local network

10. Which of the following network problems would generally affect services other than Internet access on a Windows-based network?

    a. ISP connection failure

    b. Backbone failure

    c. DNS failure

    d. T1 failure

APPENDIX A

Questions and Answers

Chapter 1: Networking Basics

Lesson 1: Network Communications

Exercise 1.1: Networking Definitions

Page 12

Match the concepts in the numbered list with the definitions that follow it.

Concepts

1. Full-duplex

2. Broadband

3. Circuit switching

4. Client/server network

5. Baseband

Definitions

a. A medium that carries multiple signals simultaneously

b. A network in which a connection is established before any data is transmitted

c. A network on which systems perform designated roles

d. A medium that carries traffic in both directions simultaneously

e. A medium that carries only one signal

1. **d**

2. **a**

3. **b**

4. **c**

5. **e**

Lesson 2: The OSI Reference Model

Exercise 1.2: OSI Model Layers

Page 25

For each of the protocols, functions, or concepts listed below, specify the OSI model layer with which it is associated.

1. Ethernet

   Data-link

2. Dialog separation

   Session

3. Transfer syntax

   Presentation

4. Routing

   Network

5. Segmentation

   Transport

6. SMTP

   Application

7. Differential Manchester

   Physical

Chapter Review

Page 27

1. Which layer of the OSI reference model is responsible for controlling access to the network medium?

   The data-link layer

2. On which type of network does each computer maintain its own permissions and security settings?

   A peer-to-peer network

3. A language that two computers "speak" while communicating over a network is called _____.

   A protocol

4. A series of LANs connected together by any means is called _____.

An internetwork

5. What kind of network is often used to connect horizontal segments on a large enterprise internetwork?

A backbone

6. Which layer of the OSI model is responsible for translating different syntaxes?

The presentation layer

7. A network in which the medium carries only one signal is called _____.

Baseband

8. An example of full-duplex communications is _____.

A telephone call

9. The address of a packet's final destination is specified in the _____ layer.

Network

10. TCP is an example of a _____ layer protocol.

Transport

11. Electrical voltages, light pulses, and infrared waves are all examples of types of _____.

Signals

12. A technology used to connect LANs at distant locations is called _____.

A wide area network (WAN)

13. The type of network in which data is split into discrete units that are transmitted over the network individually is called _____.

A packet-switching network

14. The process by which a receiving system sends messages instructing a sending system to slow down its transmission rate is called _____.

Flow control

15. A protocol that uses a handshake to establish a connection before sending data is called _____.

Connection oriented

Chapter 2: Network Hardware

Lesson 1: Network Cables

Exercise 2.1: Network Cable Types

Page 38

Match the applications in the left column with the network cable types in the right column that best suit them.

1. Uses the bus topology
2. Used for the original Token Ring networks
3. Used for Gigabit Ethernet networks
4. Contains eight wires
5. Used for LANs that span long distances
6. Uses a laser to generate signals

a. UTP
b. Singlemode fiber optic
c. Shielded twisted pair
d. Coaxial cable
e. Category 5e UTP
f. Multimode fiber optic

1. d

2. c

3. e

4. a

5. f

6. b

Lesson 2: Network Interface Adapters

Exercise 2.2: Network Adapter Functions

Page 46

1. The two hardware resources used by every network interface adapter are _____ and _____.

An interrupt request (IRQ) and an input/output (I/O) port address

2. Network interface adapters are associated with the protocol operating at the _____ layer.

Data-link

3. The network interface adapter encapsulates data by enclosing it within a _____.

Frame

Lesson 3: Network Hubs

Exercise 2.3: Network Hub Functions

Page 51   Match the concept in the left column with the definition in the right column that best describes it.

1.	Token Ring MAU	a.	Amplifies signals
2.	Intelligent hub	b.	Used to send reports to a network management console
3.	Uplink port	c.	Used to connect MAUs
4.	Loopback port	d.	Forwards packets serially
5.	Repeater	e.	Excluded from a Token Ring network
6.	Ring In and Ring Out ports	f.	Used to connect one Ethernet hub to a standard port on another Ethernet hub

1. d

2. b

3. f

4. e

5. a

6. c

Chapter Review

Page 53   1. What is the name of an Ethernet cable that contains two electrical conductors?

   a. A shielded twisted pair (STP) cable

   b. A coaxial cable

   c. A dielectric cable

   d. An unshielded twisted pair (UTP) cable

b

2. What are the names of the two most common conditions that degrade the signals on copper-based cables?

Crosstalk and attenuation

3. Which topology requires the use of terminators?

   a. Bus

   b. Star

   c. Ring

   d. None of the above

a

4. Which of the following topologies is implemented only logically, not physically?

   a. Bus

   b. Star

   c. Ring

   d. All of the above

   c

5. How many wire pairs are actually used on a typical UTP Ethernet network?

   a. One

   b. Two

   c. Three

   d. Four

   b

6. What is the name of the process of building a frame around network layer information?

   a. Data buffering

   b. Signal encoding

   c. Media access control (MAC)

   d. Data encapsulation

   d

7. Which of the connectors on a network interface adapter transmits data in parallel?

   The system bus connector

8. Which two of the following hardware resources do network interface adapters always require?

   a. DMA channel

   b. I/O port address

   c. IRQ

   d. Memory address

   b and c

9. What is the name of the process by which a network interface adapter determines when it should transmit its data over the network?

   Media access control

10. Which bus type is preferred for a NIC that will be connected to a Fast Ethernet network?

    PCI

11. A passive hub does not do which of the following?

    a. Transmit management information using SNMP

    b. Function as a repeater

    c. Provide a crossover circuit

    d. Store and forward data

    b

12. To connect two Ethernet hubs together, you must do which of the following?

    a. Purchase a special crossover cable

    b. Connect the uplink ports on the two hubs together

    c. Connect any standard port on one hub to a standard port on the other

    d. Connect the uplink port in one hub to a standard port on the other

    d

13. Which term describes a port in a Token Ring MAU that is not part of the ring?

    a. Passive

    b. Loopback

    c. Crossover

    d. Intelligent

    b

14. A hub that functions as a repeater inhibits the effect of _____.

    Attenuation

15. You can use which of the following to connect two Ethernet computers together using UTP cable?

    a. An Ethernet hub

    b. A multiport repeater

    c. A crossover cable

    d. All of the above

    d

Chapter 3: Network Connections

Lesson 1: Bridging

Exercise 3.1: Bridge Functions

Page 61

1. At what layer of the Open Systems Interconnection (OSI) reference model does a bridge function?

   a. Physical

   b. Data-link

   c. Network

   d. Transport

   b

2. What does a bridge do when it receives a packet that is destined for a system on the same network segment over which the packet arrived?

   a. Discards it

   b. Relays it

   c. Broadcasts it

   d. Unicasts it

   a

3. What is a bridge called that connects network segments using different types of cable?

   a. Transparent

   b. Remote

   c. Translation

   d. Source route

   c

4. Two network segments connected by a bridge share what type of domain?

   a. Collision

   b. Broadcast

   c. Source route

   d. Unicast

   b

5. What is the technique used to prevent bridge loops called?

    a. Transparent bridging

    b. Packet filtering

    c. Translation bridging

    d. The spanning tree algorithm

    d

Lesson 2: Switching

Exercise 3.2: Switch Functions

Page 67

1. The functionality of a switch is best described as being a combination of what two devices?

    a. A router and a gateway

    b. A hub and a bridge

    c. A bridge and a router

    d. A repeater and a hub

    c

2. Which of the following effects is a result of replacing the routers in a segment/backbone network with switches?

    a. The speed of the network increases.

    b. The traffic on the backbone increases.

    c. The number of LANs increases.

    d. The bandwidth available to workstations increases.

    d

3. When you use switches instead of routers and hubs, what is the effect on the number of collisions on the network?

    a. Increases

    b. Decreases

    c. Stays the same

    b

4. When you replace the routers with switches on an internetwork consisting of three segments connected by one backbone, how many broadcast domains do you end up with?

a. None

b. One

c. Three

d. Four

b

5. What is a switch called that immediately relays signals from the incoming port to the outgoing port?

a. A cut-through switch

b. A shared memory switch

c. A bus architecture switch

d. A store-and-forward switch

a

Lesson 3: Routing

Exercise 3.3: Routing Functions

Page 75

1. At what layer of the OSI reference model do routers operate?

a. Physical

b. Data-link

c. Network

d. Transport

c

2. Multiples of what are created by connecting several LANs with routers?

a. Collision domains

b. Broadcast domains

c. Subnets

d. All of the above

d

3. What is the information in a routing table that specifies the relative efficiency of a particular route called?

   a. Metric

   b. Static route

   c. Dynamic route

   d. Hop

   a

4. With which of the following techniques are routing protocols associated?

   a. WAN routing

   b. Static routing

   c. Dynamic routing

   d. All of the above

   c

5. What is the term for a group of LANs in one building connected by routers?

   a. A WAN

   b. A broadcast domain

   c. A collision domain

   d. An internetwork

   d

Chapter Review

Page 78

1. Which of the following devices are you most likely to use to connect a LAN to the Internet?

   a. A hub

   b. A bridge

   c. A switch

   d. A router

   d

2. Which of the following devices does not read the data-link layer protocol header in incoming packets?

   a. A hub

   b. A bridge

   c. A switch

   d. A router

   a

3. Suppose that you have a 10 Mbps Ethernet LAN that consists of 45 computers connected to three standard repeating hubs. Traffic levels are getting too high, causing excessive collisions and reduced performance. Which of the following courses of action is the most inexpensive way to reduce the overall traffic level on the network?

   a. Split the network into three LANs and connect them using dedicated hardware routers.

   b. Replace the three hubs with switches.

   c. Connect the three hubs to a high-performance switch, instead of to each other.

   d. Install a transparent bridge between two of the hubs.

   d

4. Using the same scenario as in question 3, which of the following courses of action would not increase the bandwidth available to each workstation?

   a. Split the network into three LANs and connect them using dedicated hardware routers.

   b. Replace the three hubs with switches.

   c. Connect the three hubs to a high-performance switch, instead of to each other.

   d. Upgrade the network to 100 Mbps by installing Fast Ethernet NICs and hubs.

   a

5. The spanning tree algorithm is used to prevent which of the following networking problems?

   a. Excessive collisions

   b. Packet filtering

   c. Bridge loops

   d. Static routing

   c

6, Source route bridging is associated with which of the following protocols?

   a. Ethernet

   b. Token Ring

   c. FDDI

   d. TCP/IP

   b

7. On a switched network, virtual LANs are used to create multiples of what?

   a. Collision domains

   b. Broadcast domains

   c. Internetworks

   d. All of the above

   b

8. ICS enables a computer running Windows to function as what?

   a. A hub

   b. A bridge

   c. A switch

   d. A router

   d

9. Which of the following processes requires manual intervention from a network administrator?

   a. Transparent bridging

   b. Source route bridging

   c. Static routing

   d. Dynamic routing

   c

10. Which of the following devices does not have buffers to store data during processing?

   a. A repeating hub

   b. A local bridge

   c. A cut-through switch

   d. All of the above

   d

Chapter 4: Networking Software

Lesson 1: Network Operating Systems

Exercise 4.1: Network Operating System Products

Page 90

Match the network operating system in the left column with the phrase in the right column that best describes it.

1. Linux
2. Windows NT
3. UNIX System V
4. NetWare 3.x
5. Windows 2000

a. Uses a bindery to store user accounts
b. Current version of the original AT&T UNIX
c. Available in Server, Advanced Server, and Datacenter versions
d. First version of Windows not based on MS-DOS
e. Open source UNIX version

1. e

2. d

3. b

4. a

5. c

Lesson 2: Network Clients

Exercise 4.2: Network Client Concepts

Page 97

1. What is the protocol traditionally associated with NetWare networking?

   a. NetBEUI

   b. IPX

   c. TCP/IP

   d. Ethernet

   b

2. What is the Windows component that enables an application to access a network resource in the same way as a local one?

   a. A redirector

   b. A protocol

   c. A client

   d. A service

   a

3. Which of the following Windows network components is not required for client functionality?

   a. A redirector

   b. A service

   c. A protocol

   d. A network interface adapter driver

   b

4. What is the most important reason for a network administrator to use a Novell client for NetWare rather than Microsoft's NetWare?

   a. Novell's client includes a genuine version of the IPX protocols.

   b. Novell's client is faster than Microsoft's.

   c. Novell's client is less expensive than Microsoft's.

   d. Novell's client includes the NetWare Administrator application.

   d

5. Which of the following Windows 2000 networking modules do you not install from the Network And Dial-up Connections dialog box?

   a. Services

   b. Clients

   c. Protocols

   d. Network interface adapter drivers

   d

Lesson 3: Directory Services

Exercise 4.3: Directory Service Concepts

Page 106

1. Which directory service requires users to have a separate account for each server?

   a. Windows NT Domains

   b. Active Directory

   c. NetWare bindery

   d. Novell Directory Services

   c

2. What provides communication between Windows NT domains?

   a. Trust relationships

   b. Single master replication

   c. Multiple master replication

   d. Partitioning

   a

3. On an Active Directory network, a tree is composed of multiples of what?

   a. Servers

   b. Partitions

   c. Forests

   d. Domains

   d

4. The types of objects you can create in an NDS tree are determined by what?

   a. Number of partitions

   b. Directory schema

   c. Number of containers

   d. X.500 directory service

   b

5. Which of the following terms does not describe the trust relationships between Active Directory domains in the same tree?

   a. Transitive

   b. Bi-directional

   c. Automatic

   d. Single master

   d

Chapter Review

Page 108

1. Which of the following ITU standards is the basis for NDS and Active Directory?

    a. X.25

    b. X.400

    c. X.500

    d. X.5

    c

2. Which types of network clients are included in Windows 2000 Professional?

    a. Client Service for NetWare

    b. Gateway Service for NetWare

    c. Client for Microsoft Networks

    d. Client Service for UNIX

    a and c

3. What is the Windows NT and Windows 2000 file system called that enables administrators to assign permissions to individual files?

    a. Active Directory

    b. NDS

    c. FAT

    d. NTFS

    d

4. Which of the following services on a Windows NT or Windows 2000 network is responsible for configuring TCP/IP clients?

    a. DNS

    b. WINS

    c. IIS

    d. DHCP

    d

5. Which of the following network operating systems is generally considered to be the best application server platform?

    a. Windows NT

    b. Windows 2000

    c. Novell NetWare

    d. UNIX

    d

6. What is a program called that runs in the background on a UNIX system?

   a. A service

   b. A daemon

   c. An application

   d. A domain

   b

7. Which of the following directory services uses multiword names for its domains?

   a. NetWare bindery

   b. NDS

   c. Windows NT Domains

   d. Active Directory

   d

8. What is splitting an NDS tree into pieces and storing those pieces on different servers called?

   a. Replication

   b. Partitioning

   c. Establishing trust relationships

   d. Creating a tree

   b

9. What is the Windows NT and Windows 2000 service that maintains a list of shared resources on the network called?

   a. Server

   b. Client

   c. Computer Browser

   d. Messenger

   c

10. Which of the following is not a true statement?

    a. Containers are composed of objects.

    b. Trees are composed of domains.

    c. Objects are composed of attributes.

    d. Forests are composed of trees.

    a

Chapter 5: Data-Link Layer Protocols

Lesson 1: Ethernet

Exercise 5.1: CSMA/CD Procedures

Page 125

Place the following steps of the CSMA/CD transmission process in the proper order.

1. System begins transmitting data.
2. System retransmits data.
3. System detects incoming signal on receive wires.
4. System backs off.
5. System listens to the network.
6. System stops transmitting data.
7. System transmits jam pattern.
8. System detects no network traffic

   5, 8, 1, 3, 6, 7, 4, 2

Lesson 2: Token Ring

Exercise 5.2: Ethernet Standards and Technologies

Page 131

Match the standard in the left column with the most suitable technology in the right column.

1.	IEEE 802.2	a.	Gigabit Ethernet
2.	IEEE 802.3	b.	Fast Ethernet
3.	IEEE 802.3u	c.	Thick Ethernet
4.	IEEE 802.3z	d.	Logical Link Control
5.	IEEE 802.3ab	e.	10BaseT
6.	IEEE 802.5	f.	Thin Ethernet
7.	DIX Ethernet	g.	1000BaseT
8.	DIX Ethernet II	h.	Token Ring

   1. d
   2. e
   3. b
   4. a
   5. g
   6. h
   7. c
   8. f

Exercise 5.3: Selecting a Data-Link Layer Protocol

Page 132

For each of the following scenarios, specify which data-link layer protocol you think is preferable, Ethernet or Token Ring, and give reasons why. In some cases, either protocol would be suitable; the reasons you provide are more significant than the protocol you select.

1. A family with two computers in the home wants to network them in order to share a printer and an Internet connection.

   Ethernet is definitely preferable in this case, because the family's networking requirements are light, and not likely to generate a large amount of traffic; the hardware required is much cheaper; and they can even connect the two systems directly, using a crossover cable instead of a hub.

2. A small graphics design firm wants to build a 10-node network to handle the extremely large image files that they must transfer between systems and to a print server.

   Token Ring is an option here, because the large image files will generate lots of network traffic, and Token Ring doesn't diminish in performance as traffic levels increase. However, Ethernet could also be suitable, because they could install Fast Ethernet, running at 100 Mbps versus Token Ring's 16 Mbps, and because there are only to be ten systems on the network, which will result in fewer collisions than a network with twenty systems generating the same amount of traffic.

3. A company with a 50-node LAN used by their order entry staff will be going public in the near future and is expected to grow enormously over the next year.

   While Token Ring would serve, particularly because of its ability to handle high traffic levels, Ethernet provides more flexible upgrade options. The company can increase the bandwidth available to each system by upgrading the network from regular to Fast Ethernet, or by installing bridges or switches.

Lesson 3: SLIP and PPP

Exercise 5.4: PPP Connection Establishment

Page 136

Place the following steps of the PPP connection establishment process in the correct order.

1. Link Open

2. Link Termination

3. Network Layer Protocol Configuration

4. Authentication

5. Link Quality Monitoring

6. Link Establishment

7. Link Dead

   7, 6, 4, 5, 3, 1, 2

Chapter Review

Page 138

1. What is the name of the protocol that systems use to negotiate options during the PPP connection establishment procedure?

   a. CHAP

   b. LCP

   c. PAP

   d. NCP

   b

2. What does an Ethernet system generate when it detects a collision?

   a. A beacon frame

   b. An error message

   c. A jam signal

   d. None of the above

   c

3. Which of the following is not a required component of a 10BaseT Ethernet network?

   a. Network interface adapters or NICs

   b. Cables

   c. A hub

   d. Computers

   c

4. To achieve 100 Mbps speed over Category 3 cable, 100BaseT4 Ethernet uses which of the following?

   a. PAM-5 signaling

   b. Quartet signaling

   c. CSMA/CD

   d. All four wire pairs

   d

5. In which of the following standards is Gigabit Ethernet defined?

   a. IEEE 802.2

   b. IEEE 802.3

   c. IEEE 802.3u

   e. IEEE 802.3z

   d

6. The Frame Check Sequence field in a data-link layer protocol header is used for _____.

   Error correction

7. List the hardware components that you have to replace when upgrading a ten-year-old 10BaseT network to 100BaseTX.

   The components are NICs, hubs, and cable (because a 10-year-old network is most likely using Category 3 cable, and Category 5 is required for 100BaseTX).

8. How could you upgrade a ten-year-old 10BaseT network to Fast Ethernet without replacing the cables?

   Use 100BaseT4 NICs and hubs.

9. Which data-link layer protocol is preferred on a network with high levels of traffic, Ethernet or Token Ring? Why?

   Token Ring is preferable, because it can handle high traffic levels without diminished performance. Ethernet experiences more collisions as traffic levels increase, causing performance to degrade.

10. Which Fast Ethernet physical layer option is best suited for a connection between two campus buildings 200 meters apart? Why?

    100BaseFX, because fiber optic cable is better suited to outdoor installations and because the Fast Ethernet UTP cable options are all restricted to cable segments no longer than 100 meters.

Chapter 6: Network Layer Protocols

Lesson 1: IP

Exercise 6.1: IP Header Properties

Page 150

1. What does the IP header's protocol field identify?

   a. The physical layer specification of the network that will carry the datagram

   b. The data-link layer protocol that will carry the datagram

   c. The transport layer protocol that generated the information in the Data field

   d. The application that generated the message carried in the datagram

   c

2. Which of the following IP header elements is never modified during the IP fragmentation process?

   a. The Identification field

   b. The More Fragments bit

   c. The Fragment Offset field

   d. The Time To Live (TTL) field

   a

3. What does an IP address identify?

   a. A network

   b. A computer

   c. A network interface adapter

   d. A network and a network interface adapter

   d

Lesson 2: IPX

Exercise 6.2: IPX Properties

Page 154

1. In the IP header, the IPX equivalent to the TTL field is called what?

   a. Packet Type

   b. Transport Control

   c. Checksum

   d. Source Socket

   b

2. Which of the following statements about IPX is untrue?

    a. IPX routes datagrams between different types of networks.

    b. IPX has its own network addressing system.

    c. IPX uses a checksum to verify the proper transmission of data.

    d. The IPX header is larger than the IP header.

    c.

3. How many bytes long is the information that IPX uses to identify the datagram's destination computer on a particular network?

    a. 2

    b. 4

    c. 6

    d. 10

    d

Lesson 3: NetBEUI

Exercise 6.3: NBF Protocols

Page 161

For each of the NBF message types listed below, specify which of the four NBF protocols—NMP, SMP, UDP, or DMP— is primarily associated with it.

1. Datagram Broadcast

    UDP

2. Data First Middle

    SMP

3. Name Query

    NMP

4. Status Response

    DMP

5. Add Name Response

    NMP

Chapter Review

Page 163

1. Specify which network layer protocol you would use on each of the following networks, and explain why.

   a. A private internetwork with mixed Windows and NetWare systems

   IPX, because NetWare requires it

   b. A two-node home Windows-based network with individual dial-up Internet connections

   NetBEUI, because it's easier to install and configure

   c. A ten-node Windows-based network with a router connecting it to the Internet

   TCP/IP, because it's required to connect to the Internet

2. How does a NetBEUI network prevent two systems from using the same NetBIOS name?

   By registering names using NMP messages

3. Which IP header field makes the Traceroute utility possible?

   a. Version

   b. Type of Service

   c. Identification

   d. Time To Live

   d

4. Which two protocols carried within IP datagrams operate at the transport layer of the OSI model?

   a. IMCP

   b. TCP

   c. UDP

   d. IGMP

   b and c

5. Give two reasons why NetBEUI is not suitable for use on a large internetwork.

   It is not suitable because it lacks the network identifiers needed to route packets between networks and because it generates a large amount of broadcast traffic.

6. Place the following phases of a NetBEUI Frame session in the proper order.

a. Session Alive

b. Session Initialize

c. LLC session establishment

d. Name resolution

e. Session End

f. Session Confirm

d, c, b, f, a, e

7. What is the maximum number of routers that an IPX datagram can pass through on the way to its destination?

a. 0

b. 16

c. 128

d. 256

b

8. Which of the following protocols is capable of providing connection-oriented service?

a. IP

b. IPX

c. NetBEUI

d. None of the above

c

Chapter 7: Transport Layer Protocols

Lesson 1: TCP and UDP

Exercise 7.1: TCP Header Fields

Page 179

Match the TCP header field in the left column with the correct description in the right column.

1.	Source Port	a.	Specifies how many bytes the sender can transmit
2.	Sequence Number	b.	Specifies the number of bytes in the sequence that have been successfully transmitted
3.	Checksum	c.	Specifies the functions of messages used to initiate and terminate connections
4.	Window	d.	Contains information for the application layer
5.	Urgent Pointer	e.	Specifies which of the bytes in the message should receive special treatment from the receiving system
6.	Data Offset	f.	Identifies the application or protocol that generated the data carried in the TCP message
7.	Destination Port	g.	Used to reassemble segments that arrive at the destination out of order
8.	Acknowledgment Number	h.	Specifies the length of the TCP header
9.	Control Bits	i.	Contains error detection information
10.	Data	j.	Specifies the application that will make use of the data in the message

1. **f**
2. **g**
3. **i**
4. **a**
5. **e**
6. **h**
7. **j**
8. **b**
9. **c**
10. **d**

Chapter Review

Page 185

1. In TCP, what does "delayed acknowledgment" mean?

    a. A predetermined time interval must pass before the receiving system can acknowledge a data packet.

    b. Data segments are not acknowledged until the entire sequence has been transmitted.

    c. The receiving system doesn't have to generate a separate acknowledgment message for every segment.

    d. A data segment must be acknowledged before the next segment is transmitted.

    c

2. What does the Data Offset field in the TCP header specify?

    a. The length of the TCP header

    b. The location of the current segment in the sequence

    c. The length of the Data field

    d. The checksum value used for error detection

    a

3. Specify whether each of the following statements describes TCP, UDP, or both.

    a. It provides flow control.

    TCP

    b. It is used for DNS communications.

    Both

    c. It detects transmission errors.

    Both

    d. It is used to carry DHCP messages.

    UDP

    e. It divides data to be transmitted into segments.

    TCP

    f. It acknowledges transmitted messages.

    Both

    g. It is used for Web client/server communications.

    TCP

h. It requires a connection establishment procedure.

TCP

i. It contains a Length field.

UDP

j. It uses a pseudo-header in its checksums.

Both

4. What is the combination of an IP address and a port number called?

   a. A sequence number

   b. A checksum

   c. A data offset

   d. A socket

   d

5. Which of the following is not true of the SPX protocol?

   a. It is connection-oriented.

   b. It operates at the transport layer only.

   c. Clients use it to access server files.

   d. It provides flow control.

   c

6. Which of the following TCP/IP systems uses an ephemeral port number?

   a. The client

   b. The server

   c. The system initiating the TCP connection

   d. The system terminating the TCP connection

   a

7. What flag does the first message transmitted in any TCP connection contain?

   a. ACK

   b. SYN

   c. FIN

   d. PSH

   b

8. At which layers of the OSI reference model does the NCP provide functions?

The transport, session, presentation, and application layers

9. What TCP header field provides flow control?

a. Window

b. Data Offset

c. Acknowledgment

d. Sequence Number

a

10. Which of the following services does the UDP protocol provide?

a. Flow control

b. Guaranteed delivery

c. Error detection

d. None of the above

c

Chapter 8: TCP/IP Fundamentals

Lesson 1: TCP/IP Protocols

Exercise 8.1: TCP/IP Layers and Protocols

Page 199

Specify the layer of the TCP/IP protocol stack at which each of the following protocols operates.

1. DHCP

   Application

2. ARP

   Link or Internet (either is correct)

3. IP

   Internet

4. UDP

   Transport

5. POP3

   Application

6. ICMP

   Internet

7. SMTP

   Application

8. TCP

   Transport

9. DNS

   Application

10. SLIP

    Link

Lesson 2: IP Addressing

Exercise 8.2: Variable-Length Subnetting

Page 205

Specify the subnet mask value you would use for each of the following network configurations:

1. A Class C network address with a 2-bit subnet identifier

   255.255.255.192

2. A Class A network address with a 16-bit host identifier

   255.255.0.0

3. A Class B network address with a 6-bit subnet identifier

   255.255.252.0

4. A Class A network address with a 21-bit host identifier.

   255.224.0.0

5. A Class B network with a 9-bit host identifier.

   255.255.254.0

Chapter Review

Page 207

1. Match the protocols in the left column with the appropriate descriptions in the right column.

a.	DHCP	1.	Transmits e-mail messages between servers
b.	ARP	2.	Routes datagrams to their final destination
c.	IP	3.	Provides connection-oriented service at the transport layer
d.	POP3	4.	Resolves host names into IP addresses
e.	SNMP	5.	Connects two systems at the link layer
f.	ICMP	6.	Converts IP addresses into hardware addresses
g.	TCP	7.	Automatically configures TCP/IP clients
h.	DNS	8.	Provides communications between e-mail clients and servers
i.	PPP	9.	Carries network management data to a central console
j.	SMTP	10.	Carries error messages from routers to end systems

   a. 7

   b. 6

   c. 2

   d. 8

   e. 9

   f. 10

   g. 3

   h. 4

   i. 5

   j. 1

2. Which of the following fields is blank in an ARP Request message?

   a. Sender Hardware Address

   b. Sender Protocol Address

   c. Target Hardware Address

   d. Target Protocol Address

   c

3. Which ICMP message type is the basis for the Traceroute utility?

   a. Echo Request

   b. Time To Live Exceeded In Transit

   c. Host Unreachable

   d. Fragment Reassembly Time Exceeded

   b

4. Why are ARP Request messages transmitted as broadcasts?

   They are transmitted as broadcasts because the system doesn't have the destination hardware address needed to send it as a unicast.

5. Which ICMP message type performs a rudimentary form of flow control?

   a. Source Quench

   b. Router Solicitation

   c. Redirect

   d. Echo Request

   a

6. Which of the following fields in an ARP Reply message contains a value supplied by the system transmitting the message?

   a. Sender Hardware Address

   b. Sender Protocol Address

   c. Target Hardware Address

   d. Target Protocol Address

   a

7. How does ARP minimize the number of broadcasts it generates?

   It does so by caching resolved hardware addresses.

8. Which application layer protocol uses two port numbers at the server?

   a. SMTP

   b. HTTP

   c. DHCP

   d. FTP

   d

9. Which IP address class provides for the largest number of hosts?

    a. Class A

    b. Class B

    c. Class C

    d. All three classes provide the same number of hosts.

    a

10. What kind of IP address must a system have to be visible from the Internet?

    a. Subnetted

    b. Registered

    c. Class A

    d. Binary

    b

Chapter 9: TCP/IP Routing

Lesson 1: Routing Principles

Exercise 9.1: Routing Tables

Page 216

1. What type of routing is used by a packet in which the Destination IP Address and the data-link layer Destination Address values refer to different computers?

   a. The default gateway

   b. A direct route

   c. The default route

   d. An indirect route

   d

2. Place the following steps of the routing table search process in the proper order.

   a. Default gateway search

   b. Host address search

   c. Network address search

   b, c, a

3. What is a TCP/IP system with interfaces to two different networks called?

   a. A gateway

   b. Multihomed

   c. A router

   d. All of the above

   d

Lesson 2: Building Routing Tables

Exercise 9.2: Static and Dynamic Routing

Page 226

Specify whether each of the following terms is associated with static routing, dynamic routing, both, or neither.

1. *Routed*

   Dynamic

2. Default gateway

   Both

3. Convergence

   Dynamic

4. Route.exe

   Static

5. Link-state routing

   Dynamic

6. Routing And Remote Access

   Both

7. Distance vector routing

   Dynamic

8. ROUTE ADD

   Static

9. Autonomous system

   Dynamic

10. Metric

    Dynamic

Chapter Review

Page 228

1. Which of the following is not a dynamic routing protocol?

   a. OSPF

   b. RIP

   c. ICMP

   f. EGP

   c

2. What is the name for the use of metrics based on the number of hops between a source and a destination?

   a. Distance vector routing

   b. Loose source routing

   c. Link-state routing

   d. Open shortest path first routing

   a

3. What is the primary difference between OSPF and RIP?

   OSPF uses link-state routing, while RIP uses distance vector routing.

4. Which of the following fields is not included in a RIP version 1 route?

   a. Metric

   b. Subnet Mask

   c. IP Address

   d. Address Family Identifier

   b

5. What is the primary criticism leveled at RIP?

   It generates excessive amounts of broadcast traffic that consumes network bandwidth.

6. In a Windows routing table, what column contains the address of the router that should be used to reach a particular network or host?

   a. Network Destination

   b. Netmask

   c. Gateway

   d. Interface

   c

7. What is the name of the process of updating routing tables to reflect changes in the network?

   a. Divergence

   b. Link-state routing

   c. Minimal routing

   d. Convergence

   d

8. What does a router do when it fails to find a routing table entry for a particular network or host?

   It uses the default gateway entry.

9. On a Windows system, what command do you use to display the contents of the routing table?

   ROUTE PRINT

10. The Next Hop IP Address in a RIP version 2 route ends up in which column of a Windows routing table?

    a. Network Destination

    b. Netmask

    c. Gateway

    d. Interface

    c

11. In a Windows routing table, what is the Network Destination value for the default gateway entry?

    a. 0.0.0.0

    b. The address of the network to which the router is connected

    c. 255.255.255.255

    d. The address of the router's network interface

    a

Chapter 10: TCP/IP Applications

Lesson 1: TCP/IP Services

Exercise 10.1: DHCP Message Types

Page 241

1. Place the following DHCP message types in the order in which a successful IP address assignment procedure uses them.

   a. DHCPACK

   b. DHCPOFFER

   c. DHCPREQUEST

   d. DHCPDISCOVER

   d, b, c, a

2. Place the following DHCP message types in the proper order for an unsuccessful attempt to renew an IP address lease.

   a. DHCPDISCOVER

   b. DHCPREQUEST (broadcast)

   c. DHCPREQUEST (unicast)

   d. DHCPNAK

   c, b, d, a

Lesson 2: TCP/IP Utilities

Exercise 10.2: TCP/IP Utilities

Page 257

Match the utilities in the left column with the functions in the right column.

1.	FTP	a.	Provides remote control access to a UNIX system
2.	Ipconfig.exe	b.	Displays TCP/IP configuration on a Windows 98 system
3.	Tracert.exe	c.	Creates cache entries containing IP and hardware addresses
4.	Ping	d.	Configures the network interface on a UNIX system
5.	Telnet	e.	Tests communications between two computers
6.	Netstat	f.	Transfers files between two computers
7.	Winipcfg.exe	g.	Displays network traffic statistics
8.	Nbtstat.exe	h.	Lists the routers forwarding packets to a particular destination
9.	Arp.exe	i.	Releases and renews IP address assignments on Windows 2000
10.	*Ifconfig*	j.	Displays NetBIOS connection information

1. **f**
2. **i**
3. **h**
4. **e**
5. **a**
6. **g**
7. **b**
8. **j**
9. **c**
10. **d**

Chapter Review

Page 259

1. Which TCP/IP utility should you use to most easily identify which router on your internetwork is malfunctioning?

   a. Ipconfig.exe

   b. Ping

   c. Traceroute

   d. Netstat

   c

2. What does the first word in a full DNS name identify?

   a. The top-level domain

   b. The second-level domain

   c. The DNS server

   d. The host

   d

3. What happens to a DHCP client when its attempts to renew its IP address lease fail and the lease expires?

   TCP/IP communication stops and the computer begins the process of negotiating a new lease.

4. Which of the following message types is not used during the DHCP lease assignment process?

   a. DHCPDISCOVER

   b. DHCPRELEASE

   c. DHCPOFFER

   d. DHCPREQUEST

   b

5. What is the DNS resource record type that contains the basic name-to-address mapping used for name resolution?

   a. Address

   b. Pointer

   c. Canonical Name

   d. Start of Authority

   a

6. What is the name of the DNS domain that contains address-to-name mappings?

   in-addr.arpa

7. Which of the following protocols does the Ping program never use to carry its messages?

   a. Ethernet

   b. ICMP

   c. IP

   d. UDP

   d

8. Name one method other than WINS that computers running Windows can use to resolve NetBIOS names into IP addresses.

   Either by using broadcasts or an LMHOSTS file

9. What is the name of the time during the lease renewal process when a DHCP client begins broadcasting DHCPREQUEST messages?

   a. Lease identification cookie

   b. Rebinding time value

   c. Renewal time value

   d. Init value

   b

10. What is the function of a WINS server?

    a. To convert IP addresses into hardware addresses

    b. To convert host names into IP addresses

    c. To convert IP addresses into host names

    d. To convert NetBIOS names into IP addresses

    d

Chapter 11: TCP/IP Configuration

Lesson 1: Installing the TCP/IP Protocols

Exercise 11.1: Microsoft TCP/IP Client Components

Page 266

Specify whether each of the following is installed as part of the Microsoft TCP/IP client.

1. The DHCP client

   Yes

2. Route.exe

   Yes

3. The WINS server

   No

4. The ICMP protocol

   Yes

5. The DNS resolver

   Yes

6. The SNMP Protocol

   No

7. The DNS server

   No

8. The WINS client

   Yes

9. Tracert.exe

   Yes

10. The Telnet server

    No

Lesson 2: Configuring TCP/IP

Exercise 11.2: TCP/IP Configuration Requirements

Page 277

For each of the network scenarios 1 through 5 listed below, specify which of the following TCP/IP parameters (a, b, c, d, and/or e) you must configure to provide a computer running Windows 2000 with full communications capabilities.

   a. IP address

   b. Subnet mask

   c. Default Gateway

   d. DNS server address

   e. WINS server address

1. A private internetwork using Windows NT domains

   a, b, c, e

2. A single peer-to-peer LAN

   a, b

3. A corporate internetwork using Active Directory service

   a, b, c, d

4. A peer-to-peer LAN using a shared Internet connection

   a, b, d

5. A Windows NT internetwork with a router connected to the Internet

   a, b, c, d, e

Chapter Review

Page 279

1. Which of the following IP security policies does not request the use of IPSec?

    a. Client

    b. Server

    c. Secure Server

    d. All of the above

    a

2. Which of the following services is not used on a Windows 2000 Active Directory network?

    a. DHCP

    b. WINS

    c. DNS

    d. IPSec

    b

3. What is the function of a DNS suffix?

    Its function is to complete unqualified DNS names, so that a DNS server can resolve them.

4. Which utility can you use to specify a default gateway address?

    a. Tracert.exe

    b. Arp.exe

    c. Ipconfig.exe

    d. Route.exe

    d

5. Which of the Windows 2000 Control Panel selections do you use to install the Microsoft TCP/IP client?

    Network And Dial-up Connections

6. Which of the following is a valid reason for assigning more than one IP address to a single network interface adapter?

   a. To balance the network traffic load between the addresses

   b. To support multiple subnets on one network

   c. To provide fault tolerance

   d. To support both TCP and UDP traffic

   b

7. How many default gateway addresses does a computer need to function on a LAN?

   a. 0

   b. 1

   c. 2

   d. 3

   a

8. At which of the following layers does the TCP/IP filtering option operate?

   a. Physical and data-link

   b. Application and session

   c. Data-link and network

   d. Network and transport

   d

9. How does Windows 2000 supply a subnet mask for the IP address you specify?

   a. By performing a reverse DNS name resolution on the address

   b. By checking the values of the first three address bits

   c. By checking the HOSTS file

   d. By querying the directory service

   b

10. What is the function of an LMHOSTS file?

   Its function is to resolve NetBIOS names into IP addresses.

Chapter 12: Remote Network Access

Lesson 1: Using Remote Connections

Exercise 12.1: Remote Connection Technologies

Page 293

Specify which of the remote connection technologies (PSTN, ISDN, DSL, and/or CATV) discussed in this lesson are associated with each of the following concepts.

1. Asymmetrical transfer rates

   DSL, CATV

2. Uses standard telephone lines

   PSTN, ISDN, DSL

3. Slowest of the connection types discussed

   PSTN

4. Uses an NT1

   ISDN

5. Also called POTS

   PSTN

6. Uses an ATU-R

   DSL

7. Uses analog signals

   PSTN

8. Shares bandwidth with other users

   CATV

9. Uses dial-up connections

   PSTN, ISDN

10. Requires the nearest central office to be relatively close by

    ISDN, DSL

Chapter Review

Page 295

1. To communicate with its host computer, a modem does not always need which of the following system resources?

   a. A serial port

   b. An IRQ

   c. A COM port

   d. An I/O port address

   a

2. Why are "cable modems" and "DSL modems" not really modems?

   They are not really modems because they do not convert signals between analog and digital formats.

3. Which of the DSL types is most commonly used to provide Internet access to end users?

   a. HDSL

   b. ADSL

   c. SDSL

   d. VDSL

   b

4. An ISDN installation in the United States provides you with a connection using which interface?

   a. The Basic Rate Interface

   b. The S/T interface

   c. The U interface

   d. The Primary Rate Interface

   c

5. Which of the following protocols can be transmitted through a PPTP tunnel?

   a. IP only

   b. IP and NetBEUI

   c. IP and IPX

   d. IP, IPX, and NetBEUI

   d

6. Which of the following is not the name of an ISDN service?

   a. BRI

   b. 2B+D

   c. PRI

   d. IDSL

   d

7. What three new hardware components are required to install CATV Internet access on the computer of an existing cable TV customer?

   The required components are a cable splitter, a cable modem, and a network interface card.

8. Name one of the data-link layer protocols that computers can use with a PSTN connection.

   SLIP or PPP

9. Which of the following UART chips enables a modem to achieve the best possible performance?

   a. 8250

   b. 16450

   c. 16550

   d. 16650

   c

10. Which device enables you to use a computer with an ISDN connection?

    a. A terminal adapter

    b. An NT1

    c. Terminal equipment

    d. A U interface

    a

Chapter 13: Network Security

Lesson 1: Password Protection

Exercise 13.1: Password Policies

Page 305

For each of the characteristics in the left column, specify which of the policies in the right column best applies to it.

1. Specifies the number of logon attempts a user is permitted
2. Requires passwords to contain at least six characters
3. Prevents users from reusing the same passwords
4. Prevents users from defeating the Enforce Password History policy
5. Enables passwords to be recovered

a. Enforce Password History
b. Maximum Password Age
c. Minimum Password Age
d. Minimum Password Length
e. Passwords Must Meet Complexity Requirements
f. Store Password Using Reversible Encryption
g. Account Lockout Threshold
h. Account Lockout Duration
i. Reset Account Lockout Counter After

1. g

2. e

3. a

4. c

5. f

Lesson 2: Security Models

Exercise 13.2: Security Levels

Page 309

Specify whether each of the following statements applies to user-level security, share-level security, both, or neither.

1. Requires a directory service

   Neither

2. Uses the same password for all users

   Share-level

3. Provides variable degrees of access to shared network resources

   Both

4. Stores passwords on individual computers

   Both

5. Requires separate accounts

   User-level

Chapter Review

Page 316

1. Where does a peer-to-peer network that uses user-level security store its security information?

   a. On a domain controller

   b. In a directory service

   c. On each individual computer on the network

   d. On a central server

   c

2. Service-dependent packet filtering bases its decision to allow or deny access to a network based on what criterion?

   a. Port numbers

   b. IP addresses

   c. Hardware addresses

   d. Protocol identifiers

   a

3. Which type of firewall operates at the application layer?

   A proxy server

4. Which of the following is not a password characteristic enforced by the Passwords Must Meet Complexity Requirements policy?

   a. Passwords cannot contain all or part of the account's user name.

   b. Passwords must be changed weekly.

c. Passwords must be at least six characters long.

d. Passwords must include numerals or symbols, or both.

b

5. What is the maximum length of an Active Directory password?

a. 8 characters

b. 14 characters

c. 24 characters

d. 104 characters

d

6. NAT operates at which layer of the OSI model?

a. The data-link layer

b. The network layer

c. The transport layer

d. The application layer

b

7. Why does share-level security provide less protection than user-level security?

It provides less protection because all users share the same passwords.

8. What does setting the Account Lock Threshold policy prevent intruders from using to penetrate your network security?

a. Stolen passwords

b. Illegal software

c. The brute force method

d. Unencrypted passwords

c

9. What is the main drawback to using proxy servers?

You have to configure client applications to use the proxies.

10. Where is a firewall typically located?

a. At the boundary between your ISP's network and the Internet

b. On your private network

c. On the Internet

d. At the boundary between your private network and your ISP's network

d

Chapter 14: Planning the Network

Lesson 2: Providing Fault Tolerance

Exercise 14.1: Data Availability Technologies

Page 330

Which of the disk technologies (mirroring, duplexing, spanning, or striping) applies to each of the following statements?

1. Enables a server to survive a drive failure

   Mirroring, duplexing

2. Uses multiple hard drives to create a single logical hard drive

   Mirroring, duplexing, spanning, striping

3. Enables a server to survive a disk host adapter failure

   Duplexing

4. Stores a single file on multiple drives

   Mirroring, duplexing, striping

5. Causes an entire volume to be lost when one drive fails

   Spanning, striping

Chapter Review

Page 336

1. Name three physical characteristics you should evaluate during your inspection of the network installation site.

   An adminstrator should evaluate distance between components, environmental conditions, and sources of interference.

2. Name one method you can use to connect a network that uses private, unregistered IP addresses to the Internet.

   One possible method is Network Address Translation (NAT); another is a proxy server.

3. List five environmental factors that you should check while inspecting a network site.

   You should check temperature, humidity, overnight climate control, dust, and electrical power.

4. Which is the most practical network medium to use when connecting computers that are all fewer than 100 meters apart, but located in two buildings?

   a. Unshielded twisted pair cable

   b. Shielded twisted pair cable

   c. Fiber optic cable

   d. Wireless

   c

5. Which of the following storage services is not provided by RAID?

   a. Data striping

   b. Tape backup

   c. Disk mirroring

   d. Error correction

   b

6. Which service do you use to assign IP addresses to your network workstations?

   a. DHCP

   b. DNS

   c. WINS

   d. NAT

   a

7. What is the primary reason for developing standardized workstation configurations?

   A standardized configuration helps to simplify the process of supporting and troubleshooting the workstations later.

8. What services does a cluster of servers provide that Novell's NetWare SFT III does not?

   A cluster of servers provides load balancing, distributed processing, and support for more than two systems.

9. Name two applications that can cause a network to require larger than normal amounts of bandwidth.

   Real-time data feeds and full motion video

10. What additional hardware can you install to create redundant paths through the network?

   a. NICs

   b. Hubs

   c. Servers

   d. Routers

   d

Chapter 15: Installing a Network

Lesson 1: Pulling Cable

Exercise 15.1: Internal and External Cabling

Page 355

For each of the following network scenarios, state whether you would perform an internal or external cable installation, and give a reason why.

1. A 10-node UTP network installed in a temporary office space by a seasonal business

   An external installation should be performed because the cables can easily be removed when the network is disassembled, and reused when the network is later reinstalled.

2. A 100-node corporate UTP network being installed in a newly constructed office building

   An internal installation should be performed. The new construction simplifies the process of installing the data cables along with the telephone cables. The installation will gain the benefits of appearance and cable integrity at no additional cost.

3. A 50-node Thick Ethernet network being moved to a new location

   An external installation should be performed because the heaviness and inflexibility of the RG8 coaxial cable make internal installations difficult.

Lesson 2: Making Connections

Exercise 15.2: Cable Installation Tools

Page 367

Match the tools in the left column with the proper functions in the right column.

1. Telepole	a. Used to attach male RJ45 connectors to UTP cables
2. Punchdown block tool	b. Pulls cables up through walls
3. Fish tape	c. Used to attach UTP cables to jacks
4. Raceway	d. Used to pull cable through drop ceilings
5. Crimper	e. Secures and protects external cable runs

   1. d

   2. c

   3. b

   4. e

   5. a

Chapter Review

Page 369

1. Which of the following components is not required for an internal cable installation?

   a. A raceway

   b. A wall plate

   c. A patch panel

   d. A punchdown block tool

   a

2. What is the primary function of the twists in a twisted pair cable?

   a. They bundle the positive and negative wires together.

   b. They prevent the cables from catching fire.

   c. They protect the signals against crosstalk.

   d. They separate the wire pairs.

   c

3. In a crossover cable, the TD- contact at one end is connected to which contact at the other end?

   a. TD+

   b. TD-

   c. RD+

   d. RD-

   d

4. Which of the following is not a function of the punchdown block tool?

   a. To cut off the wire ends

   b. To strip the sheath off the cable

   c. To strip the insulation off the wires

   d. To push the wires down between the contacts

   b

5. What components of an internal cable network do patch cables connect?

   a. Hubs to computers

   b. Computers to patch panels

   c. Wall plates to patch panels

   d. Patch panels to hubs

   d

6. What is the name of the signal that a NIC exchanges with a hub?

   a. Link pulse

   b. Test wave

   c. Crossover circuit

   d. Punchdown block

   a

7. Why should all your cable runs use the same wiring standard?

   a. Because Ethernet can only transmit signals over wires of a certain color

   b. Because the wires in a UTP cable are different gauges and carry signals differently

   c. To ensure that all of the connections are wired straight through

   d. To prevent crosstalk

   c

8. Which tool do you use to make a patch cable?

   a. A pair of pliers

   b. A punchdown block tool

   c. A fish tape

   d. A crimper

   d

9. Why has Thick Ethernet cable rarely been installed internally?

   It is rarely installed internally because the cable itself is too heavy and inflexible.

10. What is the style of most jacks used today?

    a. 110

    b. 568A

    c. 568B

    d. RG58

    a

Chapter 16: Network Maintenance

Lesson 1: Backups

Exercise 16.1: Incremental and Differential Backups

Page 386

1. If you back up your network by performing a full backup every Wednesday at 6:00 P.M. and differential backups in the evening of the other six days of the week, how many jobs would be needed to completely restore a computer with a hard drive that failed on a Tuesday at noon?

   Two

2. If you back up your network by performing a full backup every Wednesday at 6:00 P.M., how many jobs would be needed if you performed incremental backups in the evening of the other six days of the week?

   Six

3. For a complete restore of a computer that failed at noon on Tuesday, how many jobs would be needed if you performed full backups at 6:00 A.M. every Wednesday and Saturday and incremental backups at 6:00 A.M. every other day?

   Four

Lesson 2: Anti-Virus Policies

Exercise 16.2: Virus Types

Page 391

Match the virus types in the left column with the characteristics in the right column.

1.	Executable file viruses	a.	Modify a file's directory entry size
2.	Trojans	b.	Replicate themselves, but do not infect other files
3.	Stealth viruses	c.	Load into memory when the computer starts
4.	Boot sector viruses	d.	Infect document files
5.	Macro viruses	e.	Periodically change their signatures
6.	Worms	f.	Do not replicate or infect other files
7.	Polymorphic viruses	g.	Load into memory when you run a specific program

   1. g

   2. f

   3. a

   4. c

   5. d

   6. b

   7. e

Chapter Review

Page 397

1. Which of the following types of backup jobs does not reset the Archive bits of the files it backs up?

   a. Full

   b. Incremental

   c. Differential

   d. Supplemental

   c

2. Which of the following is the criterion most commonly used to filter files for backup jobs?

   a. File name

   b. File extension

   c. File attributes

   d. File size

   c

3. Why is a worm not considered to be a true virus?

   A worm is not a true virus because it is a separate program that does not infect other files.

4. Name three reasons why a software upgrade can be an expensive proposition.

   Possible reasons are the cost of the upgrade itself, the cost of upgrading the computer hardware, the cost of paying software installers, and the cost of retraining users.

5. How does an autochanger increase the overall storage capacity of a backup solution?

   It increases capacity by automatically inserting and removing media from a drive.

6. How does a stealth virus disguise its presence?

   a. By masquerading as an innocuous file

   b. By changing the size of the infected file's directory entry

   c. By encrypting its signature

   d. By infecting the disk's master boot record

   b

7. What are the three elements in the Grandfather-Father-Son media rotation system?

   a. Hard disk drives, CD-ROM drives, and magnetic tape drives

   b. Incremental, differential, and full backup jobs

   c. Monthly, weekly, and daily backup jobs

   d. QIC, DAT, and DLT tape drives

   c

8. Which of the following software releases is a fix designed to address one specific issue?

   a. A patch

   b. An update

   c. An upgrade

   d. A Service Pack

   a

9. How does a macro virus differ from the other major types of viruses?

   a. It doesn't replicate.

   b. It infects data files.

   c. It doesn't infect other files.

   d. It hides itself using encryption.

   b

10. What drive interface is most commonly used by network backup devices?

    a. IDE

    b. SCSI

    c. USB

    d. Parallel port

    b

Chapter 17: Network Troubleshooting Procedures

Lesson 1: Identifying Network Components

Exercise 17.1: Ports and Connectors

Page 416   Match the ports listed in the left column with the connector descriptions in the right column.

1. VGA video port	a. Rectangular four-conductor connector
2. Serial port	b. Combined power and data connector
3. SCA SCSI port	c. Mini-DIN connector
4. 10BaseT Ethernet port	d. Three-row, 15-pin D-shell connector
5. USB port	e. Female DB-25 connector
6. AUI port	f. 50-pin Centronics connector
7. Keyboard/mouse port	g. Thick Ethernet connector
8. Parallel port	h. Male DB-9 connector
9. 5 MBps SCSI port	i. BNC connector
10. Thin Ethernet port	j. RJ45 connector

   1. d

   2. h

   3. b

   4. j

   5. a

   6. g

   7. c

   8. e

   9. f

   10. i

Lesson 2: Troubleshooting a Network

Exercise 17.2: Network Troubleshooting

Page 422

Place the following steps of the problem isolation process in the proper logical order.

1. Reproduce the problem using a different computer.

2. Reproduce the problem yourself.

3. Have the user reproduce the problem.

4. Reproduce the problem using a different user account.

3, 2, 4, 1

Chapter Review

Page 424

1. What is the device called that enables you to connect a Type 1 Token Ring NIC to a UTP network?

   A Token Ring media filter

2. Which of the following ports never uses a DB-25 connector?

   a. Parallel ports

   b. Serial ports

   c. Video ports

   d. SCSI ports

   c

3. Which type of SCSI connector supplies power as well as data signals?

   a. 50-pin Centronics

   b. SCA

   c. 50-pin High-Density

   d. 68-pin High-Density

   b

4. Which of the following problems would you assign the highest priority for your network support team? Explain why.

   a. The printer in the Order Entry department isn't working.

   b. The corporate e-mail server is down.

   c. A hub is malfunctioning in the Sales department.

   d. The president of the company's workstation is locked up.

   The highest priority should be assigned to b, because this is the problem that affects a vital function for the most users. However, d gets honorable mention for enabling the technician to remain employed.

5. Which type of connector has been used both for keyboards and for power connections?

a. PS/2

b. Five-pin DIN

c. USB

d. Six-pin mini-DIN

b

6. In a two-tiered network support system, what do the tiers refer to?

a. File servers storing network documentation

b. Priorities for trouble tickets

c. Problem call databases

d. Technicians of different skill levels

d

7. Which of the following devices does not typically contain a row of at least four ports?

a. A router

b. A patch panel

c. A switch

d. A hub

a

8. What is the name of the device that provides the interface between a router and a leased telephone line?

A Channel Service Unit/Data Service Unit (CSU/DSU)

9. Which type of Ethernet connector has 15 pins?

a. RJ45

b. BNC

c. AUI

d. VGA

c

10. How does a UPS protect a network?

It protects a network by providing temporary standby power in the event that building power fails.

Chapter 18:   Network Troubleshooting Tools

Lesson 1: Documentation and Resources

Exercise 18.1: Technical Resources

Page 438

Match the resources in the left column with the appropriate descriptions in the right column.

1.	PDF	a.	ASCII text file containing recent product information
2.	TechNet	b.	Internet conference containing messages on a given subject
3.	NNTP	c.	Document format used by Adobe Acrobat
4.	Readme.1st	d.	A Microsoft CD-ROM subscription service
5.	Newsgroup	e.	Protocol used by Usenet news clients and servers

1. c

2. d

3. e

4. a

5. b

Lesson 2: Logs and Indicators

Exercise 18.2: Network Indicators

Page 459

Define each of the following terms in relation to the concepts discussed in this lesson.

1. SNMP

   Simple Network Management Protocol, a query language and protocol used to carry information between network management agents and a central console

2. NLP

   Normal Link Pulse, a signal generated by 10BaseT Ethernet hubs and network interface adapters that lights LEDs on both devices to signify that they have been wired together properly

3. Trap

   A message generated by an SNMP agent, informing the network management console of a condition requiring immediate attention

4. Link code word

An additional 16-bit data packet included in the FLP signal used by Fast Ethernet devices to negotiate the speed at which they will operate

5. MIB

Management Information Base, the place where an SNMP agent stores information about the device it's monitoring pending its transmission to the network management console

Lesson 3: Network Testing and Monitoring Tools

Exercise 18.3: Network Testing Equipment

Page 465

For each of the devices listed in the left column, specify which of the faults in the right column it is capable of detecting.

1.	Crossover cable	a.	Cable short
2.	RJ45 loopback connector	b.	Split pair
3.	Tone generator and locator	c.	Malfunctioning hub
4.	Wire map tester	d.	Excessive crosstalk
5.	Multifunction cable tester	e.	Transposed wires
		f.	Faulty network interface adapter
		g.	Untwisted cables
		h.	Broken cable

1. c, h

2. f

3. a, e, h

4. a, e, h

5. a, b, d, e, g, h

Chapter Review

Page 467

1. How does the FLP signal used by Fast Ethernet equipment differ from the NLP signal used by standard Ethernet?

   FLP includes a 16-bit link code word in the signal that the devices use to negotiate their fastest common transmission speed.

2. A fox and hound tester is another term for what device?

   a. A crossover cable

   b. A tone generator and locator

   c. A wire map tester

   d. A multifunction cable tester

   b

3. Which of the following products do you need to open a .pdf file?

   a. A news reader

   b. NNTP

   c. Adobe Acrobat Reader

   d. A multifunction cable tester

   c

4. How does the performance of a network interface adapter differ while in promiscuous mode?

   The network interface adapter reads and processes all packets transmitted over the network, not just those addressed to it.

5. What protocol do Usenet news readers and news servers use to communicate?

   a. HTTP

   b. FTP

   c. SNMP

   d. NNTP

   d

6. Which of the following cabling faults can a wire map tester not detect?

   a. Open pairs

   b. Split pairs

   c. Transposed pairs

   d. Shorts

   b

7. Arrange the following Ethernet technologies in the order of priority established by the FLP signal.

   a. 100BaseT4

   b. 10BaseT Full Duplex

   c. 100BaseTX

   d. 10BaseT

   e. 100BaseTX Full Duplex

   e, a, c, b, d

8. What are the individual elements measured by the Windows 2000 Performance console called?

   a. Counters

   b. Statistics

   c. Alerts

   d. Traps

   a

9. Which of the following types of cable tester is most expensive?

   a. Fox and hound

   b. Wire map

   c. Multifunction

   d. Loopback

   c

10. Where do agents used by network management products store their information?

    a. SNMP

    b. MIB

    c. NNTP

    d. Console

    b

Chapter 19: Network Troubleshooting Scenarios

Lesson 1: "I Can't Access a Web Site"

Exercise 19.1: Network Hardware Problems

Page 494

On an internetwork consisting of several user segments connected by a backbone, with an Internet router connected directly to the backbone, specify whether the following network conditions would normally cause Internet access problems for one user only, for all of the users connected to one hub, for all of the users on one LAN, or for the entire internetwork.

1. Both ends of a cable connecting two hubs are plugged into an uplink port.

   All of the users on one hub

2. The router connecting the network to the ISP is down.

   The entire internetwork

3. The cable connecting a user's computer to the hub is cut.

   One user only

4. The ISP's connection to the Internet fails.

   The entire internetwork

5. The router connecting a user LAN to the backbone malfunctions.

   All of the users on one LAN

Chapter Review

Page 496

1. Without a DNS server, a user can still access the Internet using which of the following techniques?

   a. By using links saved as Favorites instead of typing URLs

   b. By using NetBIOS names instead of DNS names

   c. By using hardware addresses instead of DNS names

   d. By using IP addresses instead of DNS names

   d

2. A user is unable to access the shared server drive that he uses every day, where his working files are stored. Which of the following questions would you ask the user first? State your reason why.

   a. "Are you able to access any other network resources?"

   b. "Did you have any problems logging on to the network?"

   c. "Can you access the Internet?"

   d. "Is your network cable connected to the computer?"

   b. The logon process is the user's first interaction with the network after the computer starts. If the logon completed successfully, it is clear that the user's hardware is functioning properly and that the problem lies elsewhere.

3. Which of the following is not a possible cause of Internet access failure?

   a. Missing WINS server address

   b. DNS server failure

   c. ISP connection failure

   d. Mistyped URLs

   a

4. Which of the following network/transport layer problems can be caused by another computer on the network?

   a. Missing DNS server address

   b. Incorrect subnet mask

   c. Duplicate IP address

   d. Incorrect default gateway address

   c

5. A computer running the Windows operating system without a WINS server address cannot access which of the following resources?

   a. Internet Web sites

   b. Computers running the Windows operating system that are connected to the same hub

   c. Computers not running the Windows operating system that are connected to the same LAN

   d. Computers running the Windows operating system that are connected to other LANs

   d

6. Which of the following is the best solution for a case in which a user has changed the network interface adapter configuration and can no longer access the network?

   a. Replace the adapter with a new one.

   b. Delete the adapter driver and let Plug and Play reinstall it.

   c. Modify the adapter's configuration parameters using the utility supplied by the manufacturer.

   d. Modify the adapter driver's configuration parameters using the operating system interface.

   b

7. Which of the following is the easiest way to test a patch cable for a fault?

   a. Replace it with one that you know is working properly.

   b. Connect it to a multifunction cable tester.

   c. Plug the computer end of the cable into the wall plate and the wall plate end into the computer.

   d. Connect it to a computer that you know is functioning properly.

   a

8. Which of the following tools can pinpoint the exact location of a cable break?

   a. A tone generator and locator

   b. A protocol analyzer

   c. A multifunction cable tester

   d. A wire map tester

   c

9. When a computer lacks a correct default gateway address, how far do packets destined for other networks travel?

   a. As far as the Internet access router

   b. As far as the backbone

   c. As far as the hub

   d. As far as the local network

   d

10. Which of the following network problems would generally affect services other than Internet access on a Windows-based network?

    a. ISP connection failure

    b. Backbone failure

    c. DNS failure

    d. T1 failure

    b

Glossary

2B + D Alternative name for the Basic Rate Interface (BRI) service provided by the Integrated Services Digital Network (ISDN).

5-4-3 rule An Ethernet cabling guideline stating that an Ethernet LAN can consist of up to five cable segments, connected by four repeaters, with up to three of those cable segments being mixing segments.

10Base2 Shorthand name for the Ethernet physical layer specification that is also known as Thin Ethernet, thinnet, or cheapernet, which uses RG58 coaxial cable in a bus topology. The "10" refers to the network's speed of 10 Mbps, the "base" refers to the network's baseband transmissions, and the "2" refers to the network's maximum segment length of approximately 200 meters (actually 185 meters).

10Base5 Shorthand name for the Ethernet physical layer specification that is also known as Thick Ethernet or thicknet, which uses RG8 coaxial cable in a bus topology. The "10" refers to the network's speed of 10 Mbps, the "base" refers to the network's baseband transmissions, and the "5" refers to the network's maximum segment length of 500 meters.

10BaseF Collective term for the three 10 Mbps Ethernet physical layer specifications that use fiber optic cable, as defined in IEEE 802.3, including 10BaseFB, 10BaseFL, and 10BaseFP. The use of fiber optic cable for Ethernet networks was relatively rare until the advent of Fast Ethernet because the 10 Mbps speed limitation of the 10BaseF networks made them impractical.

10BaseFB Shorthand name for one of three 10 Mbps Ethernet physical layer standards defined in the IEEE 802.3 document that use 62.5/125 multimode fiber optic cable in a star topology. 10BaseFB has a maximum segment length of 2,000 meters and was intended for use as a backbone solution to connect hubs over long distances using synchronous signaling. Like the other 10BaseF specifications, it was rarely used.

10BaseFL Shorthand name for one of three 10 Mbps Ethernet physical layer standards defined in the IEEE 802.3 document that use 62.5/125 multimode fiber optic cable in a star topology. 10BaseFL has a maximum segment length of 2,000 meters and can connect two repeaters, two computers, or a computer to a repeater. Like the other 10BaseF specifications, it was rarely used.

10BaseFP Shorthand name for one of three 10 Mbps Ethernet physical layer standards defined in the IEEE 802.3 document that use 62.5/125 multimode fiber optic cable in a star topology. 10BaseFP has a maximum segment length of 500 meters and uses a passive star coupler to connect up to 33 computers. It was designed to be the desktop fiber optic solution of the 10BaseF specifications and, like the others, was rarely used.

10BaseT Shorthand name for an Ethernet physical layer specification that uses unshielded twisted pair (UTP) cables in a star topology. The "10" refers to the network's speed of 10 Mbps, the "base" refers to the network's baseband transmissions, and the "T" refers to the use of twisted pair cable. The maximum cable segment length for a 10BaseT network is 100 meters.

100BaseFX Shorthand name for a 100 Mbps Fast Ethernet physical layer specification defined in the IEEE 802.3u document that uses 62.5/125 multimode fiber optic cable in a star topology, with a maximum segment length of 412 meters and runs at 100 Mbps

100BaseT Collective term for the three 100 Mbps Ethernet physical layer specifications defined in the IEEE 802.3u document and commonly known as Fast Ethernet. The three physical layer options for Fast Ethernet are 100BaseTX, 100BaseT4, and 100BaseFX.

100BaseT4 Shorthand name for a 100 Mbps Fast Ethernet physical layer specification defined in the IEEE 802.3u document that uses Category 3 UTP cable in a star topology, with a maximum segment length of 100 meters. 100BaseT4 can achieve its high speed using a lesser grade of cable because it uses all four pairs of wires in the cable, while other Ethernet UTP specifications, such as 100BaseTX and 10BaseT, use only two pairs. Because nearly all of the UTP cable installed today is at least Category 5, 100BaseT4 is seldom used, but it remains a viable alternative for sites with older cable installations.

100BaseTX Shorthand name for a 100 Mbps Fast Ethernet physical layer specification defined in the IEEE 802.3u document that uses Category 5 or better UTP cable in a star topology, with a maximum segment length of 100 meters. 100BaseTX achieves its high speed using only two pairs of the wires in the cable because the specification insists on the use of high quality cable. 100BaseTX is the most popular of the Fast Ethernet specifications.

100BaseVG *See* 100VG-AnyLan.

100VG-AnyLan A data-link layer protocol that runs at 100 Mbps over Category 3 unshielded twisted pair (UTP) cable, using a media access control (MAC) mechanism called Demand Priority. Introduced at approximately the same time as Fast Ethernet, 100VG-AnyLAN never captured a significant market share.

1000BaseCX Shorthand name for a 1,000 Mbps Gigabit Ethernet physical layer specification defined in the IEEE 802.3z document, which runs over 150-ohm shielded copper cable with a maximum segment length of 25 meters.

1000BaseFX Shorthand name for a 1,000 Mbps Gigabit Ethernet physical layer specification defined in the IEEE 802.3z document, which runs over 62.5/125 multimode fiber optic cable with a maximum segment length of 412 meters.

1000BaseLH Shorthand name for a 1,000 Mbps Gigabit Ethernet physical layer specification defined in the IEEE 802.3z document, which runs over 9/125 singlemode fiber optic cable with a maximum segment length of 10,000 meters.

1000BaseLX Shorthand name for a 1,000 Mbps Gigabit Ethernet physical layer specification defined in the IEEE 802.3z document, which runs over either 9/125 singlemode fiber optic cable, with a maximum segment length of 5,000 meters, or 50/125 or 62.5/125 multimode fiber optic cable with a maximum segment length of 550 meters.

1000BaseSX Shorthand name for a 1,000 Mbps Gigabit Ethernet physical layer specification defined in the IEEE 802.3z document, which runs over 50/125 multimode fiber optic cable with a maximum segment length of 550 meters or 62.5/125 multimode fiber optic cable with a maximum segment length of 275 meters.

1000BaseT Shorthand name for a 1,000 Mbps Gigabit Ethernet network defined in the IEEE 802.3ab document, which uses Category 5 or 5E UTP cable in a star topology, with a maximum segment length of 100 meters.

1000BaseZX Shorthand name for a 1,000 Mbps Gigabit Ethernet physical layer specification defined in the IEEE 802.3z document, which runs over 9/125 singlemode fiber optic cable with a maximum segment length of 100,000 meters.

A

Active Directory The enterprise directory service included with the Windows 2000 Server, Advanced Server, and Datacenter Server operating systems. Active Directory is a hierarchical directory service that consists of objects that represent users, computers, groups, and other network resources. The objects are arranged in a tree display that consists of hierarchical layers ranging upward from organizational units, to domains, to trees, and to forests. Objects are composed of attributes that contain information about the resource the object represents. When users log on to the network, their user names and passwords are authenticated against the Active Directory database by a computer that has been designated as a domain controller. This one single logon can grant them access to resources anywhere on the network. *See also* directory service.

Address Resolution Protocol (ARP) A TCP/IP protocol used to resolve the IP addresses of computers on a LAN into the hardware (or MAC) addresses needed to transmit data-link layer frames to them. Before transmitting an IP datagram, TCP/IP clients broadcast an ARP request message containing the IP address of the destination computer to the local network. The computer using that IP address must then respond with an ARP reply message containing its hardware address. With the information in the reply message, the computer can encapsulate the IP datagram in the appropriate data-link layer frame and transmit it to the destination system.

ADSL *See* Asymmetrical Digital Subscriber Line.

ADSL Termination Unit-Remote (ATU-R) The hardware device located at the client side of an ADSL connection. Also called a DSL transceiver or (incorrectly) a "DSL modem." The ATU-R connects to the computer using either a universal serial bus (USB) port or a standard Ethernet network interface adapter. *See also* Asymmetrical Digital Subscriber Line (ADSL) *and* Digital Subscriber Line Access Multiplexer (DSLAM).

application layer The top layer of the Open Systems Interconnection (OSI) reference model, which provides the entrance point used by applications to access the networking protocol stack. Some of the protocols operating at the application layer include the Hypertext Transfer Protocol (HTTP), the Simple Mail Transport Protocol (SMTP), the Dynamic Host Configuration Protocol (DHCP), the File Transfer Protocol (FTP), and the Simple Network Management Protocol (SNMP).

Archive bit A one-bit flag included with all file systems that backup software programs use to determine whether or not a file has been modified. When a file is backed up, the backup software program typically resets (or strips away) its archive bit. The next time the file is modified, the archive bit is activated. The backup software can them run a job that backs up only the files with active archive its, which reduces the time and media needed to perform the backup.

ARP *See* Address Resolution Protocol.

Arp.exe A command-line utility provided by the Microsoft TCP/IP client included with the Windows operating systems, which enables you to display and manipulate the information stored in the cache created by the Address Resolution Protocol (ARP). By pre-loading the ARP cache, you can save time and network traffic by eliminating the ARP transaction that the TCP/IP client uses to resolve the IP address of each system it transmits to into a hardware address. *See also* Address Resolution Protocol (ARP).

Asymmetrical Digital Subscriber Line (ADSL) A point-to-point, digital WAN technology that uses standard telephone lines to provide consumers with high-speed Internet access, remote LAN access, and other services. The term asymmetric refers to the fact that the service provides a higher transmission rate for downstream than for upstream traffic. Downstream transmission rates can be up to 8.448 Mbps, while upstream rates range up to 640 Kbps. *See also* Digital Subscriber Line (DSL).

Attachment Unit Interface (AUI) Provides the connection between a computer and the RG8 coaxial cable used by Thick Ethernet networks. A Thick Ethernet network interface adapter has a 15-pin AUI port, which is used to connect an AUI cable that runs to the RG8 cable. The other end of the AUI cable is connected to a device called a *vampire tap*, which clamps onto the RG8 cable and has teeth that pierce its protective insulation to make an electrical connection with the conductor inside. The term *attachment unit interface* is used by the IEEE 802.3 standard; the DIX Ethernet standards refer to the same components as the *transceiver port* and the *transceiver cable*.

attenuation The progressive weakening of a signal as it travels over a cable or other medium. The longer the distance a signal travels, the weaker the signal gets, until it becomes unreadable by the receiving system. On a data network, attenuation is one of the prime factors that limits the length of network cable segments. Different types of cables have different rates of attenuation. As a rule, copper cables are more prone to attenuation than fiber optic cables, and thinner copper cables are more prone to attenuation than thicker ones.

ATU-R *See* ADSL Termination Unit-Remote.

AUI *See* Attachment Unit Interface.

authoritative server A Domain Name System (DNS) server that has been designated as the definitive source of information about the computers in a particular domain. When resolving a computer's DNS name into its IP address, DNS servers consult the authoritative server for the domain in which that computer is located. Whatever information the authoritative server provides about that domain is understood by all DNS servers to be correct. *See also* Domain Name System (DNS).

automatic allocation An operational mode of Dynamic Host Configuration Protocol (DHCP) servers in which the server permanently assigns an IP address and other TCP/IP configuration settings to a client from a pool of addresses. *Contrast with* dynamic allocation, which assigns addresses in the same way, but reclaims them when a lease of a given duration expires, and manual allocation, which permanently assigns specific addresses to clients. *See also* Dynamic Host Configuration Protocol (DHCP).

autochanger A hardware device consisting of one or more backup drives, a media array, and a robotic mechanism that inserts media into and removes it from the drives. Used to perform automated backups of large amounts of data.

B

B channel A 64-Kbps digital communications channel that is one of the fundamental units of service provided by the Integrated Services Digital Network (ISDN). B channels carry the actual data generated by the user's applications. The Basic Rate Interface (BRI) ISDN service consists of two B channels plus one 16-Kbps D channel; the Primary Rate Interface (PRI) service consists of 23 B channels and one 64-Kbps D channel. *See also* Integrated Services Digital Network (ISDN).

backbone A network used to connect a series of other networks together, forming an internetwork. Typically, a backbone is a high-speed LAN used to route traffic from one horizontal LAN to another. Client workstations are typically not connected to the backbone, although servers sometimes are.

baseband network A network that uses a medium that can carry only one signal at a particular time. *Contrast with* broadband, which is a network that carries multiple signals at once, using a technique called multiplexing. Most LANs are baseband networks; your local cable television system is an example of a broadband network.

Basic Rate Interface (BRI) An Integrated Services Digital Network (ISDN) service that consists of two 64-Kbps B channels plus one 16-Kbps D channel, enabling users to combine the B channels for a single 128-Kbps data pipe, or utilize them separately. Also called 2B+D, BRI is the primary consumer ISDN service used for Internet access and remote networking. *See also* B channel, D channel, Primary Rate Interface (PRI), *and* Integrated Services Digital Network (ISDN).

bindery The server-based, flat file directory service used in Novell NetWare versions 3.2 and earlier. The bindery is a simple directory of user and group accounts used by NetWare to authenticate user access to server resources. Unlike more advanced directory services, which provide services for the entire enterprise, the NetWare bindery is specific to a single server. If a network has multiple NetWare servers, each server has its own separate bindery, and users must have bindery accounts on each server they want to access.

bmp A file format commonly used to store graphic images in bitmap form.

BNC Short for Bayonet-Neill-Concelman, a type of cable connector used on Thin Ethernet networks.

BOOTP *See* Bootstrap Protocol.

Bootstrap Protocol (BOOTP) A server application that can supply client computers with IP addresses, other TCP/IP configuration parameters, and executable boot files. As the progenitor to the Dynamic Host Configuration Protocol (DHCP), BOOTP provides the same basic functions, except that it does not allocate IP addresses from a pool and reclaim them after a specified length of time. Administrators must supply the IP address and other settings for each computer to be configured by the BOOTP server. *See also* Dynamic Host Configuration Protocol (DHCP) *and* Reverse Address Resolution Protocol (RARP).

BRI *See* Basic Rate Interface.

bridge A network connectivity device that operates at the data-link layer of the Open Systems Interconnection (OSI) reference model and filters network traffic based on packets' destination addresses. When you connect two network segments with a bridge, packets generated by the computers on one segment are only propagated to the other segment if they are addressed to a computer on that segment. The bridge learns which computers are connected to each segment by reading the source addresses in the packets it processes and storing the information in a table; this learning process is called transparent bridging. Other types of bridges can connect networks running different media or data-link layer protocols or connect two network segments at different locations using a wide area network (WAN) link.

broadband network A network that uses a medium that can carry multiple signals simultaneously, using a technique called multiplexing. The most common example of broadband communications is the typical cable television network, which transmits the signals corresponding to dozens of TV channels over one cable. *Contrast with* a baseband network, which can only carry one signal on its medium.

broadcast A message transmitted to all of the other computers on the local network. Data-link layer protocols have special addresses designated as broadcast addresses, which means that every computer that receives the message will read it into memory and process it. Local area networks (LANs) use broadcasts for a variety of tasks, such as to discover information about other computers on the network.

broadcast domain A collection of computers that will all receive a broadcast message transmitted by any one of the other computers. All of the computers on a LAN, for example, are in the same broadcast domain, as are the computers on two network segments connected by a bridge, because bridges always propagate broadcast transmissions. Two networks connected by a router, however, are in different broadcast domains, because routers do not propagate broadcasts. *Compare with* collision domain.

brouter Short for bridge/router, a data-link layer and network layer device that functions like a combination of a bridge and a router. Brouters can route certain types of packets (such as TCP/IP packets), but they simply propagate traffic like a bridge when faced with other types of packets that they don't recognize. *See also* bridge *and* router.

C

cable television (CATV) network A private metropolitan area network (MAN) constructed and owned by a cable television company for the purpose of delivering TV signals to customers in a given region. Because the network technology they use is compatible with data networking, many CATV companies are now also in the business of providing Internet access to consumers using the same network that delivers the television service. The downstream transmission rates for a CATV Internet connection far exceed those of standard dial-ups and most other consumer Internet solutions, and the cost is usually very competitive.

Carrier Sense Multiple Access with Collision Detection (CSMA/CD) The media access control (MAC) mechanism used by Ethernet networks to regulate access to the network. Before they can transmit data, CSMA/CD systems listen to the network to determine if it is in use. If the network is free, the system transmits its data. Sometimes, another computer transmits at precisely the same time,

however, causing a signal quality error or collision. Collisions are normal occurrences on Ethernet networks, and network interface adapters are capable of detecting them and compensating for them by discarding the collided packets and retransmitting them in a controlled manner.

cat3 The Category 3 grade of unshielded twisted pair (UTP) cable that was at one time the most common medium used for telephone and data networks. New installations now use Category 5 (cat5) cable, because it supports higher transmission speeds, although there are still some protocols that are designed specifically for use on older cat3 networks, such as 100BaseT4 and 100VG-AnyLAN.

cat5 The Category 5 grade of unshielded twisted pair (UTP) cable that is the current industry standard for telephone and data networking.

cat5e Also called Category 5e or Enhanced Category 5, a relatively new grade of unshielded twisted pair (UTP) cable designed for use on data networks running at very high speeds, such as Gigabit Ethernet.

category *n* Term used to specify a grade of unshielded twisted pair (UTP) cable, using standards developed by the Electronics Industry Association/Telecommunications Industry Association (EIA/TIA).

CATV *See* cable television network.

CCITT *See* Comité Consultatif International Téléphonique et Télégraphique.

CD-R A write-once/read-many (WORM) storage medium that can hold approximately 670 MB of data on a compact disk.

CD-ROM A read-only storage medium that can hold approximately 670 MB of data on a compact disk.

CD-RW A rewritable storage medium that can hold approximately 670 MB of data on a compact disk.

Cheapernet Slang term for a Thin Ethernet (10Base2) network, which at the time of its greatest popularity was significantly less expensive than its primary competitor, Thick Ethernet (10Base5).

circuit switching A type of network communications in which two communicating systems establish a connection that remains open throughout the life of the transaction. The telephone network is an example of a circuit-switched network. After placing a call, the telephone system establishes a path through the network connecting the two telephones, and all communications follow that path until it is broken by one of the callers disconnecting. *Contrast with* packet switching.

client A program designed to communicate with a server program on another computer, usually to request and receive information, and which provides the interface with which the user can view and manipulate the server data. A client can be a module in an operating system, such as the Client for Microsoft Networks in Windows, which enables the user to access resources on the network's other computers, or a separate application, such as a Web browser or e-mail reader.

client/server networking A computing model in which data processing tasks are distributed between clients, which request, display, and manipulate information, and servers, which supply and store information. By having each individual client be responsible for displaying and manipulating its own data, the server is relieved of a large part of the processing burden. The alternative is a mainframe or minicomputer system in which one computer performs all of the processing for all of the users, who work with terminals that do not have processors (dumb terminals).

cluster A group of two or more server computers connected together so that they function as a single unified resource, for purposes of fault tolerance, load balancing, and parallel processing. Clustering enables the server array to survive the failure of one or more computers and makes it possible to upgrade the system simply by adding additional computers to the cluster.

coaxial cable A type of cable used in various types of networking, which consists of two conductors, one wrapped around the other and separated by an insulating layer, all enclosed in a protective sheath. The data signals are transmitted over the inner conductor that forms the solid core of the cable. The outer conductor is made of a wire mesh, and functions as a ground. The two types of coaxial cable used in local area networking are called RG8 and RG58, also known as Thick Ethernet and Thin Ethernet, respectively.

collision In local area networking, a condition in which two computers transmit data at precisely the same time, and their signals both occupy the same cable, causing data loss. On some types of networks, such as Ethernet, collisions are a normal occurrence, while on Token Ring networks, they are an indication of a serious problem. Also called a signal quality error.

collision domain A group of computers in which any two that transmit at exactly the same time will cause a collision. All of the computers on a LAN are in the same collision domain, for example, while the computers on two network segments connected by a bridge or a router are in two different collision domains. This is because the processing performed by routers and bridges introduces a slight delay in the time between the generation of a packet on one segment and the propagation of the packet to the other segment.

Comité Consultatif International Téléphonique et Télégraphique (CCITT) An organization (in English, the International Telegraph and Telephone Consultative Committee) that, until 1992, developed and published international communications standards, such as those that govern modem signaling, compression, and error correction protocols. The organization is now known as the Telecommunications Standardization Sector of the International Telecommunications Union (ITU-T). The CCITT also published the document that defined the OSI reference model, called "The Basic Reference Model for Open Systems Interconnection."

compression ratio The degree to which data can be compressed for storage on another medium, such as a backup medium. Compression ratios can range from 1:1 (no compression possible) to 8:1 or higher, depending on the format of the data stored in the individual files.

connectionless A type of protocol that transmits messages to a destination without first establishing a connection with the destination system. Connectionless protocols have very little overhead, and are used primarily for transactions that consist of a single request and reply. The Internet Protocol (IP) and the User Datagram Protocol (UDP) are both connectionless protocols.

connection-oriented A type of protocol that transmits a series of messages to a destination to establish a connection, before sending any application data. Establishing the connection ensures that the destination system is active and ready to receive data. Connection-oriented protocols are typically used to send large amounts of data, such as entire files, which must be split up into multiple packets and which are useless unless every packet arrives at the destination without error. The Transmission Control Protocol (TCP) is a connection-oriented protocol.

convergence The process by which dynamic routers update their routing tables to reflect the current state of the internetwork. The primary advantage of dynamic routing is that it enables routers to modify their routing information automatically as the configuration of the network changes. For example, should a router malfunction, the other nearby routers, after failing to receive regular updates from it, will eventually remove it from their routing tables, thus preventing computers on the network from using that router. The elapsed time between the failure of the router and its removal from the routing tables of the other routers is the convergence period.

counters The individual system attributes or processes monitored by the Performance console in Windows 2000 and the Performance Monitor application in Windows NT.

crossover cable A unshielded twisted pair (UTP) cable in which the transmit contacts in each connector are wired to the receive contacts in the other connector. Using a crossover cable on a UTP Ethernet network eliminates the need for a hub. Crossover cables are used on small two-node networks and as a troubleshooting tool on larger networks.

crossover connection A twisted pair network connection in which the transmit contacts at each end of a cable are wired to the receive contacts at the other end of that cable, without the use of a hub. Normally, a hub is required for a twisted pair network, because the hub crosses the transmit and receive signals, enabling computers to communicate with each other. Standard twisted pair cables are wired straight through, meaning that the transmit contacts at one end of a cable are connected to the transmit contacts at the other end of that cable, and the receive contacts to the receive contacts. To connect two computers directly using a twisted pair cable and no hub, you must use a crossover cable in which the crossover is implemented in the cable wiring.

crosstalk A type of signal interference caused by signals transmitted on one pair of wires bleeding over into the other pairs. Crosstalk can cause network signals to degrade, eventually rendering them unviable. The individual wire pairs inside a twisted pair cable are twisted at different rates because this helps to suppress the effects of crosstalk. Crosstalk is also the main reason why you should not run other signals over the two unused wire pairs in a UTP Ethernet cable.

CSMA/CD *See* Carrier Sense Multiple Access with Collision Detection.

cyclical redundancy check An error detection mechanism in which a computer performs a calculation on a data sample with a specific algorithm, and then transmits the data and the results of the calculation to another computer. The receiving computer then performs the same calculation and compares its results to those supplied by the sender. If the results match, the data has been transmitted successfully. If the results do not match, the data has been damaged in transit.

D

D channel A digital communications channel running at 16 or 64 Kbps that is one of the fundamental units of service provided by the Integrated Services Digital Network (ISDN). D channels carry control traffic only, and are not factored into the user bandwidth provided by the service. The Basic Rate Interface (BRI) ISDN service consists of two B channels plus one 16-Kbps D channel; the Primary Rate Interface (PRI) service consists of 23 B channels and one 64-Kbps D channel. *See also* Integrated Services Digital Network (ISDN).

daemon UNIX term for a computer program or process that runs continuously in the background and performs tasks at predetermined intervals or in response to specific events. Called a service by Windows operating systems, daemons typically perform server tasks, such as spooling print jobs, handling e-mail, and transmitting Web files.

data-link layer The second layer from the bottom of the Open Systems Interconnection (OSI) reference model. Protocols operating at the data-link layer are responsible for packaging network layer data, addressing it to its next destination, and transmitting it over the network. Some of the LAN protocols operating at the data-link layer are Ethernet, Token Ring, and the Fiber Distributed Data Interface (FDDI). WAN protocols operating at the data-link layer include the Point-to-Point Protocol (PPP) and the Serial Line Internet Protocol (SLIP).

DAT *See* Digital Audio Tape.

datagram A term for the unit of data used by the Internet Protocol (IP) and other network layer protocols. Network layer protocols accept data from transport layer protocols and package it into datagrams by adding their own protocol headers. The protocol then passes the datagrams down to a data-link layer protocol for further packaging before they are transmitted over the network.

default gateway The router on the local network used by a TCP/IP client computer to transmit messages to computers on other networks. To communicate with other networks, TCP/IP computers consult their routing tables for the address of the destination network. If they locate the address, they send their packets to the router specified in the table entry, which relays them to the desired network. If no specific entry for the network exists, the computer sends the packets to the router specified in the default gateway entry, which the user (or a DHCP server) supplies as one of the basic configuration parameters of the TCP/IP client.

Destination Address A 48-bit field in data-link layer protocol headers that contains a hexadecimal sequence used to identify the network interface to which a frame will be transmitted.

Destination IP Address A 32-bit field in the Internet Protocol (IP) header that contains a value used to identify the network interface to which a packet will be transmitted.

DHCP *See* Dynamic Host Configuration Protocol.

differential backup A type of backup job that employs a filter that causes it to back up only the files that have changed since the last full backup job. The filter evaluates the state of each file's Archive bit, which a full backup job clears. Creating or modifying a file sets its Archive bit, and the differential job backs up only the files that have their Archive bit set. The differential job does not modify the state of the bits, so the next differential job will also back up all of the files that have changed since the last full backup. Differential jobs use more tape or other media than incremental jobs, because they repeatedly back up the same files, but they're easier to restore in the event of a disaster. You only have to restore the last full backup and the most recent differential to completely restore a drive. *Compare with* incremental backup.

Digital Audio Tape (DAT) A data storage medium that uses cartridges containing 4-mm wide magnetic tape, most commonly for system backups.

Digital Linear Tape (DLT) A data storage medium that uses cartridges containing one-half inch magnetic tape, most commonly used for system backups.

Digital Subscriber Line (DSL) A type of point-to-point, digital WAN connection that uses standard telephone lines to provide high-speed communications. DSL is available in many different forms, including Asymmetrical Digital Subscriber Line (ADSL) and High-bit-rate Digital Subscriber Line (HDSL). The various DSL technologies differ greatly in their speeds and in the maximum possible distance between the installation site and the telephone company's nearest central office. DSL connections are used for many applications, ranging from LAN and PBX interconnections to consumer Internet access. *See also* Asymmetrical Digital Subscriber Line (ADSL).

Digital Subscriber Line Access Multiplexer (DSLAM) The hardware device located at the server side of an ADSL connection. *See also* ADSL Termination Unit-Remote (ATU-R) *and* Asymmetrical Digital Subscriber Line (ADSL).

direct route An Internet Protocol (IP) transmission to a destination on the local network, in which the Destination IP Address and the data-link layer protocol's Destination Address identify the same computer. *Contrast with* indirect route, in which the IP destination is on another network, and the data-link layer Destination Address identifies a router on the local network used to access the destination network.

directory service A database containing information about network entities and resources, used as a guide to the network and an authentication resource by multiple users. Early network operating systems included basic flat file directory services, such as Windows NT domains and the Novell NetWare bindery. Today's directory services, such as Microsoft's Active Directory and Novell Directory Services (NDS) tend to be hierarchical and designed to support large enterprise networks. *See also* Active Directory *and* Novell Directory Services.

distance vector protocol A dynamic routing protocol that rates the relative efficiency of network routes by the number of hops to the destination. This is not necessarily an efficient method, because having networks of different speeds can cause a route with fewer hops to take longer to transmit data than one requiring more hops. The most common of the distance vector routing protocols is the Routing Information Protocol (RIP). *Compare with* link state protocol.

DIX An acronym for Digital Equipment Corporation (DEC), Intel, and Xerox, the three corporations responsible for developing and publishing the original Ethernet standard.

DLT *See* Digital Linear Tape.

DNS *See* Domain Name System.

domain A group of computers and other devices on a network that are administered as a single unit. On the Internet, domain names are hierarchical constructions (such as *microsoft.com*) that form the basis for the Domain Name System (DNS). On a Windows 2000 or Windows NT network, a domain is a group of users, computers, and other resources for which information is stored in a directory service, on a server called a domain controller.

domain controller A computer running Windows 2000 or Windows NT that has been designated for storing and processing directory service information. Windows NT domains and the Windows 2000 Active Directory store their directory service databases on domain controllers, which also authenticate users accessing network resources.

Domain Name System (DNS) A distributed, hierarchical name space designed to provide TCP/IP networks (such as the Internet) with friendly names for computers and users. Although TCP/IP computers use IP addresses to identify each other, people work better with names. DNS provides a naming system for network resources and a service for resolving those names into IP addresses. TCP/IP computers frequently access DNS servers to send them the names of the computers that they want to access. The DNS server communicates with other DNS servers on the network to find out the IP address associated with the requested name and then sends it back to the client computer, which initiates communications with the destination system using its IP address.

drive spanning A process by which a computer creates a single logical storage unit called a volume by combining the disk space of two or more

drives. The volume appears to users as a single logical entity, but data is actually being stored on multiple drives. The primary drawback of this arrangement is that if one of the drives should fail, the entire volume is lost.

driver Also called a device driver, a software component that enables an application or operating system to utilize a particular hardware device.

DSL *See* Digital Subscriber Line.

DSL modem Inaccurate terminology for the hardware unit that provides ADSL client connectivity, which is correctly called an ADSL Termination Unit-Remote (ATU-R).

DSLAM *See* Digital Subscriber Line Access Multiplexer.

duplexing A data availability technique that involves storing identical copies of data on two different drives connected to different host adapters. The drives appear as a single volume to users, and all files written to the volume are copied to both drives automatically. If one of the drives or adapters should fail, the other continues to make the data available until the failed component is repaired or replaced. *Compare with* mirroring.

dynamic allocation An operational mode of Dynamic Host Configuration Protocol (DHCP) servers in which the server assigns an IP address and other TCP/IP configuration settings to a client from a pool of addresses, and then reclaims them when a lease of a given duration expires. This enables you to move computers to different subnets without having to manually release the previously allocated IP addresses from the other subnets. *Compare with* automatic allocation *and* manual allocation. *See also* Dynamic Host Configuration Protocol (DHCP).

Dynamic Host Configuration Protocol (DHCP) A service that automatically configures the TCP/IP client computers on a network by assigning them unique IP addresses and other configuration parameters. DHCP servers can assign IP addresses to clients from a pool and reclaim them when a lease of a set duration expires. Virtually all operating systems include a DHCP client, and most of the major server operating systems, such as Windows 2000 Server, Windows NT Server, Novell NetWare, and many forms of UNIX, include DHCP server software. DHCP is a cross-platform service that can support various operating systems with a single server. *See also* automatic allocation, dynamic allocation, *and* manual allocation.

dynamic routing A system in which routers automatically build their own routing tables using specialized protocols to communicate with other nearby routers. By sharing information in this way, a router builds up a composite picture of the internetwork on which it resides, enabling it to route traffic more efficiently. The two basic types of routing protocols are distance vector routing protocols, like the Routing Information Protocol (RIP), and link state routing protocols, like the Open Shortest Path First (OSPF) protocol.

E

EIA/TIA *See* Electronics Industry Association/Telecommunications Industry Association.

Electronics Industry Association/Telecommunications Industry Association (EIA/TIA) A cooperative trade association responsible for the "Commercial Building Telecommunication Cabling Standard," also known as EIA/TIA 568, which specifies how network cables should be installed in a commercial site.

e-mail A service that transmits messages in electronic form to specific users on a network.

end system On a TCP/IP network, a computer or other device that is the original sender or ultimate recipient of a transmission. The end systems in a TCP/IP transmission are identified by the Source IP Address and Destination IP Address fields in the Internet Protocol (IP) header. All of the other systems (that is, routers) involved in the transmission are known as intermediate systems.

ephemeral port A Transmission Control Protocol (TCP) or User Datagram Protocol (UDP) port number of 1,024 or higher, chosen at random by a TCP/IP client computer during the initiation of a transaction with a server. Because the client initiates the communication with the server, it can use any port number beyond the range of the well-known port numbers (which run up to 1,023). The server reads the ephemeral port number from the transport layer protocol header's Source Port field and uses it to address its replies to the client. *Compare with* well-known port.

Ethernet Common term used to describe IEEE 802.3, a data-link layer LAN protocol developed in the 1970s, which is now the most popular protocol of its kind in the world. Ethernet runs at 10 Mbps, is based on the Carrier Sense Multiple Access with Collision Detection (CSMA/CD) media access control (MAC) mechanism, and supports a variety of physical layer options, including coaxial, unshielded twisted pair (UTP), and fiber optic cables. More recent revisions of the protocol support speeds of 100 Mbps (Fast Ethernet) and 1,000 Mbps (Gigabit Ethernet). *See also* Carrier Sense Multiple Access with Collision Detection (CSMA/CD).

F

Fast Ethernet Updated version of the Ethernet LAN protocol that increases transmission speed from 10 to 100 Mbps, while preserving nearly all of Ethernet's defining elements, such as its frame format, its physical layer options, and the Carrier Sense Multiple Access with Collision Detection (CSMA/CD) media access control (MAC) mechanism. Defined in a new document published in 1995 called IEEE 802.3u, Fast Ethernet supports three primary physical layer options: 100BaseTX, for Category 5 UTP cable; 100BaseT4, for Category 3 UTP cable; and 100BaseFX, for multimode fiber optic cable.

Fast Link Pulse (FLP)   The signal generated by Fast Ethernet network interface adapters and hubs, which the devices use to signal that they have been cabled together properly and to automatically negotiate the fastest transmission speed they have in common. When an adapter or hub receives the FLP signal from the device to which it's connected, it activates a light emitting diode (LED), which indicates that communication is taking place. FLP signals are completely compatible with the Normal Link Pulse (NLP) signals used by 10BaseT Ethernet devices, differing only in that they include a link code word that specifies the transmission speeds they support.

FAT   *See* file allocation table.

FDDI   *See* Fiber Distributed Data Interface.

Fiber Distributed Data Interface (FDDI)   A data-link layer LAN protocol running at 100 Mbps, designed for use with fiber optic cable. Typically used for backbone networks, FDDI uses the token passing media access control (MAC) mechanism and supports a double ring topology that provides fault tolerance in the event of a system disconnection or cable failure. Originally the principle 100 Mbps LAN protocol, FDDI has since largely been replaced by Fast Ethernet's fiber optic options.

fiber optic   A network cable technology that uses signals consisting of pulses of light rather than the electrical charges used by copper cables. Hence

fiber optic cable is completely resistant to electromagnetic interference, and is also able to span far longer distances than copper cables, indoors or outdoors. The core conductors in a fiber optic cable are made of glass or plastic, and are surrounded by a cladding that reflects the light back on itself, keeping it in the core of the cable. The light source is a light emitting diode (LED) or a laser, depending on the type of cable. Fiber optic cable is generally more efficient than copper-based cable in almost every way, but it's more expensive than copper and more difficult to install, requiring specialized tools and skills. *See also* multimode fiber *and* singlemode fiber.

Fiber Optic Inter-Repeater Link (FOIRL)   The earliest Ethernet physical layer specification to use fiber optic cable. Defined in the DIX Ethernet II document, FOIRL uses 62.5/125 multimode fiber optic cable in a star topology, with a maximum segment length of 1,000 meters. FOIRL was rarely used, and was replaced in the IEEE 802.3 standard by the 10BaseF specification: 10BaseFL, 10BaseFB, and 10BaseFP.

file allocation table (FAT)   File system used by the DOS operating system, which is based on a table that specifies which disk clusters contain the files stored on a disk. The Windows 95, Windows 98, Windows Me, Windows NT, and Windows 2000 operating systems currently support the 16-bit version of the FAT file system. Windows 95 OSR2, Windows 98, Windows Me, and Windows 2000 also support FAT32, a newer version that uses 32-bit FAT entries, enabling the file system to support much larger disk drives. The FAT file system is sufficient for a standard workstation, but lacks the security capabilities required by server drives. For this reason, the Microsoft operating systems designed for heavier network use, Windows 2000 and Windows NT, also include the NT file system (NTFS), which has greater security capabilities.

File Transfer Protocol (FTP) An application layer TCP/IP protocol designed to perform file transfers and basic file management tasks on remote computers. FTP is a mainstay of Internet communications, and FTP client support is integrated into most Web browsers, while FTP server support is integrated into many Web server products. FTP is also an important UNIX tool; all UNIX systems support both FTP client and server functions. FTP is unique among TCP/IP protocols in that it uses two simultaneous TCP connections. One, a control connection, remains open during the entire life of the session between the FTP client and the FTP server. When the client initiates a file transfer, a second connection is opened between the two computers, to carry the transferred data. This connection closes at the conclusion of the data transfer.

firewall A hardware or software product designed to isolate part of an internetwork, to protect it against intrusion by outside processes. Typically used to protect a private network from intrusion from the Internet, firewalls use a number of techniques to provide this protection, while still allowing certain types of traffic through. Some of these techniques include packet filtering and Network Address Translation (NAT). Once intended only for large network installations, there are now smaller firewall products designed to protect small networks and individual computers from Internet intruders.

fish tape A tool used by cable installers to push or pull cables up or down inside walls. It consists of a flexible metal tape with a hook on the end wound onto a reel (much like a plumber's snake). Cable installers connect the end of a cable to the hook and draw it through a wall by unreeling a length of tape and extending it through the cavity inside the wall.

flow control A function of certain data transfer protocols that enables a system receiving data to transmit signals to the sender instructing it to slow down or speed up its transmissions. This prevents the receiving system from overflowing its buffers and being forced to discard incoming data. For example, the Transmission Control Protocol (TCP) implements its flow control mechanism by using a Windows field to specify the number of bytes that it is capable of receiving from the sender.

FLP *See* Fast Link Pulse.

FOIRL *See* Fiber Optic Inter-Repeater Link.

fox and hound wire tester Colloquial name for a simple type of cable tester, also called a tone generator and locator.

frame Unit of data constructed, transmitted, and received by data-link layer protocols such as Ethernet and Token Ring. Data-link layer protocols create frames by packaging the data they receive from network layer protocols inside a header and footer. Frames can be different sizes, depending on the protocol used to create them.

FTP *See* File Transfer Protocol.

full-duplexing A form of network communications in which two connected systems can send signals to the other system simultaneously. For example, a telephone call (in which both parties can talk at once at any time) is an example of full-duplex communication, while a citizen's band (CB) radio (on which you must depress a key to transmit signals and release the key to receive them) is an example of a half-duplex communication device.

G

gateway On a TCP/IP network, the term gateway is often used synonymously with the term router, referring to a network layer device that connects two networks together and relays traffic between them as needed, such as the default gateway specified in a TCP/IP client configuration. However, the term gateway is also used to refer to an application layer device that relays data between two different services, such as an e-mail gateway that enable two separate e-mail services to communicate with each other.

Gbps Gigabits per second, a unit of measurement typically used to measure network transmission speed.

GB Gigabyte, equal to 1,000 megabytes or 1,000,000 kilobytes or 1,000,000,000 bytes.

GBps Gigabytes per second, a unit of measurement typically used to measure the speed of data storage devices.

gif A compressed file format commonly used to store graphic images in bitmap form.

Gigabit Ethernet The latest version of the Ethernet data-link layer protocol, defined in the IEEE 802.3z and IEEE 802.3ab documents and running at 1,000 Mbps. Gigabit Ethernet is designed for backbone networks and server connections, and supports a variety of UTP and fiber optic cabling options. The UTP option uses all four of the wire pairs in the cable to carry signals, instead of the two pairs used by most of the other Ethernet types. As with the other Ethernet varieties, Gigabit Ethernet uses the Carrier Sense Multiple Access with Collision Detection (CSMA/CD) media access control (MAC) mechanism.

grandfather-father-son A media rotation scheme used by many backup software programs in which "grandfather" refers to monthly backup jobs, "father" to weekly jobs, and "son" to daily jobs.

H

half-duplexing A form of network communications in which two connected systems can only send signals in one direction at a time. For example, a citizen's band (CB) radio (on which you must depress a key to transmit signals and release the key to receive them) is an example of a half-duplex communications device, while a telephone call (in which both parties can talk at once at any time) is an example of full-duplex communication. Most LAN protocols operate in half-duplex mode, although there is a full-duplex version of Ethernet.

HDSL *See* High-bit-rate Digital Subscriber Line.

High-bit-rate Digital Subscriber Line (HDSL) A point-to-point, digital WAN technology used by telephone companies and other large corporations to transmit data at T1 speeds.

hop A unit of measurement used to quantify the length of a route between two computers on an internetwork, as indicated by the number of routers that packets must pass through to reach the destination end system. For example, if packets must be forwarded by four routers in the course of their journey from end system to end system, the destination is said to be four hops away from the source. Distance vector routing protocols like the Routing Information Protocol (RIP) use the number of hops as a means to compare the relative efficiency of routes.

HOSTS An ASCII text file used by TCP/IP computers to resolve host names into IP addresses. The HOSTS file is a simple list of the host names used by TCP/IP computers and their equivalent IP addresses. When a user or an application refers to a computer using a host name, the TCP/IP client looks it up in the HOSTS file to determine its IP address. The HOSTS file was the original name resolution method for what later became the Internet, until the number of computers on the network grew too large to manage using this technique. Eventually, the Domain Name System (DNS) was created to perform the same function in a more efficient and manageable way. TCP/IP computers still have the ability to use a HOSTS file for name resolution, but because the names and addresses of each computer must be added manually, this method is rarely used today.

HTTP *See* Hypertext Transfer Protocol.

hub A hardware component to which cables running from computers and other devices are connected, joining all of the devices into a network. In most cases, the term hub refers to an Ethernet multiport repeater, a device that amplifies the signals received from each connected device and forwards them to all of the other devices simultaneously. *See also* multiport repeater.

Hypertext Transfer Protocol (HTTP) Application layer protocol that is the basis for World Wide Web communications. Web browsers generate HTTP GET request messages containing URLs and transmit them to Web servers, which reply with one or more HTTP Response messages containing the requested files. HTTP traffic is encapsulated using the Transmission Control Protocol (TCP) at the transport layer and the Internet Protocol (IP) at the network layer. Each HTTP transaction requires a separate TCP connection.

I

IANA *See* Internet Assigned Numbers Authority.

IBM data connector (IDC) A proprietary connector used to attach Token Ring systems to multistation access units (MAUs) using Type 1 cables and to connect MAUs together. On today's Token Ring networks, Type 1 cables and IDC connectors have largely been replaced by RJ45 connectors and unshielded twisted pair (UTP) cables.

ICMP *See* Internet Control Message Protocol.

IDC *See* IBM data connector.

IDSL *See* ISDN Digital Subscriber Line.

IEEE *See* Institute of Electrical and Electronic Engineers.

IEEE 802.2 Standard document published by the Institute of Electrical and Electronic Engineers (IEEE) defining the Logical Link Control (LLC) sublayer used by the IEEE 802.3, IEEE 802.5, and other protocols.

IEEE 802.3 Standard document published by the Institute of Electrical and Electronic Engineers (IEEE) defining what is commonly referred to as the Ethernet protocol. Although there are slight differences from the original DIX Ethernet standards, such as the omission of the Ethertype field and the separation of the data-link layer into two sublayers, the Media Access Control (MAC) sublayer and the Logical Link Control (LLC) sublayer, IEEE 802.3 retains the defining characteristics of Ethernet, including the Carrier Sense Multiple Access with Collision Detection (CSMA/CD) MAC mechanism. IEEE 802.3 also adds to the physical layer options defined in the DIX Ethernet standards by including support for unshielded twisted pair (UTP) cable.

IEEE 802.3ab Standard document published by the Institute of Electrical and Electronic Engineers (IEEE) defining an implementation of the 1,000 Mbps Gigabit Ethernet protocol using Category 5 unshielded twisted pair (UTP) cable and a 100-meter maximum segment length. Released after the original Gigabit Ethernet protocol standard (IEEE 802.3z), this specification is intended to be an upgrade path to Gigabit Ethernet for existing UTP regular or Fast Ethernet networks. To achieve a transmission speed of 1,000 Mbps, this standard calls for the use of all four pairs of wires in the cable, plus a signaling scheme called PAM-5 (Pulse Amplitude Modulation-5).

IEEE 802.3u Standard document published by the Institute of Electrical and Electronic Engineers (IEEE) defining the Fast Ethernet data-link layer LAN protocol. Running at 100 Mbps, Fast Ethernet uses the same frame format and the Carrier Sense Multiple Access with Collision Detection (CSMA/CD) media access control (MAC) mechanism as standard Ethernet, and supports three physical layer options, 100BaseTX, 100BaseT4, and 100BaseFX. Many Fast Ethernet hardware products support both 10 and 100 Mbps speeds, and use an enhanced link pulse signal called Fast Link Pulse (FLP) to negotiate the fastest possible transmission speed with the connected device.

IEEE 802.3z Standard document published by the Institute of Electrical and Electronic Engineers (IEEE) defining the 1,000-Mbps Gigabit Ethernet data-link layer protocol. Designed primarily for use on backbone networks and server connections that require high speeds, IEEE 802.3z was the first Gigabit Ethernet standard published, and includes a variety of physical layer options, most of which call for various types of fiber optic cable. Like the other varieties of Ethernet, Gigabit Ethernet uses the Carrier Sense Multiple Access with Collision Protection (CSMA/CD) media access control (MAC) mechanism.

IEEE 802.5 Standard document published by the Institute of Electrical and Electronic Engineers (IEEE) defining a Token Ring-like data-link layer protocol. *See also* Token Ring.

IETF *See* Internet Engineering Task Force.

ifconfig A UNIX utility program used to configure a network interface and display the network interface's configuration parameters. The similar Ipconfig.exe is a program available in Windows 2000 and Windows NT that performs the display functions only.

IMAP *See* Internet Mail Access Protocol.

incremental backup A type of backup job that employs a filter that causes it to back up only the files that have changed since the last backup job. The filter evaluates the state of each file's Archive bit, which a full backup job or an incremental backup job clears. Creating or modifying a file sets its Archive bit, and the incremental job backs up only the files whose Archive bit is set. It then resets the Archive bits (unlike a differential job, which does not reset the bits). Incremental jobs use the least amount of tape or other medium, but the are more difficult to restore in the event of a disaster. You must restore the last full backup job and all of the incremental jobs performed since that last full backup, in the correct chronological order, to fully restore a drive. *Compare with* differential backup.

indirect route An Internet Protocol (IP) transmission to a destination on a different network, in which the Destination IP Address and the data-link layer protocol's Destination Address identify different computers. *Contrast with* direct route, in which the IP destination is on the same network, and the data-link layer Destination Address identifies the same computer as the Destination IP Address.

Institute of Electrical and Electronic Engineers (IEEE) An organization, founded in 1984, dedicated to the development and publication of standards for the computer and electronics industries. Best known in computer networking for the IEEE 802 series of documents defining the data-link layer LAN protocols commonly known as Ethernet and Token Ring.

Integrated Services Digital Network (ISDN) A dial-up communications service that uses standard telephone lines to provide high-speed digital communications. Originally conceived as a replacement for the existing analog telephone service, it never achieved its anticipated popularity, Today, ISDN is used in the United States primarily as an Internet access technology, although it is more commonly used for WAN connections in Europe and Japan. The two most common ISDN services are the Basic Rate Interface (BRI), which provides two 64-Kbps B channels and one 16-Kbps D (control) channel, and the Primary Rate Interface (PRI), which provides twenty-three 64-Kbps B channels and one 64-Kbps D channel.

intelligent hub Also called a smart hub, a LAN cabling nexus that not only functions at the physical layer by propagating traffic to all of the other computers on the network, but is also able to buffer data and retransmit it out through specific ports as needed, and in some cases to monitor the activity on all of its ports and transmit information about its status to a network management console.

intermediate system On a TCP/IP network, a router that relays traffic generated by an end system from one network to another. The end systems in a TCP/IP transmission are identified by the Source IP Address and Destination IP Address fields in the Internet Protocol (IP) header. All of the other systems (that is, routers) involved in the transmission are known as intermediate systems.

International Organization for Standardization (ISO) An organization, founded in 1946, that consists of standards bodies from over 75 countries, such as the American National Standards Institute (ANSI) from the United States. The ISO is responsible for the publication of many computer-related standards, the most well-known of which is "The Basic Reference Model for Open Systems Interconnection," commonly known as the OSI reference model. (ISO is not merely an acronym; it's a name derived from the Greek word *isos*, meaning "equal.")

International Telecommunications Union (ITU) An organization, founded in 1865, devoted to the development of treaties, regulations, and standards governing telecommunications. Since 1992, it has included the standards development organization formerly known as the Comité Consultatif International Téléphonique et Télégraphique (CCITT), which was responsible for the creation of modem communication, compression, and error correction standards.

internet *See* internetwork.

Internet A packet-switcing internetwork that consists of thousands of individual networks and millions of computers located around the world. The Internet is not owned or administered by any central managing body; all administration chores are distributed among users all over the network.

Internet Assigned Numbers Authority (IANA) The organization responsible for the assignment of unique parameter values for the TCP/IP protocols, including IP address assignments for networks and protocol number assignments. The "Assigned Numbers" Requests For Comments (RFC) document (currently RFC 1700) lists all of the protocol number assignments and many other unique parameters regulated by the IANA.

Internet Control Message Protocol (ICMP) A network layer TCP/IP protocol that carries administrative messages, particularly error messages and informational queries. ICMP error messages are primarily generated by intermediate systems that, because the packets they route travel no higher than the network layer, have no other means of signaling errors to the end system that transmitted the packet. Typical ICMP error messages inform the sender that the network or host to which a packet is addressed could not be found, or that the Time To Live value for a packet has expired. ICMP query messages request information (or simply a response) from other computers, and are the basis for TCP/IP utilities like Ping, which is used to test the ability of one computer on a network to communicate with another.

Internet Engineering Task Force (IETF) The primary standards ratification body for the TCP/IP protocol and the Internet. The IETF publishes the Requests For Comments (RFCs), which are the working documents for what eventually become Internet standards. The IETF is an international body of network designers, operators, software programmers, and other technicians, all of whom devote part of their time to the development of Internet protocols and technologies.

Internet Mail Access Protocol (IMAP) An application layer TCP/IP protocol used by e-mail clients to download mail messages from a server. E-mail traffic between servers and outgoing e-mail traffic from clients to servers uses the Simple Mail Transport Protocol (SMTP). *See also* Post Office Protocol 3 (POP3).

Internet Protocol (IP) The primary network layer protocol in the Transmission Control Protocol/Internet Protocol (TCP/IP) protocol suite. IP is the protocol that is ultimately responsible for end-to-end communications on a TCP/IP internetwork, and includes functions such as addressing, routing, and fragmentation. IP packages data that it receives from transport layer protocols into data units called datagrams by applying a header containing the information needed to transmit the data to its destination. The IP addressing system uses 32-bit addresses to uniquely identify the computers on a network, and specifies the address of the destination system as part of the IP header. IP is also responsible for routing packets to their destinations on other networks by forwarding them to other routers on the network. When a datagram is too large to be transmitted over a particular network, IP breaks it up into fragments and transmits each fragment in a separate packet.

Internet Service Provider (ISP) A type of company whose business is supplying consumers or businesses with Internet access. At the consumer level, an ISP provides users with dial-up access to the ISP's networks, which are connected to the Internet, as well as other end-user services, such as access to DNS, e-mail, and news servers. At the business level, ISPs provide high-bandwidth Internet connections using leased telephone lines or other technologies, and sometimes also provide other services, such as registered IP addresses, Web site hosting, and DNS domain hosting.

internetwork A group of interconnected local area networks (LANs) and/or wide area networks (WANs) that are connected so that any computer can transmit data to any other computer. The networks are connected by routers, which are responsible for relaying packets from one network to another. The largest example of an internetwork is the Internet, which is composed of thousands of networks located around the world. Private internetworks consist of a smaller number of LANs, often at various locations and connected by WAN links.

Internetwork Packet Exchange (IPX) A network layer protocol used by Novell NetWare networks. IPX performs many of the same functions as the Internet Protocol (IP), but instead of being a self-contained addressing system like IP, IPX is designed for use on LANs only and uses a network identifier assigned by the network administrator plus the network interface adapter's hardware address to identify the individual computers on the network. Unlike IP, IPX is not based on an open standard. Novell owns all rights to the protocols of the IPX protocol suite, although Microsoft has developed its own IPX-compatible protocol for inclusion in the Windows operating systems.

Intranet A TCP/IP network owned by a private organization that provides services such as Web sites only to that organization's users.

Ipconfig.exe A Windows 2000 and Windows NT command-line utility used to view the TCP/IP configuration parameters for a particular computer. A graphical version of the tool, called Winipcfg.exe, is included with Windows 95, Windows 98, and Windows Me. Ipconfig.exe is most useful on computers with TCP/IP clients configured automatically by a Dynamic Host Configuration (DHCP) server, because it is the easiest way to view the assigned settings for the client system. You can also use Ipconfig.exe to release and renew DHCP-assigned TCP/IP configuration parameters.

IP *See* Internet Protocol.

IP address A 32-bit address assigned to TCP/IP client computers and other network equipment that uniquely identifies that device on the network. The Internet Protocol (IP) uses IP addresses to transmit packets to the destinations. Expressed as four 8-bit decimal values separated by periods (for example, 192.168.71.19), the IP address consists of a network identifier (which specifies the network that the device is located on) and a host identifier (which identifies the particular device on that network). The sizes of the network and host identifiers can vary depending on the address class. For a computer to be accessible from the Internet, it must have an IP address containing a network identifier registered with the Internet Assigned Numbers Authority (IANA).

IP Security protocol (IPSec) A set of TCP/IP protocols designed to provide encrypted network layer communications. For computers to communicate using IPSec, they must share a public key.

IPSec *See* IP Security protocol.

IPX *See* Internetwork Packet Exchange.

ISDN *See* Integrated Services Digital Network.

ISO *See* International Organization for Standardization.

ISP *See* Internet Service Provider.

ITU *See* International Telecommunications Union.

J

Jaz Proprietary name for a magnetic cartridge drive holding one or two gigabytes (GB).

jpg A compressed file format commonly used to store graphic images in bitmap form.

K

Kbps Kilobits per second, a unit of measurement typically used to measure network transmission speed.

L

LAN *See* local area network.

late collision On an Ethernet network, a data collision between two transmitted packets that occurs after one or both packets has completely left the transmitting system. The physical layer specifications of the Ethernet protocols are designed to ensure that the first bit transmitted by a computer reaches its destination before the last bit leaves that computer. This allows the transmitting system to detect collisions when they occur. Collisions are normal on an Ethernet network, but if a cable segment is too long, or if there are too many hubs on the path to the destination, late collisions can occur after packets have left the transmitting system, which makes it impossible for the Ethernet adapter in the transmitting system to detect them. Unlike the normal type of collision, late collisions are a serious problem on an Ethernet network that should be addressed immediately. *See also* collision *and* Ethernet.

lease identification cookie A string that consists of a computer's IP address and its hardware address, which a Dynamic Host Configuration Protocol (DHCP) server uses to uniquely identify a client in its database. *See also* Dynamic Host Configuration Protocol (DHCP).

Linear Tape Open (LTO) A data storage medium that uses cartridges containing one-half-inch wide magnetic tape, most commonly used for system backups.

link code word A 16-bit data packet included in the Fast Link Pulse signals generated by Fast Ethernet devices, which contains the speeds at which the device can transmit data and whether or not the device supports full-duplex transmissions.

link segment A network segment that connects only two computers together, such as a cable that connects a computer to a hub. *Contrast with* a mixing segment, which connects more than two computers, such as a Thin Ethernet segment, which consists of cables that run from computer to computer in daisy-chain fashion. The Ethernet protocol distinguishes between mixing segments and link segments in the physical layer configuration guidelines that specify how many repeaters are permitted on a network.

link pulse A signal transmitted by Ethernet devices that is used to indicate when the devices are communicating properly. Ethernet unshielded twisted pair (UTP) network interface adapters and hubs typically have light emitting diodes (LEDs) that light up when the device receives a link pulse signal from a device to which it is connected. 10BaseT devices use a Normal Link Pulse (NLP) signal, which is used only for link integrity testing, and Fast Ethernet devices use a Fast Link Pulse (FLP) signal, which also includes a link code word that enables the devices to negotiate the fastest possible transmission speed they have in common. *See also* Fast Link Pulse (FLP) *and* Normal Link Pulse (NLP).

link state protocol A dynamic routing protocol that rates the relative efficiency of network routes by the properties of the connections providing access to the destination. *Contrast with* distance vector protocols, which use the number of hops to rate the efficiency of a network. The most common of the link state protocols is the Open Shortest Path First (OSPF) protocol.

LLC *See* Logical Link Control sub-layer.

LMHOSTS An ASCII text file used by Windows TCP/IP computers to resolve NetBIOS names into IP addresses. Like the HOSTS file used to resolve host names into IP addresses, an LMHOSTS file is a list of the NetBIOS names assigned to computers on the network and their corresponding IP addresses. LMHOSTS files can also contain special entries used to preload the computer's NetBIOS name cache or to identify the domain controllers on the network. Windows systems can use individual LMHOSTS files for NetBIOS name resolution, but they more commonly use either network broadcast transmissions or the Windows Internet Name Service (WINS).

local area network (LAN) A collection of computers that are connected to each other using a shared medium, and that communicate with each other using a common set of protocols. *Compare with* wide area network (WAN) *and* metropolitan area network (MAN).

Logical Link Control (LLC) sublayer One of the two sublayers of the data-link layer defined by the Institute of Electrical and Electronic Engineers (IEEE) 802 standards. The LLC standard (IEEE 802.2) defines additional fields carried within the data field of data-link layer protocol headers. *See also* Media Access Control (MAC) sublayer.

loopback connector A hardware tool used to test a network interface adapter by redirecting outgoing signals back into the device.

LTO *See* Linear Tape Open.

MAC *See* media access control.

MAN *See* metropolitan area network.

manual allocation An operational mode of Dynamic Host Configuration Protocol (DHCP) servers in which the server assigns clients IP addresses and other TCP/IP configuration settings specified by the server administrator for each computer. The IP addresses are not assigned randomly from a pool, as in the automatic and dynamic allocation modes. The end result is no different than configuring the TCP/IP clients by hand, but using the manual allocation mode of a DHCP server prevents the administrator from having to travel to the client computer and prevents other computers on the network from being assigned duplicate addresses. Manual allocation is typically used for clients that must have a specific IP address, such as a Web server that must be accessible from the Internet using a DNS name. *See also* Dynamic Host Configuration Protocol (DHCP).

management information base (MIB) The object-oriented database where a network management agent stores the information that it will eventually transmit to a network management console using a protocol like the Simple Network Management Protocol (SNMP). Agents are built into network hardware and software products to enable them to report the status of the product to a central console monitored by a network administrator.

MAU *See* multistation access unit.

maximum transfer unit (MTU) The largest physical packet size that a system can transmit over a network. As packets are routed through an internetwork, they might have to pass through individual networks with different MTUs. When a packet exceeds the MTU for a particular network, the network layer protocol (IP, in most cases) divides the packet into fragments smaller than the MTU for the outgoing network. The protocol then repackages each fragment into a separate packet and transmits them. If necessary, fragments can be split into still smaller fragments by other routers along the way to the destination. Packets remain fragmented for the rest of their journey, and are not reassembled until they reach the end system that is the packet's ultimate destination.

Mbps Megabits per second, a unit of measurement typically used to measure network transmission speed.

MB Megabyte, equal to 1,000 kilobytes or 1,000,000 bytes.

MBps Megabytes per second, a unit of measurement typically used to measure the speed of data storage devices.

media In networking, a term used to describe the data-carrying hardware mechanism that computers and other network devices use to send information to each other. In computers, a term used to describe a means of storing data in a permanent fashion, such as a hard or floppy disk.

media access control (MAC) A method by which computers determine when they can transmit data over a shared network medium. When multiple computers are connected to a single network segment, two computers transmitting data at the same time cause a collision, which destroys the data. The MAC mechanism implemented in the data-link layer protocol prevents these collisions from occurring or permits them to occur in a controlled manner. The MAC mechanism is the defining characteristic of a data-link layer LAN protocol. The two most common MAC mechanisms in use today are Carrier Sense Multiple Access with Collision Detection (CSMA/CD), which is used by Ethernet networks, and token passing, which is used by Token Ring and Fiber Distributed Data Interface (FDDI) networks, among others.

Media Access Control (MAC) sublayer One of the two sublayers of the data-link layer defined by the Institute of Electrical and Electronic Engineers (IEEE) 802 standards. The MAC sublayer defines the mechanism used to regulate access to the network medium. *See also* Logical Link Control (LLC) sublayer.

Metric A field in a TCP/IP computer's routing table that contains a value rating the relative efficiency of a particular route. When routing packets, a router scans its routing table for the desired destination, and if there are two possible routes to that destination listed in the table, the router chooses the one with the lowest metric value. Depending on how the routing information is inserted into the table, the metric can represent the number of hops needed to reach the destination network, or it can contain a value that reflects the actual time needed to reach the destination.

metropolitan area network (MAN) A data network that services an area larger than a local area network (LAN) and smaller than a wide area network (WAN). Most MANs today service communities, towns, or cities and are operated by cable television companies using fiber optic cable.

MIB *See* management information base.

minimal routing The process of routing IP using only the default routing table entries created by the operating system. *Compare with* static routing *and* dynamic routing.

mirroring A data availability technique that involves storing identical copies of data on two different drives connected to a single host adapter. The drives appear as a single volume to users, and all files written to the volume are automatically copied to both drives. Should one of the drives fail, the other continues to make the data available until the failed drive is repaired or replaced. *Compare with* duplexing.

mixing segment A network segment that connects more than two computers, such as a Thin Ethernet segment, which consists of cables that run from computer to computer in daisy-chain fashion. The Ethernet protocol distinguishes between mixing segments and link segments in the physical layer configuration guidelines that specify how many repeaters are permitted on a network. *Contrast with* link segment.

modem Short for modulator/demodulator, a hardware device that converts the digital signals generated by computers into analog signals suitable for transmission over a telephone line, and back again. A dial-up connection between two computers requires a modem at each end, both of which support the same communication protocols. Modems take the form of internal devices that plug into one of a computer's expansion slots, or external devices that connect to one of the computer's serial ports. The term modem is also used incorrectly, in many cases, to describe any device that provides a connection to a wide area communications service, such as a cable television or DSL connection. These devices are not actually modems, because the service is digital, and no analog/digital conversion takes place.

MSAU *See* multistation access unit.

MTU *See* maximum transfer unit.

multicast A network transmission with a destination address that represents a group of computers on the network. TCP/IP multicast addresses are defined by the Internet Assigned Numbers Authority (IANA) and represent groups of computers with similar functions, such as all of the routers on a network. *Contrast with* broadcast and unicast.

multifunction cable tester An electronic device that automatically tests a variety of network cable properties, compares the results to pre-established standards, and specifies whether or not the cable is functioning within the defined parameters for those properties.

multihomed A computer with two or more network interfaces, whether they take the form of network interface adapters, dial-up connections using modems, or other technologies. On a TCP/IP network, each of the network interfaces in a multihomed computer must have its own IP address.

multiple master replication A technique usually associated with a directory service, in which identical copies of a database are maintained on various computers scattered throughout a network. In multiple master replication, users can make changes to any copy of the database, and the changes to that copy are replicated to all of the other copies. This is a complex technique, because it is possible for different users to make changes to the same record on different masters. The system must therefore have a mechanism for reconciling data conflicts in the various masters, such as using time stamps or version numbers to assign priorities to data modifications. Microsoft's Active Directory directory service uses multiple master replication. *Compare with* single master replication.

multimode fiber A type of fiber optic cable typically used on LANs and supported by a number of data-link layer protocols, including standard Ethernet, Fast Ethernet, Gigabit Ethernet, and Fiber Distributed Data Interface (FDDI). Multimode fiber optic uses an LED as a light source, unlike singlemode fiber optic, which uses a laser. Multimode fiber has a smaller bend radius, enabling it to bend around corners more easily than singlemode. As a result, multimode is better suited for relatively short distance connections than is singlemode. However, even multimode fiber can span much longer distances than most copper-based cables. *See also* singlemode fiber.

multiplexing Any one of several techniques used to transmit multiple signals over a single cable or other network medium simultaneously. Multiplexing works by separating the available bandwidth of the network medium into separate bands, by frequency, wavelength, time, or other criteria, and transmitting a different signal in each band. LAN media carry only one signal, and therefore do not use multiplexing, but some networks, such as cable television and telephone networks, do.

multiport repeater Another name for an Ethernet hub. A repeater is a physical layer device that amplifies incoming signals and retransmits them, enabling network segments to span longer distances without suffering from the effects of attenuation. A multiport repeater is a device that accepts multiple network connections. Signals arriving through any of the device's ports are amplified and retransmitted out through all of the other ports simultaneously. All of the hubs used on Ethernet networks are multiport repeaters.

multistation access unit (MAU or MSAU) The hub used on a Token Ring network. Token Ring hubs are more complicated than Ethernet hubs, because instead of repeating incoming signals out through all ports simultaneously, a MAU sends incoming signals out through each port in turn, and waits for the signal to be returned by the connected computer. This forms the logical ring from which Token Ring networks get their name. To prevent breaks in the network, MAUs also perform an initialization process to insert each active computer into the ring.

multitasking The technique by which a computer with one processor executes multiple tasks simultaneously. By splitting the software processing into separate processes called threads, the processor in the computer can switch rapidly from one thread to another, devoting some of its clock cycles to each. There are two types of multitasking, cooperative and preemptive. In cooperative multitasking, the operating system passes control of the processor to each application in turn, and it is up to the application to return control to the operating system. A badly written application can fail to return control, causing the entire system to run inefficiently, or even crash. In preemptive multitasking, the operating system has complete control over the allocation of processor time to each application. Even if an application crashes, the rest of the processes continue to run normally.

N

name resolution The process of converting a computer or other device's name into an address. Computers communicate using numeric addresses, but humans work better with names. To be able to send data to a particular destination identified by name in the user interface, the computer must first resolve that name into an address. On TCP/IP networks, for example, Domain Name System (DNS) names and NetBIOS names must be resolved into IP addresses. There are several name resolution methods that computers can use, depending on the type of name and type of address involved, including table lookups using text files such as HOSTS and LMHOSTS, independent processes such as broadcast message generation, and network services, such as the Domain Name System (DNS) and the Windows Internet Name Service (WINS). *Compare with* Address Resolution Protocol (ARP).

NAT *See* Network Address Translation.

Nbtstat.exe A Windows command-line utility that displays information about the NetBIOS over TCP/IP connections that the system uses when communicating with other Windows computers on a TCP/IP network.

NDIS *See* Network Device Interface Specification.

NDS *See* Novell Directory Services.

NetBEUI *See* NetBIOS Extended User Interface.

NetBIOS An application programming interface (API) that provides computers with a name space and other local area networking functions.

NetBIOS Extended User Interface (NetBEUI) Transport protocol sometimes used by the Windows operating systems for local area networking. NetBEUI was the default protocol in the first version of Windows NT and in Windows for Workgroups; it has since been replaced by TCP/IP as the default Windows protocol. NetBEUI is a simplified networking protocol that requires no configuration and is self-adjusting. However, the protocol is suitable only for small networks, because it is not routable. NetBEUI identifies computers by the NetBIOS names (or computer names) assigned during the Windows installation. Because NetBIOS uses no network identifier, there is no way for the protocol to route traffic to systems on another network.

netstat A command-line utility supplied with UNIX and Windows operating systems, which displays information about a TCP/IP computer's current network connections and about the traffic generated by the various TCP/IP protocols.

Network Address Translation (NAT) A firewall technique that enables TCP/IP client computers using unregistered IP addresses to access the Internet. Client computers send their Internet service requests to a NAT-equipped router, which substitutes its own registered IP address for the client's unregistered address, and forwards the request on to the specified server. The server sends its reply to the NAT router, which then relays it back to the original client. This renders the unregistered clients invisible to the Internet, preventing direct access to them. *See also* firewall.

Network Driver Interface Specification (NDIS) A multiprotocol device driver interface used by the Windows operating systems for its network interface adapter drivers. The NDIS driver enables a single adapter and its data-link layer protocol to support traffic generated by the TCP/IP, IPX, and NetBEUI protocols, in any combination.

network interface adapter A hardware device that provides a computer with access to a LAN. Network interface adapters can be integrated into a computer's motherboard or take the form of an expansion card, in which case they are called network interface cards or NICs. The adapter, along with its driver, implements the data-link layer protocol on the computer. The adapter has one or more connectors for network cables, or some other interface to the network medium. The network interface adapter and its driver are responsible for functions such as the encapsulation of network layer protocol data into data-link layer protocol frames, the encoding and decoding of data into the signals used by the network medium, and the implementation of the protocol's media access control (MAC) mechanism.

Network News Transfer Protocol (NNTP) A TCP/IP protocol used to post, distribute, and retrieve Usenet messages to and from news servers throughout the Internet.

network layer The third layer from the bottom of the Open Systems Interconnection (OSI) reference model. Protocols operating at the network layer are responsible for packaging transport layer data into datagrams, addressing them to its final destination, routing them across the internetwork, and fragmenting the datagrams as needed. The Internet Protocol (IP) is the most common protocol operating at the network layer, although Novell NetWare networks use a proprietary network layer protocol called Internetwork Packet Exchange (IPX).

NIC *See* network interface card.

NLP *See* Normal Link Pulse.

NNTP *See* Network News Transfer Protocol.

node Any uniquely addressable device on a network, such as a computer, router, or printer.

Nominal Velocity of Propagation (NVP) The speed at which signals travel through a particular length of cable. Cable testing devices such as time domain reflectometers use the NVP to compute the length of a particular cable segment by dividing it into the measured time needed for a generated test signal to travel to the other end of the cable and back. The NVP for a particular cable is supplied by its manufacturer.

Normal Link Pulse (NLP) The signal generated by standard Ethernet network interface adapters and hubs, which the devices use to signal that they have been cabled together properly. When an adapter or hub receives the NLP signal from the device to which it's connected, it lights up an LED, which indicates that communication is taking place. *Compare with* the Fast Link Pulse (FLP) signals used by Fast Ethernet devices.

Novell Directory Services (NDS) Formerly known as NetWare Directory Services, the first hierarchical, object-oriented directory service to achieve commercial success. NDS was first released as part of NetWare 4.0 in 1993, and has matured into a robust product that now supports other platforms in addition to NetWare, such as UNIX, Windows NT, and Windows 2000. NDS provides networks with single login capabilities and the ability to support third-party applications through the use of schema extensions. *See also* directory service *and* schema.

NT1 Short for network termination, the hardware device on the client side of an Integrated Services Digital Network (ISDN) installation that provides the S/T interface used to connect equipment to the service, such as ISDN telephones, fax machines, and the terminal adapter that connects to a computer. In some cases, the NT1 is a separate piece of equipment, but it can also be integrated into a single unit along with a terminal adapter for installations where only a single computer is to be connected to the service.

NTFS Short for NT file system; one of the file systems included with the Windows 2000 and Windows NT operating systems. Compared to the file allocation table (FAT) file system also supported by Windows, NTFS supports larger volumes, includes transaction logs to aid in recovery from disk failures, and enables network administrators to control access to specific directories and files. The main drawback to NTFS is that the drives are not accessible by any operating systems other than Windows 2000 and Windows NT. If you boot the computer with an MS-DOS disk, for example, the NTFS drives are invisible.

NVP *See* Nominal Velocity of Propagation.

O

open circuit A type of cable fault in which one or more wires is not properly connected to the proper contact at the other end of the connection. Cable testing equipment typically detects the open circuits by transmitting a test signal from one end of the cable and then failing to detect it at the other end. *Compare with* short circuit.

Open Shortest Path First (OSPF) A dynamic routing protocol that exchanges information with other routers on the network to update the system's routing table with current information about the configuration of the internetwork. OSPF is a link state protocol that evaluates routes based on their actual performance, rather than using a less accurate measurement like the number of hops needed to reach a particular destination. *Compare with* distance vector protocols, in general, *and* the Routing Information Protocol (RIP), in particular.

Open Systems Interconnection (OSI) reference model A theoretical model defined in documents published by the International Organization for Standardization (ISO) and the Telecommunication Standards Section of the International Telecommunications Union (ITU-T) used for reference and teaching purposes that divides the computer networking functions into seven layers: application, presentation, session, transport, network, datalink, and physical (from top to bottom). However, the layers do not correspond exactly to any of the currently used networking protocol stacks.

operating system The primary program running on a computer, which processes input and output, runs other programs, and provides access to the computer's hardware.

organizationally unique identifier (OUI) The three-byte hexadecimal value assigned by the Institute of Electrical and Electronic Engineers (IEEE) identifying the manufacturer of a network interface adapter, which is used as the first three bytes of the adapter's hardware address.

OSI *See* Open Systems Interconnection (OSI) reference model.

OSPF *See* Open Shortest Path First.

OUI *See* organizationally unique identifier.

P

packet The largest unit of data that can be transmitted over a data network at any one time. Messages generated by applications are split into pieces and packaged into individual packets for transmission over the network. Each packet is transmitted separately, and can take a different route to the destination. When all of the packets arrive at the destination, the receiving computer reassembles them into the original message. This is the basic functionality of a packet switching network.

packet filtering A firewall technique in which a router is configured to prevent certain packets from entering a network. Packet filters can be created based on hardware addresses, IP addresses, port numbers, or other criteria. For example, you can configure a router to allow only certain computers to access the network from the Internet, or allow your network users access to Internet e-mail, but deny them access to Internet Web servers. Although typically used to prevent intrusion into a private network from the Internet, packet filtering can also be used to limit access to one of the LANs on a private internetwork.

packet switching A type of network communications in which messages are broken up into discrete units and transmitted to the destination. These units (called packets) can take different routes to the destination and might arrive there in a different order than that in which they were sent, but the receiving system is capable of reassembling them into the proper order. Packet switching is what makes it possible for the computers on a LAN to share a single network medium. If the computers transmitted entire messages at once, they could monopolize the network for long periods of time, preventing other computers from transmitting.

PAM-5 *See* Pulse Amplitude Modulation-5.

pbx Private branch exchange, a private telephone network used within an organization, which shares a number of outside telephone lines among its users.

PC Card A peripheral device standard designed for laptops and other portable computers, which enables manufacturers to create network interface cards, modems, and other devices packaged in a form approximately the size of a credit card.

PDU *See* protocol data unit.

peer-to-peer networking A networking system in which each computer is capable of functioning both as a client and a server. Each computer also maintains its own security settings, which enables it to control access to its own resources. Peer-to-peer networking is useful on small networks, because no centralized administration is needed and users can easily maintain their own security settings. On larger networks, peer-to-peer networking is inefficient because users need a separate account for every computer they want to access, and because the access control capabilities are usually less flexible and less robust than those of a centrally administered client/server network.

phantom collision A phenomenon that occurs when excessive crosstalk on a twisted pair cable causes a computer to detect signals on both the transmit and receive wire pairs at the same time. To the network interface adapter, these simultaneous signals indicate the existence of a packet collision, and the adapter takes the appropriate steps to clear the network of data and retransmit the supposedly damaged packet. In fact, no real collision has occurred, but the end result is the same as if one had.

physical layer The bottom layer of the Open Systems Interconnection (OSI) reference model, which defines the nature of the network medium itself, how it should be installed, and what types of signals it should carry. In the case of local area networking, the physical layer is closely related to the data-link layer, immediately above it, because the data-link layer protocol includes the physical layer specifications.

Ping A TCP/IP command-line utility used to test whether a computer can communicate with another computer on the network. Ping generates Internet Control Message Protocol (ICMP) Echo Request messages and transmits them to the computer specified on the command line. The target computer, on receiving the messages, transmits them back to the sender as ICMP Echo Replies. The system running Ping then displays the elapsed times between the transmission of the requests and the receipt of the replies. Virtually every TCP/IP client implementation includes a version of Ping.

Plain Old Telephone Service (POTS) Common phrase referring to the Public Switched Telephone Network (PSTN), the standard copper cable telephone network used for analog voice communications around the world.

Point-to-Point Protocol (PPP) A data-link layer TCP/IP protocol used for WAN connections, especially dial-up connections to the Internet and other service providers. Unlike its progenitor, the Serial Line Internet Protocol (SLIP), PPP includes support for multiple network layer protocols, link quality monitoring protocols, and authentication protocols. PPP is used for connections between two computers only, and therefore does not need many of the features found in LAN protocols, such as address fields for each packet and a media access control (MAC) mechanism.

Point-to-Point Tunneling Protocol (PPTP) A data-link layer protocol used to provide secured communications for virtual private network (VPN) connections. VPNs are private network connections that use the Internet as a network medium. To secure the data as it is transmitted across the internet, the computers use a process called tunneling, in which the entire data-link layer frame generated by an application process is encapsulated within an IP datagram. This arrangement violates the rules of the Open Systems Interconnection (OSI) reference model, but it enables the entire PPP frame generated by the user application to be encrypted inside an IP datagram.

POP3 *See* Post Office Protocol 3.

port A code number identifying a process running on a TCP/IP computer. Transport layer protocols, such as the Transmission Control Protocol (TCP) and the User Datagram Protocol (UDP), specify the port number of the source and destination application processes in the header of each message they create. The combination of an IP address and a port number (which is called a socket) identify a specific application on a specific computer on a specific network. Port numbers below 1,024 are called well-known port numbers, which are assigned by the Internet Assigned Numbers Authority (IANA) to common applications. The TCP port number 80, for example, is the well-known port number for Web servers. Port numbers 1,024 and above are ephemeral port numbers, which are selected at random by clients for each transaction they initiate with a server. Alternatively, a hardware connector in a computer or other network device that is used to attach cables that run to other devices.

Post Office Protocol 3 (POP3) An application layer TCP/IP protocol used by e-mail clients to download messages from an e-mail server. E-mail traffic between servers and outgoing e-mail traffic from clients to servers uses the Simple Mail Transport Protocol (SMTP). *See also* Internet Mail Access Protocol (IMAP).

POTS *See* Plain Old Telephone Service.

PPP *See* Point-to-Point Protocol.

PPTP *See* Point-to-Point Tunneling Protocol.

presentation layer Second layer from the top of the Open Systems Interconnection (OSI) reference model, which is responsible for translating the syntaxes used by different types of computers on a network. A computer translates the data generated by its applications from its own abstract syntax to a common transport syntax suitable for transmission over the network. When the data arrives at its destination, the presentation layer on the receiving system translates the transfer syntax into the computer's own native abstract syntax.

PRI *See* Primary Rate Interface.

Primary Rate Interface (PRI) An Integrated Services Digital Network (ISDN) service that consists of twenty-three 64-Kbps B channels plus one 64-Kbps D channel, providing an aggregate bandwidth equal to that of a T1 line. The B channels can be combined into a single data pipe, used individually, or in any combination. The PRI service is rarely used in the United States, but is a popular business service in Europe and Japan. *See also* B channel, D channel, *and* Integrated Services Digital Network (ISDN).

promiscuous mode Operational mode available in some network interface adapters that causes the adapter to read and process all of the packets transmitted over the local area network (LAN), and not just the packets addressed to it. Promiscuous mode is used by protocol analyzers to capture comprehensive samples of network traffic for later analysis.

protocol A documented format for the transmission of data between two networked devices. A protocol is essentially a "language" that a computer uses to communicate, and the other computer to which it is connected must use the same language for communication to take place. In most cases, network communication protocols are defined by open standards created by bipartisan committees. However, there are still a few proprietary protocols still in use. Computers use many different protocols to communicate, which has given rise to the Open Systems Interconnection (OSI) reference model, which defines the layers at which different protocols operate.

PROTOCOL An ASCII text file found on TCP/IP systems that lists the codes used in the Protocol field of the Internet Protocol (IP) header. This field identifies the transport layer protocol that generated the data carried within the datagram, ensuring that the data reaches the appropriate process on the receiving computer. The protocol numbers are registered by the Internet Assigned Numbers Authority (IANA) and derived from the "Assigned Numbers" Request For Comments document.

protocol data unit (PDU) A generic term for the data constructions created by the protocols operating at the various layers of the Open Systems Interconnection (OSI) reference model. For example, the PDU created by data-link layer protocols are called frames and network-layer PDUs are called datagrams.

protocol stack The multi-layered arrangement of communications protocols that provides a data path ranging from the user application to the network medium. Although based on the Open Systems Interconnection (OSI) reference model, not every layer in the model is represented by a separate protocol. On a computer connected to a LAN, for example, the protocol stack generally consists of protocols at the application, transport, network, and data-link layers, the latter of which includes a physical layer specification.

proxy server An application layer firewall technique that enables TCP/IP client systems to access Internet resources without being susceptible to intrusion from outside the network. A proxy server is an application that runs on a computer with a registered IP address, while the clients use unregistered IP addresses, causing them to remain invisible from the Internet. Client applications are configured to send their Internet service requests to the proxy server instead of directly to the Internet, and the proxy server relays the requests to the appropriate Internet server, using its own registered address. On receiving a response from the Internet server, the proxy server relays it back to the original client. Proxy servers are designed for specific applications, and the client must be configured with the address of the proxy server. Administrators can also configure the proxy server to cache Internet information for later use and to restrict access to particular Internet sites. *See also* firewall. *Compare with* Network Address Translation (NAT).

PSTN *See* Public Switched Telephone Network.

Public Switched Telephone Network (PSTN) The standard copper cable telephone network used for analog voice communications around the world. Also known as the Plain Old Telephone Service (POTS).

Pulse Amplitude Modulation-5 (PAM-5) A signaling scheme used in the 1000BaseT Gigabit Ethernet variant. PAM-5 is one of the elements that makes it possible for 1000BaseT to run using standard Category 5 unshielded twisted pair (UTP) cable.

Q

QIC *See* quarter-inch cartridge.

quarter-inch cartridge (QIC) A data-storage medium that uses cartridges containing quarter-inch wide magnetic tape, most commonly used for system backups.

R

RARP *See* Reverse Address Resolution Protocol.

redirector A network client component that determines whether a resource requested by an application is located on the network or on the local system and sends the request either to the local input/output system or to the networking protocol stack. A computer can have multiple redirectors to support different networks, such as a Windows network and a Novell NetWare network.

remote bridge   A device operating at the data-link layer of the Open Systems Interconnection (OSI) reference model, which is used to connect two LANs at different locations with a WAN link, such as a dial-up modem connection or a leased telephone line. By bridging the two network segments, the amount of traffic passing over the WAN is limited, which compensates for its relative slow speed and high cost. *See also* bridge.

Remote Monitoring protocol (RMON)   A network management protocol that enables hardware and software devices to transmit status information to a central network management console.

repeater   A physical layer device that amplifies network signals, enabling them to travel longer distances without suffering from the effects of attenuation. Repeaters for Ethernet networks using coaxial cable have two ports, one for incoming traffic and one for outgoing. However, most of the repeaters used today have multiple ports to support networks using a star topology. The hubs used for unshielded twisted pair (UTP) Ethernet networks today are all multiport repeaters, which amplify signals as they transmit them out through all of the device's ports simultaneously. *See also* attenuation, hub, *and* multiport repeater.

Request For Comments (RFC)   A document published by the Internet Engineering Task Force (IETF) that contains information about a topic related to the Internet or to the Transmission Control Protocol/Internet Protocol (TCP/IP) protocol suite. For example, all of the TCP/IP protocols have been documented and published as RFCs and eventually might be ratified as Internet standards. Some RFCs are only informational or historical, however, and are not submitted for ratification as a standard. After they are published and assigned numbers, RFCs are never changed. If a new version of an RFC document is published, it is assigned a new number and cross-indexed to indicate that it obsoletes the old version.

resolver   Another name for the Domain Name System (DNS) client found on every TCP/IP computer. Whenever the computer attempts to access a TCP/IP system using a DNS name, the resolver generates a DNS Request message and sends it to the DNS server specified in the computer's TCP/IP client configuration. The DNS server then takes whatever steps are necessary to resolve the requested name into an IP address and returns the address to the resolver in the client computer. The resolver can then furnish the IP address to the TCP/IP client, which uses it to transmit a message to the desired destination. *See also* Domain Name System (DNS).

resource record   The unit in which a Domain Name System (DNS) server stores information about a particular computer. The information stored in a resource record depends on the type of record it is, but typically a resource record includes the host name of a computer and its equivalent IP address. In most cases, administrators must manually create the resource records on a DNS server, but recent additions to the DNS standards define a method for dynamically updating the information in resource records as needed. This capability is central to the DNS functionality required by Active Directory directory service. *See also* Domain Name System (DNS).

Reverse Address Resolution Protocol (RARP)   Progenitor of the Bootstrap Protocol (BOOTP) and the Dynamic Host Configuration Protocol (DHCP), an alternative mode of the Address Resolution Protocol (ARP) that enables a computer to retrieve an IP address from a RARP server by broadcasting its hardware address. Designed for use on diskless workstations, RARP is limited in that it can receive only an IP address from the server, and not other TCP/IP configuration parameters, and also in that an administrator must manually configure the RARP server with a specific IP address for every RARP client.

reverse name resolution The process of resolving an IP address into a Domain Name System (DNS) name, which is the opposite of the normal name-to-address resolution performed by DNS servers. Reverse DNS name resolution is accomplished using an extension to the DNS name space consisting of a domain called *in-addr.arpa*, which contains four levels of subdomains named using the numbers 0 through 255. These subdomains contain resource records called pointers; each pointer contains an IP address and its equivalent DNS name. A DNS server looks up an IP address by locating the domain name equivalent to the address. For example, the IP address 192.168.1.15 becomes the domain name 15.1.168.192.in-addr-arpa.

RFC *See* Request For Comments.

RG8 A type of coaxial cable, also known as Thick Ethernet, which is specified by the original DIX Ethernet specification as well as the later IEEE 802.3 standard. RG8 cable is 0.405 inches thick and relatively inflexible, and is installed using a bus topology. *See also* coaxial cable *and* Thick Ethernet.

RG58 A type of coaxial cable, also known as Thin Ethernet, which is specified by the original DIX Ethernet specification as well as the later IEEE 802.3 standard. RG58 cable is 0.195 inches thick and relatively flexible, uses BNC connectors to join the ends, and is installed using a bus topology. *See also* coaxial cable *and* Thin Ethernet.

RJ11 Short for Registered Jack 11, a four- or six-pin modular connector that is used in telephone networking. *See also* RJ45.

RJ45 Short for Registered Jack 45, an eight-pin modular connector that is used in telephone and data networking. The majority of LANs today use RJ45 connectors with unshielded twisted pair (UTP) cables. *See also* RJ11.

RIP *See* Routing Information Protocol.

RMON *See* Remote Monitoring protocol.

root name server One of a handful of servers that represent the top of the Domain Name System (DNS) name space by supplying other DNS servers with the IP addresses of the authoritative servers for all of the top-level domains in the DNS. When resolving a DNS name into an IP address, a DNS server (that is unable to resolve the name itself) sends a DNS Request to one of the root name servers identified in the server's configuration. The root name server reads the top-level domain (that is, the last word, such as *com* in *www.microsoft.com*) from the requested name and supplies the requesting server with the IP address for that top-level domain. The requesting server then transmits the same request to the top-level domain server that the root name server supplied. The root name servers are also the authoritative servers for some of the top-level domains, so they can eliminate a step from the process and supply the address of the second-level domain's authoritative server. *See also* Domain Name System (DNS) *and* authoritative server.

routed A UNIX daemon, pronounced "route-dee," that was the original implementation of the Router Information Protocol (RIP), the most popular of the distance vector routing protocols. *See also* distance vector routing *and* dynamic routing.

router A network layer hardware or software device that connects two networks together and relays traffic between them as needed. Using a table containing information about the other routers on the network, a router examines the destination address of each packet it receives, selects the most efficient route to that destination, and forwards the packet to the router or computer that is the next step in its path. Routers can connect two LANs together or provide access to remote resources by connecting a LAN to a distant network, using a WAN link. One of the most common scenarios involves using routers to connect a LAN to the network of an Internet Service Provider (ISP), thus providing Internet access to all of the LAN's users.

Routing Information Protocol (RIP) A dynamic routing protocol that enables routers to receive information about the other routers on the network, which enables them to keep their routing tables updated with the latest information. RIP works by generating broadcast messages at frequent intervals, which contain the contents of the router's routing table. Other routers use this information to update their own tables, thus spreading the routing information all over the network. Routers also take the absence of RIP messages from a particular router to be a sign that it's not functioning, and remove that router from their tables after a given interval. RIP is frequently criticized for the large amount of broadcast traffic that it generates on the network, and for the limitations of its distance vector routing method, which evaluates routes based solely on the number of hops between the source and the destination. *See also* distance vector routing *and* dynamic routing.

routing table A list maintained in every TCP/IP computer of network destinations and the routers and interfaces that the computer should use to transmit to them. In a computer that is not a router, the routing table contains only a few entries, the most frequently used of which is the default gateway entry. On a router, the routing table can contain a great many entries, which are either manually added by a network administrator or automatically created by a dynamic routing protocol. When there is more than one routing table entry for a specific destination, the computer selects the best route based on a metric, which is a rating of the route's relative efficiency.

S

schema The structure of a database system. In a hierarchical directory service, such as Microsoft's Active Directory or NetWare's Novell Directory Services, the schema contains object classes, which specify what objects can be created in the directory, the relationships between the object classes in the directory tree, and the attributes that make up each object class. Third-party applications can expand the schema for these directory services, enabling the creation of new object classes or the addition of new attributes to existing object classes. In Active Directory, it's also possible to modify the schema manually using the Active Directory Schema console.

scope The pool of IP addresses on a given subnet that a Dynamic Host Configuration Protocol (DHCP) server is configured to assign to clients when using the automatic or dynamic allocation method. *See also* Dynamic Host Configuration Protocol (DHCP), automatic allocation, *and* dynamic allocation.

SCSI *See* small computer system interface.

segment A section of a network that is bounded by hubs, bridges, routers, or switches. Depending on the data-link layer protocol and type of cable being used, a segment may in fact consist of more than one length of cable. For example, a Thin Ethernet network uses separate pieces of coaxial cable to connect each computer to the next one on the bus, but all of those pieces of cable together are called a segment.

Serial Line Internet Protocol (SLIP) A data-link layer TCP/IP protocol used for WAN connections, especially dial-up connections to the Internet and other service providers. Because it is used for connections between two computers only, SLIP does not need many of the features found in LAN protocols, such as address fields for each packet and a media access control (MAC) mechanism. SLIP is the simplest of protocols, consisting only of a single End Delimiter byte that is transmitted after each IP datagram. Unlike its successor, the Point-to-Point Protocol (PPP), SLIP has no inherent security capabilities or any other additional services. For this reason, it is rarely used today.

service Windows term for a computer program or process that runs continuously in the background and performs tasks at predetermined intervals or in response to specific events. Called a daemon by UNIX operating systems, services typically perform server tasks, such as sharing files and printers, handling e-mail, and transmitting Web files.

service-dependent filtering A type of packet filtering used in firewalls that limits access to a network based on the port numbers specified in packets' transport layer protocol headers. The port number identifies the application that generated the packet or that is destined to receive it. With this technique, network administrators can limit access to a network to specific applications or prevent users from accessing specific applications outside the network. *See also* firewall, port, *and* packet filtering.

service pack (SP) A software update package provided by Microsoft for one of its products. A service pack contains a collection of fixes and enhancements packaged into a single self-installing archive file.

SERVICES An ASCII text file found on TCP/IP systems that lists the codes used in the Source Port and Destination Port fields of the Transmission Control Protocol (TCP) and User Datagram Protocol (UDP) headers. These fields identify the application process that generated the data carried within the packet, or for which it is destined. The port numbers are registered by the Internet Assigned Numbers Authority (IANA) and derived from the "Assigned Numbers" Request For Comments document.

session layer The third layer from the top of the Open Systems Interconnection (OSI) reference model. There are no specific session layer protocols, but there are 22 services that the session layer performs, which are incorporated into various application layer protocols. The most important of these functions are dialog control and dialog separation. Dialog control provides two modes for communicating systems, two-way alternate (TWA) mode or two-way simultaneous (TWS) mode, and dialog separation controls the process of inserting checkpoints in the data stream to synchronize functions on the two computers.

shielded twisted pair (STP) A type of cable used for local area networking in environments where additional shielding against electromagnetic interference is needed. The cable consists of eight copper wires twisted into four pairs, with different twist rates and foil or mesh shielding around each pair. The four pairs are then encased in an insulating sheath that provides even more protection.

short circuit A type of cable fault in which two or more of the conductors inside the cable are in contact with each other. Shorts can be caused by a faulty cable installation, in which connectors are improperly attached, or a break in the insulation surrounding the cable's conductors, due either to mishandling or a manufacturing defect. Shorts are easily detected by even the most basic cable testers.

signal quality error Technical term used in the IEEE 802.3 standard for a packet collision, which occurs when two computers on a shared network medium transmit data at precisely the same time. *See also* collision.

Simple Mail Transport Protocol (SMTP) An application layer TCP/IP protocol used to carry e-mail messages between servers and from clients to servers. To retrieve e-mail from mail servers, clients typically use the Post Office Protocol (POP3) or the Internet Mail Access Protocol (IMAP).

Simple Network Management Protocol (SNMP) An application layer TCP/IP protocol and query language used to transmit information about the status of network components to a central network management console. Components embedded into network hardware and software products called SNMP agents are responsible for collecting data about the activities of the products they service, storing the data in a management information base (MIB) and transmitting that data to the console at regular intervals using SNMP messages.

single master replication A technique usually associated with a directory service in which identical copies of a database are maintained on various computers scattered throughout a network. In single master replication, users can make changes on only one copy of the database (the master), and the master replicates those changes to all of the other copies. This is a relatively simple technique compared to multiple master replication, because data only travels in one direction. However, the system is limited in that users might have to connect to a master located at another site to make changes to the database.

singlemode fiber A type of fiber optic cable typically used for long-distance connections between networks, supported by a relatively small number of data-link layer protocols, such as Gigabit Ethernet. Singlemode fiber optic uses a laser as its light source, unlike multimode fiber optic, which uses a light emitting diode (LED). Singlemode fiber has a larger bend radius than multimode fiber, which makes singlemode more difficult to bend around corners. As a result, singlemode is better suited than multimode for long-distance connections.

small computer system interface (SCSI) A peripheral device interface that enables you to connect internal and external devices (especially storage devices) to a computer. SCSI is the preferred interface for network servers.

sliding window A technique used to implement flow control in a network communications protocol. By acknowledging the number of bytes that have been successfully transmitted and specifying the number of bytes that it is capable of receiving, a computer on the receiving end of a data connection creates a "window" that consists of the bytes the sender is authorized to transmit. As the transmission progresses, the window slides along the byte stream, and might change its size, until all data has been transmitted and received successfully.

SMTP *See* Simple Mail Transport Protocol.

SLIP *See* Serial Line Internet Protocol.

SNMP *See* Simple Network Management Protocol.

SNMP agent A software component integrated into a network hardware or software product, which is designed to gather ongoing status information about the product, store it in a management information base (MIB), and transmit it to a central network management console at regular intervals, using Simple Network Management Protocol (SNMP) messages.

socket On a TCP/IP network, the combination of an IP address and a port number, which together identify a specific application process running on a specific computer. The Uniform Resource Locators (URLs) used in Internet client applications express a socket as the IP address followed by the port number, separated by a colon, as in 192.168.1.17:80.

Source IP Address A 32-bit field in the Internet Protocol (IP) header that contains a value used to identify the particular network interface from which a packet originated.

SP *See* service pack.

SPA *See* spanning tree algorithm.

spanning tree algorithm (SPA) A protocol used by network bridges in cases where a network contains redundant bridges for fault-tolerance purposes. The presence of multiple bridges on the same network, performing the same tasks, can result in data loss when each bridge lists a computer as being part of a different network segment, or can even result in a bridge loop, in which packets are forwarded endlessly from bridge to bridge. Using the SPA, the redundant bridges communicate among themselves and select one of the bridges to process packets, while the others remain idle until the active bridge fails.

split pair A type of twisted pair cable fault in which two or more wires are connected to the wrong contacts in the same way at both ends of the cable. The cable appears to be wired correctly, because each contact in one connector is connected to the equivalent contact in the other connector, but the wires are not twisted into the appropriate pairs. If two signal-carrying wires are twisted together (instead of the normal configuration, in which each signal-carrying wire is twisted together with a ground wire), the cable generates excessive amounts of crosstalk, which can result in phantom collisions or other communication problems. Because the wiring appears to be correct, split pairs are not detectable by standard cable testing devices that transmit a signal at one end of the wire and receive it at the other end. To detect split pairs, you must measure the crosstalk produced by the cable, which requires a high-end multifunction cable tester.

S/T interface On an Integrated Services Digital Network (ISDN) installation, the interface provided by an NT1, to which you can connect ISDN devices (like ISDN telephones or faxes) or a terminal adapter (to which you can connect standard analog communications devices). In some cases, the NT1 and the terminal adapter are integrated into a single unit, eliminating the need for S/T interface connectors.

static routing A method for the creation of a TCP/IP router's routing table, in which the table entries are manually created by a network administrator. *Compare with* dynamic routing, in which routing table entries are automatically created by specialized routing protocols that exchange information with the other routers on the network.

STP *See* shielded twisted pair.

straight-through connection A twisted pair cable wiring scheme in which each of the eight wires is connected to the same contact in the connectors on both ends of the cable. This type of cable, by itself, does not permit communications between computers to take place, because the transmit signals generated by each computer are wired to the transmit contacts in the other computer. For communication to be possible, the transmit contacts in one computer must be wired to the receive contacts in the other computer, resulting in what is called a crossover circuit. Twisted-pair Ethernet networks rely on hubs to provide the crossover circuit, which enables all of the cables to be wired straight through. To connect two computers directly, without a hub, you must use a crossover cable, which provides the crossover circuit in the cable's wiring. *See also* crossover connection *and* crossover cable.

striping A data availability technique in which data is written to clusters on multiple drives in an alternating pattern (that is, one cluster is written to one drive, then the next cluster to a different drive, and so on). The drives appear as a single volume to users, but because the computer is reading data from two or more physical drives, it is possible for the heads in one drive to be moving to the next cluster while the heads in the other drive are actually reading a cluster. This speeds up the disk read process, because one of the drives is always reading data; if only a single drive were used, it would have to stop reading after every cluster so the heads could move to their next location. The drawback of the striping method is that the failure of one drive causes the loss of the entire volume.

subnet A group of computers on a TCP/IP network that share a common network identifier. In some cases, a TCP/IP network is divided into multiple subnets by modifying the subnet mask and designating some of the host identifier bits as subnet identifier bits. This enables the administrator to divide a network address of a particular class into multiple subnets, each of which contains a group of the hosts supported by the class.

subnet mask A TCP/IP configuration parameter that specifies which bits of the IP address identify the host and which bits identify the network on which the host resides. When the subnet mask is viewed in binary form, the bits with a value of 1 are the network identifier and the bits with a value of zero are the host identifier.

switch A data-link layer network connection device that looks like a hub, but which forwards incoming packets only to the computers for which they are destined. Switches essentially eliminate the medium-sharing from Ethernet networks by providing each computer with a dedicated connection to its destination. Using switches, you can build larger network segments, because there is

no contention for the network medium and no increase in collisions as the number of computers connected to the network rises. *Contrast with* a hub, which forwards incoming packets out through all of its ports.

T

T1 A dedicated telephone connection, also called a leased line, running at 1.544 Mbps. A T1 line consists of twenty-four 64-Kbps channels, which can be used separately, in combinations, or as a single data pipe. Large companies use T1 lines for both voice and data traffic; smaller companies can lease part of a T1, which is called fractional T1 service. Although it uses the telephone network, a T1 used for data networking does not use a dial-up connection; it is permanently connected to a specific location.

TCP *See* Transmission Control Protocol.

TDR *See* time domain reflectometer.

TE1 A device designed to connect directly to the S/T interface provided by an Integrated Services Digital Network (ISDN) installation.

TE2 A device that cannot connect directly to the S/T interface provided by an Integrated Services Digital Network (ISDN) installation, and which requires an intervening terminal adapter.

Telecommunications Network Protocol (Telnet) An application layer TCP/IP client/server protocol used to remotely control a computer at another location. A mainstay of UNIX networking, Telnet is a true remote control application. When you access another computer and run a program, it is the processor in the remote computer that executes that program. The Telnet service is command line-based, making it relatively useless on Windows computers, which rely on a graphical interface. However, all versions of Windows include a

Telnet client. Windows 2000 also includes a Telnet server, but compared to a UNIX Telnet implementation, there are relatively few things that you can do with it.

telepole A cable installation tool that consists of a telescoping pole with a hook on the end, used for pushing cables through ceiling and wall spaces.

Telnet *See* Telecommunications Network Protocol.

terminal adapter Hardware component used to connect a TE2 device to an Integrated Systems Digital Network (ISDN) connection. The terminal adapter plugs into the S/T interface provided by the NT1. In some cases, a terminal adapter and an NT1 are integrated into a single unit, which is specifically designed for installations where a computer will be the only device using the ISDN connection. *See also* Integrated Services Digital Network (ISDN), NT1, TE2, *and* S/T interface.

termination The connection of a resistor pack to the ends of a bus network to prevent signals reaching the end of the cable from reflecting back in the other direction. All bus networks, including Thick and Thin Ethernet and the small computer systems interface (SCSI) bus used for storage arrays in computers, must be terminated at both ends, or communications will not be reliable.

Thick Ethernet Also called 10Base5, an Ethernet physical layer specification that uses RG8 coaxial cable in a bus topology, with network segments up to 500 meters long and running at 10 Mbps. Thick Ethernet was the original Ethernet physical layer option introduced in the DIX Ethernet standard, and was maintained in the IEEE 802.3 standard. However, because of its difficult installation, it was quickly replaced by Thin Ethernet, which has now been replaced by unshielded twisted pair (UTP) cable.

Thin Ethernet Also called 10Base2, an Ethernet physical layer specification that uses RG58 coaxial cable in a bus topology, with network segments up to 185 meters long and running at 10 Mbps. Thin Ethernet was the dominant Ethernet physical layer option for several years, but it has since been replaced by unshielded twisted pair (UTP) cable, which is easier to install and maintain, and can run at faster speeds.

tif A file format commonly used to store graphic images in bitmap form.

time domain reflectometer (TDR) A cable-testing device that measures the length of a cable by transmitting a test signal and measuring the time it takes for the signal to travel to the other end and back. By supplying the cable's nominal velocity of propagation (the speed at which signals travel through the cable), the TDR can compute the length of the cable. In most cases, the time domain reflectometry function is incorporated into a multifunction cable tester, but it is sometimes a separate unit. *See also* Nominal Velocity of Propagation (NVP).

token passing A media access control (MAC) mechanism used on ring topology networks that uses a separate frame type called a token, which circulates around the network from computer to computer. Only the computer in possession of the token is permitted to transmit its data, which prevents computers from transmitting at the same time, causing collisions. Upon receipt of the token, a computer transmits a packet and either regenerates a new token immediately or waits for the packet to circulate around the network and return to its source, at which time the computer removes the packet and transmits the token frame. Unlike the Carrier Sense Multiple Access with Collision Detection MAC mechanism, no collisions occur on a properly functioning token passing network. Token passing is used by several different data-link layer protocols, including Token Ring and Fiber Distributed Data Interface (FDDI).

Token Ring A data-link layer protocol originally developed by IBM, used on local area networks (LANs) with a ring topology. Running at 4 Mbps or 16 Mbps, Token Ring networks use the token passing media access control (MAC) mechanism. Although they use a logical ring topology, Token Ring networks are physically cabled like a star, using a hub called a multistation access unit (MAU) that transmits incoming packets out through each successive port in turn. Early Token Ring networks used a shielded twisted pair (STP) cable known as IBM Type 1, but today, most Token Ring networks use unshielded twisted pair (UTP) cable.

Token Ring media filter A hardware adapter device that enables you to connect a computer with a Type 1 Token Ring network interface adapter to an unshielded twisted pair (UTP) network.

tone generator and locator Also known as a "fox and hound," an inexpensive cable testing tool that consists of a transmitter device, which you connect to a cable or a wire, which generates a test signal, and a probe that can detect the signal when you touch it to the cable or the cable sheath. You can use a tone generator to test entire cables or individual wires, but since you must test each wire individually, this is not a practical tool for the cable installer seeking to test a large number of cable runs.

top-level domain The highest level in the Domain Name System (DNS) name space, and the rightmost word in a DNS name. For example, in the DNS name *www.microsoft.com, com* is the top-level domain.

topology The method used to install network cabling and connect the network computers to the cable, which is determined by the data-link layer protocol and cable type you choose. The three basic network topologies are the bus, in which one computer is connected to the next in daisy chain fashion; the star, in which all of the computers are connected to a central hub; and the ring, in which the computers are logically connected to each other with the ends joined together.

Traceroute A TCP/IP command-line utility that displays the path that packets are taking to a specific destination. Traceroute uses Internet Control Message Protocol (ICMP) Echo Request and Echo Reply messages with varying Time To Live (TTL) values in the IP header. This causes packets to time out at each successive router on the way to the destination, and the error messages generated by the timeouts enable the Traceroute program to display a list of the routers forming the path to the destination.

translation bridge A data-link layer network connection device that connects networks using different media (such as two different types of Ethernet) or different data-link layer protocols (such as Ethernet and Token Ring). In addition to selectively propagating packets to the other network segment, this type of bridge also strips off the data-link layer protocol header and rebuilds a new one using the other protocol. *See also* bridge, router, *and* transparent bridge.

Transmission Control Protocol (TCP) A TCP/IP transport layer protocol used to transmit large amounts of data generated by applications, such as entire files. TCP is a connection-oriented protocol that provides guaranteed delivery service, packet acknowledgment, flow control, and error detection. The two computers involved in the TCP transaction must exchange a specific series of messages called a three-way handshake to establish a connection before any application is transmitted. The receiving computer also transmits periodic acknowledgment messages to verify the receipt of the data packets, and the two computers also perform a connection termination procedure after the data is transmitted. These additional messages, plus the large 20-byte TCP header in every packet, greatly increase the protocol's control overhead.

transparent bridge A data-link layer network connection device that connects two network segments and filters packets based on their hardware addresses, which it learns automatically, only forwarding packets that are addressed to the other network segment. A transparent bridge records the address of every packet it processes to build up a list of the computers on each of the network segments it connects. This prevents the network administrator from having to manually identify the computers on each network segment. *See also* bridge, router, *and* translation bridge.

transport layer The middle (fourth) layer of the Open Systems Interconnection (OSI) reference model, which contains protocols providing services that are complementary to the network layer protocol. A protocol suite typically has both connection-oriented and connectionless protocols at the transport layer, providing different types of service to suit the needs of different applications. In the TCP/IP suite, the transport layer protocols are the Transmission Control Protocol (TCP) and the User Datagram Protocol (UDP).

trap A message generated by a Simple Network Management Protocol (SNMP) agent and transmitted immediately to the network management console, indicating that an event requiring immediate attention has taken place.

tunneling A technique for transmitting data over a network by encapsulating it within another protocol. For example, Novell NetWare networks at one time supported TCP/IP only by encapsulating IP datagrams within NetWare's native Internetwork Packet Exchange (IPX) protocol. The Point-to-Point Tunneling Protocol (PPTP) also uses tunneling to carry PPP frames inside IP datagrams.

Type 1 cable A type of shielded twisted pair (STP) cable used for longer cable runs on Token Ring networks.

Type 6 cable A type of shielded twisted pair (STP) cable used for patch cable connections on Token Ring networks.

U

U interface The connection provided by the telephone company in an Integrated Services Digital Network (ISDN) installation, to which you attach an NT1. *See also* Integrated Services Digital Network (ISDN) *and* NT1.

UART *See* universal asynchronous receiver-transmitter.

UDP *See* User Datagram Protocol.

unicast A network transmission addressed to a single computer only. *Contrast with* broadcast and multicast.

universal asynchronous receiver-transmitter (UART) A component found in internal modems and computers' serial ports that is responsible for handling the systems asynchronous serial communications. High-speed external modems should always use a serial port having a 16550 UART chip. Current-production internal modems all have integrated 16550 UARTs.

universal serial bus (USB) An external peripheral bus standard that is rapidly replacing many of the other device ports commonly used on computers.

unqualified name An incomplete Domain Name System (DNS) name that identifies only the host, and not the domain in which the host resides. Some TCP/IP clients can handle unqualified names by automatically appending to them the name of the domain in which the computer is located, or by appending user-specified domain names.

unshielded twisted pair (UTP) A type of cable used for data and telephone networking that consists of eight copper wires twisted into four pairs with different twist rates, encased in a protective sheath. The twisting of the wire pairs reduces the crosstalk generated by signals traveling over the wires and minimizes their susceptibility to electromagnetic interference. UTP cables are graded by the Electronics Industry Association/Telecommunications Industry Association (EIA/TIA) using a series of categories. Most UTP cable installed today is Category 5, although Enhanced Category 5 (or Category 5e) cable is also available.

USB *See* universal serial bus.

Usenet An Internet bulletin board system consisting of tens of thousands of conferences, called newsgroups, covering a wide range of technical, recreational, and informational topics. Users access Usenet conferences by using news reader software to connect to a news server, access to which is usually provided by Internet Service Providers (ISPs).

User Datagram Protocol (UDP) A connectionless TCP/IP transport layer protocol used for short transactions, usually consisting of a single request and reply. UDP keeps overhead low by supplying almost none of the services provided by its connection-oriented transport layer counterpart, the Transmission Control Protocol (TCP), such as packet acknowledgment and flow control. UDP does offer an error detection service, however. Because it is connectionless, UDP generates no additional handshake messages, and its header is only eight bytes long.

UTP *See* unshielded twisted pair.

V

V.90 The current standard for 56-Kbps dial-up modem communications, ratified by the International Telecommunications Union (ITU) in 1998 to reconcile the competing X2 and K56 flex standards. Virtually all modems manufactured today support the V.90 standard.

virtual LAN (VLAN) A technique often used on switched networks to make a group of computers behave as though they are connected to the same local area network (LAN), even though they are physically connected to different network segments. Computers can remain in the same VLAN even when they're physically moved to a different segment.

virtual private network (VPN) A technique for connecting to a network at a remote location using the Internet as a network medium. A user can dial into a local Internet Service Provider (ISP) and connect through the Internet to a private network at a distant location, using a protocol like the Point-to-Point Tunneling Protocol (PPTP) to secure the private traffic.

virus A deliberately created, potentially damaging program or routine that infects a computer from an outside source (such as a file download or a floppy disk) and then replicates itself, enabling it to infect other computers.

VLAN *See* virtual LAN.

VPN *See* virtual private network.

W

WAN *See* wide area network.

well-known port TCP/IP port numbers that have been permanently assigned to specific applications and services by the Internet Assigned Numbers Authority (IANA). Well-known ports make it possible for client programs to access services without having to specify a port number. For example, when you type a Uniform Resource Locator (URL) into a Web browser, the port number 80 is assumed, because this is the port associated with Web servers.

wide area network (WAN) A network that spans a large geographical area using long-distance point-to-point connections, rather than shared network media as with a local area network (LAN). WANs can use a variety of communication technologies for their connections, such as leased telephone lines, dial-up telephone lines, and Integrated Services Digital Network (ISDN) or Digital Subscriber Line (DSL) connections. The Internet is the ultimate example of a WAN. *Compare with* local area network (LAN).

Windows Internet Name Service (WINS) A service supplied with the Windows NT and Windows 2000 operating systems that registers the NetBIOS names and IP addresses of the computers on a local area network (LAN) and resolves NetBIOS names into IP addresses for its clients as needed. WINS is the most efficient name resolution method for NetBIOS-based networks, because it uses only unicast transmissions. Other methods rely on the repeated transmission of broadcast messages, which can generate large amounts of network traffic.

WINS *See* Windows Internet Name Service.

Winipcfg.exe A graphical utility included with Windows 95, Windows 98, and Windows Me that you can use to view the TCP/IP configuration parameters for a particular computer. A command-line version of the tool—called Ipconfig.exe—is included with Windows 2000 and Windows NT. Winipcfg.exe is most useful on computers with TCP/IP clients configured automatically by a Dynamic Host Configuration (DHCP) server, because it is the easiest way to view the assigned settings for the client system. You can also use Winipcfg.exe to release and renew DHCP-assigned TCP/IP configuration parameters.

wire map tester A relatively inexpensive cable testing device used to detect open circuits, shorts, and transposed wires in twisted pair cable installations. The tester consists of two units that connect to the ends of the cable. One unit transmits test signals, and the other unit detects them. The wire map tester is faster and more convenient than a tone generator and locator because it tests all eight wires in a twisted pair cable run at the same time.

X

X.500 A standard published by the International Telecommunications Union (ITU) and the International Organization for Standardization (ISO) defining the structure of a global directory service. Microsoft's Active Directory directory service and NetWare's Novell Directory Services are both based on the X.500 design.

Z

zip A file format that is typically used to package multiple files into a single compressed file (called an archive) for transmission over a network.

Zip Proprietary name for a magnetic cartridge drive holding 100 or 250 MB.

Index

Test *your* readiness *for the* MCP**exam**

If you took a Microsoft Certified Professional (MCP) exam today, would you pass? With each READINESS REVIEW MCP exam simulation on CD-ROM, you get a low-risk, low-cost way to find out! The next-generation test engine delivers a set of randomly generated, 50-question practice exams covering real MCP objectives. You can test and retest with different question sets each time—and with automated scoring, you get immediate Pass/Fail feedback. Use these READINESS REVIEWS to evaluate your proficiency with the skills and knowledge that you'll be tested on in the real exams.

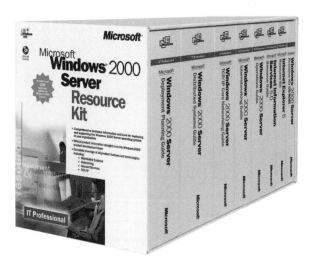

Ready solutions
for the
IT administrator

Keep your IT systems up and running with the ADMINISTRATOR'S COMPANION series from Microsoft. These expert guides serve as both tutorials and references for critical deployment and maintenance of Microsoft products and technologies. Packed with real-world expertise, hands-on numbered procedures, and handy workarounds, ADMINISTRATOR'S COMPANIONS deliver ready answers for on-the-job results.

MICROSOFT LICENSE AGREEMENT
Book Companion CD

IMPORTANT—READ CAREFULLY: This Microsoft End-User License Agreement ("EULA") is a legal agreement between you (either an individual or an entity) and Microsoft Corporation for the Microsoft product identified above, which includes computer software and may include associated media, printed materials, and "on-line" or electronic documentation ("SOFTWARE PRODUCT"). Any component included within the SOFTWARE PRODUCT that is accompanied by a separate End-User License Agreement shall be governed by such agreement and not the terms set forth below. By installing, copying, or otherwise using the SOFTWARE PRODUCT, you agree to be bound by the terms of this EULA. If you do not agree to the terms of this EULA, you are not authorized to install, copy, or otherwise use the SOFTWARE PRODUCT; you may, however, return the SOFTWARE PRODUCT, along with all printed materials and other items that form a part of the Microsoft product that includes the SOFTWARE PRODUCT, to the place you obtained them for a full refund.

SOFTWARE PRODUCT LICENSE

The SOFTWARE PRODUCT is protected by United States copyright laws and international copyright treaties, as well as other intellectual property laws and treaties. The SOFTWARE PRODUCT is licensed, not sold.

1. **GRANT OF LICENSE.** This EULA grants you the following rights:
   a. **Software Product.** You may install and use one copy of the SOFTWARE PRODUCT on a single computer. The primary user of the computer on which the SOFTWARE PRODUCT is installed may make a second copy for his or her exclusive use on a portable computer.
   b. **Storage/Network Use.** You may also store or install a copy of the SOFTWARE PRODUCT on a storage device, such as a network server, used only to install or run the SOFTWARE PRODUCT on your other computers over an internal network; however, you must acquire and dedicate a license for each separate computer on which the SOFTWARE PRODUCT is installed or run from the storage device. A license for the SOFTWARE PRODUCT may not be shared or used concurrently on different computers.
   c. **License Pak.** If you have acquired this EULA in a Microsoft License Pak, you may make the number of additional copies of the computer software portion of the SOFTWARE PRODUCT authorized on the printed copy of this EULA, and you may use each copy in the manner specified above. You are also entitled to make a corresponding number of secondary copies for portable computer use as specified above.
   d. **Sample Code.** Solely with respect to portions, if any, of the SOFTWARE PRODUCT that are identified within the SOFTWARE PRODUCT as sample code (the "SAMPLE CODE"):
      i. **Use and Modification.** Microsoft grants you the right to use and modify the source code version of the SAMPLE CODE, *provided* you comply with subsection (d)(iii) below. You may not distribute the SAMPLE CODE, or any modified version of the SAMPLE CODE, in source code form.
      ii. **Redistributable Files.** Provided you comply with subsection (d)(iii) below, Microsoft grants you a nonexclusive, royalty-free right to reproduce and distribute the object code version of the SAMPLE CODE and of any modified SAMPLE CODE, other than SAMPLE CODE (or any modified version thereof) designated as not redistributable in the Readme file that forms a part of the SOFTWARE PRODUCT (the "Non-Redistributable Sample Code"). All SAMPLE CODE other than the Non-Redistributable Sample Code is collectively referred to as the "REDISTRIBUTABLES."
      iii. **Redistribution Requirements.** If you redistribute the REDISTRIBUTABLES, you agree to: (i) distribute the REDISTRIBUTABLES in object code form only in conjunction with and as a part of your software application product; (ii) not use Microsoft's name, logo, or trademarks to market your software application product; (iii) include a valid copyright notice on your software application product; (iv) indemnify, hold harmless, and defend Microsoft from and against any claims or lawsuits, including attorney's fees, that arise or result from the use or distribution of your software application product; and (v) not permit further distribution of the REDISTRIBUTABLES by your end user. Contact Microsoft for the applicable royalties due and other licensing terms for all other uses and/or distribution of the REDISTRIBUTABLES.

2. **DESCRIPTION OF OTHER RIGHTS AND LIMITATIONS.**
   - **Limitations on Reverse Engineering, Decompilation, and Disassembly.** You may not reverse engineer, decompile, or disassemble the SOFTWARE PRODUCT, except and only to the extent that such activity is expressly permitted by applicable law notwithstanding this limitation.
   - **Separation of Components.** The SOFTWARE PRODUCT is licensed as a single product. Its component parts may not be separated for use on more than one computer.
   - **Rental.** You may not rent, lease, or lend the SOFTWARE PRODUCT.
   - **Support Services.** Microsoft may, but is not obligated to, provide you with support services related to the SOFTWARE PRODUCT ("Support Services"). Use of Support Services is governed by the Microsoft policies and programs described in the user manual, in "on-line" documentation, and/or in other Microsoft-provided materials. Any supplemental software code provided to you as part of the Support Services shall be considered part of the SOFTWARE PRODUCT and subject to the terms and conditions of this EULA. With respect to technical information you provide to Microsoft as part of the Support Services, Microsoft may use such information for its business purposes, including for product support and development. Microsoft will not utilize such technical information in a form that personally identifies you.
   - **Software Transfer.** You may permanently transfer all of your rights under this EULA, provided you retain no copies, you transfer all of the SOFTWARE PRODUCT (including all component parts, the media and printed materials, any upgrades, this EULA, and, if applicable, the Certificate of Authenticity), **and** the recipient agrees to the terms of this EULA.

- **Termination.** Without prejudice to any other rights, Microsoft may terminate this EULA if you fail to comply with the terms and conditions of this EULA. In such event, you must destroy all copies of the SOFTWARE PRODUCT and all of its component parts.

3. **COPYRIGHT.** All title and copyrights in and to the SOFTWARE PRODUCT (including but not limited to any images, photographs, animations, video, audio, music, text, SAMPLE CODE, REDISTRIBUTABLES, and "applets" incorporated into the SOFTWARE PRODUCT) and any copies of the SOFTWARE PRODUCT are owned by Microsoft or its suppliers. The SOFTWARE PRODUCT is protected by copyright laws and international treaty provisions. Therefore, you must treat the SOFTWARE PRODUCT like any other copyrighted material **except** that you may install the SOFTWARE PRODUCT on a single computer provided you keep the original solely for backup or archival purposes. You may not copy the printed materials accompanying the SOFTWARE PRODUCT.

4. **U.S. GOVERNMENT RESTRICTED RIGHTS.** The SOFTWARE PRODUCT and documentation are provided with RE-STRICTED RIGHTS. Use, duplication, or disclosure by the Government is subject to restrictions as set forth in subparagraph (c)(1)(ii) of the Rights in Technical Data and Computer Software clause at DFARS 252.227-7013 or subparagraphs (c)(1) and (2) of the Commercial Computer Software—Restricted Rights at 48 CFR 52.227-19, as applicable. Manufacturer is Microsoft Corporation/One Microsoft Way/Redmond, WA 98052-6399.

5. **EXPORT RESTRICTIONS.** You agree that you will not export or re-export the SOFTWARE PRODUCT, any part thereof, or any process or service that is the direct product of the SOFTWARE PRODUCT (the foregoing collectively referred to as the "Restricted Components"), to any country, person, entity, or end user subject to U.S. export restrictions. You specifically agree not to export or re-export any of the Restricted Components (i) to any country to which the U.S. has embargoed or restricted the export of goods or services, which currently include, but are not necessarily limited to, Cuba, Iran, Iraq, Libya, North Korea, Sudan, and Syria, or to any national of any such country, wherever located, who intends to transmit or transport the Restricted Components back to such country; (ii) to any end user who you know or have reason to know will utilize the Restricted Components in the design, development, or production of nuclear, chemical, or biological weapons; or (iii) to any end user who has been prohibited from participating in U.S. export transactions by any federal agency of the U.S. government. You warrant and represent that neither the BXA nor any other U.S. federal agency has suspended, revoked, or denied your export privileges.

6. **NOTE ON JAVA SUPPORT.** THE SOFTWARE PRODUCT MAY CONTAIN SUPPORT FOR PROGRAMS WRITTEN IN JAVA. JAVA TECHNOLOGY IS NOT FAULT TOLERANT AND IS NOT DESIGNED, MANUFACTURED, OR INTENDED FOR USE OR RESALE AS ON-LINE CONTROL EQUIPMENT IN HAZARDOUS ENVIRONMENTS REQUIRING FAIL-SAFE PERFORMANCE, SUCH AS IN THE OPERATION OF NUCLEAR FACILITIES, AIRCRAFT NAVIGATION OR COMMUNICATION SYSTEMS, AIR TRAFFIC CONTROL, DIRECT LIFE SUPPORT MACHINES, OR WEAPONS SYSTEMS, IN WHICH THE FAILURE OF JAVA TECHNOLOGY COULD LEAD DIRECTLY TO DEATH, PERSONAL INJURY, OR SEVERE PHYSICAL OR ENVIRONMENTAL DAMAGE. SUN MICROSYSTEMS, INC. HAS CONTRACTUALLY OBLIGATED MICROSOFT TO MAKE THIS DISCLAIMER.

DISCLAIMER OF WARRANTY

NO WARRANTIES OR CONDITIONS. MICROSOFT EXPRESSLY DISCLAIMS ANY WARRANTY OR CONDITION FOR THE SOFTWARE PRODUCT. THE SOFTWARE PRODUCT AND ANY RELATED DOCUMENTATION ARE PROVIDED "AS IS" WITHOUT WARRANTY OR CONDITION OF ANY KIND, EITHER EXPRESS OR IMPLIED, INCLUDING, WITHOUT LIMITATION, THE IMPLIED WARRANTIES OF MERCHANTABILITY, FITNESS FOR A PARTICULAR PURPOSE, OR NONINFRINGEMENT. THE ENTIRE RISK ARISING OUT OF USE OR PERFORMANCE OF THE SOFTWARE PRODUCT REMAINS WITH YOU.

LIMITATION OF LIABILITY. TO THE MAXIMUM EXTENT PERMITTED BY APPLICABLE LAW, IN NO EVENT SHALL MICROSOFT OR ITS SUPPLIERS BE LIABLE FOR ANY SPECIAL, INCIDENTAL, INDIRECT, OR CONSEQUENTIAL DAMAGES WHATSOEVER (INCLUDING, WITHOUT LIMITATION, DAMAGES FOR LOSS OF BUSINESS PROFITS, BUSINESS INTERRUPTION, LOSS OF BUSINESS INFORMATION, OR ANY OTHER PECUNIARY LOSS) ARISING OUT OF THE USE OF OR INABILITY TO USE THE SOFTWARE PRODUCT OR THE PROVISION OF OR FAILURE TO PROVIDE SUPPORT SERVICES, EVEN IF MICROSOFT HAS BEEN ADVISED OF THE POSSIBILITY OF SUCH DAMAGES. IN ANY CASE, MICROSOFT'S ENTIRE LIABILITY UNDER ANY PROVISION OF THIS EULA SHALL BE LIMITED TO THE GREATER OF THE AMOUNT ACTUALLY PAID BY YOU FOR THE SOFTWARE PRODUCT OR US$5.00; PROVIDED, HOWEVER, IF YOU HAVE ENTERED INTO A MICROSOFT SUPPORT SERVICES AGREEMENT, MICROSOFT'S ENTIRE LIABILITY REGARDING SUPPORT SERVICES SHALL BE GOVERNED BY THE TERMS OF THAT AGREEMENT. BECAUSE SOME STATES AND JURISDICTIONS DO NOT ALLOW THE EXCLUSION OR LIMITATION OF LIABILITY, THE ABOVE LIMITATION MAY NOT APPLY TO YOU.

MISCELLANEOUS

This EULA is governed by the laws of the State of Washington USA, except and only to the extent that applicable law mandates governing law of a different jurisdiction.

Should you have any questions concerning this EULA, or if you desire to contact Microsoft for any reason, please contact the Microsoft subsidiary serving your country, or write: Microsoft Sales Information Center/One Microsoft Way/Redmond, WA 98052-6399.

System Requirements

To view the multimedia video files on this book's compact disc, you need a computer equipped with the following minimum configuration:

- Microsoft Windows 95, Windows 98, Windows Me, Microsoft Windows NT 4 with Service Pack 3 or later, or Windows 2000

- Multimedia PC with 16-bit sound system

- 16 MB RAM for Windows 95 or Windows 98

- 32 MB RAM for Windows Me or Windows NT

- 64 MB RAM for Windows 2000

- An additional 70 MB minimum of hard disk space to install Internet Explorer 5.5 from this CD-ROM, if Internet Explorer is not already installed

- Microsoft Internet Explorer 4.01 or later

- Standard multimedia player, such as Windows Media Player or compatible software

- 4 MB of available hard drive space is required for Windows Media Player

- 110 MB of available hard drive space if you choose to copy the demonstration directory and its contents to the hard disk

- A double-speed CD-ROM drive or better

- Super VGA display with at least 256 colors

- Microsoft Mouse or compatible pointing device

OWNER REGISTRATION CARD   *Register Today!*   0-7356-1346-X

Return the bottom portion of this card to register today.

Network+ Certification Training Kit

FIRST NAME   MIDDLE INITIAL   LAST NAME

INSTITUTION OR COMPANY NAME

ADDRESS

CITY   STATE   ZIP

(   )

E-MAIL ADDRESS   PHONE NUMBER

U.S. and Canada addresses only. Fill in information above and mail postage-free.
Please mail only the bottom half of this page.

start faster go farther

For information about Microsoft Press® products, visit our Web site at **mspress.microsoft.com**

Microsoft®